Winner of the Jules and Frances Landry Award for 2014

CONFLICTING WORLDS

NEW DIMENSIONS OF THE AMERICAN CIVIL WAR

T. Michael Parrish, Series Editor

LOATHING LINCOLN

AN AMERICAN TRADITION FROM THE CIVIL WAR TO THE PRESENT

JOHN McKEE BARR

 LOUISIANA STATE UNIVERSITY PRESS   BATON ROUGE

Published with the assistance of the V. Ray Cardozier Fund

Published by Louisiana State University Press
Copyright © 2014 by Louisiana State University Press
All rights reserved
Manufactured in the United States of America
First printing

Designer: Barbara Neely Bourgoyne
Typefaces: EgyptienneD, display; Ingeborg, text
Printer and binder: Maple Press

Library of Congress Cataloging-in-Publication Data

Barr, John McKee, 1962–
  Loathing Lincoln ; an American tradition from the Civil War to the present /
John McKee Barr.
    pages cm. — (Conflicting worlds: new dimensions of the American Civil War)
  Includes bibliographical references and index.
  ISBN 978-0-8071-5383-3 (cloth : alk. paper) — ISBN 978-0-8071-5384-0 (pdf) —
ISBN 978-0-8071-5385-7 (epub) — ISBN 978-0-8071-5386-4 (mobi) 1. Lincoln, Abraham,
1809–1865—Public opinion. 2. Lincoln, Abraham, 1809–1865—Influence. 3. Presidents—
United States—Public opinion—History. 4. Public opinion—United States—History.
I. Title.
  E457.2.B23 2014
  973.7092—dc23

                                                            2013022655

Portions of chapters 1 and 4, respectively, appeared previously as "The Tyrannicide's Recep-
tion: Responses in Texas to Lincoln's Assassination," *Lincoln Herald* 91 (Summer 1989): 58–63;
and "African American Memory and the Great Emancipator," in *Lincoln's Enduring Legacy:
Perspectives from Great Thinkers, Great Leaders, and the American Experiment,* ed. Robert P.
Watson, William D. Pederson, and Frank J. Williams, 133–64. Lanham, Md.: Rowman and
Littlefield, 2011. Used by permission.

The paper in this book meets the guidelines for permanence and durability of the Committee
on Production Guidelines for Book Longevity of the Council on Library Resources. ∞

The world has never had a good definition of the word liberty, and the American people, just now, are much in want of one. We all declare for liberty; but in using the same *word* we do not all mean the same *thing*. With some the word liberty may mean for each man to do as he pleases with himself, and the product of his labor; while with others the same word may mean for some men to do as they please with other men, and the product of other men's labor. Here are two, not only different, but in-compatable [*sic*] things, called by the same name—liberty. And it follows that each of the things is, by the respective parties, called by two different and incompatable names—liberty and tyranny.

The shepherd drives the wolf from the sheep's throat, for which the sheep thanks the shepherd as *liberator,* while the wolf denounces him for the same act as the destroyer of liberty, especially as the sheep was a black one. Plainly the sheep and the wolf are not agreed upon a definition of the word liberty; and precisely the same difference prevails today among us human creatures, even in the North, and all professing to love liberty.

—ABRAHAM LINCOLN, April 18, 1864

CONTENTS

ACKNOWLEDGMENTS

In a sense this book began long ago with my parents, Charlotte Van Deren Barr and Dixon A. Barr. My mother and father were both educators and devoted readers of history and literature, a love of which I am sure in one way or another rubbed off on me. I grew up in Richmond, Kentucky, not far from Mary Todd Lincoln's and my mother's hometown of Lexington. My father was from Crown Point, Indiana, and in my boyhood home, or den, I was surrounded by his innumerable books about Abraham Lincoln, while a portrait of Robert E. Lee—a favorite of my mother—was displayed on the wall nearby. In this "North-South" marriage my parents were, in Lincoln's timeless wording, "not enemies, but friends," and my life has always been touched, and it is something for which I am continually thankful, by the better angels of their nature. It is to them, my loving mother and father, that this book is dedicated.

Since 2008 I have been fortunate to teach at Lone Star College–Kingwood. Lone Star is one of the finest community colleges in the United States and an outstanding institution of higher learning. It is also one that I think Abraham Lincoln would find admirable in its mission of helping students improve their life's prospects. I would especially like to thank my history and political science colleagues at Lone Star for their support of *Loathing Lincoln*. Our department at Kingwood is a menagerie of liberal democrats, social democrats, radicals, libertarians, and libertarian socialists and is a fun and interesting place to teach, talk, and argue. Such disparate political outlooks discredit the idea that there is some type of ideological consistency among professors on all college campuses. Our department chair, Steve Davis, embodies the best in what a history professor should be, both for his colleagues and his students, while Dr. Katherine

Persson, the president of Lone Star–Kingwood, is a key reason that our campus is such an enjoyable place to work. Both Steve and Katherine have encouraged me in writing this book. Finally, there is one colleague and friend in particular whom I especially want to thank. Dr. Amelia Keel, an English professor at Kingwood, read this entire study and offered excellent suggestions for how it might be improved. Amelia was a thoughtful and generous critic, and in addition to helping me write more clearly, she introduced my wife, Susan, and me to Virginia Woolf's novels and essays. For that alone we will always be indebted to her.

In researching this book, I have also incurred numerous debts to librarians and libraries across the United States. I would specifically like to thank Alex Simons at the University of Houston for her assistance in locating articles, journals, and additional sources relevant to my research. I am also especially grateful to Jim Birchfield and Bill Marshall at the Margaret I. King Library at the University of Kentucky, John Coski at the Eleanor Brockenbrough Library at the Museum of the Confederacy, Lynda Crist at the Jefferson Davis Papers at Rice University, Ted Jackson at the Joseph Mark Lauinger Memorial Library at Georgetown University, Nelson Lankford and Frances Pollard at the Virginia Historical Society, and Glenna Schroeder-Lein and Thomas Schwartz at the Abraham Lincoln Presidential Library in Springfield, Illinois, for their invaluable help while I was doing research for this book. With the aid of a Murray A. Miller Scholarship Grant from the University of Houston and an Andrew Mellon Scholarship from the Virginia Historical Society (VHS), I spent a wonderful week investigating the archives of the VHS in Richmond and found some excellent anti-Lincoln materials. Likewise in need of acknowledgment are the libraries in Texas I visited and all the librarians across the United States who graciously assisted me either by phone or e-mail in finding materials and then sent them to me because they knew I could not travel to their institutions in person. I would like to thank the Colorado Historical Society in Denver; the Dolph Briscoe Center for American History at the University of Texas at Austin; the Filson Historical Society in Louisville, Kentucky; the University of Wisconsin–Milwaukee, Golda Meir Library; the Harry Ransom Humanities Center at the University of Texas at Austin; the Henry Rosenberg Library in Galveston, Texas; the Herbert Hoover Institution on War, Revolution, and Peace at Stanford University; the Herbert Hoover Presidential Library in West Branch, Iowa; the Houston Metropolitan Research Center in Houston; the Houston Public Library; the Thomas D. Clark Center for Kentucky History at the Kentucky Historical Society in

Frankfort; the Southern Historical Collection at the University of North Carolina Library in Chapel Hill; the Texas State Archives in Austin; and the Jean Heard Library at Vanderbilt University in Nashville, Tennessee. This book is a testament to their contributions and the paradox of the solitary yet collaborative nature of writing and publishing.

I am likewise grateful to the people at LSU Press for agreeing to publish this work. I met my series editor, Michael Parrish, in Lexington, Kentucky, at the 2012 Society for Civil War Historians Conference. He was immediately interested in this project, and I was encouraged to hear him say that we can never have enough books about Lincoln. I am not sure if everyone would agree with Michael on that point, especially with all the books about the sixteenth president that are continually published in America, but I was certainly thrilled to hear it. Michael has been nothing less than a splendid editor. He carefully read the manuscript and tactfully offered suggestions for improvement based on his deep and wide knowledge of all matters relating to the Civil War, and his initial and ongoing support for the book was instrumental in its completion. I would also like to thank Rand Dotson, Executive Editor at LSU Press; Lee Campbell Sioles, Managing Editor; and my copy editor, Elizabeth Gratch, for their help in bringing this work to fruition. Elizabeth was a constant source of wisdom on all matters relating to *Loathing Lincoln,* and I am extraordinarily grateful for her dedication and talent.

This project on Lincoln's enemies began over twenty years ago at the University of Houston (Clear Lake) with Frank Wetta's graduate course on the Civil War and Reconstruction. His class was intellectually stimulating, inspirational even, and it was an occasion for gratification when he agreed to serve on my dissertation committee at the University of Houston in the fall of 2010. I found the history department at the University of Houston to be excellent, always challenging yet fully supportive of my endeavors. In addition to Frank, I am grateful to the other members of my committee, all of whom took the time to carefully read this study and offered constructive suggestions for improvement, not to mention encouragement: Orville Vernon Burton, Steven Deyle, James Oakes, Landon Storrs, and my advisor and chair, Eric Walther (more on Eric later). It was Jim Oakes who first suggested that I call this work "Loathing Lincoln." I subsequently was reminded that *Time* had published an article under a similar headline. So, thanks to Jim and to *Time* for the book's title!

Several other individuals and friends read and commented on the manuscript, or parts of it, and consequently made *Loathing Lincoln* a better volume. Nicholas Cox and Gregory Peek, fellow graduate students at the University of Houston, read the work in its earliest stages and always had good ideas for bettering it as we laughed and talked at Star Pizza in downtown Houston. The third chapter of the book was read by members of the Houston Area of Southern Historians (HASH), and they too offered useful criticism. The Abraham Lincoln Institute graciously invited me to speak in 2012 at its annual meeting, and I am thankful for that opportunity and encouragement. Michael Burlingame, Edna Greene Medford, and Lucas Morel of the institute were all particularly supportive in their comments. The 2012 Wepner Symposium in Springfield, Illinois, offered me a similar chance to speak, and I am grateful to the director of the symposium, Dr. Matthew Holden Jr., for his help. I would especially like to thank Larry Arnhart, Paul Blakelock, Steve Davis, Jason Jividen, James Jones, George Nash, Robert Norsworthy, Timothy Sandefur, Edward Sebesta, Jay Theis, Jennifer Weber, and Frank J. Williams for their astute observations. In addition to the historians who read early versions of this study, some of these individuals' essays and books are featured quite positively in this narrative, and I am grateful for their having taken the time to read and critique it. I would particularly like to single out Ed Sebesta for thanks. Ed is perhaps the single greatest authority on the influence of neo-Confederate ideas in modern America. He read the entire manuscript and helped find me research materials (Ed is a library unto himself), and his ongoing encouragement at some particularly low points in the process of getting this book published helped bring it to completion. Of course, all mistakes in this volume are my own.

In addition to Ed, I want to thank my advisor at the University of Houston, Eric Walther, for suggesting this topic as we were talking in his office one evening after his Comparative Slavery seminar concluded. Eric has spent an entire career studying the fire-eaters, the people who led the South out of the Union once Lincoln was elected in 1860. The historical profession, not to mention the country, has benefited immeasurably from Eric's skilled delineation of their thought. Eric nurtured this work along for several years with patience, skill, and good humor (a necessary attribute, to be sure, when researching and writing about Lincoln's enemies). He was an unwavering source of encouragement and wise criticism, and he has also become a good friend. Without Eric this book would simply not have been possible, and I hope it meets the high standards he sets for himself and his students.

Last, a word of gratitude to a few family members. My father-in-law, Tom Hanchett, read and commented thoughtfully on parts of the book.

Tom, who grew up in Illinois and spent a long and fruitful career at NASA, is the type of person for whom *Loathing Lincoln* is written, the intelligent reader who is interested in Abraham Lincoln and even more intrigued by those who continue to loathe him. Tom was raised in a large household, and that has benefited me both professionally and personally, as various members of the Hanchett family gave me lodgings as I completed my research or attended local conferences on Lincoln. I stayed with Tom's brother Mark and his wife, Anne, in Annapolis, Maryland, several times over the last few years, and while there Peter and Sally Gutierrez (Tom's sister), along with their daughter Annie and Mark and Anne's son Will, would come over from Baltimore and share family news and plenty of laughter. I learned one immutable lesson from these always enjoyable visits: when you stay with Mark and Anne Hanchett, good company, good conversation, and good food are assured. Jeanne Hanchett also took great interest in my work and never failed to ask searching questions about my project. My brother-in-law Troy Hanchett and his partner, Nikki Harbour, helped me get through some difficult days working on the book, mainly because I knew that we were meeting them at Cyclone Anaya's in west Houston on Fridays for lively talk, strong margaritas, and Tex-Mex.

I also want to thank Edward Barr and Elizabeth Masters, my brother and sister, both of whom live in Lexington, Kentucky. It was years ago, when I was in my teens, that Edward introduced me to the writings of William F. Buckley Jr. and conservatism more generally. While doing research at the University of Kentucky, I stayed with Elizabeth, her husband, Jimmy, and my niece Sarah and would return to their home after a day's work and enjoy a good meal and a restful evening. Like my parents, both Edward and Elizabeth have positively shaped my life in immeasurable ways. Finally, my wife, Susan, read every line of this rather lengthy study. She supported me every step of the way as I worked full-time and pursued my doctorate at the University of Houston and then undertook to write this book. I have been blessed by Susan's love and, in Samuel Johnson's words describing marriage, "her perpetual and indissoluble friendship; friendship which no change of fortune, nor any alteration of external circumstances, can be allowed to interrupt or weaken." In sum, it is my pleasure to express my heartfelt thanks for the professionalism, friendship, and even love of those who have made this work about the enemies of Abraham Lincoln possible. I am indebted to you all.

LOATHING
LINCOLN

INTRODUCTION

The founder of the modern conservative movement, William F. Buckley Jr., once said that Americans "shall not remember why Lincoln was loved until we come to understand why he was hated."[1] Both emotions were certainly displayed in the immediate aftermath of Abraham Lincoln's assassination by John Wilkes Booth at Ford's Theatre. On April 20, 1865, the *New Orleans Tribune,* an African American newspaper that over the course of the Civil War had periodically denounced the president for moving too slowly toward emancipation and black equality, told its readers: "Brethren, we are mourning for a benefactor of our race. Sadness has taken hold of our hearts." "No man," the paper continued, "can suppress his feelings at this hour of affliction. Lincoln and [radical abolitionist] John Brown are two martyrs, whose memories will live united in our bosoms. Both have willingly jeopardized their lives for the sacred cause of freedom."[2] On May 29, a little over a month later, shortly after Lincoln's body had been laid to rest in his hometown of Springfield, Illinois, Edgar Dinsmore, a black Union soldier stationed at Charleston, South Carolina, voiced similar sentiments, predicting that in the future "the name Abraham Lincoln will ever be cherished in our hearts, and none will more delight to lisp his name in reverence than the future generations of our people."[3] Distraught by the assassination, noted African American abolitionist Frederick Douglass in June characterized Lincoln as "the black man's president."[4] White sentiment was no different. One clergyman, Alonzo H. Quint, predicted in his Easter morning sermon that "in the story of the hard trial out of which America emerged a great and just nation, his name will be linked with its record as its martyred leader in its sufferings and its glory."[5] Such loving appreciation, voiced all over the United States that spring, reflected the deep admiration for Abraham Lincoln that had developed during the war and indicated the beginning of his heroic stature in American life.

But other Americans, especially diehard Confederates, vehemently disagreed with these laudatory assessments, and they expressed malevolent hatred for the president. Kate Stone, a Louisiana refugee living in Texas in 1865, thought Lincoln had reaped a just reward for the "torrents of blood" that he had "caused to flow."[6] Consequently, she praised Booth for killing him: "All honor to John Wilkes Booth, who has rid the world of a tyrant and made himself famous for generations." Stone hoped the famed actor and assassin would escape to the Lone Star State, where he could expect "a warm welcome." Later, after hearing of Booth's death, she added in her journal: "Poor Booth, to think that he fell at last. Many a true heart in the South weeps for his death."[7] Likewise, the *Texas Republican* contended that "there is no reason to believe that Booth in killing Lincoln was actuated by malice or vulgar ambition. He slew him as a tyrant, and the enemy of his country. Therefore we honor the deed."[8] The *Galveston Daily News* expressed essentially the same thought, predicting that in the future Booth would not be called a murderer but, instead, would be "awarded a place amongst the chivalric and heroic benefactors of mankind."[9] In La Grange, Texas, the *True Issue* editorialized that the assassination was a justifiable tyrannicide: "it is only a matter of surprise to us," the paper declared, that it took over four years to kill a president who had wielded "the scepter of tyranny and despotism thus long."[10] Lincoln's secretary of war Edwin Stanton, assuredly aware of such sentiment in 1865, proclaimed Lincoln a man for the ages, and indeed he has been as the arguments surrounding his legacy remain bitterly contested nearly 150 years after his death.

When it comes to the subject of Abraham Lincoln, it often seems that the author of Ecclesiastes was right to wearily lament, "Of making many books there is no end."[11] Yet the numerous individuals and scholars from all walks, regions, and eras of American life who have challenged accepted views of the Civil War president form a rich, controversial, and heretofore largely unexamined area of Lincoln scholarship.[12] Although historian Don E. Fehrenbacher penned a short essay on Lincoln's enemies in 1982, that was over thirty years ago, and thus far there has not been a detailed chronological investigation, which this work provides, of the numerous ways in which the negative depictions of the sixteenth president have undergone changes and mutations since the president's death and what function such varied and hostile portraits have served. Moreover, despite the celebration of the bicentennial of Lincoln's birth in 2009, the ideas of Lincoln's detractors have enjoyed something of a revival since Fehrenbacher's piece, and an updated historical analysis of their thinking is sorely needed.

Several historians have nevertheless investigated specific aspects of loathing for Lincoln. Michael Davis's excellent monograph, *The Image of Lincoln in the South* (1971), traced Confederates' view of Lincoln and how their attitudes toward the Civil War president changed both during and after the war. He argued that after military hostilities ceased, Lincoln's reputation in the South improved considerably, a claim with which this book will partially object. Davis reviewed numerous Lincoln detractors and their negative utterances about the Civil War president from the post-bellum South, but he concluded his survey with the celebration across the United States of the centennial of Lincoln's birth in 1909. Davis's study did not investigate the image of Lincoln among white southerners in the post–World War II years, nor did he investigate non-southerners who loathed Lincoln. This work, in contrast, brings criticism of Lincoln into the twenty-first century and takes into greater account how Lincoln's enemies have always used their opposition to the sixteenth president to advance a distinct political agenda. *Loathing Lincoln* demonstrates—it is in fact one of its central arguments—that more often than not, this agenda has been illiberal, even counterrevolutionary, in its aim to roll back or limit the liberty-expanding achievements of Lincoln and the antislavery movement during the Civil War and Reconstruction.[13]

Nearly a quarter-century later, Merrill D. Peterson added to Davis's study with *Lincoln in American Memory* (1994). Peterson described virtually everything that had been written, said, or commemorated about Abraham Lincoln since 1865.[14] He masterfully surveyed the various ways the president had been remembered and showed that there had been five major portrayals of Lincoln in American life: "Savior of the Union, Great Emancipator, Man of the People, the First American, and the Self-made Man." These representations coincided with concepts of "Nationality, Humanity, Democracy, Americanism, and the individual opportunity which is its essence" to form "the building blocks of the Lincoln image."[15] But because he so thoroughly covered the positive representations of Lincoln in American life, Peterson's discussion of Lincoln's critics was necessarily brief. He did not write in depth about the counterimages of Lincoln that developed alongside the more admiring portrayals in the culture at large, nor did he adequately examine why negative attitudes toward the president persisted and what political purposes they served. *Loathing Lincoln,* in contrast, will do both.

If Peterson's volume on Lincoln and memory successfully delineated the Lincoln image, then sociologist Barry Schwartz's exceptional two-volume work, *Abraham Lincoln and the Forge of National Memory* (2000) and *Abraham Lincoln in the Post-Heroic Era: History and Memory in Late Twentieth-Century America* (2008), methodically investigated it and thereby rectified one of the chief shortcomings in Peterson's book.[16] Historian James McPherson thought Peterson did "not offer an explicit answer to the big question: Why does Lincoln's image loom so large over our cultural landscape?"[17] Schwartz answered that "Abraham Lincoln is much more than a symbol, more than an idea; Abraham Lincoln is a living force" who "has always been a *lamp* illuminating the ideals of the American people as well as a *mirror* reflecting their interests."[18] The first volume, which traced the Lincoln image from 1865 through the Progressive era until the completion of the Lincoln Memorial in 1922, examined how Lincoln's image was used by various Americans as a symbol. Schwartz showed that the Lincoln image was appropriated by different groups of Americans, especially Progressives, as the country transitioned from a rural society to an industrial world power. This use of Lincoln by Progressives, as we shall see, worried the president's enemies and led to renewed efforts to denigrate him. Schwartz's main interest in the second volume was to account for the unmistakable decline in Lincoln's reputation since World War II, which he thought marked the peak of his standing in American culture. He contended that the reasons for the slow but steady demise of Lincoln's reputation included increased skepticism of government and politicians from the Vietnam War, coupled with an increasingly diversified America in which Lincoln was no longer able to serve as a unifying figure. The main contention of Schwartz's two volumes was that "the primary condition of Lincoln's apotheosis was the unique fit between his personal traits and the Progressive Era's egalitarian reforms; the primary condition of Lincoln's descent is the fading concept of greatness itself."[19]

Perhaps the most important book on Lincoln's enemies to appear in the early part of the twenty-first century was the political scientist Thomas Krannawitter's *Vindicating Lincoln: Defending the Politics of Our Greatest President* (2008).[20] In nine chapters he scrutinized what he believed to be the nine major charges made against the Civil War president, including accusations that Lincoln did not fight the war to end slavery and that he was in fact a tyrant, a racist, and the father of big government in the United States.[21] Krannawitter stressed throughout his volume that the evidence proved that Lincoln was right and his critics wrong. But the arguments that Krannawitter addressed, although vitally important, have not necessarily been the same indictments, as the following pages will demonstrate, that historically have been central to the president's foes. He did not show, for example, that Lincoln's critics have for a very long time referred to the sixteenth president as an imperialist responsible for laying the groundwork for America's overseas empire.

Notwithstanding the considerable achievements of this previous research, *Loathing Lincoln* will go beyond it by tracing the chief personalities and contentions of Lincoln's detractors from 1858 until the early twenty-first century. The philosopher Alasdair MacIntyre once said that "a tradition is an argument extended through time."[22] This volume will examine the tradition of hatred for Abraham Lincoln, a minority tradition to be sure but never a marginal one, because it has been a significant part of an important and long-standing argument about what type of nation the United States ought to be. By investigating the historical and philosophical lineage of the disparate people and groups who have hated Lincoln and drawing connections between them; what role his enemies have played in American culture and how their criticism has changed over time; what precisely their condemnations of the sixteenth president have been and how such loathing has been conditioned by changing understandings of freedom and equality as well as by shifting American political, cultural, and racial anxieties; and what their contribution has been to the decline of the Civil War president's reputation since World War II and its current standing, Americans will have a deeper understanding of why Lincoln was hated and, therefore, why he has been loved.[23] Criticism of the president is no mere historical curiosity for the reason that American public opinion regarding Abraham Lincoln has never been *only* about the man or his policies. Rather, it is more often than not a discourse about the essential nature and moral worthiness of the nation he helped to preserve. As historian Eric Foner once observed, because Abraham Lincoln "has provided a lens through which we Americans examine ourselves," the outlook of his enemies is worth serious study in order for Americans to more fully know themselves—and their country.[24] Hence, both opponents and defenders of Lincoln, indeed all Americans, will find this book valuable.

If understanding Lincoln's critics and their historical antecedents is significant as a matter of national self-understanding, it is equally impor-

tant in acknowledging a broader spectrum of political views on timeless
political problems. It is worth noting that this book will not reproduce an
exhaustive—and exhausting—list of the innumerable anti-Lincoln statements uttered over the years by the president's foes. Such a task is beyond
the scope of this work, or any work for that matter. Rather, *Loathing Lincoln* will focus on influential detractors of the president, their mind-set
and sensibility, their specific criticism, their use of the historical record,
and their impact.[25] Its themes will center around the issues Lincoln had
to face during his lifetime and as president, issues that, as James McPherson once noted, "will never become obsolete: the meaning of freedom;
the limits of government power and individual liberty in time of crisis;
the dimensions of democracy; the nature of nationalism; the problems
of leadership in war and peace; the tragedies and triumphs of a revolutionary civil war."[26] Added to McPherson's list are questions surrounding
Lincoln's personal and political ambition, natural rights, consent and
secession, political prudence and the abolition of slavery, treatment of
prisoners of war, the apparent defeat of one's ideals, definitions of freedom
and equality, and the federal government's role in linking them.[27] Ever
since Lincoln stepped onto the national stage in the 1850s to the end of
his life and beyond, the president's enemies have argued vociferously and
unceasingly that Lincoln's answers to some, or all, of these central questions were constitutionally, if not morally, wrong. If Lincoln was wrong
and his adversaries right on such vital matters of national import, then
the constitutional and moral foundation of the nation that came out of
the Civil War is called into question. Again, if the nation misunderstands
Lincoln, then in some sense it misunderstands itself. All of Lincoln's foes
believe the country has fallen prey to a calamitous historical misjudgment,
and they have regarded postwar admiration of the sixteenth president as
a threat, an obstacle, to what they perceive to be America's true national
identity and ideology. Standing on its head what the historian David Donald once said about the Lincoln legacy, critics of Abraham Lincoln hold
with unyielding certitude that there is no reason to get right with Lincoln
because Lincoln was never right to begin with.[28]

The first chapter of this book surveys the birth of hatred for Lincoln.
Such animosity began even before he was elected president and deepened
throughout his administration. Lincoln's political outlook, certainly in
contrast to the views of his slaveholding adversaries, at the very least
included several elements: it was based on Jefferson's Declaration of Independence and the idea of natural rights for all men, including the right

of African Americans to enjoy the fruits of their labor; on the idea that
slavery was economically, politically, and morally wrong, damaging to
America's reputation, and should be contained; on working closely with
the antislavery Republican Party to implement policies that would lead
to the ultimate extinction of the institution; and on the importance of
honoring the results of democratic elections, defending the indissoluble
nature of the American Union, and denying that secession was a constitutional right. Consequently, during the Civil War Lincoln was deeply
and profoundly unpopular with two major groups in the United States.[29]
Confederates viewed Lincoln (and the Republican Party he led) as a direct threat to their slaveholding interests and later as a heartless tyrant
who waged indiscriminate, inhumane, and unjust war on the southern
people. Northern political opponents, especially antiwar or peace Democrats known as Copperheads, more or less agreed with Confederates that
Lincoln's administration subverted the Constitution, especially in his
suspension of the writ of habeas corpus across the North and his issuing
the Emancipation Proclamation for broad areas of the Confederacy. Lincoln was loathed by these people chiefly for his antipathy toward slavery,
the prospect of racial equality they associated with his presidency, and
his presumed constitutional radicalism. To be sure, there were Radicals
within the Republican camp and a few abolitionists outside it who wanted
Lincoln to use his executive powers more quickly to advance the freedom
of African Americans, and they viewed him at times as an obstacle to
emancipation and vilified him for his conservatism, or tardiness. There
were also other northerners who shared President Lincoln's overall war
goals but were disappointed and at times disgusted with what they viewed
as the costly, incompetent, and perhaps corrupt execution of military
policies during the war. But these rebukes, although at times harsh and
condemnatory, were not as personally vituperative or racially charged as
those hurled by Lincoln's Confederate and Copperhead critics and thus
did not constitute deep-seated loathing for the president. They were, as
historian James Oakes has shown, "differences of style more than substance, of strategy more than goals, differences *within* the 'great movement'
against slavery."[30] Hatred for Lincoln to a large extent equaled hatred for
the antislavery movement. There nevertheless existed a small number
of abolitionists such as Lysander Spooner, who decried Lincoln's alleged
timidity in emancipating the slaves.[31] In sum the large majority of Lincoln's opponents in the 1860s were conservatives who feared that Lincoln
threatened the constitutional, economic, political, and racial status quo

that they hoped to maintain, while a far less numerous crowd of abolitionists believed that he did not move swiftly or radically enough to bring
about emancipatory change. A tradition of loathing for Abraham Lincoln,
then, emerged before 1860, intensified during the Civil War, and once the
war concluded, the intense emotions surrounding Lincoln's administration did not abate, not even after the president's assassination in 1865.

The ongoing malice for Lincoln and the shape it took after hostilities
ceased until Jefferson Davis's death in 1889, a death that signaled the
passing away of the generation that had fought the war, is described in
chapter 2. In these decades Lincoln's allegedly ignoble and sordid frontier
background, his religious beliefs or supposed lack thereof, and his conduct
of various aspects of the war to preserve the Union and abolish slavery,
all of which made possible a more racially egalitarian country, were of
primary importance to his critics, most but not all of whom were white
southerners. Spooner for one continued his vilification of the president,
refusing to accept that the war had been fought for noble, abolitionist
ends or that such ends had been secured by Union victory. Many white
southerners agreed and thought that in his use of federal power to coerce
the Confederacy to remain in the Union without its consent and relinquish
its property in slaves, the president emancipated slaves but enslaved free
men. These former Confederates constituted the large majority of Lincoln's postwar enemies, and they were almost invariably champions of
what came to be called the "Lost Cause," a term conceived after the war by
Richmond, Virginia, journalist Edward Pollard.[32] The white supremacist
advocates of this Lost Cause viewpoint, including authors Albert Taylor
Bledsoe (a former friend and colleague of Lincoln's in Illinois), William
Hand Browne, and Alexander Stephens, championed a memory of the
Civil War that denied slavery was the cause of the conflict and depicted
the Confederacy as a virtuous, glorious, Christian society whose cause
would eventually be vindicated by history. At the same time, the "disgusting" "infidel" Civil War president, the lowbred man of the people currently
popular with large numbers of Americans, was denigrated as the destroyer
of the Old Union, rather than its savior, because he had centralized power
in Washington, D.C. In short Lincoln was not the First American but the
Worst American.

Chapter 3 demonstrates that from Jefferson Davis's passing until the
Great War ended, animosity for Lincoln was promoted most effectively
by Lost Cause organizations such as the United Daughters of the Confederacy (UDC). White elites such as Mary DeButts Carter, Elizabeth Avery

Meriwether, Charles L. C. Minor, Kate Mason Rowland, and Mildred Lewis Rutherford, all associated with the UDC or other organizations that vindicated the Confederacy, penned works that defended the Old South and demonized Abraham Lincoln. Hatred for Lincoln, at least as it existed among white southerners, was more than just the work of a few disgruntled individuals. Indeed, it was part of a larger movement of irreconcilable Confederates (and those across the country who sympathized with them) who worked assiduously to ensure that their children were taught the "truths" of history about "the War between the States." They censored textbooks that did not romanticize the antebellum social order or exalt the Confederacy and placed monuments across the region glorifying their white ancestors who had fought in the war. In addition, their efforts attempted to counter the positive portrayal of Lincoln advanced by progressive presidents such as Theodore Roosevelt and Woodrow Wilson.

A crucial turning point for Lincoln's enemies developed in the 1890s, as they alleged that the consolidation of the nation that resulted from Lincoln's actions during the Civil War laid the foundation for subsequent American imperial adventures overseas. Such opposition to Lincoln and American expansionism was to an extent principled yet also grounded in racial anxieties, as the United States conquered Latin and Asian peoples and retreated from the broadly egalitarian results of the Civil War and Reconstruction into a narrower vision of American citizenship based on white supremacy.

Meanwhile, across the South, if not the entire country, through both nonviolent and violent methods, African Americans were denied their basic civil and human (i.e., natural) rights. Consequently, early in the twentieth century a few elite African Americans, such as lawyer for the National Association for the Advancement of Colored People (NAACP) Archibald Grimké and radical thinker Hubert Harrison, disappointed with Lincoln's seeming reluctance to fully embrace either emancipation or racial equality and the nation's continuing racial injustices, publicly questioned the ongoing allegiance of their race to Abraham Lincoln. Notwithstanding all his political and linguistic gifts, the president was seen as a flawed, reluctant emancipator rather than a heroic liberator. This judgment signaled the birth of a more liberal or radical dissatisfaction with Lincoln resulting from the unfulfilled egalitarian promises of the 1860s and 1870s. Such criticism scarcely equaled the loathing exhibited by the president's Lost Cause opponents, but it did reemphasize that disapproval for Lincoln across the political spectrum was inextricably linked to matters of race and the proper role of the federal government in promoting racial progress and ensuring liberty for all Americans.[33]

Chapter 4 illustrates that in the years between the Great War and the end of World War II, hatred for the sixteenth president continued among diehard Confederates such as Lyon Gardiner Tyler, the former president of William and Mary College, yet it also became something of a national, rather than strictly regional, phenomenon, as well-known journalist H. L. Mencken and Senator Albert Beveridge expressed viewpoints similar to those of previous Lincoln critics. But now a new element was emphasized by those who loathed Lincoln: he was seen as the symbol of modernity and of all that was wrong with the United States. In the midst of the Great Depression this nostalgic outlook crept into the American academy at places such as Vanderbilt University in Nashville, Tennessee, where the intellectual and political group known as the Agrarians resided, and into the work of Illinois poet Edgar Lee Masters's biography, *Lincoln: The Man* (1931). In contrast to the views of his adversaries between the wars, Lincoln's America was a nation in which one's condition in life was not fixed or based on one's social rank at birth or racial makeup.[34] As he told an audience in 1860, a free society is one in which any American "knows he can better his condition; he knows that there is no fixed condition of labor, for his whole life. . . . I want every man to have the chance—and I believe a black man is entitled to it—in which he can better his condition—when he may look forward and hope to be a hired laborer this year and the next, work for himself afterward, and finally to hire men to work for him!"[35] Lincoln thus embodied a dynamic American nation in which one's liberty and prospects in life would be determined by achievement, not familial lineage. An additional motivation for Lincoln's detractors in these decades was an escalating respect for the president by Americans, an appreciation that for a few went so far as to equate Lincoln's character with that of Jesus. His enemies termed this "Lincolnolatry," likened it to blasphemy, and believed that a "Lincoln cult" had suppressed or ignored the sixteenth president's flaws and shortcomings to the great detriment of American intellectual and political life. Hence, they saw themselves as a dedicated remnant of courageous truth tellers battling an authorized, mythical, godlike version of Lincoln propagated by the American nation-state.[36] In their various attempts to challenge the positive view of Lincoln, his critics oftentimes depicted a countermythical Lincoln that bore little relation to the historical figure they so detested. In their iconoclastic efforts to destroy what they saw as a blasphemous Lincolnolatry, the president's detractors attempted to establish, certainly in the former states of the Confederacy, an official version of the president that buttressed the entrenched political and racial interests of whites and denied blacks the chance to better their condition. Lincoln, in short, served as a "demonic Other," a man who endangered their cherished white supremacist ideals.[37] Between the Great War and World War II, more and more African Americans, including W. E. B. Du Bois, Congressman Arthur Mitchell, *Pittsburgh Courier* editor Robert Vann, Carter Woodson, and even some former slaves alive in the 1930s—a minority to be sure—joined earlier critics such as Grimké and Harrison in finding Lincoln's Emancipation Proclamation and the long-term results of the Civil War and Reconstruction to be far from satisfactory and criticized the president on that basis. Their disappointment portended the movement of African Americans' political loyalties away from Lincoln's Republican Party to Franklin Roosevelt and the Democrats.

The fifth chapter explains that such worries remained vitally significant to the president's detractors after World War II through the end of the Cold War, although disparagement of Lincoln's frontier background and his religious beliefs perhaps lost some resonance with the American public. In the midst of the Cold War, the civil rights revolution of the 1950s and 1960s, and the Vietnam War, a historic if impermanent shift occurred as public loathing for Lincoln was temporarily purged from mainstream conservatism and for the first time was just as likely to be found on the left wing of the political spectrum. Traditionally, most of Lincoln's enemies had been conservatives, reactionaries who defended the Confederacy and either downplayed or denied the inhumanity and violence at the heart of slavery. Accordingly, they advocated views that contributed to African Americans not enjoying full equality as American citizens. After 1945, however, Lincoln was vociferously defended by Harry Jaffa, a conservative political philosopher, for his moral and political courage in confronting both apologists for slavery and politicians such as Stephen A. Douglas who were indifferent to its expansion. Jaffa maintained that Lincoln's philosophy of natural rights for all, an egalitarian notion if there ever was one, was a concept that conservatives should endorse. Conservatives such as political scientist Willmoore Kendall and Texan M. E. Bradford, who was an intellectual descendant of the Agrarians and retained ongoing sympathies for the Confederacy and the Lost Cause view of the Civil War, disagreed with Jaffa. Kendall attacked Jaffa's portrayal of Lincoln's egalitarianism, while Bradford, a self-confessed reactionary, expressed his dissatisfaction with the president out of a belief that the antebellum

South had been a superior civilization, at least relative to modern America. Libertarians such as Frank Meyer and Murray Rothbard, as part of a long tradition dating back to the nineteenth-century anarchist Lysander Spooner and early-twentieth-century writers H. L. Mencken and Albert Jay Nock, advocated an antistate critique of Lincoln akin to Kendall's and Bradford's, expressing their ideas in venues such as William F. Buckley Jr.'s *National Review* and smaller outlets such as the *Libertarian Forum*. Rothbard's antistate, anti-imperialist criticism meshed nicely with literary critic Edmund Wilson's depiction of Lincoln's supposed Caesaristic ambitions and New Left historian William Appleman Williams's conviction, consistent with previous Lincoln detractors, that Lincoln's conquering of the Confederacy established the groundwork for America's overseas empire. Meanwhile, African American journalist Lerone Bennett Jr., an editor at *Ebony* magazine, alleged in a landmark essay that Lincoln was not worth emulating because of his nineteenth-century racial bigotry and timidity in pursuing a racially egalitarian society. Consequently, Lincoln's critics focused their vituperation on several, if somewhat inconsistent, allegations: Lincoln was condemned for advancing the idea that the United States was committed to equality; for his allegedly messianic rhetoric, which his opponents believed contributed to the American empire and subsequent atrocities in places such as Vietnam; for his misuse and expansion of power for the federal government and its executive branch; and for being a white supremacist, a racial bigot who was a woefully inadequate moral or political model for Americans to emulate.

Chapter 6 argues that in the post–Cold War era loathing for Lincoln more or less disappeared from critics on the left as a significant force, although criticism of the president's shortcomings, especially on race, remained widespread. At the same time, libertarian and neo-Confederate criticism of Lincoln merged into what a few of the president's detractors termed a paleolibertarian political movement designed to criticize American government power, if not discredit the American state itself. Aided by Lerone Bennett's *Forced into Glory: Abraham Lincoln's White Dream* (2000), a book that claimed that the Great Emancipator neither enthusiastically freed the slaves—in fact Bennett argued that Lincoln was an oppressor rather than a liberator—nor cared about racial equality, intellectual disciples of Lincoln detractor Murray Rothbard such as economist Thomas DiLorenzo focused their hostility on Lincoln's Whig, or statist, economic policies and what they believed was his unlawful conduct of the war. Lincoln's administration, DiLorenzo and his allies argued, was criminal in part because secession was a constitutional right, in part because of the damage the Union army did to southern civilians. At the same time, they repeated earlier criticism advanced by Confederates such as Alexander Stephens that the president had centralized too much power in Washington, D.C., at the expense of the states. In short, if for Bennett the sixteenth president was the Great Racist or Reluctant Emancipator, then for DiLorenzo and his compatriots he was also the Great Centralizer. These characterizations reinforced each other and eventually found their way back into an increasingly conservative Republican Party possessed with a deep-seated animosity for the federal government and for the forty-fourth U.S. president, Barack Obama, a liberal advocate for the necessity of federal power and an avowed admirer of Abraham Lincoln. Such attacks and their growing influence provoked several pro-Lincoln counterblasts from libertarians and conservatives and illustrated an ongoing irony of anti-Lincoln thought: it often served as a catalyst on the right for some of the most vigorous defenses of the sixteenth president ever written (the most recent work from a conservative championing Lincoln, *National Review* editor Rich Lowry's *Lincoln Unbound: How an Ambitious Young Railsplitter Saved the American Dream— and How We Can Do It Again,* was published too late for consideration in this book). Still, the cynical portrayals of Lincoln, especially after 1989, have to an extent been effective. Americans have "absorbed [arguments] and reproduced rhetoric whose history and implications they have failed to ponder," and this process has no doubt contributed to distrust for federal authority, distrust for all American politicians, and distrust for what Schwartz called the fading concept of greatness itself.[38]

It is clear that the visceral loathing of Lincoln is unlike any other presidential hostility in American history in its personal venom, philosophical disagreement, and persistence over time. It is sui generis. Although after his death Lincoln's reputation underwent a transformation in a manner similar to George Washington's, no countermyth developed criticizing Washington's personal life or presidency as it did with Lincoln. Over the course of twenty-five years Washington led the United States through its War for Independence, presided over the Constitutional Convention, and served as its first president. The Virginia planter was seen as an ideal man, a symbol of the fulfillment of the new republic's ideals he had helped create and establish. In a sense Washington's life and career *reassured* and sustained Americans' belief that self-government was possible. In contrast, Lincoln had led a disunited country through a bloody war for only four years, and although many Americans, probably a majority, viewed his background and career favorably, for countless others he *threatened* the republic Washington founded.[39]

Another president reaped similar popular hostility. Franklin Roosevelt's response to the Great Depression generated enormous controversy about the proper role of the federal government in American life. But even though people have disparaged FDR's wealth and aristocratic background, such personal criticism has never been central to a philosophical or constitutional critique of the New Deal in the way denigrating Abraham Lincoln's ancestry was for his detractors both during and after the Civil War. Nor have Americans argued much about FDR's religious beliefs, whereas the issue of whether Lincoln was a Christian has been, at least prior to 1945, fundamental for most of Lincoln's adversaries. After Pearl Harbor was attacked in 1941, the nation rallied around FDR. In contrast, when the Confederates fired on Fort Sumter and the president responded by calling for seventy-five thousand volunteers to crush the rebellion, Lincoln faced added defections within the United States, and his attempt to reunite the country by force earned him lasting enmity as a warmonger or worse, the destroyer of the Union rather than its savior. As president during the Great Depression and World War II, Roosevelt unquestionably had to confront an array of complex problems similar to those Lincoln faced, but his presidency was neither entirely encompassed by war, nor did his policies directly confront perennial American problems of race and identity in quite the same way as Lincoln's. And although Roosevelt died while in office, as did Lincoln, Roosevelt was not the recipient of murderous rage. Because of the ideas Lincoln advocated, the ideals he personified, the antislavery movement he represented and led, the nearly insurmountable problems he faced, the methods he offered for solving them, combined with the manner of his death, all guaranteed his apotheosis for most Americans and his descent into hell for others.[40]

Analogous to critics of Charles Darwin in late-twentieth- and early-twenty-first-century America, attacking and altering the image of Lincoln today is a long-term strategy for changing the nation's historical narrative, its orientation, and the nature of American political culture. The libertarian Illana Mercer published an article online entitled "'Taking America Back' Starts with Taking Lincoln Down," while Lincoln's most determined African American critic, Lerone Bennett, has written that "Lincoln is a key, perhaps the key, to the American personality, and what we invest in him, and what we hide in him, is who we are."[41] If Lincoln can be portrayed successfully as the father of big government (and he is so depicted in the writings of numerous libertarians and neo-Confederates who are opposed to President Obama's administration) or as an irredeemably flawed and racist politician who begrudgingly issued the Emancipation Proclamation, then the arguments of Lincoln's adversaries may well resonate more strongly with the American public in the future, reshape understandings of liberty, and cast doubt on the American democratic experiment. In 2007, prior to Senator Obama's election to the presidency, congressman and Republican presidential candidate Ron Paul appeared on *Meet the Press,* echoing some of libertarian author Thomas DiLorenzo's arguments from *The Real Lincoln* (2002) about the needlessness of the Civil War, and he has not retreated from that viewpoint. Indeed, in 2012 he stood in front of a Confederate flag and said that Americans have been "led to believe, and every one of our public schools since then have preached and harped and pounded it into our kids, that the only issue that was involved was slavery. And yet, that was—that was the excuse, and that was the rabble-rousing issue. And it was; you can't deny that it was an important issue. That really wasn't the issue of why the war was fought, in my estimation."[42] Two years earlier, in 2010, the Texas State Board of Education started requiring schoolchildren in the Lone Star State to read the inaugural addresses of both Abraham Lincoln and Jefferson Davis. Such a requirement makes perfect pedagogical sense if the purpose is to expose students to stances taken by important historical actors and their divergent interpretation of events. But it is another thing entirely if Davis and the cause he advocated—the perpetuation of inhuman bondage—is characterized instead as resistance to centralized government in the name of states' rights and placed on the same moral plane as Lincoln's desire to abolish the pernicious institution of slavery, ensure that *all* men enjoy the fruits of their labors, and preserve the Union from its foes.[43]

Although the vast majority of Americans love Abraham Lincoln, they are less familiar than they should be, as William F. Buckley Jr. noted, with why he has been hated or that he has been hated at all. Neither are they aware that loathing for the president remains connected to a political agenda hostile to Lincoln's political philosophy. As a result, their historical understanding of their nation's political tradition, a tradition at the center of which stands the complicated and enigmatic figure of Abraham Lincoln, is impoverished. Giving thoughtful consideration to the views of the president's critics, those who have dissented from popular veneration of Lincoln, to use Merrill Peterson's imagery, as the Savior of the Union or as the Great

Emancipator or as the First American or as the model American Democrat or as the Self-Made Man of the People, will enable Americans to comprehend more clearly the full spectrum of American political thought and enrich their understanding of the fears and anxieties that have shaped—and continue to shape—the nation's political and cultural life. Equally important, looking at Lincoln from the perspective of his enemies and empathetically considering their strongly held opinions in tandem with the historical context in which they arose will assist Americans in better understanding alternative political and moral viewpoints and serve as a safeguard against political and historical self-righteousness.[44]

It is nevertheless important to comprehend that Abraham Lincoln was a political man and that his detractors have always attempted to rewrite the American historical narrative by denigrating the person and actions of the sixteenth president and the values and hopes he (and the antislavery movement) embodied. Precisely because Lincoln exemplifies for most Americans a liberal, pluralistic, and broadly democratic America, an America of economic and social mobility and rights for all rather than a few, the attempt to alter his memory by dissenters remains a highly charged political contest that threatens to revise the past and future story of the United States. And in their peaceful attempt to understand this ongoing contest and its inextricable connection to the definition of the American nation, Americans will more fully appreciate that they too are participants in this struggle, one "not altogether for today," as Abraham Lincoln said in 1861, but "for a vast future also."[45]

1

MARKED FOR BITTERNESS

The Civil War Era, 1858–1865

The enduring contest over the memory of Abraham Lincoln in American culture began on April 15, 1865, the morning Lincoln died from a bullet fired by John Wilkes Booth the previous Good Friday evening. After a desultory breakfast the morning of the fifteenth, Secretary of the Navy Gideon Welles proceeded to the White House and encountered a poignant scene. "On the avenue in front of the White House," Welles observed, "were several hundred colored people, mostly women and children, weeping and wailing their loss. This crowd did not appear to diminish through the whole of that cold, wet day."[1] Ten days later the navy secretary wrote in his diary similar impressions of Lincoln's "imposing, sad, and sorrowful" funeral in Washington, D.C., held on April 19: "There were no truer mourners, when all were sad, than the poor colored people who crowded the streets, joined the procession, and exhibited their woe, bewailing the loss of him whom they regarded as a benefactor and father. Women as well as men, with their little children, thronged the streets, sorrow, trouble, and distress depicted on their countenances and in their bearing."[2] The subsequent two-week funeral procession of Lincoln's body from Washington, D.C., to Springfield, Illinois, which retraced the route the president-elect had taken in 1861 on the way to his first inauguration, was not only instrumental in allowing those in the northern section of the country the opportunity to mourn their dead leader, it also began and perhaps obscured the process whereby Lincoln was transformed from a deeply divisive president and politician into a national hero, if not a martyr-saint, for the new American nation re-created from the crucible of civil war.[3]

Even in the midst of such grief, there was a dissenting outlook expressed across the United States. New York diarist George Templeton Strong heard of several Irish house servants who expressed joy upon hearing of the murder, although they were "summarily discharged" for their indiscretion. Farther south, in Kentucky, Lizzie Hardin confided to her diary that "I cannot but feel glad he [Lincoln] is dead." A few days later she was even more forceful in her denunciation: "The assassination was wrong, but to one who lives in the South and has seen the thousands whose blood has been poured out on their own thresholds, the half-starved women and children wandering amid the ashes of their once happy homes, it seems a wrong for which there are many excuses." Meanwhile, as northerners mourned their slain president, across the country the *Houston Tri-Weekly Telegraph* printed an editorial written by the well-known Galveston attorney William Pitt Ballinger that expressed jubilation that Lincoln had been killed. Ballinger exulted that there was "not a soldier, nor a woman, an old man nor a lisping child . . . but feels the thrill, electric, divine, at this sudden fall . . . of the chief of our oppressors."[4] These derogatory remarks, in stark contrast to the sadness of those African Americans observed by Gideon Welles crying outside the White House after the president's death, not only reflected the loathing that had developed for Abraham Lincoln during the Civil War; they also foreshadowed a generations-long controversy surrounding the president's memory in American culture.

Decades earlier it would have been difficult for Abraham Lincoln to have imagined that his death would be the occasion for such sorrow and bitterness. As a young, obscure politician, in 1837 Lincoln had cosigned a protest to the Illinois legislature with Dan Stone that characterized slavery as "founded on both injustice and bad policy." But their complaint also said "the promulgation of abolition doctrines tends to increase rather than abate its evils."[5] Seventeen years later in Peoria, Illinois, Lincoln delivered a speech scathingly critical of slavery and the Kansas-Nebraska Act, a controversial piece of legislation sponsored by Stephen Douglas that in essence repealed the Missouri Compromise and allowed for the possibility of slavery's entrance into those western territories. In the course of his lengthy address he acknowledged uncertainty about how precisely to get rid of inhuman bondage: "If all earthly power were given me," Lincoln confessed to his audience, "I should not know what to do, as to the existing institution. My first impulse would be to free all the slaves, and send them to Liberia,—to their own native land."[6] But Lincoln thought such a policy would be disastrous, leading to the deaths of thousands, perhaps tens of thousands, of former slaves. Nor did he advocate making blacks the equals of whites: "What next?" Lincoln asked. "Free them, and make them politically and socially, our equals? My own feelings will not admit of this; and if mine would, we well know that those of the great mass of white people will not. Whether this feeling accords with justice and sound judgment, is not the sole question, if indeed, it is any part of it. A universal feeling, whether well or ill-founded, can not be safely disregarded. We can not, then, make them equals. It does seem to me that systems of gradual emancipation might be adopted; but for their tardiness in this, I will not undertake to judge our brethren of the south."[7] Still, Lincoln was absolutely clear that slavery was morally wrong, antithetical to the Declaration of Independence, and should not be extended:

> The doctrine of self government is right—absolutely and eternally right—but it has no just application, as here attempted. Or perhaps I should rather say that whether it has such just application depends upon whether a negro is *not* or *is* a man. If he is *not* a man, why in that case, he who *is* a man may, as a matter of self-government, do just as he pleases with him. But if the negro *is* a man, is it not to that extent, a total destruction of self-government, to say that he too shall not govern *himself*? When the white man governs himself that is self-government; but when he governs himself, and also governs *another* man, that is *more* than self-government—that is despotism. If the negro is a *man,* why then my ancient faith teaches me that "all men are created equal;" and that there can be no moral right in connection with one man's making a slave of another.[8]

So, when Lincoln received the senatorial nomination from Illinois Republicans four years later, in 1858, and stepped onto the national stage, the relatively unknown Springfield lawyer set his sights on defeating his more famous Democratic rival, Stephen A. Douglas, and preventing the extension of antebellum slavery westward. By the time of his contest with Douglas, it was clear from Lincoln's political career that he hated slavery and that he was steadfastly against its expansion. But in equating slavery and its possible extension with despotism, in expressing uncertainty about how to best eradicate the institution, in supporting the voluntary colonization of slaves outside the United States, in his concern about how precisely to treat the slaves if they were freed, and in his belief that abolitionism did not solve but exacerbated the institution's evils, Lincoln had laid the foundation for becoming the enemy of southern slaveholders, of Americans terrified of the prospect of racial equality, and of a few abolitionists.

The campaign against Douglas marked the beginning of Lincoln's rise to national prominence and the birth of loathing for Lincoln in American life. From 1858 until his assassination seven years later, hatred for Lincoln mostly stemmed from a conservative political tradition descended from Thomas Jefferson and Andrew Jackson. This was an American rather than exclusively southern or Confederate strain of thought, acutely suspicious of centralized federal authority (with the notable exceptions of an insistence on federal support for slavery in the states, or what was called the right of property in man, federal support for the extension of slavery into the territories, and federal support for recapturing fugitive slaves), "strict constructionists about the Constitution," and deeply opposed to emancipation or even the prospect of racial equality, in part because of a commitment to the subordination of the lower orders.[9] Consequently, Lincoln's wartime detractors in the North (e.g., northern Democrats opposed to the war, known as "Copperheads," after the poisonous snake of the same name) and South condemned the president's conduct as commander in chief, but their denunciations never veered far from matters of slavery, race, and associated issues of freedom and equality. Their attacks on Lincoln were intensely personal, racially malicious, and inextricably connected to the president's decision to fight a war to restore a Union in which "emancipation would be the *effect*" of the conflict.[10] To be sure, there were a few abolitionists who sharply criticized the president from an alternative standpoint, one devoted to slavery's immediate, constitutional abolition by the federal government.[11] But compared to Lincoln's conservative enemies, their critique of the president was relatively marginal and never matched the visceral loathing Lincoln's Confederate and Copperhead detractors exhibited. The specific aspects of a tradition of hostility to Lincoln in American life emerged even before the Civil War began, intensified during the long four years of the conflict, and then continued to be reinvigorated in every era since.

Lincoln opened his senatorial campaign against Douglas with a controversial speech about the future of the United States that a few of his friends warned might be perceived as inflammatory and perhaps ought to be excised from the address. Lincoln predicted that "a house divided against itself cannot stand" and that the United States could not "endure, permanently half *slave* and half *free*."[12] Lincoln and Douglas argued throughout their contest about slavery, the central moral and political issue of the 1850s thrust to the forefront of national politics after passage of Douglas's Kansas-Nebraska bill in 1854. Lincoln held that slavery was wrong, that it was harmful to the United States, and that all further expansion of the institution should be halted, placing it on the road to "ultimate extinction."

A fervent believer in American expansionism, Douglas countered that he did not care if slavery existed in the territories and that according to his doctrine of popular sovereignty, if the people of a territory wanted to hold slaves in bondage, they should be allowed to do so. Local control of the institution, in other words, trumped Lincoln's and the antislavery movement's aspiration to "render freedom national, and slavery sectional."[13] The two senatorial hopefuls conducted seven debates across the state of Illinois, exchanges in which each man frequently found himself on the defensive against the other's attacks. Both candidates appeared to agree on the alleged inferiority of blacks and the undesirability of social or political equality for African Americans. Lincoln nevertheless attacked Douglas for his moral indifference to the expansion of slavery, while Douglas relentlessly accused Lincoln of being an abolitionist, a "Black Republican" who wanted full political and social equality for blacks. Douglas sharply contrasted his views with Lincoln when at one debate he asserted that "in my opinion this government [the United States] was made by our fathers on the white basis. It was made by the white men for the benefit of white men and their posterity forever and was intended to be administered by white men in all time to come."[14] Throughout the debates Douglas made it clear that he had no doubt that his interpretation of the founders' sentiments was correct.

Lincoln vigorously disagreed with Douglas's interpretation of the American founding, his apathy regarding the expansion of slavery, and his belief that the indefinite future should hold absolutely no prospect of equality, however small, for African Americans in the United States. Indeed, even before the campaign against Douglas commenced in 1858, Lincoln recommended that Americans "discard all this quibbling about this man and the other man—this race and that race and the other race being inferior, and therefore they must be placed in an inferior position."[15] During their first debate at Ottawa, Lincoln exclaimed that "when he [Douglas] invites any willing people to have slavery, to establish it, he is blowing out the moral lights around us. When he says he 'cares not if slavery is voted down or up,'—that it is a sacred right of self government—he is in my judgment penetrating the human soul and eradicating the light of reason and the love of liberty in this American people."[16] As the nation increasingly attended to the campaign, Lincoln concisely declared slavery "a moral, a social and a political wrong." At the same time, Douglas's continual racial barbs led Lincoln to declare in the fourth debate at Charleston, Illinois, that he was not, "nor ever have been in favor of bringing about in any way

the social and political equality of the white and black races."[17] Perhaps
the Illinois lawyer was catering to the white supremacist prejudices of
his nineteenth-century audience in giving them the impression he shared
their racial outlook, but at Ottawa Lincoln had also claimed that "in the
right to eat the bread, without leave of anybody else, which his [the black
man] own hand earns, *he is my equal and the equal of Judge Douglas, and
the equal of every living man*," and in doing so he steadily and courageously
injected an important notion of equality, albeit limited, into the campaign.
Lincoln hated slavery in part because it permanently fixed a person's
status at birth, or what he called a "fixed condition of labor, for his whole
life," and his hope was that free labor would serve as an acid that would
gradually eat away at antebellum slavery, if not all exploitative forms of
labor.[18] Indeed, a few short years later, in the midst of the Civil War, he
publicly stated that "the perpetuation of African Slavery" was "in fact, a
war upon the rights of all working people."[19] Nevertheless, because of the
words he uttered at Charleston, Lincoln's reputation would become tainted
with the charge of racism for generations, and the accusation developed
into an important method for discrediting the sixteenth president.[20]

Although in 1858 Lincoln wanted the western territories open only
to free white labor, by condemning slavery and expressing his desire to
contain it so that it would eventually die, he was at the very least making
future racial progress in the United States imaginable, perhaps inevitable,
in the minds of many nineteenth-century white Americans—hence, the
opposition to his candidacy and ideas, even among segments of the northern population. In contrast, Douglas's indifference toward slavery and the
plight of all African Americans would have made racial progress virtually
impossible, locking in the status quo—or worse—for a generation, perhaps
longer. Lincoln lost his battle for the Illinois Senate seat in 1858 but was
undoubtedly pleased with his efforts. He told his friend Anson G. Henry
that "it gave me a hearing on the great and durable question of the age,
which I could have had in no other way." Lincoln also predicted to Henry,
perhaps a little disingenuously, that he would "now sink out of view, and
shall be forgotten."[21] Lincoln was hardly forgotten, however, for he had
acquitted himself so well against Douglas that Republican leaders across
the North began to mention his name as a potential presidential candidate
on the Republican ticket in 1860.[22]

Below the Mason-Dixon Line white southern Democrats had for the
most part paid little attention to Lincoln's utterances in 1858. They were
far more interested in Douglas's comments because he was the more

prominent political figure and could plausibly become the next Democratic nominee for president. But once Lincoln was unexpectedly nominated for the presidency by the Republican Party in 1860, white southerners examined more closely his public utterances and spotted therein an abolitionist. To many white southerners Lincoln's "House Divided" speech committed him to abolitionism, differing from abolitionists only in the timing regarding the death of their profitable institution. In Jackson, Mississippi, the *Weekly Mississippian* said as much, referring to Lincoln's "House Divided" speech in the process: "[the] doctrine of the free soil [Republican] party means the total extinction of southern institutions or it means nothing. This doctrine, dangerous, revolutionary and treasonable, was proclaimed by Abraham Lincoln of Illinois briefly in these words: 'I BELIEVE THIS GOVERNMENT CANNOT ENDURE PERMANENTLY HALF SLAVE AND HALF FREE.'" In other words, the newspaper concluded, Republicans believed that "'SLAVERY MUST BE ABOLISHED IN THE SLAVE STATES.'"[23]

The initial expressions of hatred for Lincoln across the South were impersonal, as many across the region cared little about the individual nominated by the Republican Party to be president. Rather, it was the platform of the Republican Party that proclaimed slavery wrong and mandated an end to its expansion that alarmed the white South. Their anxieties would be channeled into hatred for the Republican nominee in 1860, no matter who he was. The fire-eater Edmund Ruffin (1794–1865) explained that it was irrelevant "whether the wily, able and prominent [William Henry] Seward, or the obscure and coarse Lincoln shall be either the first or the second President of the United States, elected by the sectional abolition party of the North."[24] Alexander Stephens (1812–83), the vice president of the Confederacy and someone who was acquainted with Lincoln from their days together in Congress in the 1840s, believed Lincoln would not personally threaten the South's peculiar institution because Lincoln had a "great deal . . . [of] practical common sense. *Still his party may do mischief.*"[25] In a personal letter to Lincoln late in 1860, Stephens told the president-elect that Republican victory nonetheless dishonored the South because it placed "the Institutions of nearly half the States under the ban of public opinion and national condemnation."[26] Jefferson Davis bespoke similar thoughts shortly after Mississippi seceded in early 1861, when the future president of the Confederacy observed that Lincoln "was nothing save as he was the representative of opinions, of a policy, of purpose, of power, to inflict upon us those wrongs to which freemen never tamely submit."[27] So, it was extremely unlikely that *any* candidate nominated by the Republicans would have been viewed favorably by white southerners in the summer and fall of 1860. The Lower South was rightly fearful that any Republican president—Abraham Lincoln or William Henry Seward of New York or Salmon P. Chase of Ohio or any other Republican one could imagine—would use the powers of the executive to halt the extension of slavery in its tracks (thereby rendering freedom national and slavery local) and the powers of patronage to build a party in the region opposed to southern slaveholding interests.[28] White southerners were likewise concerned that a Republican president opposed to slavery's extension would irrevocably alter the delicate balance of power between the sections to the disadvantage of the South. Ever since the Constitution was written and ratified in the 1780s, the South had more or less dominated the politics of the United States, but now the North had a majority of the population and electoral votes. A Republican victory in 1860 threatened continued southern domination.[29]

Added to these perceived woes was the ongoing drain of slaves from the Upper South to the Lower South in the decades prior to the 1860 election, as slaveholding southerners from states such as Virginia sold their surplus bondsmen and women southward. Viewing this trend with alarm, secessionists across the cotton kingdom worried that in the future the Upper South would inevitably be less attached to the institution of slavery. Coupled with this concern was an acute anxiety that efforts to colonize Africans outside the United States would likewise serve to leave the Lower South not only as a minority within the country but an encircled and endangered minority surrounded by a "cordon of freedom" whose existence would be threatened by the abandonment of the Upper South and a supposedly dishonorable North.[30] The *Texas State Gazette* in Austin, on the eve of the 1860 election, asked its readers to think of the consequences if Lincoln, "the deadly enemy of the institution of slavery, the wicked sympathizer of [abolitionist] John Brown, the apostle of murder, arson, and servile war, the chosen chief of associated traitors, shall wield the high powers of the executive branch of the federal Government, shall control its vast patronage, and command the Army and Navy" of the United States.[31] Attacking Lincoln, the Republican nominee and the representative of a movement committed to the eventual destruction of slavery in the United States, was a useful, if not necessary, method by which white southerners discredited a "Black Republican Party" they correctly deemed opposed to their political, racial, and pecuniary interests.[32]

Consequently, many white southerners targeted Lincoln personally as the embodiment of their worst fears and spewed malice toward the antislavery candidate in the form of ad hominem attacks on his appearance. One North Carolina paper, the *Newbern Weekly Progress,* hissed that Lincoln was "coarse, vulgar and uneducated," while the *San Antonio Ledger and Texan* said he was "a bold, vulgar, unscrupulous abolitionist," and the *Houston Telegraph* described Lincoln as "the leanest, lankiest, most ungainly mass of legs, arms and hatchet face ever strung upon a single frame. He has most unwarrantably abused the privilege which all politicians have of being ugly."[33] Not to be outdone by such descriptions, in February 1861 the *Daily Delta* in New Orleans lamented Lincoln's election and sniffed "that the debasement of being ruled over by such a President—the disgust of having to look up to such a Chief Magistrate as the head of the Republic" warranted disunion.[34] The diarist Mary Boykin Chesnut repeated in her journal the comments of a friend who heard "from all quarters that the vulgarity of Lincoln, his wife, and his son is beyond credence, a thing you must see before you can believe it," while a female companion said the president was "ugly, even grotesque in appearance, the kind who are always at the corner stores, sitting on boxes, whittling sticks, and telling stories as funny as they are vulgar."[35] Such caricatures conveyed a man so ugly and uncouth that it seemed incredulous that he could win the presidency.

In a sense the personal attacks on Lincoln were unsurprising given the importance of the issues at stake in the 1860 election and the partisan nature of newspapers in nineteenth-century America. Certainly, there was an element of morale building and exhortation to resistance in the numerous remarks of white southerners. It was striking that southern writers used similar language or rhetoric to express their disapproval of the president-elect. Indeed, because of his exposure to such derogatory accounts of Lincoln's countenance, when Virginian Charles Browne Fleet witnessed the inauguration on March 4, 1861, in Washington, D.C., he noted in a letter to his brother his surprise at the president's appearance: "I wish you had been here yesterday, Old Abe was put through all right and is now our *master* (think of that). He is a much better looking man than he is represented in the papers to be, not being so extraordinarily tall, nor having such a very long neck either."[36] Words such as *disgust, vulgar,* and *coarse* were used repeatedly to describe Lincoln, words that would never be used to describe a gentleman. Editors across the South clearly believed that using such pejorative terms would sway their subscribers, demonstrating beyond all doubt Lincoln's unfitness to be president. In addition to Lincoln's views on slavery, which prospective Confederates found galling and in their view disqualified him from high office, equally prohibitive was his homely appearance, low social station, and lack of gentility, which they associated with a lack of honor.[37] White southerners were intent on denigrating Lincoln's appearance, for to do so was to disparage a man they believed would dishonor the office of president and jeopardize their region, not to mention the "Founders' white Republic."[38]

Lincoln was in essence a political symbol that threatened rather than reassured white southerners, not to mention their ideological compatriots in the North. Lincoln's frontier background in itself may have alarmed some Americans, especially slaveholders. If a man of Lincoln's ignoble upbringing could become president, overturning traditional social hierarchies, then other hierarchies based on race and gender might likewise be upended. Of course, there had been previous presidents from less than aristocratic families, namely Andrew Jackson. But Jackson was himself a slaveholder, and the Democratic Party he led was scarcely a mortal threat to either slavery or the white South's national political dominance. Lincoln, in contrast, endangered both. White southern slaveholders, if not a majority of white southerners, along with northern Democrats, opposed his election because of his ignoble background, the principles he espoused, and the potentially new American nation they correctly believed his candidacy represented. And as the war progressed and it became increasingly clear that Lincoln's policies were aligned with the cause of African American freedom, their loathing of Lincoln intensified accordingly and became more racialized.[39]

Mindful of the verbal attacks on his physical features and background, Lincoln was aware of the threat of personal violence. In rejecting a request from Samuel Haycraft in 1860 that he visit the state of his birth, Kentucky, Lincoln asked, perhaps jokingly, "Would it be safe? Would not the people lynch me?"[40] While white southerners could not actually lynch Lincoln, they did perpetrate violence on him in absentia, suggesting Lincoln was wise to sneak into Washington, D.C., before his inauguration without notice.[41] Jack Campbell of Marshall, Texas, related to a friend in January 1861 that "last night [it] rained *and* hailed . . . yet it seemed somebody was not afraid of the storms for on my arrival in the public *square this morning the* first object that greeted my eyes was a figure or manikin *hanging by* the neck to a regularly constructed gallows . . . eyes bandaged *and* labeled on the breast Abraham Lincoln."[42] Several months later, in the capital of Lincoln's birthplace, Frankfort, Kentucky, John C. Wardlaw, a senior cadet at the Kentucky Military Institute, wrote his father that "we have but little local news except the *hanging, shooting,* and *burning, of Lincoln* in effigy today, by almost the whole school." One resident of Pensacola, Florida, went so far as to send the president-elect the message: "You were last night hung in effigy in this city."[43] Lincoln's body had become a popular target for the South's hostility.

Amelia Barr was living in Austin, Texas, in 1861 when she wrote to a South Carolina friend proudly relating her response to a Texas Unionist who had told her that Lincoln was a good man who read the Bible daily: "I told him I thought him much *too good* for this wicked world," Barr drily noted, "and I prayed most sincerely that he ought to go to heaven before he went to Washington."[44] Such hostile expressions toward Lincoln, although ominous, were not surprising. Once the Confederacy had been formed, Confederates devoutly believed that theirs was a Christian nation divinely sanctioned by the Almighty. Indeed, as early as 1850, southern theologian James Henley Thornwell anticipated such a stance: "The parties in this conflict are not merely Abolitionists and Slaveholders; they are Atheists, Socialists, Communists, Red Republicans, Jacobins on the one side, and the friends of order and regulated freedom on the other. In one word, the world is the battle ground, Christianity and Atheism the combatants, and the progress of humanity the stake."[45] Consequently, in the minds of many white southerners, "Resistance to Lincoln" was to some extent "obedience to God" and in all likelihood considered a religious duty. This theological interpretation of the war as a conflict between an atheist North and Christian South would enjoy a long life and influence Lincoln's adversaries for generations.[46]

During the 1860 election derision of the president emanated from northern Democrats as well. They excoriated Lincoln and focused their sensationalistic vituperation not only on the candidate's personal characteristics but also on Lincoln's (and the Republican Party's) policies and their potential consequences. One of the most important Democratic newspapers in Illinois, the Springfield *Illinois State Register,* compared the Republican Party's platform of halting the extension of slavery into the territories to a menu and said that if the people of Illinois voted Republican, they would find "nigger in the soups, nigger in the substantials, nigger in the desert [*sic*]—Lincoln and nigger equality all through."[47] The *New York Herald* claimed the Republican Party stood for "an equalization of the

white and black races—which has never produced anything but bloodshed
in other parts of the world, and which can only result in the subjugation or
destruction of the numerically weaker race" and predicted that Lincoln's
election would lead to "anarchy, civil war, the rule of the military tyrant
and the public robber."[48] Also in New York, signs on ambulatory wagons
proclaimed the warnings:

> "Republican Principle—'The Negro better than the White Man,' Republican
> Practice—'Union of Black and White.'"
> "What 'Free Negro Suffrage' Really Means—'Amalgamation in the Military.
> Amalgamation in the Fire Department. Amalgamation in the Social Circle.'"
> "No Negro Equality." . . .
> "Free Love, Free Niggers, and Free Women!"[49]

Democrat Theodore R. Westbrook posited that the "only argument advanced by the Republicans is 'Freedom, Freedom, Freedom—Darky, darky,
darky.' Indeed, they have a darky for breakfast, darky for dinner, darky
for supper, and darky for bed-fellows."[50] Northern Democrats associated
the Republican candidate with the end of slavery and the prospect of racial
equality, coupled with the sexual mixing of races. Their fear and loathing
of Lincoln, although not precisely the same as white southern hatred, was
similar in that both viewed his election as a prelude to apocalypse.

To be sure, some abolitionists sharply criticized Abraham Lincoln before and during the campaign, but such criticism hardly amounted to a
deep-seated loathing for the Illinois lawyer. There was a broad spectrum
of antislavery opinion in the United States in 1860, and as the Republican
candidate for president, Abraham Lincoln was now the leader of an increasingly powerful and largely democratic antislavery cause. The black
abolitionist H. Ford Douglas had been bitingly contemptuous of Lincoln
during his 1858 race against Stephen Douglas, saying that he did not
"believe in the anti-slavery of Abraham Lincoln, because he is on the side
of the Slave Power," noting with considerable hostility Lincoln's earlier
refusal to sign a petition allowing black men to testify against whites in
Illinois courts.[51] Still, the abolitionist Douglas equated Lincoln's political success with that of the antislavery movement more generally.[52] And
although Wendell Phillips once called Lincoln that "slave-hound from Illinois," in reference to Lincoln's willingness to enforce the controversial
Fugitive Slave Law that had engendered considerable opposition across
the North to the South's peculiar institution, other antislavery figures had
criticized him for taking such a stance.[53] William Lloyd Garrison, the most

prominent abolitionist in the country, at first said that the Republican Party "means to do nothing, can *do nothing, for the abolition of slavery in the slave states,*" but during the 1860 presidential campaign Garrison's newspaper, the *Liberator,* altered this viewpoint, writing that Lincoln's election would "do no slight service to the cause of freedom; and to that extent, and for that reason, it has our sympathies and best wishes."[54] Others were much less optimistic than Garrison about Lincoln and the Republicans. Frederick Douglass, the noted former slave and orator, told fellow antislavery advocate Gerrit Smith, "I cannot support Lincoln" in the 1860 election, while abolitionist minister Parker Pillsbury exclaimed to an audience the same year, "I stand here to-day to give it as my deliberate opinion that in voting for Abraham Lincoln, you as effectually vote for slavery as you would in voting for [Democratic candidate] Stephen A. Douglas."[55] Yet by the election of 1860 the large majority of abolitionists had little alternative but to be firmly behind Lincoln and the Republican Party. The abolitionists and Lincoln were on the same antislavery road, even if they were not necessarily always traveling at the same speed.[56] Although they at times displayed disapproval with Lincoln, abolitionists tended to focus their criticism more on the president's seeming tardiness in implementing their shared antislavery policies and less on his personal characteristics. In contrast to Confederates and northern Democrats, their disdain for Lincoln, such as it was, diminished over the course of the war and far less often displayed the personal venom that the president's wartime opponents frequently employed.[57]

One clue about why a small fraction of abolitionists criticized Lincoln can be found in the writings of Lysander Spooner (1808–87), a radical anarchist from Massachusetts. In 1845 Spooner had written an influential pamphlet entitled *The Unconstitutionality of Slavery,* in which he argued that slavery was illegal because it violated the slaves' natural rights of life, liberty, and the pursuit of happiness mentioned in the Declaration of Independence and that the Constitution had not explicitly established bondage as legal.[58] Accordingly, slavery was unconstitutional and should enjoy no legal protection in the United States. Thirteen years later, in 1858, Spooner penned a "Plan for the Abolition of Slavery" that recommended, among other things, that slaves rebel against their masters and told whites they had a duty to assist the bondsmen in their revolt. In 1859, after John Brown had been captured during his raid at Harpers Ferry, Virginia, Spooner implored the state's governor, Henry Wise, not to execute the imprisoned abolitionist. Wise rejected Spooner's appeal, whereupon

the Massachusetts anarchist considered kidnapping Wise and trading
him for Brown.[59] Lincoln, by way of contrast, did not object to Brown's
execution; "even though he agreed with us in thinking slavery wrong," he
wrote, "that cannot excuse violence, bloodshed, and treason. It could avail
him nothing that he might think himself right."[60] Shortly after Brown's
death, in a letter written early in 1860 to Republican presidential candidate
William Seward, Spooner argued that Republicans—including, presumably, Lincoln—were naive, frauds, if they thought they could "aid liberty,
without injuring slavery; who imagine that they can even be champions
of freedom at the north, and at the same time avowedly protect slavery in
the south, 'where it is'; and that they can thus ride into power on the two
horses of Liberty and Slavery."[61] Clearly, Spooner and Lincoln agreed that
the slaves were humans who possessed basic natural rights, rights that
the institution grossly violated. Their disagreement centered on whether
the Constitution protected slavery. Spooner argued emphatically it did
not and thought the federal government could therefore constitutionally
abolish the institution, while Lincoln and the vast majority of the antislavery movement reasoned otherwise.[62] Lincoln also eschewed violence as a
method for ending slavery, although if secession occurred and as a result
war began, military emancipation would become a distinct possibility;
rather, he favored a measured, democratic approach that foresaw a role
for the state in containing the institution so that it would die, colonizing
blacks overseas, and compensating slaveholders for their loss of property.
Although Lincoln and Spooner never met, the philosophical disagreement
between the two men endured and foreshadowed criticism of the president
emanating from libertarians of an anarchist disposition.[63]

Hence, if Lincoln was too radical on the issue of slavery for northern
Democrats and white southerners, he was too hypocritical or equivocating or misinterpreted the Constitution for a minority of abolitionists.
Lincoln was nevertheless able to win the presidency because he *appeared*
to be moderate enough on slavery to be palatable for northern voters. The
president-elect took office on March 4, 1861, after winning approximately
40 percent of the popular vote across the country and 54 percent of the
vote in the North, alongside a sizable victory in the Electoral College.[64]
Lincoln was now the head of a relatively new party faced with significant
opposition in the northern states coupled with threats of secession in the
South. Indeed, seven lower southern states seceded after Lincoln's election.
Immediately after taking office, Lincoln was confronted with the problem
of what to do about the presence of Union troops in Fort Sumter, in

Charleston, South Carolina, and if they ought to be resupplied or evacuated. After much agonizing and indecisiveness in March and early April 1861, Lincoln chose to reequip the fort with nonmilitary supplies only—"food for hungry men," the president called it—and the war commenced after Confederates fired on the fort. The "counter-revolution of property" had begun.[65]

For various reasons Confederates then and later charged President Lincoln and his secretary of state, William Henry Seward, with "duplicity and treachery," all aimed at maneuvering the Confederates into beginning the war at Fort Sumter. From one Confederate standpoint, indirect communications from Seward in the spring of 1861 had led Confederate commissioners in Washington, D.C., to believe that the fort would be evacuated while he and Lincoln deceitfully plotted to resupply the garrison. Jefferson Davis said as much when he told the Confederate Congress that "the crooked paths of diplomacy can scarcely furnish an example so wanting in courtesy, in candor, and directness as was the course of the United States Government toward our commissioners in Washington."[66] Others thought Lincoln sent ships to Charleston in order to ensure federal tariffs were paid: "What about the revenue? What about the collection of duties?" Lincoln anxiously queried Virginian John B. Baldwin before the firing on Sumter.[67] To Confederates this proved that the war was not fought to preserve the Union or to eradicate slavery but for less noble, worldlier reasons: specifically, for tariffs, and more generally, to centralize power in Washington, D.C. Based on Baldwin's account of his interview with Lincoln, these Confederates also believed that Lincoln did not possess the strength to resist the will of the Radicals in his own party who wanted war, and so he proceeded to resupply the fort even though he knew it would cause the Border States to secede.[68] It is interesting that Confederates did not draw a distinction between Lincoln and the Radicals. They *equated* the two, although they viewed the president as the Radicals' dupe rather than their leader. At any rate, from the Confederate perspective Lincoln became the initiator of the terrible war that followed. As such, he served as a scapegoat for the white South in ways that no other northerner, including politicians Salmon Chase, William Henry Seward, Thaddeus Stevens, and Charles Sumner or Union officers Ben Butler, Ulysses S. Grant, and William Tecumseh Sherman, ever could. For Confederates, Lincoln embodied all the harm and hurt that came their way. Lincoln caused secession; Lincoln caused the war; Lincoln caused the emancipation of the slaves and upended the traditional social order; Lincoln caused Confederate prisoners of war to languish and die in northern prisons; Lincoln caused the untold suffering and degradation the South suffered under Butler and Sherman, for he was the commander in chief who authorized their criminal depredations.[69] These accusations of Lincoln's alleged malfeasance, born during the war, would outlive the president's administration and endure into the twenty-first century.

In the North whatever ambivalence and suspicion existed regarding President Lincoln temporarily disappeared with the Confederate attack on Fort Sumter in April 1861. Still, Lincoln's presidency was characterized by sharp and vicious attacks on his person, methods, and policies. As the war continued and casualties mounted, he found himself criticized by the same groups that had vilified him before and during his election: white southerners; northern Democrats opposed to the war, the so-called Copperheads; and a small number of abolitionists. Of course, Lincoln was condemned for different reasons by these groups. White southerners as well as northerners attacked the president for his alleged tyrannical abuse of power and for supposedly waging an inhumane war on the southern people. In the North verbal and pictorial assaults at times degenerated into racist caricatures, as it became clear that slavery would be eradicated and some measure of black equality was seen as a possibility.[70] This was perhaps most evident in an 1864 lithograph entitled *Miscegenation; or, The Millennium of Abolitionism,* which showed Lincoln mingling with an African American female in a verdant park.[71] A few abolitionists at times expressed frustration with Lincoln's alleged timidity in waging and perhaps losing the war, not to mention his apparent reluctance to strike an immediate blow against slavery, the very institution they rightly believed had precipitated the conflict. As the Radical senator Benjamin Wade of Ohio told Lincoln early in the war, "Mr. President, you are murdering your country by inches in consequence of the inactivity of the military and the want of a distinct policy in regard to slavery."[72] But as the war progressed and the permanent emancipation of the slaves became a distinct possibility, such dissatisfaction with the president, although it undoubtedly existed, faded and became relatively marginal.

Critics in the North voiced hostility to Lincoln amid accusations of tyranny, when, in April 1861, the newly inaugurated president suspended the writ of habeas corpus between the cities of Washington, D.C., and Philadelphia, engendering some of the strongest criticism of his presidency then or since. When John Merryman, a Confederate sympathizer and the grandson of Francis Scott Key, was arrested in 1861 in Baltimore,

Maryland, a hotbed of Confederate sympathizers and underground activity, Merryman sued for a writ of habeas corpus in federal court. Roger B. Taney, the chief justice of the U.S. Supreme Court, shortly thereafter issued a decision in *Ex parte Merryman* claiming that the military could not arrest civilians and that since the article of the Constitution under which suspension of the writ is allowed was specified in the legislative section of the document, Lincoln had acted unconstitutionally.[73] Lincoln, much to the chagrin of numerous northerners, simply disregarded Taney's decision.[74] Later in the war, in 1863, Lincoln, with congressional authorization, suspended the writ across the entire United States, provoking a storm of protest and outrage throughout the country. One Ohioan denounced Lincoln's administration as "a despotism, more odious than has ever disgraced the civilization of any age of the world."[75] In a public letter written in June 1863 to Erastus Corning, the president vigorously defended the broadened suspension of habeas corpus and the arrest of Clement L. Vallandigham, a notorious Ohio Copperhead, asking "Must I shoot a simple-minded soldier boy who deserts, while I must not touch a hair of a wiley agitator who induces him to desert?"[76] Still, Lincoln's suspension of habeas corpus was widely condemned, then and later, as future presidents who faced far less serious crises used Lincoln's policies to justify their own civil liberties violations.[77]

Numerous abolitionists continued to have deep misgivings about the president's public support for the voluntary colonization of blacks outside the United States, a policy that contradicted the more ethnically pluralistic nationalism to which the war pointed. In August 1862 Lincoln invited to the White House several African American leaders from Washington, D.C., the first time such an event had occurred in the nation's history. In what historian James Oakes has characterized as a "staged" performance for white "public consumption," the president told his five-man audience that they should consider colonization outside the United States, preferably to a colony in Central America. Lincoln expressed that because of white racism, blacks were suffering "the greatest wrong inflicted on any people," and "but for your race among us there could not be war." He pessimistically predicted that he saw little hope for the future regarding improved prospects for African Americans. "It is better for us both, therefore, to be separated," Lincoln concluded.[78] Lincoln's abolitionist critics were incensed and publicly expressed their anger with the president. Earlier in the war Lincoln had angered William Lloyd Garrison, as he had previously angered Lysander Spooner, for not taking the opportunity offered by the conflict to end slavery immediately, going so far as to say that although Lincoln "is 6 feet 4 inches high, he is only a dwarf in mind."[79] Lincoln's colonization proposal confirmed the abolitionist's low opinion of the president and was a consequence—and here Garrison joined Lincoln's Confederate critics in disparaging the president's background—of his previous associations, with the "white trash" of Kentucky.[80] One northern African American angrily reminded the president that "this is our country as much as it is yours and we will not leave it."[81] Members of Lincoln's cabinet and Frederick Douglass alike echoed these sentiments. Secretary of the Treasury Salmon P. Chase confided in his diary that the president's colonization proposal lacked courage and was unmanly, while Douglass exclaimed that the president's proposal was the perfect example of Lincoln's "contempt for Negroes and canting hypocrisy."[82] Much worse, according to Douglass, was that Lincoln's White House address excused "the ignorant and base, who need only the countenance of men in authority to commit all kinds of violence and outrage upon the colored people of the country."[83]

Nevertheless, after the United States army endured a series of military setbacks in the first year of the war and following a Union victory at the Battle of Antietam on September 17, 1862, Lincoln issued a preliminary Emancipation Proclamation five days later, warning Confederates that if they did not return to the Union by January 1, 1863, he would forever free their slaves. The president of the Confederacy, Jefferson Davis, worried aloud to the Confederate Congress that Lincoln's proclamation would encourage slave revolts. The *Richmond Enquirer* agreed with the Confederate president, editorializing in October 1862 that Lincoln was in essence a fiendish murderer.[84] Similarly, the *Raleigh (N.C.) Standard* called the act for which Lincoln became most famous a "monstrously wicked" edict.[85] After Lincoln signed the final Emancipation Proclamation on New Year's Day 1863, Davis told the Confederate Congress that it was "a measure by which several millions of human beings of an inferior race, peaceful and contented laborers in their sphere, are doomed to extermination, while at the same time they are encouraged to a general assassination of their masters. . . . Our own detestation of those who have attempted the most execrable measure recorded in the history of guilty man is tempered by profound contempt for the impotent rage which it discloses."[86] Davis's association of Lincoln's proclamation with excrement accords perfectly with the Confederate view of the president as vulgar and disgusting, just as the suggestion of impotence implied ungentlemanly behavior, or unmanliness, on Lincoln's part. No doubt this explains why the *Richmond Enquirer,* in its

October 1862 editorial, compared Lincoln unfavorably with Caesar, Oliver Cromwell, and Napoléon, men who, the *Enquirer* claimed, "never attempted a revolution so astounding." From the Confederate perspective Lincoln was no reluctant emancipator but "one of the smallest" men in history.[87]

Several months after Lincoln issued the Emancipation Proclamation, southern newspapers continued ranting against what they thought was the president's infamous act. *The Lincoln Catechism,* a scathing review of the president's wartime policies published in question-and-answer format throughout the South in the spring of 1863, referred explicitly to Lincoln's apparent disregard for the Constitution and supposed desire for racial equality:

Q. What is the President?

A. A general agent for Negroes.

Q. What is Congress?

A. A body organized for the purpose of appropriating funds to buy Africans, and to make laws to protect the President from being punished for any violations of law he may be guilty of. . . .

Q. What are the particular duties of a Commander-in-Chief?

A. To disgrace any general who does not believe that the negro is better than a white man.

Q. What is the meaning of the word "law?"

A. The will of the President. . . .

Q. Have the people any rights?

A. None, except what the President gives.

Q. What is the *habeas corpus?*

A. It is the power of the President to imprison whom he pleases.[88]

In the fall of 1863 the *Southern Illustrated News* published a poem about the proclamation entitled "Issued by the Tyrant Lincoln," which described Lincoln's "tyrant's blood-washed hands" petitioning for God's blessing on such heinous acts as "murder, rapine, [and] blood."[89]

The proclamation confirmed the Confederacy's worst fears, and now Lincoln was caricatured, demonized, and dehumanized across the South in poems and broadsides.[90] In a region where most whites were convinced of Lincoln's tyrannical presidency and vulgar character, it is reasonable to assume that many of the attacks on the president were not only intended to boost morale or to denigrate the enemy; they also served as a reflection of, and outlet for, Confederate rage at his person. In one broadside entitled "The Despot's Song!" published in Baltimore in March 1862, "Ole Secesh" characterized Lincoln as a liar and drunkard (even though the president more or less abstained from alcohol) and concluded with Lincoln begging the Confederate president Jefferson Davis to surrender "to all my oppression / My weakness and sin!"[91] Other poems, especially those published after the Emancipation Proclamation's issuance, elaborated on similar themes of Lincoln's dictatorship and vulgar or buffoonish character. The *Southern Literary Messenger* published "ABE'S PROCLAMATION" in response to the freeing of slaves in the Confederacy and alluded to the alleged ineffectiveness of the act:

> The slaves now under Lincoln's will,
> Continue in their bondage still;
> He only means—the tricky wretch,
> To set those free he cannot catch.[92]

White southerners insisted that only a fool would proclaim slaves to be free in areas over which he had no control.

Most Confederates nevertheless denounced the proclamation as a criminal edict and associated Lincoln with Satan for its issuance, belying the idea advanced then and later that the document was of little consequence. Significantly, some whites focused their critique on Lincoln's personal background in connection with the edict. The *Daily-Mississippian* published a lengthy piece signed by "Cicilian" on January 21, 1863, almost three weeks after Lincoln's decree went into effect, entitled "The Pedigree of Abraham Lincoln." The president's genealogist opined that "an object of so much abhorrence to the Southern people as the man or animal now disgracing the Presidency of the North must excite some curiosity as to his history—some desire to learn whence and how he came into public life, who and what he is." The author reminded his audience that both Lincoln and the Confederate president, Jefferson Davis, were born in Kentucky but emphasized their differences. Davis was characterized as noble, while Lincoln was described as coming from a family that "is one of the lowest and most disreputable in that State [Kentucky]." Following a cursory and wildly inaccurate review of Lincoln's early life, Cicilian explained that Lincoln had once been a "grocery-store keeper." This background, the author argued, was the key to understanding Lincoln and the proclamation. "Here was the schoolhouse of the future President of the United States," Cicilian noted with disgust, "this the vestibule of that Temple whose god is the Devil, whose doctrines were hypocrisy and lust, a doctrine that has culminated in the proclamation of the 1st of January, 1863, inviting servile insurrection with its train of unmentionable calamities and dark and damnable deeds, which will at least lead its votary to the fate of a Robespierre, a Marat, or a John Brown."[93] For Cicilian, as for most Confederates, the proclamation was characterized as "a stupendous crime, a curse to his [Lincoln's] name to which the infamy of a Nero or a Caligula will be light and harmless. . . . Hereafter the name of Lincoln will sound every depth and shoal of infamy and crime."[94] Denigrating Lincoln's frontier upbringing and associating the president with John Brown, French Revolutionaries, and tyrannical Roman emperors characterized the malicious commentary uttered by Lincoln's critics in the immediate aftermath of his assassination and remained a staple of loathing for Lincoln long after the war concluded.

In one well-known woodcut, published in the *Southern Illustrated News* on November 8, 1862, Lincoln was depicted as Satan, wreaking death and destruction on the South.[95] Another drawing, originally entitled "The Prince of Darkness" and published in *Southern Punch,* likewise portrayed Lincoln as Lucifer kidnapping Lady Liberty. The justification given for the illustration was that Lincoln had rebelled against the Constitution just as Satan was "the first to Rebel against constituted authority."[96] Of course, as historian Drew Gilpin Faust has noted, constituted authority and power in the antebellum South had always been exercised by white males, as part of a divinely ordained "paternalistic social order" that was supposed to protect white women.[97] The war, emancipation, and Abraham Lincoln upset this long-standing arrangement. As a result, privileged women became contemptuous of northerners and viewed the emancipated slaves—if not Lincoln himself—as diabolical. "I doubt if history affords a parallel to the deep and bitter enmity of the women of the South," General Sherman observed. "No one who sees them and hears them but must feel the intensity of their hate."[98] Such hatred extended to a potentially insubordinate slave population—"demonic invasion," Mississippi women called it—and to the black Union soldiers who actually invaded and occupied their homeland.[99] Given these wartime realities, Abraham Lincoln had become the enemy, and a satanic one at that. Indeed, some women refused to attend church because they would be required to hear prayers for their wartime adversary. "I haven't been to Church for 3 years on that account," Mary W. M. Bell told her husband.[100] Praying for President Lincoln, or even hearing such entreaties spoken aloud, could be felt as a betrayal of their religious beliefs. The elite white women of the South loathed Lincoln with an unmatched intensity. Not only had he invaded their homeland with armed forces; he had freed their slaves and destroyed their way of life. In the decades after the war concluded, these women and their descendants would become Lincoln's most vociferous detractors.[101]

It was not only white southerners who depicted President Lincoln as a demonic figure, as the German American dentist-turned-cartoonist Adalbert Johann Volck (1828–1912), an illustrator living in Baltimore, demonstrated.[102] Volck issued some of the most graphic anti-Lincoln cartoons ever made, including the preinaugural image of a frightened Lincoln scurrying into Baltimore in 1861 in the dead of night disguised in a Scotch plaid cap in order to avoid assassination. More famous, at least later, was Volck's "Writing the Emancipation Proclamation," which depicted Lincoln penning his infamous edict with a demon nearby and a slew of unsavory characters or elements in the background, including the statue of an ape, John Brown's portrait, and liquor on a table, all in close proximity to Lincoln's desk.[103] Because Volck lived in Baltimore, where Lincoln had suspended habeas corpus, and the illustrator could possibly have faced arrest for his work, his iconoclastic illustrations were probably seen by only a few hundred people.[104] They nonetheless demonstrated the intense rage that Lincoln's background and policies provoked among his contemporaries and would become an important part of postwar anti-Lincoln iconography.[105]

Not to be outdone by Confederates, some northern Democrats, whose racial beliefs had been challenged, issued their own criticism of Lincoln's Emancipation Proclamation. Democratic newspapers across the North in 1862–63 called the proclamation "a criminal wrong" and an "act of national suicide" and, in a criticism similar to that of the Confederates, noted that it would "excite the ridicule that follows impotency."[106] One Ohio newspaper, in response to the proclamation, thought that abolitionists should be hanged "till the flesh rot off their bones and the winds of Heaven whistle Yankee Doodle through their loathsome skelitonz [sic]," while Horatio Seymour, the Democratic candidate for governor of New York, said the proclamation was "a proposal for the butchery of women and children, for scenes of lust and rapine, and of arson and murder."[107] Others called for Lincoln's assassination, while newspapers in Lincoln's home state of Illinois denounced the act, with one sarcastically rejoicing, "The niggers are free!"[108] Hence, by the middle of the war Lincoln was scathingly attacked from many sides for the very act for which he would become most praised. And the criticism and threats of violence toward the sixteenth president increased as the war progressed and the birth of a new, more inclusive, and pluralistic American nation seemed more and more likely.

The mixing of races—or worse—was precisely what troubled many people about emancipation. Chauncey Burr, the editor of a magazine in New York City, the *Old Guard,* predicted that freeing the slaves would lead to a mongrel American nation "of whites, negroes, mulattoes, and sambos . . . the most degrading and contemptible people the world ever saw."[109] Farther south, in Maryland, one Catholic archbishop saw racial apocalypse as inevitable. Lincoln's Emancipation Proclamation, he averred, would let "loose from three to four millions of half civilized Africans to murder their Masters and Mistresses!"[110] Later in the war, as the military conflict drew to a close, a newspaper in the state, sneering at a black man speaking to the Maryland House of Representatives, queried: "Shall we have a civilized gorilla next? How long before Lincoln will invite them [blacks] to diplomatic dinners and lead the way with a greasy wench hanging on his arm?"[111]

The fears of Lincoln's critics were not groundless, insofar as the Emancipation Proclamation converted Union soldiers, white and black, into armies of liberation and undoubtedly led to the destruction of slavery in the United States. The advance of Union armies into Confederate territory meant freedom at once for those held nearby in inhuman bondage and the potential imposition of a totally new social order. The proclamation therefore had an incalculable effect across the country in that it was a military, diplomatic, moral, and psychological asset for the United States in its fight against the Confederacy.[112] Equally important, as contemporary comments demonstrate, the proclamation foreshadowed—or was a logical consequence of—the concept of a new American nation reborn from the war, one that included African Americans as citizens in the national community. Again, this was precisely what made the document so controversial, for when Lincoln's critics used dehumanizing language to describe the president, they were by implication dehumanizing the new freedmen as well, which would have ominous consequences for African Americans in the postwar era.[113]

People in the North as well as the South clearly understood the proclamation's importance, and Lincoln was celebrated by some as much as he was denigrated by others for issuing the document.[114] Abolitionists lauded Lincoln's proclamation and were overjoyed with what Lincoln had accomplished with a stroke of the presidential pen, even if they remained critical of the proclamation's uninspired language and limited scope. Frederick Douglass argued that Lincoln had missed a golden opportunity. "Had there been one expression of sound moral feeling against Slavery,"

Douglass lamented, "one word of regret and shame that this accursed system had remained so long the disgrace and scandal of the Republic, one word of satisfaction in the hope of burying slavery and the rebellion in one common grave, a thrill of joy would have run round the world, but no such word was said, and no such joy was kindled."[115] Similarly, black abolitionist James Hudson wrote to the editor of the *Pacific Appeal* in California, calling Lincoln "an incompetent President" and the proclamation "a halfway measure" that gave freedom to slaves "beyond the reach of our arms" concluding that if Lincoln had freed every slave in the country, Americans could "have invoked God's blessing upon our arms, and we could then have boldly claimed the services of every loyal man, white or black, in suppressing this hell-born and heaven-defying rebellion."[116] Worried about the loss of the border slave states' continued loyalty to the Union and the constitutionality of a presidential order freeing slaves, Lincoln justified the proclamation narrowly as a military measure and liberated slaves only in those areas, as William Seward had noted, not under Union control. Almost certainly Lincoln did not want to punish slaveholders who had remained loyal to the Union, yet he did want them to free their slaves and offered them financial compensation to give them an incentive to abolish the institution within their states.[117]

Despite such seeming limitations, the vast majority of abolitionists were euphoric: "At last the proclamation has come," Massachusetts senator Charles Sumner exclaimed. "The skies are brighter and the air is purer, now that slavery has been handed over to judgment."[118] Benjamin Wade, like Sumner a Radical Republican, exulted, "Hurrah for Old Abe and the *proclamation*," while William Lloyd Garrison opined in 1863 that the proclamation was "a great historic event, sublime in its magnitude, momentous and beneficent in its consequences."[119] Writing to Frederick Douglass from Tennessee, black abolitionist and Illinois soldier H. Ford Douglas declared that "Abraham Lincoln has crossed the Rubicon and by one simple act of Justice to the slave links his memory with immortality." Douglas predicted that the Civil War "will educate Mr. Lincoln out of his idea of the deportation of the Negro, quite as fast as it has some of his other proslavery ideas with respect to employing them as soldiers."[120] Notwithstanding his reservations about Lincoln's shortcomings, Douglass proclaimed in a speech at the Cooper Union in New York City that the Emancipation Proclamation was "the greatest event in our nation's history."[121]

Lincoln and the abolitionists constituted a democratic coalition that ended slavery, even as Americans agonized over the terrible casualties resulting from the conflict.[122] Although for the remainder of the war there were intermittent conflicts between the two, they were inextricably committed to ensuring that freedom for all Americans became permanent, and abolitionist criticism of the president diminished accordingly. As for the president's view of abolitionists, in May 1864 Lincoln supported a monument for Congressman Owen Lovejoy from Illinois, perhaps the most radical member of the House of Representatives. In a letter indicative of his attitude toward antislavery radicals, Lincoln wrote of his "increasing respect and esteem" for Lovejoy, adding that "he was my most generous friend" and that he deserved "the marble monument, along with the well-assured and more enduring one in the hearts of those who love liberty, unselfishly, for all men."[123] Such an expansive notion of freedom did not exist among slaveholding Confederates (a group Lincoln had only a month earlier in Baltimore likened to wolves devouring sheep), who nurtured and deepened their implacable loathing for Lincoln and the idea of universal liberty for the remainder of the Civil War—and beyond.[124]

Adding fuel to the fire of Confederate hatred was Lincoln's controversial refusal to exchange prisoners of war with the Confederacy. This was an issue that resonated with northerners as well as southerners, and the hatred exhibited for Lincoln on this point was interwoven with the subject of slavery, race, and equality. Jefferson Davis's government refused to treat black Union soldiers as legitimate prisoners of war, and if captured by the Confederate army, they could be killed or reenslaved. Black troops would therefore not be exchanged for white Confederate soldiers suffering in northern prison camps. The Lincoln administration's consistent policy was that black soldiers, along with the white officers who commanded them, must be treated equally with whites as prisoners of war and accorded all the rights that went along with such a status. Of course, Lincoln could reject prisoner trades because the Union army had more men and by 1863 was seemingly winning the war, but many Americans, especially Confederates, were furious with the president.[125] From their standpoint white men were dying because of Lincoln's stubbornness in treating captured black troops as equal to whites. In 1864 Georgian Kate Cumming saw the Union prisoner of war camp at Andersonville and encapsulated the views of many in her diary: "O, how I thought of him who is the cause of all this woe on his fellow countrymen—Abraham Lincoln. What kind of heart can he have, to leave these poor wretches here? But as sure as there is a just God, his day of reckoning will come for all the crimes of which he has been guilty against his own countrymen alone. To think of how often we have begged for exchange; but this unfeeling man knows what a terrible punishment it is for our men to be in northern prisons, and how valuable every one of them is to us. For this reason he sacrifices thousands of his own. May Heaven help us all!"[126]

As casualties from the conflict mounted, the president pondered more deeply the meaning of the war. Lincoln had opened 1863 with the Emancipation Proclamation, an "execrable measure," in Jefferson Davis's words, and he closed it with a speech at Gettysburg on November 19, 1863, eulogizing the Union dead and asking Americans to rededicate themselves to an ever more costly war in order to give birth to a qualitatively different American nation. Southern responses to the Gettysburg Address were heavily influenced by Richmond, Virginia, newspapers, in which editors made no comment on the remarks of the president at the November dedication of the national cemetery.[127] Instead, they focused on words Lincoln had extemporaneously spoken the night before, on November 18, 1863, outside the David Wills home in downtown Gettysburg, Pennsylvania. Lincoln told the crowd gathered that evening that "he had no speech to make" because he wanted to avoid saying "foolish things."[128] The *Richmond Examiner* described the president's informal comments as "a vein of comedy" mixed with "deep pathos" and an ill-mannered "deviation from classic propriety"; by careful editing, the paper made it appear it was reporting on Lincoln's Gettysburg Address the following day at the cemetery.[129] Other papers in the capital of the Confederacy dutifully followed suit, thereby leading its residents, and conceivably by extension those newspapers and people across the South who relied on Richmond journalists for their wartime news, to believe that at a solemn ceremony Lincoln had "acted the clown."[130] Perhaps Confederate newspapers were too preoccupied with military matters to comment at length on the address, as the Battle of Chattanooga out west was to begin in earnest five days after Lincoln's speech. Or perhaps they were too consumed with hatred to accurately report what Lincoln said. Whatever the case, accusations of Lincoln as a buffoon or clown resonated less and less as the Confederacy suffered previously unimaginable losses, including its soldiers, its prisoners of war, its slaves, its territory, and its identity as a superior master class destined to rule over its supposed racial inferiors.[131]

Northern reaction to Lincoln's Gettysburg Address predictably followed the same patterns regarding almost every other policy or utterance of the president during the war: Republicans praised the speech, while many Democrats condemned it. Still, Democratic criticism concentrated on

Lincoln's ideas and charged that the president was celebrating a new, more racially egalitarian American nation being born from the pain and misery of the ongoing war. The *Chicago Times* condemned the president for bringing politics into what should have been a eulogy for the slain soldiers and compared Lincoln, unfavorably, to a savage for so doing. "How dared he, then, standing on their graves," the *Times* incredulously asked, "misstate the cause for which they died, and libel the statesmen who founded the government? They were men possessing too much self-respect to declare that negroes were their equals, or were entitled to equal privileges."[132] Other Democratic newspapers struck an identical note, with the *New York World* denouncing Lincoln's proposition that the war was being fought over equality by explaining that "the Constitution . . . does not say one word about equal rights, but expressly admits the idea of inequality of human rights." One New Jersey paper, the *Hudson County Democrat,* acidly noted that what the United States needed was not "a new birth of freedom" but a "new President."[133]

Criticism of Lincoln intensified in 1864 as the United States held an unprecedented presidential election in the midst of the war to determine if the people did in fact want a new leader. The president ran on a National Union ticket against the Democratic nominee and former Union general George McClellan. The 1864 election must surely qualify as one of the most vituperative campaigns in the history of the country. Confederates, Copperheads, and some abolitionists attacked Lincoln, charging that the president was incompetent or, worse, a tyrant and dictator who sought the destruction of the Constitution in order to foist racial equality upon an unreceptive country. White southerners were of a somewhat divided mind over his reelection. Many hoped McClellan and the Democrats would defeat the president because the Democratic platform in 1864 sought to end the war "at the earliest practicable moment."[134] A McClellan victory could possibly have led to Confederate independence and the permanent division of the United States. Alexander Stephens thought McClellan's nomination by the Democrats was "the first ray of light from the North" and, despite his various misgivings about the former general's chances of victory, preferred "his election to that of Lincoln."[135] Yet if Lincoln won reelection, then white southerners could rededicate themselves to the triumph of their cause, knowing full well that four more years of Lincoln meant either ultimate victory or defeat.[136]

Most southerners thought Lincoln would win, with the *Richmond Dispatch* going so far as to predict that the president would be victorious because, the paper contended, if all else failed, the "Ape," with the help of his "beastly supporters" would use "all the means in his power—his officers, his detectives, his bribes, his military power, and his uncontrolled and irresponsible authority over all Yankeedom—to assure his own election and defeat McClellan."[137] Lincoln did win another term, and one Confederate woman, Mary Hopkins, told a correspondent, "I suppose the reelection of Lincoln will protract this dreadful struggle four years longer[;] if so it seems to me that national & individual ruin awaits us."[138] Indeed, earlier in 1864 Mary Boykin Chesnut noted that a remarkable change in attitudes toward Lincoln had occurred. "We have ceased to carp at him because he is a rough clown, no gentlemen, etc. You never hear now of his nasty fun," she observed, "but only of his wisdom. It doesn't take much soap and water to wash the hands that hold the rod of empire."[139] Chesnut's allusion to the president as an American imperialist echoed Alexander Stephens warning to Lincoln from 1860, in which Stephens told his former congressional colleague that if Lincoln coerced the South to remain in the Union, "it would be nothing short of Consolidated Despotism."[140] This charge, like the accusations of Lincoln's alleged atheism, personal vulgarity, war criminality, and tyranny, would endure for generations among his enemies.

A few abolitionists were likewise ambivalent about the reelection of Lincoln to the presidency. By 1864 William Lloyd Garrison, despite his misgivings, endorsed Lincoln against McClellan, provoking a firestorm of controversy.[141] Frederick Douglass, Wendell Phillips, and a smattering of others within the abolitionist camp called for a substitute candidate to replace the president. Lincoln faced opposition to his renomination from those abolitionists who thought the president should be replaced with a nominee who held more reliable antislavery credentials, men such as General Benjamin Butler, Salmon P. Chase (Lincoln's Treasury secretary and a longtime antislavery proponent), or John Charles Frémont, the Republican candidate for president in 1856.

At the Massachusetts Anti-Slavery Society meeting in January 1864, Phillips characterized Lincoln as "ready to sacrifice the interest and honor of the North to secure a sham peace with the Confederates" and as nothing more than "a half-converted, honest Western Whig, trying to be an abolitionist," undermining confidence in the president's candor and integrity.[142] Later that year Radical Henry Winter Davis, a congressman highly critical of Lincoln's early plans regarding Reconstruction, schemed to have Lincoln replaced as the Republican candidate. Such efforts proved fruitless once the city of Atlanta fell to General William Tecumseh Sherman's troops in September 1864. From that point forward, if not much earlier, there was little doubt that Lincoln would be the Republican standard-bearer in the 1864 presidential contest.[143] Even so, antislavery advocates such as Susan B. Anthony and Elizabeth Cady Stanton refused to support the president, and Wendell Phillips declared in one speech that he would "cut off both hands before doing anything to aid Abraham Lincoln's election."[144] The anarchist Lysander Spooner was blunter, telling the Radical Republican senator from Massachusetts Charles Sumner (a staunch proponent of Lincoln) in October 1864 that because the Republicans had conceded the constitutionality of slavery to the slaveholders, they had denied themselves a powerful moral weapon and as a result "upon yourself, and others like you . . . rests the blood of this horrible, unnecessary, and therefore guilty, war."[145] Despite such objections, the vast majority of antislavery Americans supported Lincoln's reelection. The shrinking number of Lincoln critics among the antislavery crowd reflected a significant trend. The more abolitionists moved from the periphery to the center of power in America, the more they tended to appreciate the president's political acumen and his antislavery commitment.[146]

In contrast to those with misgivings about the president and with an enthusiasm indicative of the breadth of Lincoln's popularity, there was one group of people out west decisively in favor of Abraham Lincoln's reelection. At the height of the 1864 campaign Lincoln found strong support among Latinos in California who directly linked voting for the president with opposing tyranny and larger ideas of liberty. In San Francisco a pro-Union club was established, while in one October parade various banners displayed pro-Lincoln, anti-French, and anti-Confederate viewpoints (Napoléon III had installed a client regime in Mexico under the emperor Maximilian).[147] "Honest Abe is our man—Muera Maximiliano [Death to Maximilian]" was proudly exhibited on one sign, while another harshly declared "Maximiliano el usurpador—Davis el traidor" (Maximilian the usurper, [Jefferson] Davis the traitor). More significantly, one banner proclaimed, "Dios hizo al hombre y Lincoln lo declaró libre" (God created man, and Lincoln declared him free).[148] Such sentiments indicated that by 1864, if not much earlier, Abraham Lincoln and the Union cause were associated not only with the cause of expanding freedom for all in the United States but also as a fight for its broader definition outside the nation's borders.

As with Latinos, white southerners, alongside the Democratic and Copperhead press, clearly understood that Lincoln's candidacy represented wider meanings of freedom and equality. Consequently, they were unsurpassed in their denunciations of the president's background and policies. Throughout the war and in the face of the prospect of Lincoln's reelection, the president's southern and northern opponents attempted to smear his candidacy by associating him, in shrill attacks, with the freedmen and racial equality. As noted earlier, southern newspapers publicly referred to Lincoln as "the Ape," while privately he was characterized as a "vulgar monkey."[149] Farther north, the *Cincinnati Enquirer* tried to discredit the president with the claim that Lincoln possessed "the outcrop of a remote African in his ancestry. . . . his buffoonery, superstition, and his conscientiousness—which takes no cognizance of consequences, except such as are personal, to himself—is of the purest Congo; and his negro logic and rhetoric—which we have heretofore been inclined to attribute to his negro politics—is better accounted for upon the presumption of an earlier origin."[150] Possibly the most notorious instance of the exploitation of race as a campaign issue appeared in the form of a pamphlet, published anonymously by David G. Croly and George Wakeman, two writers for the *New York World,* a staunchly Democratic newspaper. Entitled *Miscegenation: The Theory of the Blending of the Races, Applied to the American White Man and Negro,* the campaign tract introduced the word *miscegenation* into the English language. The authors used the word to describe a mixing of the races, or intermarriage between whites and blacks. They claimed—perhaps satirically—that such racial mixing would advance race relations in the United States and accused the Republican Party of being "the party of miscegenation."[151] Whether or not this was all meant as a joke is beside the point, for politicians certainly took it seriously and used it in an attempt to disgrace Lincoln and the Republicans. Congressman Samuel S. Cox of Ohio went so far as to read excerpts from the pamphlet into Congress in February 1864.[152] That such language and tactics were used to describe or taint Lincoln demonstrated the indissoluble link his white supremacist foes made between the man, his policies, and African Americans. Their loathing of Lincoln, in stark contrast to abolitionist criticism, was deeply personal and directly connected to their loathing of blacks, if not all nonwhite peoples.

A more venomous example of nineteenth-century race baiting came from one of Lincoln's most vociferous critics, Marcus Mills "Brick" Pomeroy, the editor of the *La Crosse Democrat,* in Wisconsin:

Hurrah for the nigger
The sweet-scented nigger,
And the paradise for the undertaker!
Hurrah for Old Abe.[153]

In a later issue of the *Democrat* Pomeroy called Lincoln a widow maker
and claimed that anyone who supported the president for reelection was
a traitor and murderer. With words dripping treason, Pomeroy wrote
that if Lincoln was triumphant, he hoped "some bold hand will pierce his
heart with dagger point for public good."[154] Nor was Pomeroy alone in
publishing incendiary rhetoric. In Albany, New York, the *Atlas and Argus*
encouraged Americans to recall that "Caesar had his Brutus, Charles I his
Cromwell . . . and we the People recommend Abraham Lincoln to profit
by their example."[155] It is no wonder that in 1864 Lincoln told his secretary John Hay that "it is a little singular that I, who am not a vindictive
man, should always have been before the people for election in canvasses
marked for their bitterness."[156] That Lincoln allowed such inflammatory,
murderous comments to be publicly expressed and was wearily resigned
to their inevitability in the midst of an unprecedented wartime presidential election contradicted the charge, made both in his lifetime and for
generations thereafter, that he had eradicated northern civil liberties.[157]

Despite such bitter verbal assaults, Lincoln won reelection and shortly
thereafter worked successfully with Republicans in Congress to ensure
passage of the Thirteenth Amendment abolishing slavery in the United
States forever. A little over a month later, on March 4, 1865, he delivered
his Second Inaugural Address. In that speech Lincoln reflected on the
meaning of four years of carnage and offered to the American people,
including those in the South, his opinion that the Civil War was God's
punishment for the American sin of slavery. Not everyone was pleased,
however, with Lincoln's theological reflections. The *Chicago Times* was
incredulous "that even Mr. Lincoln could produce a paper so slip shod, so
loose-joined, so puerile, not alone in literary construction, but in its ideas,
its sentiments, its grasp. He has outdone himself. . . . [his] mediocrity is
superb. Let us trust in Heaven that it is not typical of our national degeneracy."[158] Other northerners agreed, with one Pennsylvanian calling the
speech "sophomoric," while the *New York Herald* said the address consisted
of little more than "glittering generalities."[159]

Confederates were just as critical, although by March 1865 they were
in all likelihood more worried about the impending defeat of their experi-

ment in building a slaveholding republic than any speech of Lincoln's. Still, a few newspapers did comment upon the text. The *Daily Press* in Petersburg, Virginia, labeled Lincoln's Second Inaugural "a queer sort of document, being a compound of philanthropy, fanaticism and scriptural morality."[160] The *Richmond Examiner* thought Lincoln's speech "reads like the tail of some old sermon, and seems to have no particular meaning of any kind, at least, if any meaning lurks in it we fail to perceive it."[161] Indeed, Lincoln himself was perhaps aware of this criticism when he said about a week later, "I believe it is not immediately popular" because "men are not flattered by being shown that there has been a difference of purpose between the Almighty and them."[162]

Abolitionists agreed with Lincoln's assessment, for they admired and praised Lincoln's speech. Frederick Douglass told Lincoln directly that the address was "a sacred effort," while William Lloyd Garrison, after Lincoln's death, called the Second Inaugural "grandly phenomenal."[163] Some abolitionists were concerned, however, by Lincoln's closing paragraph, in which he appeared to offer leniency to the South, a leniency they considered undeserved. In South Carolina, Laura Towne thought compassion for the South might be impossible because, as she wrote in her diary, all the southerners she knew remained "bitter and spiteful and 'cantankerous' as ever, and show extreme contempt for Northerners."[164] Such contempt was quickly reciprocated. When, only six weeks after his second inauguration and less than a week after Lee's surrender at Appomattox, Lincoln was assassinated by Confederate sympathizer John Wilkes Booth, who dramatically jumped onto the stage at Ford's Theatre in Washington, D.C., and shouted the Virginia state motto, "Sic Semper Tyrannis!" (Thus ever to tyrants), much of the nation, at least initially, cried out for vengeance.

Reactions to the president's murder across the United States exemplify the almost bottomless animosity that numerous Americans, North and South, held for Abraham Lincoln.[165] To be sure, countless numbers of northerners and southerners were depressed in April and May 1865 over Lincoln's death, although for various reasons they exhibited different reactions to the shocking event. In the North the grief reflected the admiration for Lincoln that had developed across the region. Despite all the contempt articulated toward the president throughout the war, Lincoln had been elected twice by the American people, both times with a clear majority in the North.[166] After the assassination a few northern ministers remarked on Lincoln's love for all of humanity, demonstrating the association some made in the 1860s between the president and racial equality: "He believed in the brotherhood of man," one pastor told his Philadelphia congregation, "and allowed no differences in constitution, color, culture or country, to commit him to unjust discriminations against the manhood of man." Consequently, northern sorrow over Lincoln's death turned to rage against the Confederacy in the aftermath of the murder. Most sermons delivered in northern pulpits after Lincoln's death invoked the Old Testament God of wrath and vengeance and expressed the view that the South was in part to blame and deserved punishment. "We have lost all sentiment of clemency," exclaimed the New York Episcopalian minister Robert Lowry.[167]

Northern fury was also directed at fellow northerners who exulted in the assassination or at Copperheads who were held at least indirectly responsible for Lincoln's death. One Union soldier from Indiana, George W. Squier, feared that a few would "rejoice at the dire calamity which has come upon this nation."[168] But those who expressed joy over Lincoln's murder usually received quick punishment for their outbursts. Immediately after the assassination, one man exclaimed outside the Petersen House (where the president had been taken from Ford's Theatre), "I'm glad it happened," and was immediately beaten up and taken away by police for his own protection.[169] Writing in his journal, Charles A. Leuschner, a German immigrant from Victoria, Texas, and a prisoner in the North at Camp Douglas, near Chicago, described how one of the imprisoned soldiers had reacted to the death of the president: "We received new's of President Lincoln's assassination last night," Leuschner noted, "and one of our men rejoiset and said the word 'thats bully,' and a yankey happening to stand behind him commenced abusing him and kicking him about like a brute. After being through with this performan's, the yankey took the Rebell & put him on a 20 feet high out of wood & tied from 5 to 10 pound's of iron on each of one of his legg's, and done this four hour's every day for nearly two week's; & I could tell many more such cases which happens every [day]."[170] Other such incidents turned deadly. A Union soldier killed a man for expressing approval of Lincoln's killing, while still another northerner was deemed a hero for immediately shooting a man who said the assassination "served Lincoln right."[171] Out west, in San Francisco, the *Daily Dramatic Chronicle* told its readers on April 17, 1865, that "Wilkes Booth has simply carried out what the Copperhead journalists who have denounced the president as a 'tyrant,' a 'despot,' a 'usurper,' hinted at, and virtually recommended. His weapon was the pistol, theirs the pen; and though he surpassed them in ferocity, they equaled him in guilt."[172] Although Copperheads were quickly absolved of any responsibility for the assassination, such comments illustrated a deep mistrust, if not hatred, between Republicans and Democrats regarding Abraham Lincoln that would persist into the postwar era.[173]

The comments of a few Radical Republicans and abolitionists mirrored the ambivalent and complex relationship that existed between Lincoln and both groups throughout the war. George W. Julian, a congressman from Indiana, in a gathering of Radicals held immediately after Lincoln's murder, asserted that the "hostility towards Lincoln's policy of conciliation and contempt for his weakness were undisguised; and the universal feeling among radical men here is that his death is a god-send."[174] Benjamin Wade assured the new president, Andrew Johnson, "We have faith in you. By the gods, there will be no trouble now in running the government! Mr. Lincoln had too much of human kindness in him to deal with these infamous traitors," while Wade's colleague Henry Winter Davis thought the murder was certainly "a great crime, but the change is no calamity."[175] Of course, one should be careful not to make too much of such comments or to equate them to the loathing expressed by Lincoln's Confederate and Copperhead foes in the wake of the assassination. Julian's talk of Radical contempt for Lincoln's conciliation and weakness could just as easily be interpreted as impatience with the president's constitutional prudence, while Wade and Davis seemed to be saying little more than they were happily anticipating having greater sway over federal reconstruction policy. Many others, probably most, vigorously disagreed with such negative judgments of Lincoln and the positive evaluation of Johnson. William Robinson, a Massachusetts abolitionist, thought Lincoln was at the very least a known quantity, whereas "Johnson may be the tool of anybody and everybody. . . . Johnson is wholly untried."[176] Frederick Douglass was grief-stricken over the assassination and spoke extemporaneously about it in Rochester, New York, on April 15, 1865, the day of Lincoln's death. Douglass said that "a dreadful disaster has befallen the nation." He hoped Lincoln's passing would lead Americans to remember the "treason and slavery" for which the white South fought and opined that "it may be that the blood of our martyred President will be the salvation of our country."[177]

Confederates had good reason to fear such sentiments. Publicly and privately, they worried they would be blamed for the assassination, and they fearfully contemplated a Johnson presidency. Andrew Johnson had been the only southern senator in 1861 who did not join his region in seceding from the Union, and now, as president, he was in charge of the postwar reconstruction of the country. After Richmond fell to Union forces, Johnson had given a speech to an enthusiastic crowd outside Willard's Hotel in Washington, D.C., and expressed the opinion that high-ranking Confederates should be executed and that the South ought to pay reparations for the war. In a private conversation with Radical Republicans on April 15, the day of Lincoln's death, Johnson was no less harsh, telling his important audience that "*treason* is a crime; and *crime* must be punished. . . . Treason must be made infamous and traitors punished."[178]

During the war a few southern newspapers had editorialized that Lincoln ought to be assassinated and ran ads from private citizens offering to kill him.[179] The *Richmond Dispatch* argued that killing Lincoln was justified: "To slay a tyrant is no more assassination than war is murder."[180] Once Lincoln was actually slain, however, such comments took on an entirely different meaning. White southerners fretted over their future prospects under a Johnson presidency. "For an enemy so relentless in the war for our subjugation," Confederate president Jefferson Davis reflected about Lincoln's death after the war, "we could not be expected to mourn; yet, in view of its political consequences, it could not be regarded otherwise than as a great misfortune to the South."[181] Georgian Eliza Andrews, whose father had fought for the Union and brothers for the Confederacy, was devastated: "It is a terrible blow to the South, for it places that vulgar renegade, Andy Johnson, in power."[182] Still, white southerners' hatred for Johnson quickly disappeared once it became clear that he would not use the power of the executive branch to guarantee that the freedmen enjoyed equal constitutional rights. This sentiment was in stark contrast to their wartime disgust for Lincoln, who, because he had used his power as commander in chief to emancipate the Confederacy's slaves, was despised by white southerners. It might be said that after 1865 most abolitionists increasingly appreciated Lincoln and hated Johnson, while some white southerners continued to hate Lincoln and appreciate Johnson, demonstrating that loathing for Lincoln was closely, if not inextricably, connected to matters of race and federal power.

Public exhibitions of grief for Lincoln's death by Confederates were largely superficial and undoubtedly reflected the presence of Union troops in their midst. Thomas Howard Duval, a Texas Unionist living in New Orleans, observed that "nearly all the houses in the City draped in mourning [with] secesh more showy in this regard than Union. They [rebels] have been much alarmed lest the soldiers, especially negroes, should wreak vengeance on them for [the] death of President Lincoln."[183] The experience of one man in Georgia confirmed such a judgment. Mary Semmes

Clayton related to a friend an account of an unnamed individual near Marietta who was "tied up by his thumbs and a placard placed upon his back, for some remark he made about the late President of the U.S."[184] Although there was very little public approval in much of the South for Booth's crime, private exultations of joy were expressed in journals and letters.[185] Robert E. Lee's wife, Mary, for instance, gave a Baltimore friend her assessment of Lincoln's death: "The assassination of Lincoln was a dreadful act which I much regret," she wrote, "especially as I believe he was more kindly disposed towards the South than any of his party. Yet it does seem a wonderful retribution in the midst of their exultation."[186]

Confederates might well have been more jubilant over Lincoln's demise if their land had not been occupied by Union troops. In both Canada and Texas, where no large contingent of Union troops was stationed and no major battles had occurred, a significant number of Confederate sympathizers were ecstatic over the news of Lincoln's death.[187] One newspaper reported that Confederates in Montreal openly celebrated Lincoln's death, and a minister "said publicly at the breakfast table . . . that Lincoln had only gone to h[el]l a little before his time."[188] In Toronto, Confederates toasted Booth and expressed wishes for "the health of the assassin in bumpers of champagne in a public ballroom."[189] Despite such isolated expressions of joy over Lincoln's assassination, most Canadians were horrified by the murder.[190]

Meanwhile, in the Lone Star State there was little to no sympathy expressed for Lincoln as Texans distinguished themselves in their venom from their Canadian compatriots as well as the rest of the Confederacy.[191] The undisguised glee with which most Texans greeted the news of Lincoln's murder depicted the president as a tyrant and the fomenter of war and bloodshed. Dr. Gideon Lincecum, a slaveholding Texas naturalist who moved to the Lone Star State in 1848 and corresponded with the English scientist Charles Darwin, learned about the assassination on or around April 25, 1865.[192] Lincecum called Lincoln a "cold hearted tyrant" and associated the dead president with "haters of free government."[193] Such joyful reactions to Lincoln's violent death combined a healthy dose of personal invective with a belief that the assassination was God's judgment on Lincoln's character and presidency. These responses reflected an unrepentant Confederate belief in the divine and invincible nature of their cause and a deep hatred and animosity for the idea of freedom for all Americans.[194] The celebrations in the Lone Star State over the first assassination of an American president foreshadowed an ominous and violent future for the new American nation created by the Civil War. The response of Texans to the death of the president offered a clue to how some northerners, especially Copperheads, may have rejoiced at the news of Lincoln's assassination as well.[195]

Texans such as William Pitt Ballinger of Galveston and Judge Alexander W. Terrell of Austin celebrated Lincoln's murder. Ballinger received $12.50 a month to write for E. H. Cushing's paper, the *Houston Tri-Weekly Telegraph,* during the latter stages of the war. Ballinger's comments about Lincoln's death in public newspaper editorials and private diary entries are especially interesting, for they illuminate the tangled and conflicting emotional and ideological commitments the Civil War produced for innumerable Americans. Ballinger was a slaveholder and one of the most prominent lawyers in Texas. Prior to the war, in 1856, Ballinger defended a Galveston slave named Betsy Webster, who upon the death of her master, David Webster, received his entire estate and her freedom. One of Webster's relatives contested the will, however, and Betsy Webster hired Ballinger as her attorney. Despite the prospects of damage to his career as well as personal threats and insults, Ballinger won his case before the Texas Supreme Court and secured Betsy Webster her emancipation.[196] A few years later, in August 1860, just before Lincoln's election to the presidency, Ballinger gave a heartfelt but unpopular speech against secession in front of several hundred Galvestonians. Like Abraham Lincoln, Ballinger had been a member of the Whig Party virtually his entire adult life.[197] But in common with many other former Whigs in the South, Ballinger willingly transferred his loyalties to the Confederacy once his state seceded. During the war he suffered the death of three of his children and in all likelihood numerous friends.

Ballinger's editorials in the *Telegraph* regarding Lincoln's assassination were jubilant and are understandable in the context of the losses suffered over the previous four years and as an attempt to boost morale in the face of news of Lee's surrender. They also reflected the widely held belief that killing Lincoln was justifiable tyrannicide. The bitterness expressed in Ballinger's editorials about Lincoln is nevertheless stunning, offering a microcosm of negative sentiment across the country. "From now until God's judgment day," Ballinger thundered, "the minds of men will not cease to thrill at the killing of Abraham Lincoln by Booth, the actor."[198] In a passionate disquisition on Lincoln's allegedly despotic behavior throughout the war, Ballinger compared the dead president to previous tyrants, including Attila the Hun, Caesar, and, tellingly, Robespierre, but declared

Lincoln "the grimmest monster history has ever produced."[199] Expressing both disgust and wonder, Ballinger noted that Lincoln "is recognized and applauded by the people of the North today, and his name fills cathedral and church, and public places, and the voices of all, and many of them name it above the name of Washington."[200] In his diary Ballinger privately mused, "I feel that his fate is the deserved fate of tyrants," and commented on public reactions to his editorials, admitting that they have "excited considerable attention," although "some think it *too far below the patriotic high water mark.*"[201]

Judge Alexander Terrell may well have agreed that Ballinger's comments about Lincoln were too moderate. Although a loyal Unionist and supporter of Texas governor Sam Houston before the Civil War, Terrell later joined the Confederate army and served in various capacities. For years after the war ended, he kept a copy of a poem entitled "A Tribute to John Wilkes Booth," the authorship of which was incorrectly ascribed to the Texas judge. The actual author of the poem was Alfred W. Arrington, a Methodist preacher who had renounced Christianity.[202] An intermittent resident of Texas in the 1840s and 1850s, Arrington left the state seeking literary fame and was at least acquainted with such notable figures as Ralph Waldo Emerson and Henry David Thoreau. By the time the Civil War broke out, Arrington was living in Chicago and was a Copperhead sympathizer. The date of the poem's composition was probably late April 1865, around which time Arrington defiantly delivered it from the top of a table to the Union Officers' Club in Chicago and was very nearly mobbed by the audience for his act.[203] The poem, portions of which follow, makes reference to Booth's body having reportedly been carried out to sea and dumped in the ocean:

> Give him a sepulcher
> Broad as the sweep
> Of the tidal wave's measureless motion;
> In the arms of the deep
> Lay our hero to sleep
> 'Mid the pearls of the fetterless ocean.
>
> He has written his name
> In bright letters of fame
> In the pathway of Liberty's portal;
> And the serfs who now blame
> Shall crimson with shame
> When they have cursed an immortal.[204]

The poem caused considerable controversy later, when in 1893 Terrell— believed at the time to be its author—was selected as minister to Turkey by President Grover Cleveland.[205]

The gleeful reactions by some Confederates, as well as a minority of northerners, to Lincoln's assassination are certainly understandable in the context of a war that caused great loss and suffering on both sides. Considering what was at stake in the conflict and the losses all Americans endured, it would have been surprising if people had not reacted in such a manner. Between 1861 and 1865, 60,000 to 70,000 Texans served in the Confederate army or in state units, and the best estimates place the loss of life for Texas soldiers around 20 to 25 percent, or approximately 12,000 to 15,000 men.[206] Across the entire country over 600,000 Americans perished in the war, which as Drew Gilpin Faust has noted, was "more than 2 percent of the nation's inhabitants . . . the approximate equivalent of the population in 1860 of the state of Maine, more than the entire population of Vermont, more than the whole male population of Georgia or Alabama."[207] Faust calculated in 2006 that "an equivalent proportion of today's population [in America] would mean 5,500,000 dead."[208]

Still, the public and private outbursts of happiness across North America concerning the assassination of Lincoln, although certainly concentrated in the South, especially Texas, were not solely due to an absence of federal troops in various states or pervasive ideological differences with the dead president. The celebrations masked sorrow; the laughter held back tears. They were undoubtedly the result of, and intensified by, the widespread and substantial human losses and other trauma that virtually every American—men, women, soldiers, slaveholders, slaves, yeomen farmers—experienced during the war years. Americans would be accounting for this suffering for generations, and hostility for Lincoln would persist into the postbellum era. Yet those who exulted over Lincoln's murder were doing so not only because of the personal losses they had suffered but also because he had destroyed an entire way of life and their identity as a superior master class entitled to rule over their alleged racial inferiors.[209] They justified the murder—the first of an American president—as a tyrannicide precisely because Lincoln had used executive power to advance freedom for the slave. The praise heaped upon John Wilkes Booth was because he had slain the man responsible, at least in the Confederate and Copperhead minds, with the end of slavery and the idea of black equality. For these conservative enemies of Lincoln, the president had not saved the Union by reuniting North and South; instead, he had destroyed it.

Other aspects of an enduring tradition of loathing for Abraham Lincoln, none of which were ever entirely separate from matters of race and by no means confined exclusively to the Confederacy, were likewise born during the Civil War. The president was condemned for what his foes believed was his unconstitutional refusal to allow the Confederacy's right to peacefully secede from the Union. His enemies also alleged that he had caused the conflict by invading the Confederacy after Fort Sumter in order to ensure the collection of federal tariffs. Consequently, the war was fought not to end slavery but for crass financial purposes in order to consolidate power in Washington, D.C. Accusations of Lincoln as an imperialist began during the 1860s and were reinforced during the 1890s, when the United States expanded its territorial reach overseas. Such charges were almost certainly related to the wartime depiction of Lincoln as satanic, a representative man who embodied a coarse, vulgar, materialist, feminist, and atheist North imperialistically conquering a superior, honorable, paternalist, and Christian South. Resistance to Lincoln from this standpoint was nothing less than obedience to God. Added to these spiritual judgments were condemnations of a more worldly nature. Early in the conflict Lincoln was denounced by a few Radicals either for executive incompetence in waging the war or for executive hesitation in abolishing slavery, although such criticism faded away as the Union emerged victorious, with slavery dead. Conversely, he was castigated for executive high-handedness in violating American's civil liberties by suspending habeas corpus. Later in the fighting, he was lambasted for his stubborn refusal to exchange prisoners with the Confederacy. Finally, the president was criticized for the ideas contained in speeches such as the Gettysburg Address and the Second Inaugural, speeches in which he argued that the United States was at the very least dedicated to the ideal of equality and that the Civil War might reasonably be interpreted as God's righteous judgment on the American nation for the sin of slavery.[210]

The image of Lincoln in America remained bitterly contested after the war concluded, as his memory was used to advance or oppose diverse political agendas. Loathing for Lincoln developed alongside the increasing admiration for the president that arose across the nation after the assassination. Upon hearing of their emancipation in Bexar County, near San Antonio, Texas, the former slave Felix Haywood recalled that the freedmen associated Abraham Lincoln with emancipation as they sang enthusiastically:

Hallelujah broke out—
Abe Lincoln freed the nigger,
With the gun and the trigger
And I ain't going to get whipped no more.[211]

Sadly, the freedmen's joy was premature. Violence perpetrated against former slaves erupted across the South in the postwar era, as the memory of the war's sacrifice remained fresh and political struggles over the nature of the new America born of the conflict raged across the United States.[212] As historian David Blight has shown, all remembering involves some element of forgetting, and for no event in American history is this truer than for the American Civil War and its central figure, Abraham Lincoln. By identifying him as a martyr-saint in the immediate aftermath of his assassination, the majority of Americans willfully and collectively forgot the controversies and hatred that surrounded the sixteenth president in his lifetime and the nearly insurmountable odds he faced in attempting to steer the country through a war that nearly destroyed the Union that he and millions of others loved so dearly. Yet the postwar fight over Lincoln's legacy was also a form of remembering, as the ex-slaves whom Gideon Welles witnessed weeping outside the White House over Lincoln's death, the newly freed Felix Haywood, Frederick Douglass, and innumerable others praised Lincoln's leadership, which had at the very least made a different future possible for African Americans in the United States, one that included the prospect of racial equality and allowed northerners to feel absolved of the sin of slavery on their shores. Many white southerners and not a few northerners disagreed that the prospect of a biracial society was welcome (or, conceivably, that slavery was a sin from which the nation needed absolution), and they looked back with an illiberal nostalgia to the antebellum world.[213] A menacing indication about the brutal, violent nature of this postwar conflict and the ongoing war over Lincoln's memory in American life and its inextricable association with slavery was delivered on the first anniversary of the president's death, April 15, 1866, when a member of the Third Texas Cavalry named Eugene Williams offered this toast in front of his former compatriots: "Here is to the man that pulled the *Trigger* / That killed the man that freed the *Nigger*."[214]

EXPRESSIONS OF THE LIPS
VERSUS THOSE OF THE HEART

Postbellum Disgust, 1865–1889

In November 1866 the Englishman Lord Acton sent Robert E. Lee a letter soliciting the former Confederate general's views about American politics and shared with Lee his opinions on the American Civil War. Acton explained that "much of the good will felt in England towards the South" during the war "was neither unselfish nor sincere" because it stemmed from "the hope that America would be weakened by the separation." Still, Acton believed that "in State Rights the only availing check upon the absolutism of the sovereign will" could be found: "Secession filled me with hope, not as the destruction but as the redemption of Democracy." The success of the Confederacy "would have blessed all the races of mankind by establishing true freedom purged of the native dangers and disorders of Republics," he wrote. "Therefore I deemed that you were fighting the battles of our liberty, our progress, and our civilization; and I mourn for the stake which was lost at Richmond more deeply than I rejoice over that which was saved at Waterloo."[1]

Lee received Acton's missive in December 1866, just after President Andrew Johnson and the Democratic Party had been defeated in the midterm congressional elections and Radical Republicans had gained control of Reconstruction, thereby improving the prospects for the establishment of a biracial democracy in the United States. In his reply Lee contemplated not just the American past but also its future and the future of liberty everywhere—at least for whites. "I yet believe that the maintenance of the rights and authority reserved to the states and to the people," he explained, "not only essential to the adjustment and balance of the general system, but the safeguard to the continuance of a free government." The former

Confederate predicted that "the consolidation of the states into one vast republic, sure to be aggressive abroad and despotic at home, will be the certain precursor of that ruin which has overwhelmed all those that have preceded it" and informed Acton he agreed with Washington and Jefferson that such expansionism would lead "to the subversion of State Governments, and to despotism." Lee ignored here the expansion of federal and executive power that had taken place under Jefferson with his purchase of Louisiana, his war in Tripoli, and his 1807 embargo, which severely damaged the American economy.[2] Nor did he mention the imperial tendencies of white southern slaveholder presidents such as Andrew Jackson and James K. Polk in his disquisition on America's past. Continuing with his historical and philosophical ruminations, Lee reiterated to Acton that secession had once been advocated by "the New England states" but that discussion of such a right in 1866 was now "unprofitable because the judgment of reason has been displaced by the arbitrament of war, waged for the purpose as avowed of maintaining the union of the states." Lee, who two years later would publicly advocate denying African Americans the right to vote, anticipated such a stance by telling Acton he believed in "the perfect equality of rights of all the states; the exclusive right of each to regulate its internal affairs under rules established by the Constitution, and the right of each state to prescribe for itself the qualifications of suffrage." He laid the blame for the recent war squarely on the shoulders of the Republican Party and, by implication, Abraham Lincoln, for Lee's home state of "Virginia to the last made great efforts to save the union, and urged harmony and compromise . . . and that the only difficulty in the way of an amicable adjustment was with the republican party. Who then is responsible for the war?" Lee asked. He concluded by asserting that the war was finished and the South "now accepts in good faith its constitutional results, and receives without reserve the amendment which has already been made to the constitution for the extinction of slavery."[3]

The Acton-Lee correspondence, among other things, articulated the myth of the Lost Cause, its complicated connection to criticism of Abraham Lincoln, and white southern opposition after the war to the use of federal authority to ensure racial equality.[4] After 1865 leading white southerners constructed an official, white supremacist southern memory of the Civil War called the Lost Cause, a term invented by Richmond, Virginia, journalist Edward Pollard.[5] Aggressively promoted by Confederate apologists, this myth became deeply entrenched across the South, if not eventually the entire country. One of its chief tenets was the idea that the Confederacy was a

virtuous, glorious, Christian society that did not fight the Civil War to preserve slavery. Instead, ex-Confederates claimed that they had nobly battled
to preserve their constitutional rights from a centralized federal government but were overwhelmed by superior northern resources led by—at
least for Lincoln's critics—a morally inferior president. Alexander Stephens encapsulated the views of many white southerners when he asserted
that "the War, was, indeed, a contest between opposing principles; but not
as bore upon the policy of African subordination." Rather, he claimed, it
was a conflict "between the supporters of a strictly Federative Government,
on the one side, and a thoroughly National one, on the other."[6]

So, although the dream of an independent, slaveholding Confederacy
may have died at Appomattox in 1865, the idea of a white supremacist
South survived, and hating Lincoln was, for some, an essential part of that
vision.[7] The Lost Cause was, in addition to being a myth that explained
Confederate defeat, a type of "civil religion" that bound white southerners together in the aftermath of the conflict, helped them deal with their
losses from the war, and linked an increasingly nostalgic version of a
glorious antebellum Christian past and honorable Civil War experience
with the trials and tribulations of Reconstruction.[8] White Christian ministers, former Confederate soldiers, and elite women were the leaders of
this crusade, a crusade that included its own myths, theology, morality,
prophetic jeremiads, evangelists, saints, and demons, including, at least
for a few white southerners, Abraham Lincoln. The Lost Cause comforted
ex-Confederates with the sense that God remained in control, their defeat
in the Civil War was not meaningless, and eventually their region would
be vindicated and Lincoln's reputation properly discarded on the ash heap
of history—he would be seen as the destroyer of the Union rather than
its savior. As a result, the Lost Cause and its related negative portrayals
of the president contributed to the restoration of a postwar hierarchical
racial order based upon white supremacy that destroyed for decades the
rights of the very people Lincoln had helped emancipate.[9]

Neither was postwar contempt for Lincoln confined solely to the former
states of the Confederacy. Across the United States the rapid industrialization and modernization of the country contributed to a longing for the Old
South that was not entirely unrelated to negative attitudes toward Lincoln.
If the antebellum South—or the old Republic—had been a beautiful and
illustrious civilization, as was often alleged, then a few Americans thought
it was not unreasonable to blame Abraham Lincoln for its destruction.[10]
Added to this nostalgic development, as the idealism of the Civil War and

Reconstruction era gave way to the sordid and sometimes brutal spectacle of Gilded Age America, some Americans may have wondered if the recent war's carnage had been worth the price. To be sure, Lincoln's reputation certainly underwent a significant public transformation across the United States after his assassination, but it was not transformed as much, perhaps, as has previously been thought. Beneath the surface of the innumerable public displays of appreciation, there remained a significant measure of residual hatred for the dead president, even in the North, which occasionally seeped into public discourse. Still, in contrast to the war years, after 1865 denigration for Lincoln in the northern states was relatively rare and loosely organized. And although most criticism of the president continued to spring from a distinct conservative philosophical and political foundation suspicious of both federal authority and racial equality, in the North there was little or no institutional or popular base of opposition from which to malign Abraham Lincoln.

In the former slaveholding states, by contrast, hostility to Lincoln was more widespread. Although his public standing there improved somewhat, this shift conceivably occurred for tactical political reasons, as white southerners argued that the alleged horrors of Reconstruction would have never taken place had Lincoln lived. Criticism for the president was nurtured and disseminated by unreconstructed Confederates, mostly males, in journals called *The Land We Love* and the *Southern Review* and organizations such as the Southern Historical Society and its *Southern Historical Society Papers*. In the South such sentiments were to an extent the logical outgrowth of the Lost Cause memory of the Civil War and consequently had somewhat more influence than in the North. Opposition to Lincoln persisted after the war, and it was characterized by a strain of thought that denied the president's axiom that in a free society all men had certain natural rights (an idea increasingly shared by northerners). Lincoln was portrayed as a type of inverted folk hero—a folk demon perhaps, a disgusting, villainous figure associated with an ignoble lineage, vulgarity, bad character, irreligion, and tyranny.[11] If during the Civil War overt enmity for Lincoln had served to scare Americans about the *prospect* of racial equality, in the immediate aftermath of the conflict such hostility was a little more covert, given that its bold expression might have harmed the cause of all those who wanted to voice objections to the *fact* of federal enforcement of the freedmen's equality. Abraham Lincoln, it was charged, would have never advanced such an allegedly reprehensible policy. Consequently, as the United States approached the turn of the century and the idea that the federal government was obligated to advance freedom and equality gave way to the notion that Washington, D.C., had no role to play in such matters, Lincoln's name became associated more than before with racial exclusiveness rather than racial progress.[12]

The postwar fight over Lincoln's memory was inextricably tied to philosophical and political arguments over definitions of freedom, racial equality, natural rights, and American nationalism and therefore had significant consequences. Republicans found the martyred president a useful political symbol, or tool, with which to win elections, bludgeon political opponents in the immediate aftermath of the Civil War (e.g., "waving the bloody shirt"), and promote their vision of a new, powerful, and biracial American nation-state created by the Union's triumph. In contrast, after the conclusion of hostilities in 1865, former Democrats, Copperheads, and even a few Anarchists resisted this Republican memory of the war and its implications. Although they occasionally did so, they were careful about expressing their hatred for Lincoln in public as a vulgar man, an infidel, a tyrant and usurper of America's constitutional liberties. Many white southerners, perhaps even a majority, also retained a significant measure of hatred for their former adversary and likewise refused to accept the idea and promotion of Lincoln as a secular, national savior. Consequently, following the war and for decades thereafter, many Americans, especially former Confederates, contrasted Lincoln unfavorably with his Civil War counterpart, the ex-president of the Confederacy, Jefferson Davis. Much more so than in the North, there was a dispute among whites in the South, as well as between whites and African Americans, over the memory of Abraham Lincoln, pitting those who viewed him favorably against those who did not.[13] So, for many Americans a new contest over the conflict's meaning would have to be fought after the war's conclusion, and attitudes toward Lincoln were part of an ongoing clash among various groups in the United States to ensure that their interpretation of the Civil War would survive and become dominant. This argument was primarily waged between those who viewed the war's results favorably and actively sought a more racially inclusive American nation versus those who were despondent over the conflict's outcomes and struggled to preserve the continuation of a more restricted citizenship based on white supremacy. The vast majority of Lincoln's postwar critics were emphatically in the latter camp.

The struggle for control of Lincoln's image began immediately after his assassination, as his funeral train traversed the northern United States in 1865. It was continued after the president's burial by a series of admiring biographers. Ironically, these writers, some of whom were Lincoln's former friends, unwittingly supplied contemporary and future critics with abundant material with which to damage the dead president's reputation. The three most significant Lincoln biographies to appear in the immediate postwar years were Josiah Holland's *Life of Abraham Lincoln* (1866), Ward Hill Lamon's *Life of Abraham Lincoln* (1872), and finally, *Herndon's Lincoln: The True Story of a Great Life* (1889), by Lincoln's former law partner, William H. Herndon. Holland was a resident of Springfield, Massachusetts, and his volume laid the groundwork for many of the postwar Lincoln biographies. In what was perhaps the most noteworthy aspect of the book, Holland claimed Lincoln's greatness rested squarely on his Christian faith and that he would "always be remembered as eminently a Christian president."[14] Holland's biography quickly sold at least "eighty thousand copies" and was gobbled up by northern readers anxious to read of Lincoln's Christian, if not saintly, virtues.[15] The *Scioto Gazette,* published in Chillicothe, Ohio, perhaps represented the views of many, at least in the North, when it labeled Holland's book a "valuable and deeply interesting work" in a notice of a review of the volume.[16]

The question of Lincoln's religious beliefs, or possible lack thereof (the evidence lent itself to divergent interpretations), was of enormous importance in the postbellum era for numerous reasons. Lincoln had been assassinated in April 1865, on Good Friday, and numerous preachers across the northern United States gave sermons on Easter Sunday associating Lincoln with the biblical figure of Moses, who had brought the Israelites to the Promised Land but was not allowed by God to enter Canaan himself. "He stands before us, and will so stand in history, as the Moses of this Israel of ours," the Unitarian minister Charles Lowe asserted in one sermon a little over a week after the assassination.[17] Several northern ministers also explained to their audiences that although Lincoln did not formally belong to any church, he was a believer and possessed spiritual qualities that all Americans should admire and emulate. Reverend Phineas Gurley's homily at the White House on April 19, 1865, said as much when he exhorted his listeners to understand that it was "by his [Lincoln's] steady, enduring confidence in God, and in the complete, ultimate success of the cause of God, which is the cause of humanity, more than in any other way does he now speak to us, and to the nation he loved and served so well."[18] Holland's book claiming Lincoln was a Christian had substantial appeal in the triumphant North; it reassured a people who had just endured a four-year bloodletting and helped make the world intelligible; it gave the Civil

War meaning and purpose and enabled northerners to believe that God had directed recent events; it made Lincoln God's servant, or instrument, in the cause of expanding freedom for all Americans, steering the nation through its greatest crisis to a victorious conclusion; and it eventually aided Christians who sought to forgive the South and quicken reconciliation between the two sections.[19]

Innumerable Americans in the postbellum era would have found the idea of Lincoln as an unbeliever deeply troubling. If Lincoln had been an atheist or, in the parlance of the time, an infidel, what would that say about God's sovereignty and the destiny of the United States? A key tenet of Protestant Christianity, the idea that the Bible was literally, historically true, had been under attack from various quarters for several decades. American anthropologists had argued that Adam and Eve were not the only human beings created by God (monogenesis) but that there had been several other distinct, inferior races (polygenesis) created by the Almighty, while geological findings published by the scientist Charles Lyell in his *Principles of Geology* (1830–33) had established that the Earth was much older than a strict biblical literalism would allow. In addition, research on the Bible coming out of German universities, plus the theories of Charles Darwin, demonstrated that the Old Testament could not be taken as accurate history.[20] Added together, these elements make it understandable why many Americans would want—indeed would need—to believe that Abraham Lincoln had been a Christian. J. H. Wickizer caught the mood of this sentiment perfectly when he wrote to Ward Hill Lamon in 1872 regarding Lamon's biography of Lincoln. He believed that for "those who drink the milk of the Word, and 'know it is so'—to them it is cutting off their rations [if Lincoln was an unbeliever] and they will insist, if Lincoln really didn't believe their Religion, he has gone to hell."[21] In addition, because they were the dominant political party of the era, Republicans in all likelihood had no interest, political or otherwise, in Lincoln being labeled as anything but an orthodox Christian.[22]

William Herndon contributed significantly to the postwar controversy surrounding Lincoln's religious beliefs. Immediately after the president's assassination, Herndon embarked upon a quest to write an accurate biography of the man who had guided the country through the cataclysm of the Civil War. Herndon's work became enormously important for the simple reason that almost every major biography on Lincoln published in the immediate postwar era, except for Holland's, was in one way or another dependent upon the materials Herndon had unearthed in his research.

Herndon traveled back to Lincoln's boyhood haunts in Indiana and Illinois, interviewing hundreds of people about his law partner's background and upbringing, searching for illuminating anecdotes in the process. Not everyone in the country, however, was pleased with what Herndon discovered about Lincoln and made public through lectures and later in his 1889 biography. Neither did nineteenth-century Americans who virtually worshiped Lincoln appreciate Herndon's iconoclastic claim that Lincoln had not been a Christian but instead was an atheist. And because Lincoln's religious beliefs were as inscrutable as the man himself, Herndon's explosive charge of the dead president's religious infidelity was hotly debated across the United States for decades by Lincoln's friends and foes alike.[23]

Herndon was most likely motivated by Holland's characterization of his former friend and mentor as a Christian. He believed that such falsehoods about Lincoln's religion, or any falsehoods for that matter, would eventually be used against the former president by his implacable but currently quiescent foes. Herndon "dearly loved" Lincoln, but, he told one friend, "the Eulogies delivered by men on Mr. Lincoln's character made me sick sometimes." He presciently saw that portraying Lincoln as a saint virtually guaranteed that the dead president's enemies would claim Lincoln was "a perfect hellion—a high criminal—a tyrant—a despot—a child of the Devil" and perpetuate hatred for his former colleague.[24] Maybe Herndon recollected Lincoln's dismissive remark, made a decade earlier, in 1856: "Biographies as generally written are not only misleading but false," Lincoln had observed. "I've wondered why book-publishers and merchants don't have blank biographies on their shelves, always ready for an emergency; so that, if a man happens to die, his heirs or his friends, if they wish to perpetrate his memory, can purchase one already written, but with blanks. These blanks they can at their pleasure fill up with rosy sentences full of high-sounding praise. In most instances they commemorate a lie, and cheat posterity out of the truth. History is not history unless it is the truth."[25] Herndon almost certainly agreed. In the North and among the president's admirers, there was a struggle after the war between those who wanted a sanitized, saintly image to become the official version of Lincoln's life and others, such as Herndon, who favored the dissemination of a warts-and-all portrayal.

The *Chicago Times,* a newspaper that during the Civil War was decidedly antagonistic toward Lincoln, agreed with Herndon. The *Times* thought that the sanctification of Lincoln was nothing more than an attempt to "shelter the follies and criminalities of the [Republican] party which elected him"

and warned all would-be hagiographers that the deification of the former president would "provoke inquiry into his own character and that
of his administration which would not else have been made."[26] Herndon
proposed confounding Lincoln's adversaries by preempting their attacks:
"Sacred lies will not protect us. Hence as Mr. Lincoln's friend I propose
to sink and cut a counter mine. . . . Suppose all these things—Lincoln's
faults magnified by time through a want of exact truth at the right moment—mankind in time & during the ages would magnify them—swell
them out to immense dimensions and pray—who would be at fault— . . .
Lincoln's friends or who? Why Lincoln's friends, who know the truth &
told it not. Mr. Lincoln has bitter enemies—bitter deeply & thoroughly
malicious ones and they are I know biding their time. I propose to cut and
clip that by telling how all things are, so that no future lie will have any
effect upon mankind."[27]

Consequently, in order to launch a "counter mine" against the president's enemies, in December 1865 and 1866 Herndon delivered a provocative series of four lectures to Springfield, Illinois, audiences on the background, life, and character of Abraham Lincoln. In so doing, he caused a
firestorm of controversy across the North and unwittingly gave Lincoln's
foes material with which to excoriate their former enemy. The initial three
lectures—the first given on December 12, 1865, the second delivered two
weeks later, just after Christmas, on December 27, and the third held on
January 24, 1866—were talks that for the most part people in Springfield
liked and indeed praised.[28] Herndon explored topics such as Lincoln's
rough frontier background, burning ambition, secretive nature, and sad
countenance—"his melancholy dript from him as he walked"—and argued
that Lincoln's greatness lay not in his Christian faith but in "his originality
& his own thought—[it was] his own brain & toil that made him great."[29]
There were some contentious elements of Herndon's initial forays into
Lincoln biography: namely, Herndon argued that Lincoln was hardly
the tenderhearted, merciful, and forgiving Christian that biographers
such as Holland claimed. "He had no Faith," Herndon confidently told
his Springfield listeners. "Faith was unknown to his soul. 'Say-sos' he
had no respect for, coming though they might from tradition, or power
or authority."[30] Also intriguing, if somewhat less offensive, was Herndon's
judgment that the chief reason Lincoln was capable of freeing the slaves
during the Civil War was precisely because he was emotionally distant and
cold, not tenderhearted and merciful. "He loved mankind in the abstract,"
Herndon believed, "to convey a general idea, though he cared but little

for the individual."[31] If Lincoln had been too compassionate, Herndon asserted, the Union would have dissolved because such a sympathetic president could not have withstood the pressures to stop the bloodletting and end the war. "The nation—the Constitution-, the Government—the Union and the People, the end and fate of them," Herndon concluded in his third talk, "hung on a cold heartless iron will; and by it was saved. A heart now would have lost—*lost,* all, *all.*"[32] It was perhaps the great irony of Lincoln's life that the coldhearted nature Herndon described here helped the president to preserve a country that would potentially be more rather than less empathetic.

Lastly, in the fourth and final lecture, held on November 16, 1866, Herndon made the inflammatory claim that the key to his friend's character was that decades earlier Lincoln had fallen in love with Ann Rutledge of New Salem, Illinois, but that in 1835 she died prematurely and temporarily unhinged Lincoln mentally in the process. Rutledge's death and Lincoln's subsequent grief, Herndon averred, "throw their rays all over Mr. Lincoln's thoughts, acts, deeds, and life, privately, domestically, socially, religiously and otherwise."[33] Equally controversial was Herndon's assertion that Ann Rutledge was the only woman whom Lincoln had ever loved and that this explained both his former law partner's melancholy, marital difficulties, and even his decision to enter into politics.[34] Herndon was entirely unprepared for the abuse heaped upon his head for his allegations that Lincoln had not truly loved his wife or his earlier claim that the recently assassinated president had been an infidel. In short, the northern public was furious with Herndon's iconoclasm, angry with the allegation that the Great Emancipator was, at least in his heart, unfaithful to his wife and not a Christian believer. Perhaps Lincoln's son Robert expressed it best when he wrote his father's friend Judge David Davis and stated bluntly that "Mr. Wm. H. Herndon is making an ass of himself."[35]

Herndon understood perfectly that Lincoln, although physically dead, was very much alive in the public mind and still had enemies. In fact, it was Lincoln's hagiographers that Herndon thought were the deceased president's greatest long-term foes. Herndon's efforts to anticipate the attacks on his former friend that he thought were sure to come illustrate that, at least in one man's eyes, scorn for Lincoln would not go away after the Civil War. It lived on, although in submerged fashion, reemerging from time to time when Lincoln's now dormant critics saw an appropriate opportunity to attack. What Herndon found, much to his consternation, was that because he tried to tell what he saw as the truth about Lincoln,

an anti-Herndon tradition developed across the North, while individuals who persisted in their hatred of the Civil War president would use
the materials introduced in Herndon's lectures and subsequent book to
perpetuate Lincoln hatred into the twenty-first century. It had to be, at
least from Herndon's standpoint, the worst imaginable outcome, and not
until 1889, for reasons pecuniary and otherwise, did he publish his biography of Lincoln.

In the interim, between Herndon's talks and the publication of his
book, the second major biography of Lincoln appeared in 1872, and it
caused just as much controversy as Herndon's lectures. The book was
Ward Hill Lamon's *Life of Abraham Lincoln,* although the title of the volume was something of a misnomer, for the work examined only Lincoln's
pre-presidential years. A second volume depicting Lincoln's presidency
never appeared, most likely because of the negative response the first
one received.[36] Like Herndon, Lamon was Lincoln's friend. He had also
served, in an unofficial capacity, as the president's bodyguard during the
war. In desperate need of money by 1869, Herndon had sold his research
on Lincoln to Lamon for two thousand dollars. Accordingly, Lamon's book
was almost entirely dependent on Herndon's previous research and significant for that reason alone.[37] In that sense it may at least be said that the
volume was just as much Herndon's biography as Lamon's. The book was
also important in that it was published seven years after the conclusion
of the war, when, in contrast to Josiah Holland's work in 1866, emotions
from the war were perhaps a little less raw and political attitudes in the
United States were, in part a result of the Grant administration's scandals,
more hostile toward federal authority.[38] By 1872, moreover, a few southern
states had been "redeemed" and political control returned to whites sympathetic to the now defunct Confederacy. As a result, there was an opening
for more commentary on Lamon's volume—and by extension criticism of
Lincoln—in 1872 that was simply not possible in 1866. Although Lamon
claimed authorship for the work, the book was actually ghostwritten by
one of Lamon's law partners in Washington, D.C., Chauncey F. Black.
Unfortunately, from the standpoint of objectivity and Lincoln's devotees,
Black was a Jacksonian Democrat, and his biases crept into the work.
Black deemphasized, for instance, Lincoln's partisan devotion to the Whig
Party in the 1830s and instead portrayed the Lincoln of that decade, inac-
curately, as "midway between the extremes in local politics."[39]

Despite the book's authorial shortcomings, Lamon's biography was nevertheless a remarkably honest, if flawed, examination of the life and politi-

cal career of Abraham Lincoln prior to his inauguration. Whereas Holland
had stressed Lincoln's exemplary character and orthodox Christianity,
Lamon emphasized Lincoln's rough frontier background and "wonderful
thirst for distinction."[40] Lamon also examined in excruciating detail his
former friend's love for Ann Rutledge, his "frantic" grief over her death,
and his awkward, failed courtship of Mary Owens. In addition, Lamon
declared that "Mr. Lincoln was not supremely happy in his domestic relations" and his marriage to Mary Todd "was one of the great misfortunes of
his life and hers."[41] More important was Lamon's claim, similar to Herndon's earlier assertion, that Lincoln had not been a Christian but was in
fact a freethinking infidel for his entire life and hid his lack of belief for
political reasons. "While it is very clear that Mr. Lincoln was at all times
an infidel in the orthodox meaning of the term," Lamon wrote, "it is also
very clear that he was not at all times equally willing that everybody
should know it. He never offered to purge or recant; but he was a wily
politician, and did not disdain to regulate his religious manifestations
with some reference to his political interests."[42] In all likelihood Lamon's
views of Lincoln's religious beliefs were in such stark contrast to Holland's because of their differing sources. Holland had based his claim for
Lincoln's Christian faith on the unreliable account of Newton Bateman,
the superintendent of Illinois schools, while Lamon based virtually his
entire work, as noted, on materials supplied to him by Herndon.[43]

Lamon provided a frank discussion of Lincoln's views on slavery and
race. He was careful to distinguish Lincoln from the abolitionists and
instead portrayed the man northerners called the Great Emancipator
as moderate rather than radical on the issue of inhuman bondage. In a
passage reminiscent of Herndon's portrayal of the president, Lamon explained to his readers that "Mr. Lincoln was not an ardent sympathizer
with sufferings of any sort, which he did not witness with the eye of flesh.
His compassion might be stirred deeply by an object present, but never by
an object absent and unseen."[44] Accordingly, Lamon asserted, "none of his
public acts, either before or after he became President, exhibits any special
tenderness for the African race, or any extraordinary commiseration of
their lot. On the contrary, he invariably, in words and deeds, postponed
the interests of the blacks to the interests of whites, and expressly subordinated one to the other."[45] Lincoln "was no Abolitionist" and did not want
"to interfere with slavery where it had a lawful existence," although he
did desire "that the negro should be protected . . . . in life, limb, property,
reputation, and every thing that nature or law makes sacred."[46] Still, he

asserted that Lincoln would do no more for the freedmen: "He had no notion of extending to the negro the *privilege of governing* him and other white men, by making him an elector. That was a political trust, an office to be exercised only by the superior race."[47]

Lamon's book caused quite a stir in the North and, probably to a lesser degree, in the South. Josiah Holland called it a "shameless book" because it depicted the man he had argued in 1866 was a noble Christian as "a half-lunatic infidel," while Lincoln's friend Orville Hickman Browning, in utter amazement, wrote Isaac Arnold Newton: "I have just been looking over Lamon's book upon Mr. Lincoln. Many things in it shock me, as I think they do every true friend of Mr. Lincoln, when he calls him a 'wily politi-cian,' 'cold,' 'impassive,' . . . Lincoln possessed the very opposite qualities. How could he charge him with irreverence [*sic*] and infidelity when he remembers the sublime prayer with which he left Springfield, and the deep religious feeling which pervades all his writings and speeches to the day of his death? Do not you and I owe it to the memory of the dead to vindicate him from these charges?"[48] The *Chicago Tribune* concurred with Browning's assessment and warned its readers that "there are parts of the work which will shock those who have admired Mr. Lincoln, and will cause pain to his surviving relatives," all related to Lincoln's "personal history" and upbringing on the frontier in "squalid" conditions. Furthermore, the *Tribune* criticized Lamon, averring that it was unfortunate "that the work of editing the materials touching Mr. Lincoln's early life had not fallen into more discriminating hands" and that "they add nothing which any one wishes to know."[49] The *Tribune* lamented Lamon's lack of discernment in publishing what it believed to be the rather sordid and personal details of Lincoln's upbringing and love life before he met Mary Todd, concluding that Lamon's work will "leave the false impression upon the mind of the reader that Mr. Lincoln was an atheist."[50]

It was seemingly assumed that Lincoln could only be good if he had been a Christian. The *Congregationalist,* a newspaper published out of Boston, Massachusetts, declared in an editorial entitled "The Religious Character of Abraham Lincoln" that it was cruel to label Lincoln an in-fidel. The piece concluded that if any American believed Lincoln was an atheist, "all we can say is that he will incite in our minds the suspicion of being himself as base and bad a man as he would make out our martyred President to be."[51] This is not to say that the reviews of Lamon's book were uniformly negative. The *Christian Union* thought the biography "has mer-its" and that reading it "has left us with a heightened sense of Lincoln's essential greatness."[52] Nevertheless, the *Union* rightly conceded the book would be controversial, while the *New York World* went further, predicting that the regrettable result of Lamon's biography will be, for most people, a diminished "enthusiasm for the memory of the great Emancipator."[53]

Lamon was therefore quickly condemned across the North for his portrayal. Indeed, reactions to Lamon's (and Herndon's) portrait are instructive for the glimpse they provide into northern public opinion about Lincoln, acceptable biographical truths circa 1872–73, and for suggesting why enmity for the president remained somewhat muted in the immediate aftermath of the war. Decades later, in 1911, Lamon's daughter Dorothy Lamon Teillard insightfully reflected on why her father's work was vilified: "It was thought his [Lincoln's] fame would suffer if all the ugly facts were known. But it was prompted in part also by the timid and the conventional cowardly notion that opinions of the time about social standing, about education, and about religion would somehow suffer if all his experiences were frankly told. . . . The reading public regarded it as an offense to trace his wonderful growth from so humble an origin. Then there was the religious world, which was shocked that he was described as unorthodox. What may be called the sectional public took exception to the unprejudiced attitude toward the South. . . . Then there was what might be called the social public that was shocked by the truth about Lincoln's humble and hard bringing up."[54]

Of course, one reason there was a relative dearth of negative utterances in the early 1870s may be that the majority of Americans genuinely admired Abraham Lincoln. Innumerable Americans relished the Horatio Alger ideal of an individual going from rags to respectability, and Lincoln's life and career offered the quintessential example of such a rise in status. Moreover, in all likelihood Americans did not wish to speak ill of the dead, much less hear someone else do so. But it is also true that most people in the North who wished to publish or utter a derisive sentiment in the 1870s would have found the reaction to Herndon's lectures and Lamon's book a fair warning of what to expect. For instance, Charles Francis Adams, the United States diplomat to England during the Civil War, gave a speech before the New York State legislature in 1873 praising William Henry Seward, Lincoln's secretary of state. In the course of his address Adams compared Lincoln unfavorably with Seward and in the process stirred up quite a controversy. Several newspapers took issue with Adams's analysis, and former Lincoln cabinet member Secretary of the Navy Gideon Welles even went so far as to publish a small book refuting

Adams's remarks.[55] Still, the publication of Herndon's lectures and 1889 biography and Lamon's volume conclusively disprove the charge later asserted by Lincoln's adversaries that the truth about Abraham Lincoln's life and career were somehow "suppressed" in the North after the Civil War. To be sure, northerners did not want to hear what Herndon and Lamon had to say, the biographers were roundly criticized for their publications, and their works sold very poorly. But both men were able to speak freely and publish their ideas about Lincoln in a courageous yet unsuccessful attempt to counteract the deceased president's hagiographers and the quasi-official version of the Lincoln image developing across the North.[56] The deification of Lincoln taking place there, such as it was, was perhaps analogous to the Christlike image of Robert E. Lee then developing in the South.[57] Given the cataclysmic nature of the Civil War, coupled with the human aversion to hearing unpleasant truths about the icons they create, it would have been surprising if Lincoln and Lee had not been idolized and their critics demonized within their respective regions.

In fact, after the war there were northerners who vigorously and publicly perpetuated contempt for Lincoln. The Massachusetts abolitionist-turned-anarchist Lysander Spooner had been scathingly critical of the Republican Party before and during the war. Once formal hostilities ceased and the political debates of Reconstruction ensued, he continued his harsh evaluation of the violence to liberty he believed the fighting—and Abraham Lincoln—had caused. Spooner published several pamphlets between 1867 and 1870 entitled *No Treason,* all of which expounded in detail his radically anarchist political philosophy.[58] In the first pamphlet, published in 1867, Spooner argued that "the late war has practically demonstrated that our government rests upon force—as much so as any government that ever existed."[59] The war, he averred, was not fought "to liberate the slaves, but by a government that had always perverted and violated the Constitution, to keep the slaves in bondage; and was willing to do so, if the slaveholders could be thereby induced to stay in the Union."[60] Three years later Spooner was even blunter: "The pretence that the 'abolition of slavery' was either a motive or justification for the war is a fraud of the same character with that of 'maintaining the national honor.' Who, but such usurpers robbers, and murderers as they, ever established slavery? Or what government, except one resting upon the sword, like the one we now have, was ever capable of maintaining slavery? And why did these men abolish slavery?" Nor could the Massachusetts anarchist's answers to such questions have pleased northerners in 1870 as he reflected upon the bloodletting and meaning of the war. "Not from any love of liberty in general [were the slaves freed]—not as an act of justice to the black man himself, but only 'as a war measure,' and because they wanted his assistance, and that of his friends, in carrying on the war they had undertaken for maintaining and intensifying that political, commercial, and industrial slavery, to which they have subjected the great body of the people, both white and black."[61] In Spooner's view the United States government was illegitimate: it no longer existed on the basis of consent but, rather, on that of force. Accordingly, all Americans were now living in a state of "political, commercial, and industrial slavery."[62]

Once he had demonstrated, at least to his own satisfaction, that the United States government rested on force rather than consent and Americans were, as a result, enslaved, Spooner held that the Confederates had not been traitors. "The number who actually consented to the Constitution of the United States, at the first, was very small," Spooner reasoned. Consequently, "the adoption of the Constitution was the merest farce and imposture, binding upon nobody. The women, children, and blacks, of course, were not asked to give their consent. . . . Furthermore, those who originally agreed to the Constitution, could therefore bind nobody that should come after them. They could contract for nobody but themselves."[63] Confederates had therefore not committed treason in seceding from the Union and subsequently and openly withdrawing their consent from the federal government upon Lincoln's election.[64] It was clear, furthermore, from the similarity with which Spooner described the founding generation in his first pamphlet, that the Massachusetts anarchist believed that the Confederates were no different than the Americans who had broken away from England in 1776: "George the Third called our ancestors traitors for what they did at that time. But they were not traitors *in fact* . . . because they betrayed nobody, and broke faith with nobody. . . . This principle was a true one in 1776. It is a true one now. It is the only one on which any rightful government can rest. It is the one on which the Constitution itself professes to rest. It if does not really rest on that basis, it has no right to exist; and it is the duty of every man to raise his hand against it."[65] Spooner apparently agreed with Confederates such as Jefferson Davis and Robert E. Lee, who had consistently argued that they were *conserving* the revolutionary principles of 1776 when they seceded from the Union in 1860–61 and formed the slaveholding Confederacy. He nevertheless ignored a fundamental truth that vitiated this argument: in 1776 Americans had no representation in the halls of the British Parliament, an issue that for over a decade had been part of their quarrel with the English. The Confederate States of America could make no such claim in 1860–61. Indeed, white southern slaveholders had dominated the United States government since its inception, and Lincoln's election in 1860 signaled that such dominance, sooner or later, was at an end.

Lest one think that Spooner's arguments would have resonated in the white South, however, in the same pamphlet Spooner said that the South was little different than the North in that its government likewise rested on force rather than consent. "The opinions of the South, on the subjects of allegiance and treason," Spooner explained, "have been equally erroneous with those of the North. The only difference between them, has been, that the South has held that a man was (primarily) under involuntary allegiance to the *State* government; while the North held that he was (primarily) under a similar allegiance to the United States government; whereas, in truth, he was under no involuntary allegiance to either."[66] Nor would white southerners have appreciated what Spooner told one southern correspondent in 1871: southerners, he observed "seem to settle down into slavery with perfect content. . . . They seem determined either to make slaves of others, or to be slaves themselves."[67]

Given such arguments about consent, secession, and treason, it followed that Spooner would brand Lincoln a tyrant. "Abraham Lincoln did not cause the death of so many people from a mere love of slaughter," Spooner wrote in 1873, "but only to bring about a state of consent that could not otherwise be secured for the government he had undertaken to administer. When a government has once reduced its people to a state of consent—that is, of submission to its will—it can put them to a much better use than to kill them; for it can then plunder them, enslave them, and use them as tools for plundering and enslaving others. And these are the uses to which most governments, our own among the rest, do put their people, whenever they have once reduced them to a state of consent to its will."[68] From Spooner's standpoint Lincoln was a reprehensible figure, and to him "there never was and there never will be, a more gross, self-evident, and inexcusable violation of the principle that government should rest on the consent of the governed, than was the late war, as carried on by the North. There never was, and there never will be, a more palpable case of purely military despotism than is the government we now have."[69]

It is small wonder that Spooner's arguments carried little weight. In the immediate aftermath of the Civil War, Americans disagreed that the recently concluded conflict had been meaningless and fought not for idealistic reasons but, allegedly, for crass financial purposes. If Spooner was correct that the North did not at first fight the war in order to abolish slavery—a debatable point, given that preserving a Union in which slavery would be eradicated was paramount for Lincoln and the antislavery movement, which was precisely why the Confederacy seceded, began, and fought the war—he was either unable or unwilling to see that by 1865, whatever the original motives of Lincoln and the North, it had become one to end it.[70] Neither were Americans, certainly not in the North and certainly not recently emancipated African Americans, going to agree that one of the consequences of the war was that they were now slaves themselves and that the president known as the Great Emancipator was the person chiefly responsible for reducing them to bondage.[71] Also, the idea that Americans were enslaved somehow escaped the millions of immigrants who flocked to America's shores from the 1880s onward; if Spooner was right, one wonders why they came to the United States at all. Spooner's belief that the war enslaved Americans seriously underestimated the cruelty at the heart of racially based antebellum slavery, a misjudgment that would characterize nearly all future Lincoln criticism. The postwar problem, moreover, of what should be done for the ex-slave in the teeth of violent white southern hostility to their political and social advancement was incredibly challenging, and it remains difficult to see precisely how in the Reconstruction era the freedmen were going to enjoy any rights at all without state assistance in the form of a long-term presence of federal troops. It seems that only force—federal force, in fact, which Spooner for philosophical reasons consistently opposed—was going to ensure that the freedmen had a meaningful chance to enjoy their newly won liberty and pursue their happiness. For former slaves, as they and the entire nation eventually discovered, a diminished federal state meant a diminishment of their rights.[72] Spooner's arguments were a curious combination in that they joined a heartfelt love of liberty with an attack on the people who for various reasons had attempted to prevent the creation of a nation based upon the suppression of that natural right for blacks. His work, although relatively marginal in the postbellum era, nevertheless presaged a fusion of an anarchist-libertarian critique of the president's actions during the Civil War with Lost Cause defenses of the Confederacy that later became an essential element of antipathy for Lincoln.

Thomas A. Hendricks (1819–85), the governor of Indiana and Democratic candidate for vice president of the United States in 1876, also stirred the anti-Lincoln pot. In 1864 Hendricks gave a speech at the Democratic convention in Chicago praising the nomination for president of Lincoln's old military and political nemesis George B. McClellan, a speech in which Hendricks supposedly labeled Abraham Lincoln as "that smutty old tyrant."[73] The Philadelphia newspaper the *North American* was quick to condemn Hendricks's past attack upon the Civil War president. It also used the occasion to pontificate on southern opinions about Lincoln, race relations below the Mason-Dixon Line, and the upcoming presidential contest between Republican Rutherford B. Hayes and Democrat Samuel Tilden. The *North American* bitterly noted that "Booth is a heroic name in the estimation of those who tried to destroy the Union, and they emulate his example in assassinating the blacks liberated from the shackles of slavery at the cost of nearly a million of lives and billions of treasure. But then this is the surest and speediest way to make 'a solid south' for Tilden and why not adopt it?"[74] The paper ominously predicted that if Tilden and Hendricks won the election, "the life of no Republican would be safe in any State of the south."[75]

Although Tilden and Hendricks did not formally win the presidency in 1876, in the long run the *North American* turned out to be correct. Eight years later, in 1884, Hendricks was elected vice president of the United States on the Democratic ticket with Grover Cleveland. What was interesting in this political flare-up was the criticism Hendricks received for his alleged *past* attacks on the dead president, combined with the attempt by at least one northern newspaper to connect the Democratic Party with southern obsequies to John Wilkes Booth. Equally important was that Hendricks's purported negative comments did not necessarily exclude him from the vice presidency, even though his previous opposition to Lincoln had been noted in the 1884 election as well.[76] In 1885 Albion Tourgée, a Radical Republican and devoted racial egalitarian (he defended Homer Plessy in both written and oral arguments before the Supreme Court in *Plessy v. Ferguson*) who after the war lived in North Carolina and risked his life in the cause of racial equality, indirectly offered an explanation about why Hendricks's previous remarks were not seen as disqualifying, when he linked the rise of laissez-faire economic dogma, a dogma increasingly shared by Democrats and Republicans alike, with a decline in Lincoln's reputation. Lincoln, Tourgée explained, "is naturally little esteemed by an age which accounts fault-finding the test of wisdom" and influenced "by a generation of publicists to whom an economic theory outweighs in sacredness the rights of man."[77] In the postwar era, then, animosity for Lincoln was not dead, only dormant, and it was easily worth resurrecting as future political and economic squabbles allowed. At least one newspaper, the *Milwaukee Daily Sentinel,* alluded to this potential use as early as 1868 when it reprinted a comparison between Jefferson Davis and Abraham Lincoln from the *Sentinel on the Border,* published in Louisville, Kentucky. Contrasting Lincoln unfavorably with Davis, the Kentucky paper labeled the recently slain president as a "shifting, vulgar, rollicking" man "who will be execrated the more as the wheels of time roll on fanning the chaff from the wheat."[78] The *Sentinel* thought that the Louisville paper was baldly stating "just what some of the Northern organs of the same party [Democratic] in more northern localities would gladly say, did not shame and some regard for public opinion restrain them."[79]

In the South, by way of contrast, the chance of suffering retaliation for expressing hatred of Lincoln was less dangerous than in the North, chiefly because more white southerners continued loathing their Civil War adversary. In 1866, a little over a year after Lincoln's death, the *Southern Vindicator,* in Pine Bluffs, Arkansas, published an editorial on Reconstruction in which it reportedly labeled Lincoln a "tyrant" and "thanked God" that "Abraham Lincoln did not live to mock our misery."[80] To be sure, a newspaper in Macon, Georgia, rebuked the *Vindicator* because such opinions "inspire us with false hopes and false views of the political situation."[81] Even though the *Vindicator* was criticized for its stance, it was less for its opinions about Lincoln than it was for its political inexpediency in expressing such views. It is also interesting to note that the Lowell, Massachusetts, newspaper that reported these contretemps called the *Vindicator* an "ultra copperhead" sheet, thereby associating postwar denigration of Lincoln with the deceased president's northern Civil War opponents.[82] In 1868, only three years after Robert E. Lee surrendered to Ulysses S. Grant at Appomattox Court House in Virginia, an even more strident editorial was published in the Warsaw, Kentucky, *Sign of the Times.* In its shrill attack on the idea of a proposed monument to President Lincoln, the piece is an excellent summary of contempt for Lincoln in portions of the white South in 1868:

> Two hundred thousand dollars to erect a monument to Abraham Lincoln. Great God! Can it be possible? Is there a white freeman so low, so degraded, so deep in infamy as to aid or assist in erecting a monument to that beast of iniquity, that father of Jacobins, of smutty stories; a curse, a blot on the pages of humanity; a political pimp; destroyer of civil liberty; head centre of a hot bed of thieves, knaves, cowards, plunderers, murderers, houseburners, woman murderers, spoon thieves; such a crew as the father of

demons would be ashamed to associate with? A monument to Abraham
Lincoln, the defunct, sent to his father, the devil, on a Good Friday night,
from a play-house, by that lover of liberty, the great American Brutus, J.
Wilkes Booth, whose name will go down to future generations as the American Liberator—as the man who had the daring courage to destroy the first
American tyrant . . . [and] rid this unhappy country of a monster. We can
exclaim, "Well done, thou good and faithful" son of freedom![83]

The idea of a permanent monument to Lincoln being placed in the South,
even in a border state that was the site of Lincoln's birth, was simply too
much to contemplate for some white southerners. Although it is impossible to say with any certainty, perhaps the Kentucky editor was referring to a Radical Republican proposal to place a monument to Lincoln
in Atlanta, Georgia, a plan one local newspaper exclaimed was perfectly
acceptable as long as the bones and blood of dead Confederate soldiers
were used to build it.[84]

The Kentucky editor's denunciation of Lincoln as Satan's son was given
further expression in a peculiar pamphlet published in Memphis, Tennessee, entitled *Abraham Lincoln, Late President of the United States,
Demonstrated to Be the Gog of the Bible, as Foretold by the Prophet Ezekiel
in the XXXVIII and XXXIX Chapters of the Book of Prophecy* (1868). Pseu-
donymously written by "a Plain Farmer," the nearly sixty-page work equated
Lincoln with the Antichrist and claimed the former Confederate States as
a kind of new Israel. "That Abraham Lincoln is the Gog of the Bible" is not
a fact to be doubted, claimed the plain farmer. In addition to his discovery
of Lincoln as the devil made flesh, the author spoke of the happiness of
slaves in the antebellum South and the dastardly abolitionists who sought
to free them from their supposedly blissful state. The anonymous Confederate sympathizer asked readers to consider Lincoln's misdeeds: "Was
not his authority used as a cover for every species of crime and violence
that his officers and soldiers, collectively or individually, chose to exercise,
not only toward the Southern people, on whom he was making war, but,
also, over all, even of his own immediate people, who disagreed with his
policy and purposes? Was not all constitutional law set at defiance by his
adherents, and did they not violate every law of humanity against all who
opposed them?—and in so doing did they not always find in Mr. Lincoln
a sure cover of protection?"[85] Indeed, the farmer blamed Lincoln's assassination on "the bloody war which he had . . . so cruelly and relentlessly"
waged against the southern people, a war the farmer thought had justifiably led to his death at Booth's hand.[86]

Former Confederate general Daniel Harvey Hill (1821–89), editor of *The Land We Love,* a postwar journal celebrating and extolling the virtues of the antebellum South, wryly observed that the pamphlet was "interesting and readable." Still, Hill explained tongue-in-cheek, he could not agree with the farmer's thesis because it omitted any reference to Lincoln's fondness for telling stories to whomever would listen, adding, "The learned commentator fails to prove that Gog was fond of obscene anecdotes." Accordingly, although the plain farmer's work demonstrated "patient research and logical acumen," the piece was unfortunately "incomplete."[87] It is striking that Hill did not declare the thesis of the plain farmer to be nonsense or that he reviewed it at all. It is likewise interesting that these writers who resided in border states such as Kentucky and Tennessee, where the war was particularly divisive, focused their criticism on Lincoln's background and conduct of the war and expressed their hatred for him in a religious idiom. On the one hand, such language was perfectly understandable considering that Protestant Christianity was the lingua franca of nineteenth-century American public discourse. On the other hand, it is clear that Lincoln continued to be demonized after the war was over and that his reputation among some elements of the white South had not undergone much of a transformation, certainly not by 1868.

Indeed, one year later, in 1869, a twenty-six-year-old former Union soldier named Russell Conwell found much the same story when he traveled throughout the South for the *Boston Daily Evening Traveller.* Conwell witnessed continued Lincoln hostility coupled with racial hatred for African Americans, which then and later was a relatively constant element of animosity for the president. In Alexandria, Virginia, Conwell met former Confederates with "portraits" of Jefferson Davis and Robert E. Lee displayed in their homes, alongside "photographs of [John] Wilkes Booth" and "effigies of Abraham Lincoln hanging by the neck with a darkey hung at each heel, together with Confederate songs, mottoes, and keepsakes."[88] Somewhat surprised, perhaps even stunned, at finding such open bitterness toward Lincoln and the North, Conwell told his readers that similar displays of defiance would "in any other land . . . bring hundreds of them [ex-Confederates] to the gallows."[89]

For many in the South, Lincoln was seen not as God's instrument for guiding the nation through the Civil War but as the devil incarnate. It followed that God would judge the United States accordingly. Former Confederate diplomat Ambrose Dudley Mann gloated from Paris to his friend Jefferson Davis in such terms after the city of Chicago burned down in

1871. "In the destruction of Chicago there has not been such a demonstration of Divine vengeance since the destruction of Sodom and Gomorrah," Mann exulted in his letter to the former Confederate president. "It was there that the rowdy Lincoln, the prime official agent of all our woes was nominated . . . it was there that vice, politically and morally, was more honored in the breach than the observance." Mann found a certain poetic justice in that "seven years to the very day, after the laying waste of the Valley of the Shenandoah, by the fiendish Sheridan, acting under the orders of a not less fiendish superior, a conflagration occurs in the 'wicked city.'" Mann was jubilant, telling Davis that no one could, "in the presence of such convincing proof, together with the fall of Lincoln by the hand of a maniac [Booth], hesitate to cherish the opinion expressed by Horace . . .

Ravo antecedentem scelestium
Dezevuit pede Poena claudo.

This is the constant hope of my head, and, as far as is concerned, the religion of my heart."[90]

Negative judgments of Lincoln were given a similar and more serious philosophical and political expression in Alexander Stephens's *Constitutional View of the Late War between the States* (1868). A former congressional colleague of Lincoln, Stephens seemingly had no personal animus against the president, but he, like all Confederate apologists, unashamedly defended the Confederacy's right to secede, viewed slavery as incidental to the conflict, and characterized Lincoln's war as imperialistic and destructive of liberty.[91] Stephens was no less harsh in the second volume of his apologia, published in 1870, in which he characterized Lincoln not only as a man with many good qualities but also as a president who perpetrated unpardonable "errors involving not only most unjustifiable usurpations of power, but such as rise to high crimes against society and against humanity."[92] Stephens's charge that Lincoln was a war criminal anticipated by nearly 150 years similar accusations by Lincoln's twenty-first-century detractors. But at the heart of Stephens's postwar analysis were his deep-seated fear of federal power and the associated prospect of racial equality. Even allowing for Stephen's sincerity, and there is no reason to believe that he was not absolutely genuine in all he wrote, it cannot be coincidental that he expressed his fears of central authority in the midst of Reconstruction, America's unique postwar experiment at establishing a biracial democracy. Indeed, Stephens's two-volume defense of the Confederacy was published at virtually the same time as the ratification of the Fourteenth and Fifteenth Amendments to the Constitution, which conferred citizenship and the franchise on African Americans. His critique was grounded in the past, a white supremacist and narrower democratic past, coupled with a deep-seated fear that the federal government might ensure that liberty and equality were inextricably connected to one another and should be enjoyed by all Americans, regardless of race.[93] Although later in the decade Stephens expressed some kind words about Lincoln, they did not mitigate in the least his conservative philosophical and political outlook or his relevance to future criticism of the Civil War president coming from Lysander Spooner's intellectual descendants, who, like Stephens, were extremely suspicious of, if not outright hostile to, federal authority and thus loathed Abraham Lincoln.[94]

By 1872 leading white southern intellectuals responded to Lamon's—or, more appropriately, Lincoln's—biography in harsher and more personal terms than Stephens had exhibited. The Baltimore writer and editor William Hand Browne (1828–1912) penned a scathing review of Lamon's book in the journal the *Southern Magazine* in September 1872.[95] Until the Southern Historical Society began publishing its papers in 1876, the *Southern Magazine* served as its authorized mouthpiece.[96] Born in Baltimore on New Year's Eve in 1828, Browne received his M.D. degree from the University of Maryland in 1850, although he never actually practiced medicine. He later dabbled in business but found his true calling as a writer, poet, and eventual biographer of Stephens. Browne's comments about Lincoln in the early 1870s, like Stephens's earlier writings and Albert Taylor Bledsoe's subsequent fulminations, can perhaps be seen as a kind of imprimatur of the viewpoint of many, if not most, leading ex-Confederates toward their former foe, which is in opposition to the idea that they were not influential.[97] Browne thought Lincoln's biography was necessary and that one of the primary reasons Lamon's work was so important was that all previous biographies—perhaps he had Holland's book in mind—had "a palpable air of unreality" to them and were unreliable as guides to Lincoln's life and character. In fact, Browne perceptively argued, most of what had been written about Lincoln by the president's admirers "conceal[s] much that is not in accordance with the purposes, or is offensive to the tastes of the authors."[98] Browne complimented Lamon and Herndon, whom he acknowledged as the supplier of the source material for the book, because Lamon, unlike all previous biographers of the martyred president, "has acted conscientiously, indeed, even to the extent of doing violence to his feelings, is evident from the repressed disgust which, in spite of him, is manifest throughout this volume, and the open expression of which he can not always prevent."[99]

Having projected onto Lamon's biography his own antipathy toward Lincoln, Browne consequently focused his review on those aspects of Lincoln's life that he found particularly reprehensible. One, of course, was Lincoln's personal background, or low birth. "To say that Abraham Lincoln was born in 'obscurity,' or 'humble poverty,'" Browne sniffed, "is to use the language of flattery toward one who, according to his biographer, neither knew his own grandfather, nor the name which he had no legal right to bear."[100] A second flaw in Lincoln's character, in Browne's view, was his taste, if not flair, for scatological prose and poetry. Although he conceded the "clearness, simplicity, and downright directness of purpose" of Lincoln's speeches, Browne believed such gifts were irrelevant because "whether it arose from his early training, from mental constitution, or merely from a motive of policy—or, more probably, from all combined— an ineradicable love of obscenity, and that not merely of witty smut but of simple filth, was a characteristic of the late President."[101] Browne also mentioned, correctly, that Lincoln had penned a book as a young man that attempted to disprove the truths of the Bible and had nearly taken part in a duel fought over some scurrilous letters published in a Spring- field, Illinois, newspaper ridiculing James Shields. Oddly enough for an elite white southerner, Browne labeled the averted duel "ridiculous and discreditable . . . an ostentatious display of honor and valor . . . the con- summation of shabby absurdity."[102]

But what really stoked Browne's ire was Lincoln's political career, one in which, he thought, Lincoln had duplicitously and continually tacked as the political winds blew in Illinois toward the more popular position. Browne thought that in appearing to be antislavery, Lincoln "in fact wanted to keep all blacks, free or slave, out of the Territories altogether; and would have been overjoyed to discover any practicable way for deporting the whole race out of the country."[103] Browne finished his review with a flourish, oozing sadness and disbelief that a man so low of birth and clearly ignoble background could conquer his honorable but now lost Confederacy: "The whole story of his career from beginning to end is so dreary, so wretched, so shabby, such a tissue of pitiful dodging and chicanery, so unrelieved by anything pure, noble, or dignified, that even to follow it as far as we have done, has well-nigh surpassed our powers of endurance; and when, putting all partisan feeling aside, we look back at the men who were cho- sen by their countrymen to fill the places that this man has occupied—a

Washington, a Jefferson, a Madison, an Adams, or later, a Webster, a Clay, or a Calhoun—men of culture and refinement, of honor, of exalted patriotism, of broad views and wise statesmanship—and measure the distance from them to Abraham Lincoln, we sicken with shame and disgust."[104]

Browne's colleague Albert Taylor Bledsoe (1809–77) elaborated upon Browne's diatribe in the *Southern Review,* a literary journal the two men briefly coedited.[105] Born in Kentucky, Bledsoe was an intellectually gifted child with a special talent for mathematics. When he was fifteen years old, he received an appointment to West Point, where his classmates included future Confederate notables Jefferson Davis, Robert E. Lee, and Leonidas Polk. Polk later said that in thirty-eight years of friendship with Bledsoe, he "never knew him to utter a selfish or unworthy word."[106] Serving two years in the U.S. Army between 1830 and 1832, Bledsoe eventually resigned his commission and began to study law in the future capital of the Confederacy, Richmond, Virginia. After a year of reading for the bar, Bledsoe moved to Kenyon College in Ohio so that he could help prepare one of his younger brothers to become a doctor. Unfortunately, his brother died in a cholera outbreak, whereupon Bledsoe decided to study theology at Kenyon. After graduation he took orders in the Episcopal Church, served as a clergyman for a brief time in Ohio and Kentucky, but eventually left the priesthood over doctrinal disagreements regarding baptism and eventually moved to Illinois.[107]

By 1840 Bledsoe resided in the new capital of Illinois, Springfield, the perfect place for a budding lawyer to prosper. He quickly became friends with both Stephen Douglas and Abraham Lincoln and was widely recognized as a fine and able attorney throughout Illinois. In 1843 Bledsoe won more cases than any other lawyer in the state and during his career won over 50 percent of the cases that he argued before the Illinois Supreme Court. In addition, he defeated Lincoln in cases in which they opposed each other over 50 percent of the time, and although it appears that he and Lincoln never fought on the same side in the courtroom, they were deeply enmeshed in Illinois politics as friends and devoted Whigs. Bledsoe and Lincoln vigorously supported William Henry Harrison's candidacy for president in 1840 and as loyal Whigs were suspicious of executive authority, especially as exercised during Andrew Jackson's presidency. Later they opposed the Mexican War and supported the Wilmot Proviso, which would have disallowed slavery in any territories acquired as a result of the war with Mexico. Bledsoe was also a friend of Mary Todd Lincoln; he and his wife, Harriet Coxe Bledsoe, lived in the Globe Tavern with the newly married Lincolns in the early 1840s. Like no other southerner, Bledsoe was intimately involved in the political and personal world of Abraham Lincoln.[108]

After practicing law for a decade, Bledsoe moved south, returned to his love for mathematics, and became a professor in that subject at the University of Mississippi and later the University of Virginia. He produced numerous and respected works ranging in subject matter from *Theodicy, or Vindication of the Divine Glory* (1854), to *An Essay on Liberty and Slavery* (1856), and *The Philosophy of Mathematics* (1868). In the 1856 work defending slavery, Bledsoe attacked what he labeled the seventeen fallacies of abolitionists (including the idea that the Declaration of Independence was an abolitionist document) and showed, at least to his own satisfaction, that "the institution of slavery, as it exists among us at the South, is founded in political justice, is in accordance with the will of God and the designs of Providence, and is conducive to the highest, purest, best interests of mankind."[109] When war broke out between the United States and the slaveholding South in 1861, Bledsoe remained loyal to the Confederacy and his old West Point classmate Jefferson Davis by serving briefly in the Department of War. In the latter part of the conflict, according to Bledsoe's daughter Sophie, Davis asked his old friend to "undertake to prepare a book on the constitutional right of secession." Doing most of his research at the British Museum in London, where records could more easily be found, Bledsoe investigated the question of secession's constitutionality. Upon his return to the United States after Appomattox and in the midst of the bitter battles over the reconstruction of the United States, Bledsoe defended Davis with a book published in 1866 entitled *Is Davis a Traitor; or, Was Secession a Constitutional Right Previous to the War of 1861?* while the former Confederate president languished in prison for allegedly conspiring in Lincoln's assassination. The *Richmond Enquirer and Examiner* claimed that Bledsoe's volume exposed the "fallacies of the Massachusetts school of politics" and predicted, in language that foreshadowed Alexander Stephens, that the work would soon be as popular in the North as the South because its view of the Constitution and states' rights would protect all Americans "from the evils of a central despotism."[110]

Bledsoe fiercely defended the Confederacy after the war, promoted the Lost Cause, and used the *Southern Review* to advance his reactionary ideals. The *Review* was written and edited mostly by Bledsoe, although William Hand Browne helped with editorial duties for nearly two years, before leaving the journal in 1868.[111] By 1871, according to historian Richard Weaver (1910–63), the *Review* had become "the official organ of the Methodist Church."[112] For over a decade Lincoln's former colleague shared with subscribers his observations on biology, natural history, literature, poetry, classical culture, mathematics, religion, and, of course, the recent war between the North and the South. Although its subscription list "probably never exceeded three thousand," some of Bledsoe's readers consisted of the elite in the postbellum South and the journal reached an international audience.[113] Bledsoe's work reflected and contributed to a strain of Lost Cause thought coursing through the region, including the ideas that the South was justified in seceding from the Union in 1860–61, had fought nobly in the war but succumbed to overwhelming northern resources, and had nothing for which to apologize to the North now that the war was over and, finally, that Abraham Lincoln was most emphatically not a good man or president.

Equally important, Bledsoe represented, if not directed, intellectual currents in the South that saw the recent Civil War as unjust and inhumane and viewed it through a religious lens. His was a simple morality play, with Christianity and the South on one side in the conflict and atheism or infidelity allied with Lincoln and the North on the other. If war is a continuation of politics by other means, to paraphrase the Prussian military scientist Carl von Clausewitz (1780–1831), in Bledsoe's case it may be said that his writings were the continuation of the war by literary means. Destroying Lincoln's reputation was an important tenet of Bledsoe's Lost Cause theology.[114] In one January 1869 essay Bledsoe compared the French and American Revolutions, exclaiming that the essential difference between the two was that "one [France] was instigated by infidel philosophers; the other [American], by professedly religious preachers." Alas, "both Revolutions" succumbed to the erroneous belief in the perfectibility of man and were "nourished by the same fell spirit, and brought forth the same fruits of desolation and death. It was precisely this same virus," Bledsoe averred, "which convulsed and devoured France in 1789 and America in 1861. It was not as Christian divines, but as infidel dreamers and reformers, that the Beechers, the Tyngs, the Cheevers, and the McIlvaines, of the North," and by association Abraham Lincoln, "trod in the fatal footsteps of the Voltaires, the Rousseaus, and the Raynals, of France."[115] The recent conflict was from Bledsoe's standpoint not only a civil war but something even larger and more important: it was a religious and theological conflict that (to borrow a phrase from historians Elizabeth Fox-Genovese and Eugene Genovese), pitted Jerusalem and Athens and the white, Christian South against Paris and the supposedly mongrelized, Jacobin North, with Abraham Lincoln as an American version of a French Revolutionary.[116] Alongside such ideas, Bledsoe believed, as did many other Lost Cause aficionados, that the true God of the North was not the God of the Bible but money. To Bledsoe's vexation the epitome of northern civilization was the man who biographers such as Josiah Holland extolled as a virtuous Christian, Abraham Lincoln.[117]

Early in his editorial tenure Bledsoe made intermittent and derogatory comments about Lincoln. In an 1869 article entitled "Alexander Hamilton," he argued that the war proved Lincoln was Hamilton's protégé in the sense that he professed to love the Constitution but disregarded it as necessity demanded. But unlike the former Treasury secretary, Lincoln was "without the chivalry, or the conscience, or the cultivation, or the genius, of Alexander Hamilton."[118] Bledsoe bewailed that the country had made "a hero out of one who fought all his battles by proxy; a saint out of one who sacrificed his principles on the altar of success; and a martyr out of one who had made ten thousand martyrs out of braver and better men than himself." He also called Lincoln a tyrant for his treatment of southern prisoners of war and, especially, for the Emancipation Proclamation.[119] Bledsoe failed to note one essential difference between Hamilton and Lincoln: whereas Hamilton's policies consciously forged a strong connection between American elites and the infant American Republic, Lincoln's, by way of contrast, resulted in a new link between America's least fortunate and most oppressed people, American slaves, and the new nation-state created by the Civil War. Of course, this may be precisely why Bledsoe came to loathe his former friend.

So, when Lamon's biography was published in 1872, Bledsoe had already made periodic remarks about Abraham Lincoln, making him perhaps the most uniquely qualified white southerner to comment on the work. In April 1873 Bledsoe reviewed Lamon's biography as a method of public reflection about his former friend and colleague. He opened with a modest comment on his association with Lincoln during the 1840s, writing that he was pleased to have interacted with the future president on a daily basis and wanted to share his privileged, unique conclusions about "one of the most extraordinary human beings" in history. "The world will," he alerted his readers, "perhaps, know him a little better because we have known him."[120] Unlike Herndon, who Bledsoe said "had no soul, no mind, no eye for the really remarkable qualities of Mr. Lincoln," the Lost Cause "architect" led his readers to believe that they would get a much better and more insightful treatment from him into the true nature of Abraham Lincoln.[121]

Bledsoe focused his essay on Lincoln's character, inquired into the source of Lincoln's greatness, and asked whether such greatness was a deserved appellation of the Civil War president. To be sure, Bledsoe's review of Lamon's book was not entirely negative; indeed, Bledsoe conceded that Lincoln had possessed some virtues, as he remarked favorably upon Lincoln's "powerful intellect," explained that Lincoln had been "powerful in a law argument," and held that although his education was "radically deficient," Lincoln nevertheless had possessed "the power of patient thought" and had been a "formidable antagonist" as a lawyer.[122] Bledsoe informed his readers, furthermore, that Lincoln had been an effective orator who had acquired the craft of public speaking through "careful reflection and self-cultivation," and his speeches were interwoven with "simple, terse, plain, direct English" that audiences found persuasive.[123] At this point in the essay the *Southern Review*'s subscribers may have wondered if Bledsoe thought their recent antagonist in the Civil War had any poor qualities at all. They were not to be disappointed, however, as Bledsoe proceeded to quote at length from Lincoln's Lyceum Speech, given in Springfield, Illinois, in 1838, in which the future president had cautioned his audience, over two decades before he took office, to beware an American "Alexander, [or] a Caesar, or a Napoleon," who "thirsts and burns for distinction" and "will have it, whether at the expense of emancipating slaves, or enslaving freemen."[124] Bledsoe maintained that "Mr. Lincoln . . . did both"; he had emancipated the slaves but enslaved free men in order to satisfy his own political ambitions. Bledsoe advanced here an interpretation of his former friend's words that fused the recent conflict's results with speculative notions about Lincoln's Napoleonic motivations for waging the Civil War that would enjoy a long life among the president's enemies. In all likelihood, however, Lincoln was not inadvertently referring to his own thirst for distinction in the Lyceum Address but sarcastically warning his townsmen about the Caesaristic ambitions of Stephen A. Douglas, a rising Democratic star in Springfield. Neither Bledsoe nor his readers were aware of this information, but white southerners—acutely alert to their own struggles in 1873 to emancipate control of their states from ambitious and supposedly nefarious carpetbaggers, scalawags, and former slaves who favored some measure of racial equality in the postbellum South—could not have missed Bledsoe's white supremacist point that because of Abraham Lincoln, they were now enslaved by their supposed inferiors.[125]

So, Bledsoe had conceded that Lincoln possessed certain virtues and was in some ways even an honest man, but he also argued that the president was altogether too earnest in his longing to distinguish himself in the world. This burning desire for distinction, according to Bledsoe, was Lincoln's most important characteristic and led to monstrous dishonesty. Indeed, Bledsoe thought that Lincoln's ruling passion, or ambition, was precisely what "explains his career, and accounts for his success," not his "hatred of oppression, coupled with a love of freedom."[126] Indeed, "nothing is farther from the truth."[127] Bledsoe described Lincoln's upbringing as crude and deficient and claimed, in contrast to Josiah Holland, that Lincoln was an infidel. In addition, Bledsoe noted that Lincoln believed he was a superior man and hated that he "lived among pigs and pigeons."[128] Later he labeled Lincoln as "one of the most obscene men that ever lived . . . he never enjoyed his jokes so keenly, or with such a *gusto,* as when they were strongly seasoned with obscenity and filth."[129] But in order to win votes and gain lasting fame, Lincoln had suppressed the indecent aspect of his character. It was Lincoln's boundless ambition that was "the one, intense, all-absorbing, and all-consuming passion of his life. As Aaron's rod swallowed up the rods of the magicians," Bledsoe explained, "so this ruling passion of Mr. Lincoln swallowed up all the other passions and desires of his nature," which made him a "perfect monster."[130] Such a Faustian bargain, in Bledsoe's opinion, was hardly admirable or worthy of emulation. More important, although Lincoln was currently popular among some segments of the United States, "an apotheosis by the Demos, however grand and imposing in the eyes of men, is not a sure passport into the kingdom of God."[131] In keeping with wartime denunciations of the president as an abolitionist, Bledsoe concluded his excoriation of Lincoln with a brutal, devastating assessment:

> We think, on the whole, that Mr. Lincoln was "the right man in the right place." No man fitter than he, indeed, to represent the Northern Demos; or, as Wendell Phillips has it, "the party of the North pledged against the party of the South." For if, as we believe, that was the cause of brute force, blind passion, fanatical hate, lust of power, and the greed of gain, against the cause of constitutional law and human rights, then who was better fitted to represent it than the talented, but the low, ignorant and vulgar, rail-splitter of Illinois? Or if, as we also believe, it was the cause of infidelity and atheism, and against the principles and the spirit of the Christian religion, then who more worthy to muster its motley hosts, and let them slip with the fury of the

pit, than the low-bred infidel of Pigeon Creek, in whose eyes the Savior of the world was "an Illegitimate child," and the Holy Mother as base as his own.[132]

Bledsoe believed that Lincoln was a representative man, the embodiment of a section of the United States that was unchristian, heathen, one that had gained the world but in fact lost its very soul.

Bledsoe's essay was a damning indictment of the recently murdered president, one that was especially important because he, like Herndon and Lamon, had personally known Lincoln before his presidency and subsequent iconic stature in American life. Bledsoe's criticism anticipated, furthermore, the numerous attacks launched by Lincoln's enemies in its denigration of his former friend's background, character, and atheism. It was nevertheless one of the ironies of Bledsoe's life that, when he lived in Illinois, he had condemned the expansion of slavery in the territories acquired from Mexico, yet until his death in 1877 he defended a regime that had fought so ferociously to maintain and extend that same institution. It is clear that Bledsoe, despite his Christian faith, never forgave Abraham Lincoln for emancipating the slaves, allegedly enslaving whites, or defeating his beloved South. Nor could he forgive a country that venerated such a man and placed him on a pedestal equal to George Washington. In the future many Lincoln antagonists embraced these views, as much of the South transitioned into a modern industrial society. To a large degree Bledsoe's criticism of Lincoln, issued when racial boundaries were still sharply contested, was in fact a reactionary, or counterrevolutionary, assault on the new, more democratic, pluralistic, and secular American nation emerging from the war.[133]

There is no evidence that Bledsoe, or William Hand Browne for that matter, received any significant condemnation for their reviews of Lamon's biography.[134] Many white southerners may have remained silent about the authors' attacks on Lincoln because they were preoccupied with more pressing matters, such as justifying the greatness of their military in the late war and regaining control of their states from the Republican Party, or party of Lincoln. Of course, that does not mean criticism of their reviews of Lamon's biography did not exist, but Bledsoe for one never felt compelled to defend his attack on Lincoln in the pages of the *Southern Review,* something he frequently did regarding other matters that he deemed important. Bledsoe relished polemics, and if he had received significant or voluminous criticism of what he wrote about Lincoln, he would have responded to it in the pages of his journal. Without pushing the evidence too far, it seems Bledsoe's attack on his former friend circulated without much controversy or comment in the South in the early 1870s, especially among elite white southerners.

One especially intriguing aspect of the various criticisms leveled against Lincoln—both during the war and now in its aftermath— was the language his detractors used to express their disapproval. Words matter, for they yield insights into what some Americans still believed was admirable, sacred, and worthy of emulation after the war concluded, and of no individual was this perhaps more true than Abraham Lincoln.[135] So, when Pennsylvania Democrat William Bradford Reed wrote Jefferson Davis from New York City about the Lamon biography, he commented that the book was not only an interesting and true account of Lincoln's life but was also "very disgusting in its truth."[136] Browne, in the conclusion to his review of Lincoln's life, said the man's whole career caused him to "sicken with shame and disgust," while Bledsoe said Lincoln was "low, ignorant and vulgar," the editor of the Kentucky *Sign of the Times* said the president was the father of "smutty stories," and it was alleged that the governor of Indiana and future vice president of the United States Thomas Hendricks had said Lincoln was a "smutty old tyrant" in order to discredit him politically.[137] The *Milwaukee Daily Sentinel* reported as early as 1868 that a paper in Louisville, Kentucky, the *Sentinel on the Border,* had contrasted Confederate president Jefferson Davis with Lincoln, and in its comparison characterized the dead president as "an unsettled, shifting, vulgar, rollicking man."[138] Nowhere were the uses of such language and the themes of Lincoln criticism in the postbellum era better illustrated than in the Charleston poet Paul Hamilton Hayne's letter to Margaret J. Preston in 1871 commenting on a recent play about the Civil War president: "These 'Homeric lines' on *Lincoln,* for instance, *may* be good, but I see continually between each stanza, the gawky, coarse, not-over cleanly, whisky drinking, and whisky smelling Blackguard, elevated by a grotesque *Chance* (nearly allied to *Satan*) to the position for which of all others, he was most unfit;—and whose memory has been *idealized* by the Yankee fancy, & Yankee arrogance, in a way that *would* be ludicrous, were it not *disgusting,* and calculated, finally, to belie the facts of History, and hand down to future times as Hero and Martyr, as commonplace a Vulgarian as ever patronized bad Tobacco, and mistook *blasphemy* for *wit.*"[139]

Clearly, words such as *disgust, low-bred,* and *vulgar* betrayed a class-based attack on Lincoln's character. According to *Webster's Dictionary* from 1828, the word *disgust* referred to a strong dislike, "an unpleasant sensation in the mind excited by something offensive in the manners, conduct, language or opinions of others. Thus, obscenity in language and clownishness in behavior excite disgust."[140] In using such words to describe the former chief executive, Lincoln's critics were not simply expressing their dislike for the dead president or signaling to their readers in the strongest terms imaginable their aversion to Lincoln's entire life and career; nor were they simply using such language to portray Lincoln—and by extension northern civilization—in the lowest possible terms. Rather, research by the moral psychologist Jonathan Haidt at the University of Virginia has shown that the emotion of disgust is a unique feature of conservative morality, and although disgust originally contained an oral component that contributed to our ancestors' survival, it also has a socio-moral element that "is a kind of character judgment of others, especially of people who violate the basic dignity of human beings."[141] Such a socio-moral aspect of disgust, according to Haidt, allows "human societies [to] take advantage of the schemata of core disgust in constructing their moral and social lives, and in socialising their children about what to avoid."[142] This suggests that those Americans, usually white southerners, who expressed an instinctual disgust for Lincoln after the war did so not just as an insult (radical egalitarian politician, lawyer, and writer Albion Tourgée, by way of contrast, approvingly called Lincoln "the Great Uncouth") but also to draw a sharp moral distinction between the noble South and the icon whom their northern brethren venerated, who they insisted was unworthy of such reverence. Disgust is far more than finding something or someone repulsive; it is "the emotion that guards the sanctity of the soul as well as the purity of the body."[143] The postwar jeremiads about Abraham Lincoln—jeremiads issued most frequently, although not exclusively, by white southerners—and the new American nation he to an extent embodied were an attempt made by Americans of a conservative political temperament to maintain white American purity and save white American souls.

Indeed, these attacks on Lincoln were an important part of the Lost Cause, a concerted and largely successful effort of influential men and women across the South to glorify the Confederacy and the alleged righteousness of the cause for which they had fought between 1861 and 1865. Many of the leading postbellum thinkers in the South and advocates of the Lost Cause were, like Bledsoe, male ministers, skeptical of democracy and modernity, men who looked sympathetically upon what they saw as the Christian, patriarchal, and hierarchical nature of the Old South. What was especially disconcerting about the defeat of the Confederacy in the Civil War, from such a viewpoint, was that a beautiful and superior Christian civilization had been killed, or at the very least contaminated, by an inferior society led by an allegedly disgusting lowbred infidel. Because of Lincoln, the worse men now commanded the better. To these white southerners and the Americans who came to accept their interpretation of the war, Abraham Lincoln was, to stand a then prevalent image of Lincoln on its head, not the First American; rather, he was the worst American and unworthy of national adulation.[144]

Gender likewise played an important role in the attack on Lincoln. Although there is limited evidence that white southern women continued to detest Lincoln in the immediate decades after the war, in the postbellum world Lincoln hatred remained, at least in public, an overwhelmingly male preoccupation. Most elite southern women, it seems, were too busy burying and honoring the Confederate dead, and any open contempt for Lincoln, especially in the midst of nearby Union troops, would have detracted from this mission. Because they were women, it was important that their glorification of the Confederacy appear to be nonpolitical in nature. Displaying public expressions of hatred of the recently slain president would have been at the very least politically unwise.[145] In future decades, however, privileged females would nurture their hatred for Lincoln, play a central role in the public commemoration of the Lost Cause, and became some of the most prominent Lincoln detractors in the United States from the 1890s onward.[146] Alongside such latent hostility, male criticism of Lincoln, someone they frequently characterized as vulgar, base, and disgusting, was perhaps a peaceful method for former Confederates to regain a sense of honor, manhood, and patriarchy once the war was over.

Equally vital to regaining a lost sense of masculinity, the propagation of the myth of the Lost Cause, and the continuation of scorn for Lincoln was the creation of the Southern Historical Society, founded in New Orleans in April 1869. The organization was dominated by males, Virginians such as Jubal Early (1816–94), an unreconstructed Confederate officer who devoted his postwar career to defending the Confederacy and its right to secede from the Union and extolling the godlike virtues of Robert E. Lee. In 1867 Early had written in his memoir of the war that he regarded "Abraham Lincoln, his counsellors and supporters, as the real traitors who had overthrown the Constitution," which resulted in "an odious despotism."[147] It was almost as if Early and other members of the Southern

Historical Society decided that if the North was going to idolize Lincoln, they would counter that image with Lee as an alternative deity in the *Southern Historical Society Papers,* which began publication in 1876 and was a continuation of William Hand Browne's *Southern Magazine.*[148]

At first glance Lincoln seemed to be extraneous to the *Papers,* but its pages contained numerous accusations, many of which would be used by future nemeses of the president. One such criticism was that Lincoln was a weak man because he did not have the strength to resist more radical politicians to prevent war in 1860 or negotiate peace in 1865. In a review of "Memoir of a Narrative Received of Colonel John B. Baldwin, of Staunton, Touching the Origin of the War" the Rev. R. L. Dabney, D.D., gave readers his account of what Baldwin had told him in 1865 about meeting with Lincoln four years earlier, in April 1861, when the president was considering if Fort Sumter in Charleston Harbor should be reinforced and how to keep Virginia from seceding. Baldwin reportedly told the president, among other things, that Fort Sumter should be evacuated in order to conciliate states in the Upper South that had not yet seceded. According to Baldwin, the Lincoln administration was "fully aware that neither Constitution nor laws gave them any right to coerce a State to remain in the Union. The whole people, even in the imperious North, knew and recognized this truth."[149]

Baldwin believed Lincoln was manhandled by his advisors, including Secretary of State William H. Seward, and radical state governors in the North. "They had urged upon Lincoln," Baldwin claimed, "that the best way to secure his party triumph was to precipitate a collision."[150] Unfortunately, Lincoln "had not manliness enough to recede" from his commitment to northern state executives.[151] Dabney related his own litany of the consequences of Lincoln's effeminacy: the people of the North blindly gave up their rights "to the high-handed usurpations of . . . Lincoln and Seward, under pretext of subduing the seceded States, such as the suspension of habeas corpus, the State prisons, the arrests without indictment, and the martial law imposed, at the beck of the Federal power, in States called by itself 'loyal.'"[152] Lincoln was a mere pawn manipulated by radical governors and Seward, lacking the strength to resist their supposedly evil designs.

Equally important, Lincoln knew the folly of refusing to evacuate Fort Sumter but allegedly asked Baldwin, if he did not do what Seward and the Radicals wanted, "what would become of my tariffs?"[153] Dabney concluded: "Hence, when Virginia offered him a safe way to preserve the Union, he preferred to destroy the Union and preserve his tariffs. The war was conceived in duplicity, and brought forth in iniquity."[154] Consequently, for

Dabney and innumerable Lost Cause advocates, responsibility for the Civil War could not be laid at the South's doorstep; it rested exclusively on Lincoln's shoulders, was unconstitutional, fought for the preservation of tariffs (not to end slavery), and foisted upon a weak and unsuspecting president by nefarious Radical Republicans and Secretary of State Seward in order to preserve their party. It was the continuation of a wartime accusation that would persist into the twenty-first century.[155]

Portraying Lincoln as subject to the control of others was distinctly at odds with additional criticism leveled in the *Southern Historical Society Papers*. Again and again, the *Papers* asserted that once the war commenced, Lincoln waged it with indiscriminate cruelty and ferociousness by freeing the slaves; by refusing prisoner exchanges with the Confederate government, leading to the deaths of thousands of Union and Confederate soldiers; and by authorizing Ben Butler's and William Sherman's attacks on the South. In the very first issue of the *Papers* in 1876, an "Address of Congress to the People of the Confederate States (adopted in December, 1863, nearly a year after the issuance of the Emancipation Proclamation)" was reprinted in full. Contained within this wartime address was the accusation that Lincoln was a war criminal: "Disregarding the teachings of the approved writers on international law, and the practice and claims of his own government in its purer days, President Lincoln has sought to convert the South into a St. Domingo, by appealing to the cupidity, lusts, ambition and ferocity of the slave. Abraham Lincoln is but the lineal descendant of Dunmore [the colonial governor of Virginia, who offered slaves their freedom if they fought for the British in the War for Independence], and the impotent malice of each was foiled by the fidelity of those who, by the meanness of the conspirators, would only, if successful, have been seduced into idleness, filth, vice, beggary and death."[156] So, eleven years after Appomattox, unrepentant and influential ex-Confederates republished in a leading journal charges that Abraham Lincoln had broken international law, encouraged slave insurrections, and had the audacity to present slaves with the opportunity to gain their freedom if they fought for the Union army. Such forceful accusations contradict the idea that after the war concluded, Abraham Lincoln's reputation had been thoroughly transformed in the former states of the Confederacy.

Six years later an article on the Confederate prison camp at Andersonville by Edward Wellington Boate, a Union prisoner at the site, accused the former president of similar heartlessness. In essence he criticized Lincoln for refusing prisoner exchanges during the war. According to Boate, the inmates at Andersonville "called a great meeting" and agreed to formally ask Lincoln to "agree to an exchange of prisoners." Three furloughed prisoners eventually traveled North to Washington, D.C. (Boate was not among them), to meet with Lincoln. "They wrote to the President," Boate recalled, "and reported the object of their visit on three consecutive days; but it distresses me to state *that the representatives of thirty-eight thousand Union prisoners were treated with silent contempt, the President declining to see them or have any communication with them!!!*"[157] Boate said he would be "silent as to the motive of the President Lincoln in his treatment of the delegation. But I cannot help stating that the lives of some ten or twelve thousand men might have been spared had an exchange justly, I will not add generously, taken place at this period."[158] Of course, white southerners were pleased with such an assessment from a former Union soldier, for they were quick to ascribe wicked motives to Lincoln. Such actions, from their standpoint, no matter how much they contradicted other accounts within the *Papers,* were characteristic of a cruel, inhumane tyrant, not those of a weak president or a man worthy of emulation.[159]

Allegations of Lincoln's malfeasance omitted, however, the key reason that Lincoln had refused prisoner exchanges, probably because it would have reflected poorly on the Confederacy's own methods of waging war. In retaliation for Lincoln's issuance of the Emancipation Proclamation in 1863, Confederate president Jefferson Davis issued an order effectively stating that United States officers who commanded black troops would be put to death and black soldiers caught in the Confederacy would be reenslaved.[160] The Lincoln administration refused prisoner exchanges because the Confederacy would not treat all captured soldiers of the United States Army the same regardless of their race.[161] As the war dragged on into 1864, the two sides remained at an impasse over the issue, but Lincoln never backed down from his humane demand that black Union soldiers captured by the Confederacy be given the same treatment as white troops, even though this stance was an effective propaganda tool for the Confederacy and possibly damaged Lincoln during the 1864 presidential election.[162] Such nuances, unfortunately, were not adequately addressed, if at all, in the *Papers,* and the exclusion of the idea that the Confederacy was at the very least partially responsible for the deaths of imprisoned soldiers is striking. It points to a methodology of omission and distortion that has been characteristic of virtually all Lincoln opposition. Like all human beings, white southern critics, to quote Thucydides, "made their recollections fit in with their sufferings."[163]

Despite the hostility uttered toward Lincoln in the postwar era, most Americans, including southerners of all races, celebrated Abraham Lincoln's memory. Albion Tourgée described Lincoln in 1885 as "the fruit of a marvelous past, and the precursor of a future to be shaped and moulded by his aspirations."[164] Like Tourgée, African Americans, most notably the former slave and abolitionist Frederick Douglass, resisted Lincoln's opponents and fought to preserve an ideological, abolitionist, or anti-caste memory of the Civil War, a vision that contrasted sharply with alternate, racially inegalitarian currents flowing through American society that sought national reconciliation at the expense of racial equality.[165] To be sure, in his 1876 "Oration in Memory of Abraham Lincoln," delivered at the unveiling of a Lincoln statue in Washington, D.C., Douglass acknowledged that "Abraham Lincoln was not, in the fullest sense of the word, either our man or our model. In his interests, in his associations, in his habits of thought, and in his prejudices, he was a white man. He was preeminently the white man's President, entirely devoted to the welfare of white men."[166] Nevertheless, his view of Lincoln in this speech and elsewhere was, on balance, laudatory rather than condemnatory. Douglass was especially worried that in the postbellum decades Americans were in the process of forgetting the causes and consequences of the war Lincoln thought worth fighting, a war that resulted in the liberation of four million slaves from inhuman bondage. "Whatever else I may forget," Douglass said in 1883, "I shall never forget the difference between those who fought for liberty and those who fought for slavery; between those who fought to save the Republic and those who fought to destroy it."[167] More clearly than anyone else in the United States, Douglass understood that African American freedom after the war would be dependent on an accurate memory of the conflict, or to put it another way, which interpretation of the Civil War, abolitionist or reconciliationist, became dominant. Other leading African Americans, such as the former slave Booker T. Washington, in all likelihood agreed with Douglass but emphasized different themes in vigorously countering the view of Lost Cause devotees disgusted by Lincoln's background and character. Indeed, Washington found in Lincoln's upbringing much to admire because, despite his boyhood circumstances Lincoln had, by the practice of self-denial and reading, raised himself "from the humble log cabin to the Presidency of the greatest republic on earth."[168] It is possible that Douglass, Washington, and other African American leaders understood that attacking Lincoln was one way to attack the former slave, and they countered negative portrayals of Lincoln as a tyrant with their image of Lincoln as the Great Emancipator.

Still, Douglass and Washington were elite African Americans relatively free to voice their opinions about the war and Abraham Lincoln without fear of violent recrimination. More courageous were those African Americans living in the postwar South who commemorated Abraham Lincoln's memory and, by so doing, directly challenged Lost Cause interpretations of the Civil War. In fact, some celebrations of emancipation by the former slaves came before the Civil War had even concluded. In Charleston, South Carolina, on March 21, 1865, African Americans in the city held a parade and openly celebrated their freedom.[169] After the war was formally over, African Americans commemorated annually (on January 1 and July 4) their emancipation, Abraham Lincoln, the independence of the United States, and the bright prospects for the future of liberty across the globe due to Union victory in the Civil War. On July 4, 1865, fewer than three months after Lincoln's death, women in Augusta, Georgia, displayed a banner in an Independence Day parade with the words "Abraham Lincoln the Father of Our Liberties and Savior of His Country" emblazoned for all to see.[170] The annual Emancipation Day festivities often involved long treks to town so that African Americans could exult in their newfound freedom with rituals that included orators reciting aloud the Emancipation Proclamation. Such celebrations of emancipation as divinely ordained were in direct contrast to Lost Cause theology that the Confederate States of America was God's chosen nation and would eventually be vindicated by history.[171] Rather, African American Emancipation Day celebrations celebrated the past and anticipated a future of expanding freedom for all Americans. In one remarkable incident from 1867 at the Lincoln Industrial School located in Richmond, Virginia, African American students spontaneously asserted their affection for Lincoln and a sense of responsibility for the continuance of liberty in the United States when the Civil War president's image and an American flag were simultaneously hoisted aloft: "Lincoln for ever! Gone, gone for ever! Sleep, dear father, in thy grave; Union and freedom *we* will save."[172] Over twenty years later, in 1889, African Americans were still celebrating Abraham Lincoln's memory. On January 1, in New Orleans, the *Southwestern Christian Advocate* reported that during an Emancipation Day celebration to be held at New Orleans University, the unveiling of the portraits of three prominent citizens would be part of the festivities. "Bishop Gilbert Haven and Dr. R. S. Rust [and Abraham

Lincoln]. These are to hang upon the walls of New Orleans University," the
Advocate reported, "with the portrait of Lincoln in the center. The thought
is in the center. . . . It is fitting that these unique men be thus associated.
What a trinity! We shall never see their like again."[173]

To be sure, in addition to African American celebrations of Lincoln as
the Great Emancipator, there were prominent white southerners, conceivably a majority, who praised the sixteenth president in the war's aftermath.
Despite his previous literary fulminations against the president, Alexander
Stephens referred to Lincoln's "warm-hearted" magnanimity and gener-
osity in a speech given after the unveiling of Francis Carpenter's portrait
"The Signing of the Emancipation Proclamation."[174] Another southerner
who praised Lincoln in glowing terms was Henry W. Grady, editor of the
Atlanta Constitution newspaper and evangelist for a "New South," who
cast aside the idea that antebellum slavery had been a positive good and
instead advocated an industrial and modern South. Grady told a New York
audience what it wanted to hear in 1886 when he praised Lincoln as a representative man, "the first typical American" who was "the sum of Puritan
and Cavalier," one who "fused the virtues of both, and in the depths of
his great soul the faults of both were lost."[175] Lincoln was a man of whom
all Americans could justly be proud. There were other influential white
southerners, the Louisville newspaper editor Henry Watterson and future
president Woodrow Wilson being two of the more notable examples, who
at the turn of the century spoke similarly. Historian Michael Davis has
argued that such southerners found "in praising Lincoln they announced
to the North their willingness to share in those very national virtues for
which the North had canonized Lincoln as its martyr-hero."[176]

One must be careful, however, not to make too much of such a claim. As
we have seen, northern opinion remained more divided about Lincoln than
Davis argued, and some white southerners were hardly forgiving regarding
their former foe. In fact, in 1881 Albion Tourgée perceived that if there was
unanimity of white southern opinion toward Lincoln, it was an opinion
that viewed the Confederacy as right and Lincoln as criminal. "If Jeff
Davis is to be glorified as a patriot and a martyr," he observed, "Lincoln
must, of necessity, be depreciated. If the rebellion was just and righteous,
of course its suppression was a crime."[177] Many of the more generous estimates of Lincoln's character and career, moreover, came from the 1890s
onward, a time when such praise was more likely, as the United States
headed toward the centennial of Lincoln's birth and celebrated its growth
as a world power in the wake of its victory in the Spanish-American War.

Also, a close reading of many of the positive utterances about Lincoln
by white southerners reveals that they reflected the perceived severity
of the Reconstruction era, which they claimed would have been averted
had Lincoln lived. In the May 1874 issue of the *Southern Magazine,* former
Confederate Edwin De Leon published a lengthy, reflective essay entitled
"Ruin and Reconstruction of the Southern States," in which he lamented
Lincoln's death because of its impact on *whites.* "With the assassination
of Mr. Lincoln were again unchained all the evil passions engendered by
the war," De Leon exclaimed, "and a new charter of license and arbitrary
power was given to the men who had made the 'religion of hate' their creed,
and who hoped to perpetuate their lease of power by pandering to popular
passion."[178] Of course, what white southerners were complaining about
was that an attempt had been made by the federal government to ensure
some measure of equality for the freedmen after the war, an attempt they
convinced themselves would not have occurred without Lincoln's assassination. In that sense it was wise for white supremacists to claim or accept that Lincoln was a tenderhearted Christian, for that characterization
meshed quite well with similar expressions of willingness to forgive and
forget emanating from northern ministers such as Henry Ward Beecher
and Dwight Moody. Thus, one reason why public expression of opposition
to Lincoln may have been, at least on the surface, unpopular in the South
was that many detractors were calling Lincoln an atheist at the very time
it was politically useful for white supremacists to claim him as a compassionate Christian who would have never countenanced black suffrage or
equality. Many white southerners may have wished that Lincoln's more
vocal critics, although possibly agreeing with their negative stance, would
simply remain silent while they endeavored to redeem their states from
Republicans and reinstitute repressive white control of African Americans
on a different foundation than racially based slavery.[179]

The collective national amnesia willfully embraced by white Christians
in the North and South regarding why the Civil War had been fought occurred at the expense not only of an African American memory of the
war but of African Americans and their rights as American citizens.[180]
The sad, tragic, irony was that as the memory of Abraham Lincoln was
publicly celebrated across the United States as the Savior of the Union
and Great Emancipator, such celebrations eventually coincided with the
erosion of the basic freedoms African Americans had won for themselves
during the Civil War and Reconstruction. Sacrificed on the altar of white,
Christian nationalism and reunion, African Americans were denied their

freedoms. Perhaps it would have been better for African Americans after the war if Abraham Lincoln had been portrayed as a hard-hearted atheist who would not have absolved his former enemies for trying to break up the country in order to establish a slaveholding Confederacy on the North American continent. Such an image might have aided those Americans who sought a more racially egalitarian country and prevented the cheap and unsought-for forgiveness of former Confederates who continued to believe in the righteousness of their cause that instead took place. Ceremonies celebrating Emancipation and Abraham Lincoln nevertheless contributed mightily to an internal, psychological resistance on the part of African Americans to Lost Cause interpretations of the war commending the virtues of a Confederacy that explicitly denigrated their race.[181]

After Reconstruction ended, the reconciliation between the two sections of the country regarding the Lincoln image was real, but there were notable white southerners who challenged that understanding. Although the large majority of newspapers praised Henry Grady's speech praising Lincoln, there were dissenters. The editor of the *Charleston News and Courier,* Francis W. Dawson, at first ignored Grady's opinions about Lincoln but eventually used the same language that Browne and Bledsoe had earlier employed. Dawson, in contrast to Grady, described Lincoln as "coarse while kindly, vulgar though good-hearted, ill-bred while acute, awkward while amiable, and weak in act while strong in word."[182] Jubal Early wrote incredulously to Jefferson Davis about Alexander Stephens's paeans to Lincoln. "Are our leading Southern representatives, and bitterest revilers of the North," Early asked, "about to reconcile themselves into a mutual admiration society, leaving such 'irreconcilables' as you and me out in the cold?"[183] Such viewpoints as Early's, it must be emphasized, were up against powerful forces favoring reconciliation, which made the task of Lincoln's opponents extremely frustrating. While their hatred of Lincoln resonated with many white southerners, for reasons of political expediency their message was, if not ignored, submerged by an overwhelming sentiment favoring reunion.

By the end of the 1880s the outlines of a tradition hostile to Abraham Lincoln had come clearly into focus in the United States. Naturally, it was expressed with more frequency and vehemence in the South by elite white southerners. Whereas northerners tended to venerate Lincoln after his death, many former Confederates continued to hate their wartime adversary, even as some, probably most, in their midst softened their attitudes toward the deceased president in the postwar era, coming to believe that

Lincoln's death had been a terrible misfortune for the white South. Within the South, African Americans emerged as Lincoln's most devoted admirers, even if they found it increasingly difficult and dangerous to express their views because there was an outlook toward the idea of federal enforcement of racial equality (which the freedmen associated with Lincoln) that was increasingly and decidedly hostile. For them a state's right to regulate "its internal affairs," as Robert E. Lee had told Lord Acton, did not protect democracy, liberty, or equality but subverted them. Still, there were repeated personal attacks on Lincoln's freethinking atheism, his ignoble background, the vulgarity of his character, and parallel disgust with his entire life. Added to these verbal assaults were constant, if not contradictory, accusations that Lincoln was a weak president for failing to prevent the war or, conversely, that he was an imperialistic despot for coercing the Confederacy to remain in the Union, an executioner who conducted an unconstitutional, immoral, criminal war, especially in his refusal to agree to prisoner exchanges.[184] Critics also lambasted Lincoln for taking away northern liberties once the conflict began. Just as inconsistently, not a few Americans continued to lament his assassination because they believed that the president would have combined magnanimity with strength to prevent the imposition of a supposedly harsh and radical reconstruction, while there were others who thought Lincoln would have been too weak to resist the fundamental changes the more radical members of his party advocated after the war.

Jefferson Davis, for one, claimed he did not want southerners to be trapped in the past but wished for them to look toward a glorious future for the American nation. Near the end of his life Davis declared that it was his wish "that crimination and recrimination should forever cease, and then, on the basis of [white] fraternity and faithful regard for the rights of the States, there may be written on the arch of the Union, *Esto perpetua.*"[185] The former Confederate president died in the city of New Orleans on Friday, December 6, 1889. As with Lincoln, Jefferson Davis's virtues were celebrated in death in ways they had not been in life, as his body lay in state and was eventually transported from New Orleans across the South to Richmond, Virginia, where he was laid to rest.[186] A little over a week later, on December 14, 1889, the attorney general of the United States, William Henry Harrison Miller, corresponded with Kentucky abolitionist Cassius Clay regarding the obsequies to Davis and what they portended, anxiously writing: "I have been very greatly surprised at the tone of the Southern press and Southern speeches since the death of Jefferson Davis. It looks very much as if the expressions of loyalty to the old flag are expressions of the lips, while those in regard to the 'Lost Cause' are expressions of the heart. It may be, however, that these recent demonstrations mean less than would at first appear."[187] Only time would tell if Miller's prediction was correct, as Davis's death in a sense marked the passing of the generation that had fought the Civil War. Yet future generations of Americans would work assiduously over the decades to ensure that strong opposition to Abraham Lincoln remained alive and well in the new American century.

3

A NEW NATIONAL TYPE

The Great Imperialist, 1890–1918

In the midst of Venezuela's 1895 border dispute with England, Confederate veteran William Roane Aylett addressed former soldiers of the Army of Northern Virginia and Army of the Potomac in Washington, D.C., concerning Abraham Lincoln and Jefferson Davis. In his speech Aylett praised Lincoln extravagantly and linked the reunion of former adversaries with Anglo-Saxon racial expansionism. At first Aylett assured the assembled veterans that "none but Anglo-Americans could have made such a fight, and none but our kindred could have whipped us." He then recalled that when Lincoln died, he and his fellow Confederate soldiers in Lee's army "felt that we had lost a friend."[1] The grief that followed Lincoln's assassination thirty years earlier united the two sections, "victors and vanquished . . . both bleeding and weeping brothers, needing each other's sympathy and love . . . over the body of the dead president," who would have prevented the racial "horrors of reconstruction" had he lived.[2] Aylett thereafter shifted his focus overseas and spoke of the United States and Great Britain in explicitly racial terms, remarking that the recent war and its heroes would be looked upon with pride in "Anglo-Saxon history" and that everyone present was part of the "great English race," both "Puritan and Cavalier," all "representative of that Anglo-Saxon race at the front in all great deeds."[3] Warming to his theme of Anglo-American world supremacy, Aylett advocated that "the nation rebuke . . . [anyone] that seeks to renew the animosities born of our civil war, or to stir up strife between England and America. . . . Let the American Eagle and the British Lion stand together, and they can hurl defiance at a world in arms, and can command peace by the utterance of their united voices. Hate does not survive the tomb," Aylett concluded, "but love comes from Heaven and is eternal."[4]

Hatred between the North and South, coupled with loathing for Abraham Lincoln, nevertheless did survive the tomb, for from 1890 to 1918 hostility to Lincoln not only survived, but in some respects it was strengthened and institutionalized, at least in the former slaveholding states. Of course, as the speech by Aylett demonstrated, anyone who excoriated Lincoln in the early part of the twentieth century was to some extent fighting a losing battle, swimming against the tide of current events. These were extraordinary decades for the United States: in 1898 a self-confident American nation expanded overseas in the Spanish-American War, contributing to white male reconciliation between former Civil War combatants; a broad civic nationalism was replaced by a narrow ethnic one based upon white supremacy; a multifaceted reform movement known as Progressivism that was pro-Lincoln and pro–activist government emerged and reshaped American political discourse and ideals, even though Progressives rejected Lincoln's natural rights thinking; a celebration of the centennial of Lincoln's birth took place in 1909; a Virginian, Progressive, and Lincoln admirer, Woodrow Wilson, was elected to the presidency in 1912; a Great War broke out in Europe in 1914, with the United States entering the conflict three years later; a white supremacist view of Lincoln was broadcast to millions of Americans through the publication of Thomas Dixon's novels and the release of D. W. Griffith's film *The Birth of a Nation* (1915), both of which disseminated an outlook that if the president had not been assassinated, the supposed racial horrors of Reconstruction would have never occurred; and a decades-long dream of winning the elective franchise for women appeared within reach.[5] The combination of these events into such a compressed time span made it difficult, if not impossible, for Lincoln's adversaries to overcome a dominant national image of the president as the Savior of the Union, First American, and Great Emancipator. Criticism of Lincoln in this period, as in the years immediately following the Civil War, still exhibited attacks on Lincoln's atheism and ignoble background and the conduct of his presidency during the war years, but something new was also emphasized. The new element was racially based opposition to American expansionism overseas. Lincoln's critics argued that Lincoln had forced the South to remain in the Union, just as the United States was coercing former Spanish colonies such as the Philippines to become American territories without their consent. Unsurprisingly, such a viewpoint was in some circles interpreted as criticism of the growing power of the American nation-state, and Lincoln's antagonists encountered stiff opposition to their views.

Numerous individuals in the United States kept alive the Confederate critique of Lincoln in the early twentieth century. In the South, in the years between Jefferson Davis's death in 1889 and the end of the Great War in 1918, several facets of hatred for Lincoln were noticeable: leading white southerners published lengthy, if inaccurate, books criticizing almost every facet of Lincoln's life and administration, with a continued focus on his lack of religious belief and the alleged imperial despotism and cruelty of his administration. Unlike the years immediately following the Civil War, however, when white southerners were attempting to regain political control of their states and criticism of Lincoln existed but was probably considered impolitic, by the 1890s white southerners had wrested political control back from those Republicans who supported a more racially egalitarian South and who had attempted to use federal power in order to advance freedom for all Americans. Consequently, unreconstructed Confederates below the Mason-Dixon Line—especially elite white women—waxed nostalgic about the antebellum South and the Confederacy, and some of them used allegations of Lincoln's atheism as a method for resisting a burgeoning women's suffrage movement. In addition, faced with potential populist revolts from their large population of poor tenant farmers, black and white, the president's enemies in the white South aligned themselves with methods designed to keep blacks marginalized.[6] Using textbooks, schools, magazines such as the *Confederate Veteran,* and other public venues to denigrate their former adversary, champions of the Lost Cause attempted with some success to institutionalize opposition to Lincoln.

Antipathy for Lincoln also put down roots outside the old states of the Confederacy. By the end of World War I the tradition of criticizing Lincoln as a timid, reluctant emancipator reasserted itself among some intellectuals within the African American community. From 1890 to 1918 African Americans were, at least in the South, left alone by Washington, D.C., and as a result subjected to a virtual state of neo-slavery, suffering thousands of lynchings as well as nonviolent but no less debilitating forms of political, economic, and social discrimination across the entire United States. Such atrocities, when combined with demographic changes such as the Great Migration of African Americans to the North during the Great War, led a few blacks to publicly question whether Lincoln, the "Great Emancipator," had emancipated their race—or the United States—from anything at all. Disillusioned by the ongoing guerrilla war waged against their race and attendant racial atrocities committed in a country allegedly devoted to liberty and equality, a few black intellectuals voiced criticism of Lincoln and accordingly found more of an audience for their disappointment. Still, such isolated disapproval scarcely exhibited the deep-seated hatred or loathing displayed by Lincoln's white southern enemies, nor, obviously, was it tied to a reactionary political agenda that sought the continued oppression of African Americans.[7]

Confederate antagonism for Lincoln was relatively central to its conservative political philosophy and associated hostility to federal authority and racial equality. Lincoln's more radical critics, by way of contrast, might never have criticized the president at all if the United States had fulfilled the egalitarian promises from the Reconstruction era. Nevertheless, all the opponents of the sixteenth president appeared to be like Don Quixote, tilting at windmills in their condemnation of Lincoln, a man transformed into a national icon among the vast majority of Americans. If reunion between the North and the South in the 1890s and thereafter was founded upon the combination of an American empire and white racial solidarity, then Lincoln's detractors were perhaps fighting their own lost cause in attempting to convince Americans of Lincoln's personal and political wickedness. Their criticism of the Lincoln image nevertheless reached numerous and influential people, laying the foundation for even more trenchant opposition to the Civil War president in the post–World War I era.[8]

On September 10, 1894, an organization named the United Daughters of the Confederacy (UDC) was founded in Nashville, Tennessee.[9] Its purpose was to pay tribute to the Confederate States of America and instill its alleged virtues into the white children of the South. Perhaps the most important method used by the UDC for exalting the Confederacy was to build monuments to Confederate military and political heroes such as Jefferson Davis, Stonewall Jackson, and Robert E. Lee. Erecting these statues was at the very least an implicit and insolent criticism of the United States president, Abraham Lincoln, who had led the fight against such individuals.[10] Members of the UDC also worked tirelessly to make certain that Lincoln was either ignored in southern textbooks or portrayed in such a way that southern schoolchildren would not revere him in the manner of northern students. Of course, the UDC was hardly the first women's group to venerate the Confederacy. The Ladies' Memorial Associations (LMAs) that sprang up in the immediate aftermath of the war vindicated the Confederacy mainly by decorating the graves of dead soldiers or reinterring veterans into southern graveyards. But the LMAs were careful to disguise the political nature of their work.[11] By the 1890s, however, due to changing political circumstances, the UDC publicly lionized the Confederacy and disparaged Lincoln, the president who had contributed mightily to its demise.

One example of how shrines erected by the UDC implicitly criticized Lincoln was permanently engraved into the monument to the Confederacy dedicated on the grounds at Arlington National Cemetery in 1914. Arlington was the former home of Confederate general Robert E. Lee, and the shrine was both a symbol of national reconciliation and unreconstructed Confederate defiance. At the dedication ceremony President Woodrow Wilson, a well-known Lincoln enthusiast who had once characterized the Civil War president as "the supreme American of our history," spoke and lauded the efforts of the UDC, apparently unaware that emblazoned on the monument was the inscription "Victrix causea Diis placuit, sed victa Catoni."[12] According to Edward Sebesta, a writer who has studied at length neo-Confederate influence in twenty-first-century America, the phrase meant "The winning cause pleased the Gods, but the losing cause pleased Cato."[13] The inscription at the very least "implies that Lincoln was a despot and the Union cause unjust; [and that] Cato, the [Roman] stoic believer in 'freedom,' would have sided with the Confederacy."[14] At the same ceremony UDC president Daisy McLaurin Stevens called the Confederacy and its leaders "heroes," "righteous," and inspired."[15] Praising and memorializing the Confederacy, especially Lincoln's most prominent military antagonists, was a public, if somewhat covert, expression of disapproval for Lincoln himself, a method whereby white southerners created a landscape of white supremacy and nurtured their identities as virtuous.[16] The UDC's strategy was at once brilliant and subtle; as historian Kirk Savage has explained, by glorifying military heroes such as Robert E. Lee, the UDC "depoliticized the Confederacy," and "the story of the Lost Cause became a glorious military record rather than a political struggle to secure a slaveholding nation."[17]

A southern monument that displayed a more explicit criticism of Lincoln, however, resided in the noteworthy example from early in the twentieth century of Joseph Pinkney "Pink" Parker, a resident of Troy, Alabama, whose hatred of Lincoln's supposed tyranny led him to erect a small memorial honoring John Wilkes Booth.[18] Parker had served four years in the Confederate army and was in attendance at Appomattox Court House when Lee surrendered to Grant, whereupon he returned to a ruined plantation.[19] According to his obituary in the *New York Times,* Parker erected the monument in his front yard around 1901 and placed an inscription dedicated "to the memory of John Wilkes Booth for killing Old Abe Lincoln."[20] The notorious shrine forced Alabamans to frequently have to "deny reports that it was erected by public subscription."[21] Apparently, Parker's neighbors were embarrassed by the monument but, out of respect for Parker's right to do what he wished on his own property, did not ask that it be taken down.[22] In 1921, in response to a flurry of northern objections, the town council of Troy ordered Parker to remove the memorial, an order to which he acquiesced.[23] Parker died in December 1921, and the sculpture he once used to honor Booth served instead as his tombstone.[24]

In one sense it hardly seems surprising that a lone individual such as Parker would erect a shrine to America's first presidential assassin, given the hostilities engendered by the Civil War. But in another sense it is striking that the town council apparently did not receive any white southern protests regarding Parker's statue—one can only imagine what local African Americans thought—and they only ordered it removed when *northerners* protested. Maybe the town council of Troy agreed with northerners about the monument and found it an embarrassment. Or perhaps white southerners knew that defiant criticism of Lincoln would be frowned upon and they preferred a more understated approach to denigrating the former president. Still, such submission to northern judgment, even surrounding an event as deplorable as his assassination, was oftentimes the driving force behind contempt for Lincoln. Diehard Confederates did not want to be told what memorials they could raise—or what they could teach to their youngsters in schools—regarding Abraham Lincoln. Monuments to Confederate soldiers consequently became a permanent and prominent method across the southern landscape for indoctrinating all southerners, black and white, about the alleged virtues of the Confederacy.

No doubt Judge Alexander W. Terrell of Austin, Texas, shared the sentiments expressed by Parker, for decades earlier he too became embroiled in a public controversy regarding his attitudes toward Lincoln's assassin. Terrell was a former Confederate soldier, and authorship of a poem honoring John Wilkes Booth was mistakenly ascribed to him immediately after the war concluded. Terrell nevertheless kept a copy of the poem, and the verse caused problems when in 1893 Terrell was selected as minister to Turkey by President Grover Cleveland, the first Democratic president since Abraham Lincoln took office.[25] Some papers, especially Republican papers in the North, called for President Cleveland to withdraw Terrell's appointment, a request the president refused. The *Milwaukee Sentinel* noted with obvious pleasure that during the Civil War some of the very papers now desirous to see Terrell's diplomatic appointment revoked had "published much more atrocious sentiments respecting Mr. Lincoln than have ever been shown to have been uttered by Terrell."[26] Even more interesting, however, was an editorial published three years later, in 1896, in the *Memphis Commercial-Appeal* regarding atrocities committed by the Turkish government against the Armenians. Terrell had been roundly criticized in American newspapers for his tepid response to the slaughter.[27] In its editorial the *Commercial-Appeal* brought up Terrell's reputed authorship of the ode to Booth, recalling that the poem "was published after the assassination in response to a query whether the South should not give Booth an internment signifying approval of the deed—for there was in the South at that time rather more approval of it [the assassination] than the orators and writers of that section will now admit."[28] Just before reprinting the elegy in its entirety, the editorialist alleged, incorrectly, that Terrell was in fact the poem's author and expressed frustration that the judge refused to take responsibility for its creation. The unfortunate reason for Terrell's denial, according to the editorial, was that "Mr. Terrell is now thoroughly 'reconstructed.'"[29]

Two facets of this editorial were especially striking. One was that the Memphis paper claimed that sympathy for Booth was much more widespread in 1865 than anyone in the South cared to admit, suggesting that current displays of affection toward Lincoln were suspect. Two, the paper's equation of Terrell's repudiation of the poem's composition, if not its actual sentiments, pointed to an attitude widespread among Lincoln's critics across the South: namely, that only they had the courage to persist in telling the truth about Abraham Lincoln, implying that any southerner who admired or praised the president had surrendered, or "reconstructed," their critical faculties to suit Yankee propaganda.

One way to resist such indoctrination, of course, was for white southerners to tightly control what was taught in their schools and textbooks concerning Abraham Lincoln. Indeed, as early as 1881, Albion Tourgée shrewdly observed that southern textbooks "openly and ably defend the right of secession, extol the Confederacy and its leaders; assail the national government and its defenders, and, in short, tend directly to diminish the respect due to the government, and justify the action of those who sought its disruption."[30] From his perspective it was only logical that the man who led the national government during the war, Abraham Lincoln, would "of necessity, be depreciated." Tourgée anxiously and presciently concluded that such a historical portrayal was deeply problematic "for the future of the country," when "one-third of its children are being taught to despise and contemn [*sic*] that government to whose crowning effort the nation owes its existence."[31]

Generally speaking, southern textbooks took one of two approaches regarding Lincoln. They either said as little as possible about their adversary and depicted him in relatively neutral language, or, as Tourgée had ascertained, they portrayed Lincoln variously as ignoble, an illegitimate chief executive elected by a minority of voters from only the northern section of the country, an abolitionist and a threat to the South, and, finally, a president who won the war simply because he possessed more resources than Jefferson Davis. The final charge came straight out of the Lost Cause view of the Civil War that the North had won the war because it possessed superior resources, not a superior cause or superior men. Finally, textbooks uniformly expressed revulsion and outrage at Lincoln's assassination because it harmed the white South and led to the alleged horrors of Reconstruction. These textbooks, and whatever negative judgments of Lincoln were contained therein, were directly connected to a reactionary, or counterrevolutionary, political and social philosophy that defended the old Confederate regime. They also suggest what lessons elite southerners wanted schoolchildren in the region to absorb: they wanted them to learn to mistrust, if not despise, the federal government; they wanted them to learn that secession was right and their white ancestors blameless for the war; they wanted them to learn that America's experiment in creating a biracial democracy during Reconstruction had been a disaster; they wanted them to learn, therefore, that the United States government ought to play a limited, or nonexistent, role in southern—racial—affairs.[32]

Virginian Susan Pendleton Lee, who was the daughter of Robert E. Lee's chaplain, published her *School History of the United States* in 1895. Her book originally contained a relatively bland description of Lincoln, conceivably influenced by Lamon's and Herndon's earlier biographies, especially in its portrayal of Lincoln's background and character as "obscure" and his appearance as "uncouth." Lee described Lincoln's "political ambition" as "great" and complimented him on overcoming "the defects of his education by studying . . . the Bible, Shakespeare, and Euclid."[33] One year later, however, Lee had deftly altered her text and was slightly harsher in her assessment. She now described Lincoln as a politician who "in every way" was "fitted to be a successful leader of his party" but held the "strange belief that the Union was older than the States . . . or the Constitution, which they made."[34] In both versions Lincoln's background and appearance were labeled as "obscure" and "uncouth," and it was said he had "awkward manners." Lee was careful to note, however, that Lincoln overcame his initial disadvantages and became a "good speaker" and party leader. In the 1895 description Lincoln was portrayed as "at first a Whig, but had been drawn into the Republican ranks by his opposition to slavery and by his doctrine that the Union was older than the States and the Constitution made by them," but one year later he was an "ultra-Republican" because he thought "the South had no right to carry slavery into the territories, and that there must be a tariff which would protect American manufactures"[35] A year after that, in the 1897 version of the book, published for students eight to twelve years old, Lee was perhaps even more unkind in her depiction of the former president. Lincoln was now labeled as "a violent Republican" who "favored a high tariff to protect Northern manufactures."[36] It is difficult to ascertain what explains the change in Lee's description of Lincoln. Perhaps she received suggested revisions from readers, or possibly she became harsher in her assessment upon reflection. Whatever the case may be, Lee's *School History* was highly recommended in the pages of the *Confederate Veteran,* the official organ of the United Daughters of the Confederacy.[37]

Other textbooks in the region devoted less space to Lincoln's background or personal characteristics. Instead, they portrayed him in either neutral or unfavorable language, they implied his election was illegitimate, or they blamed him for the onset of the Civil War. One of Mississippi's texts described Lincoln's election as one in which "as a result of the division of the Democratic party, Abraham Lincoln, the Republican candidate, was elected, but failed to receive a majority of the votes cast," although it failed to note that when Lincoln was elected in 1860, no southerners complained that he had won the presidency unlawfully simply because he failed to win a majority of the popular vote. Everyone understood that it was victory in the Electoral College that conferred the office on the candidate, not the popular vote. Nevertheless, in Tennessee the authors wrote that Lincoln's election "was regarded by the Southern States as placing them at the mercy of a party hostile to their institutions. They began to feel unsafe in the Union." Similarly, in Florida students would learn that "when Lincoln, who had declared that the Union could not exist 'half-slave and half-free,' was elected President, they believed that the time had come to separate and form their own government." In Alabama author Joel Campbell DuBose likewise claimed that "in the campaign of 1860, the Democratic party split into three sections, and was defeated in the election. The Republican party elected Mr. Lincoln, whose open hostility to slavery led the South to believe that its rights would not be protected in the Union. History proves its conclusions to have been right."[38] In South Carolina Mary Simms Oliphant focused on a different issue, namely tariffs, claiming that the differences between the North and South "were thus economic," implying of course that they could have worked out a compromise, "until the sentiment against slavery as a moral evil began to take root in the North."[39] Oliphant, like Susan Pendleton Lee, described Lincoln as "a man of lowly birth . . . opposed to the extension of slavery." When Lincoln was elected president, "although he had not received a majority of the popular vote," South Carolina seceded, and war commenced.[40] Texan Anna J. Hardwicke Pennybacker agreed with such an assessment in her book *The New History of Texas for Schools,* writing that "most of the Southerners felt that, if Lincoln were elected, war would surely follow."[41]

It is clear that southern students, at least whites, would have learned that the South was threatened by the North because of Lincoln's election and was consequently forced to remain in the Union. But in pointing to the divisions in the Democratic Party as the cause of Lincoln's election, these textbook authors may have been alluding to the contemporary importance of white southern unity. When southern textbooks described Lincoln as a president elected by a minority of voters, furthermore, they were casting aspersion on the democratic legitimacy of his presidency and offering a justification for secession. No mention whatsoever was made of any southern culpability for the Civil War or even a shared sense of responsibility for the tragedy. No, virtually any child growing up in the South from the 1890s onward would have learned that the war was entirely the North's fault and the South blameless for the conflict. It followed that if the North were to blame for the war, the man who led the North, President Abraham Lincoln, was also to blame for its ensuing deaths. Nowhere was the innocence of the South better expressed than by DuBose, who claimed that "even after the election of Mr. Lincoln, prominent statesmen of the South tried hard to smooth over the differences between the two sections. The 'Crittenden Compromise,' offered to the Congress of 1860–61, gave to the free States three-fourth [*sic*] of all the territory of the Union, and did absolutely bind the other fourth to admit or maintain slavery. It was rejected, not by Southern Democrats, but by Northern Republicans. Jefferson Davis and Robert Toombs," DuBose continued, "whom the uninformed are disposed to charge with the responsibility for pressing the war, would have accepted and voted for the 'Crittenden Compromise' rather than bring on war. Under the circumstance it was impossible to preserve peace. The war had to come."[42]

Southern schoolbooks either ignored or touched only briefly on Lincoln's Emancipation Proclamation. The states of Florida, North Carolina, South Carolina, and Tennessee did not even deign to bring up Lincoln's freeing of the slaves in their states. Louisiana mentioned the proclamation "by which he [Lincoln] declared all slaves to be free" and told its students the Lost Cause trope that despite the prospect of freedom, "many of them [the slaves] still remained faithful to their old masters; but some ran away from the South and enlisted in the Northern armies."[43] Mississippi's description of the Emancipation Proclamation was similar, even basically accurate, when its text claimed that "the South disregarded this proclamation . . . for being out of the Union they were not bound by the proclamations of President Lincoln. But when the South was forced back into the Union at the end of the war it was generally believed that the institution of slavery was dead."[44] Earlier, in 1895, Susan Pendleton Lee had contrasted Lincoln's conduct of the war unfavorably with that of the president of the Confederacy, when she claimed that Jefferson Davis's "loyal adherence to constitutional liberty prevented him from exercising the arbitrary authority which proved so efficient in Mr. Lincoln's case."[45] In Lee's 1896 version this passage was shortened: "[Davis] was too loyal to constitutional liberty to exercise arbitrary power, as Mr. Lincoln did with great success."[46] Regarding the Emancipation Proclamation, it is unsurprising that Lee labeled it as nothing more than a confiscation of property that "gratified the hostile sentiment of much of the North, especially of New England."[47] Such books contributed to a collective amnesia about the causes and consequences of the war, a historical amnesia that Frederick Douglass and many others bemoaned in the postwar years. The idea of slavery as the cause of the war or the end of the institution as the most important result of the conflict was more or less nonexistent. What southern schoolchildren would learn instead from such texts was that the South had been wronged by the North and that the war was a calamity because of what it did to whites.

A stark example of white southern narcissism about the Civil War can be found in these writers' treatment of Lincoln's assassination and the alleged harshness of Reconstruction. Susan Pendleton Lee wrote that "when President Lincoln went to Richmond after its evacuation, the question arose as to how the conquered people should be treated, whereupon Mr.

Lincoln exclaimed: 'Let 'em up easy, let 'em up easy.'" "In his inaugural address delivered two months before this time," Lee explained, "[Lincoln] had declared that he should act 'with malice toward none, with charity for all,' and in spite of his many unconstitutional acts, and his almost reckless exercise of power, he was known to be a really kind-hearted man, who was likely after the surrender of the Southern armies, to deal as kindly as he could with the Southern people."[48] Lee declared that "Mr. Lincoln's murder excited horror throughout the civilized world" and that in "the North, rage was mingled with horror, and many believed that that the crime was instigated and planned by the Southern people." Of course, such a charge "was preposterous," for "the character of Jefferson Davis should have placed him above suspicion of anything cowardly or cruel."[49] Little was different in other texts, as they all argued, in complete disregard for what many in the South privately felt and the white southern exultation displayed in places such as Texas for Booth's murder of Lincoln, that they deplored the act and it was a disaster for their state. One of Tennessee's textbooks, for instance, described the assassination as a "deplorable event" that "strengthened the Radical wing," and "at the same time, it deprived the Confederates of a powerful and magnanimous friend."[50] Southern textbooks certainly mentioned the assassination of Lincoln and condemned the murder, but they viewed it as a tragedy because it eventually led Radical Republicans who believed in racial equality to gain control of Congress, a result they believed harmed the white South.

Why all the concern with textbooks and the image of Abraham Lincoln? To be sure, one reason was that the Civil War was the central event in American history, and few Americans were unaffected by the conflict. Still, there was more at work here, for the idea that southern children might be learning history from northerners (and most authors and publishers of textbooks did in fact come from the North) was anathema to white southerners.[51] There is evidence, furthermore, that a pro-Lincoln image was making serious inroads into the South, even among southern schoolchildren; one study showed that by the 1920s children in three Alabama towns thought Lincoln was a more worthy role model than Lee.[52] The United Daughters of the Confederacy, along with similar organizations such as the Sons of Confederate Veterans (SCV), therefore established committees to make certain that an accurate history of the antebellum South was taught, including the idea that the war was not fought to preserve slavery. "It is an awful gag for me," UDC member M. M. Birge told the Texas annual convention of the Daughters in 1915, that "my children and other people's children . . . [are taught] that the war between the states was fought to free the negro."[53] Tactics employed by Confederate apologists, in addition to the publication of proper and "truthful" textbooks, included meeting with school boards and state legislatures to make certain, as the Mississippi legislature explained, that "no history in relation to the late civil war between the states shall be used unless it be fair and impartial," and ensuring that every southern classroom had a Confederate flag and portraits of men such as Jefferson Davis, Stonewall Jackson, and Robert E. Lee adorning the walls for children to daily venerate.[54] In 1895 the Robert E. Lee Camp of the Sons of Confederate Veterans, located in Richmond, Virginia, proudly claimed to be "active in behalf of true histories for Southern schools" and found at least one book in Richmond "not fit to be taught in a southern school." The Lee Camp's wish was to "see the schools of the State given such a choice in the selection of their books from the best to be gotten as will not compel them to select histories that are obviously unfair and untrue in their statements."[55] The most tragic aspect of such thought control was, as historian Karen Cox has explained, that all these textbooks suffused with Lost Cause theology "eventually made their way into the hands of black students, since they received the cast-off books of the white schools. Thus, young African Americans were also exposed to a Lost Cause narrative [and Lincoln condemnation], which included assertions about the inferiority of their race."[56]

Irreconcilable Confederates also thought that teaching an overly positive, official view of Lincoln might contribute to the glorification of the American nation-state from which their ancestors had fought to separate themselves. Instead, they wanted to teach a different understanding of Lincoln, one that was less positive, in order to prop up a white supremacist regime that could resist federal authority on matters of race. White southerners after 1890 did everything in their power to make certain they had a monopoly over both education and violence in order to buttress their identity as superior people, and denigrating the memory of Abraham Lincoln was, for some, an essential part of that project.[57] And as the education of the young in the modern world increasingly became the responsibility of the state, controlling what children were taught about Lincoln and the Civil War in the twentieth-century South more and more reflected hostility to modernity itself.

Confederate women were continuing a long tradition in American life of females being held responsible for the moral instruction of children. In the case of the South, however, organizations such as the UDC were fulfilling a tradition of "Confederate Motherhood."[58] As Mary Singleton Slack told the Albert Sidney Johnston Chapter of the UDC in Louisville, Kentucky, in 1904, "It was through the influence of a woman that Columbus was enabled to make his voyage that led to the discovery of the New World." "Now let it be the office of the women of the South," she exhorted her audience, "working through the combined efforts of the United Daughters of the Confederacy, to teach these principles to the rising generation." If the UDC heeded her call, Slack predicted that "the Daughters of the Confederacy [will] be building the greatest of all monuments, a thought monument, to the brave men of the South . . . . A monument builded, not of stone, but of thoughts of honor and reverence in the living, pulsing hearts and active brains of their descendants. Thought is power, and will live when monuments of stone have crumbled into dust and dynasties been swept into oblivion by the wings of time."[59] These elite Confederate women, many of whom grew up during the war and Reconstruction and in all likelihood imbibed their hatred for Lincoln and the North at their parents' knees, disdained reconciliation and fought a public battle that had been denied to their gender in the 1860s and 1870s for control of the southern past—and future. Decades later the Dallas poet and Lincoln admirer Josephine Powell Beaty suggested to a correspondent why she thought white southern women perpetuated the Lost Cause. "Living in the South all these years I have learned a lot," she explained in 1947. "At last I learned why it was that the women of the South were so bitter and tended to carry on the feud long after the soldiers themselves were willing to forget it. They had been confident and eager and had urged the men on. When the men returned broken and defeated how could they say to them—even if they felt it—'It was all a mistake' or even 'let us forget and rebuild.' The only way it could be represented was as a never to be forgotten effort so noble that every sacrifice was justified."[60]

So, from the 1890s onward the white South glorified all things Confederate, and belittling Abraham Lincoln was part of this white Christian crusade to purge southern books, schools, and indeed all of white southern society of any mention of the president deemed too favorable. In this context it is understandable how and why the emancipationist memory of the Civil War (or any memory deemed unfavorable to the Confederacy) gradually withered away in the face of elite white social and political pressure as African Americans in the South immediately were socially segregated, politically marginalized, and publicly lynched.[61] Imagine, then, a typical, white, southern schoolboy or schoolgirl in the early part of the twentieth century walking to school on a fine spring April morning. Such a student might stroll through a segregated town square that in all likelihood contained a visible statue glorifying the Confederate States of America—or perhaps a recently lynched African American?—and arrive at an all-white school, where they would learn about the allegedly magnificent slaveholding Confederacy and, if the teacher or textbook even deigned to mention him, its enemy, Abraham Lincoln. Simply put, the history of the Civil War in the South, if not the entire country, became, as W. E. B. Du Bois angrily characterized it, "'lies agreed upon' and stark ignorance guides our future."[62]

No less than primary and secondary schools, higher education in the South also reflected the influence of Lost Cause advocates. In 1911 an especially conspicuous example of southern suppression of pro-Lincoln views occurred when University of Florida professor Enoch Marvin Banks published an article entitled "A Semi-Centennial View of Secession." Banks argued that, among other things, prior to the war Lincoln and the Republican Party did not want to interfere with slavery in the South and only did so later because of the onset of war. More controversially, Banks claimed that "the Northern position on the subject" of slavery was "in harmony with dictates of an advancing civilization."[63] Sadly, Banks wrote, "the tragedy of the South's past, and the tragedy of her present . . . [is] that she does not yet fully realize" this fact.[64] To make matters worse, Banks concluded by favorably comparing Lincoln's political philosophy with that of Jefferson Davis, which demonstrated the problems, or enemies, that groups such as the UDC rightly believed they faced:

> Viewing the great civil conflict . . . in the light of a broad historical philosophy, we are led irresistibly to the conclusion that the North was relatively in the right, while the South was relatively in the wrong. Lincoln for the North became the champion of the principle of national integrity and declared the time ripe for vindication of its validity; Davis for the South became the champion of the principle of particularism exprest [*sic*] in State sovereignty and declared the time ripe for its vindication. The one advocated a principle of political organization in harmony with the age in which he lived and in accord with the teachings of history; the other advocated a principle out of harmony with his age and discredited by the history of Europe during the past thousand years. The one was a statesman of the highest order . . . the other was a statesman of a distinctly inferior order in comparison, since the cause which he championed with so much ability, heroism and devotion ran counter to the true course of political and social progress.[65]

Banks was eventually pressured to resign from the University of Florida for such opinions, and he died a few short months later, in November 1911.[66]

In addition to the Banks imbroglio, there were other instances in which the United Daughters of the Confederacy and other pro-Confederate societies punished southerners making pro-Lincoln statements, thereby enforcing a particular version of the past—and present—upon white southern society. Confederate veterans in Texas condemned a book used in the states' schools that claimed Lincoln had been "one commissioned by the Most High" for his work in saving the Union.[67] Also in Texas, the head of the history department at the University of Texas, Eugene C. Barker, was questioned by the president for assigning Henry William Elson's *History of the United States of America* to students, a book that maintained, among other things, that Abraham Lincoln was God's "providential instrument . . . guiding the nation through the wilderness of threatened disunion."[68] Barker, under pressure from the board and local UDC chapters, withdrew the book from the history curriculum. A professor of history at Virginia's Roanoke College was similarly challenged for using Elson's text.[69] Conversely, white southerners howled in outrage when one of their own was punished in a school for being too critical of Lincoln. In one episode from the turn of the century, the *Confederate Veteran* reported that a schoolboy named Z. F. Barnum, a resident of Washington, D.C., was kicked out of school for writing an essay in which he described the Civil War as one Abraham Lincoln had started "by sending men South to steal niggers. These nigger thieves were called abolitionists," said the D.C. student, "and they became such a nuisance that the Southern people seceded." Once the war ended in 1865, Barnum sarcastically observed, the United States became "one, grand and glorious republic." Unfortunately, he explained to the *Veteran*'s editors, "I was expelled from school the next day, for my teacher was from New Jersey."[70]

Censorship was the weapon of choice by which the UDC and other unreconstructed Confederate groups such as the United Confederate Veterans (UCV) practiced thought control across the white South in the early part of the twentieth century. To an extent the foundation for suppression of a pro-Lincoln or anti-Confederate viewpoint on the Civil War were laid in 1893, when the *Confederate Veteran* magazine began publication out of Nashville, Tennessee, and in the following year when the UDC was established.[71] The *Veteran* became the primary vehicle for promulgating a history of the Civil War acceptable to white southerners.[72] And as a part of that project, a portrayal of Abraham Lincoln emerged that demonstrated that although Lincoln's reputation had improved by the 1890s, it was hardly the case that the former president was universally admired across white southern society. This is not to say that there were not numerous positive things said about Lincoln in the pages of the *Veteran*. He was, in fact, frequently compared to Confederate heroes such as Davis and Lee and celebrated as a great American. S. D. McCormick of Henderson, Kentucky, told the *Veteran* in 1893 that he was pleased with the new magazine, especially its "patriotism," and predicted that soon "the names of Davis and of Lincoln, of Lee and of Grant will be the common heritage of the American people, and the very terms North and South will be forgotten in a mingled admiration of the heroism and mutual sacrifices of the Anglo American race."[73]

Still, for all the praise Lincoln received in the pages of the *Veteran*, there was a significant amount of criticism that balanced such tributes, demonstrating that the contest for Lincoln's image was ongoing in the white South and that there was no unanimity of opinion regarding the Confederacy's former adversary. There were some critics of the president who believed that veneration of Lincoln was less than sincere and expressed solely for reasons of financial and political expediency. One prominent individual, Episcopal bishop of Tennessee Thomas F. Gailor, who later became chancellor of the University of the South, alluded to this attitude in 1901. "It is quite possible that there are young men in the South," Gailor declared, "sons of Confederate soldiers whose desire for commercial prosperity, or whose enthusiasm for President Lincoln's character" was leading them "to acquiesce tamely" to distorted histories of the war.[74] In fact, much of the opposition to Lincoln in the *Veteran* was expressed in the form of a complaint, usually found in articles or letters to the editor, about how some aspect of the war was being incorrectly taught or presented. Lincoln was compared to George III of England when Reverend A. T. Goodloe asked: "Did we not fight for just what Washington did our rights of life, liberty, and property: he against a tyrannical king, and we against an insufferable governing majority? Both fought, as a wronged minority, to be extricated from the unrighteous dominance of controlling powers, and for separate national independence. What if we of the South did not stand related to the Lincoln government exactly as Washington did to that of George III?"[75] Such comments by Christian ministers such as Gailor and Goodloe suggest that their crusade was in essence part of a tradition that glorified the Confederacy as Christian and demonized Abraham Lincoln, which helps explain the continued focus on Lincoln's alleged atheism in the decades after the war by the president's archenemies, not to mention their ongoing hostility. To an extent admiration of Lincoln repudiated an entire political and regional worldview that was Christian, narrowly rather than broadly democratic, hierarchical, patriarchal, and white supremacist. Those southerners Gailor deprecated, especially businessmen, needed to work with northerners in order to increase trade and profits. They may have thought the uncompromising stance of ministers to be misguided and their ongoing opposition to Lincoln a poor substitute for profits.[76]

If education constituted one battlefield for Lincoln's foes, they also set their sights on bigger game, specifically the very nature and future of the United States, including whether or not America should become a world imperialist power. In 1901 a pamphlet appeared entitled *The Real Lincoln,* the result of collaboration between two uncompromising Confederate sympathizers, Charles L. C. Minor (1835–1903) and Kate Mason Rowland (1840–1916). It was later expanded into a book of the same title, a book that for decades became a virtual bible to consult for Lincoln criticism.[77] Minor and Rowland were devoted to extolling the purported virtues of the Confederacy and disgusted with the veneration of Lincoln they believed was taking place not only in the North but also in their beloved South. Indeed, the *Confederate Veteran* highly recommended the pamphlet in its pages and claimed, with considerable understatement, that Minor was "not content with the universal deification of President Lincoln."[78] Minor had fought in the Civil War for the Confederacy, was president of Virginia A&M (later Virginia Tech), and by 1901 was in retirement, living in Baltimore and writing on matters related to the Lost Cause and the Christian religion, whereas Rowland had actually been born in Detroit, Michigan, where her uncle was the governor when it was but a territory. She was the great-granddaughter of George Mason's brother, moved to Virginia at an early age, and spent the better portion of her life in Richmond, the capital of the Confederacy, or Baltimore. She was one of the founders of the UDC, was instrumental in labeling the Civil War as the "War between the States," and received her LLD in 1916 from William and Mary College.[79] Their pamphlet was the result of an earlier correspondence that began in April 1899, one in all likelihood prompted by the recently concluded Spanish-American War and the way in which the language of emancipation—and by implication Abraham Lincoln—was used to promote and defend American expansionism. By using emancipation as a rhetorical tactic to justify territorial acquisitions overseas, American imperialists attempted to claim the moral high ground in the debate over U.S. conquest.[80]

American expansionists may have felt compelled to employ such a metaphor because the image of slavery was being used by anti-imperialists to oppose American imperialism. Critics of American adventurism overseas such as American Federation of Labor leader Samuel F. Gompers and Stanford University president David Starr Jordan held that the American worker would be damaged by U.S. territorial acquisitions. "We cannot run a republic in the West and a slave plantation in the East," Jordan proclaimed.[81] Other anti-imperialists, including descendants of the abolitionist William Lloyd Garrison, viewed themselves as standing squarely within the abolitionist tradition of opposing all forms of slavery wherever it might be practiced.[82] Southern anti-imperialists, by contrast, had another argument, explicitly white supremacist, against American conquest. If America acquired territories outside the continental United States, as South Carolina senator Ben Tillman reasoned, it would open a "Pandora's box" of racial problems for America because it would "inject . . . poisoned blood into the body politic."[83]

It was in the context surrounding American imperialism and the Spanish-American War that Minor and Rowland began corresponding, and although their arguments in opposition to American expansionism and Abraham Lincoln were couched in the language of consent, matters of race were never far from their thoughts. In beginning the letters Minor averred to Rowland that "'imperial' conquest gives too many rich prizes to be stopped," commended her for writing against U.S. imperialist ventures, and in passing noted "Lincoln's repression of criticisms [*sic*] of his administration" in connection with the *Baltimore Sun*'s critique of the McKinley administration. The irony, from Minor's viewpoint, was that McKinley's secretary of state, John Hay, had been Lincoln's private secretary decades earlier, and Minor sarcastically commented to Rowland that Hay would be the one to decide whether the *Sun* should be suppressed.[84] But what truly angered Minor was that Lincoln "has been made up for history and even Southern folk have been induced to accept him—absolutely unlike the real man."[85] Acutely aware that a UDC member would be sympathetic to such a viewpoint, Minor informed Rowland that he had compiled criticism of Lincoln made by northerners during the Civil War as a way of educating the public about the real Lincoln. In Minor's view there were several truths that needed to be told about the president. Significantly, he began with "the evidence of the sordid and degraded life of both his parents," combined with Lincoln's "blasphemous dealing with religious matters and his persistent obscenity."[86] Why Minor thought that particular truth needed to be told is somewhat of a puzzle given that they were observations made by Lamon and Herndon in their biographies and noted as well by white southern critics of the president such as William Hand Browne and Albert Taylor Bledsoe. Perhaps Minor agreed with Samuel Johnson's dictum that mankind more often needed to be reminded than instructed and so alerted Rowland to these "truths."

Moving on from Lincoln's background and religious infidelity, Minor told Rowland that Lincoln's most important achievements, "repression of 'the rebellion'" and "emancipation of the negro," were in actuality opposed by the majority of northerners during the 1860s. Notwithstanding the truth or falsity of such a claim, what was striking in Minor's comments was the evident linkage between his hatred of Lincoln with the current war in Spain and the ongoing rebellion in the Philippines. "How a war can be begun and carried on," Minor observed, "with whoop and hurrah, against the strong reprobation of almost every person who has a right to an opinion in such a matter, has been shown us in the present war."[87] Minor concluded this first missive to Rowland with his view about Lincoln hagiography and the nature of the new Union that Lincoln had saved: "All of Lincoln's biographers rest their demonstration of his excellence, in last resort, upon the assumed premise that nothing could be wrong that saved the Union and destroyed slavery. Now that the Union means a great braggard [sic], swollen with insufferable pride at victories over helpless opponents won with no more loss of life and limb than football matches cost; and now that the policy of the nation assumes that only white people are fit to be free, Lincoln will get his just deserts, as a wicked usurper who bent to his own will, against their own, a vast majority of the American people."[88] Apparently, Minor claimed that because all white Americans agreed that only their race can supposedly enjoy the fruits of democracy, Americans can finally proceed with an accurate evaluation of Abraham Lincoln.

Minor's critique was in an important sense grounded in white supremacy and represented a significant shift in criticism of Lincoln. In the immediate aftermath of the Civil War, when the status of the freedmen was somewhat unclear and contingent upon what groups gained or lost political power, Lincoln's critics also focused on his background—one they found "disgusting"—and alleged infidelity to the Christian religion. By the late 1890s, however, when the United States had clearly decided, as the 1896 *Plessy v. Ferguson* case and the subsequent suppression of the Filipino rebellion illustrated, that African Americans and other people of color would not be equal citizens, Lincoln's critics were now moving toward asking just what, exactly, Lincoln had saved. As UDC member Mary Singleton Slack said in 1904, the Lincoln administration "drifted into imperialism" and "culminated in despotism."[89] Minor seemed to be telling Rowland that because all whites now agreed blacks were not their equals, it had not been worth fighting a war that destroyed everything they held dear for a country that had become imperialist in both nature and practice.[90] The menace that conceivably worried Minor and Rowland was the prospect of a new Lincolnian tyranny being spread overseas—or at home for that matter—by an imperialist American nation, all of which might lead to the racial degradation of white southerners and the repudiation of their Confederate ideals in a Darwinian struggle for existence.[91]

Minor resumed the correspondence with Rowland several months later, on November 15, 1899, because of a piece in the *Southern Church-man* magazine, the official organ of the Episcopal Church published out of Richmond, Virginia. Stunned by a recent "astonishing editorial" that favorably grouped Washington, Lincoln, and Lee together and said in essence that all three men were good role models for southerners, Minor explained that he would pen a riposte to the *Churchman* proving them wrong. In the same manner as previous critics who had disparaged the president's background and character, Minor emphasized to Rowland that his researches had led him to find "grievous and disgusting evil traits" in Lincoln, combined with "gross indecency and immorality" and "blasphemy."[92] The letters between Minor and Rowland continued for almost three years, ending in March 1902. In that time, and in his later pamphlet and book, Minor outlined to Rowland the criticism he had collected about Lincoln, all of which became the meat and potatoes of Lincoln hostility for decades. Such condemnation included, in addition to Lincoln's alleged "indecency and irreligion," the president's refusal to exchange prisoners with the South, a policy that Minor called "barbarous and cruel"; "Lincoln's cowardly sneaking thro' Baltimore to his inauguration"; and the "military despotism" of his presidency. It was only "after his death," Minor wrote, "that people stopped describing him as he was, and the song of endless eulogy began."[93]

Minor's response to the *Churchman* apparently never appeared in that particular paper, but it was eventually published in the *Richmond Dispatch* and *Southern Historical Society Papers*. He and Rowland also produced their 1901 pamphlet, nearly seventy pages in length, entitled *The Real Lincoln*. Rowland wrote the introduction to the work, in which she observed that "to justify themselves, the Northern people glorify Lincoln, set a nimbus about his head, crown him with bays as their protagonist in the drama by which the great crime of the century was consummated— the suppression of Southern independence."[94] Rowland apparently wrote these lines without irony, completely unaware that they described a mirror image of her view of Lincoln as well; that is, in order to justify the Confederacy, she demonized the man.

Minor died two years after the pamphlet on Lincoln first came out, but it was eventually put into book form in 1904 by a Richmond publisher, Everett Waddey. *The Real Lincoln* relied almost exclusively on testimony from northern sources, especially Lamon's and Herndon's biographies, with Minor and many other unreconstructed Confederates believing this emphasis somehow proved that their view of Lincoln was correct, unbiased, and shared by all northerners. There was little that was new in *The Real Lincoln* that Minor had not discussed in his correspondence with Rowland in the preceding years.[95] Still, Minor's book was popular in the South and was eventually brought out in another edition in 1928.

The correspondence between Minor and Rowland, and their later collaboration on *The Real Lincoln*, was significant because it strengthened the foundation for a decidedly negative view of Lincoln among dyed-in-the-wool Confederates. In addition, it showed a growing willingness on the part of elite white southerners to criticize the dead president openly, without apology, and illustrated as well the increasing importance of women and the UDC in perpetuating Lincoln hatred. Of course, many northerners hated such attacks on Lincoln. Consequently, *The Real Lincoln* stirred a considerable amount of controversy, especially in Massachusetts. According to the *Boston Journal*, a Union veteran in Somerville found the book in his local library, informed the mayor about its contents, whereupon the mayor "ordered it removed from the library and destroyed."[96] A copy of *The Real Lincoln* was also found in Cambridge, and the Grand Army of the Republic (GAR) in Massachusetts campaigned successfully to have the book removed from all libraries in Boston, a fact that white southerners happily and correctly reported as an example of northern hypocrisy.[97]

Another attack on the president, published on the heels of *The Real Lincoln*, was brought out in 1904 by Elizabeth Avery Meriwether (1824–1916) from Memphis, Tennessee. Meriwether's volume was entitled *Facts and Falsehoods concerning the War on the South, 1861–1865* and was published under the pseudonym George Edmonds. Meriwether was a gifted woman who exemplified the ambiguities and contradictions of Lincoln hostility across the South. She grew up in Memphis and in 1852 married Minor Meriwether, the son of a wealthy Kentucky slave owner, Garrett Meriwether. Upon Garrett's death in 1851, Minor Meriwether, at the behest of his father's wishes, freed his father's slaves, and he and his new bride, Elizabeth, settled down to life in Memphis. As Meriwether recalled in her autobiography, her father-in-law "did not approve of setting them [the slaves] free in America; he urged that they could never be equal to the Whites, either socially or intellectually, and that consequently friction if not disaster, would result from permitting them to live in America as free men."[98] The Meriwethers supported John Bell's candidacy in the election of 1860, but both husband and wife ultimately supported secession, which shattered their heretofore serene existence. Minor eventually joined the Confederate army and by the end of the war had reached the rank of colonel.

At the beginning of the war Elizabeth Meriwether remained in Memphis, defying General Ulysses S. Grant's Special Order № 11, which stated that residents who had a family member in the Confederate army would have to be evacuated or take an oath stating that they had not aided the enemy since the city's occupation by Union forces on June 6, 1862.[99] Unfortunately for Meriwether, however, her properties were confiscated by General Sherman, and she was banned from Memphis for the remainder of the conflict, an act she bitterly resented for the remainder of her life.[100] Once the war concluded, the Meriwethers returned home, and Minor, along with their neighbor, Confederate cavalryman Nathan Bedford Forrest, reportedly helped found the Ku Klux Klan (another neighbor was none other than former Confederate president Jefferson Davis).[101] In keeping with her belief that elite white women should be allowed to vote, Meriwether defiantly cast a ballot either in the 1876 presidential election for Samuel Tilden or in a local election (the facts here are in dispute), telling her son Lee she did so "to start people thinking. Even wrong thinking is better than no thinking at all."[102] Meriwether thought the reason she was allowed to cast her ballot was simply because she was so well-known in Memphis that election officials "perhaps decided to consider me merely as a harmless 'freak.'"[103] Several years later, in 1881, she published a letter to the editor in the *St. Louis Globe-Democrat* and asked, "Are Women Slaves?" Meriwether believed so, because women were worse off than the "founders of this Government" under King George III, and the founders "called themselves slaves."[104]

Meriwether became passionately involved in the cause of women's suffrage, along with temperance reform, lecturing across the country for both causes for the rest of her life. In addition, she published several novels romanticizing the antebellum South. In light of her background, talents, and notoriety, it is striking that Meriwether did not publish her book on Lincoln under her own name but used the pseudonym George Edmonds. Clearly, she had already written and talked on controversial subjects related to suffrage and temperance, so fear of political involvement or public opprobrium could not have been a motive. Perhaps she thought that the volume would discredit her writing on other topics, although that seems unlikely. Whatever the explanation, her life was representative of those white southern women who, although progressive on some matters, married a reactionary, conservative politics to a racially based hierarchical and patriarchal order.[105]

So, in 1904, when Elizabeth Meriwether published her volume on Lincoln, *Facts and Falsehoods concerning the War on the South, 1861–1865,* she might have brought a unique viewpoint to the work, perhaps one that Charles L. C. Minor and other critics did not possess. Such was not always the case, as her book accepted Lamon's and Herndon's works uncritically, quoted from Lincoln's wartime enemies in the North, and assumed that nothing was the South's fault in the late Civil War. As with many others, there was little or no sense in her writings of the conflict's tragedy, except as it affected the South. Rather, she continually alleged that the entire war was everyone else's fault and that the South shared no culpability at all for what had happened. This was in stark contrast to Lincoln himself, who in his Second Inaugural Address ruminated on the tragedy of the war for *all* Americans. Although the book's title claimed to be about the South, the entire first part of the work was a screed against Abraham Lincoln and simply reiterated the standard contemptuous arguments, although with some important alterations. Written on the premise that "even in the South the real Lincoln is lost sight of in the rush and bustle of our modern life, and many Southerners accept the opinion of Lincoln that is furnished them ready made by writers who are either ignorant, or else who purposely falsify plain facts of history," Meriwether proceeded for ninety pages to excoriate Lincoln for his alleged misdeeds and crimes as president.[106]

Meriwether's critique fell into so many categories it is hard to enumerate them all, yet there was some semblance of order and originality to be found in her lengthy chastisement. Her essential thesis was that Lincoln was despised in life but worshipped in death because he was useful as a saintly image that propped up the Republican Party. "They [Republicans] realized the fact that if their President were known to the world as *they* knew him," Meriwether asserted, "the glory of their victory would fade; as *he* stood, so their party would stand. If *he* was despised, *they* and their party would be despised. . . . To exalt the dead President became the vital necessity of the hour. The passion of the Republican heart is to possess power. They had won power through seas of blood; to lose it now would be anguish to their very souls. To exalt to the high realm of godship the dead man they had in life despised as the dirt under their feet, was the first thought that darted on their agitated brains."[107] It was simply unimaginable to Meriwether, at least in 1904, that people could have altered their opinions of the president after the war was over or that Lincoln possessed any attributes worthy of admiration and emulation.

Meriwether also wrote disapprovingly of Lincoln's fondness for inappropriate or obscene stories. To prove her point, she quoted Lamon's account of Lincoln at the end of the war telling his cabinet—a cabinet whose members Meriwether inaccurately held despised Lincoln—a story about a boy catching coons in the night, which the president related to wanting Jefferson Davis to escape to another country. "The anguish, the agonies of four years' war, the slaughter of 700,000 men who wore the blue, and more than half as many who wore the gray," Meriwether lamented, "Lincoln could jovially liken to catching six coons, the killing of five, and the captivity of one. Not one particle of pity went out to the condition of the conquered."[108] In her view, and this too became typical, was that Lincoln, in addition to being indecent and indecorous in his use of anecdotes, was not a compassionate man and, had he lived, would not have been a friend of the South. In a sense Meriwether agreed with Herndon's earlier assessment that Lincoln was much less tenderhearted than the sentimental portrayals of the president led people to believe. But Herndon held that Lincoln's cold nature helped him withstand the rigors and suffering of the conflict and was balanced by other admirable characteristics, while Meriwether thought Lincoln cruel, inhumane, and heartless:

> Is it insanity or pure mendacity to liken a man of this nature to the gentle and loving Nazarene? . . . What act of Lincoln's life betrays tender-heartedness? Was he tenderhearted when he made medicine contraband of war? . . . Not only did Lincoln prevent medicine from going South, but when the whole South was devastated, when she was unable, properly, to feed and medicine the Union soldiers in her prisons, the Southerners paroled a Federal prisoner

and sent him a message to Lincoln informing him of the South's condition in
that respect, and telling him if he would send his own surgeons with medical
supplies they would be allowed to minister to the needs of the Union men in
prison. Lincoln refused. Was this tender-hearted? . . . And when Lincoln's
legions were devastating the South, with wanton cruelty, at the point of a
bayonet, Sherman drove 15,000 women and children of Atlanta, Georgia,
out of their homes, out of the city in ashes, did Lincoln give one thought to
the sufferings of those innocent women and children? Did he once, during
the four years of cruel war, utter or write one kind word of the people on
whom *he* had brought such unspeakable misery?[109]

From that rhetorical flourish Meriwether claimed, somewhat contra-
dictorily, that Lincoln was both a weak man manipulated by others during
the war so that the South would be punished, yet at the same time he was
supposedly a tyrant and "changed a free Republic into an imperial government."[110] She made the same argument Minor and Rowland had discussed
in their correspondence when they equated Lincoln's willingness to use
force to keep the South in the Union with American imperialism abroad.
Similarly, Meriwether voiced a judgment that many opponents already
shared in that she compared Lincoln's policies during the Civil War to
those of George III during the Revolutionary War. "Lincoln inaugurated
war from precisely the same motives which made George III of England
wage war on the colonies—conquest," Meriwether explained.[111] She also
connected, like Albert Taylor Bledsoe decades before her, Lincoln's political philosophy with Alexander Hamilton. Tragically, Lincoln's image was
used for the nefarious purposes of American expansionism. "Hamilton
made no concealment of his monarchic principles; he preferred a monarchy such as England has . . . . Until seated in the White House, Lincoln
talked Democracy and affected great esteem for Jefferson's Democratic
principles." But as soon as he took office, "no imperial despot in pagan
time ever wielded more autocratic power than did Abraham Lincoln, and
Republican writers of today are so imbued with imperialism they laud
and glorify Lincoln for his usurpation of power."[112]

One unusual idea introduced by Meriwether was that the discipline
of phrenology best explained Lincoln's personality and character. Phre-
nologists claimed that studying the shape of a person's skull would give
a window into one's personal worth or moral fiber. Relying on descriptions of Lincoln by Herndon, Meriwether told her readers that Lincoln
was a man of low character but for reasons different than those offered
by earlier Lincoln critics such as Bledsoe. "When we present the salient

features of Mr. Lincoln's mental and moral nature," Meriwether explained, "the analytical reader can compare him with his physical [traits]."[113] Meriwether proceeded to provide such analysis and quoted an unnamed lawyer—Bledsoe perhaps?—from Springfield who claimed that Lincoln, "phrenologically and physiologically" speaking, "was a sort of monstrosity."[114] In one sense Meriwether's analysis was no different than those who during and immediately after the war found themselves disgusted by the man's ignoble background and used such language to buttress their own conservative morality. But such criticism was based largely on Lincoln's allegedly illegitimate birth, whereas Meriwether grounded her claim for Lincoln's moral degeneracy on his physical characteristics and backed it up by the quack science of the day. So, in addition to the usual contentions that Lincoln was an infidel, a tyrant, cruel, despised by northerners while alive, and a president who would not have been tenderhearted toward the South had he lived, Meriwether added that the government Lincoln saved was now imperialist in nature and the real clue to Lincoln's character lay in the shape of his skull, not in the hero worship taking place across the North. She concluded her book's lengthy section on Lincoln with a series of questions, one of which would have made previous adversaries of the president such as Bledsoe and Browne proud: do the "qualities of Mr. Lincoln" she asked, show "greatness of soul, purity of heart, and unselfish devotion to principles which merit" respect, "or do they betray a man of coarse nature, a self-seeking politician, who craved high office more to satisfy his own burning desire for distinction than to use the power for the betterment of his fellow mortals?"[115] Based on the book's previous pages and a life devoted to the cause of white supremacy, her answer was obviously the latter, and it was clear that she did not include African Americans in her category of "fellow-mortals."

Intriguingly, by 1916, when Elizabeth Meriwether published her autobiography, *Recollections of 92 Years, 1824–1916,* her attitudes toward Lincoln had changed considerably, and she appeared to be somewhat embarrassed by what she had written in *Facts and Falsehoods.* Meriwether recounted Lincoln's visit to Richmond in early April 1865, after the city had been evacuated, and maintained that the people of Richmond had "received him kindly."[116] In stark contrast to her attitude toward the president in 1904, and perhaps influenced by the ascension of Virginian Woodrow Wilson to the presidency during a global war, Meriwether described Lincoln's reconstruction policy as a "merciful treatment of Virginians" that "evoked from every Southern heart the deepest appreciation; the people of the

South hoped and believed that at last the hate and bitterness of the war were to die out on both sides and a true friendship between the North and South was to make the country really one again."[117] Unfortunately, from Meriwether's standpoint what had ruined the peace was black suffrage: "It is reasonable to believe that such a travesty on sense and morals would never have taken place had Lincoln lived and enforced *his* policy instead of [Secretary of War Edwin] Stanton's."[118] She favorably quoted Lincoln's words from his 1858 debate with Stephen Douglas at Charleston, Illinois, in which Lincoln had said he was "not, nor ever have been, in favor of making voters or jurors of negroes, nor of qualifying them to hold office, nor to intermarry with white people, and I will say, in addition to this that there is a physical difference between the white and black races which I believe will forever forbid the two races living together on terms of social and political equality."[119] Meriwether regretted that Lincoln's 1858 viewpoint—she even labeled him here as the "Great Emancipator"—was not followed and as a result, she claimed, there "was untold suffering on the part of the negroes as well as the whites."[120]

What was interesting about Meriwether's change in attitude was her use of Lincoln's words at Charleston in 1858 to justify the ongoing subjection of blacks to whites in southern society, thus conceding the ongoing importance of who controlled the Lincoln image in American life. In other words, white southerners justified their oppression of blacks by claiming that Lincoln shared their racial views and that he had agreed with them about black inferiority all along. This became a common tactic of white southerners in later decades as well, especially during the civil rights movement, or "Second Reconstruction." It is ironic that some African Americans were beginning in these decades to point to the very same words of Lincoln to allege that the Great Emancipator was a racist. No one ever seemed to make the effort, certainly not Lincoln's antagonists, to understand that in the Lincoln-Douglas debates, as political scientist Lucas Morel put it, "if Lincoln played the race card, Douglas dealt the whole deck."[121] In short, Lincoln's utterances on race, even in 1858, were quite advanced compared to those of many of his contemporaries in that he consistently advanced the idea that blacks should enjoy all the natural rights mentioned by Jefferson in the Declaration of Independence. By the end of the Civil War in 1865, moreover, Lincoln expanded notions of racial egalitarianism even further when, in the last speech of his life, he advocated suffrage for black soldiers and the "very intelligent." John Wilkes Booth, who heard the president's recommendation, understood perfectly the implication of Lincoln's words, as he immediately exclaimed to David Herold that such a policy meant "nigger citizenship" and began plotting Lincoln's murder.[122]

But what was just as interesting in Meriwether's new and more charitable language was that it probably motivated other more famous critics, such as UDC historian-general Mildred Lewis Rutherford (1851–1928) and later the president of William and Mary College, Lyon Gardiner Tyler (1853–1935), to intensify their anti-Lincoln activities. If a Lincoln loather like Meriwether could change her mind, they may well have reasoned, the strength of the so-called Lincoln cult in the South was greater than they had thought, and they would need to redouble their efforts to demonize the South's former and present adversary. Indeed, even within the United Daughters of the Confederacy, and certainly in contradiction to the wishes of the likes of Rutherford, there are accounts from some of Virginia's UDC chapters of addresses on Lincoln and Davis wherein speakers depicted both presidents as "men of character and strong convictions" or as "two great and distinguished men."[123] In the same decades LaSalle Corbett Picket, the widow of Confederate general George Pickett, advocated reconciliation between the North and South, in part by touting her husband's alleged friendship with Abraham Lincoln.[124] Although groups such as the UDC claimed they did not want hostile relations between the North and South, they remained devoted to vindicating the Confederacy through their advocacy of the Lost Cause. And if women such as Pickett were influencing southern minds with what some saw as untruthful information about Lincoln, it was not unreasonable for champions of the Confederacy to worry that a "false" history of the antebellum South and the Civil War would logically follow. In other words, not hating Lincoln was, to many of the president's enemies, a betrayal of the Confederacy, a repudiation of white southern identity, and a form of historical amnesia that could not be ignored.

Historians Michael Davis and Don Fehrenbacher have argued that the president's image had improved significantly by the centennial of Lincoln's birth in 1909. While there is a large measure of truth in that argument, the reality was more complex, for even then there were considerable negative judgments expressed by influential people in the old Confederacy. In 1909 the Robert E. Lee Camp of Confederate Veterans, located in Richmond, Virginia, moved to have Judge George L. Christian give a speech "on the life and character of President Abraham Lincoln," probably as a response to the numerous celebrations of Lincoln's life taking place across the country that year.[125] Christian hardly needed any prompting to criticize Lincoln, for in a 1907 report issued by the United Confederate Veterans History Committee, he had labeled Lincoln "the great demigod of the North" and stated that the "South did right and that the North did wrong" in the late war.[126]

Two years later Christian gave his Lincoln centennial speech in October in front of Confederate war veterans and the local chapter of the United Daughters of the Confederacy.[127] He reiterated many of the typical themes of Lincoln enmity in his address: Lincoln was unchristian; Lincoln was *"secretive, crafty, cunning,"* but a weak leader; Lincoln was a tyrant; Lincoln violated the Constitution by issuing the Emancipation Proclamation; Lincoln waged inhumane warfare on the South; Lincoln's assassination was a tragedy for the South. Christian declared that all Confederate veterans *"know* that many of the things written about the cause and conduct of the North, and its leaders, *and especially about Mr. Lincoln, are false."*[128] Like many Lincoln critics before him, he challenged his audience to resist the forsaking of truth for worldly goods: "Are we so debased and cowed by the results of the conflict that we must remain silent about these for the sake of political expediency or material gain, and not tell our children *the truth,* when our *quondam* enemies have furnished us the evidences of *that truth?"*[129] Christian's speech was well received, published in pamphlet form, and sent to all who requested it, including the inveterate Lincoln critic Kate Mason Rowland.[130]

The *Confederate Veteran* also bemoaned the celebrations of Lincoln's centennial, illustrating the depth and intensity of ill will toward Lincoln among segments of the white South in 1909. "Notwithstanding the South realized the great calamity caused to it by his death," the *Veteran* told its readers, "in a general criticism Mr. Lincoln is overhonored." President Theodore Roosevelt's centennial speech in Kentucky disappointed the editors because in it he had not honored another Kentuckian, Jefferson Davis. The *Veteran* believed that the Confederate president's "career is as worthy of praise for patriotism and Christian manhood as that of any man of the generations through which he lived. The South is as loyal to the principles for which the first revolution, under the lead of Washington, was made victorious as any people of the earth to their country, but there are principles above the love of country that connect man with God, and to these principles the line will be drawn and maintained until and even after proper recognition is shown their martyr Jefferson Davis."[131]

Indeed, the *Veteran* received numerous letters, positive and negative, about the celebration of Lincoln's birth in 1909. The *Veteran* had originally planned a "brief report" on the centennial but expressed surprise that its "office was soon so surfeited with eulogies that it was impracticable to print them."[132] But there were other readers who disagreed with such eulogies and wrote to the *Veteran* to complain.[133] Consequently, the magazine printed these negative reports of Lincoln not in a "spirit of ill will," it claimed, "but [with] a desire to express the truth concerning Mr. Lincoln."[134] Mrs. A. P. Shepard's piece probably encapsulated as well as any the characteristics of Lincoln venom as it existed in the white South in 1909. She was incredulous about the "flood of eloquence, encomium, and praise it [the centennial] has brought forth from pen, pulpit, and after dinner speech!"[135] Lincoln, she drily noted, "has been set upon a pedestal and clothed with attributes that make him little less than divine. Washington has been made to step down from his long approved pinnacle of greatness, while one enthusiast in his blind fanaticism has compared him [Lincoln] most favorably with Jesus Christ himself."[136] Here Shepard noted what would become a standard complaint of Lincoln's detractors: the comparison of the president, a man they deemed unchristian in faith and practice, with Jesus.

Lincoln, in Shepard's view, was a deceitful and wicked man. She was upset, first, that Confederate commissioners in Washington had been told that Fort Sumter would be evacuated, but instead Lincoln sent ships "southward" and launched "upon the unprepared South a war unequaled for cruelty and barbarism in all modern history."[137] Accordingly, Lincoln was an unkind and heartless president. "His admirers have laid special force upon his great heart, pulsating with throbs of justice, kindness, and humanity. Did his heart pulsate with these noble qualities," Mrs. Shepard asked, "when, disregarding all the rules of civilization and humanity, he declared martial law in the States of the South, flooded the country with violence and bloodshed, and legitimatized the most atrocious form of irregular warfare? He was commander in chief of the army. Yet was he ever known to set his seal of disapproval upon the actions of his generals in their conduct of the war? General [Benjamin] Butler's treatment of the people of New Orleans was horrible almost beyond belief."[138]

Even more cruel was Lincoln's "emancipation of six millions of slaves, his exciting them to insurrection, his placing guns in the hands of negroes to murder their former masters [which] exceeded in atrocity and cruelty the tyranny of any despot in any age."[139] Moreover, she claimed, wrongly, that he gave "the ballot to ignorant negroes who had no more knowledge of the rights of suffrage than so many mules," and his malice extended to Confederate prisoners when he refused to exchange them with Union soldiers. "The Confederate government on more than one occasion sent propositions to Washington for the exchange of prisoners. No answer was given. Was Mr. Lincoln a man of high ideals? Was he a lover of the sublime, the beautiful? Was he a Christian, a gentleman?"[140] In a word, no. "What, then," she asked, "has been the basis of all this fictitious greatness? What has been the cause of thus raising him to the very pinnacle of fame accorded no other American, not excepting even the great Washington himself? We answer: 'Assassination.' Assassination placed the crown of the martyr upon his brow."[141]

The disdain for the celebration of Lincoln's centennial clearly demonstrated that scorn for the president was prevalent among segments of white southern society much earlier than when well-known Lincoln detractors Mildred Lewis Rutherford of the UDC and Lyon Gardiner Tyler of William and Mary College began their own anti-Lincoln crusade a few years later, a crusade that continued into the decades between the two world wars. Indeed, influential white southerners had begun to excoriate the martyred president from the late 1860s onward. The work of Albert Taylor Bledsoe, William Hand Browne, Charles L. C. Minor, Kate Mason Rowland, and Elizabeth Avery Meriwether, not to mention the early postwar efforts of the Southern Historical Society or the later labors of the UDC begun in the 1890s, show that Rutherford's and Tyler's Lincoln criticism, although of enormous significance to the continuation of hatred for the president in the region, for the most part built upon the foundation of numerous others' previous work.[142] Their efforts were in fact the natural result of the propagation of a reactionary strain of Lincoln hostility over several decades, and they were therefore less important, individually, to disparagement of Lincoln than has previously been believed.

Continuing unhappiness with the Civil War president so long after the war concluded certainly stemmed from a desire to vindicate the Confederacy, especially its men, but it was also a way to counteract the growing admiration of Lincoln across the country by Progressives. Lincoln was a useful symbol for Progressive intellectuals, politicians, and reformers in the early part of the twentieth century who, despite their moral blind spot on racial matters, thought they knew how to improve American society and were willing to use the federal government and the office of the presidency—with the aid of the Lincoln image—to advance their "egalitarian ideals."[143] Herbert Croly, a Progressive and founder of the *New Republic* magazine, once characterized Progressivism's political philosophy as a willingness to use "Hamiltonian [federal power] means for Jeffersonian [democratic] ends."[144] President Theodore Roosevelt agreed with Croly: "Lincoln . . . struck the right average" between Jefferson and Hamilton.[145] Indeed, in 1913, just before the outbreak of the Great War in Europe, Roosevelt delivered a speech on Lincoln's birthday in which he claimed that Lincoln was a Progressive: "We Progressives and we alone are today the representatives of the men of Lincoln's day who upheld the hands of Lincoln and aided him in the great task to which he gave his life, and in doing which he met his death. . . . Lincoln and Lincoln's supporters were emphatically the progressives of their day, and . . . it is curious to note the exact parallelism of his general attitude with the attitude that the Progressive party has now taken."[146] Although Roosevelt emphasized an important point in this speech that Lincoln and the Republicans were, as we have seen, sharply opposed by many of their contemporaries, the overall Progressive appropriation of Lincoln was to an extent a distortion of his political thought.[147] Whereas Lincoln's thinking was based on the foundational idea that all people possessed certain inviolable natural rights at birth, Progressives rejected such notions as outdated and embraced, instead, the concept that individuals possessed those rights that "progressive history" gave them.[148] On the one hand, the idea that human beings did not enjoy sacrosanct natural rights was potentially congenial to Lincoln's enemies in that such a viewpoint could be used to deny southern blacks—or women—vital economic, social, and political freedoms. On the other hand, if Progressive history *could* grant those groups expanded liberties (or even worse, if people possessed natural rights simply by being born), then such a political creed had alarming implications for entrenched interests and necessitated vigorous resistance. So, what motivated Lincoln's foes early in the twentieth century was not simply a longing to see their Confederate ancestors proved correct; they also used their critique of the sixteenth president as a method for offsetting the political ideology of Progressivism, an ideology that, however far it fell short in practice, advanced the idea of a potentially more egalitarian United States and was willing to use the federal government to achieve such goals. Attacking Lincoln was a form of opposition to Progressivism's definition of freedom being wedded to national power.[149]

When the Great War broke out in 1914, the European cataclysm led President Woodrow Wilson, a self-proclaimed Progressive, to lavish even more praise upon Lincoln, while Lincoln's nemeses responded by expanding upon the ideas introduced by Minor, Rowland, and Meriwether and equated Lincoln with Great Britain's King George III and Kaiser Wilhelm II of Germany. Woodrow Wilson, a Virginian, was the first southerner elected to the presidency after the Civil War, and he was the first Democrat to serve in that role since Grover Cleveland left office in 1897. Much to the consternation of Lincoln's rivals, Wilson, like Theodore Roosevelt before him, admired, even adored, Lincoln, and the reasons for the president's esteem in all likelihood alarmed white southern adversaries of the sixteenth president. First, Wilson had said as early as 1880 that he was glad that the Confederacy lost the Civil War; twenty-nine years later, during the celebration of the centennial of Lincoln's birth in 1909, Wilson stated that every American ought to "feel the compulsion that his example lays upon us—the compulsion, not to heed him merely but to look to our own duty, to live every day as if that were the day upon which *America was to be reborn and remade.*"[150] Second, Wilson found in Lincoln's presidency a model for Progressives, a model for transcending the political limitations of the American founders.[151] Wilson believed that the founders' view of politics was inadequate, and he instead called for "living political constitutions [that] must be Darwinian in structure and practice. Society is a living organism and must obey the laws of life," Wilson held, "not of mechanics; it must develop."[152] Wilson argued for interpreting the Constitution in "Darwinian" terms, so that the United States could adapt to modern industrial society.[153]

On the centennial of Lincoln's birth, Wilson made the connection between Lincoln and Darwin even more explicit in a speech delivered in Chicago entitled "Abraham Lincoln: A Man of the People." Wilson thought it was striking that "the struggle which determined the life of the Union came just at the time when a new issue [Darwin's theory of evolution by natural selection] was joined in the field of thought, and men began to reconstruct their conceptions of the universe and of their relations to nature, and even of their relation to God."[154] As Theodore Roosevelt had also maintained, Wilson argued in the ensuing years that the GOP had changed, regressed perhaps, and was no longer representative of the party Lincoln had steered through the Civil War. "I do not for one moment believe that Lincoln would admit that the party which is seeking to legalize monopoly was the same party he had belonged to," Wilson said on the presidential campaign trail in Springfield, Illinois, in 1912. In light of Wilson's admiration for Lincoln, it was ironic that he never risked political capital to do anything substantial to expand freedom or equality for

African Americans, whereas his Civil War predecessor eventually staked his presidency and the future of the country on emancipation. Still, that Wilson viewed himself, and the Democrats, as the new party of Lincoln, was an idea that would have been cold comfort to white southerners determined to maintain their stranglehold on southern society and the people Lincoln had helped emancipate in 1863. Discrediting Lincoln was essential to the continuation of their white supremacist project.[155]

Lincoln's archenemies were undoubtedly distressed by Wilson's use of the Lincoln image during the Great War. In his campaign for reelection in 1916, the president spoke at Lincoln's birthplace in Kentucky and said, "We are not worthy to stand here unless we ourselves are in deed and truth real democrats and servants to mankind, ready to give our lives for the freedom and justice and spiritual exaltation" of the United States.[156] Later, during the war, Wilson likened his struggles to those Lincoln had faced in the 1860s: the congressional elections of 1918 were similar to the election of 1864; the suppression of dissent during World War I was analogous to the Lincoln administration's arrest of wartime dissenters in the 1860s; the sacrifice of American soldiers in the Great War was equated to the sacrifice of Americans during the Civil War.[157] Wilson's assumption of the Lincoln mantle had global consequences because the president, according to historian Thomas Bender "more than any other single person, shaped the way Americans thought about their place in the world. Washington and Lincoln had been admired abroad, but Wilson was the first American to be a world leader."[158] In a sense Wilson's presidency legitimated the Lincoln image as it also "continued the American way of empire," a prospect that Lincoln's critics, indeed many Americans, found frightening.[159]

Consequently, O. W. Blacknall's *Lincoln as the South Should Know Him* (1915) and Lloyd T. Everett's *Davis, Lincoln, and the Kaiser: Some Comparison's Compared, 1861 and 1914* (1917) attempted to refute Wilson's image of Lincoln and its associated positive view of federal power by comparing the Civil War president with George III and the German kaiser. Certain that Lincoln's saintly reputation was undeserved, Blacknall called attention in the very first sentence of his brief twenty-five-page pamphlet to American hypocrisy in denouncing the kaiser "for the devastation of Belgium" while at the same time "we raise paeans to Lincoln, who was responsible for the far more causeless and ruthless devastation of the South by Sherman."[160] Blacknall lamented that southern schoolchildren had learned "to execrate [George III] next to Satan, and Lincoln, whom our children are being reared to venerate almost next to God, [although] both sent armies to the South."[161] Lincoln was nothing more than a man who "carried out Northern ideals of centralism, imperialism," and consequently, anyone who detested such ideas ought to detest Lincoln.[162]

Lloyd T. Everett, a Virginia attorney and unreconstructed Confederate, was similarly upset with Lincoln hagiography and likewise maintained that the Civil War president was a centralist and imperialist. Everett had argued as early as February 1914, before the Great War began, that if the Confederacy had won the Civil War, it "would have marked another glorious step forward in the laborious progress of Liberty and Self-government."[163] Like Wilson, Everett believed the nineteenth century was a turning point in world affairs. But in contrast to Wilson, Everett thought it "was an era of the predominance of the centripetal power in government, the ascendancy of the central political authority," and that the success of the Confederacy would have arrested this "dragon teeth of overweening, un-American imperialism."[164] Without any sense of irony, Everett insisted that the Confederacy stood for the ideals of "Minority Rights, Home Rule and Arbitration" and that because such principles were clearly in the ascendancy in world affairs, the South would in the future be vindicated.[165] Everett's brief pamphlet comparing Lincoln and Kaiser Wilhelm was prompted by an article in the *Saturday Evening Post* associating Lincoln's government in 1861 "with the allies of 1914."[166] Such a claim, if it took hold among the public, would have been fatal to the Confederacy's future vindication, not to mention Everett's worldview, and he therefore felt compelled to sever the link in the American mind between Abraham Lincoln and the nation's allies in the Great War, not to mention Wilson's claim that the war was fought to make the world safe for democracy.[167]

Blacknall and Everett's comparison of Lincoln with the kaiser broke new ground, but it would not be the last time Lincoln was associated with German brutality or with the idea of American imperialism more generally. Of course, two short pamphlets advancing such a viewpoint hardly compared with the presidential platform Woodrow Wilson enjoyed. Still, as we have seen, Lincoln's detractors did get their pro-Confederate viewpoint publicized and widely disseminated to significant audiences across the South by organizations such as the United Daughters of the Confederacy, which had enormous consequences not only in the early part of the twentieth century but also in the 1950s and 1960s. Indeed, federal desegregation efforts may have been seen by some white southerners previously ingrained with the conservative political philosophy propagated by Lincoln's enemies as just one more example of American, if not Lincolnian, imperialism and suggest one explanation for their deep-seated resistance to even the idea of federal enforcement of black equality.[168]

It was in the context of the recent developments in political thought, namely the Progressives' appropriation of Abraham Lincoln, combined with new scientific trends and the onset of the Great War, that one can more clearly understand the rationale for the Athens, Georgia, resident Mildred Lewis Rutherford's crusade against the Confederacy's former opponent. Equally worrisome for Rutherford and her allies was that just as advocates of American imperialism had used emancipationist rhetoric to rationalize territorial expansion overseas, women suffragettes used Lincoln's image to argue for expanding the franchise. In essence leading advocates for their cause argued that if the president's words "government of the people, by the people, for the people" were to be truly meaningful, then the United States would have to include women as full political participants in a new, more democratic polis.[169] A schoolteacher, historian-general of the UDC from 1911 to 1916, and a devoted white supremacist, Rutherford worked assiduously to oppose such ideas and make certain that a "truthful" depiction of the antebellum South, the Confederacy, and Abraham Lincoln be disseminated in southern schools and have the positive vision of Lincoln erased.[170] Indeed, if one keeps in mind Wilson's equation of Lincoln with Darwin, Progressivism, and human development or the use some suffragettes made of the president's rhetoric to advance their cause, then it becomes clearer why Rutherford was particularly worried that white southern students were being taught that Lincoln was a greater statesman than Jefferson Davis and why she labeled such veneration an "evil" that needed to be undone. A reactionary hostile to modernity, she looked back nostalgically to antebellum southern society as ideal—"the citadel of conservatism. Had she prevailed, no dangers from imperialism and centralization would have beset us," Rutherford claimed, and she consequently wanted nothing to do with any of Wilson's or any other recent ideas about progress and development. To that end Rutherford published a small volume in 1916 entitled *Jefferson Davis and Abraham Lincoln, 1861–1865.*[171] Her book made the usual comparisons between Davis and Lincoln—all to Davis's advantage, of course—but if one looks closely at how Rutherford contrasts the two men, it is striking how different her description of Lincoln was from Wilson's:

It was Jefferson Davis not Abraham Lincoln who stood for the principles as laid down by the Declaration of 1776, and the Constitution.

It was Jefferson Davis not Lincoln who stood for personal righteousness; his life private and public was one of absolute rectitude.

It was Jefferson Davis not Lincoln who stood for humanity and pleaded for those Andersonville prisoners whom Lincoln could have relieved and would not.

It was Jefferson Davis not Lincoln who was the patriot and sacrificed personal ambition for the sake of his country.

It was Jefferson Davis not Abraham Lincoln who pleaded for peace and did all to enforce it and Lincoln it was who refused four times to make it when he could.

It was Jefferson Davis not Lincoln who was a lover of his fellowmen and agonized over the suffering and dying on the battlefield, and it was Davis not Lincoln who loved the slaves too much to see them freed suddenly because so totally unprepared for freedom.[172]

A final yet significant contrast between the two men that especially disturbed Rutherford was Lincoln's alleged lack of Christian upbringing and subsequent absence of adult faith. Consequently, the Confederacy's adversary was not a proper role model for America's children. "We cannot hold him up as a 'GENTLEMAN OF REFINEMENT AND CULTURE,'" she declared.[173] In a shrewd use of the Lincoln image, and in agreement with numerous others who equated the demand for women's suffrage with atheism, Rutherford adapted the charge of Lincoln's religious infidelity to support an anti-suffragist stance.[174] Although in the immediate decades after the Civil War, Lincoln's enemies frequently characterized the president as an atheist, an American Jacobin or Robespierre, it was more often the case that ex-Confederates and their ideological allies found it politically useful to accept the increasingly popular portrayal of Lincoln as a forgiving Christian president who, if he had lived, would never have labored for black suffrage or equality. Rutherford agreed that Lincoln's assassination had been a disaster for the white South, but she publicly rejected the notion that Lincoln had been a Christian and more readily advanced the idea that he was an atheist in order to buttress support for the view that "government of the people, by the people, and for the people" should apply exclusively to white males. Of course, this is not to say that she did not concede the complexity of Lincoln's character or his political gifts; in common with the work of the president's critics, she readily granted Lincoln *some* talents. Still, it was clear to her that Lincoln "was an American, but an American of a new national type" (Darwinian or feminist, perhaps?) who "could better meet the plebeian than [Jefferson] Davis could" and an individual who "was never at home with the aristocrats" such as herself.[175] She romanticized and idealized the antebellum South and what she took to be its fixed racial and gender hierarchies, in which blacks and women were subordinate.[176] The overall effect of Rutherford's work, indeed of all the president's diehard Confederate rivals, was therefore important and served a counterrevolutionary purpose in its nostalgic, antimodern, illiberal, and narrowly democratic outlook. Indeed, of the eleven states that made up the old Confederacy, eight chose not to ratify the Nineteenth Amendment to the Constitution.[177]

Yet it would be a serious mistake to think that all hostility to Lincoln existed solely among elite white southerners. Within the African American community a slight shift in attitudes toward Abraham Lincoln and the beginnings of a negative stance occurred that echoed the small number of abolitionists who critiqued the president as a timid and weak emancipator. Since the close of the war in 1865, African Americans had courageously celebrated the memory of Abraham Lincoln in their homes and through annual public commemorations throughout the country on Emancipation Day, January 1.[178] Given the revolutionary nature of the Civil War, which led to the emancipation of four million slaves, connecting Lincoln's reputation with the fortune of African Americans was to an extent inevitable. Still, as early as 1876, on the eleven-year anniversary of Lincoln's assassination, black abolitionist leader and orator Frederick Douglass spoke with only slight misgiving about Abraham Lincoln at the unveiling of the Freedmen's Memorial Monument in Washington, D.C. Meditating on the relationship between Lincoln and the slaves freed in January 1863 by the Emancipation Proclamation, Douglass declared to the audience that Lincoln was "preeminently the white man's President" and that, in contrast, blacks were only his "step-children." Despite Lincoln's shortcomings, however, Douglass told the audience gathered in Washington that day that the "hour and the man of our redemption had somehow met in the person of Abraham Lincoln." It is possible that Douglass was making a serious point at the expense of southern fire-eaters and Confederate president Jefferson Davis. William Lowndes Yancey had said in Montgomery, Alabama, in 1861, upon Davis's ascension to the office of president of the Confederacy, that "the man and the hour have met" in Jefferson Davis. If Douglass was taking a jab at Yancey, Davis, and the former Confederacy, and it is certainly not implausible that he was, it puts his comments in a new light, one more complimentary toward Lincoln than previously thought and explicitly critical of the Confederacy. Continuing with his nuanced yet mostly sympathetic speech, Douglass contended that, "viewed from the genuine abolition ground, Mr. Lincoln seemed tardy, cold, dull, and indifferent; but measuring him by the sentiment of his country, a sentiment he was bound as a statesman to consult, he was swift, zealous, radical, and determined."[179]

In fact, in the decades after the Civil War many prominent black intellectuals such as W. E. B. Du Bois (1868–1963) and Booker T. Washington (1856–1915) drew sympathetic portraits of the sixteenth president, many of them similar to Douglass's. In 1909, the year of Lincoln's centennial, Washington gave a speech to the Republican Club in New York City, in which he regaled his listeners with stories of hearing his mother pray for Abraham Lincoln so that "she and her boy" might be free, telling the audience that Lincoln's success in life was "the success of the nation" and that Lincoln had not only freed his body but also his "soul."[180] Two years earlier, in 1907, Du Bois had characterized Lincoln as a "great man," even though—and perhaps this was a dig at those who continually harped on Lincoln's frontier background—"he did not for instance belong to the best society," but Lincoln was still great because of his "clear sightedness" and "capacity for growth" and because when he saw that "this land could not exist half slave and half free and once he realized that his was the power to break the paradox," he emancipated the slaves.[181] Finally, Carter G. Woodson, the founder of the *Journal of Negro History,* instituted Negro History Week in the 1920s during the month of February because it was the month of both Abraham Lincoln's and Frederick Douglass's birthdays.[182]

But African American celebration of Lincoln was not the entire story, for it was clear that by the turn of the century, or at the very least by the centennial of Lincoln's birth in 1909, African American admiration for the Great Emancipator had weakened.[183] In 1908 in Lincoln's hometown of Springfield, Illinois, a bloody race riot occurred in which blacks were lynched and their property destroyed, while one year later, at the city's centennial celebration of Lincoln's birth, African Americans were not allowed to participate in the official ceremonies.[184] Such heartbreaking events were unfortunately representative of the declining status of African Americans in the United States, a status too often defined by disfranchisement, segregation, and, even more tragically, homicidal violence. From Jefferson Davis's death in 1889 to the end of the Great War in 1918, thousands of blacks were lynched across the United States, extrajudicial killings that were primarily but not exclusively located in the former states of the Confederacy.[185] In such a context it is perhaps unsurprising that a few African Americans began to question if they were truly emancipated and whether Abraham Lincoln deserved the title of Great Emancipator. As one black American told the *Richmond Planet* newspaper as early as 1890: "In the first place I think that Mr. Lincoln's Proclamation didn't amount to anything from a legal standpoint. It freed nobody. Understand me that it had a very marked moral effect, but the 13th Amendment really gave freedom to the slaves."[186]

African American attorney Archibald H. Grimké, nephew of the abolitionist Grimké sisters, former American diplomat, and a prominent figure in the National Association for the Advancement of Colored People (NAACP) who opposed Booker T. Washington's compromising stance toward American white supremacy, sharply criticized Abraham Lincoln.[187] Grimké, although he admired Lincoln in certain respects, issued some tough words about the former president in 1900, and his trenchant analysis was an example of a shift in attitude within the African American community. In contrast with the abolitionists, whom Grimké venerated, Lincoln cared so little for the slave that "the right of the slave to freedom had no more practical weight . . . when set over against the peace and prosperity, or preservation of . . . [the] Union, than would have had, if such a thing was possible, the right to freedom of the imaginary inhabitants of Mars."[188] Grimké might have agreed with those who thought Lincoln's reputation was inflated, and he challenged the black community to liberate itself intellectually and rethink its admiration of Abraham Lincoln:

> It seems to me that it is high time for colored Americans to look at Abraham Lincoln from their own standpoint, instead of from that of their fellow white citizens. We have surely a point of view equally with them for the study of this great man's public life, wherein it touched and influenced our history. Then why are we invariably found in their place on this subject, as on kindred ones, and not in our own? . . . Are we to be forever a trite echo, an insignificant "me too" to the white race in America on all sorts of questions . . . ? For if we are ever to occupy a position in America other than that of mere dependents and servile imitators of the whites, we must emancipate ourselves from this species of slavery. . . . With whom can we then more appropriately begin this work of intellectual emancipation than with Abraham Lincoln, the emancipator?[189]

Grimké's view of Lincoln was clearly different from those of Du Bois and Washington, at least in 1900, in that he criticized the president's lack of moral feeling for the slave. He was just as hard, moreover, on his fellow African Americans for continuing to pay Lincoln undue homage. Still, in 1909 he called Lincoln a "great man" and the Emancipation Proclamation "the first of a series of great acts"—and here he sharply contrasted Lincoln with Alexander Stephens—"which are to establish free labor as its chief cornerstone."[190] Grimké's ambivalence, moreover, was shared by other African Americans who questioned the appellation of Great Emancipator for Abraham Lincoln.

Hubert Harrison (1883–1927) was a black political radical who, in the words of his biographer Jeffrey B. Perry, "combined class consciousness and (anti–white supremacist) race consciousness in a coherent political radicalism." Such a stance led Harrison to criticize Abraham Lincoln from a Black Nationalist, or left-wing, perspective.[191] Born in St. Croix, in the West Indies, Harrison migrated to the United States in 1900, the same year that Grimké penned his article criticizing Lincoln and two short years after America had won its "splendid little war" over Spain. Harrison was an agnostic in religion, a socialist in politics, and had what Perry labels a "'race first' political perspective."[192] By 1920 he was the editor of Marcus Garvey's *Negro World,* the magazine of the United Negro Improvement Association, and in all his writings attempted to reach the masses. Harrison was an enormously influential figure in the early part of the century among African Americans, so much so that one of his predecessors at the *Negro World,* editor W. A. Domingo, said that "all followed Hubert Harrison."[193] In 1911 he created four lectures on Abraham Lincoln, lectures he published a decade later in the *Negro World.* Entitled "Lincoln and Liberty: Fact versus Fiction," the four-part series challenged the ongoing veneration of Lincoln within the black community. Harrison persuasively argued that given the racial atrocities perpetrated against African Americans since the end of Reconstruction, blacks owed no debt of gratitude toward the Republican Party, for it had never been their steadfast ally. "This bond of serfdom, this debt of gratitude," Harrison declared in 1920, "is supposed to hinge on the love which Abraham Lincoln and his party are supposed to have borne toward the Negro; and the object of this appeal to the historical record is to show that the record demonstrates that if the Negro owes any debt to the Republican party it is a debt of execration and of punishment rather than one of gratitude."[194] Harrison nevertheless told the *World*'s readers that Lincoln "was the greatest President that the United States had up to his time": "His record still remains as that of the greatest President that America has had down to our time. But greatest and (may I coin a word?)

'goodest' are not necessarily the same."[195] Consequently, in the second installment Harrison laid out his goals:

> I shall endeavor to show that Lincoln was not an Abolitionist; that he had no special love for the Negroes; that he opposed the abolition of the Domestic Slave Trade and favored the Fugitive Slave Law: that he opposed citizenship for Negroes; that he favored making slavery perpetual in 1861; that he denied officially that the war was fought to free the slaves; that he refused to pay Negro soldiers the same wage that he paid the white soldiers; that without these Negro soldiers the North could not have won the war; that the Emancipation Proclamation was issued, not for the slave's sake, but solely as an act to cripple the army of the South; and finally, that it did not abolish slavery and was not intended to. *These are the things that I shall prove in regard to Abraham Lincoln and in regard to the men of his party.*[196]

Quoting Lincoln's own words throughout the four installments, Harrison endeavored to demonstrate each of these opinions. Ironically, Abraham Lincoln himself would probably have agreed with aspects of this criticism but would have vigorously disagreed that his policies, especially considering how closely they were aligned with the antislavery Republican Party, were in opposition to the broadened definition of freedom that Harrison's accusations implied.[197] What Harrison did not sufficiently show in his pieces was the context within which any politician in nineteenth-century America had to operate or Lincoln's personal antipathy toward slavery. Lincoln did not declare that the war was fought to free the slaves because he would have lost a good portion of the northern populace's support, not to mention the support of the border states of Delaware, Kentucky, Maryland, and Missouri, had he publicly advocated such a motivation. But the war was fought to restore a Union in which slavery would be eradicated. On this point Lincoln and the Republicans were emphatically clear. Nor did Harrison take into account that white racism explained why black soldiers were not paid as much as white troops. Indeed, Lincoln conceded as much to Frederick Douglass when they met in the White House, but he also told Douglass that eventually the pay would be equal, and that promise was kept. Moreover, Harrison did not give his readers an accurate explanation of just how radical it was in 1863 to have black troops at all, a momentous change made possible by Lincoln's Emancipation Proclamation. So, when Harrison claimed at the end of his fourth article that his essays destroyed "any claim to the Negroes' gratitude [to Lincoln and the Republican Party] on the grounds of high moral altruism and benevolence," he was stating matters too simply and harshly.[198]

Nevertheless, Harrison's and Grimké's critique signaled the beginnings of an important alternative to Lincoln criticism from those of reactionary white southerners to more radical African American thinkers. Perhaps because both men had lived abroad in the Caribbean, Grimké in the Dominican Republic as American consul, Harrison in St. Croix, their sense of America's deep-seated racial flaws were heightened and they extended this mindfulness to their hard-hitting evaluation of Abraham Lincoln.[199]

Even so, there was an important distinction, a chasm even, between African American Lincoln criticism and the loathing exhibited by irreconcilable Confederates. Lincoln's white southern opponents were scarcely likely to characterize Lincoln as a "great man" or "greatest president" or the Emancipation Proclamation as the "first of a series of great acts," as did Grimké and Harrison. Still, both men advanced an important truth with their critique: in their analysis of the president's shortcomings, they directly challenged established boundaries of thought regarding Abraham Lincoln by encouraging African Americans to emancipate themselves from all forms of dependence on whites, including the Republican Party.[200] In a manner similar to Grimké, Harrison counseled: "It is time that we Negroes should do our own historical work instead of taking our food pelican-wise from the white people's pouch. . . . For while we patter about race emancipation we will still be brain-bound to the white man's mental products and his mental interpretation of our people to the world in which they live. And that is, after all, a more hopeless slavery than physical bondage ever could be."[201] The criticism of Lincoln emanating from African Americans such as Grimké and Harrison reflected an intense desire for black liberation, issued in the context of an understandably bitter discontent with the unfulfilled egalitarian promises of the 1860s and 1870s. Lincoln's white critics in the former states of the Confederacy, in stark contrast, wanted and to a large extent reinstituted black subordination and hated the president in part because the Civil War and Reconstruction had introduced and established, however briefly, the principle of racial equality.

Condemnation of Lincoln between 1890 and 1918, although still a minority viewpoint in American life, reflected an acute dissatisfaction with Abraham Lincoln and with what had happened in the United States since the Civil War. The Russian émigré and socialist Rose Strunsky had published a perceptive and in some ways admiring biography of the sixteenth president in 1914 but claimed that because Lincoln had become all things to all people, a kind of American touchstone really, he had become irrelevant in the new nation he had helped create.[202] "Except for the inspiration of his ideal of equal economic opportunity," she declared in a statement with which Lincoln's more radical African American critics might well have concurred, "Lincoln can no longer help us."[203]

Most Americans disagreed with this assessment. Those who admired Lincoln, such as the former Confederate William Aylett, presidents Theodore Roosevelt and Woodrow Wilson, leading women suffragettes, along with countless others, believed that Abraham Lincoln was at once a model man and politician, a unique American figure who combined the best elements of the nation in the features of his life, his rhetoric, or his accomplishments or some combination of all three. Although Progressives rejected the idea of natural rights to which Lincoln had been devoted, their love for Lincoln and their country's democratic possibilities, not to mention its increasing international influence, outweighed the president's flaws. Lincoln's foes, at least those of the diehard Confederate persuasion, disagreed with his admirers, not to mention Strunsky's assertion of Lincoln's irrelevancy to American life. Indeed, for many white southerners Lincoln was an obstacle who stood for everything they had fought against in 1861 and continued to fight against in the present. Their hatred survived the tomb, and they worked strenuously and successfully to present, through monuments, schools, and books, a picture of Abraham Lincoln at odds with the memory of the country but more consistent with their white supremacist ideals. He was in their view the worst American because he emancipated the slaves, enslaved free white men, laid the basis for American imperialism, and destroyed rather than saved the Union. They agreed with the iconic Robert E. Lee, who had told Lord Acton decades earlier that northern victory would lead to "the consolidation of the states into one vast republic, sure to be aggressive abroad and despotic at home," and "to the subversion of State Governments, and to despotism."[204] As the Great War and American involvement in the conflict overseas concluded in 1918, the contest over the image of Abraham Lincoln in modern American life and what he represented would be renewed and intensified within the borders of a dynamic, modern United States of America.

4

THE SELF-PITY OF THE
DEFEATED

Contesting "Lincolnolatry," 1918–1945

In 1917, the same year the United States entered the Great War in Europe at the behest of President Woodrow Wilson, H. L. Mencken (1880–1956) published an essay excoriating the South in the *New York Evening Mail,* entitled "The Sahara of the Bozart." The South, Mencken lamented, had once been a great civilization, but "if the whole of the late Confederacy were to be engulfed by a tidal wave tomorrow," he exclaimed, "the effect upon the civilized minority of men in the world would be but little greater than that of a flood on the Yang-tse-kiang. It would be impossible in all history to match so complete a drying-up of a civilization."[1] Mencken's piece did not garner immediate attention in the region. But by 1920, with the war over and Americans returning to a supposed "normalcy" during Warren G. Harding's presidency, the essay reappeared in Mencken's collection *Prejudices: A Second Series,* and many southerners reacted with shock and horror to his characterization of their beloved South.[2]

Mencken was one of the most important and influential journalists in America in the 1920s. Yet despite being a fierce and witty critic of southern intellectual culture, he perpetuated on a national scale some of the earlier criticism of Abraham Lincoln leveled by Albert Taylor Bledsoe, William Hand Browne, Elizabeth Meriwether, Charles L. C. Minor, Kate Mason Rowland, Mildred Lewis Rutherford, and Lyon Gardiner Tyler. Mencken genuinely admired Lincoln's political and oratorical gifts, but he thought the president had become "the American solar myth, the chief butt of American credulity and sentimentality" and "a plaster saint, thus making him fit for adoration in the Y.M.C.A.'s."[3] As for Lincoln's handling of the slavery question, Mencken averred that he had dealt with it like "a politi-

cian, not a messiah" and that "an Abolitionist would have published the
Emancipation Proclamation the day after the first battle of Bull Run. But
Lincoln waited until time was more favorable."[4] Although the Gettysburg
Address was "genuinely stupendous," Mencken believed Lincoln's rhetoric
obscured the truth that it was the Confederates, not the Union, who "fought
for the right of the people to govern themselves." Confederate defeat at
Gettysburg, according to a later essay of Mencken's, unfortunately led to
"The Calamity of Appomattox."[5] Perhaps enthused by Mencken's stance,
Mary Carter of Virginia, a fervent Lincoln detractor and member of the
United Daughters of the Confederacy (UDC), penned a two-page, single-
spaced letter in 1924 to the Baltimore journalist virtually begging him
to debunk the Lincoln myth. "Where are we *at,* Mr. Editor, on this great
American myth? Surely, here is a myth worthy of your doughty pen, and I
am hoping you will take a tilt at it, and give the readers of your magazine
[the *American Mercury*] the benefit of your clinical skill."[6] Regrettably, at
least from Carter's perspective, Mencken never found the time to accede
to her request, although he contemplated doing so.[7]

Equally important, in 1917 W. E. B. Du Bois declared, like Archibald
Grimké (1849–1930) years earlier, that what had actually concerned Lincoln during the Civil War was not the freedom of the slave but saving the
Union.[8] Five years later Du Bois penned a brief description of the presi-
dent in the July 1922 issue of the magazine he edited for the NAACP, the
Crisis. His depiction of Lincoln, although it demonstrated a large measure
of admiration, was similar in language to that of previous critics. The
piece appeared soon after the Lincoln Memorial had been dedicated in
Washington, D.C., a commemoration of the Great Emancipator at which
African Americans were denied equal inclusion: "Abraham Lincoln was a
Southern poor white, of illegitimate birth, poorly educated and unusually
ugly, awkward, ill-dressed. He liked smutty stories and was a politician
down to his toes. Aristocrats—Jeff Davis, Seward, and their ilk—despised
him, and indeed he had little outwardly that compelled respect. . . . at the
crisis [Civil War] he was big enough to be inconsistent—cruel, merciful;
peaceloving, a fighter; despising Negroes and letting them fight and vote;
protecting slavery and freeing slaves. He was a man—a big, inconsistent, brave man."[9] There was also a story in the *Crisis* claiming that John
Brown "had more to do with the emancipation of the Negro than did even
Lincoln."[10] Stunned, the magazine's readers voiced their objections to Du
Bois. The African American newspaper the *Chicago Defender* labeled Du
Bois's piece a "gratuitous slur upon Abraham Lincoln," equated the essay

with "the illiterate, Negro-hating and reactionary element of the South in casting slurs upon the sacred memory of one of the greatest men our country has ever produced," and called Du Bois's comments "incomprehensible and inexcusable."[11]

Consequently, in the September issue Du Bois penned a lengthy response to his critics. It was an appreciative description but more nuanced than what he had written in 1907 or the hagiographical portraits that Booker T. Washington had drawn for audiences from the 1880s onward. Acknowledging that "many of my readers were hurt by what I said of Lincoln," Du Bois clarified that he believed "Abraham Lincoln was perhaps the greatest figure of the nineteenth century."[12] Whereas in 1907 Du Bois had extolled Lincoln's greatness because of his clear-sightedness and capacity for growth, in 1922 he cited Lincoln as fallible, great, "not because he was perfect but because he was not and yet triumphed." "I revere him more," wrote Du Bois, "because up out of his contradictions and inconsistencies he fought his way to the pinnacles of the earth and his fight was within as well as without."[13] Du Bois recognized, like many enemies of Lincoln then and since, what Lincoln had said about African American inequality in his debate with Stephen A. Douglas at Charleston, Illinois, in 1858, but unlike them, he made the important point that in 1863 the president had "declared that black slaves 'are and henceforward shall be free.' And in 1864 he was writing to [Governor Michael] Hahn of Louisiana in favor of Negro suffrage."[14] Du Bois clearly respected Lincoln—with some reservations. The swift disapproval Du Bois received for his remarks demonstrated that reverence for Lincoln remained strong within the African American community, but as Du Bois's comments also show, such veneration was by no means unambiguous.

As Abraham Lincoln's reputation reached its peak in the decades between World War I and World War II, hostility toward Lincoln, as reflected in the criticism expressed by Mencken and Du Bois, underwent important shifts. Before 1918 animosity for Lincoln had been mostly regional, a backward-looking strain of thought located, created, and institutionalized primarily, although not exclusively, in the former Confederate states among elite white southerners seeking to vindicate the Confederacy and maintain intellectual, racial, and political hegemony over their section. From 1918 to 1945, although still a minority viewpoint in the United States, contempt for the president became more of a national rather than a strictly regional phenomenon, as exemplified by the ongoing intense struggle between white southerners over Lincoln's memory and the publication of

Lincoln: The Man (1931) by Illinois poet Edgar Lee Masters (1868–1950).
Masters's book, because it was written by a famed poet, a northerner from
Lincoln's Illinois no less, garnered national attention. Equally significant,
elite and nonelite African Americans also leveled complaints against Lincoln in these decades. The rising discontent with Lincoln among African
Americans flowed in part from continuing dissatisfaction, if not outright
disgust, with their second-class status in America and the heightened expectations raised by Franklin Roosevelt's New Deal. This black southern
critique of Lincoln was scarcely a defense of the old Confederate regime,
nor did it amount to the deep-seated loathing exhibited by Lincoln's more
traditional enemies; rather, it was part of a scathing denunciation of the
federal government's failure to secure their rights as American citizens.
Another significant facet of Lincoln hatred in these decades was that it
seeped into the academy, where it gained a measure of respectability. A
group of southern writers located at Vanderbilt University in Nashville,
Tennessee, also known as the Agrarians, questioned the accelerating pace
of industrialism in the United States in their book *I'll Take My Stand: The
South and the Agrarian Tradition* (1930), and a few expressed antipathy
for Lincoln as a logical outgrowth of their agrarian, white supremacist
worldview.[15] Added to the negative stance of the Agrarians was the work of
revisionist or Progressive historians, including former senator and biographer of Lincoln Albert Beveridge, who minimized the role of slavery in
the onset of the conflict and instead argued that the war had been avoid-
able, needless, caused by fanatic abolitionists and inept statesmen. Such
a viewpoint inevitably moved "interpretation of the Civil War," according
to historian Don Fehrenbacher, in "an anti-Republican and therefore
anti-Lincolnian direction."[16] Lincoln criticism between the wars nevertheless continued to be chiefly a reactionary, antimodern strain of thought,
dripping with nostalgia, and characterized partly by the belief that federal expansionism and racial equality were a threat to white liberty. But
condemnations of Lincoln were also advanced by increasingly dissatisfied
African Americans who believed liberty and equality were inextricably
linked and that federal power should refortify that link after decades of
neglect that contributed to their ongoing oppression.

After World War I the United States found itself in the midst of substantial cultural, intellectual, and political changes that shaped the context for
the postwar battles over Abraham Lincoln's image. For the first time more
Americans lived in urban rather than rural areas, in places where traditional sexual mores were changing, and where they had ready access to

prohibited alcohol, listened to jazz music, and heard about new ideas such as Albert Einstein's theory of relativity and Sigmund Freud's constructs regarding human psychology; they perished by the hundreds of thousands from an epidemic of Spanish influenza and endured a general disillusionment with the results of the Great War, which consequently influenced their views on the Civil War and Lincoln; they feared that communism— the First Red Scare—might take over the country; they witnessed the rebirth of the Ku Klux Klan, a nascent but growing organization devoted to an America cleansed of ideas and ethnicities it deemed un-American; and they followed the Scopes Trial in Dayton, Tennessee, which showcased anti-evolution ideas, a budding Christian fundamentalist movement, and a profound discontent with modern America. Coupled with these societal upheavals were significant economic and political transformations: a booming automobile industry and the industrialization of America was more or less an accomplished fact; a general and rising level of prosperity occurred, with the disappearance of poverty discussed as a distinct possibility; a conservative political culture found expression in the policies of presidents Warren G. Harding and Calvin Coolidge, all culminating in the economic catastrophe of the crash of 1929 and the apparent decline of American capitalism. The crash was followed by the expansion of the federal government under Franklin Roosevelt's New Deal and American entrance into World War II. The decades between 1918 and 1945, although they represented the high point of Abraham Lincoln's reputation in the United States, also constituted an era in which derision for the Civil War president was characterized at least in part by its struggle with such massive changes and modernity's onslaught.[17]

Some Americans found Lincoln threatening, for his life personified the ideals of modernity from which they believed so many of society's ills sprang. Lincoln rose to the presidency from the most humble of backgrounds, one his early critics labeled as disgusting, vulgar, and base, while at the same time he embraced aspects of modernity, as many of his twentieth-century critics did not, including capitalism, industrialization, scientific progress, and an associated skepticism toward religious certitude.[18] Added to this, the president welcomed a positive role for democratic government in fostering "for a community of people, whatever they need to have done, but can not do, *at all,* or can not, *so well do,* for themselves— in their separate, and individual capacities."[19] Lincoln's America, finally, was one based upon a civic rather than ethnic nationalism, a country grounded not upon a shared geographical and racial identity but instead upon a collective belief in American constitutional democracy anchored in the natural rights ideals contained in the Declaration of Independence.[20] Such a personal background and philosophical outlook was not one that Lincoln's more conservative detractors, especially in the South, found congenial. Rather, they found it alarming, indeed menacing, to their view of an America based upon privileged birth and status, static rather than changing economic and racial hierarchies coupled with personal relationships, and in some cases an agrarian economy. Theirs was a world of religious certainties, Lincoln's one of skepticism, doubt, and uncertainty regarding the will of the Almighty. Contempt for Lincoln between the wars, at least its reactionary strain as described here, was closely allied with a desire to maintain a grip on ancient, orthodox Christian truths about America, if not all humanity.[21]

Beginning in 1920, the leading spokesman of Lincoln criticism was Lyon Gardiner Tyler. A member of one of the first families of Virginia and the son of John Tyler, former president of the United States, Tyler served as president of William and Mary University in Virginia from 1888 until his retirement in 1919, and he used his publication, *Tyler's Quarterly Historical and Genealogical Magazine* as a platform from which to denounce Abraham Lincoln.[22] An unrelenting critic, Tyler's journal provided a forum that Lincoln's foes across the country utilized in order to fulminate against the "the Lincoln myth" in American culture.[23] What particularly galled Tyler, and many of the president's enemies between the wars, was what they saw as the sacrilegious equation of Lincoln's character with Jesus's ("Lincolnolatry"). In an April 1920 essay "Propaganda and History," Tyler conceded that Lincoln possessed "real merits," including "that he did not cherish the same venom against the South as many of his party did."[24] But whatever gifts the president possessed were not, in Tyler's viewpoint, "sufficient to make him an ideal person in history."[25] In this early piece, and over the next several years, Tyler tirelessly recounted many of the typical attacks, including the president's "coarseness" and his alleged inhumanity in the methods he countenanced in waging war on the South. From Tyler's standpoint Lincoln had not saved the Union but wrecked it because "the old Union was founded on consent and the Union he had in mind was one of force." "His war," Tyler asserted, almost certainly with only white southerners in mind, "was contrary to the principles of 1776 and to the modern principle of self-determination, now the accepted doctrines of the world."[26] Tyler also maintained that Lincoln's death merely afforded the more radical members of the Republican Party the chance to carry out their supposedly dastardly plans for reconstructing the South. In Tyler's view "had Lincoln lived . . . there is little assurance that he would have successfully opposed any plan of the radicals."[27] For Tyler, Lincoln was not the savior of the Union; rather, he was its tyrannical destroyer, and for a decade and a half his periodical attacked Lincoln and defended the old Confederate regime and the white supremacist South that emerged from the dashed egalitarian hopes of the Reconstruction era.

Years later, in 1928, Tyler spearheaded a controversy that erupted over the recognition of Lincoln's birthday by the Virginia legislature. The legislature had adjourned briefly in the winter that year in order to honor Lincoln's date of birth, prompting a few notable Virginians to protest what they considered to be a current and historical injustice. Daniel Grinnan, an attorney in Richmond, wrote to the local *Times-Dispatch,* protesting that the adjournment celebrated a "manufactured" Lincoln whose "every weak and disappointing quality has been carefully covered up and wonderful qualities have been discovered and fastened together." It was this Lincoln, Grinnan groused, to whom "we are requested and even expected to do homage." Mockingly, he wondered if "miracles of healing will be made at his tomb." Grinnan recommended instead that "the proper attitude of our people in the interest of peace and harmony and of loyalty to ourselves and our fathers *is not to mention his name. This is a course that has long proved satisfactory.*"[28] Indeed, in 1930 Grinnan wrote the superintendent of Richmond's schools and enclosed a clipping from a local newspaper with the headline "Interest Grows in Lincoln's Life." The story described Jesse H. Binford's (the assistant superintendent of the schools in Richmond) visits to several elementary schools and his delight in finding "evidence of a different attitude on the part of a new generation of teachers in Virginia" regarding Lincoln. Although historically Virginia's schools "studiously avoid[ed] the mention of Lincoln," Binford noted with pleasure that "this number is very small and is gradually decreasing."[29] Grinnan was "indignant" about the story and told Binford's boss that the root cause of his employee's error was geographical: "Mr. Binford must have come from New England!" he exclaimed. "He does not talk like one of our people. The real Lincoln has been so larded over with lies and fables that he cannot be found and it is the manufactured Lincoln that it is proposed to palm off on our people as 'Second only to Jesus Christ.'"[30]

In addition to Grinnan's complaints, Tyler and Giles B. Cook, the last surviving officer of Robert E. Lee's staff, even published a pamphlet requesting the birthday resolution be overturned. Cook's opposition to adjournment was grounded in his belief that "Abraham Lincoln was the leader of the Northern fanatics who brought on the war," who "adopted and favored a policy of exterminating the Southern people by the most cruel and merciless measures and means."[31] Tyler branded the action "a great mistake," while G. W. B. Hale of Rocky Mount, Virginia, suggested adjourning in favor of John Brown rather than Lincoln, for Lincoln was just a "second edition of John Brown, without his brains or religion."[32] All this was to no avail, however, for the resolution was not repealed. In fact, some newspapers in Richmond agreed with the legislature's idea, with the *Times-Dispatch* going so far as to get in a dig at Tyler by writing that "whoever abuses Lincoln sinks himself."[33]

Time magazine took the opportunity provided by this controversy to ridicule Tyler and his dead father, labeling the former president "historically a dwarf."[34] Tyler responded with a brief book entitled *John Tyler and Abraham Lincoln, Who Was the Dwarf? A Reply to a Challenge,* published in Richmond, Virginia. In response to *Time*'s claims of Lincoln's greatness, Tyler emphasized that the war was Lincoln's fault and the North won solely because it "had all the wealth and power, and so the enormous propaganda which rose in his favor made Lincoln out to be a saint for Christianity, a Solomon for wisdom, and a Julius Caesar for war, when he was no one of the three." Instead, Lincoln was a tyrant who "adopted the rules of despotism and autocracy, and under the fiction of war powers virtually suspended the Constitution."[35]

Consequently, Tyler loathed comparison of Lincoln with Confederate luminaries. In 1930 Dr. Milton H. Shutes of California goaded the former William and Mary president by writing that "the South might easily have won if Davis had been only one third of the man that Lincoln was."[36] Incredulous, Tyler told Shutes that Lincoln was "a pitiful failure" who "sat around juggling with words and doing nothing, making incompetent appointments" to lead the United States Army. Tyler had kind words, however, for General George McClellan, who "would have been justified in slapping his [Lincoln's] face after his base treatment of him."[37] Repeating an earlier argument but with a new, racial twist, Tyler claimed that Lincoln had all the advantages in waging war at his disposal, but he was "so incompetent . . . that he had to hire five or six hundred thousand" soldiers and "200,000 slaves of the South to beat the government created by Davis and his cabinet."[38] Indeed, Tyler characterized Lincoln's reliance on African American troops as pathetic. "Poor old Lincoln had to say that 'without the aid of the negro troops he would have had to give up the war in *three weeks*.'"[39]

Who was the real Lincoln: the tyrant who waged an inhumane war on the South or the pitiful weakling, an "incompetent" who would have been unable to resist the allegedly nefarious designs of the radicals in his own party had he lived? Like many of Lincoln's detractors, Tyler apparently never saw or resolved this fundamental contradiction in his thought, nor was he able to recognize that the old Union he claimed had relied on consent rather than force was a Union that thrived and prospered on the backs of enslaved human beings who never consented to their enslavement. So, the significance of Tyler does not necessarily reside in the originality or cogency of his arguments. Indeed, much of what he wrote had already been said decades earlier by Albert Taylor Bledsoe and William Hand Browne and institutionalized across the South by organizations such as the United Daughters of the Confederacy. Rather, as the son of John Tyler and the previous president of William and Mary, Tyler lent a patina of prestige to Lincoln hatred that it otherwise might not have possessed, and his magazine supported all of the sixteenth president's critics in providing a venue in which members of the anti-Lincoln community could publish their grievances and get their hostile views of the president reaffirmed. Tyler also used the journal to punish heretics who did not subscribe to his version of white southern history and Abraham Lincoln, thus encouraging across the region the anti-intellectual spirit that Mencken had skewered so effectively in his essay "Sahara of the Bozart." In his correspondence with Shutes, for example, Tyler had predicted that northerners "will drop Lincoln" eventually because—and note here his association of Lincoln with left-wing radicalism—"the consequences of his doctrines is Bolshevism and Bolshevism will get us both some day! Terrible times are ahead!"[40] Bolshevism never conquered Tyler, but in an ironic twist of fate the son of the former president died seven years later, in 1935, on February 12—the date of Abraham Lincoln's birthday.[41] His second wife, Sue Ruffin Tyler, a descendant of Virginia fire-eater Edmund Ruffin, continued his work as the editor of *Tyler's Quarterly* into the 1950s.

The view of Lincoln propagated by Tyler and organizations such as the UDC did not go unchallenged. If everyone in the South hated Lincoln, there would have been no need to express antipathy for the president because it would have simply been taken for granted. Indeed, during 1924–25 a public controversy over Abraham Lincoln raged in Lexington, Kentucky, the hometown of Lincoln's wife, Mary Todd Lincoln. In the October 1924 issue of the *Confederate Veteran,* a resident of Lexington, Dr. Mary Scrugham, published a lengthy article entitled "Force or Consent as the Basis of American Government."[42] A native of Lexington, Scrugham graduated from the University of Kentucky in 1906 and, given the expectations for women at the time, she later took the unusual step of completing her doctorate at Columbia University in New York City under the supervision of the esteemed historian William Dunning, who like all of Lincoln's critics believed Reconstruction had been a tragedy, especially for its "hideous crime against white womanhood which now assumed new meaning in the annals of outrage."[43] Influenced by Dunning, Scrugham authored *The Peaceable Americans of 1860–61* (1921), a revisionist work sharply critical of the president—"though the methods of Lincoln and [John] Brown were different, their aims were identical"—and one that, among other things, denied the Civil War's inevitability. Mary Scrugham was in a very real sense an accomplished and progressive woman with pro-Confederate leanings, and her essay in the *Veteran* was essentially a distillation of her argument in *The Peaceable Americans.*[44] Scrugham's brother, James G. Scrugham, was in 1925 the governor of Nevada and during World War II served as the state's senator.[45]

Like Du Bois's piece in the *Crisis,* Scrugham's *Veteran* essay was prompted by the establishment of the Lincoln Memorial in Washington, D.C., in 1922. Scrugham bluntly stated that "the glory bestowed upon Abraham Lincoln for saving the American Union is a strange paradox, for he did not save the union. The fact is, he came very near to destroying it."[46] She compared Lincoln's refusal to recognize southern secession in 1860–61 to a woman rejecting a marriage proposal, arguing that "if, regardless of 'no,' he drags her to the altar and at the point of a bayonet forces her to say 'yes,' the marriage cannot be said to be based on consent. A union based on force and a union based on consent are as different as day and night, whether in government or matrimony. Force is force; and the mailed fist is the mailed fist, whether it is raised on the field of Flanders, by the streams of Ireland, or on a 'march through Georgia.'"[47] Lincoln's presidency was illegitimate because he received no votes in "ten states of the Union" and "three-fifths of the American voters in 1860 voted against him."[48] The American people never actually consented to Lincoln's election, nor did he save the Union; *"What Lincoln saved in 1861 was the Republican party."*[49]

Scrugham's essay was well received, if the responses printed in the pages of the *Confederate Veteran* were any indication. In January 1925,

for instance, three months after Scrugham's piece appeared, Cornelius
Hite of Washington, D.C., conveyed his "high appreciation of it because
of its unusual interest and importance in presenting a new and forcefully
just viewpoint to the world of the real causes of the war of 1861–65."[50]
John Ace of Wilmington, North Carolina, also approved of the "brilliant
and remarkable article by Dr. Mary Scrugham in the October number."[51]
Then, early in 1925, Scrugham was invited by the Lexington, Kentucky,
chapter of the UDC to deliver a lecture based on her article in the *Veteran*.
Scrugham's talk was subsequently printed in the local paper, the *Lexington
Herald-Leader*, on a Sunday, and it was later published in pamphlet form.[52]

All this was too much for a local Lexington attorney and Lincolnphile
named William H. Townsend (1890–1964). Writing to the *Herald-Leader*
to rebut Scrugham, Townsend said her evidence against Lincoln was, "I
submit, insufficient to go to the jury." Townsend penned a lengthy and
detailed response to Scrugham's charges that Lincoln was an illegitimate
president or responsible for beginning the war. To her claim that Lincoln
was illegitimately elected, Townsend made the obvious point that it was
not the popular vote that decided a president's legitimacy but, rather, the
results of the Electoral College. And on this basis, Townsend stated, Lincoln was constitutionally elected president. Not without a sense of irony,
the author observed that "since South Carolina had ratified the Federal
Constitution May 23, 1788, she 'consented' that the President should be
elected in the manner therein provided. Consequently," Townsend noted,
"it is apparent that South Carolina, instead of seceding because her right
of 'consent' had been violated, actually violated her 'consent' by seceding!"[53] Townsend likewise responded to Scrugham's finding that Lincoln
had not received a majority of the popular vote by explaining that neither
had presidents Zachary Taylor, James Buchanan, James Garfield, Grover
Cleveland, Benjamin Harrison, or Woodrow Wilson. Townsend queried:
"Is it too much to ask that what was awarded Cleveland twice and Wilson
twice shall not be denied Lincoln once?"[54] All in all, it was a shattering
rejoinder to Scrugham's speech.

Scrugham did not take Townsend's arguments lightly, and she replied
the very next week in the *Herald-Leader*. She labeled Townsend's essay as
"able" and made the somewhat disingenuous claim that she had no favorite
in the election of 1860. She never directly addressed Townsend's point
about the Electoral College, although she did say that even if the election of
1860 was "in accord with the letter of the law," it "was obviously a violation
of the principle on which free government is based." In other words, "it is

conceded that the spirit of the law is of more importance than the letter of the law."[55] This was a curious admission from an apparent defender of southern secession against Lincoln's political machinations, in that many of the fire-eaters had found William Seward's comments in the 1850s about the existence of a higher law than the Constitution so provocative. No matter, though, for Scrugham plodded ahead, essentially restating her argument without refuting Townsend's evidence against her claims. One week later the controversy continued unabated, as Townsend replied to Scrugham, and after that Scrugham replied to Townsend, whereupon she remarked of her astonishment "to what lengths this hero-worship [of Lincoln] carries them."[56]

On one level these contretemps between Scrugham and Townsend may seem to be nothing more than a local tempest in a Lexington, Kentucky, teapot, but the story is more complicated and instructive than that. The controversy illustrated, first of all, that in no southern community was aversion for Lincoln so dominant that it went unchallenged. Again and again, white southerners claimed they wanted the truths of history to be known, but there would have been no point in uttering such sentiments if everyone in the South agreed that Lincoln was a tyrant, infidel, or the cause of the Civil War. Indeed, African Americans for the most part remained pro-Lincoln, and many white southerners, including Townsend, shared such views. Second, the debate between Townsend and Scrugham was published in pamphlet form and offered to subscribers of the *Confederate Veteran* for the price of fifty cents.[57] Consequently, the pro-Lincoln viewpoint clearly found an outlet in the South, although the advertisement for the pamphlet in the *Veteran* concluded with the words "The South is at last victorious!"[58] The *Confederate Veteran* and the UDC continued to be one of the primary vehicles through which ill will toward Lincoln was disseminated throughout the region. Third, in keeping with previous critics, Scrugham stressed that Lincoln had not saved the Union but, rather, the Republican Party, as if this proved that Lincoln was a political cynic and not a statesman. What Scrugham failed to consider, however, was that by equating Lincoln with the antislavery Republicans, she had demonstrated precisely the opposite point: elected on an idealistic platform of ending slavery's expansion, and eventually its existence in the United States, the president-elect had refused to compromise—"On that point hold firm, as with a chain of steel," Lincoln told one correspondent—and therefore *saved* the Union from continued control by slaveholders.[59] So, it is clear from the Scrugham-Townsend controversy that animosity for

Lincoln had altered somewhat from the immediate postwar decades, as it continued to move from an emphasis on his alleged atheism and ignoble background to Lincoln's use of force to preserve a Union in which slavery would eventually be eradicated. The idea that the federal government could be used to enhance, rather than repress, political and social rights for all Americans was in itself a relatively modern concept and one that many Americans, including white southerners, found threatening. Indeed, Lincoln's antagonists were undeniably familiar with how southern state governments denied the African American population within their midst basic human rights, and in all likelihood it alarmed them that the federal government could override their region's ongoing racial atrocities, something that may have seemed more likely if Lincoln's actions during the Civil War were seen as constitutionally legitimate. At any rate, Scrugham lived another forty years but, it seems, never published again on Abraham Lincoln, while Townsend, as we shall see, advocated in public and private a pro-Lincoln viewpoint, publishing a well-respected monograph in 1929 entitled *Lincoln and His Wife's Home Town,* a book he later expanded into a longer work, *Lincoln and the Bluegrass* (1955).

If Lincoln's willingness to use force to prevent secession and the breakup of the country became a more prominent concern in the 1920s, another worrisome matter for his archenemies, one clearly related to their hostility to modernity, were comparisons of Lincoln with Jesus. When Bruce Barton published *The Man Nobody Knows: The Real Jesus* (1925), equating the two, a storm of protest emanated from some white southerners.[60] Barton was the son of the Congregational clergyman and Lincolnphile William E. Barton, whose well-received book *The Soul of Abraham Lincoln* (1920), among other things, debunked the idea that Lincoln had been an atheist.[61] It was scarcely surprising that the young Barton juxtaposed Jesus and Lincoln as successful executives and that the book was popular in a decade of conservative politics in which Christian orthodoxy seemed under attack.[62] According to Barton's biographer Richard M. Fried, *The Man Nobody Knows* "sold more than 250,000 copies in the first eighteen months" of publication, compelling Lincoln's detractors to respond in some fashion to the book's arguments.[63]

One response to Barton's work, published in the *Southern Methodist* magazine out of Memphis, Tennessee, on September 1, 1926, exemplified this mind-set. Halpin Whitney published a lengthy, bitter, and sarcastic review because, he explained, "the favorable recognition this book is being accorded in church papers, the diligence with which it is being circulated by public libraries, and the praise it receives from those who should condemn it, that we feel moved to discuss it."[64] In essence Whitney had two complaints about *The Man Nobody Knows*. One he labeled "the belittling of Jesus," while the other, more germane to the Civil War and 1920s America, was "the Glorification of Abraham Lincoln."[65] Claiming that he had "no animus against Abraham Lincoln," Whitney complained that he was fatigued with the constant bombardment of pro-Lincoln stories, "whether the subject is history, romance, or religion, [which] is a little more than one's stomach can stand when one does not believe in the canonization of saints."[66] If northerners wanted to canonize Lincoln, that was fine with him, but "among the orthodox in the South there are some 'searchers after truth' *who have already found it*."[67] Whitney grounded his opposition to Lincoln in what he perceived to be the heretical deification of the man occurring in northern churches, if not across the South. "These [southern churches] cannot bring themselves to parallel the life of any human being with that of the Redeemer of mankind. It is a sacrilege which they dare not commit," Whitney cautioned. He delineated for *Methodist* readers some standard arguments, all heavily reliant on Lamon's and Herndon's biographies, including but not limited to Lincoln's alleged atheism and that he "defeated the South and trampled underfoot the Constitution of the United States."[68]

Whitney's complaints were in one sense typically negative, but what is interesting is that they were published in a different context, a church magazine rather than a venue such as the *Confederate Veteran*. In fact, from Whitney's viewpoint Lincoln worship was a sign of the times, "in these days of degenerate ecclesiasticism."[69] Quoting liberally from Barton's book, Whitney associated Lincoln with modernity, heterodoxy, and virtually everything that he considered wrong with modern America. Nor was Whitney alone in this assessment. Methodist J. W. Duffey wrote to a female friend and, in an attached letter to Whitney's review, wished that the essay had been harsher, so that "Barton would be compelled to believe that there is not only a future hell, but that there is a present hell and that he is now in it."[70]

UDC member Mary DeButts Carter (1871–1948) of Upperville, Virginia, was equally blunt in a communication to Dr. J. W. Kennedy of Tacoma, Washington, in which she linked her contempt for Lincoln with her love of orthodox Christianity. She told Kennedy of her plans to send Whitney's review to "our Christian workers" across the South in order to inoculate Christians against Barton's blasphemy: "This book is one of the most irreverent, subtle attacks on orthodox Christianity that I have ever read, and it is calculated to do untold harm, especially to the young people in our churches, and Halpin Whitney's protest against the religious fallacies in this book, also against the sacrilegious lining up, by the author, of the name of the Son of God, and the paralleling of the most sacred and tragic events in His life, with those of a man who wrote a book to disprove the Bible and the divinity of Christ—ought to receive the approval of every reverent Christian."[71] Even more to the point, Carter quoted R. L. Rutherford, a Baptist from Georgia, to Kennedy: "What are we to do with such men as Bruce Barton? I honestly believe that the glorification of Lincoln as next to the Nazarene and the holding him up as a model religiously, has led to this spirit of Atheism abroad in the land and is largely responsible for this Modernist movement denying that Jesus was the Son of God."[72] In the 1920s and 1930s, the evidence suggests, if someone was a Christian, it did not mean they hated Lincoln, but if they hated Lincoln, then the chances were pretty good that person was either a conservative Christian or at the very least fundamentally at odds with modernity.

It seems that one of Mary Carter's correspondents, fellow Lincoln critic David Rankin Barbee (1874–1958), associated the deification of Lincoln in schools and churches across the South with a much bigger problem. In a 1927 letter to Carter he complained that his daughter's classmates raised money to buy a picture of Lincoln for their classroom and expressed alarm that "my church, the Southern Methodist, is led by such negro-equalityists as Bishop E. D. Mouzon of South Carolina and Bishop John M. Moore of Texas. They are seeking to force a reunion of the two Methodisms, which, if it ever comes to pass, will be the entering wedge in the South, to force negro equality on our people."[73] Three years later Barbee predicted a race war in the United States, telling Carter "that in setting free the slaves he [Lincoln] let loose the engine that may one day cost several million human lives, white and black. If this comes true, what a shame will hang about his name."[74] It would be virtually impossible, Barbee apparently believed, for white southerners to continue to treat African Americans so shabbily if Lincoln was viewed as a virtual demigod in the South. By the 1920s, if not much earlier, it was evident that African Americans had been methodically and violently reduced to second-class citizens across the region, and if Lincoln was being compared to Christ, how could southerners justify such reprehensible conduct toward their fellow man? Such continued persecution could perhaps be construed as antithetical to the ideals of the very Lord they professed to worship.

Halpin Whitney's essay in the *Southern Methodist* was not the only religious publication in the 1920s and 1930s that espoused a viewpoint hostile to Lincoln, allied to the entrenched interests of whites, and expressed it in the religious idiom of orthodox Christianity. Beginning in 1929, just before the stock market crash and the onset of the Great Depression, there appeared in the *Southern Churchman* magazine, the official organ of the Episcopal Church published in Richmond, Virginia, a series of lengthy editorials and articles bitterly critical of Lincoln. Edited by Langbourne Williams, a prominent Richmond resident who obviously detested Lincoln, the essays displayed a profound discontent with American culture. Before publishing these pieces, Williams, like Lyon Gardiner Tyler, had been prominently involved in a dispute regarding Lincoln in the *Richmond Times-Dispatch* in the winter of 1928. Williams publicly suggested that "in the interest of truth, and the honor of the U.S., the Lincoln memorial at Washington should be taken down or converted into some charitable institution" because "Grant and Lincoln and Sheridan and Sherman and beast Butler were guilty of unmerciful and barbaric warfare, and they practiced the basest brutality under the cover of war."[75] The *Churchman's* opening salvo against Lincoln was fairly tame and contained a reprint from the *Montgomery (Ala.) Advertiser* of a review of the film *Uncle Tom's Cabin*. In addition to criticizing the film for maligning the South, the reviewer claimed that Lincoln's Emancipation Proclamation "was the most disastrous thing that could have befallen" the slaves because they "were left to starve," and they "were incapable of providing food, clothes, and shelter" for themselves, and the war was "indefensible" and "waged under the direction and congratulations of Abraham Lincoln—by duplicity and prevarication."[76]

The most scathing of the *Churchman* essays decrying Lincoln, however, were penned by Virginian Mary Carter. Related to the Lee family by marriage, Carter had been an active member of the UDC for a good portion of her adult life. Born in 1871, her father, she explained to Barbee, "was a Methodist minister" who "served his white congregation in the morning, and taught the slaves in the afternoon."[77] Carter's parents told her the slaves would have been gradually emancipated and repatriated back to Africa, but "this peaceful method" of emancipation never occurred. If not for Lincoln and the abolitionists, she asserted, "the negro would now be working out his own salvation in his own country, and we would be free from an ever-increasing unassimilable in the body politic."[78] "The present race problem," as Carter saw it, was "Lincoln's legacy to this country."[79]

It was unclear precisely what Carter meant by the race problem. Perhaps she was alluding to the mere existence of African Americans in the United States, or maybe she was upset by those courageous Americans, especially southerners, who pressed for racial justice. However Carter may have defined it, the idea that diverse races and ethnicities could live together peacefully on an equal basis was a relatively modern idea, at least in America, and one she staunchly resisted. It is hard to ascertain, moreover, precisely how the innumerable racial atrocities whites carried out against African Americans in the postwar decades were the fault of Abraham Lincoln, but then again, matters of racial equality were never far from the minds of Lincoln loathers.

Unsurprisingly, before penning her *Churchman* essays, Carter wrote for the *Confederate Veteran,* first appearing in 1915 with an article that asked, rhetorically, "Did the War Save the Union?" As a faithful UDC member, Carter of course answered in the negative. Instead, she told the *Veteran*'s readers, "The thing that has saved our country in the past and will continue to save it, for it has to be saved not once only but all the time, is the Christian patriotism of a majority of our people."[80] In 1925 she collaborated with Lloyd T. Everett in editing and reissuing R. G. Horton's *Youth's History of the Great Civil War in the United States [War between the States] from 1861–1865* (1866), a white supremacist, Confederate, Copperhead account of the conflict in which she and Everett stated in their introduction that the Civil War was "a war of EMPIRE against their Southern brethren."[81] Horton (1829–98), a Confederate apologist, had claimed in 1866 that the South seceded "to preserve to themselves the right of self-government, and thus save themselves from the horrible consequences of *amalgamation and social death.*" White southerners, he had written, "knew from their practical knowledge of the negro that he belonged to a distinct species of man; that his brain, his shape, his nerves, in fact that every part of his body was different from the white man's. They knew that he was liable to different diseases from the white man; that he required the care and protection of the superior race. They knew that to equalize the races was simply to follow the fate of Mexico and Central America."[82] Such was the racial viewpoint of a work that Mary Carter deemed important enough to be reprinted and distributed across the South.

In addition to reissuing Horton's theories of racial degeneration, Carter also offered prize money in the pages of the *Confederate Veteran* for essays on various topics, including "Jefferson Davis's Place in History" and "The Scrugham Address." She also helped with the publication of a new edition of Charles Minor's *Real Lincoln*.[83] Carter was an indefatigable correspondent with Lincoln's foes, not just within Virginia but throughout the United States. Indeed, her dissemination of materials to schools and newspapers advocating the Lost Cause viewpoint of the Civil War with an attendant critique of Lincoln was truly remarkable. In one letter Carter informed Joseph Eggleston, the president of Hampden-Sydney College (former home of theologian Robert Lewis Dabney, who, like James Henley Thornwell, interpreted the Civil War as one between a godless North and a Christian Confederacy), that her goal as the founder of the "Virginia-Tennessee Book Committee" was to "gradually supply all the university, college, larger High School Libraries, in these two States, with books that, in the main at least contain FACTS and give the South a square deal."[84] According to Carter, her committee had supplied "between thirty and forty libraries" with such books, along with "sets of very valuable pamphlets." Carter told Eggleston she would be more than happy to supply Hampden-Sydney with such works. Interestingly, Carter christened her activities as "missionary work."[85] To Barbee she described her calling as "to down the truth-obscuring Lincoln myth that has been used by Northern historians to put the South and her institutions in the wrong" and claimed that "in putting through this plan, in this time, I have placed in the educational centers of the country, about 9,000 books and pamphlets," including the works of Albert Taylor Bledsoe, George Edmonds (aka Elizabeth Meriwether), Lloyd T. Everett, Charles L. C. Minor, and Mildred Lewis Rutherford.[86]

Mary Carter worked assiduously to make sure that no myths would be propagated regarding Abraham Lincoln. Instead, she wanted the "facts" about Lincoln and the Civil War taught correctly. Carter explained to Eggleston that she disagreed with historian Claude Bowers's characterization of Lincoln in *The Tragic Era* (1927), his book about Reconstruction, that "Lincoln was a friend of the South." Consequently, Carter's committee placed on the inside cover of every copy of Bower's book sent to a school a lengthy statement that included the lines "We do not accept . . . that Lincoln was a friend of the South, and had he lived the South would have fared differently—far from it."[87] She likewise disparaged the claim of Robert E. Lee's esteemed biographer Douglas Southall Freeman that Lincoln fought the war to preserve the Union. "Dr. Freeman has some fine material in his book [on Lee] and it is tragic that he should tie the hands of those wishing to put it the libraries, by this Lincoln dope. This is the most dangerous, *truth-obscuring, Lee-misrepresenting phase* of the Lincoln myth we have to cope with," Carter lectured Eggleston, "for in making Lincoln a Union preserver, we automatically and *inescapably make Lee a Union-destroyer.*"[88] Carter's derision of Freeman suggests another reason why numerous detractors never conceded that Lincoln did anything but save the Republican Party. If he was saving the Union from continued domination by slaveholders, by logical implication the Confederacy was ruining it; but if he was only trying to preserve a party (never mind that party's principled antislavery stance), well, in their view that was not admirable at all, and if they could persuade Americans to agree with their position, then Lincoln's stature with the country would accordingly be diminished. The Confederacy, in contrast, would have then looked much better. Carter's nostalgic version of the past coincided with her belief in white supremacy, the righteousness of the Confederate cause, a commitment she and many other Lost Cause advocates equated with Protestant Christianity. Indeed, she frequently said she was trying to spread "Truth"—clearly a religious term—throughout the southern states. In her 1948 obituary in *Tyler's Historical Quarterly* coeditor Lloyd T. Everett accurately noted that Carter was "mighty, indeed, with her pen," compared her favorably with Mildred Lewis Rutherford, and praised her because "through a long lifetime she did splendid work for the truth of United States' history through the United Daughters of the Confederacy; devoting much time and money to the work."[89]

Carter's opening volley in her *Southern Churchman* crusade was entitled, appropriately, "Lincolnolatry in the Churches." Her piece was a copy of a letter she had sent to Bishop James E. Freeman of the Episcopal Church in Washington, D.C. She complained to Freeman that "the Mariolatry that our Protestant churches so highly condemn in the Catholic church is being paralleled by a far more insidious, objectionable Lincolnolatry in our own churches."[90] Most upsetting was "a statue of Lincoln in the Episcopal Cathedral of St. John the Divine in New York City" and that Lincoln was favorably compared "with the Redeemer of mankind—our Lord Jesus Christ, in the majority of our churches, Sabbath after Sabbath."[91] Carter used Barton's *Man Nobody Knows* as evidence of the problem with which she was concerned—"a blasphemy," she labeled it. She cited Lamon's and Herndon's biographies, among others, as evidence for Lincoln's infidelity and the chief reason no Christian should draw comparisons between Lincoln and Jesus. The next week Carter's attack continued, and she focused her wrath on a proposal to build a "'Southern Methodist Lincoln Memorial Church' at Hodgenville, Ky," near Lincoln's birthplace, which in light of Lincoln's supposed atheism, she deemed sacrilegious. Examined closely,

the way in which Mary Carter closed her second *Churchman* article was
similar to Halpin Whitney's piece. She connected admiration of Lincoln
with the decline of the Christian faith and laid the blame for such a development directly on clergymen:

> Now, Bishop Freeman, as you are aware, there is a very serious religious
> crisis on in this country, the young are drifting away from the homes and
> the churches into criminal currents . . . the conclusion is inescapable that
> one of the major causes is the absence of the drawing Christian qualities in
> many of the clergy. They fail to attract the young, because their characters
> lack the *discriminating* and compelling Christian VIRTUES.
>
> As illustrating *this lack*—Abraham Lincoln is the only *American*—who
> to my knowledge ever wrote a book to disprove the Bible and the divinity of
> Christ and called the Redeemer of mankind an illegitimate child. Yet he is
> the only man who in the history of this country has been almost universally
> singled out by the clergy of this country as preeminently fitted to be classed
> with the Christ—called a Christ and eulogized from our pulpits Sabbath
> after Sabbath. There must be something radically wrong with the spiritual
> perceptions and outlook of our clergy when a man of this type is selected
> for this superhuman placing and honor! . . . What a spectacle! The reviler
> of Christ, selected by the Ministers of Christ, as the equal of Christ![92]

Carter's epistles were well received in the pages of the *Churchman,* and
her main theme, that the veneration of a supposed atheist by Americans
demonstrated a decline in American morals, found favor with numerous
individuals. Mrs. Wade Barrier, the historian of the Tennessee Division
of the UDC, for instance, wrote to the *Churchman* in July 1930 to express
her approval of Langbourne Williams's "courageous stand . . . and the help
you are rendering in the fight to stop the dangerous wave of Lincolnolatry
that seems to be sweeping this land today in absolute contradiction of
facts," stating that "the thanks and loyal support of those who desire to
see the Christian Religion kept from this contamination are yours in full
measure."[93] Mrs. J. B. Rhoad from Austin, Texas, told the *Churchman,*
"I can't thank you enough for your work in defense of the Truth," while
from Gladstone, Oregon, Paul S. Whitcomb penned a lengthy piece supporting Carter, comparing Lincoln to Kaiser Wilhelm II of Germany and
expressing his conviction "that he [Lincoln] is the most colossal hoax of
modern history."[94] The direct connection between criticism of Lincoln and
a defense of Christianity, at least as defined by elite white southerners,
was clearly evident in the pages of the *Southern Churchman.*[95] Lincoln's
deification in America's churches presented a profound intellectual and

religious crisis for his enemies. If the Confederacy had been righteous, they must have asked themselves, how could the infidel Lincoln be extolled and venerated above a man such as Jefferson Davis? This explanation suggests one reason for their conspiratorial worldview and why many white southerners after the Civil War wrote pamphlets and books contrasting Jefferson Davis favorably with Abraham Lincoln.[96]

Carter's derogatory missives were hardly the only articles hostile to Lincoln printed in the *Southern Churchman*. Landon Carter Bell of Ohio, a graduate of Milligan College in Tennessee and the University of Virginia Law School in 1902, published some essays that ventured an important explanation about why the president's foes were unwelcome in the South, both in the immediate aftermath of the war and in the long decades after 1865.[97] He conceded that the South lagged behind the North economically but that what the North really wanted was for the South to agree to "the acceptance of and a failure to protest against an utterly false version of history," namely, the history of the Civil War from the northern perspective. Bell defiantly stated that he, unlike others, would not submit to such intellectual vassalage and described those who did so contemptuously: "It may be true there are some at the South who in effect say: 'What do we care for history? What we want is the money. The Republican party is in control of things; the North is in the saddle; there will never be another President from the South; the course for us to pursue is the one that will enable us to the most dollars. If by confessing our fathers rebels and traitors, the South wrong, the North right, we can coax the North to feed us a little more generously with the crumbs from its table, why not do so? A few dollars in our pockets now is worth more to us than all the history in the world.'"[98] Bell may have been exaggerating the viewpoint of those he was criticizing, but it is difficult to believe that some semblance of the sentiment he described did not exist among whites in the American South after 1865. Indeed, a later piece in the *Churchman* entitled "Lincoln Eulogies Merely 'Facet of Herd Psychology'" made precisely this point, while Mary Carter protested the *Richmond News-Leader*'s stance that it was "not necessary to criticize the idol of the North to establish the right of secession and the justices of the Southern cause. Personalities becloud and belittle principles."[99] But from the standpoint of Lincoln's critics, the personal and political could not be separated; they could not separate love for the Confederate cause and hatred for Abraham Lincoln. Carter and her circle believed it was not only important to criticize Lincoln—it was their duty.[100]

Consequently, what infuriated Lincoln's adversaries was their belief that they were not only losing the battle with northern historians and the approving sentiment of the country regarding Lincoln; they were in addition struggling against their own people for control of the minds of white southern schoolchildren and the future of their region. In a piece entitled "Mob Psychology," for instance, the state historian of the UDC in North Carolina, Mrs. W. S. Bernard, asked, "Strange, is it not, that there are members of the daughters of the Confederacy, an organization primarily for 'preserving the truth of southern history' who cannot bear to be told the simple truth about Lincoln?"[101] South Carolinian Julia Peterkin's 1925 letter to Oliver Barrett encapsulated perfectly what the president's rivals perceived they were fighting. "Time works miracles. When I was a little girl my dear grandmother said to me after I had learned a lesson which concerned Lincoln and his attitude to the South, she spoke so gravely that I have never forgotten it. 'Learn your lesson and recite it for your teacher as it is in the book. Then forget it and remember what I'm telling you; Lincoln hated the South, and did what he could to crush it.' For years I believed her," Peterkin concluded, "but at last I think she was mistaken. Her own suffering had blinded her to much that was true."[102] Peterkin's letter is an indication that there were various arenas of contest within southern families and southern schools contending for control over Abraham Lincoln's image. This of course meant that Lincoln's archenemies were going to have to rededicate themselves to their crusade because if they could not win the battle for Lincoln's image with white southerners, they must have wondered, what would become of their identity as a people and the white supremacist cause from 1865 onward that they so deeply cherished? Because of his children's experiences, in early March 1927 David Rankin Barbee reassured Carter of his own devotion to their crusade: "I am enlisted for the war, and as long as I live I intend fighting the infamous Lincoln myth. My children in the public schools here are being taught that Lincoln is second only to Christ. They were taught that in New Orleans, where we lived prior to coming here a year ago. And if you were to examine . . . textbooks in all the Southern states you would find that that is what is being taught everywhere."[103]

The Lincoln wars continued in the pages of the *Churchman* in November 1930, when letters Alex McBee of Greenville, South Carolina, had written eight years earlier, in 1922 and 1923, to Howard Robbins, the dean of the Cathedral of St. John the Divine in New York City, were reprinted by Williams. McBee vigorously protested to Robbins the placement of

Lincoln's picture in the cathedral and enclosed several pamphlets for the dean's perusal with his initial correspondence, including works by George L. Christian and Mildred Lewis Rutherford. McBee asked Robbins, "Will you not tell me what Christian civilization is, and some specific thing that Mr. Lincoln did as President which contributed to Christianity?"[104] Robbins replied within two weeks, saying that he found the pamphlets McBee had sent "to be of quite unequal merit," singling out Christian's 1909 address to the Robert E. Lee Camp as a "crude attempt to besmirch the character of one whom practically the whole civilized world now recognizes as one of the heroic figures of human history."[105] Robbins was incredulous that Lincoln's inclusion in the cathedral would be questioned because "the greatest progress made in Christian civilization during the nineteenth century was the abolishment of slavery throughout the civilized world, and the character who best represents the revolt of the awakened Christian conscience against this age-long evil, is our own Lincoln. His patience, his vision and magnanimity have few parallels."[106] Robbins's riposte to McBee must have struck a nerve, for Langbourne Williams felt the need to clarify a few things for his readers, and he inserted a paragraph after Robbins's response, in boldface letters, more or less accusing Lincoln of being a war criminal.[107]

McBee's rejoinder, reprinted by Williams in the same issue of the *Churchman*, filled two pages and three columns of the paper. This wordiness was characteristic of many of Lincoln's critics, perhaps reflecting the insecurity of their devoutly held views about their enemy, whereby they would reply to the briefest of letters with an avalanche of "information" in order to overwhelm their opponents. Indeed, it seems that these white southerners, in their zeal, if not desperation, to discredit Lincoln, were not so much trying to vanquish their opponents intellectually as much as they were attempting to reassure themselves. At any rate McBee defended the pamphlets he sent to Robbins as "irrefutable" and closed with a flourish about Lincoln's malignant, anti-Christian, global influence:

> I am not sure that "Christian civilization," as it is exemplified by leading nations, the United States included, is related to Christianity . . . Mr. Lincoln had over 100,000 negroes, former slaves in the South, sold to Southerners by Northerners, in his army to kill Southerners . . . the object being to devastate the South, and probably to cause insurrections, thereby murdering women and children. Yet Germans and many Americans object to French having placed negro troops on the Rhine. It may be that you know of Mr. Lincoln having influenced "Christian civilization" in some parts of the world, but

the Central Allies occupy much space, and if that war was not to enslave the balance of the world, why was that war? If he did influence such Christian civilization abroad, from the foregoing it appears to me that it was at the expense of Christianity with his admirers at home.[108]

McBee informed the dean that the "refutation of facts presented . . . will be accepted gracefully."[109]

The controversy surrounding Lincoln in the *Southern Churchman* continued on for a while, but the combination of the worsening of the Depression and the death of Langbourne Williams in 1931 brought to a close this nearly two-year-long onslaught of Lincoln loathing. Still, several important themes stand out among the views expressed by Lincoln's critics: they believed Lincolnolatry posed a mortal threat to orthodox Christianity; they associated Lincoln with modernity and all its attendant ills, including the prospect of racial equality; they believed the South was not responsible for the Civil War; they believed, instead, that Lincoln was responsible for the war because he placed the well-being of the Republican Party above that of the Union; they believed Lincoln was a tyrant and war criminal; and they believed Lincoln was an imperialist and that his admirers had exploited the president's memory in garnering support for U.S. expansionism overseas. Most worrisome, however, was the sense among Lincoln's detractors that they were losing the hearts and minds of not only northerners, one cause they assuredly deemed lost, but within their own region as well.

Indications of such fears were contained in a correspondence William Townsend and Mary Carter conducted in 1930 in the midst of the *Churchman*'s campaign. Their communications were written in the context of a key trend in Lincoln scholarship that occurred in the 1920s: the study of Abraham Lincoln's life became the subject of the work of skilled historians, some of whom were revisionists critical of the sixteenth president. To be sure, hagiography was still present, most notably in the multivolume biography on Lincoln by the noted Illinois poet Carl Sandburg, but books such as J. G. Randall's *Constitutional Problems under Lincoln* (1926) and former senator Albert J. Beveridge's *Abraham Lincoln, 1809–1865* (1928) demonstrated that serious scholarly work on the president was becoming more prevalent.[110] Although both men were revisionists regarding the needlessness of the war, Randall respected Lincoln and therefore cannot be properly characterized as a historian who hated him. Beveridge's profile, in contrast, was a more complicated matter. He never finished his projected multivolume biography, as he died before it was completed. The first two volumes did not cover the presidential years, but they were never-theless sharply critical of Lincoln's prepresidential career, characterizing it as little more than a defense "of vested interests," nearly "pettifogging" in its criticism of President Polk and the Mexican War, and one, finally, that paled in comparison to the career of Stephen A. Douglas.[111] "The Lincoln of Illinois," Beveridge asserted, "could not by any possibility, have been the Lincoln of the Second Inaugural or the Gettysburg Speech. They can exalt him all they like, but the cold fact is that not one faint glimmer appears in his whole life at least before his Cooper Union speech, which so much suggests the glorious radiance of his last two years."[112] Beveridge's book therefore constituted a landmark work in Lincoln studies that prompted a good deal of discussion among interested writers. So, alongside her original letter to Townsend, Carter sent the Lexington attorney a review of Beveridge's biography by Rupert Hughes, the uncle of the Texas billionaire Howard Hughes. Rupert Hughes had described Beveridge's book as a work that "deals ruthlessly with the popular myths concerning one of the most beloved of Americans," which pleased Carter and prompted her to send the piece to Townsend in Lexington.[113] Townsend, it seems, was amused. "The correspondence began," he later told one correspondent, "like all my tilting of lances with fellow Southerners about Lincoln, with a letter from Miss Carter saying that she had read one of my books which revealed Abraham Lincoln in a favorable light, that she very earnestly deplored the fact that a Southerner of my Confederate background and antecedents should be guilty of such reprehensible practice, and that, with my permission, she would undertake my enlightenment and ultimate regeneration."[114]

Townsend eventually expressed frustration with Carter rather than de-light, for he had looked forward to a good quarrel with her, "a rebuttal" of his views, but instead found "a putrid mass of undigested vituperation."[115] Apparently, Carter had tried to invalidate Townsend's arguments—and one must be careful here for Carter's letters are at this stage lost to history—by labeling pro-Lincoln sources such as Varina Davis and other prominent white southerners who viewed Lincoln favorably as liars. "Mrs. Davis is a weak, unstable creature with traitorous inclinations!!" Townsend exclaimed. "Everybody is either a traitor or a liar who has a good word for poor old homely, kind, tragic Abraham Lincoln!"[116] He jested that "Abraham Lincoln is as far removed from your blank cartridges as Mount McKinley is from the 'Big Berthas' on the Western Front."[117] In a fascinating aside Townsend offered reasons for the deep, persistent frustrations of the president's opponents and the ever-changing nature of Lincoln hatred in the former Confederacy:

> I am not surprised that you complain of the indifference of the south's "own son's and daughters" toward this anti-Lincoln propaganda. They do their own reading and thinking and are doubtless quite satisfied with their own impression of Lincoln. Only the day before yesterday I was talking to a lawyer now eighty years of age, one of the leading lawyers of the Nashville Bar. His father, his brothers and other relatives were all in the Confederate Army, and he himself, although only fifteen years of age, had started to enlist when the news of Appomattox came. This lawyer is wholly southern in feeling and is a life-long Democrat. He is known among his associates for his love of the south, and yet when I asked him what he thought of Abraham Lincoln, he, without knowing my own views, sitting there in his office at Nashville, replied "Abraham Lincoln is, in my judgment, America's greatest statesmen." Then he went on to say that during the War he was under the impression that Lincoln was a monster, that he was almost prepared to believe that he had a forked tail and cloven hoofs, but that when he got old enough to read for himself, he read everything that he could obtain on Abraham Lincoln, both criticism and eulogies, and that now, after all these years, it was his deliberate judgment that Lincoln was America's greatest statesman and Lee America's greatest soldier.[118]

Townsend missed entirely that Mary Carter and others of her ilk did not want people to do their own thinking about Lincoln; no, these vocal Lincoln critics wanted to do their thinking for them, or at the very least offer only those "truths" about Lincoln acceptable to their own weltanschauung. Intriguingly, Townsend told Carter that Americans needed to quit asking who was right or wrong in the Civil War, essentially repeating the reconciliationist, sentimental view of the conflict espoused at the expense of African American freedom since the Spanish-American War in 1898. "Lee and Davis and our other southern statesmen were men of sublime courage to do the right as they saw the right. I do not care whether they were actually right or wrong. It makes no difference to me, nor to the vast thinking majority of our countrymen. We honor them for what they were, and we do not dim their fame by attempting to belittle others who were also great."[119]

Townsend's dispatches yield a vital clue about why Lincoln's adversaries were unpopular in both the North and the South. They, unlike the rest of the country, wanted to actually debate who had been right or wrong in the Civil War, which the rest of the nation manifestly did not want to do. If the South had been right to secede, or justified in doing so, nearly 750,000 Americans died needlessly in a gruesome Civil War. But if the North was right and the South wrong, how would white southerners, or any American for that matter, reconcile such carnage with the Lost Cause or the ongoing horrific treatment of African Americans? No, it seemed much better for whites to forget the whole thing and believe that neither side was right or wrong in the war, congratulate themselves on the valor of white soldiers in the conflict, and move on. Remembering the Civil War like this was a way of denying or forgetting that slavery was inextricably tied to the fighting, something Lincoln's opponents and, increasingly, his admirers vehemently contested, although they obviously did not want to forget their own particular version of the conflict. Even Townsend's letters lacked serious reference to the slaves or Lincoln's Emancipation Proclamation. It was almost as if he, too, would rather forget the whole subject of race and the Civil War.

Eventually, Townsend lost all patience with Carter's imperviousness to his arguments, calling her a "sadly misguided" woman "who will frankly and candidly, as becomes her race and breeding, take it all back when she meets Abraham Lincoln in heaven."[120] As for her recommendation that he read Albert Taylor Bledsoe's Lincoln essay, Townsend wearily replied: "I have long been familiar with it, as I am with all the other venomous but pathetically impotent tirades against Abraham Lincoln. I grieve for these poor, credulous 'historical' minds that hate has warped every time I see their scurrilous handiwork on my shelves. Like the 'Facts and Falsehoods' of Miss [Elizabeth] Meriwether, who hides behind a nom de plume."[121] "I do not think you and I can agree on Abraham Lincoln," Townsend concluded, no matter what else he and Carter agreed upon, and he compared her attacks—unfairly—to John Wilkes Booth sneaking up to assassinate Lincoln in Ford's Theatre, for Mary Carter was anything but surreptitious in her attacks upon the president.[122]

If William Townsend never changed the mind of Mary DeButts Carter, and there is no evidence that he did, he was able to change the mind of a publisher of a proposed book about Lamon's biography of Abraham Lincoln. Many of the president's opponents were thrilled with Beveridge's biography, for they believed it confirmed what they had been saying for years about Lincoln's prepresidential background and career.[123] One such southerner was the journalist David Rankin Barbee, appropriately enough the son of a Methodist pastor from Tennessee, who eventually became the managing editor of the *Asheville Citizen* in Asheville, North Carolina, and a columnist for the *Washington Post*. In 1927 Barbee published "An Excursion in Southern History" in the *Citizen,* a series of five articles that were later brought out in pamphlet form and were a compilation of his correspondence with Beveridge regarding the Civil War and Abraham Lincoln.[124] Barbee's purpose, stated in the foreword, "was to determine if the time was ripe to offer the truth about the South's side of the War of the 60s to a Northern historian."[125] Barbee was a relative newcomer among Lincoln's opponents, but he would remain there for the next twenty-five years, publishing various articles and works on the assassination of Lincoln and the Confederate spy Rose Greenhow in magazines such as *Tyler's Historical Quarterly* and other venues. Like Mary Carter, Barbee was a tireless researcher for those facts that corresponded with his preconceived notions. And like most of the president's enemies, Barbee had an inflated sense of his own originality and self-importance; he wrote as if nothing negative had ever been written about Lincoln and that he, Barbee (or whatever detractor one could name), was a lone seeker on a religious quest after the truth that would enlighten and delight others about the allegedly nefarious Civil War president.

The correspondence began when Barbee heard Beveridge reacted positively to a piece he had written about Washington and Lincoln. Barbee subsequently sent Beveridge a letter outlining his views on Lincoln: he was unjustly deified; he was written about from an entirely northern viewpoint and what was sorely needed was a southern perspective; he was "responsible for the horrors of Andersonville"; he was an atheist who "never believed in Christ and never was a professed Christian"; he was "as much of a hot head as [William Lowndes] Yancey, as much of a fanatic as many of our Southern people said Jefferson Davis was"; he was a tyrant who "suppressed many Democratic papers and put their editors in prison . . . this is one of the ugliest chapters in Lincoln's life, the suppression of free speech, and the assumption of dictatorial powers by the great Emancipator."[126] In reply Beveridge asked Barbee to read the manuscript of his forthcoming biography. Of course, this was precisely what Barbee wanted, for by corresponding with Beveridge and publishing their correspondence, Barbee was legitimized, at least in his own mind, as an authority on Lincoln. Back and forth went the letters between the two, with Barbee offering Beveridge whatever assistance he could, including books such as R. G. Horton's explicitly white supremacist *Youth's History of the Civil War,* edited by Mary Carter, works by Albert Taylor Bledsoe

(Barbee was a huge fan), and "the use of my private library."[127] Barbee was a devout Christian, and in *Excursion* he claimed, in agreement with previous Lincoln critics, that the Civil War had been a theological war, "a war of Atheism in the North against Christianity in the South."[128]

Curiously, Beveridge did not take Barbee's bait in that he refused to respond point by point to the journalist's criticism of Lincoln. Two years later William Townsend would learn the futility of that exercise in his correspondence with Mary Carter. That was probably fine with Barbee, for in being published as a correspondent with Beveridge, he received the scholarly imprimatur he desired. As one letter to the *Southern Churchman* put it in 1929, after Barbee's pamphlet was published, "I thank you most heartily for the little booklets on General Lee and the 'Excursions' in Southern history. Barbee is a rare historian. I was surprised that Beveridge had never heard of Bledsoe, as an intellectual giant, he topped almost any man this country ever produced."[129]

Barbee hoped *Excursion* would open the eyes of white southerners to the truth that "Lincoln was no demi-god, but a human being of very coarse fibre, with a great brain and with many ugly spots in his character. His ambition and his vanity were no less causes of the war than the militant hatred of the Northern parsons against the South."[130] He despaired that southerners did not know their own history, an ignorance he deemed "a shame" and in dire need of correction. He embarked upon the venture of publishing a book he wanted to call "The Inside History of 'Lamon's Life of Lincoln.'" Lengthily and clumsily subtitled "The Biography of the Worst Hated and Probably the Truest and Most Accurate Book Ever Written about the Great War President from His Birth to His Presidency," Barbee hoped to get the work published through the Pioneer Press of Washington, D.C.

Unbeknownst to Barbee, however, William Townsend, in correspondence with Barbee's publisher about the proposed work, had discredited the book. Interestingly, after closely reading *Excursion,* Townsend communicated with various revisionist or Progressive historians and American notables in order to gauge whether they believed if Beveridge had lived he would have produced a biography hostile to Lincoln, as Barbee had claimed in *Excursion*. In a memorandum to himself, Townsend claimed that Supreme Court justice Oliver Wendell Holmes Jr. and the esteemed Progressive historian Charles Beard "definitely agreed with me that the last two volumes of Beveridge's 'Life,' had he lived to write them, would have shown the marvelous development of Lincoln's latent genius and the flowering of his character until he reached the pinnacle of his Second

Inaugural."[131] Correspondence from Beard and Holmes confirms that Townsend's memorandum was accurate. In one letter Beard reassured the Lexington attorney that Townsend's opinions of Beveridge's book "are correct." "They check exactly with my own impressions gained from long talks with Senator Beveridge. It is true that when he was working on Lincoln as a petty lawyer in Illinois," Beard explained, "the Senator was surprised and pained to find so many things that made Lincoln look trivial and shifty as a politician. He mentioned these things to me and I advised him to gloss over nothing. I took the position that the greatest have mean aspects and often shady spots in their careers."[132] Beard furthermore informed Townsend that Beveridge was fascinated, as had been countless Americans since 1865, by "the mysterious process by which the Illinois politician was transformed into the man who wrote the second inaugural!"[133] Apparently, Townsend gently chided Beard for his wording, for in a reply on September 27, 1932, Beard reassured Townsend that "by 'shady spots' and 'meanness,' I did not intend to impute to Lincoln anything more than the triviality and selfishness that characterize the best of mortals at times in their lives."[134] Holmes, who in his old age found writing increasingly difficult, had an assistant pen a letter to Townsend stating that the Supreme Court justice "agrees entirely with what you say of Beveridge's final view of Lincoln" and in a second note explained that "Beveridge's researches had not damaged his [Beveridge's] conviction that Lincoln emerged a great man" from the war.[135]

Such comments suggest why Beveridge's *Abraham Lincoln,* although a hugely important book in Lincoln scholarship, never resonated with the president's enemies in the same manner as Edgar Lee Masters's later biography, *Lincoln: The Man.* Beveridge's lengthy work was a more deeply researched and better written volume than Masters's, but being a multivolume profile, it was less manageable for readers than Masters's single-volume account. In addition, it did not cover Lincoln's presidency, which was of course the most important aspect of Lincoln's life. Thus it did not characterize Lincoln as an imperialist for coercing the South to remain in the Union. Such a rendering could not have been too useful to those who since the turn of the century had portrayed Lincoln in precisely such terms. Finally, although Beveridge may not have liked the prepresidential Lincoln he discovered in his researches, he apparently did not loathe him. He took for granted, moreover, Lincoln's presidential greatness, which was distinctly at odds with detractors such as David Rankin Barbee or Mary Carter. Still, in its criticism of Lincoln's life before 1861, in its labeling of the war as needless, in its depiction of Stephen Douglas rather than Lincoln as the prewar hero, Beveridge's book laid the groundwork for future animosity for the president.[136]

So, when Townsend received a request from Barbee's potential publisher, Rufus Rockwell Wilson of the Pioneer Press, "asking my opinion of Mr. Barbee's capacity to do a fair and unbiased job," he was emboldened to go on the attack by reassurances from luminaries such as Beard and Holmes.[137] Townsend subsequently wrote Wilson an eleven-page, single-spaced letter detailing the reasons Barbee was an unreliable historian for such a project. Townsend doubted the Asheville journalist could maintain "unswerving impartiality" and characterized Barbee's gifts, such as they were, harshly: "I have no doubt that Mr. Barbee is an honest, sincere gentleman, but it is my deliberate judgment that interpretation of his correspondence with Beveridge, his statements about Lincoln in his monograph and his appraisal of A. T. Bledsoe as the 'honestest' writer, make it exceedingly doubtful whether Mr. Barbee, however, conscientious he is, can accurately select the 'truest' life of Lincoln."[138] Wilson found Townsend's missive persuasive, for he replied in May 1933 that "Mr. Barbee, with all his good qualities, is very much 'set in his way' and I doubt if he will agree to the conditions I shall submit to him" (Wilson wanted to write a positive assessment of Lincoln, perhaps as a counterweight to Barbee, in the introduction to the book) and so concluded, "It will thus be made impossible for us to father his book."[139] Townsend was thrilled with Wilson's response and proudly wrote in a memo that Wilson's "decision has evidently tomahawked Barbee's brain child and nothing further has been heard of 'The Inside Story of Lamon's Life of Lincoln.'"[140]

David Rankin Barbee never published his biography of Lamon's book, and it is not at all certain if he ever discovered that Townsend had torpedoed his proposed volume.[141] Townsend continued to write, publish, and battle with all comers over the Lincoln image, while Barbee remained a prominent controversialist and continued complaining that the country's problems stemmed from African Americans. "From the first day he entered the country, at Jamestown in 1620, to now," Barbee lectured one correspondent in 1948,

> the Negro has been a disturbing factor. One million young men laid down their lives on his altar. There are able historians who trace the First World War and its sequel to our War of 1861–65. What a holocaust! The disturbing—the most disturbing—factor in all this is that the leaders of the Negro race—lawyers, doctors, ministers, and, chiefly, educators—are all Com-

munists. If the FBI were to open its files, I fear there would be a race war of the most dangerous character. So far as religion is concerned, I am not at all hopeful. It seems to me that Protestant Christianity is at a very low ebb. This, too, is due to the Negro. . . . Every issue of my church paper has a leading article on Cuffy. We get Nigger, Nigger, Nigger from our pulpits and are told how intolerant we are because we do not treat him in a Christian way.[142]

In the early 1950s he moved to Orange, Texas, and the former journalist died of stomach cancer in 1958. His previous employer, the *Washington Post,* said little in its obituary of Barbee's ideas about Lincoln or African Americans. Perhaps they were unknown to the newspaper, or if known, they surmised it was best to not speak ill of the dead, especially in the midst of the burgeoning civil rights movement.[143]

Lest one believe that all the arguments over the Lincoln image were just squabbles among fanatics, enmity for the president had clearly crept into the American academy and acquired a veneer of scholarly legitimacy. In 1930, at the beginning of the Great Depression and the perceived collapse of industrial capitalism in the United States, a group of twelve white southern intellectuals published *I'll Take My Stand: The South and the Agrarian Tradition,* a book in which they collectively reaffirmed, among other things, the superiority of the southern, agrarian way of life.[144] The twelve separate essays in *I'll Take My Stand* not only attacked industrialism and defended agrarianism; they inescapably addressed issues related to the Civil War and Reconstruction. What was especially noteworthy in this collection, and in the careers of the Agrarians more generally, is that the writers who more or less came to terms with modernity, such as Robert Penn Warren (1905–89), tended to be more understanding, if not complimentary, of Abraham Lincoln, while those who remained more unreconciled to modern America, such as Andrew Lytle (1902–95) and Donald Davidson (1893–1968), were sharply critical. The significance of *I'll Take My Stand* was not necessarily in the accuracy of its contributors' analyses of what was wrong with the South or modern America. Indeed, some southern reviewers brutally attacked the book.[145] Rather, the symposium's importance was that it laid the intellectual groundwork for the modern neo-Confederate, anti-Lincoln movement after World War II. It is important to keep in mind that the Agrarians were writing about the South and the Civil War in the midst of an intellectual shift in Civil War and Lincoln studies, a revisionism whereby historians argued, as we have seen, that the war was not caused by slavery but, rather, by a blundering generation of statesmen, including Abraham Lincoln, and thus the entire conflict was unnecessary. Even though not all revisionist scholars were hostile to Lincoln—J. G. Randall most certainly was not—a few of the Agrarians most definitely were.

Andrew Lytle was born in Tennessee in 1902, graduated from Vanderbilt University in 1925, and penned an admiring biography of Confederate general and Ku Klux Klan founder Nathan Bedford Forrest in 1931. An iconoclastic literary critic, editor of the *Sewanee Review,* and noted author, Lytle was, according to a modern and sympathetic assessment from neo-Confederate Thomas H. Landess, "a sworn enemy of modernism" who "came to believe that mankind had fallen twice, once in the primal state and a second time in history, with the rise of modern materialism and the advent of the secular state. It is this second fall, he believed, that had brought about the disintegration of the modern world and the consequent problems in twentieth-century American society."[146] Entitling his essay in *I'll Take My Stand* "The Hind Tit," Lytle evoked a romantic view of an idyllic southern past, telling southerners they were mistaken in attempting to farm by industrial methods. "A farm is not a place to grow wealthy," he famously wrote; "it is a place to grow corn."[147] Lytle held that the South had been invaded by northern corporations and banks after 1865, accompanied by a propaganda machine designed to teach southerners to "despise" their way of life. Lamenting the state of the nation in the first paragraph of his essay, Lytle wrote that "when we remember the high expectations held universally by the founders of the American Union for a more perfect society, and then consider the state of life in this country today, it is bound to appear to reasonable people that somehow the experiment has proved abortive, and that in some way a great commonwealth has gone wrong. . . . Since 1865 an agrarian Union has been changed into an industrial empire bent on conquest of the earth's goods and ports to sell them in."[148] He recommended that the agrarian southerner "deny himself the articles the industrialists offer for sale . . . throw out the radio and take down the fiddle from the wall. Forsake the movies for the play-parties and the square dances. And turn away from the liberal capons who fill the pulpits as preachers."[149]

Shortly after the publication of "The Hind Tit" in 1930, Lytle responded at length in the *Virginia Quarterly Review* to the publication of Edgar Lee Masters's book *Lincoln: The Man.* In his review, entitled "The Lincoln Myth," Lytle expressed delight with Masters's biography because "historical research demanded a reinterpretation of the struggle in the terms of modern industrial America."[150] Lytle's view of Lincoln and the Civil War were part of a much larger project to preserve an agrarian South against what he believed to be an imperialistic, corporate, rapacious, and capitalistic North. From Lytle's standpoint the greatest myth of the war was "the myth that pretends the Union is preserved . . . which made it "impossible to discuss the issues of the war realistically, to discover in its wearisome marches and bitter engagements the distress and confusion of our commercial empire."[151] Although Lincoln indeed loved the Union, "he was responsible, more than any man, for its destruction, for he consciously violated the constitution in calling out armies for the reduction of the cotton states." "The war was not a war of slavery versus freedom," Lytle declared—no, "it was a war between those who preferred a federated nation to those who preferred a confederation of sovereign states."[152] Just like Alexander Stephens, Albert Taylor Bledsoe, and their numerous successors, Lytle viewed Lincoln as a disciple of Alexander Hamilton who made certain "that Hamiltonian principles finally triumphed." Consequently, Lytle believed, "it was necessary to make the Lincoln myth in order to cover the growing centralization which would make it possible for the trusts and corporations to gobble up the substance and liberties of the people."[153] Lincoln was a gifted politician, but he was "the antithesis of all that we have been taught to believe he was. He was secretive, cold, and humorous as the wilderness understood humor . . . he attached himself to the Whig Party, the moneyed political wing. He could not have been a friend of the people. He lacked the character or the philosophical clarity to understand the connotation of the American theory of the Union between sovereign states. He was an opportunist in the purest sense, that the end justifies the means."[154] Lytle's arguments were not entirely new, but they were expressed in stirring prose, and his stature as a critic, writer, and later editor lent a certain legitimacy and felicity of expression to the arguments of Lincoln's foes. To be sure, criticizing Lincoln was not central to Lytle's career; what was central, however, was the viewpoint from which he lambasted the president: a white, conservative, agrarian, hierarchical, patriarchal stance distinctly at odds with a racially plural, commercial, corporate, and industrial America.

Other Agrarians voiced substantial criticism of Lincoln in comparable terms. Frank Owsley's essay in *I'll Take My Stand*, "The Irrepressible Conflict," claimed, among other things, that the peace after the Civil War was followed by a second Yankee invasion in order to carry out "the conquest of the Southern mind . . . to impose the Northern way of life and thought upon the South, [and] write 'error' across the pages of Southern history which were out of keeping with Northern legend."[155] Of course, one of the legends dispersed throughout the South, according to Owsley, was that "Lincoln was the real Southern hero because Lincoln had saved the Union. So they [Southerners] were told!"[156] Owsley held that southerners had been held intellectually captive by northern historians such as James Ford Rhodes and John McMaster, who had argued in the war's aftermath of slavery's inextricable connection to the outbreak of military hostilities. Not true, thought Owsley. Instead, it was a conflict that was irrepressible because there were "two fundamental differences which existed between the two sections: the North was commercial and industrial, and the South was agrarian."[157]

Once again, what was notable in Owsley's essay was the denial, or at the very least the relative absence, of the idea that slavery was the primary reason for the onset of the Civil War. In the Agrarian view slavery was nothing more than an excuse given by Lincoln, the Radical Republicans, and abolitionists to launch the war they wanted so that they could destroy the institution of slavery or, more broadly, the South. As Owsley stated years later, in 1946, the ongoing problem was that "a Lincoln cult bordering on pagan deification" obscured the causes of the Civil War and "the real Lincoln."[158] Like many revisionists, Owsley thought that Lincoln seriously misjudged how bad the war would be between the North and South—who did not?—and in his "considered opinion" Lincoln was too weak to resist the radical Republicans, "the hard core of the Republican Party . . . [who] demanded war, and Lincoln himself became convinced that war would be necessary to restore the Union."[159] For Owsley, as for other detractors, Lincoln was merely a tool of the Radicals in his party and blundered into war. Once the war concluded, however, "when one views the malice and savagery of the Radicals who succeeded Lincoln, or contemplates the fathomless hatred and savagery of the world in which we now lead a day to day existence, Lincoln as a peace statesman, assumes great stature, greater, perhaps, to a Southerner than to a Northerner."[160] Lytle and Owsley's writings reflected the mind-set of Lincoln's antagonists across the white South that southerners were by comparison blameless for the conflict and that Lincoln's death was a tragedy for their region as well as the entire country. For them, if not for all of the president's enemies, America was once a much better place, but it had taken the wrong path in the 1860s, and Lincoln was to blame for that disastrous turn. Still, it was odd for a group of men who prided themselves on holding a tragic view of existence that they could not fully see the tragedy of the Civil War except as it touched upon the losses of *white* southerners, no matter how much they protested to the contrary that the war had been a terrible misfortune for the slave as well.

Donald Davidson, who fellow Agrarian Allen Tate characterized as "the leader of the Southern Agrarians," was perhaps the most determined Lincoln critic.[161] A fierce opponent of modernity and industrialism, Davidson's *I'll Take My Stand* essay argued "that, in America, the South, past and present, furnishes a living example of an agrarian society, the preservation of which is worth the most heroic effort that men can give in a time of crisis."[162] Nearly a decade later Davidson published a collection of essays entitled *Attack on Leviathan: Regionalism and Nationalism in the United States* (1938), restating his stance against the shallow values of industrial America, which included the myth of Lincoln as an American god. In a review of Burton Hendrick's *Lees of Virginia* (1935) entitled "American Heroes," Davidson rebuked Hendrick for claiming that "the influence of the Lees is 'gone forever'" because Arlington, Lee's ancestral home, was a national cemetery from whose front porch one could see the Lincoln Memorial.[163] Davidson claimed otherwise:

> The Lincoln idea, too, has had to yield to a changed America and may be gone forever . . . the fruit of his victory, represented in sprawling, confused, industrial America, is a more pitiful sight than the desolate Lee plantations, for it is hardly even a noble ruin. However effective it may have been as a war measure, Lincoln's Emancipation Proclamation was an inept bit of civil statesmanship, for it put the Negro problem beyond the hope of any such solution as America has been able to use for the Indian problem. By letting himself be used as the idealistic front for the material designs of the North, Lincoln not only ruined the South but quite conceivably ruined the North as well; and if Fascism or Communism ever arrives in America, Lincoln will have been a remote but efficient cause of its appearance.[164]

Davidson believed the deification of Lincoln was a form of intellectual imperialism, the potential precursor of American communism or fascism, and he could not fathom why southerners should have to accept Lincoln as a "national symbol."[165] He scorned those southerners who succumbed to the Lincoln myth and betrayed their white southern identity:

> We may have considerable respect for a dissent rising from principle, but it is hard to contemplate with any great respect a surrender of native myth when it has the flavor of being done in bald accordance with self-interest only. If a Southerner who is not of Unionist and Republican antecedents

whole-heartedly adopts the Northern myth of Lincoln, he is naturally suspected of having an ax to grind, and generally he does. He is likely to be
a "progressive" Southerner, out for all the material improvement of the
Northern model that he can secure. Often he will not only take up Lincoln
but surrender Lee the soldier and adhere only to the milder, more yielding
Lee, the college president and quietist. On the Northern side, however, there
is not an equal tendency to recantation. The Northerner often appropriates
Lee, but he rarely disowns Grant or Sherman or Lincoln. Significantly, it is
most often Lee that he wants to appropriate. The Northerner reaches forth
no clutching hand toward Stonewall Jackson.[166]

Such a passage was sure to alienate those southerners who had come to
accept Lincoln as great, which suggests one reason why his foes found it
somewhat difficult to gain a majority of adherents on either a national
or regional level.

In contrast to Lytle, Owsley, and Davidson, another Agrarian, Robert
Penn Warren, a writer perhaps best known for his novel *All the King's
Men* (1946), also published some important meditations on the Civil War
years after *I'll Take My Stand,* most notably, *The Legacy of the Civil War:
Meditations on the Centennial* (1961) and *Jefferson Davis Gets His Citizenship Back* (1980). Both books, extended essays really, contained some
nuanced reflections on Abraham Lincoln that were substantially different
than Warren's Agrarian colleagues' earlier fulminations. In *The Legacy
of the Civil War* Warren coined a term, the *Great Alibi,* to describe those
southerners who blamed their postwar problems exclusively on the Civil
War. By so doing, southerners absolved themselves of any responsibility
for the current problems of their society. Conversely, northerners believed that since they had won the war and eradicated slavery, they had
established a "Treasury of Virtue," leaving them "redeemed by history,
automatically redeemed."[167] Warren also offered commentary on Lincoln
germane to the relationship between hatred for Lincoln and modernity.
He found in Lincoln an example of the "pragmatic mind," one whose ethics, in contrast to the abolitionists, was "somewhat different from that of
individual absolutism—an ethic that demands scrutiny of motive, context,
and consequences, particularly the consequences to others. This kind
of ethic," Warren explained, "[is] laborious, fumbling, running the risk
of degenerating into expediency, [one that] finds its apotheosis in Lincoln," which Warren thought was precisely why abolitionists criticized the
man.[168] There is nothing here of the virulent hostility for Lincoln expressed
by other white southerners or by some of Warren's less charitable cohorts.

Rather, Warren thought that Lincoln clearly understood the war was not a northern or southern story but "a communal story," one of "an involvement of all the unworthiness and blunderings of human nature, even of virtues perverted by being abstracted from the proper human context."[169]

Nineteen years later, in 1980, in *Jefferson Davis Gets His Citizenship Back,* Warren wrote of growing up in Guthrie, Kentucky, where he had perceived that Lincoln was "somehow a great man but misguided."[170] Significantly, Warren explained that Lincoln, while not necessarily believing in the equality of blacks, "did believe, within undefined limits, in educability and progress for the black," and acknowledged Lincoln's willingness to suspend habeas corpus in the North alongside recognition "that law and the Constitution depended ultimately on need, preference, and cold-blooded power."[171] Even more important, moreover, was that in the process of differentiating Davis from Lincoln, Warren held that in the Civil War there was "more than a contrast between Lincoln and Davis." Rather, "the contrast lay in the two societies—one embracing antique values, the other in the process of developing new ones."[172] "Poor Davis," Warren concluded, "he was not a modern man in any sense of the word but a conservative called to manage what was, in one sense, a revolution."[173] Of course, in the minds of Lincoln's rivals that was precisely the point; the modern world mortified them, and rather than accommodate themselves to it, they defiantly hurled accusations of criminality at the man they believed represented modern America, Abraham Lincoln, in order to communicate their discontent and gain attention for their views.

In 1937, a few years after *I'll Take My Stand* came out, University of Texas history professor Charles Ramsdell published an important essay in the *Journal of Southern History* entitled "Lincoln and Fort Sumter," an essay that inadvertently gave hope and succor to the president's enemies across the United States.[174] Ramsdell's essential argument was that "the actual firing of the 'first shot' [at Fort Sumter] placed the Southerners under a great moral and material disadvantage" during the war and it was Lincoln's political skill and acumen that had placed them in such a position, forcing the Confederacy to be blamed for beginning hostilities.[175] To be sure, Ramsdell did not qualify as enemy of Lincoln in the sense of a Mary Carter or Lyon Gardiner Tyler. Hating Lincoln was not central to his work or worldview, and he clearly admired Lincoln's political skills, although so did many of Lincoln's enemies. But having served as president of the Mississippi Valley Historical Association and later the Southern Historical Association, Ramsdell almost assuredly understood the potential impact of his work; coming from the pen of a distinguished professor at the University of Texas and published in an important historical journal, Ramsdell's essay delighted the president's adversaries across the country, for they believed its views validated their own.[176] Indeed, Joseph Eggleston told Ramsdell his essay was "very interesting and logical" and that Ramsdell was essentially correct: "Lincoln was just a bit too astute for the Southern leaders."[177] In private letters, moreover, Ramsdell voiced opinions similar to those of Lincoln's detractors. He responded to Professor Laura White of the University of Wyoming, the first biographer of the fire-eater Robert Barnwell Rhett, by explaining that he had "come to the tentative conclusion that there was coming to be considerable sentiment in the North for the evacuation of Sumter and this was threatening a split within the Republican party which *might* prove disastrous to Lincoln's administration."[178] To Progressive historian Charles Beard he seemed defensive and even admitted the article was full of "surmises" but claimed "the evidence seems to warrant them." Later, in September 1937, Ramsdell told Beard: "I was not attacking Lincoln, if I understand my own motives in this study, but merely trying to explain why he did what he seems to have done. (You, of course, do not intimate that I did attack him, but some others seem to think that is what I did)." Still, he held that Confederate leaders had fallen "directly into Lincoln's little trap."[179] Ramsdell explained himself more fully to Mary Carter, who could not have been altogether pleased with his analysis:

> The Lincoln myth I have little patience with. It is based upon a combination of propaganda for political purposes and sentimentalism; it is unhistorical in the sense that it has been built up since Lincoln's death with no regard for historical facts. Lincoln did a great many things that reflect no credit on him, and the main consequences of some of his policies, as Mr. [Allen] Tate well says, have been very bad. In spite of all this I must confess that I think he had many elements of greatness. He was shrewd, calculating, ambitious, secretive, but he could be both courageous and generous, and he had understanding. He did not see the drift of economic forces, but to admit that he was no prophet is not to condemn him utterly. In short, while he was very far from perfection in my eyes, I am obliged to admire him for some things. But I shall always do my feeble best to help destroy the legend that has grown up about him because, and *only* because, I think it is untrue to the facts.[180]

Notwithstanding the importance of the Agrarians and Ramsdell's essay, between the wars the most significant and negative judgment of Lincoln came not from the pen of a white southerner but from Lincoln's home state of Illinois. In 1931 Edgar Lee Masters published his biography of the Civil War president, *Lincoln: The Man*. A one-time law partner of the famous attorney Clarence Darrow, Masters was a well-known poet whose volume of verse entitled *Spoon River Anthology* (1915) had garnered national attention for its ghostly evocation of Illinois's people, countryside, and history.[181] At first glance Masters seemed to be the ideal candidate to write Lincoln's biography. His poetry was beautiful, he was from Illinois, he had grown up near Lincoln's old haunts, such as New Salem, and his father, Hardin Masters, had worked with Lincoln's former law partner and biographer William Herndon.[182] Influenced by other factors, however, Masters produced an extremely negative portrait. Afraid of war and racial amalgamation, Masters's grandfather Squire Davis Masters had voted against Lincoln in his campaigns to become a U.S. senator, and Masters's father thought enough of the South during the Civil War that he gave his son Edgar the middle name of Lee after Confederate general Robert E. Lee. Masters wanted his biography to be a completion of the unfinished work begun by the late senator and Progressive Albert Beveridge. More important, he hoped to outdo his fellow poet and interloper into Lincoln territory Carl Sandburg, whose hagiographical work on Lincoln Masters despised, with a new, complete, and accurate biography.[183] Masters also wanted his book to vindicate the Democratic Party and his political idol, Illinois Democrat Stephen A. Douglas.[184] As Masters told Agrarian Allen Tate, "The Republican Party started the [Civil War] to entrench themselves politically, so they lifted up Lincoln to keep themselves entrenched; and they did it and have done it."[185]

Masters made some extraordinary claims against Abraham Lincoln, including that he had "a lazy mind" and "was an under sexed man."[186] Masters also blamed Lincoln for virtually every problem that had arisen in America since the president's death in 1865. Dedicating the book to another political hero, Thomas Jefferson, he claimed that because "no new fact of moment about Lincoln can now be brought to light, the time has arrived when his apotheosis can be touched with the hand of rational analysis."[187] Masters called members of the Republican Party "mongrel breeds who knew nothing about liberty and constitutional government," laid at Lincoln's doorstep the charges of having been commander in chief of an army "of centralists and fanatics," the harbingers of a "sordid imperialism," and, echoing Mary Scrugham from the mid-1920s, blamed Lincoln for having distorted the Declaration of Independence. By focusing on Jefferson's words that all men were created equal, Lincoln all but "ignored and trampled its principles that governments derive their just powers from the consent of the governed," and his acts "were against liberty, and so much to the advantage of monopoly and privilege."[188] Lincoln was not only officially responsible for misconduct during the Civil War; his triumph led to the rise of an imperialistic Republican Party. "But in truth," Masters wrote, "the Congressional imperialism of Lincoln was no whit different from that of McKinley."[189]

Perhaps what was most notable about Masters's book, however, was neither the virulence of his charges nor the originality or accuracy of his claims. All in all, it was a bad book, full of overheated rhetoric and selective distortion of evidence, but the responses to his work are illustrative of the state of antipathy for Lincoln at the beginning of the Great Depression. Publicly, the viewpoints about the book were mostly negative. Charles Willis Thompson reviewed the volume in the *New York Times* and labeled it, with some accuracy, a "Copperhead, not a Confederate biography," while other reviewers ridiculed the work.[190] In private Masters received several letters excoriating his irreverent stance. A member of the Lincoln Farm Association wrote a poem entitled "Hymn of Hate" and signed it "A Master's Piece," along with skull and crossbones sketched on a picture of the Illinois poet's forehead:

> I want to be a devil,
> And with the devil's stand:
> With smut upon my tail
> A pig pen in my hand.
> I love to smirch what's good,
> To relieve my crazy head;
> It's soothing to my bowels
> To malign the dead.[191]

The Jersey City Lions Club was incredulous: "We cannot understand a citizen of the United States so completely destroying a tradition which not only arrested the enemies of democracy but gained the admiration of the entire world" and intimated the book would contribute to corrupting America's youth, who "have already ceased to reverence the judgment of their elders and shortly the parents' veracity will be questioned also."[192] Another correspondent, female and perhaps African American, concluded a poem with the lines "Hold, Warriors, Counsellors, Kings! All not give place / To this dear benefactor of the race."[193] But perhaps the most touching letter Masters received was sent by fifteen-year-old Sally Taylor of Syracuse, New York, who scolded him because he had "committed a great sacrilege."[194] In heartfelt terms Taylor revealed that Masters's book pained her and in a remarkably perceptive observation explained the difficulties Lincoln's enemies faced: "To the great army of youth he [Lincoln] stands as a symbol of all that is fine in the world; high ideals, a clean life, and belief in an only God. To us he is not a stone statue, he is a living being. It is the memory of what he stands for, what he tried to do, what he *was,* that helps us when the way is rather steep and thorny. I cannot see any reason under God's Heaven that would prompt you to try and blemish one of our few remaining ideals. If you hope to destroy the memory of Abraham Lincoln, you never, never shall. He is too firmly imbedded in the very hearts of this nation, too much a part of us, for you ever to succeed."[195] She closed her letter by asking Masters, "I wonder if you realize how much you have hurt yourself?"[196]

Still, the reviews and letters Masters received were not uniformly hostile. Indeed, as noted earlier, the Agrarian Andrew Lytle wrote an extremely positive appraisal in the *Virginia Quarterly,* while the esteemed literary critic and writer H. L. Mencken published a glowing account of the work in the *New York Herald Tribune.* In his review Mencken was harsh and cynical, calling Lincoln "a second-rater" who brought nothing "noble to either the law or politics" and sought above all else "superiority" and who, despite his agnosticism toward Christianity, used "pious phrases . . . like an Old Testament prophet. It was soon manifest that this was a device of tremendous effectiveness," Mencken regretfully declared, "and all the other American presidents have employed it ever since."[197] From Mencken's standpoint Abraham Lincoln's true significance was his federal corporatism: " [Lincoln] turned his back on the Jacksonian tradition and allowed himself to be carried out by the tide that was eventually to wash away the old Republic altogether and leave in its place a plutocratic oligarchy hard to distinguish from the Roman."[198] Mencken concluded with the assertion that Lincoln had assaulted "the Constitution, and especially the Bill of Rights" and that by the end of the Civil War the Constitution was in tatters, and "it has never recovered. Every guaranty of the Bill of Rights was heaved overboard. The American people, North and South," Mencken sorrowfully explained, "went into the war as citizens of their respective states, they came out subjects of the United States. And what they thus lost they have never got back. No President since, not even Grover Cleveland, has ever followed Jefferson. They have all tried to be Lincolns."[199] So, although

Lincoln had served his country during the Civil War "as well as any other could have served it," Mencken believed that "historians must remember also his gross and lamentable weaknesses and the evil that he did."[200]

In addition to the negative correspondence sent his way, Masters received scores of positive responses, not only from the South but from all over the United States. Such Americans were thrilled with his book and wrote the poet to tell him how glad they were that he had the courage to publish such an attack. Langbourne Williams, editor of the *Southern Churchman,* informed Masters, "Your work is a great contribution to the truth of history," while Landon Carter Bell told Masters that his volume was "a creditable and praiseworthy public service."[201] David Rankin Barbee alerted Mary Carter that Masters's biography was an unanswerable attack that Lincoln's "hero-worshippers" would hate. Barbee nevertheless had two significant misgivings about the work, telling his Virginia correspondent that the book was "spoiled by Masters's atheism or infidelity, and by his blind worship of Thomas Jefferson, who did quite as much harm to this country as Lincoln ever did. The phrase makers are the harmful chaps," Barbee opined. "Jefferson's fine phrase: 'All men are created equal, etc.' was the platform of the Abolitionists and was the platform of Lincoln and he always turned to it for justification."[202] Carter never replied explicitly to Barbee's remarks, but a couple of weeks after receiving Barbee's letter, she once again complained of "Lincolnolatry" and connected it to a "crime wave" in the United States.[203]

Such comments were probably to be expected, yet what is truly fascinating is to see the range of places and ordinary people from which Masters received thanks, and these letters indicate that the arguments of Lincoln's antagonists had indeed spread far and wide across the United States. Elizabeth Polk wrote from Memphis, Tennessee, that she was "gratified" at Masters's "courage," for Lincoln was "tricky, sly and a 'poor white' all the way thru," and informed him of her "admiration and appreciation."[204] From Tulsa, Oklahoma, a correspondent warned Masters to be ready for "considerable unfavorable comment" because the United States was "a nation of hero worship & hypocritical stamina," while in Phoenix, Arizona, Cameron Plummer said that Masters's volume reminded him of *The Real Lincoln* by Charles L. C. Minor, who was his "mother's father." "If you have not seen it," Plummer encouraged Masters, "you will find that one other scholar has felt the demand of Truth" and that "the next step is to correct the lies told in our public and other school textbooks."[205] Belle Inge from

Mobile, Alabama, said that she was "delighted" that Masters had "the courage to show him [Lincoln] in his true light and as I have always felt him to be a *vulgar common* old man . . . to call him a friend of the South is too absurd for discussion."[206] Meanwhile, out in San Francisco D. Ferrero told Masters, "Thank heaven, SOMEBODY—and I mean SOMEBODY—has the courage to show up the razzle-dazzle of the Lincoln halo! My puny voice has long been raised against the false God, but here in California, even as in other localities, Lincoln is 'The Lord God Jehovah Hisself.'"[207] In El Paso, Texas, Jone Howlind offered more than a letter of congratulation: "I am going to stretch out my hands across the intervening miles and grasp your hand! You have my sympathy, my admiration and my greatest respect," Howlind declared. "The free press of America has come to a pretty pass if a bill is passed in Congress forbidding it to be sent through the mails . . . . But as you know, and are sadly to learn, liberty in America is now only a farce. Whoever offends the established and entrenched power of Capital, Church, or a popular local American God, such as Lincoln, will very soon find out just what a farce American liberty is."[208] Of course, one should not make too much out of these positive responses to Masters's book. The work was largely, although not exclusively, a rehash of previous attacks, and it certainly hurt Masters's reputation with most Americans. Indeed, as Jone Howlind indicated, Congress even considered banning the book from the U.S. mails, and it was in fact banned in parts of Boston and Philadelphia, illustrating that Lincoln's critics in the South certainly had no monopoly on censorship when it came to Abraham Lincoln.[209]

Lincoln: The Man was nevertheless an important biography. Masters's attack on Lincoln expressed his love for a different America—a white, Jeffersonian America—that no longer existed, if it ever had, and had little chance of ever doing so again.[210] Masters's work reflected a continuing strain of thought, perhaps exacerbated in the era of the Great Depression, anxious about the changing racial makeup of the country, the role of the federal government in American life, alongside the disappearance of an agrarian America, replaced by a Hamiltonian Republic. It was likewise significant that Masters embraced the idea of "revisionist" Civil War historians who saw the conflict as needless, illustrating how Lincoln's enemies perhaps influenced more serious professional and academic writing on Lincoln—and vice versa. It was also noteworthy, at least from the perspective of Lincoln critics all over the United States, that Masters lived in Illinois, where Lincoln had spent his adult life, and his work certainly encouraged the president's opponents across the country, who might otherwise have viewed their cause as hopeless, of the value of convincing Americans of Lincoln's mendacity and criminality.

Masters's book was significant for two additional reasons, one of which was consistent with hostility for Lincoln up to this point, while the other, at least superficially, was not. First, *Lincoln: The Man* equated, as had Charles L. C. Minor and Mary Scrugham before him, Lincoln's policy of coercing the South back into the Union with the imperialist policies of the United States. In fact, Masters linked the fall of Rome with America's decline from its founding ideals; the nation had been betrayed by the rise of men such as Alexander Hamilton and Abraham Lincoln.[211] This would be a theme taken up, at least in part, by more talented and influential historians such as William Appleman Williams (1921–90) after the conclusion of World War II. Second, it appears at first glance that Masters's attacks upon Christianity in the book—the "Hebraic-Puritan culture," or "madness," he called it—were at odds with the president's adversaries, who believed that a supposed Lincolnolatry was threatening Christian orthodoxy in the United States. Certainly, David Rankin Barbee and Mary Carter, among others, thought that was the case. Even here, though, Masters's attacks on Christianity were linked to a distinct anti-Semitism rather than a direct assault on the truth of the Christian faith.[212] Furthermore, if one looks beneath the surface, as historian Paul Murphy has explained of the Agrarians, although "skeptical and unorthodox themselves," they nevertheless "admired the capacity of orthodox religion to provide surety in life."[213] So, even though not all of Lincoln's detractors were orthodox Christians, they saw in Lincoln a symbol of everything they hated about the United States, a serpent in the American Garden of Eden who brought about the country's fall from innocence. For his critics the president was a moral and political degenerate who caused America's decay from a purer Union of limited government and white supremacy. This was a reactionary sentiment, or disillusionment with an increasingly modern, ethnically and religiously pluralistic America, an attitude that Masters most assuredly shared with his white southern intellectual brethren.[214] Masters's book, then, was not a Progressive attack on Lincoln; certainly, those contemporaries who praised the book did not see it as such. Lincoln's twentieth- and twenty-first-century conservative and libertarian detractors, moreover, continued to praise and recommend Masters's volume, while self-styled Progressive admirers of Lincoln such as President Barack Obama never attacked the biography or even acknowledged it. Instead of being a Progressive critique of the president, *Lincoln: The Man* was an outgrowth of Masters's personal background, his nostalgia, his narrow if not white supremacist racial outlook, combined with his deep-seated suspicion of federal authority and executive power.[215] In that sense *Lincoln: The Man* was more philosophically consistent with previous Lincoln criticism emanating from Confederate sympathizers and represented a reunion, although a tenuous one, between northern Copperheads in the Jeffersonian and Jacksonian tradition with unregenerate white southern Confederates, atheist and Christian, which persisted in the post–World War II era and beyond into the twenty-first century.[216]

Diehard Confederates and neo-Copperheads, although the most prominent strains of Lincoln antagonism between the two world wars, were not the only groups with ill will toward Lincoln. In fact, both elite and nonelite African Americans expressed sharply critical attitudes toward the Great Emancipator. In the decades after Appomattox many prominent black intellectuals, including W. E. B. Du Bois, offered sympathetic yet nuanced opinions about Lincoln. Carter G. Woodson, it may be recalled, instituted Negro History Week in the 1920s during the month of February because that was the month of both Abraham Lincoln's and Frederick Douglass's birthdays.[217] But as early as 1931, Woodson had apparently altered his attitude and seemed to be aligning himself more with previous African American critics such as Archibald Grimké and Hubert Harrison: "Lincoln should be lauded by the Negro, but he has been often overrated as the savior of the race. At best Lincoln was a gradual emancipationist and colonizationist who hoped by methods of compensation to free all Negroes by 1900 and deport them to some neglected part of the earth. He doubted that the two races could dwell together in peace. Lincoln originally had no more idea of issuing the emancipation proclamation than King John had of issuing the Magna Carta. He was forced to this position."[218] Woodson's viewpoint reflected a deep dissatisfaction with the current status of African Americans in the United States. Indeed, he said as much in 1932, when he averred, like Grimké, that veneration of Lincoln was useless, even harmful. "Admiring others will hold the Negroes forever in bondage," Woodson declared. "Abraham Lincoln did not 'set my people free.' They are still in chains."[219] Woodson nonetheless cautioned after the 1932 presidential election that "while he [Lincoln] said and did some things which we condemn today, he must be judged by the standards of his time."[220]

Lincoln had other critics among elite African Americans as well, including black newspapers and politicians, all of whom used the Lincoln

image to mock the stark contrast between the Republican Party's claim
to be the vehicle of Lincoln's ideals and America's painful lack of accom-
plishment in matters of racial progress. The editor of the black newspaper
the *Pittsburgh Courier,* Robert Vann, encouraged African Americans to
"go turn Lincoln's picture to the wall" and vote for the Democratic Party
rather than the Republicans, or "Party of Lincoln," in the 1932 presidential contest between Herbert Hoover and Franklin Delano Roosevelt.[221]
Four years later Arthur W. Mitchell, the first African American Democrat
elected to Congress and from the state of Illinois, criticized Lincoln on the
floor of the House of Representatives, stating that the Great Emancipator
was "no real foe of slavery."[222] Later that year, according to contemporary
accounts, Mitchell visited Lincoln's tomb in Springfield, Illinois, and at
the local fairgrounds told an audience of over three thousand that while
he appreciated "the sacrifices made by Lincoln," he lambasted the Republican Party because it "tells us to support their candidates, because
Lincoln, who freed our race, was a Republican. But today Lincoln is dead
and his party has forgotten his ideals and principles. We are interested
in accomplishments, not promises."[223] Abraham Lincoln remained quite
popular among most African Americans, but by the middle of the Great
Depression, after enduring decades of lynchings, not to mention a nearly
total lack of economic, political, or social equality in the United States,
there were increasingly strong currents within the African American
community sharply critical of the Great Emancipator.[224]

Such negative judgments were evident in the remarks of some of the
former slaves interviewed in the 1930s by the Works Progress Administration (WPA).[225] For the most part black southerners interviewed by the
WPA during the Great Depression viewed Abraham Lincoln positively
but not without a degree of misgiving or even outright hostility. The WPA
narratives offer a view of the Great Emancipator from the nonelite, ordinary people, rather than African American intellectuals, and provide
a microcosm of a shifting African American opinion about Lincoln in a
transitional moment: a period in the midst of the Great Migration north-
ward and just prior to World War II and the civil rights movement; a
period when the attitude of blacks toward the Republican Party, or Party
of Lincoln, were turning more negative; a period equidistant between the
Civil War and the early twenty-first century.[226] The attitudes of the former
slaves toward Lincoln in the 1930s is a window into African American sentiments regarding Lincoln *at that time* and are worthwhile as a historical
resource for gauging fluctuating black viewpoints toward Lincoln during

the Great Depression. They also provide a benchmark demonstrating the changes that took place between 1865 and the Great Depression in African Americans' perspective toward Abraham Lincoln.[227]

Several thousand black southerners across nineteen states talked to numerous WPA representatives about their experiences with the institution of slavery. The series ran to nineteen original volumes, with a supplemental series of another twenty-two volumes added later, for a total of forty-two volumes of interviews. The WPA field workers, or interviewers, were given suggestions by John A. Lomax, the national advisor on Folklore and Folkways for the Federal Writers Project, of a series of questions they could ask, ranging from topics about what those interviewed had expected from freedom, what they did after the war, their opinions about the Ku Klux Klan, whether or not they had ever voted, their opinions on disfranchisement, where and when they were born, and, "What do you think of Abraham Lincoln? Jefferson Davis? Booker Washington? Any other prominent white man or Negro you have known or heard of?"[228] Several opinions about Lincoln offered by the interviewees were paired with commentary about Jefferson Davis, Booker T. Washington, and, interestingly, Franklin Delano Roosevelt, president of the United States at the time of the interviews. Not all interviewers, however, adhered to the questionnaire drawn up by Lomax, which suggests why many of the former slaves made no mention of Lincoln at all in their remarks.

Over three hundred former slaves offered opinions about Abraham Lincoln in the original WPA interviews, the large majority of which were favorable. Some of them explicitly linked the names of Lincoln and the current president, Franklin Delano Roosevelt, in their observations, which showed that in the midst of the Great Depression, African Americans had begun to transfer their affection for Lincoln to Roosevelt.[229] A few of their statements, in fact, were more fulsome in their praise of Roosevelt than they were of Lincoln. Perhaps their heightened esteem for FDR opened the way for a more critical view of the Great Emancipator. Daniel Goddard, seventy-four years old and living in South Carolina, said: "Lincoln was raised up for a specific purpose, to end slavery, which was a menace to both whites and blacks, as I see it. . . . But there has been only one President whose heart was touched by the cry of distress of the poor and needy and his name is Franklin D. Roosevelt. He is one white man who has turned the bias of the Negroes from the bait of partisan politics."[230] Another South Carolinian, Ella Kelly, said of Lincoln and Roosevelt that she had "heard 'bout Lincoln and Booker T. Washington. [But] De President now in de White House, Mr. Roosevelt, have done more good for de nigger in four years than all de other presidents since Lincoln, done in fifty years. You say its been seventy-two years? Well, than all de rest in seventy-two years."[231] Reuben Rosebourough, also of South Carolina, put a religious twist on the nature of the two men when he said: "I think Mr. Lincoln was raised up by de Lord, just like Moses, to free 'culiar people. I think Mr. Roosevelt is de Joshua dat come after him. No president has done as much for de poor of both races as de one now president. God bless him and 'stain him in his visions and work to bring de kingdom of heaven into and upon de earth."[232] Ned Walker from South Carolina had an especially poignant characterization of Lincoln and Roosevelt: "What I think of Abe Lincoln? Dat was a mighty man of de Lord. What I think of Jeff Davis? He all right, 'cording to his education, just lak my white folks. What I think of Mr. Roosevelt? Oh, man! Dat's our papa."[233] Out in Oklahoma, Mattie Logan compared the two presidents, saying that she believed "Lincoln was a mighty good man" and that "Roosevelt is trying to carry out some of the good ideas Lincoln had. Lincoln would have done a heap more if he had lived."[234] Perhaps Robert Hinton of North Carolina summed up best their attitude when he said, "I think Abraham Lincoln wus a good man, but I likes Mr. Roosevelt; he is a good, good man."[235] Again, such remarks are especially interesting, for they signify the beginning of a turn in the African American community away from the Republican Party, and perhaps Abraham Lincoln, toward the Democratic fold during the Great Depression. FDR, like most politicians in America (Woodrow Wilson, e.g., or Barack Obama) was an astute exploiter of the Lincoln symbol, with important political consequences for the United States in the remainder of the twentieth and indeed twenty-first century. The African American embrace of FDR and the Democratic Party, in turn, may have helped lay the basis for a white southern exodus from the same party decades later.[236]

Another set of interesting recollections from the interviewees were the legendary tales they related about Abraham Lincoln having visited the South prior to the war and talked with some of the slaves. Most of these accounts portray Lincoln quite positively, even reverentially.[237] But not all of the stories of Lincoln traveling in the South are positive in nature. One story has Lincoln freeing the slaves after getting drunk, while a different tale has it that the Liberty Bell in Philadelphia cracked because of Lincoln's racial attitudes: "Do you know how they got the crack in the Liberty Bell? Well, it happened this way. The whites were mad at Abraham Lincoln for all he'd done to free the Negro. They told him about it and Lincoln told them, 'I'd wade up to my neck in blood before I'd forget my race.' When the whites heard that good news they rang the Liberty Bell 'till it cracked."[238] Such a story suggests several things: the disillusionment of black southerners with their postwar status; Lincoln's ambiguous public statements on postwar racial equality; and the persistent racism in the North, which was at the very least a contributing factor in the failure of Reconstruction to bring about full equality for blacks after the Civil War.

Several former slaves recalled that they had been afraid of the Yankees and Abraham Lincoln. James Bolton, from Athens, Georgia, said that "we didn't talk much 'bout Abbieham Lincum endurin' slavery time kazen we was skeered of him atter the war got started."[239] Tempe Pitts of North Carolina remembered, "De maddest I eber git, an' de only time dat eber I cuss bad wuz when de Yankees come. Dey stold de meat an' things from de smoke house, an' eber thing else dat dey can git. Dey ain't done nothin' ter me, but de way dey done my white folkses made me mad, an' I jumps straight up an' down and I yells, 'Damn dem Yankees an' damn ole Abraham Lincoln too!'"[240] Such comments are not too surprising, however, for Lincoln had been demonized by the South during the war and was the commander in chief of an army that southern planters often claimed, with some accuracy, was going to bring desolation and death to the region. Interestingly, the majority of accounts relating to either fear of the Yankees or Lincoln came from those living in North and South Carolina, where General William Tecumseh Sherman's army had wreaked havoc, although there were some slaves who did not believe Lincoln was at fault for the violence committed. Chana Littlejohn of Raleigh, North Carolina, exculpated Lincoln to her interviewer when she said that "when de Yankees comed dey jist about cleaned us out. Dey kills pigs, turkeys, calves an' hens all over de place, de gits de beserves an' a heap o' de lasses an' dey sass mis' betsy. All dis wus dem bad-mannered soldiers fault. Abraham Lincoln ain't mean't for it ter be dis way; I know."[241]

There were some black southerners who expressed a bitingly critical outlook toward the man formerly celebrated as the Great Emancipator, which suggests that Lost Cause loathing of Lincoln had reached African Americans. Still, most of the unflattering comments were directly related to the frustrated hopes and ensuing disappointments of the Reconstruction era, coupled with justifiable bitterness at the ongoing poor lot of their race due to white oppression. They clearly illustrated, furthermore, the contested nature of the image of Abraham Lincoln within the African American community. Hannah McFarland, eighty-five years old and living in Oklahoma City, averred that she "didn't care much 'bout Lincoln. It was nice of him to free us, but 'course he didn't want to."[242] Eli Coleman, from Texas, bluntly stated that "since the nigger been free it been Hell on the poor old nigger. He has advance some ways, but he's still a servant and will be, long as Gawd's curse still stay on the Negro race. He was turnt loose without nothin' and done been under the white men rule so long we couldn't hold no job but labor."[243] In fact, being freed "without nothin'" was a recurrent motif running through the African American interviewees' commentary about the postwar era—and Abraham Lincoln. Jacob Thomas, from North Carolina, put it bluntly: "I always thought a lot of Lincoln 'cause he had a heap of faith in de nigger ter think dat he could live on nothin' at all."[244] But it was Thomas Hall, also from North Carolina, who best explained black discontent with Abraham Lincoln and by implication the United States: "Lincoln got the praise for freeing us, but did he do it? He give us freedom without giving us any chance to live ourselves and we still had to depend on the southern white man for work, food, and clothing, and he held us through our necessity and want in a state of servitude but little better than slavery. Lincoln done but little for the negro race and from living standpoint nothing. White folks are not going to do nothing for negroes except keep them down. Harriet Beecher Stowe, the writer of Uncle Tom's Cabin, did that for her own good. She had her own interests at heart and I don't like her, Lincoln, or none of the crowd. The Yankees helped free us, so they say, but they let us be put back in slavery again."[245] By the 1930s there was unquestionable bitterness among African Americans about the shabby, violent treatment they had endured at the hands of whites since the 1860s. Such unfulfilled hopes and expectations go a long way in explaining the reasons for their harsh comments, as few as there are, in the WPA narratives. Their attitudes were consistent with previous criticism by previous African Americans, and it anticipated a decidedly negative view of Lincoln that would reemerge decades later within the black community and the country at large, during the civil rights movement, especially in Lerone Bennett's seminal 1968 essay claiming that Abraham Lincoln was a white supremacist.

For the most part, however, African Americans continued to celebrate the memory of Abraham Lincoln. Blacks throughout the South, in contrast to the Ladies' Memorial Associations, Sons of Confederate Veterans, and United Daughters of the Confederacy, all of whom glorified the antebellum South and established monuments to the men of the Confederacy who had tried to perpetuate slavery, continued their Emancipation Day celebrations after the war and revered the memory of Abraham Lincoln. Additionally, in contrast to the unreconstructed Confederates of the Lost Cause who glorified the Confederacy, they did not remember Lincoln uncritically, nor did they have any use for the alleged heroes of Confederacy or their apologists.[246] Indeed, in 1930 African American poet Sterling Brown insightfully described Lost Cause apologists as "pathetic," full of "the self-pity of the defeated," motivated by the "evils of modern life [which] furnish the impulse to an easy romantic escape in dreams of a pleasanter past," all in the service of "the buttressing of ancient prejudices."[247] African Americans who voiced criticism of Lincoln were doing so because they rightly believed that the federal government should have done more since the end of Reconstruction to ensure a new birth of freedom for their race, while Lincoln's white critics claimed they were enslaved because the president had allegedly centralized power in Washington, D.C. It was apparent, finally, that in the 1930s Lincoln was still a haunting presence in the hearts of many black Americans.

Eighty years after Abraham Lincoln's death, World War II ended with the bombing of Hiroshima and Nagasaki in 1945, and although Lincoln's reputation with Americans may have been at its peak at that time, contempt for the president was also well established, even nationalized, especially but not exclusively among whites, in its portrayal of Lincoln as a vulgar atheist, of low birth, despotic, tyrannical, imperialistic, inhumane, and representative of a modernity in thought and methods of war that were abhorrent to his critics.[248] These diehard Confederates, or neo-Copperheads, were almost invariably advocates of the Lost Cause and championed a memory of the Civil War that depicted the Confederacy as a virtuous, glorious, Christian society whose ideas would eventually be vindicated by history.[249] From 1865 to 1945 hostility to Lincoln was effectively promoted by organizations such as the United Daughters of the Confederacy and authors such as David Rankin Barbee, Albert Taylor Bledsoe, William Hand Browne, Mary Carter, Elizabeth Avery Meriwether, Charles L. C. Minor, Kate Mason Rowland, Mildred Lewis Rutherford, and Lyon Gardiner Tyler, along with innumerable others, all sympathetic to the goals of defending the Confederacy, demonizing Abraham Lincoln, and denying African Americans their basic civil and human rights. Enmity for Lincoln, at least in the South, was more than just the work of a few disgruntled individuals; indeed, it was part of a larger movement of irreconcilable Confederates and those across the nation who sympathized with their antimodern views. Other opponents of Lincoln alleged from the 1890s onward that the consolidation of the nation that resulted from Lincoln's presidency laid the foundation for subsequent American imperialism, domestic and foreign. Such opposition to Lincoln and American expansionism was to an extent principled, yet it was also grounded in racial anxieties, as the United States conquered and exploited Latin and Asian peoples in ways similar to the exploitation of African Americans throughout its history. This viewpoint was expressed most clearly on a national scale by the Illinois poet Edgar Lee Masters in 1931 with his derisive biography *Lincoln: The Man*. Masters's work also reflected a trend in Civil War scholarship that minimized the role slavery had played in bringing on the conflict, emphasizing instead that military hostilities could have been avoided with better statesmanship. This outlook meshed with previous Lincoln criticism, not to mention Senator Albert Beveridge's two-volume biography, and Lincoln's reputation suffered accordingly. Equally important, before World War II concluded, a few African Americans, such as lawyer Archibald Grimké, radical thinker Hubert Harrison, Congressman Arthur Mitchell, editor Robert Vann, and even some former slaves alive in the 1930s—a minority to be sure—found Lincoln's Emancipation Proclamation and the long-term results of the Civil War and Reconstruction to be far from satisfactory and criticized the president on that basis. After World War II, however, the United States would find itself forced by the descendants of those whom Lincoln had emancipated to come to terms with its own shortcomings on race, which meant that Abraham Lincoln's reputation would undergo new scrutiny as the country reexamined its egalitarian ideals in the wake of the worst war in human history.

5

AN INFINITELY COMPLICATED FIGURE

Is Freedom Enough? 1945–1989

On June 2, 1947, the same summer in which African American Jackie Robinson broke the color line in professional baseball, foreshadowing the Freedom Struggle of the 1950s and 1960s, historian Charles Callan Tansill of Georgetown University gave an address in the Capitol's Statuary Hall extolling the virtues of the man who had led an unsuccessful attempt to ensure the perpetual enslavement of members of Robinson's race—Confederate president Jefferson Davis. An acquaintance of the Washington, D.C., Lincoln critic David Rankin Barbee, Tansill was a prominent American isolationist and the author of several works of diplomatic history, which included *America Goes to War* (1938) and later the noted work *Back Door to War: Roosevelt's Foreign Policy, 1933–1941* (1952).

Entitling his speech "Jefferson Davis, Ardent American," Tansill asserted that the Civil War's chief villain was none other than Abraham Lincoln. In keeping with previous critics, he portrayed Lincoln as a tool of the abolitionists, "misguided men" from whom emanated "anvils of hate" that found their way into "the utterances of so-called statesmen like Lincoln," who spoke "with unaccustomed fire of a Civil War that was just around the corner of a new election."[1] Lincoln's 1858 "House Divided" speech was "equivalent to a declaration of war against the South," and the South was right in 1860 to see Lincoln as an "incendiary" who would, if elected, wage war against slavery. From Tansill's viewpoint Lincoln was to blame for the beginning of the conflict because he rejected Kentucky senator John J. Crittenden's proposal, one that Jefferson Davis had favored, to extend the Missouri Compromise line all the way to the Pacific Ocean and protect slavery indefinitely through an unalterable amendment to the Constitution.

So, when Lincoln "blocked this Southern plan for conciliation he cleared the decks of the Federal Ship of State for War," and as a result, "the responsibility for the Civil War rests securely upon only one pair of shoulders and those shoulders belonged to Abraham Lincoln."[2] Tansill finished his address by asserting that the so-called Lost Cause was not truly lost, "for the South did not fight for a lost cause," and the Confederate fight "gave inspiration to brave people the world over to rise and fight for the right to determine their own destinies."[3] Consequently, Jefferson Davis "was not a failure" because after the war such men stood up to the alleged horrors of Reconstruction and preserved, Tansill declared, "a government of the people, by the people, for the people."[4] Not everyone in the audience, however, agreed with Tansill; Mississippi congressman John Rankin left toward the end of the address, upset, he said, with the lack of "charity" in Tansill's remarks.[5] Tansill nevertheless received various letters complimenting his speech, and it was later published in the *Alabama Lawyer,* whose editor, Tansill was later informed, "gloried in your spunk in the Washington address."[6]

One year later Richard Hofstadter (1916–70) published *The American Political Tradition and the Men Who Made It* (1948), a book that achieved fame, in part, for its harsh characterization of Lincoln's Emancipation Proclamation.[7] The Lincoln chapter was of seminal importance in that it laid the groundwork for postwar criticism of the Great Emancipator from the more liberal side of the political spectrum.[8] In epigrammatic style Hofstadter argued that there was a consensus in American history about certain political ideas. "However much at odds on specific issues," he maintained, "the major political traditions have shared a belief in the rights of property, the philosophy of economic individualism, [and] the value of competition."[9] Hofstadter's Lincoln essay was written in this intellectual context and, although critical, was hardly a diatribe. He undeniably respected Lincoln, the "preeminent example of that self-help which Americans have always so admired."[10] Yet Hofstadter perceptively noted that Booth's assassination may not only have spared Lincoln the difficulties of facing the complexities of Reconstruction but also kept him from seeing "the generation brought up on self-help . . . build oppressive business corporations, and begin to close off business opportunities for the little man. Further, he would have seen his own party become the jackal of vested interests, placing the dollar far, far ahead of the man."[11] He averred, moreover, that Lincoln was unique in that he had amassed more power than any president yet remained essentially uncorrupted. As for politics,

"Lincoln was no maverick," Hofstadter asserted, and "in his public career and his legal practice he never made himself the advocate of unpopular reform movements."[12] Lincoln's basic conservatism was reflected in the document for which he became most famous, the Emancipation Proclamation. Echoing the arguments of a few of Lincoln's contemporary detractors, Hofstadter provocatively claimed that the proclamation "had all the moral grandeur of a bill of lading" and that it "did not in fact free any slaves."[13] Lincoln, therefore, "had turned liberator in spite of himself."[14] Hofstadter's analysis of the proclamation was not necessarily original, for it repeated the accusations of many previous Lincoln detractors; it was in some ways a victory of style over substance. Still, his essay signaled an important reevaluation of Lincoln on the Left and influenced future Lincoln opponents in the postwar era who unfortunately would not possess Hofstadter's even-tempered historical acuity.

Tansill's address and Hofstadter's Lincoln chapter, although distasteful to some Americans, came out in the immediate aftermath of a war fought against explicitly racist regimes in Germany and Japan and illustrated certain themes of antagonism to Lincoln as it existed in the postwar years between 1945 and the close of the Cold War in 1989. Hostility to Lincoln remained alive and well in the postwar era, as both men to an extent parroted many of the standard charges made by Lincoln's enemies since 1865. Just as clearly, such arguments had penetrated deep into the halls of academe. Originally from Texas, Tansill was an Old Right historian, opposed to Franklin Roosevelt's New Deal and American expansionism overseas. He was part of a revisionist school of American historical thought that questioned standard accounts of U.S. foreign policy, including American motives for involvement in World War I, accused FDR of deceit with the American public in foreign policy matters prior to the attack on Pearl Harbor, and doubted whether the Soviet Union was responsible for beginning the Cold War or if it was even capable of waging such a conflict after 1945.[15] Hofstadter, in contrast, was more a man of the Left who had little use for Jefferson Davis, but like the revisionists, he wanted to defy prevailing historical orthodoxies, conservative and liberal, that encouraged complacency about America's past and present.[16] Despite their ideological differences, Tansill's and Hofstadter's characterizations of Lincoln would be challenged by conservatives and nonconservatives alike after World War II, illustrating that the Lincoln image remained a sharply contested memory in American life.

Essentially, what made hostility to Lincoln unique after 1945 was not necessarily the originality of the arguments employed by its proponents but the emphasis given to different aspects of Lincoln's life and career, aspects that, especially Lincoln's nineteenth-century views on race, were of somewhat less concern to previous foes. Indeed, in the years from 1865 to 1945 Lincoln's frontier background and religious beliefs, or supposed lack thereof, and his conduct of various aspects of the war, including the use of force to preserve a Union in which slavery would eventually be eradicated and as a consequence racial equality was seen as a possibility, made him the embodiment of a modern America with which many of his critics were deeply unhappy. After 1945, in the midst of the civil rights movement, or "Second Reconstruction," conservatives' dissatisfaction with Lincoln stemmed primarily from their never-ending anxieties about racial equality and their claim that the president had accrued too much power for the federal government and its executive branch. Such an expansion of federal power, they thought, set an ominous precedent. Accordingly, their loathing of Lincoln served as a defense of entrenched white interests in the South opposed to the ongoing Freedom Struggle of African Americans. In an intellectual and political shift of historic proportions, however, conservatives waged a deep and robust intellectual debate over Lincoln after World War II, and by the end of the Cold War and the subsequent breakup of the Soviet Union, public hostility to Lincoln was momentarily expunged from mainstream conservatism.[17] For some on the Left, meanwhile, Lincoln was no longer a role model because of his racial views and his supposed timidity in pursuing emancipation. So, at the very time conservatives were coming to terms with Lincoln as a figure they should embrace, a few liberals found in the president a figure to reject. Some of Lincoln's adversaries on the Right and the Left temporarily merged their contempt for the president over disillusionment with American imperial ambitions overseas. Conflicts over Abraham Lincoln's legacy on different sides of the political spectrum therefore reflected contemporary fissures within both political philosophies, if not the essential nature of America's experiment in democracy. Indeed, many implicitly or explicitly asked if America was a "force for good in the world" and thought perhaps the world would have been better off if the United States had split apart during the 1860s.[18] Given American malfeasance in places ranging from Latin America to Vietnam, such ideas—and Lincoln's critics—gained a certain currency in American public life from the end of World War II to the end of the Cold War. As always, discourse about Lincoln was never exclusively about him; rather, it was a much broader argument about America itself.

As an emerging postwar movement attempting to acquire power, American conservatism consisted of several strands of thought, coupled with something of a shared outlook regarding postwar America. One strain was traditionalist and personified by Russell Kirk's *Conservative Mind* (1953) and Richard M. Weaver's *Ideas Have Consequences* (1948) and *The Southern Tradition at Bay: A History of Postbellum Thought* (1968). Such conservatives admired the antebellum South, were the intellectual descendants of the Agrarians, and sought a renascence of the Christian West in the fight against communism abroad and what they believed was an increasingly decadent, shallow, and morally relativist culture at home.[19] Not all members of this group hated Lincoln—Kirk and Weaver certainly did not—but many, perhaps most, did not consider Lincoln a conservative and were sharply critical of him. A second group of conservatives, if they can be labeled as such, were the classical liberals, or libertarians, iconoclasts such as Frank Meyer (1909–72) and Murray Rothbard (1926–95), who believed America was on the road, allegedly begun by Abraham Lincoln in the 1860s, to a socialist, if not totalitarian, state.[20] Third were conservatives such as the founder of *National Review* magazine, William F. Buckley Jr. (1925–2008), along with numerous others, who viewed executive power and Abraham Lincoln somewhat more favorably as they contemplated a long, bitter struggle against international communism. Also allied with Buckley, at least after the 1960s, were "neoconservatives," former liberal intellectuals and academics with a much less jaundiced view of federal authority than traditional conservatives or libertarians, and, finally, devotees of the political philosopher Leo Strauss, one of whom was Lincoln admirer Harry Jaffa, a former student of Strauss. From Alexander Stephens onward, Lincoln's conservative and libertarian foes had advanced the argument that Lincoln's presidency was the turning point toward centralism in the federal government, a centralism they keenly resisted once African Americans renewed their Freedom Struggle in the 1950s. More than any other conservative after World War II, Jaffa directly challenged this anti-Lincoln position, and in the process he helped reshape American conservatism's public stance toward Abraham Lincoln. Jaffa advocated the idea of Lincoln as America's greatest statesman, the most prominent American defender of natural rights, freedom, and equality, political principles he argued in numerous, controversial writings that conservatives should embrace.[21]

So, in addition to being animated by these shared attitudes or dispositions, conservatives were clearly influenced by various European and

American intellectuals (the following list is by no means exhaustive), who in turn helped shape their views on Abraham Lincoln. As noted, one fundamental idea that conservatives held in common, an idea clearly articulated during Franklin Roosevelt's New Deal and later, was their belief that the federal government, or statism, was a threat to liberty.[22] Central to this libertarian or classical liberal worldview were the works of two Austrian economists who had emigrated from Europe either during or after the war, Friedrich A. Hayek (1899–1992) and Ludwig von Mises (1881–1973), both of whom were alarmed by the growth of the state. A professor at the University of Chicago, Hayek published his most influential book, *The Road to Serfdom* (1944), before he arrived in America. In it he argued that the Western world, especially Great Britain and the United States, was "in some danger of repeating" Germany's mistakes because "we have progressively abandoned that freedom in economic affairs without which personal and political freedom has never existed in the past."[23] In Hayek's view the enlargement of the state would not lead to an enhancement of freedom but to its diminishment. Hayek's book sold well and became an instant classic within a conservative community already predisposed to be suspicious of the exercise of federal power.

The second Austrian to shape postwar conservatism was Hayek's "mentor," Ludwig von Mises. Mises came to America in 1940 and after the war taught at New York University for over twenty years.[24] A prolific economist, Mises published his magnum opus, *Human Action,* in 1949, a thousand-page-long manifesto for capitalism and, among other things, an attack upon central economic planning.[25] For neither Hayek nor Mises was Abraham Lincoln central or even a subject worthy of serious study; they were, in fact, primarily concerned with opposing economic planning and the accompanying growth of government, which they believed led to freedom's diminishment, if not outright eradication. In fact, Mises more or less equated the welfare state with fascism or Nazism. "'Paternal' care of the 'Welfare State' will reduce people to the status of bonded workers bound to comply," he wrote, "without asking any questions, with the orders issued by the planning authority. Neither is there any substantial difference between the self-styled 'progressives' and those of the Italian Fascists and the German Nazis."[26] Mises, unsurprisingly, was quite critical of the institution of slavery and defended the right of secession as important to the preservation of liberty. "No people and no part of a people shall be held against its will in a political association that it does not want," Mises declared as early as 1919.[27] Both economists provided conservatives, few if any of whom were talking about secession from the United States in the immediate aftermath of World War II, with a theoretical and intellectual defense of the free market, yet it would be the disciples of Mises in particular who would become some of the most vocal critics of Abraham Lincoln in the postwar era, especially for what they saw as Lincoln's centralization of power in the executive branch of the federal government at the expense of the states.

A third European immigrant of long-lasting significance to American conservatives was Leo Strauss, a political philosopher who, like Hayek, taught at the University of Chicago. Born in Germany at the turn of the twentieth century, Strauss arrived in the United States during the Great Depression, and after the war he migrated to the Midwest. As a professor at Chicago, Strauss was the decisive intellectual influence on numerous students, arguing in various works that there was a "crisis of liberalism," a "crisis of modernity," or a "crisis of the West."[28] This crisis resulted from "the contemporary rejection of natural right [which] leads to nihilism—nay, it is identical to nihilism."[29] For Strauss "natural right in its classic form is connected with a teleological view of the universe. All natural beings have a natural end, a natural destiny, which determines what kind of operation is good for them. In the case of man, reason is required for discerning these operations: reason determines what is by nature right with ultimate regard to man's natural end."[30] So, Strauss maintained that a return to the idea of natural right was necessary in order for the West to stave off the current crisis, especially the disastrous effects of "historicism," the modern, nihilistic idea that there were no permanent, fixed truths guiding mankind—and thus no genuine natural right—because people believed that "all human thought belongs to specific historical situations, all human thought is bound to perish with the situation to which it belongs and to be superseded by new, unpredictable thoughts."[31] The ancients, Strauss believed, could provide Americans a rational defense of the idea of natural right, not to mention their regime, in their fight against the Soviet menace. It was no accident, then, that it was one of Strauss's students, Harry Jaffa, who became Abraham Lincoln's staunchest defender among conservatives in the Cold War era.

Conservatives were similarly influenced by American authors. In 1948 yet another University of Chicago instructor, English professor Richard Weaver, published an important book, *Ideas Have Consequences,* a work that, among other things, defended Agrarianism and lamented the "decadence" of modern culture, a condition he traced all the way back to

the Middle Ages, when the English philosopher William of Occam "pro-
pounded the fateful doctrine of nominalism, which denies that universals
have a real existence."[32] Weaver's book contributed to the idea that conservatives were going to be instrumental in saving Western civilization from
extinction.[33] *Ideas Have Consequences* sold relatively well but did not, considering Weaver's affection for antebellum southern civilization, contain
any specific criticism of Abraham Lincoln. Indeed, it seems that Weaver
was not a Lincoln detractor at all; in one essay entitled "Abraham Lincoln
and the Argument from Definition," published in the 1950s, it appears
that Weaver genuinely admired the president, labeling him at one point
"the father of the nation even more convincingly than Washington."[34] Of
course, even Lincoln's enemies said as much; they simply lamented what
America had become since the 1860s and held the president responsible
for the nation's decline.

Still, the stance from which Weaver wrote was significant for the conservative Lincoln critique and evident in *The Southern Tradition at Bay*
(1968), originally his doctoral dissertation. Weaver described an America
in which "everywhere crassness, moral obtuseness, and degradation are
on the increase" and pronounced the antebellum South an "ethically superior" civilization that viewed "science as a false messiah."[35] He mourned
the passing of the feudal, chivalric, gentlemanly, and religious (i.e., Christian) virtues of the Old South, a civilization he believed was admirable
for numerous reasons, including its literature, thought, and way of life.[36]
Through an examination of its leading white, postbellum thinkers (including Lincoln detractor Albert Taylor Bledsoe), many of whom were skeptical of modernity and defended the antebellum South, Weaver offered a
mythical, idealized, indeed nostalgic version of the region. Perhaps the
most remarkable section of the book was its conclusion, in which Weaver
asserted that the slaveholding South was "right without realizing the
grounds of its rightness"—it was "*the last non-materialist civilization in
the Western World*"—and argued for a restoration of patriarchy, coupled
with a suggestion for the abolition of women's suffrage.[37] *Ideas Have Consequences* and *The Southern Tradition at Bay* had important ramifications
for the way conservatives viewed themselves and Abraham Lincoln.

Another American writer essential for conservatives after World War II
was Russell Kirk, who brought out *The Conservative Mind* in 1953. Kirk
traced the major thinkers and ideas of conservative thought going all the
way back to Edmund Burke, the eighteenth-century Irish politician and
member of British Parliament who defended the Old French Regime and

predicted the Terror of the French Revolution in *Reflections on the Revolution in France* (1790). *The Conservative Mind* delineated several "canons of conservative thought": a "belief in a transcendent order, or body of natural law"; a belief that "political problems, at bottom, are religious and moral problems"; a belief in "affection for the proliferating variety and mystery of human existence, as opposed to the narrowing uniformity, egalitarianism, and utilitarian aims of most radical systems"; a belief "that civilized society requires orders and classes" and "that freedom and property are closely linked"; and a belief "in prescription and distrust of 'sophisters, calculators, and economists' who would reconstruct society upon abstract designs." Finally, Kirk thought conservatives, unlike liberals, had a "recognition that change may not be salutary reform: hasty innovation may be a devouring conflagration, rather than a torch of progress."[38] Surprisingly, the book became a best seller. Later, in 1957, Kirk founded the academic quarterly *Modern Age* as an avenue to explore the elements of what he called the "permanent things." Abraham Lincoln was mentioned infrequently in Kirk's best-selling survey of conservative thought and was not classified as a conservative, even though he helped conserve the American Union. Kirk nevertheless thought Lincoln was an enormously important figure in American history. In fact, in a 1954 review essay of Weaver's *Ethics of Rhetoric* alongside Benjamin Thomas's 1953 biography of Lincoln, he averred that Lincoln's election to the presidency in 1860, as opposed to the Civil War itself, was "the great line of demarcation of history in America" and that "Abraham Lincoln was a conservative statesman of a high order."[39] So, although thinkers such as Hayek, Mises, Weaver, and Kirk did not loathe Abraham Lincoln, or in Hayek's and Mises's cases even pay much attention to him, they nonetheless contributed to the propagation of various elements of a political philosophy that was congenial to Lincoln's conservative detractors, including suspicion if not outright hostility to state authority, especially at the federal level; pro-antebellum South; pro-Agrarian; illiberal and antimodern in outlook; wary of change; and, last, pessimistic about the America that Abraham Lincoln had helped conserve, or re-create, with Union victory in the Civil War.[40]

It was the achievement of William F. Buckley Jr., son of a Texas oilman, Yale graduate, and *enfant terrible* of the liberal establishment in America in the 1950s and 1960s, to provide a forum in which conservatives could propagate and debate their ideas about significant issues and people, including Abraham Lincoln. In 1955 Buckley founded the weekly magazine *National Review,* editorializing in the first issue his goal of standing "athwart history, yelling Stop" to the forces he believed were destroying the United States. For Buckley such forces included an ever larger and more intrusive federal government and the inability, if not unwillingness, of Americans to evaluate properly the threat communism posed to the nation.[41] It was in the pages of *National Review* that conservatives' attitudes toward Abraham Lincoln, and by implication America itself, would be most publicly and vigorously contested. The diverse sentiments expressed toward Lincoln in the magazine no doubt reflected the philosophical differences—or unity—within the conservative movement as a whole regarding the role of the federal government in ensuring racial equality.[42]

In 1954, one year before Buckley founded *National Review,* Chief Justice Earl Warren's Supreme Court, in the *Brown v. Board of Education of Topeka, Kansas* decision, overturned the 1896 *Plessy v. Ferguson* case, which allowed for racially segregated public facilities across the South. The Warren Court's overturning of *Plessy* sparked a firestorm of controversy within the region and among conservatives. The *Brown* decision—"a rape of the Constitution," *National Review* writer Frank Meyer termed it—forced Americans to confront directly the problem of racial inequality in the United States and what role, if any, the federal government should play in attempting to eradicate or ameliorate racial oppression.[43] Because these questions were inextricably bound up with the Civil War and Reconstruction era, it was inevitable that conservatives would voice their opinions about Abraham Lincoln in the immediate aftermath of the *Brown* case. Moreover, by 1957 African Americans were effectively using the Lincoln Memorial as a venue with which to connect their Freedom Struggle to Lincoln's legacy as the Great Emancipator. That year President Dwight Eisenhower sent troops to Little Rock, Arkansas, guaranteeing that nine African American students could attend classes at all-white Central High School. In this context Buckley penned an editorial in *National Review* in 1957 entitled "Why the South Must Prevail" that illustrated the racial concerns of many conservatives in terms that would have pleased diehard Confederates and Lincoln critics: "The central question that emerges . . . is whether the white community in the South is entitled to take such measures as are necessary to prevail, politically and culturally, in areas in which it does not predominate numerically. The sobering answer is *Yes*—the white community is so entitled because, for the time being, it is the advanced race. . . . The question, as far as the white community is concerned, is whether the claims of civilization supersede those of universal suffrage. . . . *National Review* believes that the South's premises are correct."[44] Eventually, at least for strategic political reasons, *National Review* repudiated such sentiments. In *Southern Tradition at Bay,* Richard Weaver clearly saw that "considerations of strategy and tactics forbid the use of lost causes. There cannot be a return to the Middle Ages or the Old South under slogans identified with them. The principles must be studied and used, but in such presentation that mankind will feel the march is forward." Jeffrey Hart, an editor at the magazine, agreed, and in his memoir of *National Review* said "the myth of the Lost Cause" was poisonous "as a political recommendation." Thus, it is unsurprising that conservatives, including Buckley, became amenable to a more positive view of Abraham Lincoln.[45]

Many white southerners of whom Buckley spoke nevertheless agreed with his opinions. Indeed, it probably confirmed their own sense of racial superiority, and there were individuals and groups who selectively used Lincoln's words from his debates with Stephen Douglas in 1858 to bolster their white supremacist outlook. Marvin C. Mobley of Decatur, Georgia, sold tiny pamphlets with words by Lincoln on the inside and variously entitled *Abraham Lincoln Said This, More Words of Abraham Lincoln That the Race-Mixers Never Quote,* and *The Little-Known Words of Abraham Lincoln.* Mobley's pamphlets supported the segregationist viewpoint and sold at a rate of five dollars for one hundred copies. "There are white men enough to marry all the white women," Mobley quoted Lincoln in one pamphlet, "and black men enough to marry all the black women." Mobley alleged that communists—in his mind probably civil rights advocates—hated Lincoln's First Inaugural Address, in which the newly sworn-in president had said, "The candid citizen must confess that if the policy of government upon vital questions effecting the whole of the people is to be irrevocably fixed by decisions of the Supreme Court the people will have ceased to be their own rulers, having to that extent practically resigned their government into the hands of that eminent tribunal."[46] From the segregationist standpoint this statement proved Lincoln would have supported the massive resistance of white southerners to the *Brown* decision. But the portion of Lincoln's Inaugural Address in which the president plainly stated that disobeying the laws of the land was unconstitutional was absent from Mobley's pamphlet. Mobley's leaflets illustrated that some whites clearly understood the importance of countering the argument of many civil rights leaders that Lincoln, if he were still alive, would have sympathized with their movement. This explains why Mobley never brought out any pamphlets citing Lincoln's idea that the natural rights Jefferson had mentioned in the Declaration of Independence applied to all men, an idea his senatorial opponent Stephen Douglas had opposed. Nor did Mobley deign to mention Lincoln's public support at the end of the war on behalf of limited suffrage for blacks. Segregationists selectively quoted the late president in order to support the continuation of white supremacist policies. Still, Mobley was just one figure putting out a few brochures with which many white southerners already concurred and had repeatedly heard from organizations such as the United Daughters of the Confederacy (UDC) and other Lincoln contrarians over the past few decades.[47]

More substantial in its influence was the official newspaper of the segregationists, the *Citizens' Councils*. The Citizens' Council, an organization whose views "on states' rights" Buckley approved, consisted of middle-class whites, and they likewise used the Lincoln image to advance their segregationist agenda.[48] In the second issue of the paper the *Councils* reported on an address of Dr. W. M. Caskey, who taught at Mississippi College and had quoted Abraham Lincoln to the effect that just as Lincoln said he would not abide by the 1857 *Dred Scott* decision, white southerners were not obliged to obey decisions of the Warren Court requiring integration of their schools.[49] The May 1956 issue contained Lincoln's words from the August 1862 gathering with an African American delegation, in which Lincoln had told his audience, among other things, that the two races could not live together and blacks should be colonized outside the United States. The headline to the piece in the *Citizens' Councils* exclaimed, "Eternal Truth Never Changes!"[50] Other issues included short pieces for southern schoolchildren averring that "Lincoln Was against Race-Mixing" and "Lincoln Did Not Believe the Races Could Live Together."[51] In 1957, when the crisis in Little Rock, Arkansas, was in full swing, words eerily similar to Marvin Mobley's pamphlets made their way into the *Councils*. "Abe Said: More words of Abraham Lincoln that the race-mixers never quote," declared the headline, followed by Lincoln's 1859 assertion in Cincinnati, Ohio, that "the people of the United States are the rightful masters of both Congress and Courts, not to overthrow the Constitution, but to overthrow the men who pervert the Constitution."[52] To be sure, there were hardly a slew of articles quoting Lincoln in the *Citizens' Councils*, but when Lincoln was quoted, it was usually done selectively, ignoring speeches from later in his presidency and in such a way as to bolster the white segregationist position on race and resistance to the federal government. It may seem odd that white southerners would cite a president some of them traditionally despised for using force to preserve the Union, but as all sides in the civil rights argument were well aware, the Lincoln image in American culture was important, and whoever could capture or control that image was going to have a very powerful weapon indeed in their arsenal.[53]

African American civil rights leaders had no illusions about the strength of the opposition they faced in their quest for racial equality. As a result, they used the icon of Abraham Lincoln as a method for combating the idea of their white supremacist enemies that Lincoln had been on the side of the segregationists. As early as 1939, the African American opera singer Marian Anderson sang a version of "America" to a crowd of over seventy-five thousand people in front of the Lincoln Memorial, after the Daughters of the American Revolution (DAR) had refused to allow her to sing at Constitution Hall solely on account of her race.[54] Anderson's concert was only the first in a series of demonstrations held in front of the Lincoln Memorial between 1939 and 1963 that helped garner sympathy and support for the civil rights movement across the country. Just as segregationists used the Lincoln image in their fight against racial equality, African Americans likewise employed "Lincoln's memory and monument as political weapons" in their Freedom Struggle.[55] Of course, there had never been complete unanimity of opinion about Abraham Lincoln within the African American community. To be sure, most African Americans from the Civil War onward displayed great affection for Lincoln, but after World War II such admiration had waned somewhat.[56] The leaders of the movement nevertheless understood the power of the Lincoln image in white America and used rallies in front of the Lincoln Memorial as a way to communicate their egalitarian aspirations to the rest of the country in a historical and democratic language everyone would understand.[57] In other words, segregationists appealed to Lincoln's memory to hinder steps toward equality in the United States, while civil rights leaders shrewdly used the same image to advance their race on the same path.

So, the attacks on Lincoln from within postwar conservatism inescapably addressed the ongoing domestic controversy over the relationship between the federal government and racial equality. The conservative Lincoln wars that erupted after 1945 stemmed in part from the publication of an important, laudatory book by Harry V. Jaffa entitled *Crisis of the House Divided: An Interpretation of the Issues in the Lincoln-Douglas Debates* (1959). Jaffa was a political philosophy professor at Claremont McKenna College and the reputed author of Barry Goldwater's famous aphorism, uttered at the 1964 Republican convention in San Francisco, "that extremism in the defense of liberty is no vice! And let me remind you

also that moderation in the pursuit of justice is no virtue!"[58] *Crisis* was
written, at least in part, to counter Richard Hofstadter's debunking portrait of Lincoln given in *The American Political Tradition,* but the impact
of Jaffa's book and subsequent pro-Lincoln essays was felt more strongly
on the Right.[59] In *Crisis* Jaffa concluded, among other things, that in 1858
Lincoln was right and Douglas wrong in the debates over the fundamental
nature of the Union. Directly challenging all revisionist historians who
argued that the Civil War was unnecessary, caused by a inept generation
of politicians, Jaffa maintained that the "Lincolnian case for government
of the people and by the people meant being for a moral purpose that
informs the people's being," and as a result, "had not Lincoln challenged
Douglas in 1858, there would probably have been no subsequent crisis,
or at least none of the same nature." Jaffa furthermore claimed that "by
effectively destroying Douglas as the leader of a national political coalition, by dividing him from both the Republicans and from the South,
Lincoln made morally certain that the nation would be constitutionally
committed to his view of national political responsibility, a view which
he well knew most of the South believed incompatible with its dearest
interests."[60] Lincoln's "moral purpose," if not America's, was for Jaffa the
idea contained within the first paragraph of Jefferson's declaration "that
all men are created equal."[61] Jaffa's Lincoln, then, was no political cynic or
scheming politician but a philosopher statesman of the highest order. In a
way Jaffa's thesis that Lincoln had to destroy Douglas anticipated George
Forgie's psychobiography, *Patricide in the House Divided: A Psychological
Interpretation of Lincoln and His Age* (1979) by twenty years, but whereas
Forgie believed that Lincoln had a psychological need to "symbolically
murder" Douglas, Jaffa's interpretation was moral and political and held
that Lincoln, with his emphasis on equality, fulfilled, perhaps even tran-
scended, the framers' ideals.[62]

Jaffa's book, not to mention his subsequent writings, threw a gauntlet
down to conservative theorists such as Willmoore Kendall (1909–68)
and Frank Meyer, both writers at Buckley's recently established *National
Review,* if not mentors of Buckley himself. In his insistence that political
equality was a conservative principle, Jaffa directly challenged a fundamental conservative tenet, the idea that, as Russell Kirk put it in *The
Conservative Mind,* "civilized society requires orders and classes."[63] In a
review of Jaffa's volume entitled "Source of American Caesarism" Kendall
readily acknowledged the importance of Jaffa's work and said he hoped
that the number of people who read the book "will be legion."[64] But Ken-

dall thought the adoption of Jaffa's Lincolnian political philosophy of natural right would be potentially disastrous, leading to "an endless series of Abraham Lincoln's, each persuaded that he is superior in wisdom and virtue to the Fathers, each prepared to insist that those who oppose this or that new application of the equality standard are denying the possibility of self-government, each ultimately willing to plunge America into Civil War rather than concede his point."[65] He concluded with the assertion that it was "the Southerners," not Lincoln, "who were the anti-Caesars of pre–Civil War days." Kendall's great fear—and given how the president's rhetoric had been previously appropriated by Progressives such as Woodrow Wilson or liberals such as Franklin Roosevelt and Lyndon Johnson, his anxiety was not altogether unwarranted—was that Jaffa's Lincoln would be used, or misused perhaps, to further political goals conservatives would find objectionable: "Lincoln was the Caesar Lincoln claimed to be trying to prevent; and that the Caesarism we all need to fear is the contemporary Liberal movement dedicated like Lincoln to egalitarian reforms sanctioned by mandates emanating from national majorities, a movement which is Lincoln's legitimate offspring."[66]

To be sure, Kendall admired the president in certain respects, but then again, so did almost all Lincoln critics. Later, in a piece published toward the end of his life, "Equality: Commitment or Ideal?" Kendall attacked a portion of Lincoln's reasoning in the Gettysburg Address as "heretical."[67] Although in agreement with Lincoln that the United States "was conceived in liberty" and "dedicated to an overriding purpose," Kendall forcefully confronted the idea that the nation's purpose was, as Lincoln put it in the first sentence of the address, devoted to "the proposition that all men are created equal."[68] In explicitly religious terminology Kendall argued that by consciously dating the founding of the United States from 1776—"Four score and seven years ago"—Lincoln had deliberately falsified "the facts of history, and . . . in a way that precisely *confuses* our self-understanding as a people." Lincoln was guilty of "an act of *political heresy* compounded by an *act of impiety* toward the nation's true Founding Fathers," namely, the men who wrote the Constitution in 1787. Consequently, the United States had no obligation to equality. "We have no such commitment," Kendall declared, "we have, collectively and individually, no obligation to promote the overriding purpose [of equality]; the whole business is a further Lincolnian heresy." Instead, what the United States was and must be committed to, in Kendall's view, were the six purposes laid out in the preamble to the Constitution: "Union, Justice, Domestic Tranquility, The

Common Defense, The Blessings of Liberty."[69] Curiously, Kendall did not fully explain how such goals were necessarily less subject to political abuse than Lincoln's argument that the nation, at least in a metaphorical sense, was committed to equality, nor did he adequately take into account the political context in which Lincoln had been operating since the passage of the Kansas-Nebraska Act in 1854. Stephen Douglas, along with millions of Americans, held that the Declaration of Independence applied only to white men, and Lincoln consistently and vigorously opposed this viewpoint in arguing that Jefferson's appeal to natural rights in 1776 applied to all men, regardless of race. Moreover, given all that had happened in the Civil War by November 1863, when Lincoln spoke at Gettysburg, it would have been more surprising if Lincoln had *not* referred to equality in some sense as a national goal. After all, there was still an entire section of the United States fighting and dying in large numbers in order to keep slaves in bondage—a rather unequal condition by anyone's standard—a stark reality that would have been the result of a Confederate victory in the Civil War, no matter what its apologists then or later have claimed to the contrary.

The contretemps between Jaffa and Kendall continued into the 1970s, when Kendall's *Basic Symbols of the American Political Tradition* (1970) was posthumously published (with George Carey), a book that contained a further attack on Jaffa's interpretation of Lincoln, the Declaration, and equality. "The Declaration of Independence did not," Kendall and Carey declared, "as Lincoln proclaims, establish our independence *as a nation*. Rather, what it did was to establish a baker's dozen of new sovereignties."[70] Lincoln's "internalization of the concept of equality" was pernicious because "many professional students of American government are preoccupied with the question of what equality means within our society" and because "Lincoln's interpretation" of the Declaration of Independence was predominant "among contemporary scholars."[71] Lincoln, in short, had "derailed" the American tradition. Thus, it was no wonder that Lincoln "is so congenial to modern egalitarians."[72] Jaffa, as we shall see, responded at length to this line of attack in 1975 with an essay entitled "Equality as a Conservative Principle," and in the process he intensified a decades-long quarrel over Abraham Lincoln in conservative circles.[73]

The shift in Lincoln criticism initiated by Kendall, or more accurately Jaffa, was momentous. Before World War II conservative opposition to Lincoln was largely, although not exclusively, made by Confederate sympathizers and, without ever being entirely uncontested or unconcerned with matters of equality, race, or empire, also focused on his background, lack of religion, alleged mistreatment of Union and Confederate prisoners of war, or his suspension of habeas corpus. After the war, however, as a direct result of Jaffa's controversial and vigorously defended assertion that equality was a conservative principle, some conservatives were compelled to assail Lincoln for a different reason: his notion of equality. Much of this attack, certainly, was quite old and consistent with criticism emanating from previous critics. Lincoln's contemporaries, even in the North, had in fact lambasted the president for what they believed would be the racially egalitarian consequences of his emancipatory policies. But this renewed assault on Lincoln now took place in a different historical and political context, and it was not accidental—or incidental to conservative political theory—that Kendall and other conservatives were critiquing Lincoln's egalitarianism in terms pleasing to *Brown's* opponents in the immediate aftermath of the Court's decision and amid the contemporary African American Freedom Struggle.[74] Their image of Lincoln countered the one civil rights leaders effectively used in advocating for federal protection of the human and constitutional rights denied to their race since the end of Reconstruction.

Kendall's hostility may have led Jaffa years later to reemphasize Lincoln's philosophical advocacy of natural rights, not to mention the president's basic agreement with, rather than transcendence of, the founders, in his turn-of-the century sequel to *Crisis,* entitled *A New Birth of Freedom: Abraham Lincoln and the Coming of the Civil War* (2000).[75] In that volume Jaffa, among other things, penned a lengthy philosophical attack on the Progressive historian (and the Progressive appropriation of Lincoln more generally) Carl L. Becker's assertion, stated in his *Declaration of Independence: A Study in the History of Political Ideas* (1922), that "to ask whether the natural rights philosophy of the Declaration of Independence is true or false is essentially a meaningless question."[76] For Jaffa, of course, this was not a meaningless but a necessary question. "If what Becker asserts is the incontrovertible truth of the matter," he reasoned, "then the conviction upon which Lincoln defended his policy of preserving the Union and justified his entire life (not to mention his death, and the deaths of 600,000 other Americans) was a delusion."[77] In short Jaffa held that "Lincoln's belief in the truth of the Declaration" was not just "emotionally evocative and persuasive, but . . . *philosophically sound.*"[78] And because Jaffa believed that "Lincoln's acceptance of the idiom of natural rights and natural law—above all his acceptance of the idea of nature not merely as a record of cause and effect but as a source of moral principles—has become alien to us," he sought to restore such thinking to the forefront of American political thought.[79] By equating Lincoln's thought with that of the founders, Jaffa, at least to his own satisfaction, addressed Kendall's aforementioned worries of "an endless series of Abraham Lincoln's, each persuaded that he is superior in wisdom and virtue to the Fathers." In other words, Jaffa used what he believed was Lincoln's timeless natural rights philosophy to combat "the idea of history," or historicism, cited by Strauss and utilized by some Progressives, who had seized the Lincoln image to advance their cause of ameliorating or eradicating ongoing injustices in American life.[80]

Jaffa and Kendall, indeed all conservatives, were treading in old historical and philosophical waters here, yet both men made important points. On the one hand, Jaffa was correct to stress Lincoln's idealism, his deep-seated agreement with the Declaration's emphasis on mankind's natural rights, and his staunch opposition to slavery. He was also right in reintroducing the idea that the Civil War, far from being needless, may have been unavoidable. *Crisis* was an important, provocative counterweight to traditional conservative hostility toward Lincoln, not to mention Hofstadter's earlier and somewhat cynical interpretation of the sixteenth president. On the other hand, Kendall and Carey were correct in claiming that Lincoln *had* derailed the American political tradition. He and the Republicans broadened that tradition and made it more egalitarian. They had, in the words of political scientist Rogers M. Smith, "generated a period of liberalizing civic reforms unmatched in the nation's history," reforms that might include "equal citizenship for blacks and possibly women."[81] Although those reforms were short-lived, the *idea* of a more egalitarian and pluralistic America unleashed by the war and Reconstruction could not forever be squelched. Consequently, Kendall was rightly worried over the potential consequences of Jaffa's Lincoln, for it was a principled, Janus-faced portrait that looked backward in its association of Lincoln with the founders yet looked forward in its depiction of the president, with his emphasis on natural rights for all, as realizing, if not transcending, their ideals.

If Willmoore Kendall attacked Harry Jaffa and Abraham Lincoln from a more traditional conservative perspective, in a series of *National Review* articles Frank Meyer appeared to challenge Jaffa's egalitarian notions from a classically liberal, or libertarian, standpoint. It was nevertheless remarkable how closely Meyer's analysis aligned with Kendall's. There had been a clear and consistent libertarian strain or critique of Lincoln's

Whig political philosophy dating all the way back to the Jacksonian era, although it had become rather submerged in the immediate aftermath of the Civil War. H. L. Mencken, Edgar Lee Masters, and the anarchist Albert Jay Nock (like Albert Taylor Bledsoe, a former Episcopal priest) revived this tradition between the wars, although Mencken was never all that preoccupied with Lincoln, and Masters's book was not well received. Mencken for one hated all politicians, and he had, in a sense, other gods to slay with his brilliant and witty attacks on Puritanism in American literature and culture. Nock, one of William F. Buckley's intellectual heroes, revitalized the libertarian's negative evaluation of Lincoln. In his book *Our Enemy, the State* (1935) Nock asserted that Lincoln's closing peroration in the Gettysburg Address asking for a "new birth of freedom" and continuation of government "of the people, by the people, for the people," was "the most effective single stroke of propaganda ever made in behalf of republican State prestige."[82] Nock disparaged Lincoln's administration as a "monocratic military despotism" and alleged "Lincoln ruled unconstitutionally throughout his term." In reference to Lincoln's suspension of habeas corpus and wartime blockade of the South, Nock echoed the words of previous enemies: "In fact, a very good case could be made out for the assertion that Lincoln's acts resulted in a permanent radical change in the entire system of constitutional 'interpretation'—that since his time 'interpretations' have not been interpretations of the constitution, but merely of public policy . . . . A strict constructionist might indeed say that the constitution died in 1861, and one would have to scratch one's head pretty diligently to refute him."[83] Such commentary demonstrates that Nock's negative judgment of the president's actions as having led America down the path to perdition was virtually indistinguishable from that of Lincoln's previous Lost Cause detractors.

Frank Meyer added to Kendall's criticism with a vengeance in June 1965, three months after the first American ground troops arrived in Vietnam and in the midst of congressional debate on the Voting Rights Act. In a brief review of the book *Freedom under Lincoln* (1965) Meyer complimented the author for demonstrating that Lincoln's administration "was, in terms of civil liberties, the most ruthless in American history."[84] Some readers disagreed with Meyer's assessment, including, somewhat surprisingly considering his affection for Nock, the editor of the magazine, William F. Buckley Jr.[85] Meyer consequently felt compelled to respond at greater length regarding his views. "The issue is not really the one my critics raise; whether Lincoln was or was not a humanitarian," he argued.

"So far as this is concerned, suffice it say that against Lincoln's magnificent language and personal acts of individual kindness there must be placed in the balance the harshness of his repressive policies and his responsibility for methods of waging war approaching the horror of total war."[86] Meyer blamed Lincoln for destroying the old Union by disallowing the question of whether a state had a right to secede, which made "nugatory the autonomy of the states."[87] In addition, Meyer maintained: "It is on his [Lincoln's] shoulders that the responsibility for the war must be placed. Had he been less of an ideologue, he could have let the seven states [of the Deep South] go, and thus hold Virginia (the key to future unity) and the others in the Union . . . . [Lincoln] waged it to win *at any cost—and by winning he meant the permanent destruction of the autonomy of the states.*"[88] The real tragedy was that "were it not for the wounds that Lincoln inflicted upon the Constitution, it would have been infinitely more difficult for Franklin Roosevelt to carry through his revolution."[89] It seemed that it was not so much Lincoln whom Meyer was complaining about but the consequences of U.S. victory in the war, which he believed had led to Franklin Roosevelt's New Deal and Lyndon Johnson's Great Society. And although conservatives disagreed on many things, on the necessity of overturning the New Deal and opposing the Great Society, they more or less were in consensus. Attacking Lincoln, then, was to an extent part of a much larger argument about the nature of freedom and equality, whether they were inseparably linked, and if the federal government rather than the states could best protect that connection. Kendall, Meyer, and Lincoln's conservative critics clearly believed not. The charges against the Civil War president leveled by Meyer and Kendall, along with Harry Jaffa's spirited ripostes, appeared in conservative forums just as the nation was debating the proper role of the federal government in, as Abraham Lincoln once said in another context, "assuring freedom to the free."

Meyer's hostile stance provoked a rebuttal by Harry Jaffa in *National Review* on September 21, 1965. Jaffa was incredulous, although he should not have been, because it was a standard omission of most who denigrated Lincoln, that Meyer "has written a critical essay on Abraham Lincoln and the Civil War without mentioning or even alluding to the subject of slavery."[90] To Meyer's argument that Lincoln had harmed the tension in the Constitution between the states and the federal government, Jaffa wrote that the writers of the Constitution were at least as guilty as Lincoln for destroying such a tension, for they had replaced the Articles of Confederation with the Constitution to address precisely those problems.

As for whether or not a state had a right to lawfully secede, Jaffa quoted Andrew Jackson from the Nullification Crisis of 1832 to startling effect, noting that Jackson had foreshadowed the arguments of Lincoln's First Inaugural Address when he said state nullification of federal law was "incompatible with the existence of the Union, contradicted expressly by the Constitution, unauthorized by its spirit, inconsistent with every principle on which it was founded, and destructive of the great object for which it was formed."[91] Jaffa asked Meyer (along with *National Review*'s readers), a devout libertarian who supposedly abhorred tyranny: "Is not slavery the most unlimited of all forms of government? How can one identify theories devised to protect slavery with the cause of limited government?"[92] In Jaffa's view, and to an extent he appears to have conceded some of Meyer's argument here, slavery justified Lincoln's waging of the Civil War and subsequent repression of civil liberties: "Whatever the debit side of the ledger might show, certainly the credit side must show a mighty entry: the destruction of that reproach to everything sacred to the American mission in the world, American Negro Slavery."[93] Ordinary readers of *National Review* were impressed and weighed in on the controversy, with their published remarks divided between Meyer and Jaffa. Henry Paolucci of New York City was "disturbed" by Meyer's article because he believed it showed "American conservatives" are not "united in their determination to preserve this American national union of ours *at all costs,*" while William J. Gill of Pittsburgh, Pennsylvania, thought "Lincoln's total war policy *was* unforgivable" and asserted, with typical anti-Lincoln hyperbole, that "Lincoln's reign was the beginning of the end of constitutional government in the United States."[94]

Meyer was not finished with Lincoln or Jaffa, however, for he responded in January 1966 to Jaffa's September piece. He did not address one of Jaffa's central points, the issue of slavery and the Civil War, because, as he said, "Lincoln himself and most of his defenders deny (including Professor Jaffa in this essay) that the abolition of slavery was ever Lincoln's intent." Instead, Meyer focused his counterattack on the issue of divided sovereignty between the states and federal government, once again telling *National Review*'s readers that the sovereignty of the states, even in a divided system such as the United States, "implies the right to secede" and Jaffa's problem was that he "does not begin to grasp the incalculable damage for which Lincoln is responsible. . . . The freedom of the individual from government, not the equality of individual persons, is the central theme of our constitutional arrangements. . . . *Freedom and equality are*

opposites."[95] Given the atrocities that African Americans had suffered in
the United States since being declared "forever free" by Lincoln in 1863,
especially in the former states of the Confederacy, where white residents
were left alone by the federal government to oppress, terrorize, and lynch
blacks virtually at will, it seems certain that African Americans would
have agreed with Meyer on the latter point.

Other libertarians also challenged the pro-Lincoln view promulgated
by Jaffa and to greater long-term effect. The libertarian-turned-anarchist
Murray N. Rothbard recalled Meyer's Lincoln critiques as important because "Meyer clearly saw that changes Lincoln wrought in American society
were the decisive shift toward the centralizing and despotic nation-state,
changes that were built upon by the Progressive era, by Woodrow Wilson,
and finally by the New Deal."[96] A keen student of Ludwig von Mises, the
iconoclastic and unceasingly optimistic Rothbard was perhaps the foremost exponent of Austrian economics in the United States, an economist
who specialized in the causes of the Great Depression but commented
on all manner of issues. A staunch advocate of natural rights in the anarchist tradition of Lysander Spooner, Rothbard argued that "the great
failing of natural-law theory—from Plato and Aristotle to the Thomists
and down to Leo Strauss and his followers in the present day—is to have
been profoundly statist rather than individualist."[97] Consequently, he was
philosophically at odds with Jaffa's idea (or the Progressives or FDR or
Lyndon Johnson, for that matter) that the "Lincolnian case for government of the people and by the people meant being for a moral purpose"
because for him the state itself was unjustifiable, if not immoral. In other
words, the best regime for protecting an individual's natural rights was
not Lincolnian but no regime at all. Rothbard drew a sharp distinction
"between a man's right and the morality and immorality of his exercise of
that right." So, for example, although parents might be morally obligated
to care for their children, they should have no "legal obligation to feed,
clothe, or educate" them.[98] Because Rothbard defined libertarianism as
"a *political* philosophy, confined to what the use of violence should be in
social life," and because he hated the state (which he believed war always
enlarged), a position he consistently advocated over his lifetime, Rothbard
loathed Abraham Lincoln and his elevated status in American culture.[99]

Rothbard expressed his antipathy for Abraham Lincoln to Buckley as
early as 1959, when Soviet premier Nikita Khrushchev visited the United
States. The Khrushchev visit, Rothbard happily anticipated, was "an exciting and welcome sign of a possible détente, of a break in the Cold War dike,

of a significant move toward ending the Cold War and achieving peaceful coexistence" with the Soviet Union.[100] What particularly incensed Rothbard was that Buckley and *National Review* had organized a campaign—"a demagogic argument," he labeled it—that President Eisenhower, and by extension the United States, should not "Shake the Hand of the Bloody Butcher of the Ukraine (Khrushchev)."[101] Apparently, he and Buckley had "a tart exchange of letters" over the subject, and in one missive Rothbard suggested Khrushchev should visit the White House and sleep "in the sainted Lincoln's bed, but this would surely be more than apt, considering that Mr. K's deeds in Hungary were precisely equivalent to Mr. Lincoln's butchery of the South."[102] One distinction Rothbard failed to make here between Hungary's oppression by the Soviet Union was that Hungarians had never consented to be part of the Soviet empire, while white southern slaveholders such as George Washington and Thomas Jefferson were instrumental in the creation of the United States, and the white South had benefited in numerous ways from its membership in the American Union. In fact, in the early 1960s Rothbard was critical of white southern slaveholders. He thought that "the basic root of the controversy over slavery to secession . . . was the aggressive, expansionist aims of the Southern 'slavocracy.'"[103] Rothbard nevertheless broke with Buckley and the New Right after the Khrushchev visit, concluding that "the entire right wing had been captured from within by its former enemy: war and global intervention," and he instead sought an antiwar alliance with the Left. "By consistently following an antiwar and isolationist star," he wrote, "I had shifted—or rather been shifted—from right-wing Republican to left-wing Democrat."[104] As a result, Rothbard was virtually alone in libertarian circles, and even Frank Meyer eventually wrote him out of the conservative movement.[105] Rothbard's condemnation of Lincoln nevertheless continued. His critique also anticipated historian William Appleman Williams's ideas by several years, and although his attempted fusion with the Left ended in failure and disappointment, he persisted in his advocacy of anarcho-capitalist ideals.

For the next several decades Rothbard criticized American imperialism ("empirically," he wrote in 1973, "taking the twentieth century as a whole, the single most warlike, most interventionist, most imperialist government has been the United States"), defended the right of secession down to where "the individual may secede," and criticized the Lincoln administration for economic and military misconduct. Rothbard's antipathy demonstrated once again that argument about Lincoln was more often than not a discussion about the nature of the American nation itself: "The Civil War, in addition to its unprecedented bloodshed and devastation, was used by the triumphal and virtually one-party Republican regime to drive through its statist, formerly Whig, program; national government power, protective tariff, subsidies to big business, inflationary paper money, resumed control of the federal government over banking, large-scale internal improvements, high excise taxes, and, during the war, conscription and an income tax. Furthermore, the states came to lose their previous right of secession and other states' powers as opposed to federal government powers."[106] Abraham Lincoln was not necessarily the person most central to Rothbard's intellectual work, but criticizing Lincoln was an important vehicle with which to advance his ideas. If praising Lincoln served the interests of the state, as Rothbard believed and argued, then attacking him could serve his own antistatist inclinations and interests. In 1969 Rothbard founded the bimonthly newsletter of the libertarian movement, the *Libertarian Forum,* which he edited until 1984. In 1979 the *Forum* contained a fairly lengthy attack on Lincoln by Lance Lamberton, who cited Lincoln's high standing in American polls as "indicative of a collectivist and statist mind-set that permeates the thinking of the American public and the historical profession," a mind-set that was "a sad and depressing commentary on the American people and the ideals that most Americans espouse that they have chosen to venerate that American who was most successful in oppressing them."[107]

Also published in 1979, in the *Journal of Libertarian Studies,* yet another journal edited by the indefatigable Rothbard, was Joseph Stromberg's "War for Southern Independence: A Radical Libertarian Perspective."[108] Stromberg, who later held the JoAnn B. Rothbard Chair in History at the Ludwig von Mises Institute in Alabama, offered "a libertarian assessment" of the Civil War regarding "other options and might-have-beens for contrast" from what he believed to be nationalist, pro-Unionist, interpretations of the conflict.[109] Arguing that "self-determination" is a "revolutionary right," Stromberg alleged that it would have been better for the North—and the slaves—to have let the South secede and form a slaveholding republic. "Indeed," Stromberg wrote, perhaps in reference to Lincoln's First Inaugural Address, "the fact that secession implies 'anarchy' is an argument in favor of secession, not against it. Consistent application of self-rule to the Confederate case demands recognizing that it would have been more correct morally and practically to let the South go. . . . To accept this is not at all to disparage the equal right of Black Americans to use any means necessary to establish *their* freedom from the slaveholders (and from political oppression South *and* North). The issues, however, are separable, and Southern independence was the issue in 1860–61; the internal institutions of the CSA did not justify a war of conquest any more than the issue of feudalism, free markets or socialism in Vietnam."[110] Although Stromberg did not deny that slavery was "an issue in 1860–61," he disagreed it was "*the* issue."[111] It was clear that he found secession to be both a constitutional and moral right and believed that when Abraham Lincoln opposed southern secession with a "policy of war and subjugation," it was a deeply immoral act that had innumerable unfortunate consequences. Such consequences included an enhancement of the federal government at the expense of the states, "the entire long-standing Federalist/Whig program of neo-mercantilism and subsidies to Northern industry," and, quoting William Appleman Williams, "no end of empire except war and more war."[112] Stromberg's essay assumed more than it proved, especially in its claim that allowing southern secession would have been the constitutionally and morally correct course for Lincoln to follow—millions of Americans alive in 1860–61, probably a majority, disagreed with such a notion. In addition, Stromberg's assertion that the slaves had the right to revolt against their masters was true but beside the point because, as he almost assuredly knew, a slave revolt was hardly equivalent to Confederates seceding and waging war against the United States government. The Confederates were literate, could seek alliances with other nation-states, and, most important, had weapons. The slaves possessed few or none of these assets, and if they had tried to rise up and slay their owners in order to win their right to "self-determination," they would have been promptly slaughtered. Still, Stromberg's piece was a harbinger of an intellectual union between libertarian disciples of Rothbard and robust defenders of the Confederacy, united in their hatred for Abraham Lincoln.

The establishment in 1982 of the Ludwig von Mises Institute in Auburn, Alabama, was a significant development for the propagation of Rothbard's ideas, not to mention the long-standing tradition of hostility to Lincoln. Founded by Llewellyn Rockwell Jr., a friend and intellectual compatriot of Rothbard, the institute's purpose was "to place human choice at the center of economic theory, to encourage a revival of historical research, and to advance the [Ludwig von] Misesian tradition of thought through the defense of the market economy, private property, sound money, and peaceful international relations, while opposing government intervention as economically and socially destructive."[113] Rothbard served as the institute's "academic vice-president," and he and the Mises Institute reached thousands of students through the organization's various educational outreach programs. The institute later became the intellectual nerve center of radical libertarian political thought associated with modern Confederate sympathizers.[114] By the early 1980s, then, an aggressive movement of opposition to Lincoln independent of the mainstream conservative movement had been launched. With Murray Rothbard as its intellectual founder, and remaining its guiding spirit long after his death in 1995, it emerged onto the national political scene in the last decade of the twentieth century and laid the groundwork for one of the most important books of Lincoln criticism published in the post–Cold War era, Thomas DiLorenzo's *Real Lincoln* (2002).

Quarrels about Abraham Lincoln within the conservative community were much more than an academic dispute between different intellectual strains of conservatism.[115] *National Review* was the flagship publication of an increasingly influential political movement, and it is fascinating that Buckley allowed such a robust debate to take place in his relatively new magazine. There may have been some risk in allowing anti-Lincoln statements such as Kendall's and Meyer's to get out to the public at large and thereby discredit the nascent conservative crusade with Americans. But this was precisely the point, for what took place within the pages of *National Review* was an important debate about Abraham Lincoln and whether American conservatives could shed their historically pro-Confederate leanings. It was a necessary and spirited argument about what American conservatism meant in the postwar era, especially regarding racial equality and the role of federal authority in such vital matters.

But what was William F. Buckley's attitude regarding Abraham Lincoln? Unquestionably, Buckley had a libertarian strain of thought in his political philosophy. As noted earlier, he had been an ardent admirer of Albert Jay Nock since his youth, and he was a fan of both Willmoore Kendall and Frank Meyer. Notwithstanding such highbrow and libertarian affinities, Buckley's views of Lincoln were less condemnatory than those of his intellectual predecessors or *National Review* colleagues, although in some respects his opinions reflected traditional opposition to the president. Of course, what made Buckley's opinions on Lincoln significant was precisely that he reflected the tensions within conservatism toward the president who had conserved the Union but resorted to extraordinary measures such as emancipation in order to prevail. In the long run Harry Jaffa exerted a greater influence on Buckley's stance concerning the sixteenth president than either Nock or Meyer.

In one of his earliest books, *McCarthy and His Enemies: The Record and Its Meaning* (1954), Buckley compared criticism of himself and coauthor L. Brent Bozell to the vitriol Lincoln had been subjected to during the Civil War, while in *Up from Liberalism* (1959) Buckley commended Lincoln for freeing the slaves and labeled him "pragmatic."[116] Buckley exhibited his own form of political pragmatism in his 1965 New York City mayoral campaign, when he used Lincoln's views on the necessity of government to justify solving some of the Big Apple's environmental problems.[117] Despite sharing the political outlook of previous Lincoln critics, Buckley was no hardened Lincoln hater, and attacking the president was not uppermost in the editor's mind as he attempted to combat liberals and midwife the birth of the modern American conservative movement.

Still, remarks about Lincoln crept into Buckley's writings, as they almost inevitably would for anyone who thought seriously about American political history. Buckley's most extended foray into Lincoln commentary came in reflections published soon after his electorally unsuccessful (in other respects it was a boon to Buckley's career) 1965 mayoral campaign in New York City. Published after passage of the Civil Rights Act of 1964 and the Voting Rights Act of 1965 and following a subpar debate performance against the African American writer James Baldwin at Oxford University in England, his book *The Unmaking of a Mayor* (1966) contained a lengthy disquisition on Abraham Lincoln's relationship to conservatism and the use of his "legacy" by politicians.[118] Buckley's ruminations are particularly significant because in his quixotic campaign he attacked the ideas of the more liberal Republican candidate, John Lindsay (if not liberalism itself), who attempted to equate his ideas and policies with Lincoln's. Lindsay frequently referred to the Republican Party as the "Party of Lincoln," the implication being of course that Lindsay—and moderate Republicans— stood squarely in the tradition of Abraham Lincoln's politics and leadership. Clearly irritated by such a stance, Buckley questioned Lindsay's contention at length in *The Unmaking of a Mayor*. At first Buckley forgave Lindsay his Lincoln "name-dropping," for that, Buckley wearily conceded, "is standard practice among politicians."[119] Nevertheless, Buckley opined, "serious students of politics will want, if only for the academic exercise, to go beyond political opportunism to probe the nexus that allegedly binds the old hero and his presumptive heir."[120]

Buckley challenged Lindsay's claim to be Lincoln's political heir on several grounds. "Abraham Lincoln was an infinitely complicated figure," he conceded, "and learned debate still rages about the exact nature of his

contributions to the formulation of American political philosophy."[121] Of
course, Buckley was keenly aware of this raging debate because some of
it took place within the pages of the magazine he founded and edited, *National Review.* In Buckley's view it was not exactly clear what politicians
meant when they claimed to be heirs to the Lincoln tradition, and Buckley
was, if nothing else, a stickler for precision in language. He questioned
whether Lincoln was a politician "whose thought, at whatever moment
in history it is consulted, immediately suggests an appropriate approach
to a contemporary problem." He therefore doubted if Lindsay, or any
politician for that matter, could legitimately claim to stand in the Lincoln
tradition because it was such a protean phenomenon. To be sure, Buckley
wrote, "one thing a self-professed Lincolnian cannot be, is a defender of
slavery."[122] He referenced the recent dispute between Meyer and Jaffa in
National Review as evidence that if two such self-proclaimed conservatives
disagreed so vehemently about Lincoln's place within the conservative
pantheon, any politician, including John Lindsay, had to show precisely
where he stood in the Lincoln tradition. At this task, Buckley held, Lindsay
had failed miserably.

Buckley drew a sharp distinction between Lindsay, a moderate Republican, and conservatism. He did so by associating Lincoln, and by inference
Lindsay, with Democrats. He described Lindsay's assertions to be Lincoln's
heir "proprietary, historically snobbish, diffuse, and sentimentalized . . .
not a little evasive [and] intellectually incoherent."[123] Buckley contrasted
Lindsay's political positions with the historical Lincoln by writing that
"Lincoln's party is not the party of civil rights, according to the modern
understanding of civil rights—the Democratic party clearly deserves the
title."[124] Moreover, he declared, no conservative could be pleased with
"Lincoln's executive highhandedness during the Civil War" in suspending
habeas corpus or the methods he used to free the slaves "without either
compensation or due process."[125] Nor, according to *National Review's* editor, was Lincoln "an avid protector of the person and his liberties against
the majority," although he thought Lincoln could conceivably be forgiven
on this point because "he was perhaps the most powerful advocate in
history of human equality as the necessary basis for self-government."[126]
Finally, Lincoln was simply too busy trying to win the war—a point many
of Lincoln's antagonists often ignored—to "concern himself with the . . .
threat of big business, or, in any systematic way, with the federal bureaucracy, and its bearing on human rights. And certainly Lincoln had no opportunity to weigh the rights of individuals over against those of labor

union monopolies."[127] At this point Buckley quoted words attributed to Abraham Lincoln (words in fact Lincoln never uttered, although Buckley was perhaps unaware of this) to the effect that Lincoln would oppose "redistributionism" and "compulsory welfarism."[128] In Buckley's view the attempts by Lindsay to portray himself and, by implication, the contemporary Republican Party as Lincoln's rightful heirs in matters of civil rights, executive power, majority rule, and the rights of labor were nothing more than "a romantic pursuit."[129] Still, in disassociating American conservatism from Lincoln, Lindsay, and moderate Republicanism, Buckley conceded that the Lincoln image was of continuing significance in American life, and it appears he thought that linking the sixteenth president with the Democratic Party, at least on matters of race and federal power, was an effective tactic. Given the political realignment that occurred in the United States after 1965 as the white South allied itself more with the Republican rather than the Democratic Party on such issues, Buckley no doubt was correct.

Indeed, Buckley asserted that Lincoln's racial attitudes "must be an embarrassing memory for Lindsay." To be sure, Buckley repeated the idea that "as a defender of the metaphysical proposition that men are equal, Lincoln was the greatest postbiblical political philosopher." But then, anticipating by two years some of the Lincoln criticism offered by African American writer Lerone Bennett, Buckley cited Lincoln's words from the Charleston debate with Stephen Douglas as evidence that "concerning the big contemporary issues, Lincoln was not only, according to current terminology, a segregationist but also a racist" and averred that if there were a Lincoln tradition on race and segregation, it "clearly suggests that the states should retain a measure of authority respecting at least some of the questions nowadays pre-empted in the various civil rights bills by the federal government."[130] Like many of Lincoln's previous foes, especially unreconstructed Confederates, Buckley froze Lincoln's racial utterances in 1858 in order to reinforce opposition to recent federal civil rights laws. In addition, he inexcusably failed to cite Jaffa's argument in *Crisis* (an argument with which he was almost certainly familiar, as editor of *National Review*) that the evidence for Lincoln being a racist was more ambiguous than the president's opponents had previously allowed. Nor did the former mayoral candidate discuss Lincoln's advocacy of black suffrage, albeit limited, in 1865. Still, at the end of his reflections Buckley maintained that "at the profoundest level, Lincoln was a moralist; and as such outside the positivist and relativist tradition of contemporary social thought and jurisprudence . . . Lincoln's principal metapolitical insight was that for *transcendent reasons* logically explicable, men cannot be considered *other* than equal." Buckley quoted Richard Weaver's essay "The Ethics of Rhetoric" to conclude that Lincoln was a statesman of a high order and "fell in the tradition of natural law, rather than of the positivism that modern liberalism absolutely depends upon." "Beyond that towering point," Buckley declared, "Lincoln is up for grabs and has been claimed as a patron by any number of ideological opportunists," among them John Lindsay.[131]

Buckley's reflections were the most extended public disquisition conservatives had ever received (or ever would receive) about Abraham Lincoln from the father of their movement. Although he was at times harsh, inaccurate, and imperceptive in his assessment of the sixteenth president or the need for federal civil rights legislation, in the ensuing decades Buckley sensed that public loathing of Lincoln was politically toxic. Influenced by Harry Jaffa, whose emphasis on Lincoln's natural rights thinking meshed nicely with his devout Catholicism and its natural law philosophy, Buckley's attitude toward Lincoln moderated with age, and he became more appreciative of the president's political and linguistic gifts. His anthology of American conservatism, *Did You Ever See a Dream Walking? American Conservative Thought in the Twentieth Century* (1970), contained hardly a negative word about Lincoln. Indeed, a piece by Jaffa entitled "On the Nature of Civil and Religious Liberty" praised Lincoln, while there was nothing from Frank Meyer that offered an opposite viewpoint. An updated anthology published in 1988 contained Jaffa's essay "Equality as a Conservative Principle," and the new introduction, penned by Charles R. Kesler, reflected Jaffa's influence. Buckley's collected volume of speeches, *Let Us Talk of Many Things: The Collected Speeches* (2000), exhibited no Lincoln hatred, nor did his autobiography *Miles Gone By: A Literary Autobiography* (2004). And shortly before his death, Buckley granted that "I once believed we could evolve our way up from Jim Crow. I was wrong: federal intervention was necessary," an outlook that may have contributed to his softened stance on Lincoln.[132] Still, if Buckley had somehow managed in the Cold War era, to a large extent at the behest of Frank Meyer's urging, a type of fusion between traditionalists and libertarians within the conservative movement, then that union would break apart in the early years of the Reagan administration, once conservatives acquired power. Abraham Lincoln would in fact be at the center of why traditional conservatives, libertarians, and neoconservatives were unable to maintain an intellectual and political union in the Reagan years. With Reagan's ascension to the presidency, open criticism of Lincoln within the conservative movement became less acceptable, as Lincoln's detractors, to their vexation, discovered.

The story of the breakup of conservative unity begins in the 1970s, when Harry Jaffa crossed intellectual swords over Lincoln with a southern conservative, M. E. Bradford (1934–1993), a professor of literature at the University of Dallas, a Catholic institution. Bradford began attacking Lincoln that decade, and he directly challenged Jaffa's ideas a few short years later, with Jaffa vigorously counterpunching in a decades-long exchange over the Lincoln legacy in American life. In addition to being one of the most prominent Lincoln critics in the postwar era, Bradford was a proud intellectual descendant of the Agrarians, especially Donald Davidson, a notable Faulkner scholar, and much esteemed by his intellectual compatriots.[133] He was the author of numerous books, including *A Better Guide than Reason: Studies in the American Revolution* (1979), *Generations of the Faithful Heart* (1982), *Remembering Who We Are: Observations of a Southern Conservative* (1985), and *The Reactionary Imperative: Essays Literary and Political* (1990). Indeed, Bradford proudly labeled himself a reactionary: "Reaction is a necessary term in the intellectual context we inhabit late in the twentieth century. Merely to conserve is sometimes to perpetuate what is outrageous."[134]

Bradford launched his fusillade upon Lincoln's legacy in 1971 with an article in *Triumph* magazine, a Catholic periodical edited by L. Brent Bozell, William F. Buckley Jr.'s brother-in-law and coauthor of *McCarthy and His Enemies*. Bradford focused his Lincoln criticism, then and later, on the harmful consequences of Lincoln's rhetoric. Writing in the context of the controversies over the civil rights movement, Vietnam, and the apparent breakdown of the heretofore racially based American social order, Bradford claimed: "We have reached a point where easy assumptions about our nature and destiny [American exceptionalism] are no longer convincing. . . . We are, in short, prepared as never before to doubt our secularized eschatology."[135] What better way to express such skepticism, Bradford apparently thought, than to attack the central figure of American history, Abraham Lincoln? In his *Triumph* essay Bradford, like Willmoore Kendall before him, concentrated his intellectual onslaught on Lincoln's Gettysburg Address, declaring that "what the Emancipator accomplished by confirming the nation in (or 'institutionalizing') an erroneous understanding of the Declaration of Independence made possible that ultimate elevation of that same error in Mrs. Julia Ward Howe's 'war song' and set us forever 'trampling out the grapes of wrath.'"[136] He compared Lincoln's leadership to an "Oriental despotism" and called his Gettysburg speech "an advance from discourse of what is *believed to be* into an assertion of what *must be and yet forever remain in the process of becoming.*"[137] Bradford thought a good part of the address's power came from its biblical rhetoric, but that was also its chief problem, for "Lincoln's strategy in the first sentence at Gettysburg is to lift beyond discourse, away from the political and into the 'moral' order, what stands in the Declaration (despite its reference to the Deist's 'Creator') to be proved and argued."[138] From Bradford's standpoint Lincoln had founded a "political religion," with ghastly consequences for the United States.

Later in 1971, in a continuation of his first *Triumph* article, Bradford stressed the link between the Gettysburg Address and Howe's "Battle Hymn of the Republic."[139] Echoing Edmund Wilson's argument in *Patriotic Gore,* Bradford claimed "total power" characterized the "Battle Hymn," which, in his words, contained "a touch of hysteria," if not blasphemy, in its linkage of a "socio-political goal ('freedom' for blacks, evidently) with the sacrifice of the Cross."[140] According to Bradford, it was a tragedy that "we are at ease in this Zion because she and Lincoln, and the trends they bespoke, accomplished their objectives . . . the 'Battle Hymn' . . . is now *our* 'orthodoxy'—even in the most conservative circles."[141] This should make us all "shudder" because "the rhetoric of gnostic hope can produce only the politics of discontent," as recent events in America, he believed, proved to be the case.[142]

A few years later, in a more direct attack on Harry Jaffa, Bradford wrote of "Lincoln's lasting and terrible impact on the nation's destiny," again for his distortions of the Declaration of Independence and Jefferson's phrase "all men are created equal." Bradford was responding to the article published by Jaffa in the *Loyola Law Review* in 1975 entitled "Equality as a Conservative Principle," a piece that Bradford accurately described as "itself a critique of *The Basic Symbols of the American Political Tradition* by Willmoore Kendall and George W. Carey."[143] In that essay Jaffa had conceded that the North and the South fought for certain principles, which was of course part of the inherent tragedy of the conflict, but he also provocatively stated, "Let us have no foolishness about both sides being right," and made it clear he agreed with Frederick Douglass in thinking the South wrong in the Civil War.[144] Regarding Kendall's earlier suggestion that Lincoln should have proposed compensated emancipation in 1860, Jaffa explained that "to have proposed emancipation in 1860 or 1861, would have been regarded as an act of bad faith . . . it would have been a firebrand."[145] In addition, Jaffa observed, correctly, that Lincoln *did* propose compensated emancipation plans during the war and such plans were decisively rejected by white slaveholders in the border states. Finally, regarding secession, "it was the Northern Democrats no less than the Republicans who shared" the Republican attitude toward secession, and "the overwhelming majority of Democrats, led by Douglas, opposed secession as much as Lincoln."[146]

But Jaffa's arguments in 1975 were mere preliminaries to his main point, which was that equality was a principle that conservatives could embrace without betraying the American founders. Slavery, he maintained, was especially pernicious because it treated all members of "a certain class as having their worth determined by their membership in that class. This is equally the root of contemporary totalitarianism. To be elevated, or regarded as worthy, because one is white, proletarian, or Aryan, or to be degraded and scorned as a Negro, a capitalist, or a Jew, does not involve any distinction of principle."[147] From Jaffa's standpoint it was not Lincoln who was the real totalitarian, or centralizer, but rather southern slaveholders intent on holding men as property based on their membership in an allegedly inferior race of human beings: "Do not all the totalitarian slave states of our time rest upon theoretical propositions in which race or class differences delude some men to consider themselves superhuman?" Jaffa asked his fellow conservatives. "And does not this delusion lie at the root of their bestiality? Is it not this that makes them think that, for the sake of the classless society, or the thousand year Reich, everything is permitted to them? Surely Abraham Lincoln was right when he said that the doctrine of human equality was 'the father of all moral principle [among] us.'"[148] It was at once a forceful attack on decades of Lost Cause apologetics and a complete reordering of conservative philosophical and political priorities about Abraham Lincoln, if not conservatism itself.

Bradford could not let Jaffa's remarks go unanswered without his strain of conservatism, if not his entire neo-Confederate worldview, being discredited. He chose the pages of *Modern Age,* Russell Kirk's highbrow conservative quarterly, for his counterblast: "Let us have no foolishness indeed. . . . Equality, with the capital 'E'—is the antonym of every legitimate conservative principle . . . there is no man equal to any other, except perhaps in the special and politically untranslatable, understanding of the Deity. *Not intellectually or physically or economically or even morally. Not equal!*"[149] In his dual assault on Jaffa and Lincoln, Bradford argued that their misinterpretation of the Declaration resulted in part "from the

habit of reading legal, poetic, and rhetorical documents as if they were
bits of revealed truth or statements of systematic thought. My objections
derive primarily from those antirationalist realms of discourse."[150] Accordingly, he wrote, "it is my view that the Declaration of Independence is not
very revolutionary at all. Nor the Revolution itself. Nor the Constitution.
Only Mr. Lincoln and those who gave him support both in his day and
in the following century."[151] Continuing his verbal onslaught, Bradford
exclaimed that Lincoln's interpretation of the Declaration was "moralistic,
[a] verbally disguised instrument which Lincoln invented may indeed be
the most revolutionary force in the modern world: a pure gnostic force."
Bradford fervently believed, as did Kendall before him, that Lincoln was
an American Caesar and called his 1858 "House Divided" speech "a Puritan
declaration of war" that was "in league with Satan" and "that what Lincoln
did to preserve the Union by expanding and enshrining equality" left a
horrific legacy for the nation.[152]

Bradford persisted with such rhetoric for over a decade, charging that
Lincoln was as bad as any modern dictator. "The final Lincoln is the worst,"
he asserted. "For by him the real is defined in terms of what is yet to come,
and the meaning of the present lies in its pointing hither. This posture,
when linked to one of the regnant abstractions of modern politics, can
have no other result than a totalitarian order. In its train it has left us, as a
nation, with a series of almost insoluble problems in our social, economic,
and political policy, to say nothing of our foreign affairs: with a series of
promises impossible to keep."[153] In one of the footnotes to his "Heresy of
Equality" essay, Bradford made the rather extraordinary claim that Lincoln should be compared to Otto von Bismarck, Vladimir Lenin (literary
critic Edmund Wilson [1895–1972] had first compared Lincoln to these
two men in 1962), and Adolf Hitler.[154] No doubt, such rhetorical comparisons were remarkable, but what stunned Jaffa was Bradford's affection
for the antebellum South and his infrequent references to the institution
of slavery in his essays. It was almost as if the antebellum South was not
based upon slave labor—as Jaffa said, a totalitarian form of government
if there ever was one—but upon a moonlight and magnolias version of the
region drawn from *Gone with the Wind* and similar nostalgic versions of
antebellum southern society. Bradford's hatred for Lincoln, in addition to
his unoriginal defense of an antebellum South that had never truly existed,
coupled with his repetition of the arguments of previous adversaries of
the president, was contemptuous of the modern, pluralistic America tak-

ing shape by the 1980s. Such an illiberal nostalgia, at least from Jaffa's viewpoint, was the very antithesis of conservatism.[155]

Relishing the controversy, Jaffa countered Bradford's essay with a lengthy piece in *Modern Age* entitled "Equality, Justice, and the American Revolution: In Reply to Bradford's 'The Heresy of Equality.'"[156] At first Jaffa went on the philosophical attack, claiming that "equality is a conservative principle because justice is conservative, and equality is the principle of justice. Where exchanges are just—that is, where one party does not over-reach the other—and where distributions are just—that is, where rewards are proportioned to merit—men tend to become friends."[157] Moving from the philosophical to the historical realm, Jaffa argued that the American Revolution was indeed radical in the sense that it intended to get rid of "the rule of priests and kings, and of priestly kings, and the legal privileges of hereditary orders generally, [and] were regarded by our Founders as elements of unjust inequality in all European constitutions, including the British."[158] Such a hierarchical—and racially based—order was of course precisely what antebellum slaveholders, and possibly Bradford, wanted to conserve. Warming to his theme, Jaffa said Bradford's view of the Dec-laration was no different than "the Marxist and Black Power historians of recent years, who have all along maintained that the Declaration was a bourgeois or racist document, never intended to be understood in the universalistic sense in which it is expressed."[159] At this point, and by way of contrast, Jaffa closely examined Alexander H. Stephens's "Cornerstone" speech, an address Jaffa described as "a comprehensive reply" to Lincoln and the most "authentic" view of Confederate political philosophy ever given because it was issued in the full "flush of its confidence" that they would win independence and establish a slaveholding republic. As Jaffa made clear, not one of the founders of the Confederacy had any problem with equality "as far as white men are concerned," but what distinguished the Confederacy was its insistence that the United States' founders were wrong and did not intend for the Declaration to include blacks. Stephens had insisted the new Confederate nation discovered for mankind the truth of "the inferiority of the Negro race" and was consequently based on the most modern and scientific principles. Jaffa therefore concluded it was not Lincoln who should be compared to Hitler but Stephens and other Confederate leaders, for whom natural rights were "primarily and essentially the rights of the master race. And the Confederate States of America represented the first time in human history that a doctrine of a master race was fully and systematically set forth as the ground of a regime. More precisely, it was the first time that such a doctrine was set forth on the authority of modern science. It was this authority that made it so persuasive and so pernicious."[160]

A few years later, in 1981, Bradford's excoriations of Lincoln had personal and public consequences when he was nominated by President Ronald Reagan to be the chairman of the National Endowment for the Humanities (NEH). According to the *New York Times,* Bradford's appointment was seen as "a concession to conservative supporters of President Reagan . . . angered by his choice of Judge Sandra Day O'Connor as an Associate Justice of the Supreme Court."[161] Sponsored for the NEH post by Republican senators Jesse Helms from North Carolina and John Tower from Texas and supported by Harry Jaffa, Bradford's nomination ran into immediate trouble with conservatives, or neoconservatives, upset with his views on Abraham Lincoln and possibly for his previous support of Alabama governor George Wallace's campaign for president.[162] Neoconservatives, many of whom were former liberals, staunchly anticommunist, and not reflexively antigovernment, had no use for Bradford's critique. Consistent with the American tradition of groups holding divergent viewpoints toward Lincoln within their own movement, Bradford's writings were scrutinized and sharply criticized by such conservatives.[163] Although not a neoconservative himself, the influential *Newsweek* columnist and television commentator George Will encapsulated the views of many about Bradford after the University of Dallas professor's nomination had been derailed. In a *Washington Post* column entitled "A Shrill Assault on Mr. Lincoln," Will questioned if someone with Bradford's opinions was fit to be chairman of the NEH. "Bradfordites should contritely retire to a quiet corner and consider the entertaining enquiries that would have enlivened any confirmation hearings of their choice," Will advised. He imagined senators questioning the Texan on such matters as why Bradford compared Lincoln to Hitler or how exactly blacks having their inalienable rights protected "undermined our inherited constitutional system."[164] Of course, Will failed to note that the second point was precisely what Americans, especially conservative opponents of Lincoln, had argued for years regarding black equality. Bradford's view of Lincoln, Will thought, "involves . . . a profoundly mistaken moral judgment about what Lincoln did."[165] Although Will clearly disagreed with Bradford's views, he also foresaw that the controversy required conservatives to eradicate public criticism of Lincoln from their movement. "Political eccentrics can contribute to the public stock of harmless pleasure," he counseled, "but it is not harmless for a great political party to mock its noble past."[166] William Bennett, who held a doctorate in political philosophy from the University of Texas, received the nomination, to considerable controversy, instead of Bradford.[167]

Bradford may have been denied the NEH post, but he was not going to cut and run to Texas without responding to his critics. In the *Washington Post* he unapologetically delivered a hostile parting shot to George Will, citing past and present enemies of Lincoln as authorities for his stance:

> Most of his quotations from my work on Lincoln are reflections of academic commonplaces—the books and essays of Edgar Lee Masters, Donald W. Riddle, Willmoore Kendall, Edmund Wilson, Gottfried Dietze, and Will's one-time editor [at *National Review*], the late Frank Meyer. My contribution to the critique has been an analysis of Lincoln's rhetoric, an idiom that contributed to the death of 600,000 American boys. I have also spoken of Lincoln's use of troops to win elections, the graft of his administration, his abuse under the war powers of his political opponents in the North, his claims to intimacy with the divine will (a limited link to such political demigods as Napoleon, Lenin and Hitler) and his willingness to waste Northern lives in search of a Republican general to command his armies.[168]

The brouhaha over the Bradford nomination was an interesting and illuminating controversy, for it pointed to a basic and perhaps irresolvable tension within conservatism itself. As historian Eric Foner astutely put it, the dispute was not simply an argument about Lincoln but a larger one about "states' rights, morality in government, and race" and some fundamental problems within conservatism that the controversy exposed.[169] Mainstream conservatives were suspicious of exercising state power at home but not abroad in the Cold War fight against communism. Similarly, they extolled the virtues of capitalism yet to an extent ignored how it undermined traditional communities. "Rather than freeing the nation from Lincoln's legacy," Foner maintained, "modern conservatism has embraced the worst parts of Lincoln's heritage while abandoning the best. After all, the aspiring Illinois politico of the 1850s who pandered to the racial prejudices of his audience had, by the end of the Civil War, arrived at a remarkable sensitivity to the plight of blacks in American society. The growth of Lincoln's vision was the hallmark of his Presidency. Will his Republican descendants prove as capable of a broadening and humanizing of their own views," Foner asked, "or will they irrevocably cut themselves loose from the heritage Lincoln bequeathed them?"[170] Like their godfather William F. Buckley Jr., most conservatives indeed broadened and humanized their stance toward Lincoln—and federal power—but not without consequence to their political unity.

In fact, Bradford's denial of the chairmanship of the NEH caused long-lasting bitterness within the conservative movement. It foreshadowed, if not caused, a future split within conservatism itself between, as English professor Benjamin B. Alexander observed, "the thinkers of the old right like Bradford, who were rooted in the prescriptive conservatism of Edmund Burke and Samuel Johnson, versus the neoconservative thinkers, who enshrined Lincoln as the paragon of presidents and extended the adoration to the mythic iconography of Martin Luther King."[171] In his collection of essays *Beautiful Losers: Essays on the Failure of American Conservatism* (1993) traditional conservative and newspaper columnist Samuel Francis, who later maintained that "neither 'slavery' nor 'racism' as an institution is a sin," explained that "the bitterness felt by many Old Rightists at Bennett's finally winning the nomination was due not so much to losing the post for their own candidate as to what they regarded (accurately, in my view) as a neoconservative smear campaign against Bradford that insinuated he was, among other things, a Nazi sympathizer rather than an unreconstructed southern conservative who publicly and repeatedly criticized Abraham Lincoln."[172] Paul Gottfried, a conservative historian, remarked upon the Texan's death that "the attacks leveled against Bradford probably prompted the conservative wars." Later he bemoaned Buckley's intervention with Reagan to nominate Bennett instead of Bradford.[173] What these conservatives—or "paleoconservatives," as they came to be called—did not understand, it seemed, were the political realities under which Reagan had to maneuver and the way political capital must be conserved. Reagan had frequently been accused by his critics of being a racist, or at the very least as a candidate who stoked racial fears (he had launched his 1980 presidential campaign from Philadelphia, Mississippi, located in the county where three civil rights workers had been murdered in the 1960s), and he wanted to implement an agenda seemingly at odds with nearly a half-century of federal fiscal and social policy. There was simply no way the newly elected president was going to supply his enemies with the political ammunition with which to attack him by nominating such a critic of Abraham Lincoln to a relatively insignificant post within the federal government.[174]

Although Bradford remained unapologetic about his views, there are clear indications he was stung by the whole affair.[175] He nevertheless continued criticizing Lincoln until his death in the 1990s, although in venues other than *National Review.* Indeed, at one Lincoln conference held in Gettysburg, Pennsylvania, in 1984, Bradford claimed that Lincoln's "way of freeing the slaves—at bayonet point, in the midst of war, confined in a South angry and without means, with no federal plan for an intermediate period of apprenticeship in freedom in some respects is to blame for the nation's continuing racial problems."[176] One year later, in 1985, he renewed his ongoing spat with Harry Jaffa in the pages of the *American Spectator,* another conservative journal, with a spirited response to Jaffa's criticism that it was the Confederates who were racist and based their views on new science; rather, he thought, such views were more likely to be found in the North than the South. Moreover, Alexander Stephens's "Cornerstone" speech, Bradford averred, was hardly representative of southern public opinion, for Jefferson Davis had allegedly condemned it. What Bradford failed to point out was that leading Confederates did not disagree with the substance of what Stephens said as much as they considered it impolitic.[177] After undergoing heart surgery in March 1993, Bradford died unexpectedly and received accolades from colleagues for being a "first-rate scholar" and a "popular professor with black students" at the University of Dallas.[178] Jeffrey Hart called his death "a very large loss to American letters" and thought his criticism of Lincoln was "long and valuable" because he was asking essential questions about "whether Lincoln was a revolutionary who had fundamentally changed the Constitution" and doing so "with great good humor and intellectual skill."[179] Harry Jaffa also wrote a generous review of Bradford about their Lincoln wars, one he hoped they could continue in another life.[180]

The Bradford controversy was significant for another reason: namely, Bradford was but one figure, a particularly notable one to be sure, in a long, continuous, antiliberal tradition of white southern Christians, many of whom were Lincoln critics, all of whom interpreted the Civil War as a war between a Christian Confederacy and an allegedly atheist or unorthodox North. From southern antebellum theologians Robert Lewis Dabney, James Henley Thornwell, and Benjamin Morgan Palmer to Albert Taylor Bledsoe, Mary Carter, Mildred Lewis Rutherford, David Rankin Barbee, to Bradford, such thinkers portrayed the Confederate States of America in reverential, even Christian, terms while the North, and Abraham Lincoln, were depicted negatively as American Jacobins, fanatics, and atheists.[181]

A few years after the Bradford affair concluded, Mississippian Trent Lott told *Southern Partisan* magazine that "the 1984 Republican platform, all the ideas we supported there—from tax policy, to foreign policy; from individual rights, to neighborhood security—are things that Jefferson Davis and his people believed in."[182] But by the end of the Cold War in 1989, or shortly thereafter, Bradford's brand of ill will toward Lincoln had been largely eliminated or, more accurately, momentarily driven underground from mainstream conservatism. Conservatism had been redefined, at least in its public stance toward Lincoln, by Harry Jaffa.[183] Indeed, although *National Review*'s cover in December 1989 displayed Lincoln's visage with the caption "Dishonest Abe: A New Look at the Lincoln Myth," accompanied by a hard-hitting analysis of Lincoln's speeches by Thomas Fleming, the piece was rebutted by Jaffa a little over a month later, and Bradford disassociated himself from Buckley and the magazine in 1991, when his critical review of James MacPherson's *Abraham Lincoln and the Second American Revolution* (1991) was not published, according to Bradford, out of fear that "it might be taken as an expression of the magazine's editorial philosophy."[184] Fleming and Bradford subsequently published their hostility to Lincoln in other periodicals, such as *Chronicles: A Magazine of American Culture* and *Southern Partisan,* and found other allies such as the anarcho-capitalist Murray Rothbard. On the centennial of Lincoln's birth in 2009, *National Review* pictured Lincoln on its front cover with an admiring article inside the magazine by historian Allen Guelzo extolling Lincoln's conservative virtues.[185] Still, as Lott's comments showed, ideas that displayed sympathy with the Confederacy were never eliminated entirely from the conservative movement, if for no other reason than "considerations of strategy and tactics."[186] Indeed, Lott became the Senate majority leader *after* equating Jefferson Davis's political philosophy with the Republican Party's, suggesting that it remained acceptable to privately hold and express negative opinions about the Civil War president. Public expression of hatred for Lincoln would not be tolerated unless the political atmosphere altered considerably.

Changing political realities contributed to another historic shift in postwar opposition to Lincoln, as some liberals, or the New Left, reevaluated Lincoln's presidency in light of ongoing American poverty, the civil rights movement, and the Vietnam War. Their criticism pointed to a tenuous merger of conservative Lost Cause views of the Civil War as the first in a long line of American imperialist wars with leftist disenchantment with the American empire, the basis for which, some believed, was laid in the North's victory over the Confederacy. Postwar Lincoln criticism on the Left dated from Richard Hofstadter's 1948 essay delineating the Emancipation

Proclamation's shortcomings and historian Ralph Korngold's *Two Friends of Man: The Story of William Lloyd Garrison and Wendell Phillips and Their Relationship with Abraham Lincoln* (1950), in which Korngold argued that the real heroes of the Civil War were just as much—if not more—abolitionists such as Garrison and Phillips rather than Abraham Lincoln. Indeed, Korngold's book held that Lincoln was not a friend of the slave; he was, in fact, a colonizationist until the end of his life and therefore was little more than a timid and reluctant emancipator.[187] A few short years later, in 1957, Donald Riddle published a sharply critical volume entitled *Congressman Abraham Lincoln*. Even though it is difficult to ascertain Riddle's precise political leanings, his book nonetheless contributed to the overall negative view of Lincoln being adopted by his detractors (recall that M. E. Bradford had cited Riddle's work). He described Lincoln as a cynical, scheming, politician who did not truly care about slavery's eradication but capitalized on the controversy surrounding it in the 1850s as a way to satiate his political ambitions. "He was using the slavery issue," Riddle averred, "conveniently presented by the Kansas-Nebraska Act, to advance his own political standing. He was using the act to run for office."[188] Such contemptuous portrayals of Lincoln's political and racial inadequacies gave license to authors on the Left to explore Lincoln's allegedly pernicious legacy in domestic and foreign matters.

In the middle of the Civil War centennial, noted literary critic Edmund Wilson (1895–1972) published *Patriotic Gore: Studies in the Literature of the Civil War* (1962), one of the most original works ever published on the conflict. Wilson's father was a lawyer, subject to fits of depression, and a great admirer of Abraham Lincoln, apparently giving speeches from time to time on Lincoln as the "Great Commoner."[189] Wilson himself wrote for various magazines upon graduating from Princeton University, including *Vanity Fair,* and he helped edit the *New Republic* from 1925 to 1931, after previously serving in Europe during World War I.[190] A prolific author and critic and a man of the Left, by 1962 Wilson was disillusioned with the Cold War and with American militarism and adventurism abroad, and these disillusionments were evident in his treatment of Abraham Lincoln in *Patriotic Gore.* The book also symbolized how Lincoln's critics on both the Right and the Left found common cause in their opposition to American imperialism. Wilson's book was not a standard narrative history; rather, it was a brilliant portrait, or thirty portraits to be more exact, of northerners and southerners before, during, and after the conflict and the literature and myths they created about the Civil War.[191]

In the introduction to *Patriotic Gore* Wilson delineated the major themes
of the volume. First, of course, was Wilson's admiration for the artistic
quality of the people under the examination of his literary microscope.
"Has there ever been another historical crisis of the magnitude of 1861–65
in which so many people were articulate?" Wilson queried.[192] Second,
although Wilson was captivated by the era's writers, he also thought that
"having myself lived through a couple of world wars and having read a
certain amount of history, I am no longer disposed to take very seriously
the professions of 'war aims' that nations make."[193] Wilson's readers were
alerted early to his cynicism and that this volume—among the hundreds,
if not thousands, that have been written about the Civil War—might be
different, if for no other reason than the author would perhaps bring a
certain skepticism to Lincoln's writings. Third, Wilson took a biological
view of the conflict, writing that what distinguished man from other
species was "that man has succeeded in cultivating enough of what he
calls 'morality' and 'reason' to justify what he is doing in terms of what
he calls 'virtue' and 'civilization.' Hence the self-assertive sound which he
utters when he is fighting and swallowing others: the songs about glory
and God, the speeches about national ideals, the demonstrations of logical ideologies."[194] Clearly, Wilson was speaking here not only of the Civil
War and its centennial but of his disenchantment with Cold War America,
the American empire, the country's general historical amnesia regarding
American expansionism, and its sham conflict with the Soviet Union.[195] It
was difficult to label Wilson as an unreconstructed Confederate, although
Patriotic Gore in places echoed the arguments of Albert Taylor Bledsoe.
In fact, it contained an incredibly sympathetic chapter—some thought it
bordered on a spirited defense—on Alexander Stephens.[196]

Wilson's introductory observations about Lincoln and the comparisons
he made with political leaders from countries outside the United States
were intriguing, if somewhat unoriginal. Claiming that the eradication of
slavery was a "pseudo-moral" issue for the North in the Civil War, Wilson
preferred to see the Confederacy's defeat as just another form of American
imperialism. "The North's determination to preserve the Union was simply
the form that the power drive now took," he declared.[197] Accordingly, Wilson argued that in order to truly understand Lincoln, Americans must see
him "in connection with the other leaders [around the world] who have
been engaged in similar tasks."[198] Who did Wilson have in mind? "The chief
of these leaders have been Bismarck and Lenin. They with Lincoln have

presided over the unifications of the three great new modern powers."
Wilson made several striking comparisons between the three men:

> Each became a hero for the people who gave their allegiance to the state he
> established. (I remember how shocked I was when, on a visit in my child-
> hood to my Virginia cousins, I heard them refer to Lincoln as a "bloody
> tyrant."). . . . Lincoln and Bismarck and Lenin were all men of unusual
> intellect and formidable tenacity of character, of historical imagination
> combined with powerful will. They were all, in their several ways, ideal-
> ists, who put their ideals before everything else. . . . None liked to deal in
> demagogy and none cared for official pomp. . . . Each established a strong
> central government over hitherto loosely coordinated peoples. . . . Each of
> these statesmen was confident that he was acting out the purpose of a force
> greater than himself. Each of these men, through the pressure of the power
> which he found himself exercising, became an uncompromising dictator,
> and each was succeeded by agencies which continued to exercise this power
> and manipulate the peoples he had been unifying in a stupid, despotic and
> unscrupulous fashion, so that all the bad potentialities of the policies he had
> initiated were realized, after his removal, in the most undesirable way.[199]

Ignoring those enemies before him who *had* argued that Lincoln was a
dictator, Wilson held that Americans had never thought of Lincoln in precisely this way, and in a decade of historical forgetting about the tragedy of
the conflict, he claimed he was going to make Americans remember what
the Civil War was truly about by examining its major military, political,
and literary figures.[200]

Of course, Abraham Lincoln unified all three categories in his role as
commander in chief, a democratically elected president attempting to
persuade Americans—with unprecedented literary skill among American politicians—that they needed to continue fighting a war that was not
only dividing but also slaughtering the country. The essay on Lincoln in
Patriotic Gore was a central part of the work. Wilson began his Lincoln
chapter by noting Alexander Stephens's postwar remark that for Lincoln
the Union "had risen to the sublimity of religious mysticism."[201] Wilson
noted the irony of Stephens's observation because for most of his life, at
least prior to the Civil War, Lincoln had been a "free-thinker" more associated with skeptics such as "Voltaire, Volney and Tom Paine" rather
than Jesus and Christianity.[202] Wilson contrasted such skepticism with
Lincoln's later speeches, especially the Second Inaugural, in which Lincoln meditated openly and ambivalently about the purposes of God in

the bloody war. Wilson observed the change in Lincoln, writing that "it is nevertheless quite clear that he himself came to see the conflict in a light more religious, in more and more Scriptural terms, under a more and more apocalyptic aspect" than before. Or, more acutely, "we are far here from Herndon's office, closer to Harriet Beecher Stowe."[203]

But this was all really a preliminary to Wilson's unique, if not central, contention that Lincoln understood the Civil War as *the* crisis in American history and saw himself as the central figure in the crisis—and had thought so for a very long time indeed. Wilson, unlike virtually every Lincoln scholar who preceded him but somewhat in keeping with Bledsoe's stance, believed the key to Lincoln's self-understanding lay in a heretofore little-investigated speech Lincoln gave in January 1838, twenty-three years before Confederates fired on Fort Sumter, to the Young Men's Lyceum of Springfield, Illinois, entitled "The Perpetuation of Our Political Institutions." Shortly after the murder of abolitionist Elijah Lovejoy in Alton, Illinois, in 1837, Lincoln told his audience that there was certainly no external threat to the United States: "At what point then is the approach of danger to be expected? I answer, if it ever reach us, it must spring up amongst us. It cannot come from abroad. If destruction be our lot, we must ourselves be its author and finisher. As a nation of freemen, we must live through all time, or die by suicide."[204] What clearly concerned Lincoln was that because the American Revolution was finished, successfully established, and the founding generation dead, what could his generation do to build on the success of the founders? It was at this point, Wilson believed, that Lincoln surprised the audience and unwittingly described himself:

> Towering genius disdains a beaten path. It seeks regions hitherto unexplored. It sees no distinction in adding story to story, upon the monuments of fame, erected to the memory of others. It denies that it is glory enough to serve under any chief. It scorns to tread in the footsteps of any predecessor, however illustrious. It thirsts and burns for distinction; and, if possible, it will have it, whether at the expense of emancipating slaves, or enslaving freemen. Is it unreasonable then to expect, that some man possessed of the loftiest genius, coupled with ambition sufficient to push it to its utmost stretch, will at some time, spring up among us? And when such a one does, it will require the people to be united with each other, attached to the government and laws, and generally intelligent, to successfully frustrate his designs.[205]

According to Wilson, "Lincoln has projected himself into the role against which he is warning them [his Illinois audience]."[206] With the onset of the Civil War, Lincoln possessed "his heroic role, in which he was eventually seen to tower—a role that was political through the leadership of his party; soldierly through his rank of commander-in-chief of the armies of the United States; spiritual . . . as the prophet of the cause of righteousness. And he seems to have known that he was born for this."[207]

From this point forward Wilson scrutinized Lincoln's character and found much to admire in the man's mental and moral makeup. Wilson thought that he had significant damage to undo here, especially because Lincoln's personality had been obscured by mythmakers. "The cruellest thing that has happened to Lincoln since he was shot by Booth has been to fall into the hands of Carl Sandburg," Wilson drily noted.[208] In keeping with Edgar Lee Masters's 1930s biography, Wilson rejected Sandburg's hagiographical portrayal and instead offered a Lincoln who was "intent, self-controlled, strong in intellect, tenacious of purpose," a man who "created himself as a poetic figure, and . . . imposed himself on the nation."[209] One of the chief methods Lincoln used to so impose himself, according to Wilson (and this was precisely what many of Lincoln's critics over the years thought they were battling), was that he determined for the country the "conception of the course and the meaning of the Civil War." Wilson also thought Lincoln omitted important economic matters, such as the importance of the tariff and the growing power of industrial monopolies at the war's end, and concluded with this dramatic, if hyperbolic, sentence. "He must have suffered far more than he ever expressed from the agonies and griefs of the war," Wilson averred, "and it was morally and dramatically inevitable that this prophet who had crushed opposition and sent thousands of men to their deaths should finally attest his good faith by laying down his own life with theirs."[210]

Patriotic Gore elicited a good deal of acclaim and controversy, although oddly enough, it did not seem to resonate among Lincoln's foes the way it did within the Lincoln community and among scholars more generally. Historian Henry Steele Commager took notice of the controversial introduction to the volume in which Wilson claimed, as Murray Rothbard had previously argued to William F. Buckley, that Lincoln's suppression of the South was no different than the Russians invading and crushing the Hungarian rebellion in 1956, but he did not attack the idea that Lincoln, Lenin, and Bismarck were similar statesmen or shared many personal and political qualities. Perhaps the entire subject was too uncomfortable and controversial to touch. Nevertheless, Commager was puzzled by Wilson's sympathy with southern accounts of how Lincoln—and by extension Grant, Sherman, and Sheridan—conducted the war, bluntly stating that "if you start a war you must expect to get hurt." Regarding the alleged harshness of Reconstruction, Commager acidly stated, "The defeated rebels in Russia, Spain, France and Cuba would be pretty happy to settle for so mild a punishment" as the South received after the war concluded.[211]

Irving Howe, in the pages of the left-wing journal *Dissent,* likewise devoted his analysis to Wilson's introduction and in a biting critique called attention to Wilson's "disenchantment" with America, perceptively noting that (like virtually all of the president's detractors) "Edmund Wilson is not at home in the modern world" and contending the essays "convey a criticism of modern society [and dare I say modern politics] with which many radicals sympathize."[212] Howe astutely observed that there were serious political implications to Wilson's contemptuous outlook: "Wilson's reflections upon American history is [sic] often shared by people who find themselves disenchanted with the Cold War and who therefore turn to a kind of absolutist emotional radicalism, a radicalism without or even against politics, a radicalism of nausea."[213] He had little use, if not outright disdain, for Wilson's cavalier dismissal of professed "Northern idealism" and inadvertently offered a biting assessment of all Lincoln hostility: "The Civil War did mark the victory of modern capitalism and let loose those tendencies toward a centralized state which Wilson deplores; but also, the Civil War brought to an end the system by which one man could own another and therefore, despite all the necessary discounts, it represents a major turning in the moral development of the United States. . . . The point needs to be added that while the victory of the North did help to speed the growth of the bureaucratic state, it was surely not the *source* of that growth. . . . Northern politicians may have been hypocritical and Northern publicists self-righteous, but the slaves were freed. Had the South won, they would not have been. There can be no evading this central fact."[214] Finally, Howe was especially puzzled by Wilson's affinity for Alexander Stephens. "If we cannot do better than Alexander Stephens," he fretted, the United States was in dire trouble indeed.[215]

Wilson's analysis of Lincoln, therefore, was significant, if at times one-dimensional. Like Bledsoe before him, Wilson saw the Lyceum Speech as important, perhaps key, in understanding Lincoln, and his psychological or Freudian interpretation of the address, moreover, would in the late 1970s and early 1980s be developed more fully in two psychobiographies: George B. Forgie's aforementioned *Patricide in the House Divided* and Dwight Anderson's *Abraham Lincoln: The Quest for Immortality* (1982).[216] Anderson's was the more critical of the two books, with the author at one point labeling the president an American "Robespierre."[217] In essence Anderson argued that Lincoln's gigantic ambition, combined with ongoing frustrations with an apparently failed political career, led him to use the issue of slavery coupled with dictatorial methods during the Civil War to gain enduring fame and transcend George Washington as the greatest American, tragically accomplished by assassination.[218] Forgie's earlier book inadvertently pointed out a weakness in Wilson's psychological interpretation of the Lyceum Speech. Forgie, it may be recalled, plausibly claimed that the towering genius warned about in Lincoln's address was none other than Stephen A. Douglas, his political opponent in Illinois.[219] Still, Lincoln psychobiography, intriguing though it was, was relatively disconnected from any political influence and perhaps simplistic in ascertaining Lincoln's motives for combating slavery and waging the Civil War. When Wilson claimed at the end of the Stephens chapter, moreover, that "there is in most of us an unreconstructed Southerner who will not accept domination as well as a benevolent despot who wants to mold others for their own good," he seemed to be talking solely about whites. Consequently, his vision of the conflict, for all its literary brilliance, was on this point narrow and exclusive rather than broad and pluralistic. The Civil War was full of gore, to be sure, but as historian David Blight has accurately written, it was "*about something . . .* more than gore."[220]

The American Civil War, no matter what its purpose was in 1861, when the war began, was by 1865 about the permanent end of slavery, the meaning of freedom and equality, and the role of the federal government in ensuring the substance of both for *all* Americans. Since the federal government had manifestly failed in that task since Reconstruction, by the mid-1960s Americans, especially African Americans, were beginning to judge Abraham Lincoln harshly. Malcolm X put it bluntly: " [Lincoln] probably did more to trick Negroes than any other man in history."[221] In 1965, furthermore, Martin Duberman edited a collection of essays entitled *The Anti-Slavery Vanguard: New Essays on the Abolitionists,* including pieces by noted historians such as David Brion Davis, Leon Litwack, and James McPherson. The concluding chapter, by Howard Zinn, was entitled "Abolitionists, Freedom-Riders, and the Tactics of Agitation" and, like Ralph Korngold's book fifteen years earlier, compared Lincoln to the abolitionists—unfavorably. Indeed, he argued that Lincoln had been pushed into emancipation by the agitation of the abolitionists just as John F. Kennedy had been made to support the Freedom Struggle of African Americans by the broad-based appeal of the civil rights movement. The stage was therefore set for a major reevaluation of Lincoln as the Great Emancipator.[222]

The foremost proponent for questioning Lincoln's bona fides as the Great Emancipator came from Lerone Bennett Jr., an African American historian, senior editor of *Ebony* magazine, and author of a landmark 1968 essay entitled "Was Abe Lincoln a White Supremacist?" Bennett had once admired Lincoln, but his attitudes about him began to change during his childhood in 1930s Mississippi. He told one interviewer, "I was a child in whitest Mississippi reading for my life when I discovered for the first time that everything I'd been taught about Abraham Lincoln was a lie."[223] According to Bennett, he read Lincoln's words from his debate with Stephen Douglas at Charleston, Illinois, where Lincoln had said that he did not have any desire to see blacks made the equals of whites in the United States, and "I read it and I—and I was just—just absolutely shocked. And from that point on, I started to—researching Lincoln and trying to find out everything I could about him. . . . I was trying to save my life because I find it difficult to understand how people could say this man was the great apostle of brother—brotherhood in the United States of America."[224] Bennett attended Morehouse College in Atlanta and was a classmate of Martin Luther King Jr. He graduated in 1949 and went to work for the *Atlanta Daily World* shortly thereafter. He eventually moved to *Ebony* magazine, where he later became its editor.[225] Historians often write as if Bennett exploded unannounced onto the scene in 1968, when in fact he had been writing and publishing in the United States for a long time on the centrality of African Americans to the American experience.[226] Still, Bennett's essay was a surprise, and many reacted in shock and horror to what he wrote and, conceivably, that an African American had written it.

By February 1968, when Bennett's essay appeared, the civil rights movement had achieved some important legislative victories, but much remained to be achieved in terms of economic and social equality. In addition, rioting in places such as Watts in Los Angeles in 1965 had occurred, and Martin Luther King Jr. had come out against the Vietnam War in 1967, a war in which blacks and the poor were disproportionately being drafted and killed in Southeast Asia. Americans from all walks of society were wondering if their country was unraveling, and it would not have been unusual in such a context for them to wonder what Lincoln might have done to address such dilemmas. But it was Bennett's view, analogous to William F. Buckley's expressed a few years earlier, that Lincoln provided no guidance at all regarding current dilemmas because he was in fact a large part of America's racial problems.

Bennett leveled numerous and explosive accusations against Lincoln in his article. Given the state of American race relations in 1968, he thundered, it was clear that "Abraham Lincoln was *not* the Great Emancipator." Indeed, Bennett believed the edict was extremely limited in its impact and that Lincoln would have preferred not to even issue it but was forced by events to do so. More troubling, Bennett believed, was that Lincoln was a racist who "had profound doubts about the possibility of realizing the rhetoric of the Declaration of Independence and Gettysburg Address on this soil; and he believed until his death that black people and white people would be much better off separated—preferably with the Atlantic Ocean or some other large and deep body of water between them."[227] In substantial agreement with historians such as Richard Hofstadter, Bennett contended that the Emancipation Proclamation had "all the moral grandeur of a real estate deed" and, echoing Frederick Douglass's words from 1863, claimed it did "not enumerate a single principle hostile to slavery."[228] He believed the act for which Lincoln was most famous, indeed revered, did not free a single slave and "on the basis of the evidence one can make a powerful case for the view that Lincoln never intended to free the slaves, certainly not immediately."[229] Nor did Bennett think that if Lincoln had lived to serve out his second term, Reconstruction would have been substantially different, for Lincoln's version "was going to be a Reconstruction of the white people, by the white people and for the white people."[230] Bennett ended the essay with a harsh evaluation of Abraham Lincoln and the American political tradition, a tradition that, unlike Willmoore Kendall, he assuredly wanted derailed: "For, in the final analysis, Lincoln must be seen as the embodiment, not the transcendence, of the American tradition, which is, as we all know, a racist tradition. In his inability to rise above that tradition, Lincoln, often called 'the noblest of all Americans,' holds up a flawed mirror to the American soul. And one honors him today, not by gazing fixedly at a flawed image, not by hiding warts and excrescences, but by seeing oneself in the reflected ambivalences of a life which calls us to transcendence, not imitation."[231]

Reaction to Bennett's piece was swift. In the *New York Times,* to cite one example, author and critic Herbert Mitgang wrote a scathing response, arguing that Lincoln had been opposed to slavery, even when it was politically unpopular to be so opposed, and although Mitgang did not deny the truth of Lincoln's statements in his debates with Douglas, he argued that Lincoln was making tactical concessions while remaining consistent in his overall goal of stopping slavery's expansion. In contrast to Bennett,

Mitgang thought that Lincoln's racial views changed during the conflict, to the point that he was advocating by the end of his life integrated schools in Louisiana and limited suffrage for African American males.[232] Bennett was having none of it, however, and he responded a few weeks later, claiming that Mitgang had answered "facts with smears" and never addressed his point that Lincoln had been opposed to "sudden and general emancipation" all his life. Bennett found Mitgang's defense of Lincoln's statements at places such as Charleston weak, for in his view they made Lincoln a "liar and hypocrite," which was at the very least "curious," if not "pathetic." With some justification Bennett accused Mitgang of "McCarthyism" for claiming that his views on Lincoln were no different than those of the White Citizens' Councils of Mississippi, whose leaders selectively used Lincoln's utterances from 1858 to allege that the Great Emancipator was a racist and in fact agreed with them on the need for a segregated United States.[233] Bennett's attacks on Lincoln were of course much different than those of the White Citizens' Councils; Bennett, obviously, was no segregationist, and he criticized the president because in his view Lincoln had not truly embodied the ideals of freedom and equality that Americans professed to hold, while the White Citizens' Councils that distorted Lincoln's racial views did so in order to advance an anti-egalitarian, white supremacist agenda.

The quarrel between Bennett and Mitgang in the *New York Times* was hardly the only reaction to Bennett's essay, although it was perhaps the most prominent. The African American newspaper the *New York Amsterdam News* in a brief notice said, "*Ebony* magazine should be congratulated" for publishing Bennett's piece, an essay it claimed "does much to destroy an American myth," and that "Mr. Bennett's research ranks at the highest level" and "shows the need for a re-evaluation of the man Lincoln."[234] Another African American newspaper, the *Pittsburgh Courier,* commented at much greater length, telling its readers that "the Negro and a large body of the American people have been deceived for a long time by historians who deliberately concealed the true facts about the Civil War president."[235] The *Courier* did not question Bennett's analysis and thought it was an outstanding piece of historical scholarship. The paper also noted that long before Lincoln issued his Emancipation Proclamation, thousands of slaves had already been freed by the Confiscation Acts of 1861 and 1862 and thousands more had freed themselves by running away from southern plantations to Union lines, which foreshadowed a future debate among scholars over the question of who really freed the slaves.

Lerone Bennett's essay was an especially significant, if at times inaccurate, critique of Lincoln (see chapter 6 for a detailed analysis), for in addition to perpetuating hostility toward the president, it challenged the central and most lasting legacy of Abraham Lincoln, that of Great Emancipator. Equally important, and this may suggest one reason why the reaction to Bennett's essay was so harsh, was that Bennett confronted the standard narrative of American history that the United States was a place of ever-expanding freedom for all who arrived on its shores and that Abraham Lincoln's presidency represented the culmination of that freedom narrative.[236] In fact, what Bennett's essay really challenged was the idea that noble and powerful whites were responsible for the emancipation of ignoble and powerless blacks. His piece was part of a long and rich tradition of Lincoln criticism by African Americans who saw an excessive veneration of the sixteenth president as a not-so-subtle form of intellectual subservience to whites.[237] By attacking the legitimacy of Lincoln as the Great Emancipator, then, Bennett was doing more than simply engaging in a piece of historical scholarship. He was taking on the entire story of the American past and using animosity toward Abraham Lincoln as a vehicle for his ideas. In that sense the accuracy of Bennett's charges of Lincoln's racism were beside the point, for he was attacking American exceptionalism and critiquing the interests American power had served both at home and abroad. In other words, if by 1865 the Civil War was a contest over the question of whether American nationalism would remain based solely upon white, male ethnicity or if it would be based upon something larger and more inclusive, Bennett maintained that Lincoln was in the former camp and it was time for Americans to drop the fiction that the so-called Great Emancipator had believed in freedom and equality for all.

Postwar discourse about Abraham Lincoln was an argument not only about Lincoln but also one about the complicated relationship between modern notions of freedom, equality, race, and federal power. On an even larger scale, moreover, these Cold War arguments regarding Lincoln were about America's role in world affairs. Lincoln had once characterized the United States as "the last best hope of earth." But in the postwar era, Americans asked themselves, was this really true? Was America really a force for good? If so, precisely how did the United States become such a world behemoth, and how should America exercise its power across the globe? Among historians, if not all Americans, there was a vigorous debate about the roots of American imperialism and the nation's rise to world prominence, with all participants operating under the assumption that a deeper understanding of the historical basis of American expansionism would contribute to better decision making in the middle of the Cold War. Some scholars argued that the Spanish-American War or World War II was the key turning point on the American road to imperialism. Lincoln's Confederate enemies held, of course, that the expansionist path began with Lincoln's invasion of the South. Others maintained, in contrast, that there was no single event in American history that one could pinpoint to mark when America unequivocally became an imperialist power. Rather, such historians maintained that the United States had always been an expansionist nation or became one due to an interlocking set of factors, including but not limited to the desire of American policy makers to build the country into a worldwide economic and cultural hegemon.

At the height of the Cold War, New Left historian William Appleman Williams published his seminal book, *The Tragedy of American Diplomacy* (1959).[238] Manifestly discontent with American policy, domestic and foreign, Williams's critique of Lincoln offered an opportunity for a merger between detractors of the president on the Left and Right. In the 1970s Williams faulted Abraham Lincoln for America's woes when he took Edmund Wilson's argument about Lincoln's Lyceum Speech and applied it to American foreign policy. In *America Confronts a Revolutionary World, 1776–1976* (1976), Williams directly challenged Lincoln's legacy as positive for either the United States or the world. Like many who questioned the prevailing view of Lincoln, Williams was clearly impressed with the president's gifts: "He was graced with an unusually powerful mind, driven by vaulting ambition, and quick to learn the shrewd expertise of politics; and he revealed exceptional skill with the language, a persistent taste for the mystical, and disturbingly sly habits."[239] In the Lyceum Address, according to Williams, Lincoln's claim that his generation would have to expand upon the work of the founders, along with his warnings against potential American Caesars who might require "free speech (hence self-determination)," was in essence "a majestic statement of the imperial ethic—my way is better than yours and I will therefore impose my way—masked in the rhetoric of law and order."[240] Williams also briefly referenced Lincoln's recommendation to temperance advocates that one would win more converts with honey than condemnation and claimed that Lincoln's "true object is to reform everyone—America first and then the world. To rid mankind of booze is good, but as nothing compared to giving the American Present to the rest of mankind."[241] It was quite a stretch to equate twentieth-century American imperialism with Lincoln's advocacy of voluntary temperance reform, but Williams pressed on, later calling Lincoln a "Houdini with words" who used magnificent speeches "to mask the truth that he was abroad upon a grand voyage to honor his slyly limited commitment to the revolutionary right of self-determination."[242]

If Lincoln had at best a limited commitment to the right of self-determination—and his critic denied that he had such a commitment—Williams proceeded to unmask the consequences of Lincoln's presidency in stark and unforgiving terms. Lincoln was, in Williams's view, a conservative, "the personification of the antislavery mentality as opposed to the spirit of egalitarian abolitionism. . . . Honest Abe can realistically be called the prophet of segregation. Leave them [blacks] alone, he advised. Which means in practice abandoning them to the terrors of a marketplace dominated by whites."[243] According to Williams, Lincoln denied white southerners the right of self-determination (i.e., the right to own, exploit, beat, and rape African Americans and their descendants—forever) and was in opposition to the principles of 1776. No critic of Abraham Lincoln from Alexander Stephens to M. E. Bradford could have put it better. "The act of imposing one people's morality upon another people is an imperial denial of self-determination," Williams declared. "Once begin the process of denying it to others in its own name and there is no end of empire except war and more war."[244] Williams concluded that

> the soul-wrenching truth of it is that Lincoln played a double game. He wanted to transcend the Founding Fathers, free the slaves, and expand America's power throughout the world. But he lacked the courage to take his chances on that program . . . we have to face the truth that he steered a counter-revolutionary course. Hence the myth is dangerous because it obscures the truth . . . Lincoln's American present was the possessive individualism of marketplace capitalism, and he riveted it upon America. That not only perpetuated the sense that expansionism was vital to America's well-being, but also reinforced the sense of unique mission to reform the world. And in the process he consolidated and extended all the earlier precedents for the President to use any and all powers at his discretion.[245]

Later Williams even went so far as to claim that the Israelis had used Lincoln's arguments to justify their denial of statehood to the Palestinian cause: "You are perfectly free [Israel told the Palestinians] to self-determine yourselves into an increasingly irrelevant minority within our Present. And American leaders said Amen."[246]

Four years later, in *Empire as a Way of Life: An Essay on the Causes and Character of America's Present Predicament along with a Few Thoughts about an Alternative* (1980), Williams more explicitly linked his negative evaluation of Lincoln with his anti-imperial stance. Noting that Lincoln was more moderate on slavery because he wanted it ended "slowly" rather than "cataclysmically," like the abolitionists sought to do, Williams agreed, in contrast to some of his predecessors in the community of Lincoln detractors, that slavery was wrong, even "evil. But that truth," Williams emphatically declared, "fails to define either the question or the answer. For so is empire. The irreducible issue is whether or not one uses one evil, empire, to destroy another evil, slavery."[247] Williams simply could not differentiate between Lincoln having won a relatively democratic election—an election in which the people whom Williams alleged the president had imperialistically conquered willingly participated—and American malfeasance overseas after 1945. Williams's alternative to America's Lincolnian imperialism was a return to the Articles of Confederation and a breaking up of the United States. How such a national dismemberment was to advance the cause of freedom around the world or how in 1861 Lincoln's having allowed the Confederacy the right of self-determination to enslave others permanently would have better served liberty, Williams did not say, but considering that he was writing in the aftermath of the Vietnam War and other American misadventures overseas, it is easy to see the source of his animosity and why his views appealed to individuals such as Murray Rothbard. As the libertarian Lincoln critic Joseph Stromberg has written, "It is probably among libertarians and anti-imperialist conservatives that Williams now finds his true following." Although Williams is often associated with the New Left, in his hostility toward American expansionism and Abraham Lincoln, he could plausibly be placed squarely in alliance with Old Right libertarians such as Murray Rothbard.[248]

It is in the context of Williams's linkage of American imperialism with Abraham Lincoln that one can best understand the charges leveled against the president by Gore Vidal (1925–2012), renowned writer and author of the historical novel *Lincoln* (1984). Vidal admired William Appleman Williams and, too, Lincoln's political skills. "The real Lincoln was a superb politician," Vidal wrote in 1981. "He knew when to wait; when to act. He had the gift of formulating, most memorably, ideas whose time had, precisely, on the hour, as it were come. He could also balance opposites with exquisite justice."[249] Still, like Williams and many other detractors, Vidal thought that America, unfortunately, had been transformed during the

Civil War into "the American nation-state," or, more appropriately from Vidal's viewpoint, "the National-Security State."[250]

Published in the aftermath of the Vietnam War and only a few years after Williams's musings on the Civil War president, Vidal's *Lincoln* was one volume in a series of excellent historical novels that both chronicled and revised the history of the United States from its inception to Vidal's day. As noted, Vidal admired Lincoln's political skills and cunning, but he could also be quite critical. Lincoln, as portrayed by Vidal, cared merely about saving the Union and emancipated the slaves only when forced to do so, wanted blacks to be colonized outside the United States until his death, and used tyrannical methods—including the suspension of habeas corpus—in order to keep the Union together.[251] Of course, the charge that Lincoln cared only about saving the Union was fallacious. Lincoln and the Republicans wanted to save a Union in which slavery would be restricted and eventually eradicated, while his white opponents in the South left the Union in order to perpetuate the institution indefinitely. This was a substantial difference and one that the president's detractors continuously ignored when they charged that Lincoln cared only about the Union and not at all about ending slavery. In containing and eventually eradicating slavery, Lincoln had said as early as 1854, he wanted to save the Union *and* make it worth saving.[252] White southern secessionists, indeed all of Lincoln's contemporary enemies, understood more clearly than Lincoln's latter-day critics that his presidency was a threat to their slaveholding interests, which was one reason—indeed the primary reason—they seceded in the first place.[253] At any rate, perhaps Vidal's most controversial claim in the book, based on the testimony of Lincoln's law partner William Herndon, was that Lincoln had contracted syphilis as a young man and had passed that disease on to his wife, Mary.[254]

There was hardly anything new in such charges, but with his portrayal of the sixteenth president Vidal infuriated scholars and revealed some sympathies with Lincoln's enemies.[255] To be sure, there were numerous effusive reviews of *Lincoln*. Literary critic Harold Bloom called the work "masterly" and "powerful" and its depiction of the president as "plausible and human," in addition to being "grand entertainment."[256] In the *Wall Street Journal,* Ellen Wilson Fielding was disappointed that "Mr. Vidal eliminates almost entirely his subject's opposition to slavery" but believed the Lincoln contained in the book's pages was nevertheless "lovable," while in a somewhat critical review in the *New York Times* Christopher Lehmann-Haupt said that despite the book's flaws, "it is a very well-founded, complex, very nearly heroic portrait of Lincoln that Mr. Vidal presents."[257] Such tributes to *Lincoln* may help explain why it was later turned into a NBC television miniseries in 1988, four years after publication.

That Vidal's work was so popular and could therefore reach the masses through the venue of television prompted some negative essays by Lincoln scholars and witty ripostes from Vidal in the *New York Review of Books* and the *American Historical Review*. Historian Richard Nelson Current penned an unsympathetic review in which he characterized *Lincoln* as "fictional history" rather than historical fiction.[258] When the miniseries came out on NBC, historian Mark Neely Jr. penned a harsh but perceptive evaluation of the show—and Vidal's *Lincoln*—with two key complaints: first, "why deny his [Lincoln's] well-documented and sincere antislavery convictions?"[259] Second, Neely noted the resemblance between Vidal's portrayal of Lincoln with the one given to the country by Alexander Stephens (not to mention Edmund Wilson and William Appleman Williams). Vidal concurred with Wilson's Freudian interpretation of the war; that Lincoln had waged the conflict in order to achieve fame greater than that of the framers. So, when the critic Herbert Mitgang asked if "Lincoln really wanted the Civil War, with its 600,000 casualties, in order to eclipse the Founding Fathers and insure his own place in the pantheon of great presidents," Vidal readily agreed that was his view.[260] "Yes, that is pretty much what I came to believe," Vidal wrote, "as Lincoln got more and more mystical about the Union, and less and less logical in his defense of it, and more and more appalled at all the blood and at those changes in his country, which, he confessed—with pride?—were 'fundamental and astounding.'"[261] From Alexander Stephens to Albert Taylor Bledsoe to Edmund Wilson to Gore Vidal, it seemed that the controversy over Vidal's *Lincoln* illustrated the old adage that the more things change, the more they remain the same.

But to an extent the back-and-forth between Vidal and his critics was rather beside the point. Vidal's *Lincoln* was a hugely entertaining, if at times factually incorrect, book. Lincoln *was* an exceedingly complex and mysterious human being, and Vidal may be allowed some mistakes in his portrayal of the man who, along with Thomas Jefferson, remains the country's most enigmatic president. Less forgivable was Vidal's essentially neo-Confederate portrayal of Lincoln, pointed out by Neely in his analysis. Vidal, however, was after bigger game with his historical novels than being correct about what he might term "historical minutiae," in that he was trying to demystify the American—imperial?—past, and debunking the so-called Lincoln myth was a central part of that project. Vidal alluded to this endeavor in one of his essays for the *New York Review of Books,* when he labeled historians as "workday bureaucrats of the History Departments [who] are solemnly aware that *their* agreed-upon facts must constitute—at least in the short term—a view of the republic that will please their trustees. Since all great Americans are uniquely great, even saints, those who record the lives of these saints are hagiographers."[262] Vidal believed that he was delivering a needed dose of realism to an imperialistic nation that worshipped Abraham Lincoln and the American empire he helped create by having preserved the Union. Perhaps this was why Vidal's next novel in his American chronicles series was entitled, appropriately enough, *Empire.*

Ever since his arrival on the national scene in 1858 Lincoln had been denigrated from the conservative side of the political spectrum, but after 1945 he was condemned more often for his emphasis on equality and use of state and executive power than his lack of faith or hardscrabble, frontier background. Such critiques were almost assuredly related to Harry Jaffa's defense of Lincoln's natural rights philosophy, coupled with the large-scale transformations taking place in American life, including the civil rights movement and the decades-long conflict with the Soviet Union. Once the conservative movement attained power in 1980, with Ronald Reagan's election, it made peace with an expansive federal government in both domestic and foreign matters, and Lincoln criticism was more or less eliminated, or driven underground, from mainstream conservatism by the end of the Cold War in 1989. Conservatives, it might be said, unwittingly accepted advice the poet Josephine Powell Beaty gave to Lincoln opponent David Rankin Barbee in 1947, the same summer Barbee's acquaintance Charles Tansill had berated Lincoln in his Statutory Hall address. In a beautiful and tactful letter Beaty pitied Barbee for his Lincoln hatred. "I am genuinely sorry that you feel as you do [about Lincoln] for I think you are missing so much. . . . Only couldn't you let a seam in your heart and take in a little more of your country?"[263] Within conservatism, a political philosophy allegedly devoted to the principle of limited government in the service of *liberty* (at least for some), there had always been a fundamental dilemma over how to view Lincoln's presidency, a presidency that significantly expanded the powers of the office and enhanced the power of the federal government at the expense of the states, in the service of some measure of *equality* for African Americans (and potentially other marginalized groups). The dilemma was, given the political philosophy of conservatism, perhaps unresolvable. Still, many on the Right opened the seam in their heart, and loathing for Lincoln diminished among conservatives after 1945. Denigration of Lincoln, however, became for the first time a significant, if relatively temporary, aspect of left-wing criticism in the United States. There was an evolving attitude on the Left that Lincoln had in actuality accomplished very little as president, even in matters of slavery or racial equality, except to preserve and justify a capitalist, imperial, and racist state that was little more than a scourge in world affairs.[264] On this point at least, there was agreement among individuals with divergent political viewpoints, including the New Left historian William Appleman Williams, libertarians such as Murray Rothbard, and writer Gore Vidal.[265] But their tenuous alliance could not be maintained, and Lincoln's critics would have to forge and maintain new alliances in the post–Cold War era.

6

A LITMUS TEST FOR
AMERICAN CONSERVATISM

The Great Centralizer, 1989–2012

In April 2003, 138 years after he had first visited the capital of the Confederacy, Abraham Lincoln still haunted Richmond, Virginia. The occasion was the dedication of a sculpture depicting Lincoln and his son Tad seated on a bench outside Richmond's Tredegar Iron Works, engraved with the words "To Bind Up the Nation's Wounds." Commissioned years earlier by the United States Historical Society, the monument commemorated Lincoln's visit in April 1865, shortly after Confederates evacuated the city. That spring, as Lincoln walked through the streets, he was greeted as a savior by the city's African American population, as Confederate residents remained in their homes, peering from behind their windows. Nearly 140 years later, it was evident that for some Americans honoring Lincoln remained controversial indeed. Brag Bolling, a member of the Sons of Confederate Veterans (SCV), thought the statue was a mark of "insensitivity," a "not-so-subtle reminder of who won the war and who will dictate our monuments, history, heroes, education and culture." "Why here?" Bolling asked.[1]

On one level, most people were stunned by the brouhaha Lincoln's statue sparked. The dedication ceremonies were picketed by several dozen protestors with banners comparing Lincoln to Adolf Hitler and demanding that Lincoln be indicted for war crimes. Overhead flew a plane with a banner displaying the words John Wilkes Booth uttered after assassinating Lincoln: "Sic Semper Tyrannis" (Thus Ever to Tyrants). Few in Richmond seemed to share such extreme reactions. Tim Kane, Virginia's lieutenant governor and former mayor of Richmond, characterized the demonstrators as "wrong": "We claim Abraham Lincoln as a brother. We claim

Abraham Lincoln as a Virginian."[2] One woman, Marsha Hunt, brought her ten-year-old son Daniel to the event and told a reporter, "I think Abe Lincoln was a good person, and I'm glad that the slaves were freed."[3] Her outlook would have been extremely upsetting to previous Lincoln critics, especially that Hunt would praise their traditional historical villain in the presence of her child.

On another level, although the Richmond protesters were a minority viewpoint, diehard Confederate sympathizers who refused to accept the massive emancipatory social changes that had taken place in the United States over the past forty years, they nevertheless represented the views of an increasingly outspoken and influential segment of Americans. Across the country Lincoln's opponents were a dedicated, vocal group of people, "passionate outsiders" who had the potential to shape public opinion in the United States about the president, the Civil War, and related political matters. The president's detractors had been quite busy since the end of the Cold War in 1989 and the subsequent breakup of the Soviet Union in 1991, forming white southern nationalist organizations such as the League of the South, publishing books and essays with an unambiguously hostile stance toward Lincoln, and using the Internet to propagate their dissenting view about one of America's most revered statesmen. Lincoln's enemies were part of a broader political movement, a neo-Confederate movement, defined by its antagonism toward modernity, equality, democracy, and the secularization of American society and well connected to many leading conservative figures and Republican politicians.[4]

The president's diverse critics were profoundly discontent with America for various reasons: they condemned what they saw as an intrusive federal government and continued their rhetorical advocacy of nullification or secession as constitutional and morally sound solutions to centralization in Washington, D.C.; they condemned historians who, they believed, demonized the antebellum South by focusing on the institution of slavery as the cause of the Civil War and argued, instead, that the war was fought over tariffs and the rights of the states to resist federal tyranny; they condemned a godless, materialistic nineteenth-century North which, they believed, had fought an unjustified war against a Christian South; they condemned ongoing attacks on the Confederate flag, a flag they held to represent orthodox Christianity and limited, small government; they condemned Franklin Roosevelt's New Deal and Lyndon Johnson's Great Society; they condemned continued American military involvement overseas, even though the Cold War had ended and the Soviet Union had broken apart; they condemned the nation's changing demographics resulting from immigration; they condemned the increased emphasis on multiculturalism and diversity in American life; and they condemned the political, racial, and sexual egalitarianism, or radicalism, resulting from the liberation movements of the post–Cold War era.[5] These disgruntled and dissatisfied Americans, who included a diverse mix of anarcho-capitalists, radical libertarians, and traditional conservatives ("paleoconservatives") sympathetic to the antebellum South, the Confederacy, and the worldview of the Vanderbilt Agrarians, sought to "repeal the twentieth century."[6] By 1989, if not long before, these widely disparate groups shared a heartfelt contempt for Abraham Lincoln. Although ideological differences certainly existed between these various crowds, they read, recommended, and incorporated the ideas of each other's essays and books and attacked Lincoln with similar arguments in like-minded venues.

The president's enemies used Abraham Lincoln as a method to bring attention to their political and cultural agenda, an agenda that they themselves characterized as reactionary. One particularly influential aspect of Lincoln hostility was inaugurated in 1990 in the pages of *Liberty* magazine, a small libertarian journal, with a manifesto by Llewellyn H. Rockwell Jr., founder of the Ludwig von Mises Institute, former chief of staff for Texas congressman Ron Paul, and devoted friend of anarcho-capitalist Murray Rothbard. Rockwell challenged libertarians and traditional conservatives to join forces around a defense of the free market against the "intrusions" of the federal government, intrusions that included "the 1964 Civil Rights Act and all subsequent laws that force property owners to act against their will," with a cultural conservatism based on Christianity.[7] Later, in a different venue, Rockwell defined this outlook more specifically: "libertarian anti-government economics, decentralist local patriotism, anti-war isolation, and a reactionary cultural outlook that saw government as the key to the loss of the Old Republic."[8] These paleolibertarians held that Confederate secession had been justified, legally and morally, and would have preserved liberty and that Lincoln's war was unnecessary, unconstitutional, and conducted immorally because of his suspension of habeas corpus and authorization of Sherman's March across Georgia and the Carolinas. From their standpoint Abraham Lincoln was not the Union's savior but its destroyer and a war criminal that set the precedent for twentieth-century expansion of federal power such as the New Deal and the Great Society. They criticized Lincoln in order to attack the federal government and its ongoing support for civil rights and civil liberties for formerly marginalized groups against local efforts to oppose the same. Publicly loathing Lincoln was one way to attract attention for their vision of a vastly different America, one more hierarchical and less pluralistic but, at least at the federal level, one more liberated from government constraints. Between 1989 and the bicentennial of Lincoln's birth in 2009, this reactionary political philosophy, and the neo-Confederate movement more generally, had once again become a part of the conservative movement from which it had been temporarily exiled in the 1980s.[9] Consequently, such ideas were vigorously challenged by opposing libertarians and conservatives, including Harry Jaffa, some of his students, and others, and the conservative wars surrounding Abraham Lincoln were again under way. And whoever emerged victorious in this contest would have a decisive advantage in defining American conservatism and the Republican Party, if not America itself, for future generations.

Indictments against Lincoln, however, did not come solely from paleo-libertarians or neo-Confederates more broadly. If Lincoln's self-confessed reactionary critics accused him of being a dictator and war criminal and castigated the president for centralizing power in the federal government, a much different and unmistakably negative assessment came from African Americans, including Lerone Bennett Jr., who advanced a detailed argument that Lincoln was a timid president and a scheming politician who never really wanted to free the slaves but was instead forced into authorizing emancipation. Neither side seemed to recognize that their critiques canceled each other out, that Lincoln could not have been despotic and timid at the same time. Nor did they seem to sense that if Lincoln could be blamed for everything wrong with modern America, it was just as logical to give him credit for all that was right. All of Lincoln's critics shared a propensity to focus their debunking efforts on Lincoln's prewar statements, in which the future president told Illinois audiences he did not favor racial equality, statements that proved, they believed, that Lincoln was not a racial egalitarian and was therefore unworthy of American's adulation. They thought such comments reflected Lincoln's true racial views and confirmed that for his entire political career he had been a white supremacist who wanted to rid the country of blacks permanently by colonization. Consequently, for them Lincoln never really cared about emancipation; freeing the slaves, if he should even receive credit for so doing, they argued, was simply a tactic a typical politician would use in order to advance his real agenda, which was to maintain and aggrandize power and/or rid the country of blacks.

To be sure, after 1989 Lincoln's adversaries did not drop entirely the traditional reasons for loathing the president (e.g., his ignoble background, his atheism, his imperialist tendencies, and his messianic rhetoric), but in several important essays and books they emphasized different themes: neo-Confederates, especially paleolibertarians, argued that Lincoln was the Great Centralizer and destroyer of the Union, while Bennett found in the sixteenth president the Great Equivocator or Great Racist or Reluctant Emancipator. Consequently, this contemptuous portrayal of Lincoln contributed to an atmosphere of public distrust in the United States, a sense that in the 1860s Lincoln had been wrong and the South right and that the nation's existence was somehow morally dubious. Such an outlook helped delegitimize the nation's government and made effective governance, at least at the federal level, less likely, if not impossible, to achieve.[10] Those who believed freedom, equality, and the federal government were inimical to one another embraced such an outcome, and their aversion to Lincoln received a boost perhaps with the inauguration of the nation's first black president in 2009, which took place, coincidentally, on the two hundred-year anniversary of Abraham Lincoln's birth. At the same time, Lerone Bennett's critique of Lincoln received greater attention but was used by the president's more conservative enemies to advance their decidedly negative portrait of Lincoln. For Bennett, whose writings indicated a belief that freedom and equality were inextricably linked and necessitated a strong federal government and that because of the "Lincoln myth" there had been neither a consistent national commitment to racial equality nor a "real emancipation proclamation" in the United States, such a result must have been bittersweet indeed.[11]

Beginning in the early 1990s, on the heels of his friend Lew Rockwell's manifesto, Murray Rothbard published two essays that launched Lincoln criticism in the post–Cold War era from an openly paleolibertarian stance. Rothbard laid the intellectual foundation for the reemergence of loathing for Abraham Lincoln into Republican circles—and America more generally—in the early twenty-first century. One piece sharply attacked Lincoln's career in the context of the "secession" of the Baltic republics from the USSR, while the other contained Rothbard's analysis of what made a war morally acceptable and precisely which wars in American history met his criteria.[12] In the first essay Rothbard celebrated the Soviet Union's disintegration, a development that showed national boundaries were not forever fixed. He lamented that Americans were "puzzled and disturbed rather than delighted at the re-emergence of the nationalities question."[13] One group hostile to these developments, he wrote, were pro-Lincoln "global democrats," including the neoconservatives he believed had treated M. E. Bradford so shabbily in 1981. In the course of his pro-secession essay rejoicing over the Soviet Union's collapse, Rothbard anticipated virtually every argument of Thomas DiLorenzo's *Real Lincoln* (2002), one of the most significant Lincoln critiques to emerge in the post–Cold War era:

> And so didn't Lincoln use force and violence, and on a massive scale, on behalf of the mystique of the sacred "Union," to prevent the South from seceding? Indeed he did, and on the foundation of mass murder and oppression, Lincoln crushed the South and outlawed the very notion of secession (based on the highly plausible ground that since the separate states voluntarily entered the Union they should be allowed to leave).
>
> But not only that: for Lincoln created the monstrous unitary nation-state from which individual and local liberties have never recovered: e.g., the triumph of an all-powerful federal judiciary, Supreme Court, and national army; the overriding of the ancient Anglo-Saxon and libertarian right of *habeas corpus* by jailing dissidents against the war without trial; the establishment of martial rule; the suppression of freedom of the press; and the largely permanent establishment of conscription, the income tax, the pietist "sin" taxes against liquor and tobacco, the corrupt and cartelizing "partnership of government and industry" constituting massive subsidies to transcontinental railroads, and the protective tariff; the establishment of fiat money inflation through the greenbacks and getting off the gold standard; and the nationalization of the banking system through the national Banking Acts of 1863 and 1864.[14]

At a 1994 conference in Atlanta, Rothbard lambasted Lincoln as part of a talk entitled "Just War."[15] "The two just wars in American history were the American Revolution, and the War for Southern Independence," not the nation's efforts to eradicate slavery or defeat Nazism.[16] Rothbard claimed that a just war occurs "when a people tries to ward off the threat of coercive domination by another people, or to overthrow an already-existing domination." An unjust conflict, by contrast, ensues "when a people try to impose domination on another people, or try to retain an already coercive rule over them."[17] Accordingly, the South was justified in seceding in 1861, just as Americans were correct in seceding from the British Empire, and the Civil War was as much about tariffs and their collection as it was about slavery. Consistent with previous critics, Rothbard faulted the North for the Civil War, calling northerners "the Jacobins, the Bolsheviks of their era," whose "fanatical spirit" was "summed up in the pseudo-Biblical and truly blasphemous verses of that quintessential Yankee Julia Ward Howe, in her so-called 'Battle Hymn of the Republic.'"[18]

In language with which Lerone Bennett Jr. would have agreed, Rothbard claimed that "Abraham Lincoln's conciliatory words on slavery cannot be taken at face value." He was, according to Rothbard, a "master politician," a "consummate conniver, manipulator, and liar," who "maneuvered the Southerners into firing the first shot" in the Civil War.[19] Lincoln was, from Rothbard's viewpoint, a horrible man, "a typical example of a humanitarian with a guillotine." Lincoln not only conducted the Civil War inhumanely and criminally, but along with "Grant and Sherman," he "paved the way for all the genocidal honors of the monstrous 20th century." Citing Lord Acton, Rothbard exhorted his audience: "We must always remember, we must never forget, we must put in the dock and hang higher than Haman, those who, in modern times, opened the Pandora's Box of genocide and the extermination of civilians: Sherman, Grant, and Lincoln. Perhaps, some day, their statues, like Lenin's in Russia, will be toppled and melted down; their insignias and battle flags will be desecrated, their war songs tossed into the fire. And then Davis and Lee and Jackson and Forrest, and all the heroes of the South, 'Dixie' and the Stars and Bars, will once again be truly honored and remembered."[20] Rothbard no longer spoke of the "aggressive expansionist aims of the Southern 'slavocracy,'" as he had in 1961. Such legitimate criticism of the imperialistic aims of the white South prior to secession were, if not entirely absent from Rothbard's thinking, much more muted in the wake of the end of the Cold War, as he attempted to build a political coalition with neo-Confederates on the right.[21]

Extreme as Rothbard's rhetoric was, his argument was part of a broader effort to legitimize the idea of secession, 130 years after the fact. The conservative Emory University philosopher Donald Livingston wrote two years after Rothbard's address that Americans might learn to accept secession if such attacks on Lincoln continued: "[Americans] are still under the spell of the centralized modern state founded in the Lincoln myth. Ours is the uphill task of refuting that myth both as an historical account of the American polity and as a *moral and philosophical* account of the best form of political association. That form is and has always been some form of federative polity with the right of secession. . . . As Mel Bradford has taught us, we must refute also the blasphemous puritan ideology of the Lincoln myth which pretends to speak the speech of God and, in the

Cromwellian 'Battle Hymn of the Republic,' teaches slaying and waste in the name of the Lord. The Union was not in 1861 and is not now the last best hope on earth."[22]

Why focus on Lincoln, when in fact the federal government, or national security state, expanded significantly and in far more permanent ways as a result of World War II than it did because of the Lincoln administration? One would think the president's libertarian or anarcho-capitalist adversaries would take note that most Americans were brought into the modern income tax structure as a result of the fight against Hitler. And the methods used to wage World War II, including not just atomic weapons but the indiscriminate bombing of civilians in Europe and Japan as well, were far more barbarous than any atrocities perpetrated by Sherman. Granted, they argued that the Lincoln administration had set the precedent for such policies, that Lincoln was the precursor of progressivism and what they characterized as the expansionist, regulatory, and murderous federal government in Washington, D.C. When Rothbard and Livingston uttered such sentiments in the mid-1990s, however, there was in the United States a relative unanimity that World War II was a just war, worthy of American lives and expenditures, with some positive transformative effects, not least in that it served as a catalyst for the civil rights movement. But attacking Abraham Lincoln might gain traction for a nascent, reactionary political movement that was in general anti-Washington in nature. Rothbard shrewdly recognized that there was a readily available political, if not regional, constituency in America for criticizing Lincoln. Undermining the Lincoln myth was one method for bringing down "the current system," one described by Rothbard in 1992 as "an unholy alliance of 'corporate liberal' Big Business and media elites, who, through big government, have privileged and caused to rise up a parasitic Underclass, who, among them all, are looting and oppressing the bulk of the middle and working classes in America."[23] It is unsurprising that in 1994, the same year he delivered his speech excoriating the Civil War president, the League of the South, a pro-Confederate organization with secessionist goals, hostile to Lincoln and the federal government, was formed in Tuscaloosa, Alabama, with Rothbard as one of this group's key intellectual leaders.[24]

One year later, in October 1995, Michael Hill and Thomas Fleming, both of whom possessed doctorates, Hill in history and Fleming in classics, published a "New Dixie Manifesto" in the *Washington Post* explaining the league's formation and some of its goals.[25] Comparing themselves with ethnic groups such as the "Scots and Welsh in Britain, the Lombards and

Sicilians in Italy and the Ukrainians in the defunct Soviet Union," Hill and Fleming argued that southerners had seen their "loyalty" reciprocated by the United States "with exploitation and contempt."[26] After listing some of the contributions made by southerners in fields as diverse as literature, music, politics, and religion, they claimed the league was "calling for nothing more revolutionary than home rule for the states established by the U.S. Constitution."[27] Denying any hatred for the United States, the authors said the league's motivation was "a concern for states' rights, local self-government and regional identity [which] used to be taken for granted everywhere in America." "The United States," they lamented, "is no longer, as it once was, a federal union of diverse states and regions. National uniformity is being imposed by the political class that runs Washington, the economic class that owns Wall Street and the cultural class in charge of Hollywood and the Ivy League. . . . What had been a genuinely federal union has been turned into a multicultural, continental empire, ruled from Washington by federal agencies and under the thumb of the federal judiciary." Accordingly, the authors believed it was time "for the people of the South to take control of their own governments, their own institutions, their own culture, their own communities, and their own lives." Fearful of the consequences over the "war that is being waged against the Southern identity and its traditional symbols," the authors angrily described a world in which "legislatures in Southern states are under pressure to rename streets and destroy monuments that honor Confederate soldiers": "Corporations headquartered in Southern states have refused to fly state flags that contain a Confederate emblem; public schools have forbidden the display of the Confederate battle flag as if it were an example of gang colors . . . we utterly repudiate the one-sided and hypocritical movement to demonize Southerners and their symbols." Claiming "we prefer not to think of ourselves as victims," Hill and Fleming wrote that "if Southerners were any other people in the world, the campaign to rob them of their symbols, their history and their cultural identity would be termed cultural genocide," and they asked for "the right to be let alone to mind our own business, to rear our own children and to say our own prayers in the buildings built with our own money."[28] In 1995, after a young white man in Kentucky was murdered by blacks for flying a Confederate flag in the back of his truck, Hill declared to a white audience that "the South represents the only remaining stumbling block to the imposition of an American police state." In a phrase reminiscent of earlier Lincoln hatred, Hill worried that the United States was becom-

ing "mongrelized."[29] According to a 2000 Southern Poverty Law Center
Intelligence Report, the League of the South had at least nine thousand
members "organized into 96 chapters in 20 states," although it was damaged significantly when Hill celebrated the September 11, 2001, attacks
on the Pentagon and World Trade Centers as, tellingly, "the natural fruits
of a regime committed to multiculturalism and diversity."[30] Although the
league's national credibility was harmed by such comments, the ideas it
represented and advocated did not disappear. Instead, they moved into
mainstream American political discourse.

So, by the mid-1990s there were important people advocating a sharp
critique of Lincoln from both a libertarian and neo-Confederate perspective, although at times it was hard to distinguish between the two. Their
negative account of the sixteenth president was part of an open expression
of enmity toward the federal government and included the idea that secession was constitutionally and morally right. Of course, given Abraham
Lincoln's opposition to secession, any movement in the United States advocating its right was going to be, more likely than not, hostile to Lincoln in
its intellectual orientation. Although these critics were at this time outside
the mainstream of the modern conservative movement (to be sure, many
of them would have claimed that *they* were the authentic conservatives
and had been wrongly expelled from venues such as William F. Buckley's
National Review), the Internet was becoming available in American homes,
which allowed for widespread access to their ideas. And there were leading
conservatives, such as columnist and ABC political analyst George Will,
who wrote sympathetically about some of their notions.[31] Finally, with
men as divergent ideologically as anarcho-capitalist Murray Rothbard
and paleoconservative Thomas Fleming as leading figures in what might
be labeled an anti-Lincoln movement, or alliance, the president's enemies
had a certain intellectual heft that could appeal to various malcontents.
Such men could not be easily dismissed as ignorant or unintelligent; many
were respected academics and influential figures in American culture
and politics.[32] Although some of Lincoln's critics from the libertarian or
conservative side of the spectrum agreed with the Republican Party in
certain respects—recall then congressman Trent Lott's comment equating the 1984 Republican platform with "things that Jefferson Davis and
his people believed in"—they were also quite critical of them in other
ways. They nevertheless shaped public opinion, not just on the subject
of the Civil War but on what they saw as related matters, including but
certainly not limited to the proper role of government in American soci-

ety.[33] Indeed, Thomas Fleming was in a group that met in 2006 with Texas senator John Cornyn about immigration, while Mises Institute founder Llewellyn Rockwell Jr. claimed that Rothbard's essays, published in the *Rothbard-Rockwell Report* in the 1990s, influenced "a surprising number of players, for good and evil, on the right." When philosopher Donald Livingston held a conference on secession in 1991, he reported that "nobody showed up." But by 2010 the Abbeville Institute that Livingston founded in Atlanta, which was named in honor of antebellum proslavery advocate John C. Calhoun, had "64 associated scholars from various colleges and disciplines."[34] Their 2005 summer conference was devoted to "Re-thinking Lincoln: The Man, the Myth, the Symbol, the Legacy."[35] Attacking Lincoln was part of a long-term intellectual and manifestly political strategy to educate—or reeducate—the American public and reshape debate not only about Americans' understanding of Lincoln but about their understanding of the means and ends of American democracy as well. Lincoln's critics knew, as Lincoln himself stated in 1858, that "he who moulds public sentiment goes deeper than he who enacts statutes or pronounces decisions. He makes statutes and decisions possible or impossible to be executed." Two years earlier he had declared: "Our government rests in public opinion. *Whoever can change public opinion can change the government.*"[36]

Two magazines edited at different times by Fleming, *Southern Partisan* and *Chronicles: A Magazine of American Culture,* propagated a decidedly negative view of Lincoln—and post–Cold War America.[37] *Chronicles* was the more intellectually serious and offered a forum for many of Lincoln's adversaries, including Bradford, Livingston, Rockwell, Rothbard, the notable journalist and presidential candidate Pat Buchanan, and historian Clyde Wilson. Founded "in the bicentennial year of 1976" as part of the Rockford Institute in Rockford, Illinois, *Chronicles* and the institute's subjects, according to its spring 2013 fund-raising letter, "are the survival of the West, the challenges to Christendom, and the ways in which we might revive regional cultures and decentralist practices in America." The obstacles they faced included "a huge, blundering, intrusive federal government that is hostile to Christian men and women and no longer restrained by the Constitution . . . [and] mass media that glorify, even sanctify, perversion while mocking decency and any who practice it."[38] Fleming published numerous pieces hostile to Lincoln from the 1990s onward, culminating in an entire issue dedicated to the president's allegedly negative legacy on the bicentennial of his birth in 2009.[39] In 1997 *Chronicles* examined the "Imperial Presidency." In the essay from his monthly "Hard Right" column, Fleming emphasized the traditional themes of Lincoln enmity, declaring that "the racial attitudes espoused by Lincoln and his colleagues are closer to those of the KKK than to those of the NAACP." The sixteenth president was a political and religious hypocrite who violated the Constitution to save the Union, "like the man who beats his wife in order to save the marriage," and "a nonbeliever who loved to misuse religious language." But "Lincoln's worst bequest," according to Fleming, was the one he left to the very slaves he had supposedly freed: "The best historians of slavery [Fleming left such historians unnamed] have shown that, on average, black slaves were better off than contemporary white workers in the North and better off than their own free children after emancipation." And for Fleming, Lincoln was the progenitor of virtually everything that was wrong with America: "Today, many wars after Mr. Lincoln's and with trillions of dollars of debt, the American people are bondslaves to great multinational interests who send our sons into foreign wars in which we have nothing to gain, who openly bribe our political leaders with campaign contributions from foreign governments, and who have created a vast government apparatus that tells us how to bring up our children, where to send them to school, how to provide for our elderly parents, what we can eat and drink, what we can smoke, and what we can say or think. If George Washington and Thomas Jefferson had known what lay ahead, they would have put on red coats and suppressed the secessionists of 1776."[40]

Former Nixon and Reagan administration official, presidential candidate, and well-known political pundit Patrick J. Buchanan resurrected the idea that the Civil War had been a blunder that could have been easily avoided if not for Lincoln's poor statesmanship. Buchanan downplayed the interests at stake in 1860–61 and furthermore claimed, as with all Confederate apologists, that the war was not about ending slavery. Buchanan, like other Lincoln critics, seemed either unable or unwilling to understand that Lincoln and the Republicans wanted to preserve a relatively democratic Union so that slavery could eventually be eradicated, while the Confederacy wanted to destroy that Union in order to ensure its indefinite perpetuation. The South had a perfect right to secede from the Union, Buchanan wrote, because it was "a separate civilization and wished to be a separate country" from the North. In his view the war had been fought over tariffs, not slavery, and Lincoln had waged the war as a dictator, unjustly and even criminally.[41]

In the same issue Lew Rockwell's loathing for Lincoln was extended to the office of the presidency. Rockwell, who was a relatively infrequent contributor to *Chronicles,* declared that the presidency itself "must be destroyed": "It is the primary evil we face, and the cause of nearly all our woes. . . . It is the chief mischief-maker in every part of the globe, the leading wrecker of nations, the usurer behind Third World debt, the bailer-out of corrupt governments, the hand in many dictatorial gloves, the sponsor and sustainer of the New World Order, of wars, interstate and civil, of famine and disease."[42] Rockwell's favorite president was William Henry Harrison because "he keeled over shortly after his inauguration."[43] In Rockwell's view the problem with the presidency, which meshed nicely with the stance of conservative Christians antagonistic to Lincoln, lay in its pseudoreligious trappings and symbolism. The president, rather than being seen as an executive or federal officeholder, is oftentimes viewed as a religious figure. Accordingly, "the structure of the presidency, and the religious aura that surrounds it, must be destroyed. The man is merely a passing occupant of the Holy Chair of St. Abraham. It is the chair itself that must be reduced to kindling."[44] After his more general criticism of the presidency, Rockwell leveled some specific condemnations of Lincoln that were in keeping with previous detractors, calling him "a Caesar, in complete contradiction to most of the Framer's intentions."[45]

In contrast to his hatred for Lincoln and the American presidency, Rockwell was a consistent supporter of Texas congressman Ron Paul's political career, including the congressman's presidential ambitions, and reportedly authored some of Paul's controversial newsletters in the 1980s and 1990s. Paul recommended both the Rockwell and Mises Institute websites in his book *Liberty Defined: 50 Essential Issues That Affect Our Freedom* (2011), a book he dedicated to, among others, Murray Rothbard.[46] Indeed, Rockwell's website, LewRockwell.com, contains a lengthy "King Lincoln" file of paleolibertarian criticism. Even the most cursory perusal of that collection will alert the reader to articles such as Thomas DiLorenzo's "What Lincoln's Army Did to the Indians," Joseph Stromberg's "Sherman the Exterminator," and Clyde Wilson's "War Crimes Trial of Abraham Lincoln."[47]

The significance of such negative analyses was far more than just the typical ventilation of hatred for the Civil War president; rather, they represented the intellectual vanguard of a movement that wanted to change the political course of the United States in a more conservative, or as they said, reactionary, direction. According to reporters Julian Sanchez and

David Weigel from *Reason* magazine, a libertarian monthly, the alliance forged by Rockwell, Rothbard, and Paul "was of a piece with a conscious political strategy" to create "a schismatic 'paleolibertarian' movement" that "they hoped would midwife a broad new 'paleo' coalition."[48] Rothbard viewed this coalition as a potential reincarnation of the "Original Right, the right wing as it existed from 1933 to approximately 1955 . . . formed in reaction against the New Deal, against the Great Leap Forward into the Leviathan state that was the essence of the New Deal."[49] As part of this political strategy, Rothbard advocated, a "right-wing populism: exciting, dynamic, tough, and confrontational, rousing, and inspiring not only the exploited masses, but the often shell-shocked right-wing intellectual cadre as well." His political models were Senator Joseph McCarthy and fellow *Chronicles* contributor and Republican presidential candidate Pat Buchanan, and it is easy to see a prescient description of the early-twenty-first-century American Tea Party movement in his language. Rothbard suggested the term *radical reactionaries* for this crusade and detailed its goals: "With the inspiration of the death of the Soviet Union before us, we know that it *can* be done. We shall break the clock of social democracy. We shall break the clock of the Great Society. We shall break the clock of the welfare state. We shall break the clock of the New Deal. We shall break the clock of Woodrow Wilson's New Freedom and perpetual war. We *shall* repeal the twentieth century."[50] Clearly, attacking Lincoln was consistent with Rothbard's description of a populist conservatism that was, "tough, and confrontational," a useful method for advancing a proudly reactionary and inegalitarian political and cultural agenda.[51] Although Rothbard died early in 1995, he remained an enormously influential figure in paleolibertarian circles long after his passing.

Southern Partisan also worked assiduously to advance authors such as Bradford, DiLorenzo, Wilson, historian Ludwell Johnson, and Thomas Woods, author of *The Politically Incorrect Guide to American History* (2004) and *Nullification: How to Resist Federal Tyranny in the 21sth Century* (2010), all of whom were hostile to Lincoln in one way or another. During the Clinton presidency, the *magazine* promoted the sale of Edgar Lee Masters's classic anti-Lincoln biography, *Lincoln: The Man.* Masters's book was reissued by the Foundation for American Education, the same organization that funded the publication of *Southern Partisan,* with an advertisement: "If you think Bill Clinton Has a Character Problem." It also sold T-shirts showing a picture of Lincoln on the front with the words "Sic Semper Tyrannis" underneath his visage, while on the back of the shirt were the words of Thomas Jefferson, "The tree of liberty must be refreshed from time to time with the blood of patriots and tyrants." Timothy McVeigh, the American terrorist who bombed the Oklahoma City federal building in 1995, killing 168 people, was wearing this shirt when he was arrested.[52]

Southern Partisan celebrated all things Confederate and emphasized the rights of local communities to define standards of behavior and morality without federal interference. So, although the magazine was not itself libertarian, its philosophy of local control was perfectly consistent with libertarian disdain for the federal government and the reactionary outlook advocated by Rockwell and Rothbard. It featured interviews by Republican luminaries such as Texas congressman Dick Armey, associated with the early-twenty-first century Tea Party movement, George W. Bush's attorney general John Ashcroft, Reverends Jerry Falwell and Pat Robertson, Senators Trent Lott and Phil Gramm, and conservative activist Phyllis Schlafly. *Southern Partisan* was edited for a brief period by Thomas Fleming, but South Carolinian Richard Quinn, who co-owned the magazine, took over editorial duties in 1981 and stayed in that position until 1999.[53] Quinn proudly touted his work "as media consultant for Governor Ronald Reagan" in the 1980 South Carolina primary election, and he was reportedly paid substantial sums of money by John McCain's 2008 presidential campaign for similar labor.[54] Quinn also worked for influential South Carolina politicians, including Republican senators Strom Thurmond and Lindsay Graham and Congressman Joe Wilson, and he endorsed the eventual winner of the 2012 Republican South Carolina primary, Newt Gingrich.[55]

The *Partisan*'s associate editor during Quinn's tenure, Richard T. Hines, was likewise intimately involved in Republican Party circles. A relatively insignificant member of the Reagan administration, in 2000 Hines was a key reason George W. Bush won the Republican South Carolina primary over John McCain. In order to ensure Bush's victory, Hines reportedly issued "250,000 fliers that he signed with his own name accusing McCain of 'changing his tune' on the Confederate flag and describing Bush as 'the [only] major candidate who refused to call the Confederate flag a racist symbol.'"[56] It is no wonder, then, that the *Partisan* lamented the death of segregationist Strom Thurmond and gave a "Scalawag Award" monthly to individuals who they believed betrayed the neo-Confederate cause. Such recipients of this award included Texas governor Ann Richards, whose "booze-wasted voice and coarse laugh . . . can be heard across barrooms in Southwestern America": "We have been charmed by her sharp tongue, her massive application of lipstick and her frozen albino hair. Even watching her on television, you can almost smell the cheap perfume." Governor Richards's sin? She had, at an Austin picnic, chosen to narrate "an Ode to Abraham Lincoln," demonstrating that she did not share the magazine's hostility to the sixteenth president. So, the *Partisan* awarded her the honor of being "our very first female Scalawag."[57] The *Partisan's* circulation was only a couple of thousand people in the early 1980s but had grown to over fifteen thousand in the middle of the Clinton administration. By 2005 it had declined to only six thousand subscribers. *Southern Partisan* nevertheless "acted as Hines's instrument for connecting sympathetic political movers and shakers to the neo-Confederate base."[58] The *Partisan* reflected and propagated a strain of reactionary political thought that gave voice to numerous Lincoln detractors alongside significant Republican figures, including a future Senate majority leader and attorney general of the United States, and therein laid the magazine's significance.[59]

Letters to the editor from *Partisan* readers demonstrated the intricate, if not inextricable, connection between their enmity for Lincoln, political discontent, and the cultural and political stance that characterized paleolibertarianism. Some letters were relatively innocuous but revealed a dreadful hatred of Lincoln and insensitivity to the seriousness of the issues he had dealt with. A couple of South Carolinians sent in photographs proudly displaying a Confederate flag in front of the seated statue of the president inside the Lincoln Memorial. A resident of Lincoln County, North Carolina, wrote to let *Partisan* readers know that his county was named for Revolutionary War hero Benjamin Lincoln, not Abraham.[60] A thief in Maryland and Virginia, according to the *Partisan,* had robbed several stores in 1999 dressed as the president, which the magazine's editors thought was apt because they had long "been trying to warn people" that Lincoln was untrustworthy. The *Partisan* suggested that the local police "look at the faculty members of college history departments around the area" for the culprit.[61] Other letters were more ominous. Greg Hobson wrote in from Bedford, Virginia, to thank the *Partisan* for the quality of its magazine but also to decry the condition of a country that "officially reveres Lincoln" but unfortunately "now has a president [Clinton] who wants to free the gays, lesbians, transvestites, and all other sexual perverts, and let them in our military, schools, and public offices."[62] At home Hobson proudly flew his Confederate flag and challenged "liberal fascists" to try to take it down, all the time worrying that Clinton would pursue his "agenda" and force "it down our throats whether we like it or not."[63]

Chronicles and *Southern Partisan* were not the only magazines that promoted Lincoln bashing as part of a broader decentralist cause. In 2002 the Sons of Confederate Veterans (SCV) was taken over by racial extremists. With its membership rolls estimated between eighteen and thirty thousand, according to the Southern Poverty Law Center, combined with "$5 million in reserves and a number of very prominent members" and "real political pull in some places," the SCV was "a tempting prize for racists."[64] The same year as the takeover of the SCV, the *Confederate Veteran,* the official publication of the organization, published an article on the Emancipation Proclamation by John Weaver, the "chaplain in chief" of the SCV who once called blacks "a retrograde species of humanity."[65] In loathsome language Weaver argued that "Lincoln did not emancipate the slaves—he enslaved free men with his centralized, socialized, protectionist, and mercantilistic form of government. He did not destroy slavery—he merely enlarged the plantation. He destroyed a society and a republic of free men and gave us what we have today—a centralized, bureaucratic, power hungry, dictatorial democracy that steals from the working man and gives to the indolent, the criminal, the pervert, and the enemies of liberty, freedom and righteousness."[66] One year later, just after Lincoln's statue had been dedicated in Richmond, Virginia, the *Veteran* published in its July–August issue a page-length poem entitled "Richmond Air Corps," about a pigeon defecating on the sculpture of the president seated with his son Tad:

So, why the hell is Lincoln there?
He disgraced this Southern land.
To Remove this blight and reclaim our pride,
together we must band.

The seating of this ugly man,
was something forced on us.
The sight of him and his little brat, too,
Only makes me cuss.

I gathered my nerve and went to see,
how Yankees had shown their ass.
While viewing old Abe, I also saw,
many spots upon the brass.

With closer look, I noticed they were,
the work of pigeon's best.
On Lincoln's head, a proud bird struts,
a Rebel flag upon his breast![67]

The *Veteran* offered advertisements to its readers for both old and new attacks on Lincoln, including such classics as Lyon Gardiner Tyler's *Confederate Catechism,* Elizabeth Avery Meriwether's *Facts and Falsehoods concerning the War on the South, 1861–1865,* John S. Tilley's *Lincoln Takes Command: How Lincoln Got the War He Wanted,* and the two central books of Lincoln criticism from the early twentieth and twenty-first centuries, Charles L. C. Minor's and Thomas J. DiLorenzo's works of the same name, *The Real Lincoln.*[68] One would look in vain for any balanced treatment of Lincoln in the *Veteran*'s pages, which was ironic for a group of people who continually decried the influence of the "Lincoln cult." But balance was not the point: the point of their Lincoln loathing was to undermine the legitimacy of the national government by demonstrating that, in refusing to concede the Confederacy's right to secede and establish a slaveholding republic, the president had brought federal tyranny to the United States.[69] Consequently, ongoing animosity for Lincoln and the federal government was related to a larger political purpose: as one leader of the SCV, Larry Salley, put it in another context, the organization's goal was "to decentralise political power to the extent that no central politician has the power to tell me, or my son, when or where he can pray, or what firearm he can own, or whether we can ban abortion."[70]

As the turn of the century approached, Lincoln's enemies had created an intellectual and political infrastructure for their movement that was at the very least linked indirectly, if not directly, to the larger conservative movement as a whole. With the Ludwig von Mises Institute, LewRockwell.com, *Chronicles, Southern Partisan,* the SCV, and influential Republican strategists and politicians sympathetic to and willing to advance their ideas, they were provided with several crises and historic events that aided their anti-Lincoln crusade: the impeachment of President Clinton contributed to an overall cynicism toward Washington, D.C., if not all federal officeholders; the 2001 attacks on the World Trade Center and Pentagon and America's domestic and foreign response to the "War on Terror" brought renewed scrutiny to the role of the United States in world affairs and the role of the presidency in American life; the bloated spending of the Bush administration, followed by the Great Recession of 2008, seemed to discredit other branches of conservatism found in publications such as *National Review,* which in 2009 had published an essay by historian Allen Guelzo extolling the president's conservative virtues during the bicentennial of Lincoln's birth; the federal government's inept response to Hurricane Katrina tarnished the national government; the historic inauguration of the first African American and deft user of the Lincoln image, Barack Obama, to the presidency during Lincoln's bicentennial focused the nation's attention on Lincoln and the Civil War; and the increasing federal debt and deficit under President Obama, coupled with an expansion of the federal role in health care with the 2010 passage of the Patient Protection and Affordable Care Act (so-called Obamacare), confirmed for many that the federal government was either out of control or too controlling. These happenings assisted in bringing public loathing for Abraham Lincoln ever closer into mainstream conservative circles. Indeed, even as early as 1996, journalist Peter Applebome thought "it's hard to know these days where the Confederacy ends and the Republican Party begins."[71]

At the same time, the cause of destroying Lincoln's stature was aided by Lerone Bennett Jr.'s six-hundred-page magnum opus, *Forced into Glory: Abraham Lincoln's White Dream* (1999).[72] Issued three decades after he first accused Lincoln of racism, *Forced into Glory* was "a political study of the uses and abuses of biography and myth." Bennett argued that "your identity, whatever your color, is based, at least in part, on what you think about Lincoln, the Civil War, and slavery."[73] And in Bennett's view this was vitally important "because Abraham Lincoln is not the light, because he is in fact hiding in the light, hiding our way."[74] *Forced into Glory* not only attempted to discredit Lincoln; it indicted the entire American historical profession for portraying Lincoln as a Great Emancipator when he was actually an oppressor. Lincoln scholars had argued that the white supremacist statements Lincoln uttered and the colonization plans he pursued were just attempts to cater to nineteenth-century voters, but Bennett argued that Lincoln's great speeches were words that hid his real agenda: to deport every black out of the United States and create a less pluralistic country, one exclusively for whites.[75] From Bennett's standpoint Lincoln scholars were complicit in shrouding this truth from Americans and thus hindered racial progress. "The issue posed by all this is not the state of the soul of Abraham Lincoln but the state of the soul of the Republic," Bennett declared, "which finds its deepest moral values in a White supremacist who opposed integration and wanted to deport all Blacks. One can say that the Republic has been unfortunately deluded by scholars who have systematically hidden the truth in one of the most extraordinary episodes in the history of scholarship."[76] Bennett shared at least one characteristic with all of Lincoln's enemies in that he presented himself as an intellectual pioneer, an iconoclast, a debunker of myths devoted to the truth that had been suppressed by an allegedly nefarious Lincoln cult blind to the reality about its flawed idol. Bennett's numerous charges, despite the intense criticism of Lincoln that had circulated throughout the United States since 1858, made more plausible those libertarian and neo-Confederate accusations that the Civil War was not fought over slavery, or was even Lincoln's real concern, but was instead waged, as both groups vociferously argued, to expand federal power over the states.

Forced into Glory elaborated in much greater depth and more strident rhetoric Bennett's central contention that the Emancipation Proclamation freed no slaves. The proclamation "enslaved and/or continued the enslavement of a half-million slaves, more slaves than it ever freed. Let's rephrase it and put it another way: *On January 1, 1863, Abraham Lincoln reenslaved and/or condemned to extended slavery more Blacks than he ever freed.*"[77] In Bennett's view Lincoln never wanted to end slavery. Instead, it was the abolitionists who pressured Lincoln to rid the nation of slavery, Congress through its Confiscation Acts (bills Lincoln signed into law), the slaves who ran away from the farms and plantations during the conflict, and those who played a role in passing the Thirteenth Amendment who truly deserved acclaim for abolition.

The idea that Lincoln was forced by events to emancipate the slaves was hardly original. Carter Woodson had made the same point decades earlier. Nor was it shocking that a politician in a democracy might be influenced by public opinion to enact a policy he long favored. Indeed, in 1864 Lincoln said as much in a letter to Albert Hodges of Kentucky: "I claim not to have controlled events, but confess plainly that events have controlled me."[78] What made Bennett's claim extraordinary was not simply that Lincoln was coerced into freeing the slaves but that he was an actual *hindrance* to their emancipation. His argument was to an extent in opposition to previous African American critics of the president. Although men such as Archibald Grimké, Hubert Harrison, and W. E. B. Du Bois had expressed decidedly negative opinions about Lincoln, their stance did not necessarily constitute loathing, for they had also called Lincoln "great," America's "greatest president," and "perhaps the greatest figure of the nineteenth century."[79] Bennett, however, sharply disagreed with such characterizations. In his view the United States would have been better served had Lincoln not been president: "Lincoln was at best an incidental, accidental rider of a liberating wave that probably would have crested sooner—and higher—without him."[80] He cited philosopher Sidney Hook's argument in *The Hero in History* (1943) that throughout history there are two types of men: "The *eventful* man in history is any man whose actions

influence subsequent developments along a different course than would
have been followed if these actions had not been taken." In contrast, "the
event-making man is an eventful man whose actions are the consequence
of outstanding capacities of intelligence, will, and character rather than
accidents of position."[81] Bennett made it very clear that he believed Lincoln
was the former, "the beneficiary of events that he neither shapes and, in
Lincoln's case, opposed."[82]

If Lincoln did not really believe in freeing the slaves, or only did so because he had to, then according to Bennett, what Lincoln truly advocated
was white supremacy coupled with the colonization of blacks outside the
United States. Here Bennett made his most controversial claims about Lincoln (and really about the country that venerated him). He maintained that
Lincoln as much as anyone else in nineteenth-century America did not subscribe to the idea of a multiracial nation and that if his colonization policies
had been fulfilled, America would have remained racially exclusive:

> For if Lincoln had been a strong and effective leader, there would be no
> Blacks here, not even the Blacks who say he was the strongest and best U.S.
> president . . . . At the same time, we ought to remember, if only for perspec-
> tive, that if Lincoln had succeeded there would be no Broadway, no musi-
> cal comedy, no American music, no Grammy and Rock 'n' Roll, no Beatles
> or Gershwin or Copland or Fred Astaire, no American athletics to speak
> of, no Jim Brown or Michael Jordan or Dr. J., a thin White gruel of pale
> religion and food, and a Constitution and a democracy lacking the ballast
> of the Fourteenth and Fifteenth amendments and the singing summons of
> Thurgood Marshall, Martin Luther King, Jr., Earl Warren, and Bill Clinton,
> an America, in short, without color, rhythm, and soul—Australia with a
> Mississippi River.[83]

Like Lincoln's neo-Confederate opponents, Bennett thought Lincoln's
presidency was *the* turning point in American history, not because he
succeeded in winning the war or freed the slaves or centralized power
in Washington, D.C., but because his white supremacist policies failed.

From Bennett's standpoint Lincoln was an indecisive leader morally
indifferent to slavery and oppression. Lincoln was "the archetype of the
sensitive, suffering, ineffectual, *fence* figure—in America, in the Third
Reich, in Algeria, in South Africa—who is born on a fence and lives and
dies on a fence, unable to accept or reject the political evil that defines
him objectively."[84] Unlike those critics who saw Lincoln as Hitleresque in
his expansion of executive power and his war crimes, Bennett claimed
that Lincoln was a compromiser, a racist like those Germans who stood

idly by while the Nazis carried out the Holocaust. "Lincoln was in and of himself, and in his objective being, an oppressor," a conservative, when "to be a conservative at a time of extreme oppression, as in South Africa, as in the Third Reich, as in the Slave South, at a time when to be moderate is to be culpable, and to be a conservative is to be an accomplice, is to be a different kind of person."[85] Historians who defended Lincoln (or even tried to make his policies explicable), it followed, were no better than intellectuals in Nazi Germany who joined the Nazi Party and became apologists for Hitler's regime.[86] Bennett held that "with rare exceptions, you can't believe what any major Lincoln scholar tells you about Abraham Lincoln and race."[87]

But what about the Confederacy? Many of Lincoln's enemies maintained that the Confederacy was a "morally sound" cause—the words are philosopher Donald Livingston's—and that it would have hastened the end of slavery had it won the war. Bennett, by contrast, had no patience with that argument. A little more than midway through *Forced into Glory,* Bennett observed that "few modern scholars notice the similarities between the Third Reich and the Confederacy, and almost no one arraigns it or its leaders for crimes against humanity."[88] Elsewhere Bennett implied that Confederate president Jefferson Davis, General Robert E. Lee, and other high-ranking Confederates were war criminals who should have been severely punished after the war.[89] Nonetheless, Bennett associated Lincoln with the Confederacy's views, attributing Lincoln's failure to answer Alexander Stephens's "Cornerstone" speech, despite being encouraged to speak out against it, inasmuch as "he was fighting for the old Union, for the Constitution as it was, *with its slave clauses,* for South Carolina as it was, with mint juleps, cotton and slaves, and for Illinois as it was, with Black Laws and a constitution barring Black settlers."[90] In fact, Lincoln rarely reacted publicly to anything said by Confederate officials. It was part of his overall strategy of avoiding any form of recognition of a regime he considered illegitimate.

Bennett's true heroes were Illinois senator Lyman Trumbull and abolitionists such as Wendell Phillips: "Trumbull is virtually unknown to White Americans who have worked night and day for more than 140 years to perpetuate the memory of a White separatist who wanted to deport all African Americans and who provides, moreover, the greatest example in all history of the wisdom of standing idly by in a great national crisis like slavery or apartheid or the Third Reich."[91] Bennett maintained that for most of his political career Lincoln had not been in the forefront of the movement for racial justice. It was here that Bennett was particularly hard on scholars who defended Lincoln by claiming that everybody in the nineteenth century was a white supremacist. He cited Phillips, among others, as a prominent example of whites from that era who were, unlike Lincoln, racial egalitarians. Bennett believed it was no defense to say that Lincoln pandered to contemporary racist sentiment to get elected. "For a man who race-baits in order to get elected and who supports man-hunting, woman-hunting, and children-hunting because of his ambition has nothing to say to us," Bennett thundered, "no matter how many historians sing his praises."[92] From Bennett's standpoint "most major Lincoln scholars—comfortable, conservative, cautious White males—make themselves academic accomplices of the oppression and the slavery Lincoln supported."[93] In his defense of Trumbull and Phillips, Bennett made an important point in emphasizing that there were whites who did speak up and try to end slavery and that Lincoln was not initially one of slavery's more vocal opponents. But few modern, pro-Lincoln scholars have ever claimed otherwise, and it was a serious omission not to point out the extent to which Lincoln, Trumbull, and Phillips were all part of the same broad movement in the United States to end slavery and make freedom national.[94]

Notwithstanding Lincoln's private and public advocacy of limited suffrage for African Americans, Bennett claimed that the president remained to his dying day an unapologetic racist who wanted America cleansed of all African Americans.[95] Yet Bennett acknowledged one moment when the president came tantalizingly close to embracing racial equality. He quoted approvingly the section of the Second Inaugural Address in which Lincoln resolved that if the war lasts "until all the wealth piled by the bondman's two hundred and fifty years of unrequited toil shall be sunk, and until every drop of blood drawn with the lash, shall be paid by another drawn with the sword, as was said three thousand years ago, so still it must be said, 'the judgments of the Lord, are true and righteous altogether.'"[96] Bennett characterized these lines as the "one electric moment" in the speech.[97] But "from this great (rhetorical) height, Lincoln descended to the valley" of racist policies by stating on April 11, 1865, the last speech of his life, that he preferred that the franchise was "conferred *on the very intelligent* [blacks], and on those who serve our cause as soldiers."[98] From that day forward Booth planned to assassinate Lincoln, in the hopes of reviving the Confederacy's fortunes, for uttering the very words Bennett argued proved Lincoln was a racist: "He [Lincoln] believed until his death the Negro was the Other, the Inferior, the Subhuman, who had to be—Lincoln said it was a NECESSITY—subordinated, enslaved, quarantined to protect the sexual, social, political and economic interests of Whites. Everything he did in his last one hundred days, everything he said, even the speeches his defenders are always praising, was based on this racist idea, which defined his life, his politics, and his Gettysburgs."[99] Abraham Lincoln, Lerone Bennett concluded, "must be seen as the embodiment, not the transcendence, of the American Tradition of racism. In his inability to rise above that tradition, Lincoln, often called 'the noblest of all Americans,' holds up a flawed mirror to the American soul."[100]

Forced into Glory struck a nerve in the Lincoln community and also among the public at large. The former director of the Lincoln Museum in Fort Wayne, Indiana, historian Gerald J. Prokopowicz, wrote in one review that *Forced into Glory* was "easily the most controversial Lincoln-related publication of this generation" and said that although it quoted Lincoln selectively and oversimplified the political context in which he operated, it was a book with which all Americans "will need to come to terms."[101] Michael Lind, author of *What Lincoln Believed: The Values and Convictions of America's Greatest President* (2004), said Bennett's book contained "irrefutable" scholarship.[102] Yet two of America's most reputable scholars, Eric Foner and James M. McPherson, felt compelled to respond, to refute the irrefutable, in reviews published in the *Los Angeles Times* and *New York Times,* respectively. Foner thought Bennett's "book deserves attention" if for no other reason than it "presents compelling evidence of how historians have consistently soft-pedaled Lincoln's racial views."[103] Despite the volume's merits, however, Foner labeled Bennett's assertion that Lincoln was a supporter of slavery and an oppressor "totally unfounded" and said "Bennett is guilty of the same kind of one-dimensional reading of Lincoln's career as the historians he criticizes."[104] McPherson agreed that *Forced into Glory* "must be taken seriously," but while acknowledging that "Lincoln did share the racial prejudices of his time and place" and advocated "the idea of colonizing blacks abroad," he concluded that "Bennett gets more wrong than he gets right," especially in his "distortions in interpretation" and "distortion by omission."[105] McPherson made the obvious and unanswerable point that if Lincoln was not hostile to slavery, as Bennett maintained, then it was impossible "to understand why seven slave states seceded in response to Lincoln's election."[106] Finally, Bennett's idea that Lincoln's Emancipation Proclamation "freed not a single slave" is one that McPherson stated "could not be more wrong": "From Jan. 1, 1863, freedom would march southward with the Union Army, which became an army of liberation."[107]

As for Lincoln's allegedly undying wish for colonizing blacks beyond the North American continent, when Bennett claimed that "Lincoln believed that deporting Blacks and creating an all-White country was a *moral* imperative," he ignored available scholarship that contradicted his thesis.[108] Although he was correct that for much of his career Lincoln—along with many other Americans—wanted to colonize blacks outside of the United States, a result that certainly would have meant a less racially pluralistic future for the country, Bennett was incorrect to use the term *ethnic cleansing,* a twentieth-century term denoting murder or the forced removal of populations from their homes. Lincoln's colonization plans were to have been *voluntary,* an important distinction that seems to have escaped Bennett's attention. As for the idea that Lincoln tenaciously held on to his wish for colonization, Bennett based his case on the testimony of General Benjamin Butler, who claimed that in a meeting with Lincoln in the spring of 1865, the president told him he feared "a race war" could ensue once the military hostilities ended. Butler asserted that Lincoln wanted him to examine the practicality of removing blacks from the United States, but Butler answered that colonization was not feasible. Bennett acknowledged that Butler's story has "been questioned by some scholars," but he did not let his reader know that historian Mark Neely Jr. damaged, perhaps irreparably, Butler's account of this incident as early as 1979.[109] Neely's article in the journal *Civil War History* did not even appear in Bennett's notes or bibliography; instead, Bennett quoted scholars who agreed with him, but he did not adequately alert his readers that there were others, such as Neely, who had challenged and perhaps discredited Butler's story.[110] Possibly the omission was because the information did not fit Bennett's preconceived notions about Lincoln's supposed pathological racism and because it would have destroyed one of the book's chief arguments, that Lincoln was a racist who never changed his views about African Americans. Regrettably, this was a characteristic that all of Lincoln's rivals shared, which was a tendency to claim the president was a racist when in fact the evidence for such a charge remains to a certain degree ambiguous, especially considering that Lincoln was the leader of a broad-based social movement that was not only attempting to end slavery but also struggling mightily to widen notions of American citizenship to include African Americans. To be sure, Lincoln was in some ways a typical nineteenth-century American who shared many of the racial assumptions of the age, but he fought hard to transcend them, which was a far cry from those Confederates and Copperheads who strenuously resisted Lincoln's and the Republicans' efforts.[111] In fact, it would not be too much of an exaggeration, considering that it was Lincoln's recommendation in April 1865 of limited suffrage for male African Americans that prompted Booth to assassinate him, to say that Lincoln was a white American who, whatever his motives, tried to do and did some good things for blacks in the United States and was killed for it.

Still, early in the twenty-first century some excellent work was published on Lincoln and colonization that possibly vindicated Bennett's point about Lincoln holding onto the idea of colonization but at the same time discredited the idea that there was some type of "Lincoln cult" among professional historians. In 2008 Phillip Magness published a partial rebuttal to Mark Neely's 1979 *Civil War History* article entitled "Benjamin Butler's Colonization Testimony Reevaluated."[112] Magness's carefully worded and measured conclusion was that "sufficient evidence exists to merit additional consideration of Lincoln's colonization views later in life, and tends to caution against the conclusiveness that many scholars have previously attached to the view that Lincoln fully abandoned this position. The Butler anecdote remains an imperfect example, yet some of its more plausible details may indicate that Lincoln retained an interest in colonization, even if limited, as late as 1865."[113] Although the evidence remains inconclusive, if not insubstantial, and certainty about Lincoln's views on colonization in 1865 may forever elude historians, Bennett may have been partially correct. But despite the claims of Bennett and indeed all Lincoln foes about a so-called Lincoln cult that ignored or suppressed unpleasant truths about the president, Magness's important and critical article was published in the flagship journal of Lincoln studies—the *Journal of the Abraham Lincoln Association*.[114]

Bennett omitted additional relevant information in *Forced into Glory*. He asserted that Lincoln was an obstacle to slavery's immediate abolition but never specifically named the politician who was electable on a national scale in nineteenth-century America who would have hastened slavery's demise faster and more fully than Lincoln. If Lincoln had been the despicable figure Bennett portrayed, or an actual hindrance to emancipation, then it is hard to ascertain how the antislavery Republican Party that nominated him for the presidency did not see it. Bennett also failed to inform the reader, to cite another example of his omitting important evidence, that the primary reason Lyman Trumbull became a senator in the mid-1850s was because of Abraham Lincoln. At a time when senators were chosen by state legislatures, Lincoln was not able to win enough votes in the Illinois legislature to secure the senatorial seat, so he told his supporters that Trumbull would be a suitable replacement because although Trumbull was a Democrat, he opposed the 1854 Kansas-Nebraska Act that allowed for the expansion of slavery into those territories. Lincoln's support for Trumbull was hardly the action of an unprincipled politician or one who cared not at all if slavery existed. In fact, by telling his supporters to vote for Trumbull, Lincoln engaged in a principled antislavery act, unfortunately one absent from Bennett's narrative of Lincoln's career. Nor did Bennett reveal that during the Lincoln-Douglas debates Senator Douglas repeatedly linked Trumbull with Lincoln by claiming that they had conspired "to abolitionize the old Whig party and the old Democratic party."[115] In other words, Douglas drew no distinction between Lincoln and Trumbull but saw both men as equally villainous for their antislavery stances. In addition, Trumbull had made statements about African Americans that were perhaps as offensive, if not more so, to Bennett's moral sense as Lincoln's words at Charleston. On the floor of Congress in 1859, Trumbull had said: "When we say that all men are created equal, we do not mean that every man in organized society has the same rights. We do not tolerate that in Illinois. I know there is a distinction between these two races because the Almighty himself has marked it upon their very faces; and, in my judgment, man cannot, by legislation or otherwise, produce a perfect equality between these two races, so that they will happily live together."[116] Finally, in citing philosopher Sidney Hook, Bennett argued that Lincoln was not a heroic man worthy of imitation. Perhaps true, except that Hook himself had great admiration for Lincoln, and in a lecture delivered in India that was perhaps available to Bennett as the editor of *Ebony* magazine, called the abolitionists Bennett admired "fanatics of virtue . . . God's angry men, . . . who think they have a mandate from on high to impose virtue upon others at any cost" and "are usually blind to the virtues of any other way than their own." In the same address Hook favorably compared Lincoln and Mahatma Gandhi: "Lincoln is unique among the statesmen not only of the United States but of *the entire world* in that he represents a fusion of idealism and intelligence."[117]

Bennett's lapses were unfortunate but all too characteristic of the scholarship, such as it was, of all Lincoln critics. When confronted by an honest examination of their contentions, they simply refused to allow that they might have been wrong, that their work was riddled with selective use of the historical record, and that as a result, their contentions were perhaps not as original or worthy of consideration as they believed. Instead, in a form of inoculation against historians who they anticipated would condemn their frequently unsubstantiated arguments, Lincoln's antagonists unceasingly attacked their opponents as either dishonest or under the sway of some wicked Lincoln cult. The truth is, however, that the historical profession in the United States, for all its numerous shortcomings and despite being likened to Hitler apologists for Nazism by Lerone Bennett Jr., has been far more considerate and diligent in examining Lincoln's flaws and the claims of his enemies than his rivals have been in willing to concede Lincoln's virtues and achievements.

The overall effect of Bennett's work has been significant, although perhaps not in the way that many have believed. African American historian Gerald Horne has described Bennett's popularity among blacks as "stratospheric," and Lincoln biographer Allen Guelzo thought *Forced into Glory* symbolized "one of the most dramatic transformations in American historical self-understanding in the past century, and that is the slow, almost unnoticed withdrawal of African Americans from what was once the great consensus of blacks' admiration for Abraham Lincoln."[118] That consensus had always been somewhat fragile and contested, but Guelzo was right that there were significant political consequences to Bennett's (and neo-Confederate) loathing of Abraham Lincoln. From 1858 onward Lincoln's critics, especially that small minority of abolitionists and those who fashioned themselves their intellectual descendants, shared with twenty-first-century Americans a disdain for the slow, untidy compromises endemic to democratic politics and all too characteristic of politicians. This was not an attitude that Abraham Lincoln shared. He gloried in democratic politics. It is here, in the president's enlightened, prudential approach to emancipation—a *constitutional* approach that favored concrete results over pure motives as the criterion for successful policy—that one will find an important reason why some people loathe Abraham Lincoln.[119] Contempt for Lincoln, historically speaking, has often coincided with contempt for sluggish, messy democratic government and the flawed politicians who embrace it. Sadly, the work of the president's critics in the post–Cold War era contributed to Americans' cynical discontent with the political system Lincoln fought a war to preserve "so that *all* should have an equal chance."[120]

It was impossible to claim, furthermore, that Bennett's work remained as shocking as it had been in the 1960s, or that it was necessarily representative of black opinion, when one considered the comments of other African Americans who admired Lincoln. Thomas Sowell, an influential conservative economist with libertarian leanings at the Hoover Institution, a conservative think tank, reviewed Guelzo's book *The Emancipation Proclamation* in 2005, saddened there was even a need for such a volume. The book was necessary, and here the economist conceded the increasing influence of Lincoln's detractors, Sowell wrote, "because of the completely unrealistic view of the world—past and present—that prevails, not only among the ignorant but among the intelligentsia as well."[121] Writing as if he had all of Lincoln's adversaries in mind, Sowell declared that "since the 1960s, it has been fashionable in some quarters to take cheap shots at Lincoln, asking such questions as 'Why didn't he free all the slaves?' 'Why did he wait so long?' 'How come the Emancipation Proclamation didn't just come right out and say that slavery was wrong?'"[122] Sowell failed to acknowledge that such questions have been asked of Lincoln since the 1860s, but he correctly noted that the "people who indulge in this kind of self-righteous carping act as if Lincoln was someone who could do whatever he damn well pleased, without regard to the law, the Congress, or the Supreme Court."[123] Sowell explained that when Lincoln issued his Emancipation Proclamation, he had to do so with the Supreme Court in mind, a Supreme Court "still headed by Chief Justice Roger Taney," who in the *Dred Scott* case had argued that blacks in the United States "had no rights which the white man needed to respect." It was precisely for this reason that the proclamation was issued in language that was dry and uninspiring, for it was a military and legal document issued by the commander in chief during war, which meant it had to apply to those "slaves in territory controlled by enemy forces."[124] Finally, Lincoln's issuance of the proclamation took political courage because there was "no big political support in the North for freeing slaves." Many northerners opposed it, fearing that it would strengthen the resolve of secessionists.[125] The country should be grateful to have had a leader like Lincoln in such "turbulent times," but unfortunately there were detractors who, in Sowell's judgment, "reduce other times—including our own—to cartoon-like simplicities that allow us to indulge in cheap self-righteousness when judging those who carry heavy responsibilities."[126]

Also in 2005, an African American politician of a more liberal persuasion, Barack Obama from Illinois, published an essay in *Time* magazine honoring Lincoln's strengths while recognizing his limitations. Obama encapsulated why Lincoln's story continued to move Americans, yet at the

same time the future president of the United States unwittingly gave voice
to Bennett's influence, if not additional elements of previous anti-Lincoln
thought. Lincoln's rise from poor obscurity and his strength in the face of
tragic loss were reminders "of a larger fundamental element of American
life—the enduring belief that we can constantly remake ourselves to fit our
larger dreams." Nevertheless, "as a law professor and civil rights lawyer
and as an African American," Obama could not "swallow whole the view of
Lincoln as the Great Emancipator." He was cognizant of Lincoln's "limited
views on race" and saw the Emancipation Proclamation as "more a military
document than a clarion call for justice."[127] Obama's comments here were
somewhat equivocal: most Americans admired Lincoln's rise from poverty, and the Illinois senator's praise for the Emancipation Proclamation
was somewhat tepid. Nevertheless, echoing the voice of W. E. B. Du Bois,
Obama thought it was "precisely those imperfections" that made Lincoln
"so compelling": "For when the time came to confront the greatest moral
challenge this nation has ever faced, this all too human man did not pass
the challenge on to future generations."[128] Senator Obama launched his
presidential candidacy, moreover, from Lincoln's hometown of Springfield, Illinois, in 2007, and as president of the United States he has been
complimentary of Lincoln, averring at the 2009 Abraham Lincoln Association Banquet in Springfield that "it's fair to say that the Presidency of
this singular figure who we celebrate in so many ways made my own story
possible."[129] President Obama's embrace of Lincoln signaled an important
post–Cold War shift in anti-Lincoln sentiment: namely, that a politically
influential dissatisfaction with the sixteenth president emanating from
the left wing of the political spectrum, a dissatisfaction that only emerged
in the twentieth century from the unfulfilled egalitarian promises of the
Civil War and Reconstruction, was on the decline, if not dead altogether.[130]

Still, by 1999 Lerone Bennett's arguments appeared to be accepted into
the mainstream or at the very least recognized as important enough to be
taken into account in any assessment of Abraham Lincoln. In fact, one
could even detect his influence in popular culture. A 2004 film, a counterfactual documentary called *C.S.A.: The Confederate States of America*,
operated on the premise that the Confederates had won the Civil War and
perpetrated one of Bennett's main contentions: Lincoln was portrayed as a
weak, vacillating president, a president relatively unconcerned about slavery and whose most significant act, the Emancipation Proclamation, the
narrator of the film claimed, "did not free a single slave."[131] So, it is difficult
to say whether Bennett's influence has been felt primarily inside or outside

the black community. Certainly, his arguments have carried weight there, but the drop in Lincoln's standing with African Americans has also been caused by other factors, including the overall loss of prestige among all political leaders in the post-Watergate and post-Vietnam era.[132] Most important, if the most prominent African American politician in U.S., if not world, history finds in Lincoln a positive, useful image, the most significant impact of Bennett's work may reside outside the black community. Its illiberal, unintended effect—especially considering Bennett's comparison of the Confederacy to the Third Reich—was to give succor to Lincoln's opponents, who claimed that Lincoln was the father of big government, a warmongering imperialist, a liar, and probably a racist and that a nefarious, professional Lincoln cult suppressed such unpalatable truths.[133]

By the turn of the century and aided by Lerone Bennett Jr., loathing Abraham Lincoln had once again become what *Chronicles* called a "Litmus Test for American Conservatism." In the ensuing decade public criticism of the sixteenth president reemerged more fully into mainstream conservatism. As Donald Livingston explained: "Abraham Lincoln is thought of by many as not only the greatest American statesman but as a great conservative. He was neither. Understanding this is a necessary condition for any genuinely American conservatism."[134] Indeed, in a 2002 symposium on "The War between the States" held in the pages of Murray Rothbard's former periodical, the *Journal of Libertarian Studies* (posted at the Mises Institute website, Mises.org), Livingston claimed "that the 1860 attempt to dismember the Union by peaceful secession was morally sound, and that the North's invasion to prevent secession and to create a consolidated American state was morally unsound."[135] In his essay Livingston argued that the history of the Civil War needed to be rewritten in a deliberate attempt to change America's entire historical narrative. He cited four books in particular that he believed "worth mentioning" in such endeavors: Jeffrey Rogers Hummel's *Emancipating Slaves, Enslaving Free Men: A History of the American Civil War* (1996), Charles Adams's *When in the Course of Human Events: Arguing the Case for Southern Secession* (2000), Thomas DiLorenzo's *Real Lincoln: A New Look at Abraham Lincoln, His Agenda, and an Unnecessary War* (2002), and John Remington Graham's *Constitutional History of Secession* (2002).[136] Historian Thomas Woods, who penned the introduction to the 2002 symposium and later authored *The Politically Incorrect Guide to American History* (with an illustration of Confederate general James Longstreet by Civil War artist Mort Künstler on the cover), a *New York Times* best seller and available through the Conservative Book

Club, popularized some of the notions contained in these books for larger audiences.[137] Others, including George Mason University economist Walter Williams and sometime guest host of Rush Limbaugh's radio show, Fox News legal analyst Judge Andrew P. Napolitano, and Congressman Ron Paul, did likewise. The ideas about Abraham Lincoln and the Civil War voiced by these influential figures provide a window into their political philosophy and rhetoric—a reactionary strain of thought at the very least indirectly connected with influential Republican politicians and leading figures within the conservative movement intent on decentralizing power away from Washington, D.C.—and they are therefore extraordinarily significant and worth examination for that reason alone.

Except for Hummel's *Emancipating Slaves,* which was a reputable and scholarly work by an American historian, these individuals articulated a critique of Lincoln, either individually or in toto, that recalled many of the traditional themes of hostility for the president for modern audiences: that southern secession was legally and morally justified; that secession would have aided rather than hindered the antislavery cause; that slavery would have withered away had not war occurred and thus the war was unnecessary; that secession—and the Confederacy itself—was of a piece with the American tradition of limited government and that the Union victory had centralized power in Washington, D.C.; that the war was not fought to end slavery but to preserve tariffs; and that Lincoln's war to prevent secession was a war of conquest, unjust and immoral, and the methods by which he waged it were incompetent, unconstitutional, barbarous, and criminal. In a relatively new twist they also emphasized that the Union victory had led to a neo-mercantilist American government—according to DiLorenzo, it had established the system of "tax-funded subsidies to politically well-connected businesses and industries . . . protectionism" and "nationalized banking"—and the subsequent creation of the federal welfare bureaucracy of the New Deal. Lincoln was therefore the cause, as Hummel (and Rothbard before him) put it, of "the welfare-warfare State of today."[138]

An attorney by trade, Graham in his *Constitutional History of Secession* held that secession was a constitutional right, while DiLorenzo, an economics professor at Loyola College in Baltimore, claimed that the founding fathers had considered secession "the most fundamental principle of political philosophy."[139] In fact, DiLorenzo had an entire chapter on Americans, including northerners, who had favored secession prior to the beginning of the war. Graham wrote at length about British history, especially the Glorious Revolution of 1688, whereby the crown of England was transferred from James II to William of Orange in a relatively peaceful manner.[140] The American colonists were aware, Graham contended, of the peaceable nature of this revolution and later incorporated the right of secession and nullification in the 1787 Constitution.[141] Graham, DiLorenzo, and Woods claimed that when Virginia, New York, and Rhode Island ordained the new Constitution, they reserved the right to leave the Union in their ordinances of ratification. Woods, who received "useful suggestions" and "vetting" from DiLorenzo and neo-Confederate historian Clyde Wilson for his *Politically Incorrect Guide to American History,* claimed the South had a right to secede under the Tenth Amendment to the Constitution. "The Constitution is silent on the question of secession. And the states never delegated to the federal government any power to suppress secession. Therefore," Woods concluded, "secession remained a reserved right of the states."[142] Congressman Paul praised Woods's volume ("[Woods] heroically rescues real history from the politically correct memory hole. Every American should read this book") and claimed in *Liberty Defined* that "the question was never raised that the states didn't have a right to secede." He likewise asserted that "the Constitution would have never been ratified" if states knew they would not be allowed to secede.[143]

In a sense these critics were attempting to claim the mantle of Lysander Spooner or William Lloyd Garrison by asserting that secession or, as libertarian Joseph Stromberg once called it, "*de facto* independence," would have hastened the end of slavery. "For one thing," Stromberg argued, "there would have no longer been any certainty of recovering runaway slaves after they had escaped into the North. This alone would have constituted a major problem for the slave regime."[144] Consequently, "the new Confederate government," for economic, constitutional, and ideological reasons, "would have been a weaker protector of slavery than the old Federal government."[145] DiLorenzo agreed, claiming that "slavery was on its way out" and would have been dead "long before the end of the century." Slavery was economically inefficient and would never have survived in the Confederate States of America.[146] Paul cited the abolitionists as "supporters of secession" and averred that "many people who favored secession also believed, and rightly, that the modern industrial state would eventually work to eliminate slavery."[147] Woods and Hummel thought northern secession from the South, as Garrison had advocated, would have been a superior antislavery strategy because it would have meant that northerners could disobey the controversial federal fugitive slave law, which required them to subsidize the costs of returning escaped slaves. Still, Hummel had no use for those who thought that slavery was not the cause of secession or that white southerners were not trying to defend the institution; he nevertheless argued that allowing southern secession—a right Hummel supported unconditionally—would have been the better antislavery policy.[148]

These critics defended secession as an antislavery strategy in order to ennoble their own antigovernment cause, and discrediting Lincoln was a key element in that endeavor. As part of this effort, they claimed the president had no real commitment to racial equality. Indeed, DiLorenzo had an entire chapter entitled "Lincoln's Opposition to Racial Equality," and in writing that Lincoln was, on racial matters, a "textbook example of a masterful, rhetorically gifted, fence-straddling politician," he called to mind Murray Rothbard's and Lerone Bennett's earlier accusations.[149] Woods cited Lincoln's 1858 Charleston quote denying he was in favor of black equality, while Graham argued that Lincoln, in his 1854 Peoria address, had "articulated the same basic thought" as Alexander Stephens, who believed that blacks were inferior to whites.[150] Less emphasized, however, was the letter Lincoln wrote to Stephens in December 1860, in which the president-elect said, "You think slavery is *right* and ought to be extended; while we think it is *wrong* and ought to be restricted."[151] To be sure, Lincoln denied in his Peoria speech that the black man was equal to the white man, but Graham for one left unmentioned that in the same speech Lincoln had argued that the issue was irrelevant: "If the negro is a man, is it not . . . a total destruction of self-government to say that he shall not govern *himself*? When the white man governs himself that is self-government; but when he governs *another* man, that is more than self-government—that is despotism. . . . there can be no moral right in connection with one man's making a slave of another."[152] To say the least, this was not a viewpoint with which few, if any white, southern slaveholders would have concurred. It was a tactic of distortion by omission all too characteristic of those who sought to tarnish Lincoln's reputation by whatever means available. But the point was not historical accuracy. Rather, it was to demonstrate for their audiences that neither secession nor the war was about slavery and that Lincoln had no commitment to racial justice; therefore the president must have had another agenda in mind.

Graham did, however, cite Lincoln's 1858 speech in which he argued that African Americans were "entitled to all the natural rights enumerated in the Declaration of Independence." But then, in the nostalgic manner of virtually all Lost Cause devotees, he claimed that "in historical fact, the

condition of slaves was very good in the old South. The peculiar institution of the Dixie States had been woven into a cultural fabric of gentle and
quiet beauty. And the personal relations between whites and blacks were
in excellent order. A civilization of high and noble bearing had evolved
throughout the region. The architecture was graceful. The landscapes
were magnificent. Education focused on classical knowledge. Traditions
were honored. Modern innovations improved but did not dictate the style
of life. The old South was a society graced by good manners, radiant
with happiness."[153] Graham's description of the Old South echoed those
of historian Charles Adams, who, in his discussion of Charles Dickens,
England, and the Civil War, had called slavery evil but also claimed "there
were other evils at home that deserved equal if not higher rank among the
social cruelties of his time. A baby born into slavery had the right to be
taken care of from cradle to grave." In contrast, a "child of the slums had
a much more miserable life—one of hunger, cold, homelessness, disease,
illiteracy, and little chance of rising above this deplorable condition."[154]
As for Graham, he was not only factually wrong in his nostalgic depiction
of antebellum slavery, but his romantic portrayal possibly served another
purpose: by describing inhuman bondage in such a sentimental manner
and omitting the violence that lay at the heart of the institution, he had
implicated Lincoln in the destruction of a supposed Garden of Eden. This
rendering leaves the reader puzzled about why anyone would want to do
away with such an allegedly fine society and suggests that any president
who did such a thing must have been a reprehensible tyrant, which of
course was what many of Lincoln's foes wanted their readers to believe.
What was even more alarming and bewildering—until one considered the
goals of such adversaries and the minimization of slavery's horrors that
has historically coincided with antipathy for Lincoln—was that a respected
philosopher such as Donald Livingston recommended Graham's volume,
Woods cited it regarding the *Dred Scott* case in *Politically Incorrect,* and
historian Clyde Wilson praised the book by claiming that "nowhere is
there a truer and more thorough treatment of the real origins and nature
of freedom and self-government [to be found]."[155]

   If for Lincoln's detractors ending slavery was not the reason for secession or war, then the conflict was an unjustified invasion of the southern
states. The point here was to remove Lincoln's waging of war to restore a
Union without slavery from the moral high ground and claim, instead, that
it was the Confederate cause that was morally correct, thereby delegiti-
mizing the federal government. According to economist Walter Williams,

"The problems that led to the Civil War are the same problems today—big, intrusive government." But there will be no war today because Americans "don't have yesteryear's spirit of liberty and constitutional respect."[156] Charles Adams, who specialized in the history of taxation in the United States, argued in *When in the Course of Human Events* that secession in 1861 was precisely the same as the colonists' secession in 1776 from the British Empire. Like every Lincoln opponent who has made this argument since the 1860s, Adams seemed unable to understand that in 1776 the colonists had no representation in the British Empire from which they were allegedly seceding—launching a *revolution*—while in 1861 white southern slaveholders had dominated the federal government for decades, voted in elections, and were well represented in the United States Congress, the Supreme Court, and the American presidency. Of course, this point was of no importance to Adams, who in a chapter on business interests and the war claimed that "slavery was a nonissue" for northern financial interests and that "the tariff was *the* issue."[157] According to Adams, the reason the tariff was so vital to northerners was that the Confederacy had adopted "a low tariff [that] was instituted immediately, essentially creating a free trade zone in the South," which northerners quickly saw "meant disaster for Northern commerce."[158] Woods echoed Adams, writing that "if the South were allowed to secede and establish freed trade, foreign commerce would be diverted from Northern ports to Southern ones, as merchants sought out the South's low-tariff or free-trade regime."[159] Adams cited Abraham Lincoln asking southerner John B. Baldwin about Fort Sumter possibly falling into Confederate hands: "What then will become of my tariff?"[160] To such paleolibertarian critics this relatively isolated utterance of Lincoln's—as late as October 1859, Lincoln told one correspondent that "I have not thought much upon the subject [of tariffs] recently," while in March 1860 he related to a Connecticut audience that subjects such as the tariff "cannot even obtain a hearing, . . . the question of Slavery is the question, the all absorbing topic of the day"—was of the utmost importance and revealed the real significance of Fort Sumter and the cause of the Civil War: the fort guarded the port of Charleston, where the United States government collected customs duties. DiLorenzo added to Adams's argument by claiming that "to Lincoln, slavery was just another political issue subject to compromise. But protectionist tariffs—the keystone of the Republican Party platform—were nonnegotiable. He promised to wage war on any state that refused to collect enough tariff revenue, a truly bizarre stance."[161] Accordingly, Lincoln's First Inaugural Address was not about reassuring southerners that the federal government would not attack them but about Lincoln "saying to Southerners that if they refused to pay this increased rate of tribute, they would face an invasion by a federal army."[162] Williams unequivocally stated that the war was not "fought to free slaves" but over tariffs. According to Williams, the South seceded "after Lincoln's election" because "Congress passed the highly protectionist Morrill tariffs." He thought it was wonderful that the slaves were freed, but when the president "destroyed the states' right to secession, Abraham Lincoln opened the door to the kind of unconstrained, despotic, arrogant government we have today."[163] Congressman Paul was blunter: "The Civil War was fought to keep all the states under the thumb of a powerful central government."[164]

These individuals deemphasized, or ignored, an entire edifice of modern scholarship that demonstrated conclusively that even if one conceded that slavery was not the primary issue for the North—although preventing the expansion and working for the eventual abolition of the institution was assuredly central for both Lincoln and the antislavery movement—it most certainly was for the Confederacy. Even the most cursory reading of the Declaration of the Causes of Secession issued from states that joined the Confederacy (from which the issue of tariffs is almost entirely absent) or of Alexander Stephens's "Cornerstone" speech" supports such a conclusion.[165] As the libertarian Timothy Sandefur wrote in addressing this argument:

> Southern Democrats were not committed to free markets, either. The Democratic platform of 1860 also called for railroad subsidies and other interventions in the market, and the slave power was hostile to free markets for economic and social reasons. George Fitzhugh, one of the leaders of the "positive good" school of slavery, advocated a hierarchical agrarian modeled on the Middle Ages because he believed that the slaves, if freed, would be unable to fend for themselves and needed a paternalistic helping hand to protect them. When South Carolina Governor James Hammond engaged English Abolitionist Thomas Clarkson in some famous open letters, he made clear that his defense of slavery was rooted in a fundamental hostility to industrial capitalism: wage workers, he said, were worse off with freedom than slaves were without it. Republicans may have embraced certain mercantilist elements in their platform, but Democrats called for the perpetual subordination of the black race to the status of human property, precisely because anything else threatened to replace their Society of Status with a Society of Contract.[166]

Still, in agreement with libertarian Jacob Huebert, these critics argued that although slavery was undoubtedly a monstrous institution, "all governments do things that harm their citizens."[167] Congressman Paul would, it seems, concur: "Think of the draft, confiscatory taxation, laws and mandates against home schooling, speech controls, or any number of impositions of life and property, and regulations designed to control our social and business associations. There is a sense in which these can all be considered forms of slavery."[168] Comparing if not equating routine government operations and regulations that can be altered or eliminated by democratic methods with racially based antebellum slavery was at the very least historically obtuse. It also does not acknowledge that neither free blacks nor slaves had *any* prospect of becoming citizens in the Confederate States of America. This was in stark contrast to their markedly improved prospects for racial equality in the United States once the Civil War was over and northern victory secured.

As for how the war was actually conducted, Adams, DiLorenzo, Woods, and even Hummel emphasized additional aspects of Lincoln's malfeasance: he was incompetent; he unconstitutionally and dictatorially suspended habeas corpus and suppressed political dissent; he encouraged slave insurrection with the Emancipation Proclamation; he refused prisoner exchanges and approved the barbarous methods of Union generals William Tecumseh Sherman and Philip Sheridan. Hummel, a former tank commander in the U.S. military, thought that Lincoln's apologists in the historical profession had obscured the view that the president was not, at least early in the war, an effective military leader. Indeed, Hummel wrote that the "blame for early Union reverses" in the conflict rested squarely on the shoulders of "Abraham Lincoln."[169] Donald Livingston agreed but added: "Having failed to win the war after two years, Lincoln broke the international code of war and turned it against civilians. Sherman acknowledged that he was guilty of war crimes punishable by death according to the laws of war taught at West Point. Vast areas of the South were turned into desert, and two-thirds of Southern property was destroyed, not counting the cost of slaves."[170] DiLorenzo and Adams were no less harsh, each devoting entire chapters to Lincoln's war crimes, while Woods had a section in his chapter on "The War between the States" entitled "The Rise of Total War."[171] Adams claimed that "most academic historians, without legal training, have played down the war crimes issue," an omission he aimed to correct, arguing that Lincoln, Sherman, and northern generals violated the laws of war but have been excused "because they won."[172]

The basis for the accusations of Lincoln as a war criminal stemmed from the charge that he violated the Lieber Code. Designed by Francis Lieber, a professor at Columbia University, who spent much of his life at South Carolina College before moving north, the code found formal expression when Abraham Lincoln issued General Order № 100 on April 24, 1863. Captured soldiers were not to endure "any suffering, or disgrace, by cruel imprisonment, want of food, by mutilation, death or any other barbarity," and "the unarmed citizen is to be spared in person, property, and honor as much as the exigencies of war will admit."[173] The president's detractors charged Abraham Lincoln and the Union army with violating this humane policy. Adams and DiLorenzo argued that by tolerating cruelty toward southerners, Lincoln laid the groundwork for the extermination of the Indians in the West after the Civil War, if not the entire concept of total war. In fact, DiLorenzo pointed out one prominent postwar example of "empire-building and war-mongering," leading to disastrous consequences: the destruction of the Plains Indians. One little remembered piece of legislation signed into law by President Lincoln was the Pacific Railway Act of 1862, providing for the building of a transcontinental railroad across North America paid for in essence by government subsidies. As the railroad advanced into Indian Territory, their way of life was threatened, and the native inhabitants responded by waging war. And it was the luminaries of the Civil War—at least northern luminaries Sherman and Sheridan—who, according to DiLorenzo, conducted "a campaign of ethnic genocide against the Plains Indians to make way for the government-subsidized railroads."[174] DiLorenzo averred that the real reason for both the Civil War and the destruction of the Plains Indians were that "the Southern Confederates and the Indians stood in the way of the Whig/Republican dream of a North American economic empire, complete with a subsidized transcontinental railroad, a nationalized banking system, and protectionist tariffs. Consequently, both groups were conquered and subjugated by the most violent means," and Lincoln's war crimes laid the basis for the American economic and military empire. Indeed, Graham held that northern victory in the war "has produced imperial power, imperial militarism, imperial conquest, imperial oppression, and imperial ruin."[175] From their perspective, conceivably, it would be more appropriate to call Lincoln the Great Imperialist rather than the Great Emancipator.

DiLorenzo indicted Lincoln and those historians who admired Lincoln's war management but refused to label him a war criminal on the grounds that Lincoln was unaware of the atrocities his generals committed. Discounting that the Confederates instigated the Civil War by firing on Fort Sumter, DiLorenzo argued in Rothbardian fashion that the "only just war" was a war fought in self-defense, and as a result, "Lincoln's invasion of the South surely makes him the aggressor."[176] Noting Lincoln's frustration with General George McClellan, who Lincoln believed was far too passive, DiLorenzo claimed, without clear attribution, that "Lincoln wanted Southern civilians to suffer, which required him to abandon international law and the U.S. military's own code as he began to wage total war. And it was total war waged against fellow citizens—mostly women and children and old men—not an invading army." Indeed, according to DiLorenzo, "it is not an exaggeration to say that Lincoln's entire battle plan, from the very beginning, was to wage war on civilians as well as the armed rebels. . . . Hundreds of Southern churches were put to the torch, and priests and ministers were imprisoned for not saying prayers for Abraham Lincoln. The devastation of Southern churches was so pervasive that one gets the impression that the invasion of the South was, among other things, a kind of medieval holy war."[177] Disregarding that the Union army liberated thousands of slaves from slavery, DiLorenzo nevertheless argued that "the slaves suffered as much as anyone else at the hands of Sherman's army." Consequently, at least according to DiLorenzo, the consequences of Lincoln's actions were horrific: "The victors are never charged as war criminals, of course; only the losers are. This was true in 1865 and it is true today. Lincoln's abandonment of the internationally agreed upon rules of war as codified by the Geneva Convention of 1863 and his demolition of constitutional liberties . . . established precedents that would provide countless excuses and rationalizations for empire-building and war-mongering politicians throughout the world in the decades to come. Politicians of all parties would routinely invoke the name of the martyred Lincoln to 'justify' their own schemes to run afoul of the Constitution, international law, and commonly accepted norms of morality."[178]

Another important aspect of such criticism, especially evident in DiLorenzo's and Adams's books and in one part of Woods's discussion, was their attempt to place the Civil War in an international context. *When in the Course of Human Events* included a chapter entitled "British Scholars Speak," which, oddly, cited only one author, Charles Dickens, as a scholar who saw slavery as not the cause of the war. This claim supposedly refuted English philosopher John Stuart Mill's assertion to the contrary. DiLorenzo maintained that the United States was unique in that it took a war to end slavery in America, whereas "dozens of countries, including the possessions of the British, French, and Spanish empires, ended slavery *peacefully.* Only in the United States was warfare associated with emancipation. . . . In virtually every other country of the world, slavery ended through either manumission or some form of compensation."[179] Lincoln, from DiLorenzo's standpoint, "was not particularly supportive of emancipation," and "his real objective" was "the consolidation of state power."[180] Williams wrote an admiring foreword to DiLorenzo's *Real Lincoln* echoing this claim, stating that "Lincoln's Emancipation Proclamation was little more than a political gimmick" and that the "more appropriate title for Abraham Lincoln is not the Great Emancipator, but the Great Centralizer."[181] As a result, because it took a war to end American slavery, with ghastly costs for the United States in terms of lives lost and the idea of limited government, Abraham Lincoln cannot be labeled a great statesman; in fact, he was in this particular instance a rather poor one. Congressman Paul summarized this viewpoint in 2010: "No, I don't think he [Lincoln] was one of our greatest presidents. I mean, he was determined to fight a bloody civil war, which many have argued could have been avoided. For 1/100 the cost of the war, plus 600 thousand lives, enough money would have been available to buy up all the slaves and free them. So, I don't see that is a good part of our history. Besides, the Civil War was to prove that we had a very, very strong centralized federal government and that's what it did. It rejected the notion that states were a sovereign nation."[182]

DiLorenzo's chief contribution in *The Real Lincoln,* and it is perhaps the most important of these books for Lincoln loathers, was that it took the long-standing arguments criticizing the president that had been in circulation among their circle and placed them into an accessible, easily readable volume. *The Real Lincoln* was highly praised by libertarians and conservatives alike, who thought the author's arguments irrefutable. "Things will never be the same again," Clyde Wilson exulted on the back of the paperback edition.[183] Perhaps, but even among what Jeffrey Rogers Hummel called "favorably inclined reviewers," there were serious misgivings about the work. Indeed, Hummel himself called Adams's and DiLorenzo's works "amateurish neo-Confederate books" in a brutally critical review of Woods's *Politically Incorrect Guide to American History* published in the *Journal of Libertarian Studies.*[184] Richard Gamble of Palm Beach Atlantic University thought DiLorenzo was "essentially correct" in his accusations but called the book "a travesty of historical method and documentation": "Exasperating, maddening, and deeply disappointing, *The Real Lincoln* ought to have been a book to confound Lincoln's apolo-

gists and to help *rebuild the American historical consciousness.*"[185] Nor did
The Real Lincoln fare much better in other venues. In 2012 it was voted
as one of the "five least credible books of history in print" by readers at
the History News Network.[186] DiLorenzo by then had already published a
second book on Lincoln in 2006, dedicated to former Lincoln detractor
M. E. Bradford, entitled *Lincoln Unmasked: What You're Not Supposed
to Know about Dishonest Abe,* and he became the most prominent of all
Lincoln critics. This collection of essays elaborated on themes presented
in *The Real Lincoln,* although it was harsher in tone and more critical of
what DiLorenzo repeatedly called "the Lincoln Cult." DiLorenzo asserted
that Adolf Hitler had admired Lincoln for crushing states' rights, and he
labeled conservative and liberal defenders of Lincoln such as William F.
Buckley Jr. and Eric Foner as "Lincoln Totalitarians."[187]

These indictments of Lincoln did not remain cloistered within a small
network of like-minded individuals but migrated into venues that reached
larger audiences. In addition to Paul's influence, a good example of their
impact can be found in the work of Fox News legal commentator Judge
Andrew P. Napolitano, who has leaned heavily on their arguments. Judge
Napolitano called Lincoln a "racial supremacist" and "tyrannical," and his
book *The Constitution in Exile: How the Federal Government Has Seized
Power by Rewriting the Supreme Law of the Land* (2006) included a chapter on Abraham Lincoln's presidency entitled "Dishonest Abe."[188] In this
book Napolitano asserted that "in order to increase his federalist vision
of centralized power, 'Honest' Abe misled the nation into an unnecessary
war." The president "could have simply paid the slave owners to set their
slaves free," but Lincoln "chose not to compensate" slaveholders, "blatantly
ignored" that states had a constitutional right to secede, and as a result,
"tore apart the Constitution." Judge Napolitano made additional claims,
all consistent with previous accusations: Lincoln supported "a large federal government"; he "did not have much concern for the slaves"; he "was
more concerned about the failure of states to collect tariffs than he was
about slavery"; he authorized the "murdering of civilians, declaring [of]
martial law, suspending habeas corpus, seizing of vast amounts of private
property without compensation (including railroads and telegraphs),
conducting a war without the consent of Congress, imprisoning nearly
thirty thousand northern citizens without trial, shutting down several
newspapers, and even deporting a congressman (Clement L. Vallandigham
from Ohio) because he objected to the imposition of an income tax"; he
was a "dictator"; he "destroyed federalism through the Civil War"; his

policies were precursors to the New Deal and War on Terror due to his acts of "economic protectionism, erosion of civil liberties during wartime, and violations of the separation of powers."[189] Napolitano not only quoted DiLorenzo in this chapter; he relied almost exclusively on his work. If one goes to the back of the book, one can see that Judge Napolitano included twenty-four endnotes for his assertions about "Dishonest Abe." Of those twenty-four references, twenty-three are from DiLorenzo (to be sure, many of DiLorenzo's citations come from respected Lincoln scholars), and the twenty-fourth note is from one of Lew Rockwell's essays. Judge Napolitano's work was highly praised on the back of the book by then Fox News commentators Bill O'Reilly, Sean Hannity, and Alan Colmes (a liberal), conservative radio host Rush Limbaugh, and respected civil liberties advocate Nat Hentoff, demonstrating that such loathing for Lincoln and its associated hatred for the federal government reached influential public figures. In the spring of 2012 Judge Napolitano was placed on the Cato Institute's board of directors, a libertarian think tank, with the assistance of influential billionaires sympathetic to libertarian ideas Charles and David Koch. Later that fall, for undisclosed reasons, he resigned from Cato's board.[190]

Several accounts have been offered for this continuing hatred of Abraham Lincoln. Clearly, one explanation is that disgust for Lincoln is linked to an evident hostility toward federal power and the associated diminishment of the power of state and local governments such enlargement of federal authority supposedly entailed. For libertarians their nonaggression, antiwar proclivities are likewise significant, if not determinative.[191] Sandefur has argued that the Vietnam War was "the formative event in the lives of many libertarians," and the lesson they "drew from that experience" was "that war is *never* justified."[192] Added to this is a fundamental philosophical disagreement over the nature of democracy. Ludwig von Mises believed (and it seems fair to think that his followers would agree) that "anonymous forces operating on the market are continuously determining anew who should be entrepreneur and who should be capitalist. The consumers vote, as it were, for those are to occupy the exalted positions in the setting of the nation's economic structure."[193] Free markets, in short, were far more democratic—and efficient—than elections. As a result, they were much more likely to destroy an economically inefficient institution such as slavery.[194] This philosophy was at odds with Lincoln's faith in the importance of democratic elections and his position as a politician who for various reasons, most of them having to do with increasing economic opportunity for all Americans, supported protectionist tariffs, internal improvements, and public education. Lincoln would have agreed with Mises that free labor was superior to slave labor, but faced with the events of the 1850s, he came to the conclusion that slavery would never end of its own accord:

> All the powers of earth seem rapidly combining against Him [the slave]. Mammon is after him; ambition follows, and philosophy follows, and the Theology of the day is fast joining the cry. They have him in his prison house; they have searched his person, and left no prying instrument with him. One after another they have closed the heavy iron doors upon him, and now they have him, as it were, bolted in with a lock of a hundred keys, which can never be unlocked without the concurrence of every key; the keys in the hands of a hundred different men, and they scattered to a hundred different and distant places; and they stand musing as to what invention, in all the dominions of mind and matter, can be produced to make the impossibility of his escape more complete than it is.[195]

Ending slavery would consequently require concerted political action for its containment and eventual abolition—hence, the creation of the antislavery Republican Party, Lincoln's devotion to its success, and his utter contempt for those who believed that "the liberty of one man to be absolutely nothing, when in conflict with another man's right of property. Republicans, on the contrary, are for both the man and the dollar; but in cases of conflict, the man before the dollar."[196] In other words, for Mises consumer preferences *were* democracy, the best guarantee for the eventual, nonviolent end of slavery, while for Lincoln American democracy was larger than consumer preferences, especially given that some American consumers preferred permanent slaveholding to liberty. The United States therefore needed a democratic movement of "all Americans" to "join in the great and good work" of peacefully containing and ultimately extinguishing the institution.[197]

Such interpretations for the continuation of loathing for Lincoln, although certainly accurate, are nevertheless incomplete. In 2009 historian Clyde Wilson offered an additional reason for the persistence of Lincoln criticism from his intellectual compatriots:

> For a long time [white] Americans North and South observed a truce. It was agreed that the war was a great tragedy with good and bad on both sides, from which a stronger and better country had emerged. In this scenario, Lincoln is the great martyred Peacemaker who would have "bound

up the nation's wounds" and avoided the evils that followed the War. This is a dubious estimate of Lincoln, but one in which it was useful for all parties to believe.

Things have changed in the last few years. There is a concerted effort to banish the South into one dark little corner of American history labeled "slavery" and "treason." Here in the Lincoln bicentennial, we can note there has been an accompanying literature that celebrates Lincoln not as the Peacemaker but as the great Hero of Democracy who was justified in using any means necessary to destroy evil (i.e., kill recalcitrant Americans). This accompanies and justifies America's turn toward a mission to impose "global democracy" by unlimited force and preemptive war. Even General Sherman is once more being celebrated as a great military hero for his ruthless campaigns against civilians.[198]

Although Wilson failed to mention that the "truce" of which he wrote was resisted by Lincoln's postwar detractors and one that took place at the expense of the freedoms of African Americans, not white southerners, he had a valid point here in that Lincoln's critics had powerful rivals.[199] Their conservative and libertarian opponents, aligned with think tanks such as the Ashbrook Center, Cato Institute, Claremont Institute, Hoover Institution, and Heritage Foundation, not to mention *National Review* and the vast majority of American politicians, subscribed to an irreconcilably different view of Abraham Lincoln than that of the Mises or Abbeville Institute. After the September 2001 attacks on the Pentagon and World Trade Center, a few of them conceivably saw in Lincoln's presidency a model for how the War on Terror ought to be waged. So, while Lincoln's detractors maintained that the sixteenth president was a lesson in how not to conduct a presidency or fight a war, a few of their opponents argued precisely the opposite. Both sides played a chess match with Lincoln's image as a pawn, demonstrating once again the significance and malleability of that image and how Lincoln's presidency could be used for divergent political agendas, even within groups that shared certain ideological affinities. This pliability suggests why the dispute surrounding Lincoln remained such a fiery topic: both groups were arguing not only about the sixteenth president but about the essential nature of conservatism, libertarianism, and the American founding, if not the future definition and orientation of the American nation-state.

As economist Thomas Sowell's aforementioned defense of Lincoln indicated, the charges against Lincoln often assumed more than they proved and demonstrated a recurring and disturbing methodology: namely, the oversimplification and distortion of extraordinarily difficult historical problems. Of their challengers, paleolibertarians certainly asked important, tough questions about the causes, conduct, and results of the Civil War, but their answers to such significant historical problems seemed ideologically predetermined to discredit Lincoln. In addition, they omitted scholarship that disagreed even slightly with their own viewpoint, especially regarding the hideousness of the institution of slavery on the North American continent, and demonstrated an inability, if not unwillingness, to accurately render a nuanced description of Lincoln's thought on slavery and race. In addition to Sowell, there were conservatives and libertarians who, in essays and books of their own, reprised the battle Harry Jaffa had conducted with M. E. Bradford, Willmoore Kendall, and Frank Meyer after World War II and vigorously contested this decidedly negative portrait of Abraham Lincoln. It is indicative of the increasing influence of Lincoln's enemies within these political ideologies that these individuals felt the need to respond at all and defend Lincoln's administration.

In 2002 and 2006 Timothy Sandefur of the Pacific Legal Foundation, and later an adjunct scholar at the Cato Institute, published two essays that directly challenged the assertion that secession was an obvious constitutional right. Sandefur argued that the "states have no constitutional authority to secede unilaterally from the union. Nor were southern states engaged in a legitimate act of revolution, because they initiated force rather than act in defense of individual rights."[200] To Sandefur it was a vital matter of national self-understanding for Americans to realize that the Civil War was not an instance of might (the Union) conquering right (the Confederacy) but its exact opposite. It was worrisome that "a majority of libertarians agree" with arguments castigating Lincoln.[201] He held that libertarians and their intellectual ancestors were mistaken in two key matters: in their interpretation of the Declaration of Independence and in their interpretation of the Constitution as a compact between the states. In refuting Jeffrey Rogers Hummel's assertion that "as a revolutionary right, the legitimacy of secession is universal and unconditional," Sandefur argued to the contrary that "The Declaration of Independence actually says exactly the opposite: only a *defense of individual rights* will justify an act of revolution." As such, and because the antebellum South believed the Declaration of Independence to be false—"there is not a word of truth in it," claimed the proslavery senator from South Carolina John C. Calhoun—Sandefur called the Confederacy's waging of war against the North nothing less than "a large criminal conspiracy" fought to enslave and exploit millions of human beings.[202] Fellow libertarian Tibor Machan expressed a similar viewpoint on the Cato Institute website, opining that when the Confederacy was formed, white southerners were, "in effect, kidnapping millions of people—most of whom would rather have stayed with the union that held out some hope for their eventual liberation—[thus] the idea of secession no longer seems so innocent." (DiLorenzo vigorously challenged Machan's analogy in the afterword to the paperback edition of his book.) Still, it is a testament to the impact of Lincoln's detractors that Machan's essay opened with his confession that he was "obsessed" with the question of whether or not "Abraham Lincoln [was] a good American."[203]

In addition, Sandefur forcefully maintained that secession was unconstitutional. The Confederates' decision to leave the Union was therefore not "a legitimate act of revolution" because the southern states had resorted to force and were not acting "in defense of individual rights." In citing numerous founders to prove that there was no unilateral right to secede, Sandefur concluded that "the federal union was an agreement between the *people,* not the *states.*" Added to this, he pointed out that if the states were in fact supreme over the federal government, "it would make little sense to require state officials to take an oath to support the U.S. Constitution, since their allegiance to the federal union would depend wholly on whether the state decided to remain in the Union or not." Dispensing with the assertion that the war was not about slavery, Sandefur stressed that "the Confederates fought for the (literally absolute) right of *white people* to govern *black people,* without the black people's consent."[204]

Lincoln's defenders noted that other matters related to secession were ignored by the president's enemies. They failed, for example, to consider that if secession was an obvious constitutional right, then nobody would have questioned the Confederacy's right to leave the Union. Even northern doughfaces such as President James Buchanan and Jeremiah Black, proslavery politicians who supported the South, said states had no right to secede, although to be sure they did not think the South could be coerced to remain in the Union. Sandefur addressed the contention that New York, Rhode Island, and Virginia had reserved the right to leave the Union when they ratified the Constitution by arguing that there "can be no conditional assent to the Constitution, just as . . . there can be no new terms in agreeing to a contract. Either the people of a state ratify the Constitution—and accept that it is the supreme law of the land—or they do not." In addition, a reservation expressed by a state, Sandefur explained, was not the same thing as a right of secession being explicitly written into the Constitution itself. Such reservations, he thought, may have had more to do with re-serving a right to revolution than a right to secede.[205] Reading the books of Lincoln's foes, furthermore, one would forget rather quickly, as Harry Jaffa pointed out, it was not only Lincoln and the Republicans who op-posed secession but millions of northern Democrats as well. Nor do the president's detractors—except Hummel, who again has been a sharp critic of their works—acknowledge that the Confederacy itself was hardly unified on either secession or war; indeed, as with the American founders, the men who wrote the Confederate Constitution did not explicitly incorporate the right of secession into the document, which may explain why Judge Napolitano felt the need to assert that in the U.S. Constitution the right was "implicit . . . since it was the *states* that ratified the Constitution."[206] In addition, innumerable white southerners opposed separation, including tens of thousands of white southerners who fought for the Union, not to mention the slaves themselves, who wanted the Confederacy to lose and were in fact demonstrably overjoyed by its defeat.[207] It was simply not as clear as many have claimed that the thirteen original states were sovereign and had a right to secede. In agreement with Sandefur, Thomas Kran-nawitter, a former student of Harry Jaffa's, argued in his book *Vindicating Lincoln: Defending the Politics of Our Greatest President* (2008) that "states do not possess a constitutional right of secession, while human beings do possess a natural right of revolution."[208] Certainly, innumerable Americans alive in 1860–61 did not think the southern states had a right to secede; otherwise, there would have been no Civil War.[209] For those like Thomas Woods, who claimed secession as a right reserved to the states under the Tenth Amendment, Sandefur said the amendment "*reserves* powers to the states—it does not create them." Article 6 of the United States Constitu-tion, unlike the alleged right to secede that many claim was implicit in the document, explicitly states that "this Constitution, and the Laws of the United States which shall be made, in Pursuance thereof; and all Treaties made, or which shall be made, under the Authority of the United States, shall be the *supreme Law of the Land*."[210] Accordingly, because it was the people who created the Constitution and not the states, the states had no unilateral right to secede.

In contrast to Sandefur's essays, Krannawitter's *Vindicating Lincoln* was a book-length critique of libertarian and conservative arguments denigrat-ing the president. At the time of publication Jaffa's protégé was a political scientist at Hillsdale College in Michigan, an institution of higher learning highly praised by many conservatives. Krannawitter examined what he believed to be the key contentions used to belittle Lincoln, ranging from "Was Lincoln a Racist?" to "Do States Possess a Constitutional Right of Secession?" to "Was the Civil War Caused by Slavery or Big Government?" Six years prior to his book's publication, Krannawitter had penned a sharp evaluation alongside a brutally personal attack on DiLorenzo's *Real Lincoln* in the *Claremont Review of Books,* a conservative quarterly, calling it "a compendium of misquotations, out-of-context quotations, and wrongly attributed quotations—one howler after another, yet none of it funny. . . . His unreal Lincoln inhabits an unreal world, so crudely and tendentiously drawn as to beggar belief. One wonders if the libertarian neo-Confederates have run out of front-line troops. In this screed, at any rate, they have sent a giddy, careless, half-educated boy to do a man's job."[211] Understandably, DiLorenzo did not take such words kindly, and in the afterword to the paperback version of *The Real Lincoln,* he said Krannawitter's review was "an egregious collection of falsehoods."[212] In *Vindicating Lincoln* Krannawitter acknowledged the increasing importance of Lincoln's critics: "growing numbers of prominent scholars dismiss Lincoln's principles as irrelevant," while "others openly attack his politics, arguing that he was a traitor to the cause of free society and constitutional government."[213] Like Sandefur, Krannawitter held that misunderstanding Lincoln was in some sense a matter of civics, for if Americans misunderstand Lincoln, he believed, they misunderstand their country and "the very possibility of democratic greatness."[214] Krannawitter's aim, similar to Jaffa's, was to restore Lincoln's natural rights principles to American political discourse and restore such greatness.

In addition to being a professor, Krannawitter was a senior fellow with the Claremont Institute in Claremont, California, and his intellectual mentor, Harry Jaffa, was listed on the institute's website as a "distinguished fellow."[215] The Claremont Institute is without question pro-Lincoln. Its stated purpose was "to restore the principles of the American Founding to their rightful, preeminent authority in our national life. These principles are expressed most eloquently in the Declaration of Independence, which proclaims that 'all men are created equal and are endowed by their Creator with certain unalienable rights.'" Furthermore, Claremont sponsors "Lincoln Fellowships for rising young conservative leaders" and publishes a quarterly review, the *Claremont Review of Books,* as a conservative alternative to the more liberal *New York Review of Books.*[216] The institute was undoubtedly influential in conservative circles. Just as the Mises Institute served as an intellectual nerve center for paleolibertarian, anti-Lincoln thought, the Claremont Institute fulfilled a similar role for conservatives allied with Jaffa's positive view of the sixteenth president. In 2009, in keeping with the institute's pro-Lincoln stance, the *Claremont Review* published a "Lincoln Bicentennial Issue" consisting of seven laudatory essays on the sixteenth president, while one of its senior fellows, John Eastman, the dean of Chapman University Law School, hosted a 2009 symposium on "Lincoln's Constitutionalism in Time of War: Lessons for the War on Terror?" The controversial Bush administration attorney John Yoo, author of several post-9/11 memos that sanctioned torture against suspected terrorists ("enemy combatants") served on one panel, while Jaffa delivered the keynote address.[217]

One essential difference between Lincoln's enemies at the Mises Institute and their Claremont Institute rivals was that the former were far more suspicious of the national government. The anti-Lincoln crowd held, among other things, that secession would be a check on federal authority and would therefore enhance liberty. But what was not addressed in their books was the work of scholars who investigated the idea of secession in the wake of the USSR's breakup in 1991 and showed how it could easily benefit anti-liberty causes. Allowing state withdrawal as a constitutional right could, as liberal legal scholar Cass Sunstein observed, "increase the risks of ethnic and factional struggle; reduce the prospects for compromise and deliberation in government; raise dramatically the stakes of day-to-day political decisions; introduce irrelevant and illegitimate considerations into those decisions; create dangers of blackmail, strategic behavior, and exploitation; and, most generally, endanger the prospects for long-term self-governance."[218] Even if a constitutional right to secession would foster greater freedom, its advocates should at least acknowledge the potential difficulties that would follow from separation rather than dogmatically asserting it to be an unqualified good. Americans, one would think, would be especially alert to the unforeseen consequences of secession; advocating such a course prior to 1860 was not quite the same as being in favor of it after 1865. In their advocacy of secession as a fundamental constitutional and moral right, one of course finds a major reason many people loathe Abraham Lincoln. But in their inability to consider adequately viewpoints that differ from their own, or to even mention such viewpoints, one also finds justification for questioning their doctrinaire assertions.[219]

One piece of history that these Lincoln contrarians ignored, and one that libertarians such as Sandefur thought should give them pause, was that a virtual secession *was* carried out by the South in the years after the country abandoned Reconstruction. By 1900, once African Americans were effectively disfranchised across the region, the white South was in effect in local control of its own internal affairs. The real tragedy of Reconstruction, notwithstanding the assertions of Lincoln's detractors, was not that it enhanced federal power at the expense of the states but that the country eventually turned a blind eye to homicidal violence and racial oppression for almost another century after the president's death.[220] The link between freedom and equality forged by the Declaration of Independence and vindicated in the Civil War and Reconstruction was severed by the turn of the century. The consequence was that a broad anti-caste, civic nationalism was replaced by a narrow, ethnic nationalism based upon white supremacy. Democracy was in effect dead, certainly for blacks, in the southern United States until the stunning achievements of the civil rights movement in the 1960s, whose legislative successes were anathema to Lincoln's foes. The de facto secession of the former Confederacy after Reconstruction on racial matters did not enhance freedom; rather, it diminished freedom and tarnished American lives and ideals.[221]

Likewise misleading, at least from Sandefur's viewpoint, was the relatively unsubstantiated assertion that a slaveholding Confederacy (or northern secession from the South) would have eventually emancipated the slaves without federal intervention. Following Mises's emphasis on slavery's economic inefficiency, DiLorenzo maintained that "the market economy and the advance of industrialization were in fact eating away at the institution of slavery." This trend, together with the repeal of the Fugitive Slave Act, "would have caused the price of slaves to plummet by dramatically increasing the cost to slave owners of enforcing the system, thereby quickening the institution's demise."[222] Such speculation ignored that slaveholders wanted the Fugitive Slave Law enforced and would never have consented to its repeal and that in an independent, slaveholding regime such as the Confederacy, there would have been strong economic and cultural incentives to preserve the institution and to acquire more slaves by whatever methods necessary. Slavery was extraordinarily profitable, and it is difficult to see why white southerners would have voluntarily abolished the institution. Indeed, if slavery was such an inefficient, unproductive form of labor that would have some day perished, then one wonders why it had not withered away by the twenty-first century.[223] As Sandefur concluded in a 2012 lecture: "Slavery was efficient to southerners, if not as a purely financial matter, at least as a means of perpetuating White Supremacist social institutions. Proslavery leaders sought to address those economic problems that did plague slavery—escape, manumission, and the need for land—through government subsidies and crackdowns on civil liberties."[224] So, at the very least it was debatable whether northern secession would have led to large numbers of slaves running away to freedom, although perhaps that would have been the case. Still, southern fire-eaters such as Robert Barnwell Rhett, Edmund Ruffin, and William Lowndes Yancey all thought slavery would be better protected in an independent slaveholding Confederacy because such a republic could deport abolitionists and their sympathizers, provide greater domestic surveillance of slaves, build an elaborate border patrol system, and use railroads and telegraph lines to deliver a more rapid response to runaways and potential rebellions.[225] Once the Confederacy had been formed, these fire-eaters thought, the importance of cotton to the northern economy would force the United States government to make treaties promising to return or pay for runaways. "Our treaties would protect our slaves," explained Yancey.[226]

If the Civil War led to "an enhancement of the federal government at the expense of the states," it is worth noting that during the conflict, according to Hummel, "Confederate war socialism was more economically centralized than the Union's neo-mercantilism."[227] The leaders of the Confederacy therefore had no principled objection to using their own central government to protect their most valuable institution—slavery—should future circumstances force them to do so. Indeed, even before the Civil War, some southern states encouraged slaveholding among greater numbers of whites, which was not exactly a libertarian stance toward the economy or a description of people who thought slavery was a dying institution.[228] Consequently, as Krannawitter explained, the Confederacy "was *not* defending limited self-government against an oppressive federal government" but sought instead "to secure the Southern way of life, a way of life that revolved in many ways around the institution of slavery."[229] In point of historical fact, even after the Civil War and Reconstruction were over, many white southerners worked assiduously, and successfully, to reinstitute oppression of blacks on a different, if less tyrannical, basis than what had existed during antebellum slavery.[230]

Following Krannawitter, and in the tradition of Harry Jaffa's post–World War II defense of Lincoln, Gettysburg College historian Allen Guelzo continued to argue that Abraham Lincoln was a president conservatives could and should claim as one of their own. In a tightly argued paper delivered to the Heritage Foundation, a prominent conservative think tank in Washington, D.C., Guelzo examined the paleolibertarian claim that Lincoln was the father of big government whose real agenda was to centralize power in the national government rather than preserve a Union that one day would be rid of slavery. He examined in painstaking economic and statistical detail three areas of the federal government in Lincoln's administration—its "size," "budget," and "reach"—to ascertain if the centralization that paleolibertarians claimed had occurred under Lincoln's watch actually happened. Guelzo's conclusion? "Abraham Lincoln's presidency undertook no permanent reconstitution of the federal government on Leviathan-like proportions, and this was largely because it had never intended to do so." He maintained that it was the Progressives, especially Woodrow Wilson, who were the *"real* father of big government" and encouraged conservatives not to disdain Lincoln but to "embrace him."[231] What was especially significant here about Guelzo's essay was that he challenged libertarian assertions on their own intellectual turf. DiLorenzo is a trained economist, Adams a historian on taxation, and Congressman Paul an important voice on intrusive, centralized government, yet Guelzo's piece (in addition to its denigration of Progressives) seemed to be written to make the point that in their own fields of expertise, they were wrong. It begged the question that if Lincoln's rivals were mistaken about the president being the father of big government, a matter on which they were supposedly authorities, on what other matters might their conclusions be suspect?

In truth, certainly with regard to permanently protecting the institution of slavery, it was the Confederacy that favored big government. But this point was often ignored or denied in the writings of Lincoln's enemies, for it contradicted the idea that the president had embraced centralized government and that *only* the federal government can be oppressive. As noted earlier, it is difficult, if not impossible, to believe that slaveholders would not have used the power of the Confederate state to protect and enhance their investment and thus an independent Confederacy may well have strengthened rather than weakened the institution. In other words, slaveholders seceded to form a slaveholding republic that served their financial as well as psychological interests, and it is improbable that they would not have formulated policies to protect those interests. As Lincoln put it in 1860, "this two thousand million of dollars, invested in this species of property, all so concentrated that the mind can grasp it at once—this immense pecuniary interest, has its influence upon their [the slaveholders'] minds."[232] It also seems likely that births of new slaves would have greatly exceeded the number of runaways in any Confederate republic, as had been true in the Union since 1776. If the institution of slavery would have been weakened in a slaveholding Confederacy, as Lincoln's detractors claimed, it is hard to see why any slaveholders in the South would have supported secession. They would all have seen that to leave the Union after Lincoln's election in 1860 was going to undermine their peculiarly profitable institution, and they would have opposed dismembering the country. To be sure, some slaveholders thought secession would lead to war, emancipation, and, potentially more worrisome, race war. But the large majority of owners favored the creation of a slaveholding republic precisely because they were certain their beloved institution was endangered by Lincoln and the Republican Party. They believed that enslaved labor would be better protected in a new Confederacy rather than in the old Union.[233] Thus, it is likely that slavery would have been made more secure by the existence of a slaveholding republic on the North American continent, a Confederate republic that would have sought and attained diplomatic and economic relations with other slaveholding countries in the hemisphere such as Brazil and Cuba. And even if inhuman bondage were eventually abolished in an independent Confederacy, the historical record makes it clear that it would have been succeeded by an apartheid regime, not a post–Civil Rights Act of 1964 government.

Lincoln's defenders also challenged DiLorenzo's assertion, and it is an assertion that virtually all Lincoln detractors have embraced, that "in virtually every other country in the world, slavery ended through either manumission or some form of compensated emancipation." As Sandefur (and Guelzo) pointed out in 2011, "It was the Lincoln Administration that planned to do away with slavery peacefully, and it was the Confederacy that would not allow that to happen. If one believes it would have been preferable to find some political method of peacefully eliminating slavery, then your only candidate has to be Abraham Lincoln. It was Lincoln's plan to ban slavery, by law, from spreading into the western territories, so as to set the foundation for its ultimate extinction—a perfectly constitutional and peaceful plan. It was this that the south would not stand for, and what they initiated force to prevent. So while the war was ultimately worth the cost in that it brought about the end of slavery, the blame for the fact that it took a war to do it—that rests entirely on the Confederacy."[234] Regarding the onset of the Civil War and emancipation, DiLorenzo maintained Lincoln should have sought compensated emancipation (something he proposed to the border slave states during the war, although his proposal was rebuffed) instead of fighting a war that cost nearly 750,000 American lives. But it was the point of secession to preserve slavery forever, not to use it as leverage to win financial compensation for abolishing the institution. Slaveholders wanted to keep their slaves, not sell them so that they could be free to enjoy the fruits of their labor, to which Lincoln, for one, said they were entitled. Even Murray Rothbard, who saw himself as perpetuating Garrison's and Spooner's criticism of the president, believed that "there was only one possible moral solution for the slave question: immediate and unconditional abolition, with no compensation to the slavemasters. Indeed, any compensation should have been the other way—to repay the oppressed slaves for their lifetime of slavery."[235]

In addition, slavery ended in the French colony of Haiti because of a massive and violent slave rebellion in the 1790s and early 1800s, which DiLorenzo mentioned only briefly. Nor did DiLorenzo acknowledge that Haiti's experience, combined with Britain's state-sponsored and state-enforced emancipation scheme, strengthened the will of southern slaveholders to resist *any* scheme of emancipation.[236] The *Economist* magazine editorialized in the late 1850s that "with the example of West Indian emancipation before them, it could not be expected that Southern statesmen [in the United States] would ever risk the liberation of their slaves on such conditions."[237] DiLorenzo mentioned Lincoln's allegedly clumsy attempt at compensated emancipation but argued, without citing any evidence, that Lincoln was not really serious about such a policy; it was something to which he paid "lip service" because what he really wanted was "the consolidation of state power."[238] Guelzo vigorously contested the accuracy of these contentions in his paper at the Heritage Foundation and in his book *Lincoln's Emancipation Proclamation: The End of Slavery in America* (2004), a book that was listed as recommended reading on the website of the Claremont Institute and one labeled by fellow conservative and Naval War College professor Mackubin T. Owens as "magnificent," a "tour de force."[239] During the Civil War Lincoln tried to compensate slaveholders in border slave states such as Delaware, but to Lincoln's consternation, they refused the offer.[240] In fact, when Lincoln proposed payment for emancipating their slaves, it was done as a peace measure, one that he thought would end the increasingly bloody war more quickly and scarcely the action of a president whose adversaries labeled a war criminal.

Furthermore, DiLorenzo's claim that slavery ended peacefully "in virtually every other country of the world" or Paul's assertion that the war was "needless" and that "it was tragic that the abolishment of slavery was

not achieved as it had been with all other Western nations, peacefully,"
overlooked entirely the resistance even to the *idea* of emancipation among
white slaveholders, even in border slave states. In fact, what was truly
unique to the United States was that by 1860 many American slaveholders
had come to the erroneous and tragic conclusion that their slaves loved
them, that slavery was divinely sanctioned and good for the slave and for
their society (not to mention the pocketbooks and sexual proclivities of the
slaveholder). They were willing to fight to the death to preserve the institution. Although slavery brought enormous profits, violence lay at the
heart of inhuman bondage, and it was brought down, at least in part, by
the innumerable, courageous acts of violent and nonviolent resistance
on the part of the enslaved, and in that sense slavery neither began nor
ended peacefully anywhere on earth. In other words, the claim made by
Lincoln's opponents of the conflict's needlessness is, as historian James
Oakes put it in another context, "an evasion of the moral dilemma of the
Civil War, not a serious engagement with it."[241]

  . Related claims were likewise challenged by conservatives and libertarians. As we have seen, the president's detractors maintained that Abraham
Lincoln did not care about racial equality (a somewhat odd charge for
these conservatives and libertarians to make given that they hold that
any truly free society would be justly inegalitarian), but it was the Union
victory in the Civil War—a needless and unjustified war to paleolibertarians—that even made racial egalitarianism a possibility. Historically, the
president's enemies have been quick to cite statements of Lincoln's that
they think demonstrate that he was not in favor of racial equality, especially the 1858 quote from Charleston in his debate with Douglas, but it is
difficult if not impossible to find an equivalent emphasis on those aspects
of Lincoln's career when he defended natural rights for all and expanded
freedom: that Lincoln, as early as 1854, maintained that slaves were men
who were more than "free horses and free cattle" and told white southerners that "it is your sense of justice, and human sympathy, continually
telling you, that the poor negro has some natural right to himself—that
those who deny it, and make mere merchandise of him, deserve kickings,
contempt and death"; that Lincoln signed into law the First and Second
Confiscation Acts, bills passed by an antislavery Congress and ones that
were important steps in the emancipation process; that Lincoln was the
only president to sign legislation abolishing slavery—in Washington, D.C.;
that Lincoln issued the Emancipation Proclamation, in Guelzo's words "the

most revolutionary pronouncement ever signed by an American president, striking the legal shackles from four million black slaves and setting the nation's face toward the total abolition of slavery within three more years"; that Lincoln vigorously supported and signed the Thirteenth Amendment ending slavery in the United States forever, even though presidents did not normally sign amendments; that Lincoln was the first president in American history to recommend the vote for *any* African Americans.[242] It was during Reconstruction, in the face of white southern opposition to such a potentiality, that African Americans, with federal assistance, became American citizens who could vote and hold public office. And one of the reasons that the United States became a more racially inclusive nation after World War II was due to the Civil Rights Act of 1964, a federal law opposed by many whites and one that paleolibertarians still condemn. Indeed, Ron Paul said on the floor of Congress in 2004, the forty-year anniversary of the legislation, that "the Civil Rights Act of 1964 did not improve race relations or enhance freedom. Instead, the forced integration dictated by the Civil Rights Act of 1964 increased racial tensions while diminishing individual liberty."[243] In defending his fellow paleolibertarian from conservative attacks during the 2012 presidential campaign, DiLorenzo called the 1964 legislation "*inequality* under the law in the form of institutionalized discrimination against white males, which is what 'civil rights regulation' became immediately upon passage of the Civil Rights Act of 1964."[244]

It is in such remarks that one can detect additional elements of what continues to drive animus for Lincoln: the acute sense that his elevated stature advances a political and cultural agenda—in the minds of Lincoln's self-confessed reactionary enemies an egalitarian, broadly democratic, multicultural, multiracial, and secular agenda—that they believe Americans have been forced to accept, a type of intellectual imperialism. Since 1964, as the historical profession, alongside the rest of the United States, has become more racially diverse and formerly marginalized groups more powerful, American historians, as Clyde Wilson noted, have rewritten the nation's historical narrative in a direction that Lincoln's detractors think unduly stresses the evils of antebellum southern slavery and characterizes the Confederacy as treasonous.[245] "Some people who have wrapped up their identity in white history feel challenged," historian David Goldfield has observed of this trend, "if not disregarded and neglected. They realize the tide of history is rolling very heavily."[246] Indeed it is, and in their so-called discovery of a Lincolnian turn toward tyranny in American history, Lincoln's foes resemble a fundamentalist religion nostalgically looking back to a political Garden of Eden before the supposed original sin of Abraham Lincoln's presidency.[247] This impulse has made an ironic contrast to the views of those living in Victorian America who believed slavery was the country's original sin and mourned the sacrifice of the Great Emancipator, who was killed on Good Friday 1865. Their loathing of Lincoln therefore had little affinity with nineteenth-century abolitionism or even Lerone Bennett's critique. The vast majority of abolitionists did not loathe Lincoln. And for those who did, such as Lysander Spooner, their efforts, while admirable, paled in comparison to the achievement of the antislavery movement of which Abraham Lincoln was an indispensable part. In addition, indefensible as some of his attacks were, Bennett was motivated by a dream of a more racially egalitarian United States, and he despised the Confederacy, while many of Lincoln's post–Cold War opponents were antagonistic to racial egalitarianism and found in the Confederacy a beloved cause. The historical revisionism to which Goldfield alluded was a mortal threat to the outlook of Lincoln's detractors. If the Confederacy was indelibly scorned, or Lincoln esteemed too highly, then their entire worldview was in danger of ultimate extinction.

Accordingly, the image of Abraham Lincoln as a model American democrat had to be taken down. Mises Institute distinguished fellow, Lincoln critic, and monarchist Hans-Hermann Hoppe alluded to this precondition when he encouraged his intellectual compatriots to understand that "above all, the idea of democracy and majority rule must be delegitimized" and replaced by locally controlled, homogeneously ethnic communities, in which "voluntary transactions between various property owners" will lead to "decidedly nonegalitarian, hierarchical, and elitist" social arrangements, all of which will be seen as natural. "Owing to superior achievements of wealth, wisdom, bravery, or combination thereof," Hoppe explained, "some individuals [will] come to possess 'natural authority,' and their opinions and judgments [will] enjoy widespread respect. Moreover, because of selective mating and marriage and the laws of civil and genetic inheritance, positions of natural authority are more likely than not passed on within a few noble families."[248] Or consider Rothbard's description of an ideal social order: "In a country or a world, of totally private property, including streets, and of private contractual neighborhoods consisting of property owners, these owners can make any sort of neighborhood-contracts they wish. In practice, then, the country would be a truly 'gorgeous mosaic,' . . . ranging from rowdy Greenwich Village–type contractual neighborhoods, to socially homogeneous WASP neighborhoods. Remember that all deeds and covenants would once again be totally legal and enforceable, with no meddling government restrictions upon them."[249]

These comments extolling the virtues of decentralized, homogeneous communities led by naturally superior individuals and living apart from each other explains why one sees in Lincoln loathers' circles constant propagation of the idea that the Civil War was a fight against tariffs (i.e., taxes) or a fight against a despotic, Lincolnian, centralized government in Washington, D.C., or a fight for states' rights or a fight during Reconstruction to redeem the states from Yankee rule—the "Southern holocaust," as *Southern Partisan* labeled it. In addition to their genuine antiwar proclivities, Lincoln's conservative and libertarian enemies have advanced an alternative historical narrative that serves, and to an extent has always served, entrenched interests at the state and local level. It is a conservative—or as Rothbard put it, a radically reactionary—political philosophy rooted in local control, hierarchy, patriarchy, and, at least historically speaking, white supremacy, one that would inevitably reward the well-to-do and involuntarily subordinate the underprivileged to their economic and political power.[250] The consequences of such economic and political power being seen as "natural" by subordinates would be, and indeed have been, materially and psychologically devastating (as post–Reconstruction era race relations in the South, if not all of world history, amply demonstrate).[251] Carter Woodson once alluded to the effects of such social arrangements in analyzing segregation, but his words seem particularly apt here: "When you control a man's thinking you do not have to worry about his actions. You do not have to tell him to stand here or go yonder. He will find his 'proper place' and will stay in it. You do not need to send him to the back door. He will go without being told. In fact, if there is no back door, he will cut one for his special benefit."[252] In short, as Ed Sebesta, an author who studies neo-Confederate influence in American society, put it: "They believe in what they call 'ordered liberty.' As far I can tell, ordered liberty means they're going to order you around, and they'll be at liberty to do so because there'll be no central authority."[253] For the president's detractors Abraham Lincoln, the president who staked the nation's future on ultimately ending slavery—and slaves were easily the most marginalized group in American society—and the quintessential symbol of American democracy and the American state, was in the way. His iconic status and the supposed "Lincoln cult," which included Lincoln's conservative and libertarian defenders, therefore had to be destroyed. This suggests why the most sustained and deep defenses of Lincoln after 1945, ironically, came from conservatives and libertarians such as Harry Jaffa, followed by Guelzo, Krannawitter, and Sandefur. They all maintained that Lincoln's defense of natural rights, the indivisible nature of the American Union, and the waging of the Civil War had been morally right and any movement that continually denigrated the president was fundamentally at odds with the American democratic experiment in liberty, not to mention conservatism or libertarianism.

Hence, the accusation that Lincoln was a war criminal and would have been prosecuted as such if the United States had lost the war had to be countered. This charge implied Lincoln was admired by contemporaries either because of Union victory or assassination, or both, but not for merit. To be sure, northern success and the manner of the president's death were significant factors in Lincoln's elevated stature with nineteenth-century Americans. But Lincoln *was* elected twice in free and fair elections and was well respected by his compatriots (even loved, if one considers African American attitudes) before his death, and that appreciation increased after his demise. In opposition to the president's foes, the libertarian Sandefur thought that "the right side did prevail in that war, and libertarians should stop doing themselves the great disservice of defending a cruel and oppressive slave society," while conservative Krannawitter's entire book was premised on the idea that Lincoln was a great statesman whose political principles were *"true."*[254] Lincoln's defenders did not see the president's iconic status as entirely contingent upon Union success in the war, although clearly there has always been an element of that judgment; rather, they would have agreed, to paraphrase Joseph Addison's *Cato,* that Lincoln not only commanded success; he *deserved* it.[255]

Related to this point, scholarship regarding the Civil War being a total war, or for that matter a war criminally conducted by Lincoln and his generals, is far from settled. One of the books DiLorenzo cited for his allegation of Lincoln as a war criminal was historian Mark Grimsley's *Hard Hand of War* (1995). But Grimsley actually concluded (a conclusion with which DiLorenzo and other critics clearly disagreed) that Lincoln's army used methods "roughly proportional to legitimate needs."[256] Equally important, Grimsley perceptively argued that the attention given after the war to the alleged barbarities of the North had more to do with the desire of white southerners to absolve themselves for the decision to secede and begin the war in the first place rather than any other factor.[257] Lincoln's adoption of the Lieber Code, moreover, was not a license for

Lincoln's generals to wage total war, although central to its purpose was Lieber's belief that "the more vigorously wars are pursued, the better it is for humanity."[258] Rather, "Lincoln's Code," as legal scholar John Fabian Witt has termed it, "crafted a common vocabulary, a way of talking about war's grave moral stakes that could be shared by war's fiercest defenders and its most uncompromising humanitarian critics alike."[259] The consequence of this common vocabulary has not been the sanctioning of total war; rather, according to Witt, it has "helped constrain U.S. presidents a century and a half later" and served as an inspiration around the world for "men and women [who] have worked ever since to preserve the framework he [Lincoln] helped establish."[260] Finally, the Civil War was arguably less brutal than the Mexican War—a war launched by a southern, slaveholding Democrat, James K. Polk, and one that Lincoln had opposed as a freshman congressman from Illinois—or the behavior exhibited toward Indians on the North American continent from the country's inception. This is not to say that the Civil War was not a total, criminal war; perhaps it was. But it is to say that Lincoln's enemies asserted something to be manifestly true when in fact it was very much contested within the scholarly community, not to mention the public at large, illustrating once again their selective use of the historical record and proclivity to cherry-pick scholarship that agreed with their viewpoint and neglect aspects of work (e.g., Grimsley's) that did not.[261]

In their speculation that Lincoln would have been prosecuted as a war criminal if the South had won the war, moreover, the president's critics ignored historical reality in order to tarnish Lincoln's reputation. After 1865 scarcely any Americans were prosecuted for war crimes. The Confederacy lost the war, but only one individual, Henry Wirz, the commander of Andersonville prison in Georgia, was tried and executed for his wartime malfeasance. Lincoln's detractors seemed to be arguing that if the Confederacy had won the war, they would have tried a former president for war crimes and thus been harsher than their northern counterparts. In point of historical fact, despite their failed attempt to break up the United States in order to establish a slaveholding republic, many former Confederates enjoyed successful postwar political careers and the esteem of their region, if not the entire country, as honorable men. The peace that followed the war was not harsh but lenient, except for the former slaves, whose freedom and lives were endangered as the nation's commitment to racial equality retreated in the teeth of white southern resistance to the idea of a more egalitarian America. It is difficult to imagine, furthermore, had the Americans lost their War for Independence with Great Britain, a war that Lincoln's critics over the years have argued was a war of secession, that George Washington or Thomas Jefferson would have been allowed to return to Virginia and serve out the remainder of their days in like manner to Robert E. Lee or Jefferson Davis, lionized by Americans as heroes with monuments raised to their memories once they were dead. Here the president's enemies appeared to hold that if the United States had lost its so-called war of secession in 1776, in the aftermath of the conflict the British would have been as magnanimous as the Union. But the American revolutionaries knew precisely what was at stake when they declared independence from England: not only their honor and fortunes were on the line if they lost; their very lives were endangered by defeat.

The related charge that Abraham Lincoln laid the foundation for the postwar American empire loses its initial plausibility when examined more closely. The United States was militantly expansionist long before Lincoln became president, as antebellum treatment of Native Americans and Mexicans confirms. Indeed, prior to the Civil War, white southerners as well as white northerners wanted to migrate and conquer the West, while not a few southerners had designs on Cuba or South America. The white South favored expansion, moreover, so that slavery could spread and thrive, while the white North desired such territory remain free on the theory that slavery should be contained and eventually die. Antebellum southerners were no less imperialistic than were their northern brethren. Influential northerners such as Stephen Douglas, furthermore, viewed Lincoln and the Republicans, because of their insistence on keeping the western territories closed to slavery, as an obstacle to, rather than advocate for, American expansionism. "Whenever it becomes necessary in our growth and progress to acquire more territory," Douglass explained in one of his debates with Lincoln, "I am in favor of it without reference to the question of slavery."[262] Native Americans, meanwhile, were perhaps doomed even if the Civil War had never occurred; therein, of course, lay the tragedy. Even if the Confederacy had won the war, finally, there is no reason to suppose that it would have been less imperialistic than postbellum America. In fact, C. L. R. James, an esteemed African American historian and author of *The Black Jacobins: Toussaint L'Ouverture and the San Domingo Revolution* (1938), went even further, maintaining in a 1959 essay that praised Lincoln "as one of the greatest statesmen the world has ever known," that the breakup of the United States would have been a disaster for the West Indies. "All who live in the Americas are better able to understand the perils we would have been in if America had gone the way of Europe, and the outlying territories had become, as they certainly would have become, a hunting ground and cockpit for two or three powerful American states. One of them is giving us enough trouble as it is. Two or three of them would have reduced us to the fate of Belgium and Holland, Malta and Cyprus."[263]

In addition, for his entire career Abraham Lincoln rejected opportunities for American expansionism. While serving as a congressman in the 1840s, he opposed the invasion of Mexico, and his speeches are riddled with the idea that the glory of the American Union lay not in its military or its Manifest Destiny but in the principles of the Declaration of Independence and the idea and *"love of liberty."*[264] To be sure, the Lincoln administration's colonization proposals were a potential method for projecting American interests overseas, but these plans, in the end, never amounted to much. Lincoln overruled Secretary of State William Seward's pre–Fort Sumter recommendation that the president launch a European war so as to reunite Americans, during the conflict he freed Confederate diplomats James Mason and John Slidell in the *Trent* affair in order avoid war with Great Britain, and he gave absolutely no credence to an unofficial end-of-the-war proposal by Francis J. Blair that the North and South re-create national unity by invading Mexico in order to overthrow a French client state established by Napoléon III south of the Rio Grande.[265] Consequently, blame for the postwar American empire can no more be attached to Abraham Lincoln's name than to those previous adversaries of the president who unjustly faulted him for the racial atrocities carried out by white southerners against African Americans in the decades after Appomattox.

Abraham Lincoln, other conservatives held, was no imperialistic dictator who emancipated slaves yet enslaved freed men. Dictators may hold elections, but they do not worry much about losing them, as Lincoln believed he would in August 1864, when the Union's military fortunes were at low ebb. Nor do tyrants tolerate the type of vitriol and hatred that was leveled against the president throughout the war. Without question Lincoln's suspension of the writ of habeas corpus remains rightly controversial, and his sometimes heavy-handed suppression of political opposition was unprecedented. In his book about presidential power, *Crisis and Command: The History of Executive Power from George Washington to George W. Bush* (2009), Bush administration and Justice Department attorney John Yoo defended Lincoln's presidency as great, or transformative, precisely because he used executive power so forcefully: "Lincoln's greatness is inextricably linked to his broad vision of presidential power"[266] Moreover, Yoo described Lincoln's presidency in language that seemed to justify Bush's actions in the War on Terror, writing that "the Unique nature of the Civil War forced the Lincoln administration to reduce civil liberties in favor of greater security."[267] Meanwhile, conservative historian Mackubin Owens, a Naval War College professor and adjunct fellow with the Ashbrook Center at Ashland University, a conservative think tank, penned several columns defending Lincoln—and President Bush.[268] Lincoln's critics are right to recall the president's civil liberties violations (although they are not as quick to note that the Confederacy likewise suppressed their people's liberties). Libertarians oppose war for just this reason: they believe that war, in addition to its horrific violence and violation of Rothbard's nonaggression axiom, permanently enlarges the state and leads to a diminishment of freedom. Nevertheless, the situation Lincoln faced as president was unprecedented, as Lincoln himself acknowledged: "I can be no more persuaded that the government can constitutionally take no strong measure in time of rebellion, because it can be shown that the same could not be taken lawfully in time of peace, than I can be persuaded that a particular drug is not good medicine for a sick man, because it can be shown not to be good food for a well one."[269] Today's leaders abuse the historical record when they invoke Lincoln as precedent for their own domestic or foreign malfeasance. Even Yoo said as much: "Not every President is a Lincoln, and not every crisis rises to the level of the Civil War."[270] Still, Yoo was being somewhat disingenuous here in that he imprudently saw relatively few, if any, constitutional limits on executive power (i.e., the unitary executive), whereas Lincoln prudently stressed those same constitutional limits on his own presidential office. Americans should therefore remind themselves of Lincoln's words of the unparalleled nature of the crisis he faced in the 1860s and resist the more boundless claims of his successors whenever they use the sixteenth president to justify their own civil liberties violations.[271]

On the heels of Barack Obama's inauguration in January 2009, the demonization of Lincoln—and the modern, multicultural, and relatively egalitarian America born from the ashes of the Civil War—only seemed to intensify. *Chronicles* devoted its February issue to criticizing the sixteenth president, reviving all the themes of antagonism for Lincoln. Thomas Fleming, the magazine's editor, thought that the Civil War indeed represented a second American Revolution, but he bemoaned its legacies:

> We went from being a confederation of republics that minded their own business, and permitted farmers, merchants, and manufacturers to mind theirs, to a global empire run by stockjobbers, moneychangers, and Transcendentalist do-gooders, a Leviathan with wings that is forever busybodying at home and abroad. From a fairly homogenous ethnic base—a British core with Northern European accretions—we have morphed into a multiethnic, multilingual, multicultural population in which no one, not even descendants of the oldest stock, knows or cares who he is. Leftists now rejoice that the White House will be presided over by someone whose middle name is Hussein actually run by someone whose middle name is Israel.[272]

In language similar to previous detractors of the president, Fleming said Lincoln was a "mixture of ambition and incompetence" whose rhetoric "cloaked his political agenda in a lofty religious language," all leading to the deaths of hundreds of thousands of Americans, including, he claimed, "hundreds of thousands of dead slaves."[273] Thus, the *Chronicles* editor echoed the complaint of 1870s Lincoln critic Albert Taylor Bledsoe by comparing Lincoln's rhetoric to "the French Jacobin who treated mass murder as the noblest part of statecraft. It is in the French Revolution and its aftershocks that ideology began to take the place of religion as the formative rhetoric of Europe and North America."[274] In a way Fleming reintroduced the old charge of Lincoln as an infidel when he equated him to "Robespierre" and "Lenin and Stalin, and Hitler and Mussolini," all of whom "were anything but Christian, and it is the rejection of Christianity that is the hallmark of modern ideology."[275]

So, on the two hundredth anniversary of Abraham Lincoln's birthday, all the charges leveled against the president dating back to the nineteenth century had once again reentered American political debate. There were competing organizations, scholars, television personalities, even political figures, articulating very different conceptions of the American founding, Abraham Lincoln and the Civil War, and the United States' role in the world. Considering the intellectual firepower and political connections of some of the individuals involved in this contest, this was no mere academic or think tank squabble. On one side were those who believed that in opposing secession Lincoln caused the United States to take a disastrously wrong turn in the 1860s; that the Confederate cause was morally sound because of its alleged hostility to what they called a centralized government in Washington, D.C.; that the worst consequence of Lincoln's war, in addition to its horrendous casualties, was that the idea of limited, decentralized government in America was tarnished, perhaps irreparably; and that the federal government became an imperialist behemoth in both domestic and foreign imperialist policy. On the other side were those who believed that in opposing secession Lincoln acted in a manner consistent with and in a fulfillment of the American founding tradition of natural rights and limited government; that in so doing the president preserved the idea of democratic government; that right triumphed in the war; that whatever centralization occurred in the 1860s was temporary; that limited, decentralized government remained an essential aspect of American political practice, much to the chagrin of blacks; and that the United States was, on balance, a force for good in the world. Given the stature of Abraham Lincoln in American culture, it seemed that the quest of Lincoln's detractors was quixotic. "If you want to tilt at windmills," David Goldfield has explained, "Lincoln's the biggest windmill around."[276]

But it was evident that those who persisted in their project of taking down, or at the very least altering, the president's image in order to serve their political agenda had made some progress. By Lincoln's bicentennial in 2009 his standing in American life, although secure, had weakened somewhat since World War II, and negative judgments of the president had resurfaced into mainstream conservatism and the Republican Party.[277] It is unsurprising that in the South, geographically a Republican stronghold, many states reported their celebrations of Lincoln's bicentennial to be muted and "low-key."[278] Part of the decline in Lincoln's reputation was probably inevitable. After World War II, as the country became more pluralistic, more egalitarian, and more skeptical of authority and tradition, Americans were less likely to venerate any political figure, including Lincoln.[279] Vietnam, Watergate, Reagan's War on Drugs, Iran-Contra, Clinton-Lewinsky, and the controversies surrounding President Bush's War on Terror further discredited national authority, if not all political figures, and it would have been surprising if Lincoln's reputation had remained altogether immune to such cynicism. But surely it did not help the president's image that his enemies were relentlessly outspoken in their criticism.

Lincoln's detractors in the post–Cold War era have subtly shaped the way Americans view Lincoln, the Civil War, and American democracy. There remains a type of dogmatic mentality harshly critical of Lincoln's racial views, views linked to his understanding of freedom, equality, and federal power, a mentality that demands a moral perfectionism of intention that none of the nation's leaders will ever attain. This unbending critique breeds cynicism for the democratic political system that Lincoln helped preserve. Lincoln's racial views may fall far short of twenty-first-century standards, but the idea that there was no substantial difference between Lincoln, the Republican Party, and the United States, who struggled to contain slavery so it would eventually die, and, say, Jefferson Davis and the Confederacy, who struggled to expand slavery so that it would live, remains prevalent. Indeed, a "Jefferson Davis Presidential Library" is being rebuilt with federal dollars in Biloxi, Mississippi, at Beauvoir, the home where the Confederate president spent his last years. The library is not meant as a place of serious research but as a symbol that by its very existence equates Davis's presidency with that of other American presidents, including, presumably, Abraham Lincoln. The library's bookshop sells the neo-Confederate volume *Was Jefferson Davis Right?*, the publisher of which, Pelican Publishing, brought out John Remington Graham's book on secession along with other anti-Lincoln works.[280] During the Lincoln bicentennial the writer Adam Gopnik dispelled any notion of moral equivalency between Davis and Lincoln, or Lerone Bennett Jr.'s view that the president was an oppressive racist: "Liberals who struggle with their own prejudices are somehow equal in prejudice to those who never took the trouble to make the struggle. Imperfect effort at being just is no different than perfect indifference to it. Lincoln's equivocations on race are somehow equivalent to the outright racism of his opponents, then and later, as though the whole point is not that Lincoln was doing everything in his power to end the agony and assist the emancipation of an oppressed group, while those on the other side were doing everything in their power to prolong the agony and prevent the emancipation."[281] In misunderstanding this basic point, Americans not only ignore the vast personal and political difficulties Lincoln and his allies faced in eradicating the deeply entrenched institution of slavery; they are insufficiently attentive to the president's twenty-first-century libertarian and conservative detractors, who have utilized this argument from moral equivalence to delegitimize the federal government in Washington, D.C.

Given the work of the president's critics, it is no surprise that although reputable historians the world over are in virtually unanimous agreement with Abraham Lincoln, as he said in his Second Inaugural Address, that the conflict was somehow caused by slavery, the American public to an extent disagrees with that viewpoint. According to the Pew Research Center, in 2011, 48 percent of the American public believed that the war was "mainly about states' rights," while another 9 percent thought it was equally about slavery and states' rights. Only 38 percent of those polled believed the war was "mainly about slavery." Over a third, 36 percent, thought that it was "appropriate for public officials today to praise Confederate leaders."[282] In addition, when CNN asked Americans in 2011 if they sympathized more with the Union or the Confederacy, 25 percent said the Confederacy.[283] In such a context, Lincoln (and the Republicans) may be seen less as a president who justifiably preserved the Union, eradicated slavery, and maintained the integrity of democratic elections and more as one who violated the rights of the states by opposing their so-called right to secede, thereby centralizing government in Washington, D.C. Equally significant is how different age groups perceived the war: "Young people are more likely than older Americans to say that the war's main cause was states' rights—60% of those younger than age 30 express this view, the highest percentage of any age group. Those ages 65 and older are the only age group in which more say that slavery, rather than states' rights, was the main cause of the Civil War (by 50% to 34%). While 48% of whites view states' rights as the war's main cause, so too do 39% of African Americans."[284]

These demographics suggest that Lincoln's enemies have already influenced public attitudes and will continue to do so in the future. Congressman Ron Paul has made it clear that he does not believe Lincoln was a great president. Given his ideological affinities and the admirable consistency with which he has held his stances throughout his political career, this is unsurprising. If nothing else, his esteem for Murray Rothbard and strong connection to the Mises Institute substantiate that Paul has little or no affection for Abraham Lincoln, and he has publicly affirmed that stance.[285] Thomas DiLorenzo's statement in 2010 to a group of Tenth Amendment advocates at a conference in Atlanta that he thought "Abraham Lincoln an enemy of the Constitution" did not prevent him from testifying one year later before Congressman Paul's House Financial Services Committee on monetary policy.[286] Although it would not be appropriate to say that Paul shares all of DiLorenzo's views, or vice versa, they have written and spoken in similar language about Lincoln, and they apparently share the same basic political philosophy. Also, Paul has enthusiastically recommended Thomas Woods's *Politically Incorrect Guide to American History* and in his own book *Liberty Defined* suggested Woods's *Nullification: How to Resist Federal Tyranny in the 21st Century* (2010) for further reading.[287] And Woods is no marginal figure. According to one historian of libertarianism, Brian Doherty, Woods is the "biggest speaking-circuit superstar in the Paul world who isn't named Paul."[288] Given Woods's popularity and Congressman Paul's extraordinary appeal to younger voters, it is inconceivable that such voters will not be exposed to their views about Abraham Lincoln and the Civil War. Paul's candidacy has been compared to Barry Goldwater's in that although he did not win the presidency, he has already influenced future voters, young people who are already predisposed to believe that the Civil War was about "states' rights." On the one hand, it is unlikely that the Texas congressman's decidedly negative stance toward Lincoln will triumph. Americans continue to venerate Lincoln, and Goldwater won the Republican nomination, which the Texas congressman failed to do. But Paul's failure, if it can even be considered as such, may have been due more to the congressman's antiwar and anti-imperialistic foreign policy views than his emphasis on local control in domestic matters. On the other hand, although the Texas congressman retired from the House of Representatives in 2012, he will continue in his attempts to shape the long-term orientation of the Republican Party and the entire United States.[289] His son, Kentucky senator Rand Paul (R), who has spoken highly of Murray Rothbard, may continue his father's mission to move the country in a direction that will be more hostile to Abraham Lincoln's understanding of the Constitution and American democracy.

In a political trend ideologically sympathetic with the Ron Paul phenomenon, there are some indications this move has already occurred. In response to President Obama's Affordable Care Act, at least ten states from all over the country contemplated passing nullification ordinances to repeal Obamacare. Other states have considered nullifying gun control laws. In addition to the idea of nullification, Texas governor and 2012 Republican presidential candidate Rick Perry has openly voiced secessionist sentiments, while in two Minnesota congressional districts Republican conventions attempted to pass secession resolutions. In fact, the Fifth Congressional District convention passed such a resolution, stating, "Be it resolved the Republican Party of Minnesota supports nullification of unconstitutional federal laws and secession as options to enforce state sovereignty."[290] It should have been no surprise that another 2012 presidential candidate, Minnesota congresswoman Michele Bachmann, has, like her congressional colleague Paul, equated antebellum slavery with economic enslavement or that her intellectual mentor, Oral Roberts University law professor John Eidsmoe, has claimed that "Jefferson Davis and John C. Calhoun understood the Constitution better than did Abraham Lincoln."[291] Congresswoman Bachmann has also praised a biography of Robert E. Lee by Steve Wilkins, a Louisiana pastor who has defended antebellum slavery and been critical of Abraham Lincoln's religion, or supposed lack thereof.[292] According to a 2011 Rasmussen poll, 21 percent of Americans believe states should have the right to secede, and 12 percent see that as a possibility in the future.[293] The *Daily Kos* reported in a 2009 poll that only 63 percent of southerners were sure they wanted to stay in the United States, while 29 percent responded they were unsure they wanted to remain.[294] So, although Congressman Paul has correctly conceded that "no constitutional amendment will be passed to explicitly permit nullification or secession," he is nevertheless confident that "through a new relationship evolving out of current economic and political chaos, *something approaching this goal is about to come.*"[295]

At the very least, such a result would change the relationship between the states and the federal government and jeopardize current understandings of American democracy and majority rule.[296] Americans would do well to remember that limited government, or states' rights, has historically been invoked in opposition to civil rights for minorities and in support of governments that disenfranchised both whites and blacks and resulted in those governments supporting privileged whites. Decentralizing power away from Washington, D.C., may be rhetorically appealing, if not in certain respects necessary, but it can also mean, in effect, local control of the less fortunate by an already locally powerful elite and lead to a diminishment of freedom and equality.[297] If what Congressman Paul predicts comes true, in certain areas of the country opposition to Lincoln and its associated reactionary views may develop and take hold among segments of the American population. Indeed, that already seems to be happening in Texas, where the Lone Star State's history standards have been rewritten in such a way that slavery as a cause of secession and the Civil War are minimized, thus providing a context and a forum whereby the Confederacy and its leaders could be glorified.[298] These trends, none of which, it must be emphasized, are historically unprecedented in the United States, might negatively influence how Americans think about Lincoln, a president who maintained that "a majority, held in restraint by constitutional checks, and limitations, and always changing easily, with deliberate changes of popular opinions and sentiments, is the only true sovereign of a free people. Whoever rejects it does, of necessity, fly to anarchy or to despotism. Unanimity is impossible; the rule of a minority, as a permanent arrangement, is wholly inadmissible [*sic*]; so that, rejecting the majority principle, anarchy, or despotism in some form, is all that is left."[299] In short, in a democracy "there can be no successful appeal from a fair election, but to the next election."[300]

Unlike those 2003 protestors of the Lincoln statue in Richmond, Virginia, with their "malice toward one," Americans continue to remember Lincoln as a great statesman, one who courageously advanced the cause of freedom and equality during the Civil War.[301] But there has always been an alternative narrative of those who loathe Lincoln who argue that he hindered its cause and set the country on a tyrannical course. Although it appears unlikely that this narrative will ever predominate in American life, it could become more influential. If the historical narrative of Lincoln's enemies becomes more influential, the constitutional and moral foundations of the country's existence will be less secure, or established on a different basis; nullification and secession may be more commonly used as a rhetorical method for advocating limited government and resistance to all federal authority, thereby casting doubt on the legitimacy of democratic elections; larger areas of the United States might accept the Confederacy's war goals as noble rather than malevolent, overturning if not inverting the meaning of freedom and equality, thereby making hierarchy and inequality more acceptable in American life; it may become increasingly difficult to accept that political parties led by figures such as Abraham Lincoln can, with eloquent, persuasive language and gradual, ameliorative measures, enlarge freedom, and Americans' skepticism toward democratic politics could degenerate into an unhealthy cynicism that would reinforce the political and social status quo; and Americans may become hopelessly pessimistic that the federal government has *any* role to play in addressing national or international problems, many of which require national and international solutions.

The historical narrative of Lincoln's enemies has habitually masked or evaded the Civil War's serious moral issues in euphemisms such as states' rights, tariffs, and centralization. This inclination has degraded American political discourse and hampered the nation's ability to face squarely the impact of slavery and emancipation, not to mention obscuring the contribution of the millions of Americans, white and black, who devoted their lives to liberty, equality, and justice in order to eradicate inhuman bondage. It has also obscured the contribution of Lincoln himself, a flawed human being to be sure but a politician who, with the assistance of innumerable others in the concrete pressure of a struggle for national survival, insisted at all times on the moral wrongness of slavery, the necessity of its extinction, and the importance of honoring the results of democratic elections. Understanding these details of the past will mean that it is not inevitable that the historical narrative of Lincoln's enemies will become more influential. If Americans clearly comprehend their arguments, their historical antecedents, and, more often than not, their elitist temperament and inegalitarian goals, then they can take heart from Lincoln's life and work, and they will be better equipped to fight peacefully against his enemies' contentions. They can likewise take heart from the president's struggles as they make their own contribution to improve a country for which Lincoln, alongside countless others, gave his life to preserve, a nation whose devotion to liberty and equality made it a country "forever worthy of the saving."[302]

CONCLUSION

In the aftermath of the Civil War, Alexander Stephens strenuously denied that the military conflict had been fought over slavery. Instead, he claimed it was a war "between the opposing principles of Federation, on the one side, and Centralism, or Consolidation on the other."[1] Although Stephens expressed kind words for Abraham Lincoln personally, he also stated that in his "official position" Lincoln had committed "errors involving not only [the] most unjustifiable usurpations of power, but such as rise to high crimes against society and against humanity." He compared the late president to Julius Caesar, who "by the general consent of mankind [is] looked upon as the destroyer of the liberties of Rome!"[2] Nearly seventy years later, in the midst of the Great Depression, Edgar Lee Masters echoed the former Confederate vice president: "The Union that he [Lincoln] mystically adored, the Union under the Constitution of 1787, perished with the war. . . . With consolidation came imperial America." Lincoln, Masters explained, had "crushed the principles of free government."[3] Seventy-one years after Masters informed Americans of their enslavement, economist Thomas J. DiLorenzo reiterated their claims. DiLorenzo said "the war created the highly centralized state that Americans labor under today. The purpose of American government was transformed from the defense of individual liberty to the quest for empire."[4] Neo-Confederate historian Clyde Wilson, in a 2011 essay extolling the virtues of South Carolina politician and proslavery apologist John C. Calhoun that barely mentioned the word *slavery*, labeled the Civil War simply "the War of Consolidation."[5] In their never-ending argument that Abraham Lincoln had consolidated power in Washington, D.C., that slavery was not the issue that provoked secession or the war, that Lincoln had destroyed the American people's liberties—emancipating slaves but enslaving free men—and that he had laid the basis for an American empire, these individuals were part of a 150-year tradition of loathing for Lincoln and for the results of the United States' victory in the American Civil War.

Most Americans consider Abraham Lincoln one of the greatest presidents in the history of the United States. But in Lincoln's lifetime and since, numerous Americans have vilified the sixteenth president. Immediately after the 1860 election, rather than remain under his influence and authority, seven states seceded from the Union, followed by four more states after Confederate forces fired upon Fort Sumter. He was the first president to die at the hands of an assassin—a murderer who won accolades from many in the defeated Confederate States. And the hatred for Lincoln that commenced even before his presidency began has persisted, with tactical adaptations to changing circumstances, into the twenty-first century. In 1858, when he concluded his debates with Stephen Douglas, Lincoln himself anticipated the essential nature of the fight that would continue over his name:

> That is the issue that will continue in this country when these poor tongues of Judge Douglas and myself shall be silent. It is the eternal struggle between these two principles—right and wrong—throughout the world. They are the two principles that have stood face to face from the beginning of time; and will ever continue to struggle. The one is the common right of humanity and the other the divine right of kings. It is the same principle in whatever shape it develops itself. It is the same spirit that says, "You work and toil and earn bread, and I'll eat it." No matter in what shape it comes, whether from the mouth of a king who seeks to bestride the people of his own nation and live by the fruit of their own labor; or from one race of men as an apology for enslaving another race, it is the same tyrannical principle.[6]

Lincoln was more right than he could have possibly known at the time. To a large extent the struggle over Lincoln's image has always been rooted in contesting visions of America, one envisioning freedom and equality for all, the other envisioning freedom and equality for some, with subordination to authority, or their so-called natural superiors, for the rest. With few exceptions loathing for Lincoln has meant loathing for an expanded notion of freedom and equality joined in direct opposition to the idea, as the assertions from Stephens, Masters, DiLorenzo, and Wilson illustrate, that the Civil War was fought over such notions or that the federal government should play any role in maintaining a link between these two

American ideals. Abraham Lincoln's enemies have always tried to define who he was, but in in their loathing for the president, they have more often than not defined themselves.[7]

During his presidency Lincoln and the antislavery Republican Party were hated mainly by two large groups: Confederates and northern peace Democrats known as Copperheads. A few Radical Republicans and abolitionists strongly critiqued Lincoln from time to time, but as a whole their attacks were scarcely equivalent to the racially based hatred expressed by the president's far more populous opponents and did not descend to the level of genuine loathing. Confederates and Copperheads believed Lincoln was a tyrant because he used federal power to emancipate slaves in parts of the Confederacy, suspended habeas corpus across the North, and waged what they claimed was a brutal, inhumane war on the seceded states. Their opposition to Lincoln sprang from a deep-seated belief that freedom and equality should remain forever limited to white men, and they expressed their disgust for the president in rhetoric especially fearful of the prospect of increased racial egalitarianism. To be sure, there were some in the antislavery camp, such as Lysander Spooner, who believed that the natural rights ideals of the Declaration of Independence and the Constitution itself authorized the president to abolish slavery.[8] Hence, at times Lincoln was criticized for not using his executive powers forcefully enough or quickly enough to end the pernicious institution. This was nevertheless a minority viewpoint within the broad antislavery movement, and it became increasingly marginal with the likelihood of Union victory in the war, with passage of the Thirteenth Amendment abolishing slavery, and with the idea of increased racial equality ensured by federal power seeming a distinct possibility.

In the decades after Lincoln's murder, condemnations of the president continued to emanate from his wartime enemies. Although their denunciations were relatively muted in the immediate aftermath of the conflict, the president's opponents refused to accept Lincoln's iconic stature with the majority of Americans. Lincoln was attacked by relatively marginal figures in the North such as Lysander Spooner and more influential white southerners such as Alexander Stephens for centralizing power in Washington, D.C., both of whom denied that ending slavery had been the cause of the war or one of its goals or even one of its results. Others, such as William Hand Browne and Albert Taylor Bledsoe, were in agreement with these views, but they also denounced Lincoln for his "coarse" or "vulgar" or "disgusting" frontier background, for being an unbeliever who did not fully embrace Christianity, and for wartime atrocities such as refusing prisoner exchanges with Confederates. Consequently, criticism of Lincoln persisted, but it was oftentimes reactionary in nature and rhetoric and involved a spirited philosophical defense of the old Confederate regime in what came to be called the Lost Cause. Loathing for Lincoln came from those, mostly in the South, who accepted that slavery and the Confederacy were dead but bemoaned their not inconsiderable losses from the war and refused to consent to the revolutionary idea that the new American nation should be based upon the idea of liberty and equality of opportunity for all or that the federal government, especially through the Fourteenth Amendment to the Constitution, should ensure that such an egalitarian principle of *national* citizenship be fulfilled.[9] So the counterrevolutionary claim was made that Lincoln was unworthy of emulation, for he had emancipated the slaves but enslaved free white men to federal power, and his detractors accordingly viewed him (and the section of the country he represented) as the destroyer rather than savior of the Union. He was for these critics, in short, an American Jacobin. Still, most Americans, especially African Americans, celebrated Lincoln as the embodiment of American democratic ideals, the Great Emancipator and Savior of the Union, and they enthusiastically accepted the portrayal of the president as a compassionate, forgiving, and Christian figure. Sadly, this kindhearted depiction contributed to a national reconciliation between the North and South that eventually diminished the rights of the people Lincoln had helped emancipate.

As the generation that actually fought the war passed away and northerners withdrew from their commitment to liberty and equality for African Americans and the use of federal power to ensure their maintenance, white southerners more openly challenged the idea that Lincoln had saved the Union or was a model American. Between 1890 and 1918 individuals in the former states of the Confederacy, including Mary DeButts Carter, Elizabeth Avery Meriwether, Charles L. C. Minor, Kate Mason Rowland, and Mildred Lewis Rutherford, allied themselves with organizations such as the United Daughters of the Confederacy (UDC) and publicly disagreed with their northern counterparts who praised the new, expansionist American nation and lauded Lincoln; instead, they glorified the Confederacy and accused Lincoln of laying the groundwork for American imperialism. They disseminated their pro-Confederate outlook throughout the former states of the Confederacy in monuments, schools, textbooks, and other publications. No doubt Lincoln was celebrated by the vast majority of Americans, not least Progressive presidents Theodore Roosevelt and Woodrow Wilson, but this viewpoint was directly and indirectly challenged by the UDC and other privileged southerners. And even for those white southerners who had come to view the president more favorably, their appreciation had less to do with being in agreement with Lincoln's political philosophy of federal supremacy (at least regarding secession) and natural rights for all and more to do with their claim that Lincoln, too, was a white supremacist. Their stance was racially repressive, sometimes violently so, and stemmed from a desire to maintain white control over African Americans; it was also, tragically, compatible with the racial outlook of most of the country, as the United States receded from the possibility of a multiracial society with expanded opportunities for shared power to a more narrow one based exclusively upon white rule. A few elite African Americans, such as Archibald Grimké and Hubert Harrison, in light of the nation's retreat from its Civil War era commitment to racial equality, forcefully and publicly questioned allegiance to the Great Emancipator and held that continued veneration of Lincoln was in fact a hindrance to their race. Still, one must be careful here not to characterize too quickly their stance as loathing for the president; what they truly loathed was that in a country supposedly devoted to liberty and equality, the oppression of blacks was countenanced, even at times encouraged, by their fellow Americans.

Between the Great War and the end of World War II, criticism of Lincoln became more widespread, even as the president's reputation reached its zenith among the majority of Americans. The denunciations of Lincoln emanating from men such as Lyon Gardiner Tyler did not vary too significantly from that of previous decades, although now there was a distinct opposition to modernity alongside their traditional attacks because Lincoln was seen by his adversaries as modernity's embodiment or at the very least as someone who had aided its advance. Of course, because one aspect of modernity entailed an enhanced authority for state—that is, federal—power, especially during the Great Depression and Franklin Roosevelt's New Deal, opposing Lincoln was one way to oppose such power and its potentially worrisome consequences for continued white supremacy. Lincoln's detractors found a measure of national respectability as their arguments were expressed, at least in part, by well-known figures such as Senator Albert Beveridge, the journalist H. L. Mencken, and some of the Southern Agrarians connected to Vanderbilt University, including Donald Davidson and Andrew Lytle, and in famed Illinois poet Edgar Lee

Masters's biography *Lincoln: The Man*. Heartened by FDR's presidency and understandably discouraged with the nation's departure from even the ideal of racial equality, there was a widening of criticism for Lincoln within the African American community from leaders such as W. E. B. Du Bois, Congressman Arthur Mitchell, *Pittsburgh Courier* editor Robert Vann, and Carter Woodson to ordinary African Americans, some of which was shared by former slaves in the Works Progress Administration (WPA) interviews. This reappraisal signaled the beginning of a historic shift in attitude among blacks away from the Republican Party, the "Party of Lincoln," and toward the Democrats as the party that would best guarantee their basic constitutional and human rights. It also presaged Lerone Bennett Jr.'s, postwar disapproval, which at the very least reflected bitter disillusionment with Lincoln, if not actual loathing.

After 1945, in a society more disposed to accept racial equality, more disdainful of white supremacy, and more secular and attentive to merit rather than birth, Lincoln was attacked far less for his background or religious beliefs and more for his expansion of executive power, allegedly messianic wartime rhetoric, and shortcomings on race. In opposition to the civil rights movement, or "Second Reconstruction," Lincoln was criticized by conservatives and libertarians alike for executive overreach, in part because he was so ably and vigorously defended by the conservative political philosopher Harry Jaffa. Later African American critics such as Lerone Bennett Jr. indicted the president for having done too little to advance emancipation and racial equality. In keeping with previous African Americans who had questioned Lincoln's bona fides as the Great Emancipator, Bennett held that American veneration for the sixteenth president was a continuing obstacle to such humanitarian goals. Accordingly, one was as likely to find deep-seated criticism of the president coming from liberals as conservatives. To a degree they found a common enemy in Lincoln, their animosity merging in the Cold War era over distaste for American adventurism overseas. By the time the Cold War ended in 1989, public condemnations of Lincoln were seen as politically poisonous and temporarily purged from mainstream conservatism.

Libertarians such as Murray Rothbard and his intellectual disciples at the Ludwig von Mises Institute nevertheless continued their hostility and, in tandem with conservative Lincoln detractors such as M. E. Bradford, advanced similar, or at least compatible, anti-Lincoln views. Between the end of the Cold War and the commencement of the War on Terror in 2001, these libertarian and conservative critics were part of a larger neo-Confederate or paleolibertarian movement that continued the standard charges against Lincoln but also stressed that he had been a war criminal and the precursor to the "warfare-welfare state" that they believed was destroying America's limited constitutional government. Their arguments and outlook, although vigorously challenged by pro-Lincoln conservatives and libertarians, were associated with influential Republican figures such as Congressman Ron Paul of Texas. This self-confessed reactionary judgment of Lincoln intensified with the election in 2008 of the first African American president (and Lincoln admirer), Democrat Barack Obama. Bennett's negative analysis remained publicly visible with his book *Forced into Glory: Abraham Lincoln's White Dream* (2000) but drifted into relative political insignificance on the Left, in part because it was judged incompatible with the historical record, in part because Obama's inauguration during the bicentennial of Lincoln's birth in 2009 was to an extent seen as a fulfillment of the Civil War president's ideals.

Again, the contest over Lincoln's image from the nineteenth century onward has been nothing less than part of a struggle over whether freedom and equality are for the many, particularly people of color, or the few. Abraham Lincoln was the democratically elected leader of those Americans who were in the former camp, and with the assistance of the antislavery movement, not to mention the movement of the slaves themselves away from their masters, he staked his presidency—indeed the nation's very existence—on ending American slavery forever. As Frederick Douglass put it in 1876, eleven years after the president's assassination: "Abraham Lincoln was at the head of a great movement, and was in living and earnest sympathy with that movement, which, in the nature of things, must go on until slavery should be utterly and forever abolished in the United States."[10] Because of their starkly contrasting answers to the fundamental political dilemma about the scope of freedom and equality, alongside questions of whether a link between these ideals even exists or if the federal government should guarantee that such a link should be maintained or if such ideals should be extended to others previously outside "the boundaries of justice" in American life, antipathy for Lincoln has, historically speaking, been more central to conservatism and libertarianism than liberalism (although necessitated by neither, as the defense of the president launched by Harry Jaffa and carried on by Allen Guelzo, Thomas Krannawitter, and Timothy Sandefur attests). It is conceivable that if the country had fulfilled its commitment to expanded notions of freedom and equality for African Americans in the aftermath of the Civil

War, then there might never have been the intermittent opposition to Lincoln that later came from liberals, whereas it was precisely because the country had tried to honor that commitment at all that hatred for the president immediately and constantly emanated from more reactionary conservatives and libertarians deeply unhappy with the war's results, modernity, and the American nation-state, intellectually duty bound in their loathing for Abraham Lincoln.[11]

If the past 150 years are any indication, disgust with Lincoln will remain a permanent feature of the American political landscape, and his image will continue to be twisted and turned for different political ends. Of course, the form that such loathing takes will be determined by the specific discontents that exist in a particular historical era, as attitudes toward Lincoln have always been shaped by contemporary understandings of freedom, equality, and federal power. The centralization that Lincoln's reactionary opponents have always decried has never been entirely disconnected from the idea that federal authority was being used or might potentially be used (or in Lerone Bennett's case was not being used forcefully enough) in the service of greater racial equality. To the degree that the national government uses its power in the service of a wider egalitarianism—it is irrelevant whether that egalitarianism is racial, sexual, or some other essential aspect of expanded autonomy—there will continue to be hatred for Abraham Lincoln emanating from some conservatives and libertarians as a way to oppose such a goal or the means of achieving it. On this point it might be worth noting Congressman Paul's language in opposition to the 2003 Supreme Court decision in *Lawrence v. Texas* overturning *Bowers v. Hardwick* (1986), which had criminalized homosexual acts: "The Court determined that Texas had no right to establish its own standards for private sexual conduct, because gay sodomy is somehow protected under the 14th amendment 'right to privacy.' Ridiculous as sodomy laws may be, there clearly is no right to privacy nor sodomy found anywhere in the Constitution. There are, however, *states' rights*—rights plainly affirmed in the Ninth and Tenth amendments. Under those amendments, the State of Texas has the right to decide for itself how to regulate social matters like sex, using its own local standards."[12] To the degree that inequalities persist and the federal government is perceived as doing too little to address ongoing inequities, or indeed as having caused them, there will be loathing for Lincoln coming from liberals or radicals who argue that Lincoln is either irrelevant to improving their lot or that veneration of his memory is an obstacle to meaningful progress toward greater equality.

Given America's ongoing racial inequities, especially the incarceration rates of African Americans in U.S. prisons, there could potentially be a vast subculture of individuals understandably receptive to such views on these points. Whatever the future holds, it is likely that whether Lincoln's enemies make deeper inroads or have diminishing influence in American life will to an extent be based upon questions of political power, for as the English writer George Orwell once explained, "Who controls the past controls the future: who controls the present controls the past."[13]

As a result, although Lincoln's reputation among Americans seems relatively secure, his enemies can and will continue to shape debate about his legacy in order to move the country in a different political direction. The president's adversaries have been relentless in their attempt to replace the nation's historical understanding of Lincoln with their more sinister image. One thing that Lincoln's defenders and detractors have agreed on over the years has been that what Americans think of Lincoln is very much related to what Americans think of themselves—and their country. The writer Sarah Vowell wittily alluded to this outlook when she said: "Lincoln is like one of those novelty mirrors with a beard painted on the glass. Americans tend to see themselves in him. If you're a gay Republican, you think he's a gay Republican. If you're mopey, you get relatively excited that he was depressed, too."[14] Vowell was right, but what she perhaps minimized was the political dimension of how Lincoln's enemies have toiled, in some times and places successfully, in most times and places less so, to influence or eradicate entirely the image of Lincoln Americans see in the mirror. The president's antagonists have never been excited, indeed they have been horrified, that Americans see themselves in Lincoln, and they have worked assiduously—and will continue to do so—to ensure that their countrymen see Jefferson Davis or Robert E. Lee or Lysander Spooner or Martin Luther King Jr. or some other figure of their liking reflected back instead. Lincoln's detractors are very much like the enemies of Charles Darwin in late-twentieth- and early-twenty-first-century America. Darwin's theory of evolution is the unifying concept of all biology, yet it has been vigorously challenged as untrue and pernicious by fundamentalist Christians, as well as a few others, over the past several decades. These individuals have not proven false the theory of evolution, but they have been successful in making Americans think there is a robust argument over the truth of Darwin's theory, when in fact there is no such debate among reputable biologists. As a result, they have cast doubt not only on the theory of evolution but in a number of ways on the entire scientific enterprise. Similarly, Lincoln's enemies have cast doubt on his commitment to ending slavery, the constitutionality of his actions as president, and his overall legacy. By so doing, they have cast doubt not only on Abraham Lincoln but in certain respects on the American experiment in democracy. They have tried to give the appearance that in some fundamental manner the United States took the wrong fork in the road in the 1860s and that the country, if not the world, has paid a steep price ever since for its erroneous choice.

Despite the ongoing work of his enemies, Americans continue to revere, even love, Abraham Lincoln and all that he stood for and accomplished. If nothing else, the popularity of the Steven Spielberg biopic *Lincoln* demonstrates the truth of this claim. Like Lincoln, Americans believe in equality of opportunity, the idea that a person's status or role in life should not be fixed at birth. The vast majority of the United States, unlike the president's longstanding critics, find Lincoln's rise from frontier rags to the Oval Office inspiring rather than disgusting. Attacks on Lincoln's supposed irreligion also ring hollow, in part because religious imagery pervades Lincoln's speeches, which appeals to Americans of a religious persuasion, and in part because charges of Lincoln's "infidelity" are simply not going to resonate as much in an increasingly secular and religiously diverse nation. Added to this, Americans are in deep-seated agreement with the Lincolnian conviction that all people have certain rights that should never be violated and that democracy, for all its considerable flaws, is the best form of government, especially when it protects such rights and, by so doing, empathetically "expresses equal respect for all."[15] Finally, there is a deeply shared sense in the United States that the federal government has *some* role to play in doing things for the national community, or even the international community, that Americans or others cannot do for themselves. Although one can never be too certain, those aspects of loathing for Lincoln opposed to such viewpoints could become increasingly irrelevant in American life or perhaps disappear altogether. What the president said in 1858 of British reactionaries may also apply to his American counterparts: "Though they blazed, like tallow-candles for a century, at last they flickered in the socket, died out, stank in the dark for a brief season, and were remembered no more, even by the smell."[16]

In all likelihood, loathing for Lincoln will nonetheless persist as the president's enemies contend against the modern world and the pluralistic, egalitarian, and democratic ideals unleashed by the United States' victory in its terrible Civil War.[17] The essayist Lewis Lapham once said that his fellow citizens would "squander the truth of our inheritance if we don't know how or why it was accumulated, against what odds, with what force of the human imagination and which powers of expression."[18] For Americans to fall prey unwittingly without a struggle to the arguments of Lincoln's foes would be to squander, if not outright reject, a fundamental part of their democratic inheritance and place themselves on the road to becoming a less empathetic nation. As Lincoln once asked in a different context: "Have we no *tendency*" to neither condition?[19] It is therefore important that Americans fully comprehend the seriousness of "the Sisyphus work of morally assassinating Abraham Lincoln and the great republic he headed" on which Lincoln's enemies embarked in the 1860s and one from which they will not retreat.[20] Although they clearly understand the enormity of their task in undermining Lincoln's stature with their fellow countrymen—they may actually be inspired by its difficulty—the president's opponents do not see their efforts as futile.

Americans need to remind themselves that Lincoln's principled stand against the monstrous injustice of slavery and the slaveholders' advocacy for its perpetuation "in all future time," combined with his belief that recurrent elections as opposed to secession were the best, most peaceful method for solving political disagreements, were not only the hallmarks of democratic politics and Lincoln's political career but essential aspects of "the better angels of our nature."[21] Consequently, Lincoln's aim in asking Americans to fight a war to preserve a relatively democratic Union eventually cleansed of slavery was courageous and noble, perhaps even necessary, and the country remains indebted to those who fought to ensure that the United States was not forever split apart in the 1860s. This is not to say that Lincoln was either a god or a saint; obviously, he was neither, and he would in fact have been the first to scoff at such a notion.[22] Nor was the president a demon, the progenitor of all of America's ills. Both views are an oversimplification of an extraordinarily complex man and movement dedicated to ending slavery in America. In fact, there is no shame in saying that Lincoln was a gifted, prudent politician who, with the help of millions of antislavery Americans, including the slaves themselves, enthusiastically issued the Emancipation Proclamation and, in public letters and speeches that contained some of the most beautiful language ever written, explained why the United States should attempt to fulfill the better ideals of its founders. And because of the war those ideals were, at least for a time, realized. The "new birth of freedom" of which Lincoln expectantly spoke at Gettysburg occurred, as African Americans became citizens in the new American nation born from the conflict, with ratification of the Fourteenth Amendment to the Constitution.[23] In this particular instance federal power broadened rather than diminished freedom, and it became another of the war's heartbreaking tragedies (in addition to its hundreds of thousands of casualties) that human liberty shrank as the nation's commitment to a more pluralistic democracy withered in the face of state and local resistance to the postwar era's egalitarian possibilities. Such inegalitarian consequences persisted for far too long yet were thankfully impermanent because Americans, especially African Americans, realized they were inconsistent with the nation's increased commitment to freedom and equality forged in the 1860s and 1870s. As they have in the past, so will Americans in the future continue to grapple with the Civil War and the president who led the nation through that conflict. But to loathe Abraham Lincoln would be to lose, or loathe, an essential part of the nation that he thought should allow all its inhabitants "an open field and a fair chance for . . . industry, enterprise and intelligence," one that would give his fellow Americans "equal privileges in the race of life," a country Lincoln hoped would become, as he said in his last written words, "a Union of hearts and hands as well as of States."[24]

NOTES

INTRODUCTION

1. William F. Buckley Jr., quoted in foreword to Jaffa, *American Conservatism and the American Founding,* xii.

2. *New Orleans Tribune,* quoted in McPherson, *Negro's Civil War,* 312.

3. Edgar Dinsmore, quoted in McPherson, *Negro's Civil War,* 312.

4. Frederick Douglass, quoted in Hampson, "200 Years Later, a More Complex View of Lincoln."

5. Alonzo H. Quint, quoted in Chesebrough, *"No Sorrow like Our Sorrow,"* 89.

6. Anderson, *Brokenburn,* 333.

7. Ibid., 333, 341.

8. *Texas Republican,* May 5, 1865.

9. *Galveston Daily News,* April 27, 1865.

10. *La Grange (Tex.) True Issue,* April 29, 1865.

11. Ecclesiastes, quoted in Geary, *Geary's Guide to the World's Great Aphorists,* 231.

12. For the most recent and detailed historiographical essay on Abraham Lincoln, see Pinkser, "Lincoln Theme 2.0," 417–40.

13. Davis, *Image of Lincoln in the South.*

14. Peterson, *Lincoln in American Memory.*

15. Ibid., 27.

16. Schwartz, *Abraham Lincoln and the Forge of National Memory;* Schwartz, *Abraham Lincoln in the Post-Heroic Era.*

17. James McPherson, quoted in Schwartz, *Abraham Lincoln and the Forge of National Memory,* 8.

18. Schwartz, *Abraham Lincoln in the Post-Heroic Era,* preface, x–xi.

19. Ibid., xii.

20. Krannawitter, *Vindicating Lincoln.*

21. Ibid., vii. See Krannawitter's table of contents for other topics.

22. Alasdair MacIntyre, quoted in Holmes, *Anatomy of Antiliberalism,* 111.

23. *Cultural anxieties* is Christopher Hitchens's phrase.

24. Foner, *Fiery Trial,* xv.

25. The terms *mind-set* and *sensibility* come from Holmes, *Anatomy of Antiliberalism,* 5.

26. McPherson, *Abraham Lincoln and the Second American Revolution,* preface.

27. Foner, *Story of American Freedom,* xiii–xxii.

28. Donald, *Lincoln Reconsidered.*

29. Fehrenbacher, *Lincoln in Text and Context,* 197–215. Fehrenbacher included Radical Republicans and abolitionists among those who hated Lincoln, but he overstated their disagreements.

30. Ibid., 198; Oakes, *Freedom National,* xxi.

31. Oakes, *Freedom National,* 5.

32. Pollard, *Lost Cause.*

33. Fehrenbacher, *Lincoln in Text and Context,* 197; Jost, Federico, and Napier, "Political Ideology," 307–37.

34. Howe, *Making the American Self,* 136–56.

35. Basler, Dunlap, and Pratt, *Collected Works of Abraham Lincoln,* 4:24–25.

36. Hirschman, *Rhetoric of Reaction,* 36; Bodnar, *Remaking America.*

37. Malik, *From Fatwa to Jihad,* 24.

38. Holmes, *Anatomy of Antiliberalism,* xiii.

39. Edelman, *Symbolic Uses of Politics,* 1–7.

40. Dirck, *Lincoln and Davis,* 2–4; Anderson, *Imagined Communities,* 1–7; McPherson, *Is Blood Thicker than Water?,* 27–69; Potter, "Lincoln Theme and American National Historiography," 151–76; Blum, *Reforging the White Republic;* Hague, Beirich, and Sebesta, *Neo-Confederacy,* 50–75; Neely, *Lincoln and the Triumph of the Nation,* 49–50.

41. Mercer, "'Taking America Back' Starts with Taking Lincoln Down"; Moser, "Conflicts Arise over Lincoln Statue in Richmond, Va., Cemetery"; Bennett, *Forced into Glory,* 627–35.

42. "AOL Lincoln Poll"; Conant, "Rebranding Hate in the Age of Obama," 31–33; RonPaul.com, "Hearings"; Guelzo, "Abraham Lincoln or the Progressives." See video of Congressman Paul speaking on the Civil War at www.youtube.com/watch?v=B85TJJyKyKw (accessed 5/29/12). Ron Paul, quoted in Sandefur, "Texas Lincoln Talk," 2.

43. The term *inhuman bondage* is from Davis, *Inhuman Bondage.*

44. Haidt, *Righteous Mind,* 49; Hogan, *Lincoln, Inc.,* 154–55; Warren, *Legacy of the Civil War.*

45. Basler, Dunlap, and Pratt, *Collected Works of Abraham Lincoln,* 5:53.

1. MARKED FOR BITTERNESS: THE CIVIL WAR ERA, 1858–1865

1. Beale, *Diary of Gideon Welles,* 2:290–93.

2. Ibid.

3. Schwartz, "Mourning and the Making of a Sacred Symbol," 343–64; Peterson, *Lincoln in American Memory,* 3–35; Schwartz, *Abraham Lincoln and the Making of National Memory,* 29–65; Turner, *Beware the People Weeping,* 77–89; Steers, *Blood on the Moon,* 268–93.

4. Nevins and Thomas, *Diary of George T. Strong,* 3: 584–86; Clift, *Private War of Lizzie Hardin,* 233–35; *Houston Tri-Weekly Telegraph,* April 26, 1865; Moretta, *William Pitt Ballinger,* 150–51.

5. Basler, Dunlap, and Pratt, *Collected Works of Abraham Lincoln,* 1:75.

6. Ibid., 2:255.

7. Ibid., 2:255–56; Oakes, *Radical and the Republican,* 121–22.

8. Basler, Dunlap, and Pratt, *Collected Works of Abraham Lincoln,* 2:265–66; Sandefur, "Texas Lincoln Talk," 23–24. I am indebted to Timothy Sandefur for pointing out the importance of this quote to me.

9. Weber, *Copperheads,* 4–23; Robin, *Reactionary Mind,* 7; Oakes, *Freedom National,* 1–34.

10. Oakes, *Freedom National,* 129; Blum, *Reforging the White Republic;* Donald, *Lincoln,* 122–26; Fehrenbacher, *Lincoln in Text and Context,* 197–213; Weber, *Copperheads,* 4–23; Allitt, *Conservatives,* 67–96. As a freshman Whig congressman from Illinois, Lincoln had spoken out against the Mexican War in the 1840s, but his speeches lambasting President James K. Polk and the spot resolutions he introduced demanding to know the precise piece of American soil on which Polk claimed that American blood had been shed were little noticed. Illinois Democrats were upset with Lincoln, but there was little *national* controversy surrounding Lincoln's criticism of Polk.

11. Oakes, *Freedom National,* 5.

12. Basler, Dunlap, and Pratt, *Collected Works of Abraham Lincoln,* 2:461; Donald, *Lincoln,* 209.

13. Isaac Arnold, quoted in Oakes, *Freedom National,* ix; Ceaser, *Nature and History in American Political Development,* 49; Sandefur, "Texas Lincoln Talk," 23.

14. Davis and Wilson, *Lincoln-Douglas Debates,* 184; Jaffa, *Crisis of the House Divided,* 363–86; Guelzo, *Lincoln and Douglas,* 7; Hummel, *Emancipating Slaves, Enslaving Free Men,* 114–17.

15. Basler, Dunlap, and Pratt, *Collected Works of Abraham Lincoln,* 2:501.

16. Davis and Wilson, *Lincoln-Douglas Debates,* 34.

17. Ibid., 131.

18. Ibid., 21; Basler, Dunlap, and Pratt, *Collected Works of Abraham Lincoln,* 4:24; Guelzo, *Lincoln as a Man of Ideas,* 93, 99. Notice what Lincoln said in the sixth debate at Quincy, Illinois: "I only refer to this matter to say that I am altogether unconscious of having attempted any double dealing anywhere, that upon one occasion I may say one thing and leave other things unsaid, and *vice versa.* But that I have said anything on one occasion that is inconsistent with what I have said elsewhere, I deny. At least I deny it so far as the intention is concerned." Davis and Wilson, *Lincoln-Douglas Debates,* 217–18. Lincoln might be silent about some things, in other words, but he was not going to lie. Or what Lincoln said about race in the debates may have led—or misled—the people of Illinois to believe that he shared their views about African Americans. I am indebted to Larry Arnhart for pointing out this passage and its significance. For a lengthy discussion of Lincoln's alleged racial inconsistency, see Jaffa, *Crisis of the House Divided,* 363–86; Guelzo, *Lincoln and Douglas,* 192–93.

19. Basler, Dunlap, and Pratt, *Collected Works of Abraham Lincoln,* 7:259; Nichols, *The "S" Word,* 92.

20. Guelzo, *Lincoln and Douglas,* 190–202; Morel, "Lincoln, Race, and the Spirit of '76," 3.

21. Basler, Dunlap, and Pratt, *Collected Works of Abraham Lincoln,* 3:339; Burton, *Age of Lincoln,* 550; Guelzo, *Lincoln and Douglas,* 302.

22. Guelzo, *Lincoln and Douglas,* 296–97.

23. *Weekly Mississippian,* quoted in Reynolds, *Editors Make War,* 23; Foner, *Free Soil, Free Labor, Free Men,* 214–15.

24. Edmund Ruffin, quoted in Walther, "Fire-Eaters and ~~Seward~~ Lincoln," 19; Wakelyn, *Southern Pamphlets on Secession,* 89; Walther, *William Lowndes Yancey,* 260.

25. Alexander H. Stephens, quoted in Davis, *Image of Lincoln in the South,* 24, emphasis mine.

26. Stephens, *Constitutional View of the Late the War between the States,* 2:268; Davis, *Image of Lincoln in the South,* 27.

27. Jefferson Davis, quoted in Davis, *Image of Lincoln in the South,* 39.

28. Stewart, *Holy Warriors,* 177–80; Brown, *Southern Outcast,* 170–75.

29. McPherson, *Battle Cry of Freedom* 859–60; Hummel, *Emancipating Slaves, Enslaving Free Men,* 129–33.

30. Oakes, *Freedom National,* 1–83; Walther, *Fire-Eaters,* 181–88; Freehling, *Road to Disunion,* 269–342; Freehling, *Reintegration of American History,* 105–37; Deyle, *Carry Me Back,* 60–61.

31. *Texas State Gazette,* quoted in Reynolds, *Texas Terror,* 171.

32. McPherson, *Battle Cry of Freedom,* 861; Freehling, *Reintegration of American History,* 138–57; Deyle, *Carry Me Back,* 60–61; Hummel, *Emancipating Slaves, Enslaving Free Men,* 51–52. Hummel shows that the slaves were worth approximately "$2.7 and $3.7 billion" and quotes James Henry Hammond to striking effect: "Were any people civilized or savage, persuaded by any argument, human or divine, to surrender voluntarily two thousand millions of dollars?" Davis, *Image of Lincoln in the South,* 7–40; Walther, *Fire-Eaters,* 220–22; Dew, *Apostles of Disunion,* 74–103; McCurry, *Confederate Reckoning,* 11–37.

33. *Newbern Weekly Progress* and *San Antonio Ledger and Texan,* quoted in Reynolds, *Editors Make War,* 55–56; *Houston Telegraph,* quoted in Holzer, *Lincoln Seen and Heard,* 130–31.

34. *New Orleans Daily Delta,* quoted in Dumond, *Southern Editorials on Secession,* 470–71.

35. Martin and Avary, *Diary from Dixie,* 12, 19.

36. Charles Browne Fleet to Alexander Frederick Fleet, March 5, 1861, Mss3 K5893 a 1–68, King and Queen County Historical Society Papers, Virginia Historical Society (VHS); original underlining in the letter appears here in italics.

37. Wyatt-Brown, *Southern Honor,* 88–114; Walther, *Fire-Eaters,* 173–81; Bushman, *Refinement of America,* 390–98; David Demaree, "Lincoln's Relationship with Gentility in America," in Watson, Pederson, and Williams, *Lincoln's Enduring Legacy,* 179–96.

38. Greenberg, *Honor and Slavery,* 15–16; Wilson, *Evolution for Everyone,* 115–24; Hirschman, *Rhetoric of Reaction,* 7; McCurry, *Confederate Reckoning,* 28. The term *Founders' white Republic* is from Blum, *Reforging the White Republic.*

39. Edelman, *Symbolic Uses of Politics,* 7.

40. Basler, Dunlap, and Pratt, *Collected Works of Abraham Lincoln,* 4:70; Davis, *Image of Lincoln in the South,* 18.

41. Davis, *Image of Lincoln in the South,* 14.

42. Jack Campbell Letters, Dolph Briscoe Center for American History, University of Texas at Austin. The signature on the letter is illegible, but the date for the communication is January 24, 1861; original underlining in the letter appears here in italics.

43. John C. Wardlaw to his father, March 4, 1861, John C. Wardlaw Letters, Margaret I. King Library, Special Collections, University of Kentucky, Lexington (original underlining in the letter appears here in italics); Pensacola, Fla., resident, quoted in Holzer, *Lincoln, President-Elect,* 71.

44. Amelia Barr Papers, Dolph Briscoe Center for American History, University of Texas at Austin (original underlining in the letter appears here in italics); Davis, *Image of Lincoln in the South,* 13–14.

45. Faust, *Creation of Confederate Nationalism,* 22–40; Rable, *Confederate Republic,* 75–77; Rubin, *Shattered Nation,* 11–42; Davis, *Image of Lincoln in the South,* 14; James Henley Thorn-

well, quoted in Eugene D. Genovese, "Religion in the Collapse of the American Union," in Miller, Stout, and Wilson, *Religion and the American Civil War,* 80.

46. Sebesta and Hague, "U.S. Civil War as a Theological War," in Hague, Beirich, and Sebesta, *Neo-Confederacy,* 50–75. According to Davis, the phrase "'Resistance to Lincoln is obedience to God' was the proposed motto of a young men's club" in Montgomery, Ala. Davis, *Image of Lincoln in the South,* 14.

47. *Illinois State Register,* quoted in Burlingame, *Abraham Lincoln,* 1:551.

48. *New York Herald,* quoted in Burlingame, *Abraham Lincoln,* 1:664–65.

49. New York banners, quoted in Burlingame, *Abraham Lincoln,* 1:664–65; McPherson, *Battle Cry of Freedom,* 860–61.

50. Theodore R. Westbrook, quoted in Burlingame, *Abraham Lincoln,* 1:665.

51. H. Ford Douglas, quoted in Guelzo, *Lincoln as a Man of Ideas,* 889; Norman, "Other Lincoln-Douglas Debate," 1–21; Walther, *Shattering of the Union,* 36–38; Donald, *Lincoln,* 207–9.

52. Foner, *Fiery Trial,* 141–42.

53. Wendell Phillips, quoted in Foner, *Our Lincoln,* 176; Hanchett, *Lincoln Murder Conspiracies,* 8; Foner, *Fiery Trial,* 141.

54. William Lloyd Garrison, quoted in McPherson, *Struggle for Equality,* 13–15; Mayer, *All on Fire,* 507–14.

55. Frederick Douglass, quoted in Oakes, *Radical and the Republican,* 89; Parker Pillsbury, quoted in Robertson, *Parker Pillsbury,* 120–21.

56. I heard Eric Foner make this point on March 24, 2012, in College Park, Md., at the Abraham Lincoln Institute annual symposium.

57. Oakes, *Radical and the Republican,* 298; Foner, *Fiery Trial,* 141–42.

58. DiLorenzo, *Lincoln Unmasked,* 52–61; Oakes, *Freedom National,* 5; Perry, *Radical Abolitionism,* 195–97; Colaiaco, *Frederick Douglass and the Fourth of July,* 100–101; Shone, *Lysander Spooner,* 77–93. I am especially indebted to the work of Thomas DiLorenzo in pointing out the importance of Spooner for abolitionist criticism of Lincoln.

59. Shone, *Lysander Spooner,* 90–91; DiLorenzo, *Lincoln Unmasked,* 53.

60. Basler, Dunlap, and Pratt, *Collected Works of Abraham Lincoln,* 3:502.

61. Lysander Spooner to William H. Seward, January 22, 1860, www.lysanderspooner.org/ letters/SESP012260.htm (accessed 1/1/10) (original underlining in the letter appears here in italics); Watner, "Radical Antislavery Tradition in Libertarian Thought," 321–24; DiLorenzo, *Lincoln Unmasked,* 52–61; Perry, *Radical Abolitionism,* 194–208.

62. Oakes, *Freedom National,* 5.

63. Ibid., 34–42.

64. McPherson, *Battle Cry of Freedom,* 232. The charge of Lincoln as "equivocating" has been made by Lerone Bennett Jr. and is his word. Guelzo, "Prudence, Politics, and the Proclamation."

65. Current, *Lincoln and the First Shot;* Current, *Speaking of Abraham Lincoln,* 61–78; McClintock, *Lincoln and the Decision for War;* W. E. B. Du Bois, quoted in Oakes, *Freedom National,* 397.

66. Jefferson Davis, quoted in Davis, *Image of Lincoln in the South,* 56. See also *New Orleans Daily Delta,* quoted on 55.

67. Abraham Lincoln, quoted in Davis, *Image of Lincoln in the South,* 59.

68. Davis, *Image of Lincoln in the South,* 50–61.

69. Ibid., 62–63.

70. Holzer, *Lincoln Seen and Heard,* 118–19.

71. Ibid., 122–23. To view the lithograph, see the Library of Congress website, www.loc .gov/pictures/item/2008661680/ (accessed 3/15/2012).

72. Benjamin Wade, quoted in Donald, *Lincoln,* 332.

73. Neely, *Fate of Liberty,* 186–209; Farber, *Lincoln's Constitution,* 157–95; Manber and Dahlstrom, *Lincoln's Wrath;* White, *Abraham Lincoln and Treason in the Civil War.*

74. Weber, *Copperheads,* 31; McPherson, *Battle Cry of Freedom,* 287–88.

75. Ohioan, quoted in Weber, *Copperheads,* 92–93.

76. Basler, Dunlap, and Pratt, *Collected Works of Abraham Lincoln,* 6:266

77. Foner, *Story of American Freedom,* 98–99; Neely, *Fate of Liberty,* 222–35.

78. Oakes, *Radical and the Republican,* 193–94; Basler, Dunlap, and Pratt, *Collected Works of Abraham Lincoln,* 5:370–72; Foner, *Fiery Trial,* 221–30; Oakes, *Freedom National,* 308–10.

79. William Lloyd Garrison, quoted in Guelzo, *Lincoln as a Man of Ideas,* 90.

80. Mayer, *All on Fire,* 538–39.

81. Anonymous African American, quoted in McPherson, *Battle Cry of Freedom,* 508–9.

82. McPherson, *Battle Cry of Freedom,* 509; Frederick Douglass, quoted in Foner, *Our Lincoln,* 156.

83. Frederick Douglass, quoted in Neely, "Colonization and the Myth That Lincoln Prepared the People for Emancipation," 51; Masur, "African American Delegation to Abraham Lincoln," 117–44.

84. *Richmond Enquirer,* quoted in Mitgang, *Lincoln as They Saw Him,* 316.

85. *North Carolina Standard,* quoted in Burlingame, *Abraham Lincoln,* 2:17.

86. Jefferson Davis, quoted ibid., 472; Hirschman, *Rhetoric of Reaction,* 7.

87. Mitgang, *Lincoln as They Saw Him,* 317.

88. *The Lincoln Catechism,* quoted ibid., 343–44.

89. Poem, quoted, ibid., 351.

90. Moss, *Confederate Broadside Poems,* 30–37; Collection of Confederate Broadsides at Wake Forest University, http://zsr.wfu.edu/collections/digital/broadsides/access/50p1.jpg (accessed 12/24/09); Wilson, *Lincoln in Caricature.*

91. Moss, *Confederate Broadside Poems,* 152; Davis, *Image of Lincoln in the South,* 61–86.

92. Harwell, "Confederate Anti-Lincoln Literature," 22–40.

93. *Daily Mississippian,* January 21, 1863, Confederate Scrapbook, MS 2566, Colorado Historical Society.

94. Ibid.

95. Holzer, *Lincoln Seen and Heard,* 136–37.

96. *Southern Punch,* quoted in Phillips, *Diehard Rebels,* 57–58.

97. Faust, *Mothers of Invention,* 59.

98. General William Tecumseh Sherman, quoted in Commager, *Blue and the Gray,* 764.

99. Faust, *Mothers of Invention,* 59.

100. Ibid., 185.

101. Holzer, *Lincoln Seen and Heard,* 119; Phillips, *Diehard Rebels,* 74–75; Smith, *Less than Human.*

102. Holzer, *Lincoln Seen and Heard,* 143; Neely, Holzer, and Boritt, *Confederate Image,* 44.

103. Holzer, Boritt, and Neely, *Lincoln Image,* 128–29.

104. Holzer, *Lincoln Seen and Heard,* 143; Neely, Holzer, and Boritt, *Confederate Image,* 44–54.

105. Ibid.

106. Democratic newspapers quoted in Mitgang, *Lincoln as They Saw Him,* 315–16.

107. Ohio newspaper and Horatio Seymour, quoted in Weber, *Copperheads,* 63–64.

108. Burlingame, *Abraham Lincoln,* 2:415–16; Illinois newspaper, quoted in Guelzo, *Lincoln's Emancipation Proclamation,* 159.

109. Chauncey Burr, quoted in Hanchett, *Lincoln Murder Conspiracies,* 13.

110. Catholic archbishop, quoted in Burlingame, *Abraham Lincoln,* 2:471.

111. Maryland editor, quoted in Hanchett, *Lincoln Murder Conspiracies,* 13.

112. Guelzo, *Lincoln's Emancipation Proclamation,* 215–22.

113. Richard Striner, "Abraham Lincoln and the Antislavery Movement," in Fornieri and Gabbard, *Lincoln's America,* 163; Oakes, *Freedom National,* 353–60.

114. Guelzo, *Lincoln's Emancipation Proclamation,* 183–235.

115. Frederick Douglass, quoted in Guelzo, *Lincoln's Emancipation Proclamation,* 160.

116. James Hudson, quoted in Ripley, *Black Abolitionist Papers,* 5:184–85.

117. Oakes, *Freedom National,* 293.

118. Charles Sumner, quoted in Guelzo, *Lincoln's Emancipation Proclamation,* 158; Masur, *Lincoln's Hundred Days,* 205–18.

119. Benjamin Wade and William Lloyd Garrison, quoted in Burlingame, *Abraham Lincoln,* 2:470.

120. H. Ford Douglas, quoted in Ripley, *Black Abolitionist Papers,* 5:166–67; Magness and Page, *Colonization after Emancipation.*

121. Frederick Douglass, quoted in Burlingame, *Abraham Lincoln,* 2:470–71; Arnhart, "Biopolitical Science," 248; Guelzo, "Prudence, Politics, and the Proclamation."

122. Guelzo, *Lincoln as a Man of Ideas,* 99–101; Foner, *Free Soil, Free Labor, Free Men,* 11–39; Guelzo, *Lincoln's Emancipation Proclamation*; Oakes, *Freedom National.*

123. Basler, Dunlap, and Pratt, *Collected Works of Abraham Lincoln,* 7:366. I am indebted to James Oakes for alerting me to this beautiful letter.

124. Dirck, *Abraham Lincoln and White America,* 129.

125. Cloyd, *Haunted by Atrocity,* 8–10.

126. Kate Cumming, quoted in Davis, *Image of Lincoln in the South,* 77; Harwell, *Kate,* 228–29.

127. Peatman, "Virginians Respond to the Gettysburg Address," 28–46; Schwartz, "New Gettysburg Address," 160–86.

128. Abraham Lincoln, quoted in Donald, *Lincoln,* 463.

129. *Richmond Examiner,* quoted in Peatman, "Virginians Respond to the Gettysburg Address," 34.

130. Ibid. See also 48–76.

131. Davis, *Image of Lincoln in the South,* 80.

132. Mitgang, *Lincoln as They Saw Him,* 359–60.

133. *New York World,* quoted in Burlingame, *Abraham Lincoln,* 2:576–77; *Hudson County Democrat,* quoted in Boritt, *Gettysburg Gospel,* 141.

134. Democratic platform, quoted in Long, *Jewel of Liberty,* 283–84; Weber, *Copperheads,* 170–82.

135. Alexander Stephens, quoted in Davis, *Image of Lincoln in the South,* 87.

136. Ibid., 87–88.

137. Mitgang, *Lincoln as They Saw Him,* 401–3.

138. Mary E. Hopkins to Thomas E. Bartlett, December 23, 1864, Mss1 B6117 a 265–69, Blanton Family Papers, VHS. Bartlett was serving as a Captain in the 13th Arkansas Regiment, CSA. See also Robert E. Lee letter to Mary Lee, November 12, 1864, Mss1 L51 c 547–61, Lee Family Papers, VHS. "We must therefore make up our minds for another four years of war," Lee explained.

139. Williams, *Diary from Dixie by Mary Chesnut,* 344; Davis, *Image of Lincoln in the South,* 80.

140. Stephens, *War between the States,* 2:270.

141. Mayer, *All on Fire,* 562–69.

142. Wendell Phillips, quoted in Mayer, *All on Fire,* 562; Oakes, *Radical and the Republican,* 225–29.

143. McPherson, *Struggle for Equality,* 281–85; Oakes, *Radical and the Republican,* 227.

144. McPherson, *Struggle for Equality,* 281–85.

145. Lysander Spooner to Charles Sumner, October 12, 1864, quoted in Richman, "Anti-War Abolitionists," 335.

146. Mayer, *All on Fire,* 563; McPherson, *Struggle for Equality,* 285; Oakes, *Radical and Republican,* 227.

147. David Hayes-Bautista, "Southwest's Mexican Roots: The Untold Stories; Mexicans, Lincoln, and Obama," *Los Angeles Eastside Sun,* February 12, 2009, 1.

148. All parade banners and translations quoted in David Hayes-Bautista, "Southwest's Mexican Roots: The Untold Stories; Mexicans, Lincoln, and Obama (Continued)," *Los Angeles Eastside Sun,* Thursday, February 19, 2009, 1.

149. Mitgang, *Lincoln as They Saw Him,* 401–3; Hanchett, *Lincoln Murder Conspiracies,* 11.

150. *Cincinnati Enquirer,* quoted in Burlingame, *Abraham Lincoln,* 2:696.

151. Weber, *Copperheads,* 160; Kaplan, "Miscegenation Issue in the Election of 1864," 234–337; Neely, "Miscegenation," no. 1635, 1–4, and no. 1636, 1–2; Long, *Jewel of Liberty,* 153–76.

152. Neely, "Miscegenation," no. 1635, 4.

153. *La Crosse Democrat,* quoted in Burlingame, *Abraham Lincoln,* 2:696.

154. Marcus Mills "Brick" Pomeroy, quoted in Weber, *Copperheads,* 159; Klement, "'Brick' Pomeroy: Copperhead and Curmudgeon," 106–13, 156–57; Nutter and Abrams, "Copperhead Newspapers and the Negro," 131–52; Klement, "Copperheads and Copperheadism in Wisconsin," 182–88.

155. *Atlas and Argus,* quoted in Burlingame, *Abraham Lincoln,* 2:698.

156. Abraham Lincoln to John Hay, quoted in Holzer, *Lincoln Anthology,* 91.

157. Neely, *Fate of Liberty,* 222–35; Farber, *Lincoln's Constitution,* 144–75.

158. *Chicago Times,* quoted in Mitgang, *Lincoln as They Saw Him,* 426; and Burlingame, *Abraham Lincoln,* 2:771; White, *Lincoln's Greatest Speech,* 186–95.

159. Quoted in Burlingame, *Abraham Lincoln,* 2:770–71.

160. *Daily Press,* quoted in Mitgang, *Lincoln as They Saw Him,* 428.

161. *Richmond Examiner,* quoted in White, *Lincoln's Greatest Speech,* 193.

162. Basler, Dunlap, and Pratt, *Collected Works of Abraham Lincoln,* 8:356; White, *Lincoln's Greatest Speech,* 199.

163. Frederick Douglass, quoted in White, *Lincoln's Greatest Speech,* 199; William Lloyd Garrison, quoted in Mayer, *All on Fire,* 587.

164. Laura Towne, quoted in McPherson, *Struggle for Equality,* 311.

165. Davis, *Image of Lincoln in the South,* 62–63; Steen, "Texas Newspapers and Lincoln," 199–212; Barr, "Tyrannicide's Reception: Texans Respond to Lincoln's Assassination," 30–73.

166. Trefousse, *"First among Equals."*

167. Philadelphia minister Reuben Jeffery, quoted in Blum, *Reforging the White Republic,* 44; Robert Lowry, quoted in Chesebrough, *"No Sorrow like Our Sorrow,"* 53, introduction xiv–xxi.

168. Indiana soldier George W. Squier, quoted in Weber, *Copperheads,* 215.

169. Turner, *Beware the People Weeping,* 26.

170. Spurlin, *Civil War Journal of Charles A. Leuschner,* 52.

171. Turner, *Beware the People Weeping,* 49.

172. *Daily Dramatic Chronicle,* quoted in Burlingame, *Abraham Lincoln,* 2:813.

173. Weber, *Copperheads,* 215–16.

174. George W. Julian, quoted in Burlingame, *Abraham Lincoln,* 2:820.

175. Ibid., 2:820–21.

176. William Robinson, quoted in McPherson, *Struggle for Equality,* 314–15.

177. Frederick Douglass, quoted in Oakes, *Radical and the Republican,* 243–44.

178. Trefousse, *Andrew Johnson,* 192–98.

179. Burlingame, *Abraham Lincoln,* 2:812–13.

180. *Richmond Dispatch,* quoted ibid.

181. Turner, *Beware the People Weeping,* 94.

182. Ibid.

183. Thomas Howard Duval Diary, April 1865, Thomas Howard Duval Papers, Dolph Briscoe Center for American History, University of Texas at Austin.

184. Mary Semmes "Mamie" Clayton to Marion, n.d., Mss1 C5796a 7273, Clayton Family Papers, VHS.

185. Phillips, *Diehard Rebels,* 174; Turner, *Beware the People Weeping,* 96.

186. Mary Anne Lee to Mrs. L. in Baltimore, April 23, 1865, John Hunt Morgan Papers, box 17, Margaret I. King Library, Special Collections, University of Kentucky, Lexington. The date on the letter is illegible but appears to be the twenty-third; because the letter mentions Lincoln's death, it seems reasonable to conclude that it was written in April 1865.

187. Wells, "Mourning the President."

188. Unidentified minister, quoted ibid., 9.

189. *Evening Times,* April 17, 1865, quoted ibid., 10.

190. Ibid., 11.

191. Barr, "Tyrannicide's Reception: Texans Respond to Lincoln's Assassination," 50–73; Davis, *Image of Lincoln in the South,* 62–63; Steen, "Texas Newspapers and Lincoln," 199–212; Turner, *Beware the People Weeping,* 25–52, 90–99; Chesebrough, *"No Sorrow like Our Sorrow,"* xix.

192. Lincecum, Phillips, and Redshaw, *Gideon Lincecum's Sword,* 4–12.

193. Gideon Lincecum, quoted ibid., 325–26; Burkhalter, *Gideon Lincecum,* 84–85.

194. Phillips, *Diehard Rebels,* 182.

195. Davis, *Image of Lincoln in the South,* 62–63; Barr, "Tyrannicide's Reception: Texans Respond to Lincoln's Assassination," 50–73; Steen, "Texas Newspapers and Lincoln," 199–212; Turner, *Beware the People Weeping,* 96.

196. Moretta, *William Pitt Ballinger,* 112–17, 150–51; Thomas, "Rebel Nationalism," 343–55.

197. Moretta, *William Pitt Ballinger,* 120–21, 160; Donald, *Lincoln,* 110.

198. *Houston Tri-Weekly Telegraph,* April 26, 1865.

199. Ballinger, quoted in Moretta, *William Pitt Ballinger,* 166.

200. *Houston Tri-Weekly Telegraph,* April 26, 1865.

201. William Pitt Ballinger diary, April 1865, William Pitt Ballinger Papers, Henry Rosenberg Library, Galveston, Tex., emphasis mine.

202. Worley, "Story of Alfred W. Arrington," 315–39.

203. Ibid., 336.

204. Gould, *Alexander Watkins Terrell,* 50, 181. Terrell's entire poem is quoted in Wilson, *John Wilkes Booth,* 303–4. Worley, "Story of Alfred W. Arrington," 315–39; Evans, *Legend of John Wilkes Booth,* 103; Turner, *Beware the People Weeping,* 97.

205. *Portland Morning Oregonian,* July, 2, 1893, 4; *Milwaukee Sentinel,* July 2, 1893, 12; *Raleigh News-Observer-Chronicle,* July 6, 1893, *Memphis Commercial Appeal,* February 16, 1896; Turner, *Beware the People Weeping,* 97.

206. Campbell, *Gone to Texas,* 261–62.

207. Faust, *This Republic of Suffering,* 266; Neff, *Honoring the Civil War Dead.*

208. Faust, quoted in Neely, *Civil War and the Limits of Destruction,* 212. New estimates place the number of dead Americans higher, at approximately 750,000; Hacker, "Census-Based Count," 307–48. The higher estimate is used in the remainder of this volume.

209. Robin, *Reactionary Mind,* 55–57.

210. Foner, *Story of American Freedom,* 98–99.

211. Tyler and Murphy, *Slave Narratives of Texas,* 113.

212. Rable, *But There Was No Peace;* Crouch, "Spirit of Lawlessness," 217–32.

213. Blight, *Race and Reunion,* 5; Fahs and Waugh, *Memory of the Civil War in American Culture,* 123; Potter, *Authenticity Hoax,* 15.

214. Eugene Williams, quoted in Hale, *Third Texas Cavalry in the Civil War,* 278.

2. EXPRESSIONS OF THE LIPS VERSUS THOSE OF THE HEART: POSTBELLUM DISGUST, 1865–1889

1. Fears, *Essays in the History of Liberty,* 361–66. See also "The Acton-Lee Correspondence," 1866, www.lewrockwell.com/orig3/acton-lee.html (accessed 3/23/13).

2. Steele, "Thomas Jefferson, Coercion, and the Limits of Harmonious Union," 823–54; Novak, "Myth of the 'Weak' American State," 752–72.

3. Fears, *Essays in the History of Liberty,* 361–66; LewRockwell.com (accessed 8/31/10); Freeman, *Lee: An Abridgment in One Volume* by Harwell, 533–36; Flood, *Lee: The Last Years,* 143–44; Loewen and Sebesta, *Confederate and Neo-Confederate Reader,* 254–56.

4. Lears, "Concept of Cultural Hegemony," 567–93.

5. Pollard, *Lost Cause.*

6. Alexander Stephens, quoted in DiLorenzo, *Real Lincoln,* 125.

7. Wilson, *Baptized in Blood,* 1.

8. Ibid., 8; Foster, *Ghost of the Confederacy,* 8.

9. Wilson, *Baptized in Blood,* 8; Davis, *Image of Lincoln in the South,* 105–34.

10. Anderson, "Down Memory Lane," 105–36; Glazer and Key, "Carry Me Back," 1–24; Fritzsche, "Specters of History," 1587–1618.

11. Schwartz, "Reconstruction of Abraham Lincoln," 81–106; Sands, *American Public Philosophy and the Mystery of Lincolnism,* 71–75; Frederickson, *Inner Civil War,* 183–98; Marshall, *Creating a Confederate Kentucky.*

12. Foner, *Story of American Freedom,* 119–20.

13. Peterson, *Lincoln in American Memory,* 3–81; Schwartz, *Abraham Lincoln and the Forge of National Memory,* 1–103; Davis, *Image of Lincoln in the South,* 105–34; Schwartz, "Reconstruction of Abraham Lincoln," 81–106.

14. Josiah Holland, quoted in Angle, *Shelf of Lincoln Books,* 19–20; Peterson, *Lincoln in American Memory,* 68–70; Boritt, *Lincoln and the Economics of the American Dream,* 291–311.

15. Donald, *Lincoln's Herndon,* 212–13; Peterson, *Lincoln in American Memory,* 68. Donald claims one hundred thousand copies of Holland's book were sold, while Peterson, quoted here, places it at eighty thousand.

16. Editorial, *Scioto Gazette,* March 27, 1886, www.houstonlibrary.org/newspapers (accessed 7/26/09). To access the Houston Public Library newspapers, go to www.houstonlibrary .org. Click on "research," then scroll down and click on "newspapers," then click on "19th Century U.S. Newspapers Digital Archive." You may need to register for a library card in order to access this database.

17. Chesebrough, *"No Sorrow like Our Sorrow,"* 35–37; Turner, *Beware the People Weeping,* 77–89; Maas, "Battle over Lincoln's Soul," 1–21 (paper in possession of author). Maas's Wheaton College website, www.wheaton.edu/History/faculty/maas.html, states that this paper was "presented October 2, 2009, 11th Annual Conference on Illinois History, Springfield, Illinois."

18. Chesebrough, *"No Sorrow like Our Sorrow,"* 28–29.

19. Noll, *Civil War as a Theological Crisis,* 90; Blum, *Reforging the White Republic.*

20. Turner, *Without God, without Creed,* 141–67.

21. J. H. Wickizer, quoted in Teillard, "Lincoln in Myth and Fact," 14043.

22. Basler, *Lincoln Legend,* 10; Donald, *Lincoln's Herndon,* 272.

23. William H. Herndon and Jesse W. Weik, in Wilson and Davis, *Herndon's Lincoln,* xvi; Mark Noll, "American Religion, 1809–1865," in Fornieri and Gabbard, *Lincoln's America 1809–1865,* 72–93; Maas, "Battle over Lincoln's Soul," 1–21.

24. Donald, *Lincoln's Herndon,* 198–215. Herndon is directly quoted on 198–99 and 215.

25. William H. Herndon and Jesse W. Weik, in Wilson and Davis, *Herndon's Lincoln,* 264–65.

26. *Chicago Times,* quoted in Donald, *Lincoln's Herndon,* 215–16.

27. William H. Herndon, quoted ibid., 216.

28. Herndon's first, second, and third lectures were published in the *Abraham Lincoln Quarterly:* "Analysis of the Character of Abraham Lincoln," 343–83 (first lecture); "Analysis of the Character of Abraham Lincoln," 403–41 (second lecture); "Facts Illustrative of Mr. Lincoln's Patriotism and Statesmanship," 178–203 (third lecture); the fourth lecture was reprinted as Herndon, "Abraham Lincoln, Miss Anne Rutledge, New Salem, Pioneering, and the Poem: A Lecture," 1–67; Donald, *Lincoln's Herndon,* 197–241.

29. Herndon, "Analysis of the Character of Abraham Lincoln," 364.

30. Ibid., 366.

31. Herndon, "Analysis of the Character of Abraham Lincoln," 414.

32. Herndon, "Fact Illustrative of Mr. Lincoln's Patriotism and Statesmanship," 202–3; Paludan, "Lincoln and Negro Slavery," 1–23.

33. Herndon, "Abraham Lincoln, Miss Anne Rutledge, New Salem, Pioneering, and the Poem," 11; Donald, *Lincoln's Herndon,* 218–41.

34. Ibid., 29–30, 56–57.

35. Herndon, "Abraham Lincoln, Miss Anne Rutledge, New Salem, Pioneering, and the Poem," 1–67; Robert Todd Lincoln, quoted in Donald, *Herndon's Lincoln,* 230; Prokopowicz, *Did Lincoln Own Slaves?,* 42–43; Simon, "Abraham Lincoln and Ann Rutledge," 13–34; Gannett, "Anne Rutledge Story," 21–60.

36. Davis, introduction to Lamon, *Life of Abraham Lincoln,* v–xv.

37. Ibid.; Donald, *Lincoln's Herndon,* 250–53; Wilson and Davis, introduction to *Herndon's Lincoln,* xxiii.

38. Donald, *Lincoln's Herndon,* 263.

39. Lamon, *Life of Abraham Lincoln,* 127; Donald, *Lincoln's Herndon,* 266–67; Davis, *Life of Abraham Lincoln,* vii.

40. Lamon, *Life of Abraham Lincoln,* 237.

41. Ibid., 473.

42. Ibid., 497.

43. Peterson, *Lincoln in American Memory,* 68–69; Fehrenbacher and Fehrenbacher, *Recollected Words of Abraham Lincoln,* 24–26. According to the Fehrenbachers, Bateman's testimony "must be regarded as dubious biographical material."

44. Lamon, *Life of Abraham Lincoln,* 344.

45. Ibid., 344–45.

46. Ibid., 345–46.

47. Ibid.

48. Teillard, "Lincoln in Myth and Fact," 14040–42; letter from Isaac Newton Arnold to Orville Hickman Browning, November 22, 1872, in *Abraham Lincoln and Mary Owen,* 12.

49. *Chicago Tribune,* "The Objectionable Nature of Lincoln's Sensational Biography," reprinted in *Daily Arkansas Gazette,* June 14, 1872, www.houstonlibrary.org/newspapers (accessed 7/26/09).

50. Ibid. See also *Cleveland Morning Daily Herald,* June 28, 1873, www.houstonlibrary.org/newspapers (accessed 7/26/09).

51. "The Religious Character of Abraham Lincoln," *Congregationalist,* July 18, 1872, www.houstonlibrary.org/newspapers (accessed 7/26/09); "Abraham Lincoln: His Memory Defended against Ward H. Lamon–The Legitimacy of His Birth and the Nature of His Religious Belief," *Cleveland Morning Daily Herald,* June 28, 1873, www.houstonlibrary.org/newspapers (accessed 7/26/09).

52. *Christian Union,* quoted in Teillard, "Lincoln in Myth and Fact," 14043.

53. Ibid.

54. Ibid.; Basler, *Lincoln Legend,* 10.

55. Duberman, *Charles Francis Adams,* 388–89; Wills, "Henry Adams on Lincoln," 297–310; Peterson, *Lincoln in American Memory,* 82–83.

56. Donald, *Herndon's Lincoln,* 264–65; Peterson, *Lincoln in American Memory,* 68–81; Schwartz, *Abraham Lincoln and the Forge of National Memory,* 98.

57. Connelly, *Marble Man,* 27–98; Gallagher, *Lee and His Generals in War and Memory,* 199–226.

58. Martin, *Men against the State,* 167–201; Perry, *Radical Abolitionism,* 282–85; Weicek, *Source of Antislavery Constitutionalism in America,* 249–75; Barnett, "Was Slavery Unconstitutional before the Thirteenth Amendment?," 977–1014. Pieces by Barnett, Martin, and Weicek can be found at LysanderSpooner.org. See also Rothbard, introduction to Spooner, *Vices Are Not Crimes;* DiLorenzo, *Lincoln Unmasked,* 52–61; Shone, *Lysander Spooner,* 77–92.

59. Lysander Spooner, "No Treason: № 1," in *Collected Works of Lysander Spooner,* ed. Shively, 1:5. Pages are unfortunately not numbered in consecutive order. Numbers refer to the page number in the pamphlet cited.

60. Ibid., iii.

61. Lysander Spooner, "No Treason: № 6, The Constitution of No Authority," *Collected Works of Lysander Spooner,* ed. Shively, 1:56–57; DiLorenzo, *Lincoln Unmasked,* 59.

62. Ibid.

63. Lysander Spooner, "No Treason: № 2: The Constitution," *Collected Works of Lysander Spooner,* ed. Shively, 1:4.

64. Ibid., 8.

65. Spooner, "No Treason: № 1," *Collected Works of Lysander Spooner,* ed. Shively, 1:13–14; DiLorenzo, *Lincoln Unmasked,* 57.

66. Spooner, "No Treason: № 1," *Collected Works of Lysander Spooner,* ed. Shively, 1:13.

67. Lysander Spooner to John A. Thomson, March 5, 1871, quoted in *Collected Works of Lysander Spooner,* ed. Shively, 1:5.

68. Spooner, "Forced Consent," *Word* 2 (December 1873), http://praxeology.net/LS-FC .htm (accessed 1/30/10).

69. Ibid.

70. Oakes, *Freedom National.*

71. Shone, *Lysander Spooner,* 78.

72. Holmes, *Passions and Constraint,* 19.

73. *North American,* October 18, 1876, www.houstonlibrary.org/newspapers (accessed 6/26/09).

74. Ibid.

75. Ibid.; *Bangor Daily Whig and Courier,* July 13, 1876, www.houstonlibrary.org/news papers (accessed 6/26/09), also contains criticisms of Hendricks.

76. *North American,* September 26, 1884, www.houstonlibrary.org/newspapers (accessed 6/26/09).

77. Elliott and Smith, *Undaunted Radical,* 186, 296–339; Foner, *Story of American Freedom,* 119.

78. *Milwaukee Daily Sentinel,* February 3, 1868, www.houstonlibrary.org/newspapers (accessed 6/26/09).

79. Ibid.

80. *Southern Vindicator,* editorial reprinted in *Lowell Daily Citizen and News,* December 28, 1866, www.houstonlibrary.org/newspapers (accessed 7/1/09).

81. Ibid.

82. Ibid.

83. *Sign of the Times,* reprinted in editorial, "Satanic Journalism," *Daily Evening Bulletin* (San Francisco, Calif.), June 5, 1868, www.houstonlibrary.org/newspapers (accessed 6/26/09).

84. Peterson, *Lincoln in American Memory,* 46.

85. Plain Farmer, *Abraham Lincoln, Late President of the United States,* 22. The identity of the "Plain Farmer" remains unknown at this time. Davis, *Image of Lincoln in the South,* 123.

86. Plain Farmer, *Abraham Lincoln, Late President of the United States,* 43.

87. *Land We Love* 6 (January 1869): 258–59.

88. Conwell, *Magnolia Journey,* 5–6; Blight, *Race and Reunion,* 154–55.

89. Ibid.

90. Ambrose Dudley Mann to Jefferson Davis, December 5, 1871, in Rowland, *Jefferson Davis,* 7:299. The Latin phrase to which Mann refers comes from Horace. It is literally translated as "Rarely has Punishment, though halt of foot, left the track of the criminal in the way before her." Norbert Guterman, ed., *Anchor Book of Latin Quotations with English Translations* (New York: Anchor Books, 1966), 162–63. I would like to thank Brenda Pearson, a retired Latin teacher at Kingwood High School, Kingwood, Tex., for help with this translation. According to Pearson, the basic sense of the lines is that bad deeds are punished—eventually.

91. Stephens, *Constitutional View of the Late War between the States.*

92. Alexander H. Stephens, quoted in Wilson, *Patriotic Gore,* 421.

93. Schott, *Alexander H. Stephens of Georgia,* 456–57.

94. Ibid., 458; DiLorenzo, *Real Lincoln,* 124–25; Wilson, *Patriotic Gore,* 380–437.

95. Browne, "Review of *The Life of Abraham Lincoln,*" 368–74.

96. Connelly, *Marble Man,* 70.

97. *Dictionary of American Biography,* 2d ed., s.v. "Browne, William Hand"; Foster, *Ghosts of the Confederacy,* 49–50. Foster argued that Bledsoe's utterances were of "very limited public influence at the time."

98. Browne, "Review of *The Life of Abraham Lincoln,*" 368.

99. Ibid.

100. Ibid.

101. Ibid., 373–74.

102. Ibid., 372.

103. Ibid., 373.

104. Ibid., 374; William Hand Browne, also quoted in Davis, *Image of Lincoln in the South,* 118.

105. Barnhart, *Albert Taylor Bledsoe,* 189; Barnhart, "Albert Taylor Bledsoe," 3–30; Davis, *Image of Lincoln in the South,* 113–20. This section on Albert Taylor Bledsoe is heavily indebted to the work of Barnhart and Davis.

106. Pratt, "Albert Taylor Bledsoe," 153–83.

107. Barnhart, *Albert Taylor Bledsoe,* 10–21.

108. Ibid., 22–38.

109. Bledsoe, *Essay on Liberty and Slavery,* 8.

110. *Richmond Enquirer and Examiner,* January 7, 1868.

111. Barnhart, *Albert Taylor Bledsoe,* 190.

112. Weaver, *Southern Tradition at Bay,* 119–26.

113. Barnhart, *Albert Taylor Bledsoe,* 207.

114. Gaines M. Foster, "The Legacy of Confederate Defeat," in Ford, *Companion to the Civil War and Reconstruction,* 434–35; Barnhart, *Albert Taylor Bledsoe,* 169–210.

115. Bledsoe, "Great Error of the Eighteenth Century," 18.

116. Genovese and Genovese, *Mind of the Master Class;* Noll, *Civil War as a Theological Crisis,* 90. In addition to reading Bledsoe and other Lincoln critics, I am indebted to Timothy Sandefur for stressing that the president's detractors viewed him as a type of French Revolutionary.

117. Herrick, "Albert Taylor Bledsoe," 1–6; Pratt, "Albert Taylor Bledsoe,"153–83; Davis, *Image of Lincoln in the South,* 113–20; Barnhart, "Albert Taylor Bledsoe," 3–30. See also "Chivalrous Southrons," *Land We Love* 5 (October 1869): 456–77.

118. Bledsoe, "Alexander Hamilton," 18.

119. Ibid., 21.

120. Bledsoe, "Review of *The Life of Abraham Lincoln,*" 328–64.

121. Ibid., 329. The phrase *Lost Cause architect* is from the subtitle of Barnhart, *Albert Taylor Bledsoe.*

122. Ibid., 329–32.

123. Ibid., 334.

124. Basler, Dunlap, and Pratt, *Collected Works of Abraham Lincoln,* 1:114.

125. Bledsoe, "Review of *The Life of Abraham Lincoln,*" 335. To an extent Bledsoe's citation of the Lyceum Speech and his explanation of its significance anticipated by almost one hundred years Edmund Wilson's argument in *Patriotic Gore.* Wilson, *Patriotic Gore,* ix–xxxii, 99–130. For a quick refutation of Wilson's speculation, see Burlingame, *Inner World of Abraham Lincoln,* 365–67. I am indebted to Larry Arnhart for the phrase *Caesaristic ambitions.*

126. Bledsoe, "Review of *The Life of Abraham Lincoln,*" 339–40.

127. Ibid.

128. Ibid., 343–45.

129. Ibid., 346–47.

130. Ibid., 349, 352–54.

131. Ibid., 362.

132. Ibid., 364; Albert Taylor Bledsoe, also quoted in Davis, *Image of Lincoln in the South,* 120.

133. Barnhart, "Albert Taylor Bledsoe," 24, 206; Davis, *Image of Lincoln in the South,* 119–23.

134. Davis, *Image of Lincoln in the South,* 113–20.

135. Weaver, *Southern Tradition at Bay,* 145.

136. William B. Reed to Jefferson Davis, June 24, 1872, Jefferson Davis Collection, Alabama Department of Archives and History, Montgomery.

137. Browne, *Southern Magazine,* 374; Bledsoe, *Southern Review,* 364; *Sign of the Times* reprinted in editorial, "Satanic Journalism," *Daily Evening Bulletin* (San Francisco), June 5, 1868, www.houstonlibrary.org/newspapers (accessed 6/26/09); *North American,* October 18, 1876, www.houstonlibrary.org/newspapers (accessed 6/26/09).

138. *Milwaukee Daily Sentinel,* February 3, 1868, issue 28, col. C.

139. Paul Hamilton Hayne, quoted in Basler, *Lincoln Legend,* 57; Davis, *Image of Lincoln in the South,* 123.

140. *Webster's Dictionary,* 1828, http://1828.mshaffer.com/ (accessed 6/25/09); Lears, "Concept of Cultural Hegemony," 589.

141. Haidt, Rozin, McCauley, and Imada, "Body, Psyche, and Culture," 118. See also Jonathan Haidt's website, http://people.stern.nyu.edu/jhaidt/home.html; Miller, *Anatomy of Disgust,* 18; Haidt, *Righteous Mind,* 146–54. In addition to Haidt, I am indebted to Larry Arnhart for the phrasing of disgust as a "unique feature of conservative morality."

142. Haidt, Rozin, McCauley, and Imada, "Body, Psyche, and Culture," 124.

143. Elliott and Smith, *Undaunted Radical,* 175; Rozin, Haidt, and McCauley, "Disgust," 644 (see online version at http://faculty.virginia.edu/haidtlab/articles/rozin.haidt.2000.disgust .pub017.pdf).

144. Lears, "Concept of Cultural Hegemony," 589; Hays, "Polemics and Philosophy," 480; Weaver, *Southern Tradition at Bay;* Foster, "Legacy of Confederate Defeat," 434–36; Peterson, *Lincoln in American Memory,* 27–35; Robin, *Reactionary Mind,* 16. I have inverted Robin's sentence about a world before emancipation "where the better man commands the worse."

145. Janney, *Burying the Dead but Not the Past,* 1–14; Blair, *Cities of the Dead,* 77–106.

146. Blair, *Cities of the Dead,* 97.

147. Jubal Early, quoted in Weaver, *Southern Tradition at Bay,* 170–71.

148. Gary W. Gallagher, "Jubal A. Early, the Lost Cause, and Civil War History: A Persistent Legacy," in Gallagher and Nolan, *Myth of the Lost Cause and Civil War History,* 35–59.

149. Dabney, "Memoir of a Narrative Received," 449–50; Harris, "Southern Unionist Critique of the Civil War," 50–51; McPherson, *Battle Cry of Freedom,* 270–72; McClintock, *Lincoln and the Decision for War,* 240–44.

150. Dabney, "Memoir of a Narrative Received," 451.

151. Ibid.

152. Ibid.

153. Abraham Lincoln, quoted ibid., 454–55.

154. Ibid.

155. Hunter, "The Peace Commission of 1865," 173–74.

156. "Address of Congress to the People of the Confederate States (adopted in December, 1863)," *Southern Historical Society Papers* 1, no. 1 (January 1876): 32–33.

157. Boate, "True Story of Andersonville," 31.

158. Ibid.

159. Cloyd, *Haunted by Atrocity,* 1–83.

160. McPherson, *Tried by War,* 204.

161. Ibid.

162. Ibid., 247–48; Cloyd, *Haunted by Atrocity,* 1–83.

163. Thucydides, quoted in Blight, *Race and Reunion,* epigraph.

164. Elliott and Smith, *Undaunted Radical,* 185.

165. The term *anti-caste* is from Horton, *Race and the Making of American Liberalism,* 32–35.

166. Douglass, "Oration in Memory of Abraham Lincoln."

167. Blight, "For Something beyond the Battlefield," 1156; Oakes, *Radical and the Republican,* 247–88.

168. Harlan, *Booker T. Washington Papers,* 2:73, 3:93, 3:130.

169. Clark, *Defining Moments,* 33–34.

170. Ibid., 28.

171. Ibid., 44.

172. Ibid., 89. Clark also noted that this event concluded with a call for a monument of Lincoln to be constructed in Richmond, Va. The wish of these African Americans was finally fulfilled in 2003, when a Lincoln statue was placed in the city commemorating the president's visit in April 1865, after the fall of Richmond. See also *Richmond Times,* April 16, 1867, "Anniversary of the Death of Abraham Lincoln," which reported over two thousand freedmen gathered to commemorate Lincoln.

173. *Southwestern Christian Advocate,* issue 51, December 19, 1889, 4, col. C.

174. Davis, *Image of Lincoln in the South,* 139.

175. Henry W. Grady, quoted ibid., 159; Davis, *Henry W. Grady's New South,* 178–79.

176. Davis, *Image of Lincoln in the South*, 170; Watterson, "Abraham Lincoln," in Watterson, *Compromises of Life and Other Lectures and Addresses*, 137–80.

177. Elliott and Smith, *Undaunted Radical*, 84.

178. de Leon, "Ruin of Reconstruction of Southern States," 458.

179. Blum, *Reforging the White Republic*, 87–145; Blackmon, *Slavery by Another Name*.

180. Ibid.; Blight, "For Something beyond the Battlefield," 1167; Davis, *Image of Lincoln in the South*, 109.

181. Clark, *Defining Moments*, 214; Davis, *Image of Lincoln in the South*, 170.

182. Francis W. Dawson, quoted in Davis, *Henry W. Grady's New South*, 178.

183. Jubal Early to Jefferson Davis, February 16, 1878, in Rowland, *Jefferson Davis*, 8:82; Cooper, *Jefferson Davis, American*, 622.

184. Gopnik, *Angels and Ages*, 120. The word *executioner* is Gopnik's.

185. Jefferson Davis, quoted in Cooper, *Jefferson Davis, American*, 658; "We Should Be Trying to Understand Davis and the Confederacy: An Interview with Prof. William J. Cooper, Jr.," *Museum of the Confederacy Magazine* (Spring 2008): 7–13.

186. Daniel, "Life, Services and Character of Jefferson Davis," 113–59.

187. William Henry Harrison Miller to Cassius Clay, December 14, 1889, Cassius Clay Papers, Special Collections and Digital Programs, University of Kentucky Margaret I. King Library, Lexington.

3. A NEW NATIONAL TYPE: THE GREAT IMPERIALIST, 1890–1918

1. William Roane Aylett Papers, Speech before Veterans of Army of Northern Virginia and Army of the Potomac, 1895, 2–3, VHS. There is no specific date given for Aylett's speech, although the Virginia Historical Society and evidence internal to the address strongly suggest it was given in 1895.

2. Ibid., 5–6.

3. Ibid., 7–8.

4. Ibid., 8–10; Silber, "Emancipation without Slavery: Remembering the Union Victory," in Cooper and McCardell, *In the Cause of Liberty*, 105–25.

5. Blum, *Reforging the White Republic*, 207–49; Davis, *Image of Lincoln in the South*, 149–52.

6. James M. McPherson, "Long-Legged Yankee Lies: The Lost Cause Textbook Crusade," in McPherson, *This Mighty Scourge*, 93–106; Bailey, "Textbooks of the 'Lost Cause,'" 507–33; Bailey, "Free Speech at the University of Florida," 1–17; Bailey, "Free Speech and the 'Lost Cause' in Texas," 453–77; Bailey, "Free Speech and the Lost Cause in the Old Dominion," 237–66; Bailey, "Mildred Lewis Rutherford and the Patrician Cult of the Old South," 509–35; Case, "Historical Ideology of Mildred Lewis Rutherford," 599–628; Monroe, "Lincoln the Dwarf," 32–42; Lowenthal, "Past Time, Present Place," 1–36; Glazer and Key, "Carry Me Back," 1–24; Anderson, "Down Memory Lane," 105–36; Heyse, "Rhetoric of Memory-Making," 408–32.

7. Blackmon, *Slavery by Another Name*.

8. Williamson, *Crucible of Race*; Smith, *Old Creed for the New South*; Litwack, *Trouble in Mind*; Blackmon, *Slavery by Another Name*; Lasch, "Anti-Imperialists, the Philippines, and the Inequality of Man," 319–31; Kramer, "Empires, Exceptions, and Anglo-Saxons," 1315–53; Kramer, "Race-Making and Colonial Violence in the U.S. Empire," 169–210.

9. Cox, *Dixie's Daughters,* 1–7.

10. Ibid., 3.

11. Janney, *Burying the Dead but Not the Past.*

12. Woodrow Wilson, quoted in Davis, *Image of Lincoln in the South,* 161; Edward H. Sebesta, "Letter to President Barack Obama, 2009," May 8, 2009, www.templeofdemocracy .com/2009ObamaLetter.pdf (accessed 2/22/10); Hague, Beirich, and Sebesta, *Neo-Confederacy;* Cox, *Dixie's Daughters,* 53–56.

13. Sebesta, "Letter to President Barack Obama." http://arlingtonconfederatemonument .blogspot.com/2010/03/2009-letter-to-president-obama.html (accessed 7/20/2010).

14. Ibid.

15. Ibid.

16. Nora, "Between Memory and History," 7–24.

17. Savage, *Standing Soldiers, Kneeling Slaves,* 131.

18. Turner, *Beware the People Weeping,* 97; Bryan, *Great American Myth,* 385; Hanchett, *Lincoln Murder Conspiracies,* 134–35. See also "(Former) John Wilkes Booth Monument," www.exploresouthernhistory.com/boothmonument.html (accessed 3/30/13).

19. Hall, "Pink Parker's Tombstone," 8–9.

20. Obituary, *New York Times,* December 15, 1921, 19.

21. Ibid.

22. Hall, "Pink Parker's Tombstone," 9.

23. Ibid.; *New York Times,* July 14, 1921, 6; Hall, "Pink Parker's Tombstone," 9; Bryan, *Great American Myth,* 385.

24. Hall, "Pink Parker's Tombstone," 9.

25. Gould, *Alexander Watkins Terrell,* 50–51, 181; Worley, "Story of Alfred W. Arrington," 315–39; *Portland Morning Oregonian,* July, 2, 1893, 4; *Milwaukee Sentinel,* July 2, 1893, 12; *Raleigh News-Observer-Chronicle,* July 6, 1893; *Memphis Commercial Appeal,* February 16, 1896; Turner, *Beware the People Weeping,* 97.

26. *Milwaukee Sentinel,* July 2, 1893, 12.

27. *Memphis Commercial-Appeal,* February 16, 1896, 4; Gould, *Alexander Watkins Terrell,* 137–38.

28. *Memphis Commercial-Appeal,* February 16, 1896, 4.

29. Ibid.

30. Elliott and Smith, *Undaunted Radical,* 83.

31. Ibid., 84.

32. Textbooks surveyed for this study included: King and Ficklen, *History of Louisiana;* Lee, *Lee's School History of the United States;* Pennybacker, *The New History of Texas for Schools;* Garrett and Goodpasture, *History of Tennessee;* Riley, *School History of Mississippi;* Brevard, *History of Florida;* Elson, *History of the United States of America;* Hill, *Young People's History of North Carolina;* Magill, *Magill's First Book in Virginia History;* DuBose, *Alabama History;* Simms, *The History of South Carolina,* revised by Mary C. Simms Oliphant. I am indebted to historian Fred Bailey's articles for the list of these textbooks.

33. Lee, *Lee's School History of the United States* (1895 version), 347–48.

34. Ibid.

35. Ibid.

36. Lee, *Lee's Primary School History of the United States* (1897 version), 174.

37. *Confederate Veteran* 3 (November 1895): 333.

38. King and Ficklen, *History of Louisiana,* 213; Riley, *School History of Mississippi,* 221–22; Garrett and Goodpasture, *History of Tennessee,* 202; Brevard, *History of Florida,* 155; DuBose, *Alabama History,* 132.

39. Simms, *History of South Carolina,* rev. Mary C. Simms Oliphant, 258.

40. Ibid., 258–59.

41. Pennybacker, *New Texas History for Schools* (1895), 261.

42. DuBose, *Alabama History,* 132.

43. King and Ficklen, *History of Louisiana,* 229.

44. Riley, *School History of Mississippi,* 279.

45. Lee, *School History of the United States* (1895 version), 352–53.

46. Lee, *School History of the United States* (1896 version), 225.

47. Ibid., 435.

48. Ibid., 533.

49. Ibid., 533–34.

50. Garrett and Goodpasture, *History of Tennessee,* 244; Hale, *Making Whiteness,* 81.

51. McPherson, "Long-Legged Yankee Lies," 93–106.

52. Foster, *Ghosts of the Confederacy,* 197.

53. Mrs. M. M. Birge, quoted in Bailey, "Free Speech and the 'Lost Cause' in Texas," 458.

54. Mississippi legislature, quoted in McPherson, "Long-Legged Yankee Lies," 99; Cox, *Dixie's Daughters,* 121.

55. *Confederate Veteran* 3 (October 1895): 317.

56. Cox, *Dixie's Daughters,* 161.

57. Gellner, *Nations and Nationalism,* 33; Hague, Beirich, and Sebesta, *Neo-Confederacy,* 202–25; McPherson, "Long-Legged Yankee Lies," 97.

58. Cox, *Dixie's Daughters,* 122.

59. Slack, "Causes That Led to the War between the States in 1860."

60. Josephine Powell Beaty to David Rankin Barbee, December 12, 1947, box 14, folder 727, David Rankin Barbee Papers, Joseph Mark Lauinger Library, Georgetown University, Washington, D.C.

61. Clark, *Defining Moments,* 227; Kachun, *Festivals of Freedom.*

62. W. E. B. Du Bois, "The Lie of History as It Is Taught Today (The Civil War: The War to Preserve Slavery)," February 15, 1960, in Paschal, *W. E. B. Du Bois: A Reader,* 115–20.

63. Banks, "Semi-Centennial View of Secession," 301–2; Bailey, "Free Speech at the University of Florida," 1–17.

64. Banks, "Semi-Centennial View of Secession," 302.

65. Ibid., 303; Enoch Banks, quoted also in Bailey, "Free Speech at the University of Florida," 1–17.

66. Bailey, "Free Speech at the University of Florida," 1–17.

67. Texas textbook, quoted in Bailey, "Textbooks of the Lost Cause," 507–33; Bailey, "Best History Money Can Buy," 28–48; McMichael, "'Memories Are Short but Monuments Lengthen Remembrances': The United Daughters of the Confederacy and the Power of Civil War Memory," in Cantrell and Turner, *Lone Star Pasts,* 95–118; Mendoza, "Causes Lost but Not Forgotten: George Washington Littlefield, Jefferson Davis, and Confederate Memories at the University of Texas at Austin," in Grear, *Fate of Texas,* 155–79.

68. Henry W. Elson's textbook, quoted in Bailey, "Free Speech and the 'Lost Cause' in Texas," 464–66.

69. Ibid.; Bailey, "Free Speech and the Lost Cause in the Old Dominion," 237–66.

70. *Confederate Veteran* 9 (August 1901): 370.

71. Cox, *Dixie's Daughters,* 95–96.

72. Ibid., 95; Blight, *Race and Reunion,* 277–78; McPherson, "Long-Legged Yankee Lies," 93–106.

73. *Confederate Veteran* 1 (March 1893): 81.

74. *Confederate Veteran* 9 (June 1901): 244–45.

75. *Confederate Veteran* 2 (August 1894): 230. Lincoln was criticized for other things in the *Veteran.* He was frequently denigrated for refusing prisoner exchanges with the Confederate government during the war. I am indebted to historians at the Southern Historical Association for the point about businessmen needing to cooperate with northerners. I heard this idea in a panel discussion at the annual meeting in Baltimore 2011 and thought it apt in this context.

76. Wilson, *Baptized in Blood,* 8.

77. Davis, *Image of Lincoln in the South,* 123–25; Coski, "Early 20th Century Pamphlets," 10.

78. *Confederate Veteran* 9 (September 1901): 421.

79. Davis, *Image of Lincoln in the South,* 123–24; obituary, "Miss Kate Rowland," *Southern Historical Society Papers* (Richmond, Va.: Broadfoot Publishing Co., 1991), 41:113–14; Coski, "Early 20th Century Pamphlets," 9–12; Cox, *Dixie's Daughters,* 30.

80. Silber, "Emancipation without Slavery," 119; Schwartz, *Abraham Lincoln and the Forge of National Memory,* 117–20; Kramer, "Empires, Exceptions, and Anglo-Saxons," 1315–53.

81. David Starr Jordan, quoted in Silber, "Emancipation without Slavery," 117.

82. Ibid., 117–18.

83. Ben Tillman, quoted in Kantrowitz, *Ben Tillman and the Reconstruction of White Supremacy,* 263.

84. Charles L. C. Minor to Kate Mason Rowland, April 10, 1899, Kate Mason Rowland Collection, Museum of the Confederacy, Richmond, Va. Rowland's replies to Minor, unfortunately, are at this writing unknown. Many thanks are due to John Coski at the Museum of the Confederacy for the location and transcription of these letters. Dr. Coski kindly sent me these letters before he published his "Early 20th Century Pamphlets," 9–12.

85. Ibid.

86. Ibid.

87. Ibid.

88. Ibid.

89. Slack, "Causes That Led to the War between the States in 1860."

90. Karp, *Politics of War,* 109.

91. Lasch, "Anti-Imperialists," 321.

92. Minor to Rowland, November 25, 1899; Coski, "Early 20th Century Pamphlets," 11.

93. Minor to Rowland, November 25, 1899; Minor to Rowland, December 18, 1899; Minor to Rowland, December 29, 1899; Coski, "Early 20th Century Pamphlets," 11–12.

94. Coski, "Early 20th Century Pamphlets," 12; Kate Mason Rowland, quoted on the same page.

95. Ibid.; Davis, *Image of Lincoln in the South,* 124–25.

96. "The Real Lincoln to Be Suppressed," *Boston Journal,* June 27, 1905.

97. Ibid.; Davis, *Image of Lincoln in the South,* 125.

98. Meriwether, *Recollections of 92 Years,* 43; Berkeley, "Elizabeth Avery Meriwether," 390–407; Frank, "Meriwethers of Memphis and St. Louis"; Davis, *Image of Lincoln in the South,* 125–26. I am indebted to Fred Arthur Bailey for alerting me to the importance of Elizabeth Meriwether's writings.

99. Berkeley, "Elizabeth Avery Meriwether," 394–96.

100. Ibid.; Meriwether, *Recollections,* 74–75.

101. Berkeley, "Elizabeth Avery Meriwether, 397.

102. Meriwether, *My Yesteryears,* 83–84; Berkeley, "Elizabeth Avery Meriwether," 403. According to Berkeley, at the meeting organizing the Klan in the Meriwether home, "Elizabeth . . . suggested that the men consider enfranchising 'respectable' Southern white women to counterbalance the votes of black and white men targeted by the Klan."

103. Meriwether, *Recollections,* 205.

104. Elizabeth Avery Meriwether, "Are Women Slaves?" *St. Louis Globe-Democrat,* July 17, 1881, 6.

105. Faust, *Mothers of Invention,* 253.

106. Meriwether, *Facts and Falsehoods,* 1–90.

107. Ibid., 4.

108. Ibid., 5–6.

109. Ibid., 49–50; Elizabeth Avery Meriwether, also quoted in Davis, *Image of Lincoln in the South,* 125–26.

110. Meriwether, *Facts and Falsehoods,* 33.

111. Ibid., 166.

112. Ibid., 136.

113. Ibid., 35.

114. Ibid.

115. Ibid., 90.

116. Meriwether, *Recollections of 92 Years,* 163.

117. Ibid.

118. Ibid.

119. Ibid.

120. Ibid., 164–65.

121. Morel, "Lincoln, Race, and the Spirit of '76," 3; Davis, *Image of Lincoln in the South,* 135–70.

122. John Wilkes Booth, quoted in Kauffman, *American Brutus,* 210.

123. Mrs. J. G. Hughes, "Jefferson Davis vs. Abraham Lincoln," address given before the United Daughters of the Confederacy, Hanover Chapter, Ashland, Va., 1914–15, Eleanor S. Brockenbrough Library, Museum of the Confederacy, Richmond; Mrs. William Marshall Tredway, "Jefferson Davis, Abraham Lincoln: A Contrast," address given before the United Daughters of the Confederacy, Riley Martin Chapter, ca. 1922, Eleanor S. Brockenbrough Library, Museum of the Confederacy, Richmond, Va.

124. Pickett, "President Lincoln: Intimate Personal Recollections," 555–60; Janney, "'One of the Best Loved, North and South,'" 370–406.

125. Minutes of Grand Camp of Confederate Veterans, Robert E. Lee Camp, № 1, Richmond, Va., April 9, 1909, 326, VHS.

126. *Confederate Veteran* 15 (July 1907): 314–16.

127. Minutes of Grand Camp of Confederate Veterans, Robert E. Lee Camp, № 1, Richmond, Va., October 1, 1909, 364, and October 29, 1909, 368, VHS.

128. George L. Christian, "Abraham Lincoln," address delivered before Robert E. Lee Camp, № 1, October 29, 1909 (Richmond, Va.: Richmond Press, 1927), 9, 32, VHS.

129. Ibid.

130. Minutes of Grand Camp of Confederate Veterans, Robert E. Lee Camp, № 1, Richmond, Va., November 19, 1909, 374, and December 17, 1909, 381, VHS.

131. *Confederate Veteran* 17 (March 1909): 104.

132. *Confederate Veteran* 17 (April 1909): 153–55. Unless otherwise indicated, the following discussion draws on this source.

133. Ibid.

134. Ibid.

135. Ibid.

136. Ibid.

137. Ibid.

138. Ibid.

139. Ibid.

140. Ibid.

141. Ibid.

142. See Davis, *Image of Lincoln in the South,* 127–34; Fehrenbacher, *Lincoln in Text and Context,* 205–8.

143. Schwartz, *Abraham Lincoln and the Forge of National Memory,* 124; Neely, "Progressive Admiration," 1–3; Jividen, *Claiming Lincoln.* I am especially indebted to Larry Arnhart and Jason Jividen for their insights on the appropriation of Lincoln by Progressives.

144. Herbert Croly, quoted in Richard Striner, "Lincoln, the Roosevelts, and Herbert Croly's America," in Watson, Pederson, and Williams, *Lincoln's Enduring Legacy,* 165.

145. Theodore Roosevelt, quoted ibid., 166.

146. Roosevelt, "Heirs of Abraham Lincoln."

147. Jividen, *Claiming Lincoln,* 32; Arnhart, DarwinianConservatism.com.

148. Jividen, *Claiming Lincoln,* 175; Krannawitter, *Vindicating Lincoln,* 295; Schulten, "Barack Obama, Abraham Lincoln, and John Dewey," 807–18. The term *foundational idea* comes from Ceaser, *Nature and History in American Political Development.*

149. Foner, *Story of American Freedom,* 139–61.

150. Woodrow Wilson, quoted in Davis, *Image of Lincoln in the South,* 161.

151. Jividen, "Woodrow Wilson's Abraham Lincoln," paper prepared for the Western Political Science Association Annual Meeting, Las Vegas, March 8, 2007, 3; Jividen, *Claiming Lincoln,* 64–96; Gaughan, "Woodrow Wilson and the Legacy of the Civil War," 225–42.

152. Woodrow Wilson, quoted in Jividen, "Woodrow Wilson's Abraham Lincoln," 3.

153. Ibid., 4.

154. Ibid., 11.

155. Gaughan, "Woodrow Wilson and the Legacy of the Civil War," 235.

156. Woodrow Wilson, quoted in Stockwell, "Lincoln's Bridge to the World," 19.

157. Gaughan, "Woodrow Wilson and the Legacy of the Civil War," 238–41; Peterson, *Lincoln in American Memory,* 198.

158. Bender, *Nation among Nations,* 241.

159. Ibid., 243.

160. Blacknall, *Lincoln as the South Should Know Him,* 2.

161. Ibid., 8.

162. Ibid., 22.

163. Lloyd T. Everett, "Living Confederate Principles: A Heritage for All Time," address delivered at the reception of Washington Camp of the Confederate Veterans of Washington, D.C., February 14, 1914, 34.

164. Ibid., 37.

165. Ibid., 40.

166. Everett, *Davis, Lincoln, and the Kaiser,* 3.

167. Ibid., 12.

168. Cox, *Dixie's Daughters,* 161.

169. Anna Howard Shaw, "Equal Suffrage—A Problem of Political Justice," *Annals of the American Academy of Political and Social Science* 56 (1914): 94. I am indebted to a paper delivered by the political scientist Rogers M. Smith at the 2012 Wepner Symposium in Springfield, Illinois, for these insights about the use of Lincoln's rhetoric by suffragettes to advance their cause. Rogers M. Smith, "Emancipators' Dilemmas: The Lincoln Legacy and Struggles for African American and Women's Rights, 1895–1945," 1–34. Smith's paper can be found at https://edocs.uis.edu/ggiannot/www/Wepner%202012/Smith%20-%20Emancipators%27%20 Dilemmas.pdf (accessed 11/24/12). See also Silber, "Emancipation without Slavery," 115.

170. Blight, *Race and Reunion,* 279–84; Bailey, "Mildred Lewis Rutherford and the Patrician Cult of the Old South," 509–37; Case, "Historical Ideology of Mildred Lewis Rutherford," 599–628.

171. Rutherford, *Jefferson Davis and Abraham Lincoln,* 45.

172. Ibid., 16.

173. Ibid., 34.

174. McRae, "Caretakers of Southern Civilization," 825; Case, "Historical Ideology of Mildred Lewis Rutherford," 615.

175. Rutherford, *Jefferson Davis and Abraham Lincoln,* 41.

176. Case, "Historical Ideology of Mildred Lewis Rutherford," 628.

177. See the "Order of Ratification of the 19th Amendment" map at http://law2.umkc.edu/faculty/projects/ftrials/anthony/ratifmap.html (accessed 11/24/12).

178. Clark, *Defining Moments;* Peterson, *Lincoln in American Memory,* 171–75.

179. Frederick Douglass, quoted in Christopher N. Breiseth, "Lincoln and Frederick Douglass," in Schwartz, *"For a Vast Future Also,"* 80–81.

180. Booker T. Washington, quoted in Holzer, *Lincoln Anthology,* 397–404. See also James L. Curtis, "Abraham Lincoln," in Dunbar, *Masterpieces,* 227–29; Abraham Walters, "Abraham Lincoln and Fifty Years of Freedom," in Dunbar, *Masterpieces,* 230–37.

181. Sundquist, *Oxford W. E. B. Du Bois Reader,* 248–56.

182. Frederickson, *Big Enough to Be Inconsistent,* 2–3; Smith, "Black Images of Lincoln in the Age of Jim Crow," 3–4; Horton and Horton, *Man and the Martyr,* 36; Guelzo, *Lincoln's Emancipation Proclamation,* 244; Peterson, *Lincoln in American Memory,* 173.

183. Peterson, *Lincoln in American Memory,* 170.

184. Crouthamel, "Springfield Race Riot of 1908," 164–81; Smith, "Black Images," 1.

185. Litwack, *Trouble in Mind,* 306; Williamson, *Crucible of Race,* 118; Smith, "Black Images," 1–4.

186. Unnamed African American man, quoted in Blair, *Cities of the Dead,* 163.

187. Smith, "Black Images," 3–4. This section on Grimké is heavily indebted to Smith's excellent essay. Bruce, *Archibald Grimké*.

188. Archibald H. Grimké, quoted in Smith, "Black Images," 4; Blair, *Cities of the Dead*, 144–70.

189. Archibald H. Grimké, quoted in Smith, "Black Images," 4.

190. Grimké, "Abraham Lincoln and the Fruitage of His Proclamation," 51–53.

191. Perry, *Hubert Harrison Reader*, 1–2.

192. Ibid., 5.

193. W. A. Domingo, quoted ibid., 1.

194. Perry, *Hubert Harrison Reader*, 152.

195. Hubert Harrison, "Lincoln and Liberty—Fact versus Fiction," *Negro World*, March 5, 1921, 8.

196. Hubert Harrison, quoted in Perry, *Hubert Harrison Reader*, 130–31, emphasis mine.

197. Oakes, *Freedom National*.

198. Hubert Harrison, quoted in Perry, *Hubert Harrison Reader*, 136.

199. Bruce, *Archibald Grimké*, 72–73; Smith, Black Images, 3–4.

200. Hogan, *Lincoln, Inc.*, 93, 154. Hogan, quoting Edward Herman and Noam Chomsky, calls this challenging boundaries of "thinkable thought."

201. Hubert Harrison, "Chapter Four: A Crooked Deal for the Black Patriot," *Negro World*, March 26, 1921, 7. See the National Negro Committee's 1909 letter expressing bitter disappointment with American race relations and proposing a national conference. Du Bois was among its signers. *The African American Odyssey: A Quest for Full Citizenship*, Library of Congress, http://memory.loc.gov/cgi-bin/ampage?collId=ody_mssmisc&fileName=ody/ody0609a/ody0609apage.db&recNum=0&itemLink=/ammem/aaohtml/exhibit/aopart6b.html@0609&linkText=9 (accessed 3/26/13).

202. Strunsky, *Abraham Lincoln*, 257–61; Peterson, *Lincoln in American Memory*, 163.

203. Rose Strunsky, quoted in Peterson, *Lincoln in American Memory*, 163.

204. Fears, *Essays in the History of Liberty*, 361–66. See also "The Acton-Lee Correspondence," 1866, www.lewrockwell.com/orig3/acton-lee.html (accessed 3/23/13).

4. THE SELF-PITY OF THE DEFEATED: CONTESTING "LINCOLNOLATRY," 1918–1945

1. Mencken, "Sahara of the Bozart," 69–82.

2. Hobson, *Serpent in Eden*, 11–32.

3. Mencken "Abraham Lincoln," 77–80, 197–200.

4. Ibid.

5. Ibid.

6. Mary D. Carter to H. L. Mencken, November 20, 1924, David Rankin Barbee Papers, box 11, folder 599, Georgetown University Library, Special Collections Division, Washington, D.C.; original underlining in the letter appears here in italics.

7. Forgue, *Letters of H. L. Mencken*, 256.

8. Frederickson, *Big Enough to Be Inconsistent*, 2.

9. W. E. B. Du Bois, quoted in Holzer, *Lincoln Anthology*, 435.

10. Horton and Horton, *Man and the Martyr*, 41.

11. "The Week," *Chicago Defender* (National Edition), July 15, 1922, 16.

12. W. E. B. Du Bois, quoted in Holzer, *Lincoln Anthology,* 436; Frederickson, *Big Enough to Be Inconsistent,* 436.

13. Holzer, *Lincoln Anthology,* 437.

14. Ibid., 438.

15. Twelve Southerners, *I'll Take My Stand;* Janney, "War over a Shrine of Peace," 91–120.

16. Fehrenbacher, *Lincoln in Text and Context,* 191–92; Guelzo, "Does Lincoln Still Belong to the Ages?," 6–7.

17. Johnson, *Modern Times,* 1–48; Ecksteins, *Rites of Spring,* xii–xvi; Kennedy, *Freedom from Fear,* 1–42; Schwartz, *Abraham Lincoln in the Post-Heroic Era,* 1–19.

18. Wolfe, *Future of Liberalism,* 253; Carwardine and Sexton, *Global Lincoln,* 22.

19. Basler, Dunlap, and Pratt, *Collected Works of Abraham Lincoln,* 2:266.

20. Dirck, *Lincoln and Davis,* 245.

21. Ibid., 244; Singal, *War Within,* 7–8; Johnson, *Modern Times,* 1–11; Carwardine and Sexton, *Global Lincoln,* 22–23.

22. Fehrenbacher, *Lincoln in Text and Context,* 197–205; Davis, *Image of Lincoln in the South,* 128–34.

23. Lyon Gardiner Tyler, "Propaganda in History," *Tyler's Quarterly Historical and Genealogical Magazine* 1 (April 1920): 223.

24. Ibid., 224.

25. Ibid.

26. Ibid., 230.

27. Lyon Gardiner Tyler, "Propaganda Again," *Tyler's Quarterly Historical and Genealogical Magazine* 2 (January 1921): 150.

28. Daniel Grinnan to *Richmond Times-Dispatch,* "The Lincoln Birth-Day Resolution," February 29, 1928, Grinnan Family Papers, VHS, emphasis mine.

29. Albert Hill Hudgins Papers, box 19, folder 1, Richmond, VHS.

30. Daniel Grinnan to Albert Hill Hudgins, February 17, 1930, Albert Hill Hudgins Papers, box 19, folder 1, Richmond, VHS.

31. Giles B. Cook, "An Open Letter" advertisement, February 19, 1928, 3. The letters of Cooke, Hale, and Tyler were eventually collected and published in pamphlet form. Peterson, *Lincoln in American Memory,* 252.

32. Giles B. Cook, "An Open Letter," 12.

33. *Richmond Times-Dispatch,* quoted in Peterson, *Lincoln in American Memory,* 252.

34. Ibid., 254.

35. Tyler, *John Tyler and Abraham Lincoln,* 4–5.

36. Lyon Gardiner Tyler to Milton H. Shutes, November 11, 1930, William H. Townsend Papers, box 6, folder 7, Townsend Correspondence, Margaret I. King Library, University of Kentucky, Lexington. Tyler quoted Shute's comparison of Davis and Lincoln back to Shutes.

37. Ibid.

38. Ibid.

39. Ibid.; original underlining in the letter appears here in italics. See also the letter that Milton Shutes of California sent in 1950 to William H. Townsend of Lexington, Ky., in which he described Tyler's writings as "prime examples of how the degree of blindness parallels the depth of prejudices." William H. Townsend Papers, box 6, folder 7, Townsend Correspondence, Margaret I. King Library, University of Kentucky, Lexington.

40. Ibid.

41. Peterson, *Lincoln in American Memory,* 254; Davis, *Image of Lincoln in the South,* 134.

42. Scrugham, "Force or Consent as the Basis of American Government," 376–78.

43. William A. Dunning, quoted in Novick, *That Noble Dream,* 77.

44. Scrugham, *Peaceable Americans of 1860–1861,* 13–17; Braeman, "Albert J. Beveridge and Demythologizing Lincoln," 16–17; Cox, *Dixie's Daughters,* 74–75; Faust, *Mothers of Invention,* 248–54. Faust describes such women as "an almost inexplicable paradox of progressivism and reaction."

45. Obituary, *Lexington Herald-Leader,* April 10, 1965.

46. Scrugham, "Force or Consent," 376.

47. Ibid.

48. Ibid.

49. Ibid.

50. Cornelius B. Hite, "Statue of the Wrong Man," *Confederate Veteran* 33, no. 1 (January 1925): 6.

51. "Letters of Appreciation," *Confederate Veteran* 33, no. 3 (March 1925): 118.

52. Scrugham, *Force or Consent as the Basis of American Government,* 12. All subsequent quotations from Mary Scrugham and William H. Townsend are from this pamphlet.

53. Ibid., 13.

54. Ibid.

55. Ibid., 21–22.

56. Ibid., 30.

57. *Confederate Veteran* 33, no. 6 (June 1925): 242.

58. Ibid.

59. Basler, Dunlap, and Pratt, *Collected Works of Abraham Lincoln,* 4:151; Levine, review of *We Have the War upon Us;* Oakes, *Freedom National.*

60. Barton, *Man Nobody Knows,* 1–31.

61. Angle, *Shelf of Lincoln Books,* 117–18; Peterson, *Lincoln in American Memory,* 221–26.

62. Peterson, *Lincoln in American Memory,* 221–22; Fried, *Man Everybody Knew,* 102–10.

63. Fried, *Man Everybody Knew,* 102.

64. Whitney, "Bruce Barton's Babblings."

65. Ibid.

66. Ibid.

67. Ibid.; underlining in the original letter appears here in italics.

68. Ibid.

69. Ibid.

70. J. W. Duffey to "Miss Daisy," n.d., David Rankin Barbee Papers, Joseph Mark Lauinger Memorial Library, Special Collections Division, box 11, folder 598, Georgetown University, Washington, D.C.

71. Mary D. Carter to Dr. J. W. Kennedy, January 13, 1927, David Rankin Barbee Papers, box 11, folder 598.

72. Ibid.; Mary D. Carter to David Rankin Barbee, May 31, 1927, David Rankin Barbee Papers, box 11, folder 598, in which Carter told Barbee that comparisons of Lincoln with Jesus were "driving people away from church."

73. David Rankin Barbee to Mary DeButts Carter, March 21, 1927, David Rankin Barbee Papers, box 11, folder 598.

74. Barbee to Carter, September 7, 1930, David Rankin Barbee Papers, box 11, folder 599.

75. Langbourne Williams, letter to editor, *Richmond Times-Dispatch,* January 6, 1928.

76. Ed M. Harris, "Commander of Confederate Veterans Aroused at Hatreds of 'Uncle Tom's Cabin,'" *Southern Churchman,* June 8, 1929, 24. The Virginia Historical Society in Richmond has an extensive and fairly complete collection of the *Southern Churchman* in its archives.

77. Carter to Barbee, May 17, 1927, David Rankin Barbee Papers, box 11, folder 598.

78. Ibid.

79. Ibid.

80. Mary D. Carter, "Did the War Save the Union?" *Confederate Veteran* 23 (1915): 61.

81. Carter and Everett, *Youth's History of the Great Civil War [War between the States] from 1861–1865,* by Horton, vii. See the positive comments the book received in the pages of the *Confederate Veteran* 34 (1926): 118, 158, 238.

82. R. G. Horton, quoted in Loewen and Sebesta, *Confederate and Neo-Confederate Reader,* 243, emphasis mine.

83. *Confederate Veteran* 34 (1926): 72.

84. Mary D. Carter to Joseph Eggleston, November 30, 1934, Eggleston Family Papers, VHS; Hughes, "Civil Theology for the South," 447–67.

85. Carter to Eggleston, May 21, 1935, Eggleston Family Papers.

86. Carter to Barbee, February 28, 1927, David Rankin Barbee Papers, box 11, folder 598.

87. Ibid.; Carter to Eggleston, May 10, 1935, Eggleston Family Papers.

88. Ibid.; original underlining in the letter appears here in italics.

89. Lloyd T. Everett, "Miss Mary D. Carter," *Tyler's Quarterly Magazine* (October 1948): 138–39.

90. Mary D. Carter, "Lincolnolatry in the Churches," *Southern Churchman* 95, May 24, 1930, 24.

91. Ibid.

92. Mary D. Carter, "Lincolnolatry in the Churches (Continued)," *Southern Churchman* 95, May 31, 1930, 24; words originally in boldface type appear here in italics.

93. Mrs. Wade Barrier, letter to the editor, *Southern Churchman* 95, July 12, 1930, 11.

94. Mrs. J. B. Rhoad, letter to the editor, *Southern Churchman* 95, July 19, 1930, 12; Paul S. Whitcomb, "Most Colossal Hoax of Modern History," *Southern Churchman* 95, August 9, 1930, 23–24, and September 13, 1930, 21.

95. Wilson, *Baptized in Blood.*

96. Rutherford, *Contrasted Lives of Jefferson Davis and Abraham Lincoln—Jefferson Davis: The Home of a Christian Gentleman; Abraham Lincoln: The Home of an Unbeliever.*

97. Landon Carter Bell, "A. Lincoln and His Co-Mate in Crime, General 'Beast' Butler, of Silver Spoons, Hill," *Southern Churchman* 95, no. 35, August 30, 1930, 24; Landon Carter Bell to Joseph Eggleston, August 25, 1942, Eggleston Family Papers.

98. Bell, "A. Lincoln and His Co-Mate in Crime," 24.

99. John T. Goolrick, "Lincoln Eulogies Merely 'Facet of Herd Psychology,'" *Southern Churchman* 95, October 4, 1930, 24; Mary D. Carter, "History Minus Personality," *Southern Churchman* 95, October 11, 1930, 24.

100. Carter, "History Minus Personality," 24; Peterson, *Lincoln in American Memory,* 251.

101. Mrs. W. S. Bernard, "Mob Psychology," n.d., Laurence Foushee London Papers, Collection no. 4958, Southern Historical Collection, University of North Carolina, Chapel Hill.

102. Julia Peterkin to Oliver R. Barrett, March 6, 1925, Oliver R. Barrett Papers, Collection no. 4114, Southern Historical Collection, University of North Carolina, Chapel Hill.

103. David Rankin Barbee to Mary Carter, March 2, 1927, David Rankin Barbee Papers, box 11, folder 598.

104. Alex McBee, "No Excuse for Lincoln Idolatry Especially in the Christian Churches Which He Attacked Openly," *Southern Churchman* 95, November 1, 1930, 14–24.

105. Ibid., 14.

106. Ibid.

107. Ibid.

108. Ibid., 23.

109. Ibid.

110. Angle, *Shelf of Lincoln Books,* 53–54; Fehrenbacher, *Lincoln in Text and Context,* 192; Braeman, "Albert J. Beveridge and Demythologizing Lincoln," 1–24.

111. Albert J. Beveridge, quoted in Braeman, "Albert J. Beveridge and Demythologizing Lincoln," 12–18.

112. Ibid., 14.

113. Rupert Hughes, "Rupert Hughes Appraises Year's Biographies," *Chicago Daily-Tribune,* December 8, 1928.

114. William H. Townsend to Edward C. Stone, June 7, 1944, William H. Townsend Papers, box 8, folder 2.

115. William H. Townsend to Mary D. Carter, August 29, 1930, Abraham Lincoln Presidential Library, Springfield, Ill. Many thanks to Professor Stephen Berry at the University of Georgia and Glenna Schroeder-Lein at the Abraham Lincoln Library in Springfield for alerting me to the existence of Townsend's letters to Carter. Unfortunately, Carter's responses to Townsend must be inferred from Townsend's comments.

116. Ibid.

117. Ibid.

118. Ibid.

119. Ibid.

120. Ibid.

121. Ibid.

122. Ibid.

123. Braeman, "Albert J. Beveridge and Demythologizing Lincoln," 14–15; Peterson, *Lincoln in American Memory,* 284.

124. Barbee, *Excursion in Southern History.* Subsequent quotations are from Barbee's pamphlet.

125. Ibid., foreword.

126. Ibid., 7–23.

127. Ibid., 11–19.

128. Ibid., 42.

129. J. C. Hooks, "Letter to the Editor," *Southern Churchman,* June 20, 1929, 12.

130. Barbee, *Excursion in Southern History,* 53.

131. Townsend, "Memorandum on Barbee's 'An Excursion in Southern History' and Beveridge's and Lamon's Biographies of Abraham Lincoln," William H. Townsend Papers.

132. Charles A. Beard to William H. Townsend, September 4 [probably 1932].

133. Ibid.

134. Beard to Townsend, September 27, 1932, William H. Townsend Papers.

135. Horace Chapman Rose to William H. Townsend, September 14, 1932; Rose to Townsend, September 18, 1932, both in William H. Townsend Papers.

136. Braeman, "Albert J. Beveridge and Demythologizing Lincoln," 1–24; Boritt, *Lincoln and the Economics of the American Dream,* 295–98; Fehrenbacher, *Lincoln in Text and Context,* 185–87; Guelzo, "Does Lincoln Still Belong to the Ages?," 1–13.

137. Townsend, "Memorandum." Townsend apparently wrote this memorandum sometime in 1933, as his letter to Rufus Wilson is dated in that year, although Townsend could have written it upon reflection years later. Wilson's first letter to Townsend is dated April 18, 1933, with Townsend responding on April 27, 1933, nine days later.

138. William H. Townsend to Rufus Rockwell Wilson, April 27, 1933, William H. Townsend Papers.

139. Rufus Rockwell Wilson to William H. Townsend, May 5, 1933, William H. Townsend Papers.

140. Townsend, "Memorandum."

141. Peterson, *Lincoln in American Memory,* 284. I found no reference in Barbee's voluminous writings that Barbee knew what Townsend had written to Wilson.

142. David Rankin Barbee to Robert A. Meek, July 25, 1948, box 11, 634, David Rankin Barbee Papers.

143. Obituary, "David Rankin Barbee Is Dead at 83," *Washington Post,* March 9, 1958, B2.

144. Singal, *War Within,* 198; Roland, "South of the Agrarians," 269–83; O'Brien, *Idea of the American South, 1920–1941;* Malvasi, *Unregenerate South;* Murphy, *Rebuke of History.*

145. Murphy, *Rebuke of History,* 64–66.

146. Landess, "Andrew Lytle, RIP," 52–54.

147. Andrew Lytle, in Twelve Southerners, *I'll Take My Stand,* 205.

148. Ibid., 242–45, 201–2.

149. Ibid., 244.

150. Lytle, "Lincoln Myth," 620–26. Lytle's review was republished in 1997 in a reprint edition of the Edgar Lee Masters's biography of Lincoln from the Foundation for American Education.

151. Ibid.

152. Ibid.

153. Ibid.

154. Ibid.

155. Owsley, "Irrepressible Conflict," 63. Owsley also wrote that after the war the former states of the Confederacy were "turned over to the three millions of former slaves, some of whom could still remember the taste of human flesh and the bulk of them hardly three generations from cannibalism." Murphy, *Rebuke of History,* 21.

156. Ibid., 66.

157. Ibid., 67. For a contrary argument to Owsley's that the two sections were irreconcilably different, see Pessen, "How Different from Each Other Were the Antebellum North and South?," 1119–49.

158. Frank J. Owsley, "Southerner's View of Abraham Lincoln," address delivered before the Illinois Historical Association, May 1946, 1, Vanderbilt University Library, Frank J. Owsley Papers, Nashville, Tenn.

159. Ibid., 11.

160. Ibid., 4, 18.

161. Allen Tate, quoted in Twelve Southerners, *I'll Take My Stand,* 373; Winchell, *Where No Flag Flies.*

162. Davidson, "Mirror for Artists," in Twelve Southerners, *I'll Take My Stand,* 30; Murphy, *Rebuke of History,* 99–113.

163. Davidson, *Attack on Leviathan,* 217; Blair, *Cities of the Dead,* 171–207.

164. Davidson, *Attack on Leviathan,* 216–17.

165. Ibid., 218.

166. Ibid., 224–25. Murphy, *Rebuke of History,* 251; Malvasi, *Unregenerate South,* 153–219.

167. Warren, *Legacy of the Civil War,* 53–59. Warren, *Jefferson Davis Gets His Citizenship Back;* Blight, *American Oracle,* 31–79.

168. Warren, *Legacy of the Civil War,* 32–33. *The Legacy of the Civil War* was dedicated to Sidney Hook.

169. Ibid.; Blight, *American Oracle,* 51.

170. Warren, *Jefferson Davis,* 9.

171. Ibid., 40–41, 63.

172. Ibid.

173. Ibid., 68.

174. Ramsdell, "Lincoln and Fort Sumter," 259–88.

175. Ibid., 259–60; Fehrenbacher, *Lincoln in Text and Context,* 208.

176. Stephenson, "Charles W. Ramsdell," 501–25.

177. J. D. Eggleston to Charles W. Ramsdell, September 11, 1937, Charles Ramsdell Papers.

178. Charles Ramsdell to Laura White, January 18, 1936, Dolph Briscoe Center for American History, Charles Ramsdell Papers; original underlining in the letter appears here in italics.

179. Charles Ramsdell to Charles Beard, September 21, 1937, Charles Ramsdell Papers.

180. Charles Ramsdell to Mary D. Carter, April 1, 1937, Charles Ramsdell Papers; original underlining in the letter appears here in italics.

181. Masters, *Spoon River Anthology;* Russell, *Edgar Lee Masters,* 65–76.

182. Russell, *Edgar Lee Masters,* 269; Norman, "Illinois Iconoclast," 43–57; Neely, "Lincoln and the Hateful Poet," 1–4.

183. Russell, *Edgar Lee Masters,* 270–73.

184. Norman, "Illinois Iconoclast," 45–48.

185. Edgar Lee Masters to Allen Tate, quoted in Russell, *Edgar Lee Masters,* 275.

186. Masters, *Lincoln: The Man,* 115, 145; Russell, *Edgar Lee Masters,* 268–79; Neely, "Lincoln and the Hateful Poet," 1–4.

187. Masters, *Lincoln: The Man,* 1.

188. Ibid., 3–9.

189. Ibid., 3.

190. Charles Willis Thompson, "A Belittling Life of Lincoln by Edgar Lee Masters," *New York Times,* February 8, 1931; Norman, "Illinois Iconoclast," 52–53; Russell, *Edgar Lee Masters,* 277; Neely, "Lincoln and the Hateful Poet," 3.

191. Edgar Lee Masters Papers, "Lincoln the Man" file, Harry Ransom Humanities Center, University of Texas, Austin. There are over 150 letters to Masters in this file praising or condemning his work, although the vast majority of the letters expressed gratitude for the book's publication.

192. Jersey City Lions Club to Edgar Lee Masters, February 12, 1931, Edgar Lee Masters Papers, "Lincoln the Man" file.

193. Mrs. Harold P. Brewster to Edgar Lee Masters, February 12, 1931, Edgar Lee Masters Papers, "Lincoln the Man" file.

194. Sally Taylor to Edgar Lee Masters, February 26, 1931, Edgar Lee Masters Papers, "Lincoln the Man" file.

195. Ibid.; underlining in the original letter appears here in italics.

196. Ibid.

197. Mencken, "Birth of Order." Mencken's review is reprinted at the back of the 1997 edition of Masters, *Lincoln: The Man.* Also noteworthy is a comment Mencken made in a letter to Benjamin De Casseres in 1932, in which he called Lincoln, along with the philosopher Baruch Spinoza and clergyman Henry Ward Beecher, "one of the worst scoundrels who ever lived." Quoted in Forgue, *Letters of H. L. Mencken,* 350.

198. Mencken, "Birth of Order" (page numbers are not given in the back of this new edition).

199. Ibid.

200. Ibid.; Neely, "Lincoln and the Hateful Poet," 3.

201. Langbourne Williams to Edgar Lee Masters, February 10, 1931; Landon Carter Bell to Edgar Lee Masters, February 14, 1931, both in Edgar Lee Masters Papers, "Lincoln the Man" file.

202. Barbee to Carter, June 3, 1932, David Rankin Barbee Papers, box 11, folder 599.

203. Carter to Barbee, June 20, 1932, David Rankin Barbee Papers, box 11, folder 599.

204. Elizabeth P. Polk to Edgar Lee Masters, n.d., "Lincoln the Man" file.

205. H. Nagle (signature illegible) to Edgar Lee Masters, February 24, 1931; Cameron W. Plummer to Edgar Lee Masters, February 14, 1931, both in Edgar Lee Masters Papers, "Lincoln the Man," file.

206. Belle Inge to Edgar Lee Masters, February 10, 1931, "Lincoln the Man" file; underlining in the original letter appears here in italics.

207. D. Ferrero to Edgar Lee Masters, February 12, 1931, "Lincoln the Man" file.

208. Jone Howlind to Edgar Lee Masters, February 26, 1931, "Lincoln the Man" file.

209. Russell, *Edgar Lee Masters,* 277–79; Norman, "Illinois Iconoclast," 53–57; Neely, "Lincoln and the Hateful Poet," 4. Russell reports that the book sold seventy-one hundred copies in the United States.

210. Russell, *Edgar Lee Masters,* 97–98; Neely, "Lincoln and the Hateful Poet," 4.

211. Norman, "Illinois Iconoclast," 47, 49.

212. Neely, "Lincoln and the Hateful Poet," 4; Masters, *Lincoln: The Man,* 103–4.

213. Murphy, *Rebuke of History,* 5.

214. The phrase *serpent in the Garden of Eden* is from "Long-Legged Yankee Lies," 93–106.

215. Neely, "Lincoln and the Hateful Poet," 4.

216. Guelzo, "Does Lincoln Still Belong to the Ages?," 1–13.

217. Frederickson, *Big Enough to Be Inconsistent,* 2–3; Smith, "Black Images of Lincoln in the Age of Jim Crow," 3–4; Horton and Horton, *Man and the Martyr,* 36; Guelzo, *Lincoln's Emancipation Proclamation,* 244. An extended version of the following discussion can be found in my essay "African American Memory and the Great Emancipator," 133–64.

218. Carter Woodson, quoted in Schwartz, "Limits of Gratitude," 27.

219. Carter Woodson, "Does the Negro Really Know His Race? Do Leaders Study the Negro?" *Atlanta Daily World,* May 2, 1932, 2.

220. Carter Woodson, "Abolitionists Worried Lincoln," *Atlanta Daily World,* November 24, 1932, 2. See also Carter Woodson, "Lincoln as a Friend of Man," *Chicago Defender* (National Edition), November 19, 1932, 14.

221. Robert Vann, quoted in Medford, "Imagined Promises, Bitter Realities," 45; Robert Vann, "This Year I See Millions of Negroes Turning the Picture of Abraham Lincoln to the Wall," *Pittsburgh Courier,* September 17, 1932, 12.

222. Arthur W. Mitchell, quoted in "Solon Mitchell Praises Lincoln," *New York Amsterdam News,* September 26, 1936, 2; Congressmen Arthur W. Mitchell, *Congressional Record,* 74th Cong., 2d sess., April 22, 1936, pt. 6, 5886–88.

223. Arthur W. Mitchell, quoted in "Cong. Mitchell Says Lincoln Not Real Foe of Slavery," *Atlanta Daily World,* September 28, 1936, 2; "House Cheers as Mitchell Scores Republican Party," *Pittsburgh Courier,* May 2, 1936, 18.

224. Even the most cursory reading of African American newspapers such as the *Atlanta Daily World,* the *Chicago Defender,* the *New York New Amsterdam News,* and the *Pittsburgh Courier* reveals that there was still great affection for Lincoln among African Americans. Indeed, Mitchell was criticized for his speech in the pages of the *Chicago Defender.* "Attorney Gives New Views on Lincoln's Life," *Chicago Defender* (National Edition), July 11, 1936. Still, as early as the 1932 election, Carter Woodson had alluded in two separate pieces that African Americans were critical of Lincoln "for his inaction and hesitancy in matters respecting the emancipation and recognition of the race." Woodson, "Lincoln as a Friend of Man," 14; Woodson, "Abolitionists Worried Lincoln," 2.

225. Guelzo, "How Abraham Lincoln Lost the Black Vote," 1–22; Horton and Horton, *Man and the Martyr,* 1–52; Jones, "Who Was More Important," 30.

226. See the essay by Shaw, "Using the WPA Ex-Slave Narratives to Study the Impact of the Great Depression," 623–58, for an excellent discussion of how the slave narratives can be used as a resource by historians for studying conditions during the Great Depression. Jones, *Roosevelt's Image Brokers;* Sitkoff, *New Deal for Blacks;* Weiss, *Farewell to the Party of Lincoln;* Topping, *Lincoln's Lost Legacy.*

227. For an extended discussion of the problems of the WPA narratives, see Yetman, "Background of the Slave Narrative Collection," 534–53; Woodward, "History from Slave Sources," 470–81; Blassingame, "Using the Testimony of Ex-Slaves," 473–92; Escott, *Slavery Remembered;* Yetman, "Ex-Slave Interviews and the Historiography of Slavery," 181–210; Spindel, "Assessing Memory," 247–61; Shaw, "Using the WPA Ex-Slave Narratives," 623–30.

228. See the appendix to Rawick, *From Sundown to Sunup,* 169–79, for a detailed list of suggestions and questions for the WPA interviewers.

229. Schwartz, "Limits of Gratitude," 28.

230. Rawick, *American Slave,* vol. 2: *South Carolina Narratives,* pt. 2, 151.

231. Ibid., vol. 3: *South Carolina Narratives,* pt. 3, 82.

232. Ibid., vol. 3, pt. 4, 47.

233. Ibid., vol. 3, pt. 4, 178.

234. Ibid., vol. 7: *Oklahoma Narratives,* 191.

235. Ibid., vol. 14: *North Carolina Narratives,* pt. 1, 440.

236. Weiss, *Farewell to the Party of Lincoln,* 225; Peterson, *Lincoln in American Memory,* 316–21; Donald, *Lincoln Reconsidered,* 12–16.

237. Barr, "Lincoln in the WPA Narratives."

238. Ibid. The Liberty Bell story is quoted in Wiggins, *O Freedom,* 71–72.

239. Rawick, *American Slave,* vol. 12: *Georgia Narratives,* pt. 1, 102.

240. Ibid., vol. 15: *North Carolina Narratives,* pt. 2, 175.

241. Ibid., vol. 15, pt. 2, 75.

242. Ibid., vol. 7: *Oklahoma Narratives,* 211.

243. Ibid., vol. 4: *Texas Narratives,* pt. 1, 239.

244. Ibid., vol. 15: *North Carolina Narratives,* pt. 2, 351.

245. Ibid., vol. 14: *North Carolina Narratives,* pt. 1, 361.

246. J. A. Rogers, "Rogers Denounces 'The Robert E. Lee' Postage Stamp," *Pittsburgh Courier,* April 17, 1937, 14. See the scathing review of some contemporary books on the Civil War, especially two by the Agrarian Allen Tate on Stonewall Jackson and Jefferson Davis, by Brown, "Unhistoric History," 134–61.

247. Brown, "Unhistoric History," 134.

248. See Schwartz, *Abraham Lincoln in the Post-Heroic Era,* 59–90, for Lincoln's reputation during World War II.

249. Pollard, *Lost Cause.*

5. AN INFINITELY COMPLICATED FIGURE: IS FREEDOM ENOUGH? 1945–1989

1. Charles C. Tansill, "Jefferson Davis, Ardent American," Charles C. Tansill Papers, Herbert Hoover Presidential Library, West Branch, Iowa; Fehrenbacher, *Lincoln in Text and Context,* 197–213.

2. Tansill, "Jefferson Davis."

3. Ibid.

4. Ibid.

5. John Rankin, quoted in Fehrenbacher, *Lincoln in Text and Context,* 208; *Time,* June 16, 1947, 29.

6. James R. O'Daniel to Charles C. Tansill, June 3, 1947; and John S. Tilley to Charles C. Tansill, July 18, 1947, both in Charles C. Tansill Papers, Herbert Hoover Presidential Library, West Branch, Iowa.

7. Brown, *Richard Hofstadter,* 50.

8. Ibid.

9. Hofstadter, *American Political Tradition,* xxxvi–xxxvii; Brown, *Richard Hofstadter,* 50–56.

10. Hofstadter, *American Political Tradition,* 121–23.

11. Ibid., 137.

12. Ibid., 126, 139.

13. Ibid., 169–71.

14. Ibid.

15. Novick, *That Noble Dream,* 208–24; Riggenbach, *Why American History Is Not What They Say,* 37–38, 71–78; Bacevich, *American Empire,* 7–31; Barnes, *Perpetual War for Perpetual Peace* (Tansill's essay in this collection is entitled "The United States and the Road to War in Europe," 79–186); Stromberg, "Harry Elmer Barnes (1889–1968)."

16. Brown, *Richard Hofstadter,* 54–56.

17. My interpretation here parallels DiLorenzo, *Lincoln Unmasked,* 149–55.

18. The question of whether the United States is a "force for good in the world" is from Neuhaus, *Naked Public Square,* 72.

19. Hague, Beirich, and Sebesta, *Neo-Confederacy,* 24.

20. Even though many libertarians would eschew the label *conservative,* there was a certain "fusion"—the word is attributed to Frank Meyer—of traditional conservatives with libertarians after the war, and they will be grouped together here in this analysis of Lincoln critics. Freeman, "Illiberal Libertarians," 105–51.

21. Nash, *Conservative Intellectual Movement,* xx–xxi; Gottfried and Fleming, *Conservative Movement;* Allitt, *Conservatives,* 165. On neoconservatives, see Norton, *Leo Strauss and the Politics of American Empire;* Zuckert and Zuckert, *Truth about Leo Strauss,* 217–27; Thompson, with Brook, *Neoconservatism;* Arnhart, "Krannawitter on Lincoln and Limited Government"; Doherty, *Radicals for Capitalism;* Boaz, *Libertarianism;* Rothbard, *Betrayal of the American Right;* Rothbard, *For a New Liberty.*

22. Nash, *Conservative Intellectual Movement,* 1–49; Gottfried and Fleming, *Conservative Movement,* 1; Critchlow, *Conservative Ascendancy,* 1–40.

23. Hayek, *Road to Serfdom,* 2–13.

24. "Biography of Ludwig von Mises (1881–1973)," http://mises.org/page/1468/Biography-of-Ludwig-von-Mises-18811973 (accessed 12/8/12).

25. Nash, *Conservative Intellectual Movement,* 15.

26. Mises, *Socialism,* 13; Tilman, *Ideology and Utopia,* 25.

27. Ludwig von Mises, quoted in McGee, "Secession Reconsidered," 1.

28. Leo Strauss, quoted in Holmes, *Anatomy of Anti-Liberalism,* 62.

29. Strauss, *Natural Right and History,* 5.

30. Ibid., 7.

31. Ibid., 19; Zuckert and Zuckert, *Truth about Leo Strauss,* 30–35; Critchlow, *Conservative Ascendancy,* 18–19.

32. Weaver, *Ideas Have Consequences,* 3.

33. Nash, *Reappraising the Right,* 103–5; Haddigan, "How Anticommonism 'Cemented' the American Conservative Movement," 1–18.

34. Weaver, "Abraham Lincoln and the Argument from Definition," in Weaver, *Ethics of Rhetoric,* 86. For a contrary view regarding Weaver's admiration of Lincoln, see Dimock, "Rediscovering the Heroic Conservatism of Richard M. Weaver: Part One," 301–10; Dimock, "Rediscovering the Heroic Conservatism of Richard M. Weaver: Part Two," 13–21; Meyer, "Richard M. Weaver," 243–48; Bradford, "Agrarianism of Richard Weaver," 249–56; Murphy, *Rebuke of History,* 151–78.

35. Weaver, *Southern Tradition at Bay,* 15–19.

36. Ibid., 31–32.

37. Ibid., 372–80.

38. Kirk, *Conservative Mind,* 8–9.

39. Kirk, "Measure of Abraham Lincoln," 197–206.

40. Hague, Beirich, and Sebesta, *Neo-Confederacy,* 29.

41. William F. Buckley Jr., quoted in Bogus, *Buckley,* 141; Nash, *Conservative Intellectual Movement,* 228; Judis, *William F. Buckley, Jr.*

42. MacLean, *Freedom Is Not Enough,* 45.

43. Frank Meyer, quoted ibid.

44. William F. Buckley Jr., quoted in Judis, *William F. Buckley, Jr.,* 138–39. For an illuminating discussion of the relationship of *National Review* to the civil rights movement, see Hart's fine book *The Making of the American Conservative Mind,* 97–108. Hogeland, *Inventing American History,* 69–87, offers a harsh assessment of Buckley's editorial.

45. Weaver, *Southern Tradition at Bay,* 378; Hart, *Making of the American Conservative Mind,* 104.

46. The Virginia Historical Society possesses these pamphlets. The pamphlets were unprocessed as of May 2009 but are located in the Virginia Historical Society, unprocessed papers, MSSIr54956, miscellaneous Lincoln, Richmond.

47. Loewen and Sebesta, *Confederate and Neo-Confederate Reader,* 337–65. See also www.confederatepastpresent.org (accessed 8/10/10).

48. William F. Buckley Jr., quoted in Critchlow and MacLean, *Debating the American Conservative Movement,* 187; MacLean, *Freedom Is Not Enough,* 46.

49. "Educator Says We Must Save South's Youth," *Citizens' Councils* 1, no. 6 (March 1956): 11. The complete online version of this newspaper can be found at www.citizenscouncils.com; an independent scholar of modern neo-Confederates, Edward Sebesta, has made these papers available online to the public for research.

50. "Eternal Truth Never Changes!" *Citizens' Council* 1, no. 8 (May 1956): 3.

51. "Manual for Southerners," *Citizens' Council* 2, no. 2 (April 1957): 3.

52. "Abe Said," *Citizens' Councils* 3, no. 3 (December 1957): 3.

53. Davidson, "New South and the Conservative Tradition," 141–46.

54. Sandage, "Marble House Divided," 135; Arsenault, *Sound of Freedom.*

55. Sandage, "Marble House Divided," 136.

56. Schwartz, *Abraham Lincoln in the Post-Heroic Era,* 254–68; Davidson, "New South and the Conservative Tradition," 146.

57. Sandage, "Marble House Divided," 150. See also Martin Luther King Jr.'s "Letter from Birmingham Jail," in which he speaks of Lincoln quite positively.

58. Hart, *Making of the American Conservative Mind,* 150.

59. Jaffa, *How to Think about the American Revolution,* 2–4.

60. Jaffa, *Crisis of the House Divided,* v, 2. For a critique of Jaffa's book, see Zuckert and Zuckert, *Truth about Leo Strauss,* 217–27.

61. Nash, *Conservative Intellectual Movement in America,* 345.

62. Jaffa, *Crisis of the House Divided,* 318; Zuckert and Zuckert, *Truth about Leo Strauss,* 240–41; Forgie, *Patricide in the House Divided,* 250; Fehrenbacher, *Lincoln in Text and Context,* 222.

63. Kirk, *Conservative Mind,* 8.

64. Kendall, "Source of American Caesarism," 461–62.

65. Ibid.; Nash, *Conservative Intellectual Movement,* 345–47.

66. Kendall, "Source of American Caesarism," 462; Zuckert and Zuckert, *Truth about Leo Strauss,* 240–41; Jividen, *Claiming Lincoln.*

67. Kendall, "Equality," 95–103.

68. Ibid.

69. Ibid., 99–103.

70. Kendall and Carey, *Basic Symbols of the American Political Tradition,* 90.

71. Ibid., 156.

72. Ibid., xxi.

73. Jaffa, "Equality as a Conservative Principle," reprinted in *How to Think about the American Revolution,* 13–48.

74. MacLean, *Freedom Is Not Enough,* 35–75.

75. Zuckert and Zuckert, *Truth about Leo Strauss,* 247–52.

76. Becker, *Declaration of Independence,* 277; Jaffa, *New Birth of Freedom,* 73.

77. Jaffa, *New Birth of Freedom,* 76.

78. Ibid., 75, emphasis mine.

79. Ibid., xiii.

80. Jaffa, *How to Think about the American Revolution,* ix; Jaffa, *Crisis of the Strauss Divided,* 241–69; Jividen, *Claiming Lincoln.*

81. Smith, *Civic Ideals,* 285.

82. Nock, *Our Enemy, the State,* 57.

83. Ibid., 171.

84. Meyer, "Review of *Freedom under Lincoln,*" 520.

85. DiLorenzo, *Lincoln Unmasked,* 151.

86. Meyer, "Lincoln without Rhetoric," 725.

87. Ibid.

88. Ibid.

89. Ibid.

90. Jaffa, "Lincoln and the Cause of Freedom," 827–28, 842.

91. Andrew Jackson, quoted ibid., 827.

92. Ibid., 828.

93. Ibid., 842.

94. Letters to the editor, *National Review* 17, no. 40, October 5, 1965, 850, 852.

95. Meyer, "Again on Lincoln," 71, emphasis mine.

96. Murray N. Rothbard, "Frank S. Meyer: The Fusionist as Libertarian Manqué," in Carey, *Freedom and Virtue,* 152–53.

97. Rothbard, *Ethics of Liberty,* 21.

98. Ibid., 24, 100; Pearce, "Libertarianism Ancient and Modern," 73–94.

99. Rothbard, "Frank Meyer," 141; Rothbard, "Negro Revolution," 29–37; Rothbard, *Ethics of Liberty,* 22; Raimondo, *Enemy of the State;* Doherty, *Radicals for Capitalism;* Gordon, *Essential Rothbard;* Veyser, "Murray Rothbard: In Memoriam," 41–45. See also Kantor, "Murray Rothbard's Copperhead Abolitionism."

100. Rothbard, *Betrayal of the American Right,* 173; Raimondo, *Enemy of the State,* 103–4.

101. Rothbard, *Betrayal of the American Right,* 173.

102. Rothbard, quoted in Raimondo, *Enemy of the State,* 104.

103. Murray N. Rothbard, "Slavery and War," www.lewrockwell.com/rothbard/rothbard 175.html (accessed 8/21/10). According to the website, Rothbard wrote this in "a 30,000-word memo to the Volker Fund" in 1961.

104. Rothbard, *Betrayal of the American Right,* 174.

105. Payne, "Rothbard's Time on the Left," 9–10; DiLorenzo, *Lincoln Unmasked,* 151.

106. Rothbard, *For a New Liberty,* 338; Rothbard, quoted in Kantor, "Murray Rothbard's Copperhead Abolitionism," 7. Rothbard's interpretation here parallels Eric Foner's analysis in *Reconstruction.*

107. Raimondo, *Enemy of the State,* 178–79; Lamberton, "Abraham Lincoln," 2.

108. Stromberg, "War for Southern Independence," 31–53; Pressly, "Emancipating Slaves, Enslaving Free Men," 254–65.

109. Stromberg, "War for Southern Independence," 31.

110. Ibid., 34–35.

111. Ibid.

112. Ibid., 36.

113. Pamphlet, *About the Ludwig von Mises Institute,* 1; Raimondo, *Enemy of the State,* 259–60. See also Mises.org.

114. *About the Ludwig von Mises Institute,* 2; Zengerle, "Paleo Wacko," 5–6. Zengerle labeled the Mises Institute "Paleolibertarianism's intellectual hub." Doherty, *Radicals for Capitalism,* 607–8.

115. Nash, *Conservative Intellectual Movement,* 345–50.

116. Buckley and Bozell, *McCarthy and His Enemies,* 304; Buckley, *Up from Liberalism,* 191. Buckley's title *Up from Liberalism* is a play on Booker T. Washington's *Up from Slavery.* This gives the reader a clue about Buckley's attitude toward the relative status of conservatism and liberalism in late-1950s America. Judis, *William F. Buckley, Jr.,* 167.

117. Bogus, *Buckley,* 273.

118. Blight, *American Oracle,* 237–40.

119. Buckley, *Unmaking of a Mayor,* 84–90.

120. Ibid., 85.

121. Ibid.

122. Ibid.

123. Ibid., 86.

124. Ibid.

125. Ibid.

126. Ibid.

127. Ibid.

128. Ibid.

129. Ibid.

130. Ibid., 87–88.

131. Ibid., 89.

132. Bogus, *Buckley,* 173; Hogeland, *Inventing American History,* 82–83; Robin, *Reactionary Mind,* 27.

133. Wilson, "Lost Causes Regained," 1–16. Bradford also ensured that Weaver's book, *The Southern Tradition at Bay,* was posthumously published in 1968.

134. Bradford, *Reactionary Imperative,* viii; Bailey, "M. E. Bradford," 291–313.

135. Bradford, "Lincoln's New Frontier," pt. 1, 11–13, 15–17.

136. Ibid., 12.

137. Ibid.

138. Ibid.

139. Bradford, "Lincoln's New Frontier," pt. 2, 15–17.

140. Ibid., 16. Bradford's language here reflects the influence of the conservative political philosopher Eric Voegelin, who wrote Bradford in 1970 that in his view Lincoln's "of, by, and for formula is even more a millenarian blasphemy than becomes apparent in your analysis. [Lincoln] transposed a cosmological formula into a millenarian formula for politi-

cal action." This letter is quoted by Bradford in his May 1971 piece on Lincoln at the bottom of page 13.

141. Ibid., 17.

142. Ibid.

143. Bradford, "Heresy of Equality," 62–77; Jaffa, "Equality as a Conservative Principle," reprinted in *How to Think about the American Revolution,* 13–48.

144. Ibid., 18.

145. Ibid., 24–25.

146. Ibid., 31.

147. Ibid., 36.

148. Ibid., 43.

149. Bradford, "Heresy of Equality," 62–77.

150. Ibid., 64.

151. Ibid., 66.

152. Ibid.

153. Bradford, "Dividing the House," 10–24.

154. Bradford, "Heresy of Equality," 77.

155. Bailey, "M. E. Bradford," 292–93.

156. Jaffa, "Equality, Justice, and the American Revolution: In Reply to Bradford's 'Heresy of Equality,'" reprinted in *How to Think about the American Revolution,* 140–61.

157. Ibid.

158. Ibid.

159. Ibid.

160. Ibid.

161. Irvin Molotsky, "Texan Set to Get Endowment Post," *New York Times,* September 20, 1981.

162. *New York Times,* September 24, 1981; Bailey, "M. E. Bradford," 296–300. For Jaffa's support of Bradford, see Bridges and Coyne, *Strictly Right,* 253.

163. *New York Times,* September 20 and 24, 1981; Allitt, *Conservatives,* 203–14.

164. George F. Will, "A Shrill Assault on Mr. Lincoln," *Washington Post,* November 29, 1981.

165. Ibid.

166. Ibid.

167. *New York Times,* December 27, 1981.

168. Bradford, "It's George Will Who's Being Shrill," A13.

169. Foner, "Lincoln, Bradford, and the Conservatives."

170. Ibid.

171. Benjamin B. Alexander, "The Man of Letters and the Faithful Heart," in Wilson, *Defender of Southern Conservatism,* 31.

172. *Washington Post,* October 19, 1995, D01; Francis, *Beautiful Losers,* 14.

173. Paul Gottfried, quoted in Larry Witham, "Southern Scholar M. E. Bradford Dies" (obituary), *Washington Times,* March 4, 1993; Gottfried, *Conservatism in America,* 66–67.

174. It might also be added that Reagan genuinely admired Lincoln. See some of his comments about Lincoln at the American Presidency Project's website, www.presidency.ucsb.edu/ws/index.php#axzz1Q8D2UDsj (accessed 6/24/11).

175. Jeffrey Hart, "M. E. Bradford, R.I.P.," *National Review,* March 29, 1993, 19–20.

176. M. E. Bradford, "Against Lincoln: An Address at Gettysburg, Commentary on 'Lincoln and the Economics of the American Dream,'" in Boritt, *Historians Lincoln,* 113. This was a conference on Abraham Lincoln hosted at Gettysburg College at which Bradford was invited to speak. That Bradford was invited to address such a gathering at all is evidence that the so-called Lincoln cult that Lincoln's critics continually deride is a convenient myth.

177. Jaffa, with a reply by Bradford, "Bradford and Jaffa: Once More on Lincoln," 22–27; Rable, *Confederate Republic,* 52.

178. Larry Witham, "Southern Scholar M. E. Bradford Dies," *Washington Times,* March 4, 1993.

179. Hart, "M. E. Bradford, RIP," 19–20.

180. Jaffa, "In Abraham's Bosom," 50–51.

181. Edward H. Sebesta and Euan Hague, "The U.S. Civil War as a Theological War," in Hague, Beirich, and Sebesta, *Neo-Confederacy,* 51; Bailey, "M. E. Bradford," 299.

182. Trent Lott, quoted in Critchlow and MacLean, *Debating the American Conservative Movement,* 202.

183. Rothbard, *Betrayal of the American Right;* Schwartz, *Abraham Lincoln in the Post-Heroic Era,* 147–218.

184. Fleming, "Lincoln's Tragic Heroism," 38–40; Jaffa, "Lincoln's Character Assassins," 34–38; Bradford, "From the Family of the Lion," 30–31.

185. Allen C. Guelzo, "Our Lincoln: Obama, He Was Not," *National Review,* February 23, 2009, 25–28.

186. Weaver, *Southern Tradition at Bay,* 378.

187. Korngold, *Two Friends of Man.*

188. Riddle, *Congressman Abraham Lincoln,* 249; Boritt, *Lincoln and the Economics of the American Dream,* 298.

189. Lynn, "Right to Secede from History," 21–24; Blight, *American Oracle,* 129–81.

190. Scialabba, "Great Deal of Work."

191. Fehrenbacher, *Lincoln in Text and Context,* 220–21; Peterson, *Lincoln in American Memory,* 382–83. See also Neely, "Lincoln's Lyceum Speech."

192. Wilson, *Patriotic Gore,* ix.

193. Ibid., xi.

194. Ibid., xii.

195. Cook, *Troubled Commemoration,* 11.

196. Wilson, *Patriotic Gore,* 380–437; Blight, *American Oracle,* 165.

197. Wilson, *Patriotic Gore,* xvi.

198. Ibid.

199. Ibid., xvii–xix.

200. Cook, *Troubled Commemoration.*

201. Ibid., 99.

202. Ibid.

203. Ibid., 106.

204. Basler, Dunlap, and Pratt, *Collected Works of Abraham Lincoln,* 1:109.

205. Ibid., 114.

206. Wilson, *Patriotic Gore,* 108.

207. Ibid., 115.

208. Ibid.

209. Ibid., 117–23.

210. Ibid., 123–30.

211. Commager, "Myths, Morals and a House Divided," 309.

212. Howe, "Edmund Wilson and the Sea Slugs," 70–74.

213. Ibid., 72.

214. Ibid., 73.

215. Ibid., 74; Blight, *American Oracle,* 167–68.

216. Fehrenbacher, *Lincoln in Text and Context,* 214–27.

217. Anderson, *Quest for Immortality,* 61; Neely, "Lincoln's Lyceum Speech," 3.

218. Fehrenbacher, *Lincoln in Text and Context,* 222–23.

219. Ibid.

220. Wilson, *Patriotic Gore,* 435; Warren, "Edmund Wilson's Civil War," 151–58. Warren believed Wilson's term *unreconstructed Southerner* was "one of his devices of shock." Blight, *American Oracle,* 168; Fehrenbacher, *Lincoln in Text and Context,* 223.

221. Malcolm X, quoted in Fehrenbacher, *Lincoln in Text and Context,* 100.

222. Duberman, *Antislavery Vanguard.*

223. Interview of Lerone Bennett Jr. by Brian Lamb, C-SPAN, *Booknotes,* September 10, 2000, transcript at www.booknotes.org/Watch/158187-1/Lerone+Bennett.aspx (accessed 11/19/08).

224. Ibid.

225. Bennett, *What Manner of Man.* See the preface and introduction for Bennett's biographical details.

226. Cook, *Troubled Commemoration,* 168–69.

227. Lerone Bennett Jr., "Was Abe Lincoln a White Supremacist?" in Holzer, *Lincoln Anthology,* 738–39.

228. Ibid., 749.

229. Ibid., 750.

230. Ibid., 751.

231. Ibid., 752.

232. Mitgang, "Was Lincoln Just a Honkie?"

233. Lerone Bennett Jr., "In Search of the Real Lincoln," letter to the editor, *New York Times,* March 3, 1968.

234. "The Man Lincoln," *New York Amsterdam News,* February 10, 1968, 16.

235. "A New Lincoln," *Pittsburgh Courier,* February 17, 1968, 6.

236. Horne, "Toward a Transnational Research Agenda for African American History," 288–303, esp. 293.

237. Ibid., 293; Hogan, *Lincoln, Inc.,* 154.

238. Williams, *Tragedy of American Diplomacy.*

239. Williams, *America Confronts a Revolutionary World,* 89.

240. Ibid., 90.

241. Ibid., 91.

242. Ibid., 111.

243. Ibid., 112.

244. Ibid., 113.

245. Ibid., 119, 121.

246. Ibid., 174.

247. Williams, *Empire as a Way of Life,* 91.

248. Stromberg, "William Appleman Williams"; Payne, "Rothbard's Time on the Left."

249. Gore Vidal, "First Note on Abraham Lincoln," in Vidal, *United States,* 668. This essay by Vidal first appeared in the *Los Angeles Times,* February 8, 1981.

250. Ibid.; Vidal, "First Note on Abraham Lincoln," 672.

251. Bloom, "Central Man"; Riggenbach, *Why American History Is Not What They Say It Is,* 54–58.

252. Basler, Dunlap, and Pratt, *Collected Works of Abraham Lincoln,* 2:276.

253. Oakes, "War of Northern Aggression," 45–47.

254. Current, "Fiction as History," 82.

255. Neely, "Lincoln Gored by Television," 1–4.

256. Bloom, "Central Man."

257. Fielding, "Honest, Yes, but No Pushover," 32; Lehmann-Haupt, "Review of *Lincoln: A Novel,*" C20. The reviewer for the *Washington Post Book World,* Shelby Coffey III, took a contrary view when he opened his piece asking, "Can Abraham Lincoln really have been such a monster?" Nevertheless, Coffey thought Vidal's book was "entertaining." Coffey, "Gore Vidal's Lincoln Log," 1.

258. Current, "Fiction as History: A Review Essay," 77–90.

259. Neely, "Lincoln Gored by Television," 3–4.

260. Herbert Mitgang, quoted in Vidal, *United States,* 683.

261. Vidal, *United States,* 683.

262. Ibid., 674. See also "Gore Vidal—Surrealism and Patriotism: The Education of an American Novelist," *New Left Review* 149 (January–February 1985): 95–107.

263. Josephine Powell Beaty to David Rankin Barbee, July 17, 1947, box 14, folder 727, David Rankin Barbee Papers, Joseph Mark Lauinger Memorial Library, Special Collections Division, Georgetown University, Washington, D.C.

264. Horton, *Race and the Making of American Liberalism,* 180.

265. Schwartz, *Abraham Lincoln in the Post-Heroic Era,* 254–68; Schwartz, "Limits of Gratitude," 27–31.

6. A LITMUS TEST FOR AMERICAN CONSERVATISM: THE GREAT
CENTRALIZER, 1989–2012

1. Brag Bolling, quoted in Steve Clark, "Yes, Lincoln; Yes, Here," *Richmond Times-Dispatch,* December 26, 2002.

2. Shear and Whoriskey, "Lincoln Statue Heightens Old Pains."

3. Jeremy Redmon and Lindsay Kastner, "Lincoln Returns," *Richmond Times-Dispatch,* April 6, 2003.

4. The term *passionate outsiders* is John Stauffer's description of abolitionists and is quoted in Stewart, "Reconsidering the Abolitionists in an Age of Fundamentalist Politics," 10; Hague, Beirich, and Sebesta, *Neo-Confederacy,* 8.

5. Willis, "What's the Matter with Tom Frank," 10; Sebesta, "Overview of the Neo-Confederate Movement," 1–25.

6. The words are Rothbard's. See Rothbard, "Strategy for the Right," http://mises.org/daily/3931 (accessed 5/20/10).

7. Rockwell, "Case for Paleo-Libertarianism," 34–37.

8. Rockwell, *Irrepressible Rothbard,* xiv.

9. Hague, Beirich, and Sebesta, *Neo-Confederacy,* 8. On the decline in Lincoln's reputation, see Schwartz, *Abraham Lincoln in the Post-Heroic Era.*

10. Critchlow and MacLean, *Debating the American Conservative Movement,* 170. I am indebted to Timothy Sandefur for the phrase *morally dubious.*

11. Bennett, *Forced into Glory,* 42.

12. Murray N. Rothbard, "The Nationalities Question," *Rothbard-Rockwell Report* (August 1990), http://mises.org/daily/2437 (accessed 9/17/09); Rothbard, "Just War" (based on talk given in 1994), LewRockwell.com, www.lewrockwell.com/rothbard/rothbard20.html (accessed 9/17/09); Gordon, *Secession, State, and Liberty.*

13. Rothbard, "Nationalities Question," 1.

14. Ibid., 4.

15. Rothbard, "Just War"; Denson, *Costs of War,* 119–33. Rothbard's speech was included here under the title "America's Two Just Wars: 1775 and 1861."

16. Rothbard, "Just War," 1.

17. Ibid.

18. Ibid., 6.

19. Ibid.

20. Ibid., 9–10. The phrase *humanitarian with the guillotine* comes from an important early-twentieth-century libertarian writer, Isabel Paterson. www.lewrockwell.com/mcelroy/mcelroy66.html (accessed 9/1/10).

21. Rothbard, "Slavery and War," www.lewrockwell.com/rothbard/rothbard175.html (accessed 8/21/10).

22. Livingston, "Secession and the Modern State," December 1996, www.lrainc.com/swtaboo/taboos/dwliv01.html (accessed 9/9/09).

23. Rockwell, *Irrepressible Rothbard,* 40; Zengerle, "Paleo Wacko," 6.

24. Kantor, "Murray N. Rothbard's Copperhead Abolitionism," http://mises.org/pdf//asc/2002/asc8-kantor.pdf (accessed 5/26/10), 8.

25. Beirich and Potok, "The Ideologues," www.splcenter.org/get-informed/intelligence-report/browse-all-issues/2004/winter/the-ideologues?page=0,0 (accessed 6/2/12).

26. Hill and Fleming, "New Dixie Manifesto."

27. Ibid.

28. Ibid.

29. Michael Hill, quoted in Horwitz, *Confederates in the Attic,* 112–13; Horton, *Youth's History of the Great Civil War in the United States [War between the States] from 1861–1865.* Horton claimed that the Civil War was a "revolution from a White Man's government to that of a mongrel nation, in which negroes should have the same rights as white people." Horton, quoted in Loewen and Sebesta, *Confederate and Neo-Confederate Reader,* 246.

30. Southern Poverty Law Center, *Intelligence Report,* no. 99 (Summer 2000), www.splcenter.org/get-informed/intelligence-report/browse-all-issues/2000/summer (accessed 10/13/09); Hill, quoted in Southern Poverty Law Center, Intelligence Files, "League of the South," www.splcenter.org/get-informed/intelligence-files/groups/league-of-the-south (accessed 8/11/11). Donald Livingston quit the league because of Hill's comments.

31. Hague, Beirich, and Sebesta, *Neo-Confederacy,* 2.

32. Goldfield, *Still Fighting the Civil War,* 302; Hague, Beirich, and Sebesta, *Neo-Confederacy,* 7.

33. Trent Lott, quoted in Critchlow and MacLean, *Debating the American Conservative Movement,* 202.

34. Hague, Beirich, and Sebesta, *Neo-Confederacy,* 313; Rockwell, *Irrepressible Rothbard,* xiv; Terris, "Scholars of the Old South," December 6, 2009, http://chronicle.com/article/Secretive-Scholars-of-the-Old/49337/ (accessed 6/28/10).

35. Ibid.; www.abbevilleinstitute.org/index.php/2012-04-15-09-16-38 (accessed 4/24/13).

36. Davis and Wilson, *Lincoln-Douglas Debates,* 32; Basler, Dunlap, and Pratt, *Collected Works of Abraham Lincoln,* 2:385, emphasis mine; Rothbard, "Strategy for the Right."

37. For more on Thomas Fleming's background, see Murphy, *Rebuke of History,* 224–27.

38. Thomas Fleming to John Barr, fund-raising letter, Rockford Institute, Spring 2013. Copy in possession of author. See also www.chroniclesmagazine.org for more information.

39. *Chronicles,* 33.2 (February 2009); Allitt, *Conservatives,* 248–49.

40. Fleming, "From White House to Blockhouse," 10–12. Neely, in "Emancipation Proclamation as an Act of Foreign Policy," 1–4, disputed the claim that Lincoln issued the proclamation for anything other than domestic and military considerations.

41. Buchanan, "Mr. Lincoln's War," 13–22.

42. Rockwell, "Down with the Presidency," 27–32. See also Healy, "Cult of the Presidency."

43. Ibid., 29. See also Rothbard, "Generalissimo Washington."

44. Ibid.

45. Ibid., 30.

46. Sanchez and Weigel, "Who Wrote Ron Paul's Newsletters?"; Kirchik, "Angry White Man"; Paul, *Liberty Defined,* 328. For Ron Paul's newsletters, see *New Republic* website, see www.tnr.com/article/politics/ron-paul-newsletter (accessed 1/3/12).

47. "King Lincoln" archive, www.lewrockwell.com (accessed 8/21/10).

48. Sanchez and Weigel, "Who Wrote Ron Paul's Newsletters?" Kentucky senator Rand Paul (R), Ron Paul's son, has said he remembers riding in the car with Rockwell and his father and heard them discuss various intellectual topics. See Zengerle, "Paleo Wacko," for Rand Paul's account.

49. Rothbard, "Strategy for the Right."

50. Ibid.

51. Ibid. See also the introduction by Hans-Hermann Hoppe to Rothbard, *Ethics of Liberty,* xxxix; Sebesta, "Overview of the Neo-Confederate Movement," 4–12.

52. Moser, "Conflicts Arise over Lincoln Statue in Richmond, Va., Cemetery"; see www.thesmokinggun.com/mugshots/celebrity/killers/timothy-mcveigh, for McVeigh's mug shot; Loewen and Sebesta, *Confederate and Neo-Confederate Reader,* 370.

53. Loewen and Sebesta, *Confederate and Neo-Confederate Reader,* 366.

54. Richard Quinn, quoted in "McAllister and Quinn Endorse Gingrich"; "Hesiod," "McCain Campaign Paid $50,000 to a White Supremacist."

55. "McAllister and Quinn Endorse Gingrich"; Conason, "Joe Wilson's Confederate Cronies"; Loewen and Sebesta, *Confederate and Neo-Confederate Reader,* 366.

56. Blumenthal, "Lobbyist for the Lost Cause."

57. "Scalawag Award," *Southern Partisan* 12 (3d quarter 1992): 9.

58. Blumenthal, "Lobbyist for the Lost Cause."

59. Hague, Beirich, and Sebesta, *Neo-Confederacy,* 37–48, 312.

60. Letter to the editor, *Southern Partisan* 14, no. 4 (July–August 2004), but published July 2005, 5; Richard M. Palmer, letter to the editor, *Southern Partisan* 14 (2d quarter 1994): 4.

61. "Partisan Letters," *Southern Partisan* 19 (3d quarter 1999): 10–11.

62. Letter to the editor, *Southern Partisan* 13 (2d quarter 1993): 4.

63. Ibid.

64. Blumenthal, "Lobbyist for the Lost Cause"; Beirich, "Infighting at Sons of Confederate Veterans." According to Beirich, because of the SCV's drift into racial extremism, membership declined from 30,000 to 18,500 between 2006 and 2007. See also the organization's website, SCV.org.

65. Southern Poverty Law Center, "John Weaver," profile, www.splcenter.org/get-informed/intelligence-files/profiles/john-weaver (accessed 6/2/12).

66. John Weaver, "Chaplain's Comments," 61.

67. Kidd, "Richmond Air Corps," *Confederate Veteran* 51 (July–August, 2003): 56. This magazine is not the same one published by the United Daughters of the Confederacy (UDC) between the 1890s and the 1930s. The Sons of Confederate Veterans (SCV) began publication of this magazine in the 1980s and made its issue numbers follow those from the earlier volumes published by the UDC. Also, the volume and dating system of the *Confederate Veteran* has been inconsistent. From the mid-1990s to the early part of the twenty-first century each issue of the magazine would be given a different volume number. Later the SCV dropped this system and went back to calculating from the original *Confederate Veteran*. So, despite the volume number cited here, there are not fifty-one volumes of the *Confederate Veteran* published by the Sons of Confederate Veterans.

68. *Confederate Veteran* 1 (2001): 28; *Confederate Veteran* 51, no. 6 (November–December 2003): 62; *Confederate Veteran* 62, no. 2 (March–April 2004): 70.

69. David Blight, "The Theft of Lincoln in Scholarship, Politics and Public Memory," in Foner, *Our Lincoln,* 276.

70. Larry Salley, quoted in Blumenthal, "Lobbyist of the Lost Cause."

71. Peter Applebome, quoted in Hague, Beirich, and Sebesta, *Neo-Confederacy,* 4.

72. Bennett, *Forced into Glory.*

73. Ibid., preface.

74. Ibid., 42.

75. I heard historian Gerard J. Prokopowicz make this point, or one very close to it, in a talk given in Richmond, Va., in 2009.

76. Bennett, *Forced into Glory,* 84; see 123–27 for more of Bennett's criticism of historians.

77. Ibid., 13.

78. Basler, Dunlap, and Pratt, *Collected Works of Abraham Lincoln,* 7:269.

79. See the end of chapter 3 and the beginning of chapter 4 for a more detailed analysis.

80. Ibid., 44.

81. Hook, *Hero in History,* 154.

82. Bennett, *Forced into Glory,* 43.

83. Ibid., 51. For more on Bennett's view of Lincoln's racism, see 197.

84. Ibid., 67.

85. Ibid., 76.

86. Ibid., 131–37, 481–82.

87. Ibid., 115.

88. Ibid., 342.

89. Ibid., 406.

90. Ibid., 343.

91. Ibid., 25.

92. Ibid., 136.

93. Ibid., 137.

94. Foner, *Fiery Trial;* Oakes, *Freedom National.*

95. Lincoln, in addition to publicly suggesting limited suffrage for African Americans in April 1865, had a year earlier privately suggested the same to Governor Michael Hahn of Louisiana. See Donald, *Lincoln,* 487–88, for this account. One wonders why, if Abraham Lincoln wanted to cleanse the United States of all African Americans, would he be pondering, in both private and public, limited suffrage?

96. Abraham Lincoln, quoted in Bennett, *Forced into Glory,* 617.

97. Ibid.

98. Abraham Lincoln, quoted ibid., 618. In the next paragraph Bennett stated that "if the franchise had been confined to 'very intelligent Whites' this nation [the United States] would have perished from the earth long ago."

99. Ibid., 624.

100. Ibid., 625.

101. Prokopowicz, "Rethinking Lincoln," 2–3.

102. Lind, *What Lincoln Believed,* 15.

103. Foner, review of *Forced into Glory.*

104. Ibid.

105. McPherson, "Lincoln the Devil."

106. Ibid.

107. Ibid.

108. Bennett, *Forced into Glory,* 229; Neely, "Abraham Lincoln and Black Colonization," 77–83.

109. Bennett, *Forced into Glory,* 616; Neely, "Abraham Lincoln and Black Colonization," 77–83.

110. Bennett, *Forced into Glory,* 616–17.

111. Gopnik, *Angels and Ages,* 49.

112. Magness, "Benjamin Butler's Colonization Testimony Reevaluated," 1–28; Magness and Page, *Colonization after Emancipation;* Eric Foner, "Lincoln and Colonization," in *Our Lincoln,* 135–66. For a nuanced view on the subject of Lincoln's racism, see James Oakes, "Natural Rights, Citizenship Rights, States' Rights, and Black Rights: Another Look at Lincoln and Race," in Foner, *Our Lincoln,* 109–34.

113. Magness, "Benjamin Butler's Colonization Testimony," 28.

114. Bennett spoke quite critically of Lincoln at the Sixth Annual Lincoln Forum in Gettysburg, Pa., on November 17, 2001. I was in attendance at this speech, and it is my recollection that although members of the forum were not pleased with the substance of Bennett's speech and the historians in attendance challenged his ideas, he was given a respectful—some people thought too respectful given the charges he leveled against Lincoln—hearing that day. That Bennett spoke at the Lincoln Forum at all, as did M. E. Bradford at a different conference on

Lincoln in the 1980s, also held in Gettysburg, demonstrated that the charge of a Lincoln cult is at the very least suspect. Cults do not invite critics to their meetings; scholars, however, do. Bennett's remarks to the Lincoln Forum at Gettysburg were excerpted in *Forced into Glory,* 627–35. See also Guelzo, Review of Magness and Page, *Colonization after Emancipation,* 78–87.

115. Davis and Wilson, *Lincoln-Douglas Debates,* 11–12.

116. Burlingame, *Abraham Lincoln,* 1:525.

117. Hook, "Lincoln and Gandhi," n.d., Sidney Hook Collection, box 34, folder 35, Hoover Institution on War, Revolution and Peace, Stanford University, emphasis mine.

118. Gerald Horne, letter to the editor, *Journal of American History* 96, no. 3 (December 2009); Guelzo, "How Abe Lincoln Lost the Black Vote," 19.

119. Ibid., 21; Guelzo, *Emancipation Proclamation,* 5–11. For a different view than Guelzo's characterization of Lincoln as an Enlightenment politician, see Winger, *Lincoln, Religion, and Romantic Cultural Politics;* Wilentz, "Who Lincoln Was," 24–47.

120. Basler, Dunlap, and Pratt, *Collected Works of Abraham Lincoln,* 4:240.

121. Sowell, "Trashing Our History: Lincoln."

122. Ibid.

123. Ibid.

124. Ibid.

125. Ibid.

126. Ibid.

127. Obama, "What I See in Lincoln's Eyes," 74.

128. Ibid.; Guelzo, "Hardly," 22.

129. Barack Obama, "Remarks at the Abraham Lincoln Association Annual Banquet," Springfield, Ill., February 12, 2009, American Presidency Project, www.presidency.ucsb.edu/ws/index.php?pid=85778&st=Abraham+Lincoln&st1=#axzz1QnUAbIUe (accessed 7/1/11).

130. Maass, "Lincoln at 200"; Blackburn, "Lincoln and Marx," 48–51. *Counterpunch* is a website with a radical leftist orientation, while Robin Blackburn edited the *New Left Review,* and his piece connecting Lincoln and Marx was published in *Jacobin* magazine, a left-wing quarterly. See also Blackburn, *Unfinished Revolution,* 1–100. Or consider Corey Robin's assessment of Lincoln's status on the left. Robin is a left-wing political theorist and author of *The Reactionary Mind,* a critical analysis of conservative thought: "My sense is that he's [Lincoln] fairly widely respected on the left. I know there's Lerone Bennett's work which probably influenced a subset of black nationalist thinkers and activists, and still does to some degree. But I think the dominant position is ambivalently positive, acknowledging his limitations but aware of his achievements. [Eric] Foner's book sort of stands in for the mainstream view of the left, I think." Corey Robin, e-mail message to author, October 6, 2011; Foner, *Fiery Trial.*

131. Gallagher, *Causes Won, Lost, and Forgotten,* 104.

132. Schwartz, *Abraham Lincoln in the Post-Heroic Era.*

133. DiLorenzo, "African-American Icon Speaks Truth to the Lincoln Cult."

134. Livingston, "Litmus Test for American Conservatism,"17.

135. Livingston, "Moral Accounting"; Terris, "Scholars of the Old South."

136. Livingston, "Moral Accounting," 1. There are many other paleolibertarian writings, of course, sharply critical of Lincoln. See Gordon, *Secession, State, and Liberty.* Others would include Denson, *Costs of War;* Cisco, *War Crimes against Southern Civilians;* Emison, *Lincoln Über Alles.* I am focusing here on the books that Livingston mentioned in the 2002 forum or the works of influential public figures as particularly worthy of study. Graham's book, as well

as Cisco's and Emison's, are all published by Pelican Publishing Company. For an interesting article on the publisher of this company, reportedly an advocate of secession named Dr. Milburn Calhoun, see Adler, "House That Dr. Calhoun Built." One of the company's best-selling books is by Kennedy and Kennedy, *The South Was Right!* See also Manber and Dahlstrom, *Lincoln's Wrath,* for a different critique of Lincoln.

137. Hague, Beirich, and Sebesta, *Neo-Confederacy,* 36, 313.

138. DiLorenzo, *Real Lincoln,* 56–59; Hummel, *Emancipating Slaves, Enslaving Freemen,* 359; Rothbard, "Strategy for the Right."

139. DiLorenzo, *Real Lincoln,* 85.

140. Graham, *Constitutional History of Secession,* 51.

141. Ibid., 73–128; Sandefur, "How Libertarians Ought to Think about the Civil War," 61–83.

142. Woods, *Politically Incorrect Guide to American History,* 62–63.

143. Paul, *Liberty Defined,* 262, 268.

144. Pressly, "Emancipating Slaves, Enslaving Free Men," 258–59; Stromberg, "War for Southern Independence," 41.

145. Stromberg, "War for Southern Independence," 41–42.

146. Ibid., 44; DiLorenzo, *Real Lincoln,* 276–78; DiLorenzo, *Lincoln Unmasked,* 52–60.

147. Paul, *Liberty Defined,* 262.

148. Hummel, *Emancipating Slaves, Enslaving Free Men,* 1–128. On page 360 Hummel stated that "my support for this revolutionary right [of secession] is unconditional." Woods, *Politically Incorrect,* 63–64.

149. DiLorenzo, *Real Lincoln,* 13.

150. Alexander Stephens, quoted in Graham, *Constitutional History of Secession,* 297.

151. Abraham Lincoln to Alexander H. Stephens, December 22, 1860, in Basler, Dunlap, and Pratt, *Collected Works of Abraham Lincoln,* 4:160.

152. Ibid., 2:266–67.

153. Graham, *Constitutional History of Secession,* 300–301.

154. See also Adams, *When in the Course of Human Events,* 86. There is no better response to Graham's romantic portrayal of slavery than Abraham Lincoln's: "The ant, who has toiled and dragged a crumb to his nest, will furiously defend the fruit of his labor, against whatever robbers assails him. So plain, that the most dumb and stupid slave that ever toiled for a master, does constantly *know* that he is wronged. So plain that no one, high or low, ever does mistake it, except in a plainly *selfish* way; for although volume upon volume is written to prove slavery a very good thing, we never hear of the man who wishes to take the good of it, *by being a slave himself.*" Basler, Dunlap, and Pratt, *Collected Works of Abraham Lincoln,* 2:222.

155. Ibid.; Livingston wrote an admiring foreword to Graham's volume. See the back of the book for Wilson's positive comments. Woods, *Politically Incorrect,* 55, 57.

156. Williams, "Civil War Wasn't about Slavery."

157. Adams, *When in the Course of Human Events,* 64.

158. Ibid., 63–64.

159. Woods, *Politically Incorrect,* 68.

160. Abraham Lincoln, quoted in Adams, *When in the Course of Human Events,* 27.

161. Basler, Dunlap, and Pratt, *Collected Works of Abraham Lincoln,* 3:487, 4:14; DiLorenzo, *Real Lincoln,* 237.

162. DiLorenzo, *Real Lincoln,* 237.

163. Williams, "Civil War Wasn't about Slavery."

164. Paul, *Liberty Defined,* 270.

165. For a start, see the documents at the American Civil War Homepage, http://sunsite.
utk.edu/civil-war/reasons.html (accessed 6/28/10), for why white southerners said they
seceded from the Union. Foner, *Free Soil, Free Labor, Free Men;* Genovese, *Political Economy
of Slavery;* Roark, *Masters without Slaves;* Oakes, *Ruling Race;* Faust, *Creation of Confederate Nationalism;* Levine, *Half Slave and Half Free;* Walther, *Fire-Eaters;* Cooper, *Liberty and
Slavery;* Dew, *Apostles of Disunion;* Walther, *William Lowndes Yancey and the Coming of the
Civil War;* Oakes, *Freedom National.*

166. Sandefur, "Texas Lincoln Talk"; Sandefur, "Springtime for Jeff Davis and the
Confed'racy," 2; Krannawitter, *Vindicating Lincoln,* 205–61.

167. Huebert, *Libertarianism Today,* 190. Huebert's book is highly touted by people at the
Mises Institute.

168. Paul, *Liberty Defined,* 261.

169. Hummel, *Emancipating Slaves, Enslaving Free Men,* 174.

170. Livingston, "Moral Accounting of the Union and Confederacy," 95. See Grimsley,
Hard Hand of War, 219–25, for a contrary and more nuanced view than Livingston's on the
supposed war crimes of the Union army.

171. Woods, *Politically Incorrect,* 71.

172. Adams, *When in the Course of Human Events,* 111–12; DiLorenzo, *Real Lincoln,* 171–99.

173. Read, "Francis Lieber, Abraham Lincoln, and the American Contribution to International Law."

174. DiLorenzo, *Real Lincoln,* 198, 220.

175. Ibid., 223; Adams, *When in the Course of Human Events,* 120; Clyde N. Wilson, "The
Lincoln War Crimes Trial: A History Lesson," in Wilson, *From Union to Empire,* 201–7. Wilson's counterfactual essay is also posted online in the "King Lincoln" archive at LewRockwell.
com, www.lewrockwell.com/orig2/lincoln-arch.html. For an examination of the charges of
Lincoln as a war criminal, see Carnahan, *Lincoln on Trial;* Graham, *Constitutional History
of Secession,* 303.

176. DiLorenzo, *Real Lincoln,* 174.

177. Ibid., 179–80; McPherson, *Tried by War,* 267.

178. DiLorenzo, *Real Lincoln,* 199.

179. Ibid., 48–49.

180. Ibid., 53.

181. Ibid., x, xiii.

182. Hawkins, "Interview with Ron Paul"; Guelzo, "Abraham Lincoln or the Progressives."
Thanks to Allen Guelzo for unearthing this interview with Congressman Paul.

183. Simply take note of the blurbs on the back of the paperback volume to *The Real Lincoln*
or look at www.lewrockwell.com to get a sense of the importance of this book to Lincoln's
foes.

184. See Hummel, "Review Essay of *The Politically Incorrect Guide to American History,*"
65–86. The quote on Adams and DiLorenzo can be found on page 72.

185. Gamble, review of *The Real Lincoln,* 611–14, emphasis mine; Majewski, "Review of
The Real Lincoln," 60–62; Feller, "Libertarians in the Attic," 184–95. Feller, a well-respected
historian whose political leanings are unknown to this writer, called DiLorenzo's book a
"soapbox tirade."

186. Walsh, "What Is the Least Credible History Book in Print?"

187. DiLorenzo, *Lincoln Unmasked,* 81–84, 149–55. Another example of the sloppy scholarship Gamble and Hummel lament can be found in Graham's book. He implied at the end of the volume that Secretary of War Edwin M. Stanton was complicit in Lincoln's assassination; see Graham, *Constitutional History of Secession,* 380–81. Listed in his bibliography is the work that perpetuated this calumny on Stanton, by David Balsiger and Charles Sellier, *The Lincoln Conspiracy* (Los Angeles: Schick Sunn Classic Books, 1977). The book was later made into a film. William Hanchett demolished the claims of Balsiger and Sellier in *The Lincoln Murder Conspiracies.* Hanchett's book, unfortunately but not unsurprisingly, was not listed in Graham's bibliography. Neither are two other classic works on the assassination, Turner, *Beware the People Weeping,* and Steers, *Blood on the Moon.*

188. Napolitano, "Presidency and Mythology." See the video of Judge Napolitano calling Lincoln tyrannical, to Ralph Nader, at SkepticalEye.com, www.skepticaleye.com/2011/02/judge-andrew-napolitano-abraham-lincoln.html; Napolitano, *Constitution in Exile,* 61–76.

189. Napolitano, *Constitution in Exile,* 61–76.

190. Welch, "More Details on the Increasingly Bitter Koch/Cato Lawsuit and Feud"; "Judge Napolitano Resigns from the Cato Board." Lew Rockwell wondered: "Could it be because of the neocon-like warmongering and Republican establishment politics? Or that all board members and top execs are personally liable under DC law if the shenanigans, on which the kibosh has definitely not been put, continue?"

191. Rothbard, *For a New Liberty,* 27. Rothbard called this the "nonaggression axiom."

192. Sandefur, "How Libertarians Ought to Think about the U.S. Civil War," 28, http://papers.ssrn.com/sol3/papers.cfm?abstract_id=933676 (accessed 5/17/12).

193. Ludwig von Mises, quoted in Jones, *Masters of the Universe,* 56.

194. On this point, see DiLorenzo, *Real Lincoln,* 294–98.

195. Basler, Dunlap, and Pratt, *Collected Works of Abraham Lincoln,* 2:404.

196. Ibid., 3:375.

197. Ibid., 2:276.

198. Wilson, "Treasury of Counterfeit Virtue," 14–15.

199. Blight, *Race and Reunion.*

200. Sandefur, "Liberty and Union, Now and Forever," 33–39, 54; Sandefur, "How Libertarians Ought to Think about the U.S. Civil War," 61–83.

201. Sandefur, "Liberty and Union, Now and Forever."

202. Ibid.

203. Machan, "Lincoln, Secession, and Slavery." See DiLorenzo's response to Machan in DiLorenzo, *Real Lincoln,* 298–300.

204. Sandefur, "How Libertarians Ought to Think about the U.S. Civil War," 66, 74, 79.

205. Timothy Sandefur, "Liberty and Union—and Their Critics." MS in possession of author.

206. Napolitano, *Constitution in Exile,* 62.

207. Thomas, *Confederate Nation,* 63; Current, *Lincoln's Loyalists.*

208. Krannawitter, *Vindicating Lincoln,* 198.

209. Farber, *Lincoln's Constitution,* 44, 92–114; Sandefur, "How Libertarians Ought to Think about the U.S. Civil War," 61–83. See also Sandefur, "Liberty and Union, Now and Forever," 33–39.

210. Sandefur, "Liberty and Union—and Their Critics," 2; U.S. Constitution, quoted in Amar, *America's Constitution,* 489, emphasis mine.

211. Krannawitter, "Dishonest about Abe."

212. DiLorenzo, *Real Lincoln,* 287.

213. Krannawitter, *Vindicating Lincoln,* 5.

214. Ibid., 9.

215. Claremont.org.

216. Ibid.

217. Elias, "John Yoo." For the Lincoln Bicentennial Issue, see *Claremont Review of Books* 9 (Winter 2008–9), 48–69. For the conference schedule, see *Chapman Law Review 2009 Symposium,* www.chapman.edu/law/publications/chapman-law-review/annual-symposium/2009-symposium.aspx (accessed 5/21/12). Although videos of the conference are available online, Harry Jaffa's address keynote address is not.

218. Sunstein, "Constitutionalism and Secession," 634; Buchanan, *Secession;* Buchanan, "Toward a Theory of Secession," 322–42; Buchanan "Theories of Secession," 31–61; Patten, "Democratic Secession from a Multinational State," 558–86. It is not clear if Graham had access to Patten's work, but Buchanan's book and essays, as well as Sunstein's, were most certainly available for his perusal, and their arguments are not even addressed in his work, nor are they cited in his brief bibliography. Nor does Graham cite the work of Livingston, *Philosophical Melancholy and Delirium,* 358–82, in which Livingston, a noted philosopher of David Hume, defended secession. For a more nuanced and detailed view of the secessionist viewpoint, see Livingston's book on Hume and Gordon, *Secession, State, and Liberty.* This work, incidentally, was dedicated "to the Memory of Those Who Gave Their Lives That Others Might Be Free."

219. Sandefur, "How Libertarians Ought to Think about the U.S. Civil War," 81.

220. Noll, *God and Race in American Politics,* 92–93; Adams, *When in the Course of Human Events,* 149–65; DiLorenzo, *Real Lincoln,* 200–232; Woods, *Politically Incorrect,* 92.

221. Sandefur, "How Libertarians Ought to Think about the U.S. Civil War," 81–82; Horton, *Race and the Making of American Liberalism,* 3–119.

222. DiLorenzo, *Real Lincoln,* 297, 295.

223. McNally, "There Are More Slaves Today."

224. Sandefur, "Texas Lincoln Talk."

225. Walther, "Course to Freedom," 28–32.

226. William Lowndes Yancey, quoted ibid., 48–52.

227. Hummel, *Emancipating Slaves, Enslaving Free Men,* 238.

228. Oakes, *Ruling Race,* 231–32; Krannawitter, *Vindicating Lincoln,* 222–23.

229. Krannawitter, *Vindicating Lincoln,* 291–92.

230. Blackmon, *Slavery by Another Name.*

231. Guelzo, "Abraham Lincoln or the Progressives."

232. Basler, Dunlap, and Pratt, *Collected Works of Abraham Lincoln,* 4:16.

233. Oakes, *Ruling Race,* 225–42.

234. DiLorenzo, *Real Lincoln,* 49; Sandefur, "Make Sure the Tables Are Turned the Right Way"; Guelzo, *Lincoln's Emancipation Proclamation,* 21–26.

235. Rothbard, *Ethics of Liberty,* 75; Oakes, *Freedom National.*

236. Rugemer, *Problem of Emancipation;* Davis, *Inhuman Bondage,* 231–49: Oakes, *Freedom National,* 67.

237. *Economist,* quoted in Davis, *Inhuman Bondage,* 231.

238. DiLorenzo, *Real Lincoln,* 52–53.

239. Claremont.org (accessed 5/18/12); Owens, "Abraham Lincoln Saved the Union."

240. Guelzo, *Lincoln's Emancipation Proclamation,* 54–58, 67–69, 92.

241. DiLorenzo, *Real Lincoln,* 49; Paul, *Liberty Defined,* 261–62. Oakes, *Freedom National,* xvi.

242. Basler, Dunlap, and Pratt, *Collected Works of Abraham Lincoln,* 2:265; Guelzo, *Lincoln's Emancipation Proclamation,* 1; Oakes, *Freedom National.*

243. Paul, "Trouble with the '64 Civil Rights Act."

244. DiLorenzo, "Will Ron Paul Destroy the 'Party of Lincoln'?"

245. Wilson, "Treasury of Counterfeit Virtue," 14–15; Moser, "Conflicts Arise over Lincoln Statue in Richmond, Va., Cemetery."

246. David Goldfield, quoted in Moser, "Conflicts Arise over Lincoln Statue in Richmond, Va., Cemetery"; Krugman, *Conscience of a Liberal,* 3–14, 83–100.

247. Haworth, *Anti-Libertarianism;* Boaz, "Up from Slavery."

248. Hoppe, *Democracy,* 70–71; Rothbard, *Egalitarianism as a Revolt against Nature and Other Essays;* Hague, Beirich, and Sebesta, *Neo-Confederacy,* 130.

249. Murray N. Rothbard, quoted in Hoppe, *Democracy,* 212.

250. Chait, "Why Romney Loves the States and Hates the Feds"; Drum, "Soaking the Poor, State by State"; Citizens for Tax Justice, "Who Pays Taxes in America?" The term *involuntary subordination* is philosopher Donald Livingston's.

251. Freeman, "Illiberal Libertarians," 135–36; Woodward, *Strange Career of Jim Crow,* 98–101.

252. Woodson, *Mis-Education of the Negro,* 6–7. I am indebted to the writer Nathan McCall for alerting me to this quote when he spoke at Lone Star College in February 2013.

253. Edward H. Sebesta, quoted in Blumenthal, "Lobbyist of the Lost Cause."

254. Sandefur, "How Libertarians Ought to Think about the Civil War," 83; Krannawitter, *Vindicating Lincoln,* 126.

255. Cato, quoted in Miller, "America's Greatest Play."

256. Grimsley, *Hard Hand of War,* 219–20.

257. Ibid.

258. Francis Lieber, quoted in Witt, *Lincoln's Code,* 235.

259. Ibid., 365.

260. Ibid., 373.

261. Witt's book was published long after the works considered here, and therefore Lincoln's critics could not have taken his volume into account when making their argument. See also Neely, *Civil War and the Limits of Destruction,* 4, 108, and 197; Neely, "Was the Civil War a Total War?" 5–28; Royster, *Destructive War.* For a view contrary to Neely's, see Sutherland, "Lincoln, John Pope, and the Origins of Total War," 567–86; Janda, "Shutting the Gates of Mercy," 7–26; Stout, *Upon the Altar of the Nation;* Wei-Siang Hsieh, "Total War and the American Civil War Reconsidered," 394–408; Rosenberg-Smith, *This Violent Empire.*

262. Stephen A. Douglas, quoted in Ceaser, *Nature and History in American Political Development,* 43, 49.

263. C. L. R. James, "Lincoln, Carnival, George Padmore: Writings from *The Nation,*" in Grimshaw, *C. L. R. James Reader,* 281–82. For more on Lincoln's career-long opposition to expansionism, see Boritt, *Lincoln and the Economics of the American Dream,* 137–42, 259.

264. Basler, Dunlap, and Pratt, *Collected Works of Abraham Lincoln,* 3:95; Richard Carwardine, "Lincoln's Horizons: The Nationalist as Universalist," in Carwardine and Sexton, *Global Lincoln,* 38.

265. Jones, *Abraham Lincoln and a New Birth of Freedom,* 40–41, 56–62, 184–85; Foner, *Fiery Trial,* 314–15.

266. Yoo, *Crisis and Command,* 201.

267. Ibid., 224.

268. Owens, http://ashbrook.org/page/2/?s=Mackubin+Thomas+Owens (accessed 3/28/13).

269. Basler, Dunlap, and Pratt, *Collected Works of Abraham Lincoln,* 6:267.

270. Yoo, *Crisis and Command,* 249.

271. Hummel, *Emancipating Slaves, Enslaving Free Men,* 260; Neely, *Fate of Liberty,* 223–35; I am indebted to Larry Arnhart for this wording in contrasting Lincoln's constitutional prudence with John Yoo. See also Weber, "Was Lincoln a Tyrant?"; Farber, *Lincoln's Constitution.*

272. Thomas Fleming, "Rendering unto Lincoln," *Chronicles* 33 (February 2009): 10.

273. Ibid., 11.

274. Ibid.

275. Ibid.

276. David Goldfield, quoted in Moser, "Reconstructing Lincoln."

277. Schwartz, *Abraham Lincoln in the Post-Heroic Era,* 254–68.

278. Deslatte, "Southern States Low-Key for Lincoln Bicentennial."

279. Hogan, *Lincoln, Inc.,* 72; Schwartz, *Abraham Lincoln in the Post-Heroic Era,* 189–90.

280. Brook, "Unreconstructed," 40–41. For the library's website, see Beauvoir, the Jefferson Davis Home and Presidential Library, http://beauvoir.org/faq/faq.htm (accessed 6/5/12); the website is owned and operated by the Mississippi Division, Sons of Confederate Veterans.

281. Gopnik, *Angels and Ages,* 49.

282. Pew Research Center, "Civil War at 150."

283. CNN.com, "Political Ticker" blog, http://politicalticker.blogs.cnn.com/2011/04/12/civil-war-still-divides-americans/ (accessed 3/28/13); Blow, "Escaping Slavery."

284. "Civil War at 150."

285. See the video of Ron Paul explaining the Civil War while standing in front of a Confederate flag at www.youtube.com/watch?v=B85TJJyKyKw (accessed 6/6/12).

286. Avlon, "Return of the Confederacy"; www.ronpaul.com/congress/hearings/ (accessed 8/27/11).

287. Paul, *Liberty Defined,* 272.

288. Doherty, *Ron Paul's Revolution,* 153.

289. Mises.org; LewRockwell.com.

290. McKinley, "Texas Governor's Secession Talk Sparks Furor"; Sturdevant, "Secession Gaining Fans in MN GOP," www.startribune.com/opinion/90659669.html (accessed 5/25/12). Many thanks to Edward H. Sebesta for the information on nullification and secession resolutions. The information comes from a background document for a survey Sebesta sent to all 2012 presidential candidates. Edward H. Sebesta, e-mail message to author, May 9, 2012, 2. See also http://arlingtonconfederatemonument.blogspot.com/2013/01/2013-letter-to-obama-asking-him-not-to.html#.UX292LWsiSo (accessed 5/29/13).

291. Yan and Schwartz, "GOP Candidates Caught in Slavery Controversy"; Lizza, "Leap of Faith," 60.

292. Wilkins, "Yes, Mr. Minnery."

293. "21% Say States Have Right to Secede," *Rasmussen Reports,* June 2, 1011, www.rasmussenreports.com/public_content/politics/general_politics/may_2011/21_say_states_have_right_to_secede (accessed 5/25/12); "12% See Secession Attempt as Very Likely in Next 25 Years or So," *Rasmussen Reports,* June 22, 2010, www.rasmussenreports.com/public_content/

politics/general_politics/june_2010/12_see_secession_attempt_as_very_likely_in_next_25_
years_or_so (accessed 5/25/12); Guelzo, "Nullification Temptation," 28–30; Wilentz, "States
of Anarchy," 5–6. It is telling that Guelzo, a conservative, and Wilentz, a liberal, both agree
that nullification is not only unconstitutional and ahistorical but also a bad idea.

294. Benen, "Polling Secession."

295. Paul, *Liberty Defined*, 270, emphasis mine.

296. Tilman, *Ideology and Utopia*, 168.

297. Schlesinger, "In Defense of Government," A14; Alperovitz, *America beyond Capitalism*, 63–69, 152–66; Robin, "Fragmented State, Pluralist Society," 1061–93.

298. Sebesta, "Neo-Confederate Ideology in the Texas History Standards," in Erekson,
Politics and the History Curriculum. Paper in possession of the author.

299. Basler, Dunlap, and Pratt, *Collected Works of Abraham Lincoln*, 4:268.

300. Ibid., 6:410.

301. The phrase *with malice toward one* is from Holzer, *Lincoln Seen and Heard*, 103.

302. Basler, Dunlap, and Pratt, *Collected Works of Abraham Lincoln*, 2:276; Oakes, *Freedom
National*, xvi; Blight, "For Something beyond the Battlefield," 1178; Wolfe, *Political Evil*, 37.

CONCLUSION

1. Stephens, *Constitutional View of the Late War between the States*, 1:12.

2. Ibid., 2:447.

3. Masters, *Lincoln*, 482.

4. DiLorenzo, *Real Lincoln*, 3.

5. Wilson, "Society before Government," 14–17.

6. Basler, Dunlap, and Pratt, *Collected Works of Abraham Lincoln*, 3:315; Arnhart, "Biopolitical Science," 221–65.

7. Holmes, *Anatomy of Antiliberalism*, 261.

8. Oakes, *Freedom National*, 5; Foner, *Fiery Trial*, 43.

9. Horton, *Race and the Making of American Liberalism*, 33.

10. Frederick Douglass, quoted in Oakes, *Freedom National*, xviii; Douglass, "Oration in
Memory of Abraham Lincoln."

11. David Hume, quoted in Sen, "Boundaries of Justice: David Hume and Our World,"
23–26; Maas, "Lincoln at 200"; Blackburn, "Lincoln and Marx," 48–51.

12. Greenhouse, "Supreme Court: Homosexual Rights"; Paul, "Federal Courts and the
Imaginary Constitution"; Sandefur, "Texas Lincoln Talk."

13. Orwell, *1984*, 32; Alexander, *New Jim Crow.*

14. Sarah Vowell, quoted in Wheeler, "Psychic Lincoln?"

15. Wolff, *Introduction to Political Philosophy*, 102. The quotation is Wolff's, but the sentiment is Lincolnian.

16. Abraham Lincoln, quoted in Boritt, *Of the People, by the People, for the People*, 123.

17. Robin, *Reactionary Mind*, 248.

18. Lapham, "Ignorance of Things Past," 31.

19. Basler, Dunlap, and Pratt, *Collected Works of Abraham Lincoln*, 2:462.

20. "Address of the International Workingmen's Association of to President Johnson,"
May 20, 1865, quoted in Blackburn, *Unfinished Revolution*, 214.

21. The phrase *in all future time* is from the Texas "DECLARATION OF CAUSES: February 2, 1861, A Declaration of the Causes Which Impel the State of Texas to Secede from the Federal Union," Texas State Library and Archives Commission website, https://www.tsl.state.tx.us/ref/abouttx/secession/2feb1861.html (accessed 12/28/12); Basler, Dunlap, and Pratt, *Collected Works of Abraham Lincoln*, 4:271.

22. Masur, *Lincoln's Hundred Days*, 283.

23. Sandefur, "Texas Lincoln Talk."

24. Abraham Lincoln, quoted in Boritt, *Lincoln and the Economics of the American Dream*, 278; Abraham Lincoln, quoted in Cuomo and Holzer, *Lincoln on Democracy*, 349. Lincoln's words are from his last letter, dated April 14, 1865, the day he was assassinated; see Arnhart, *Darwinian Natural Right*, 161–210.

BIBLIOGRAPHY

MANUSCRIPT COLLECTIONS

Abraham Lincoln Presidential Library, Springfield, Ill.
    William H. Townsend and Mary Carter correspondence
Alabama Department of Archives and History, Montgomery, Alabama.
    Jefferson Davis Collection
Carl A. Kroch Library, Division of Rare and Manuscript Collections, Cornell University, Ithaca, N.Y.
    Amzi Wood Papers
Colorado Historical Society, Denver
    Confederate Scrapbook, MS no. 2566
Dolph Briscoe Center for American History, University of Texas at Austin
    Amelia Barr Papers
    Guy M. Bryan Papers
    Jack Campbell Papers
    Thomas Howard Duval Papers
    Andrew Jackson Hamilton Papers
    Pendleton Murrah Papers
    Williamson Simpson Oldham Papers
    Charles W. Ramsdell Papers
    Ashbel Smith Papers
Eleanor S. Brockenbrough Library, Museum of the Confederacy, Richmond, Va.
    Kate Mason Rowland Papers
    Hughes, Mrs. J. G. "Jefferson Davis versus Abraham Lincoln." Address
        given before the United Daughters of the Confederacy, Hanover Chapter,
        Ashland, Va., 1914–15.
    Tredway, Mrs. William Marshall. "Jefferson Davis, Abraham Lincoln: A
        Contrast." Address given before the United Daughters of the Confederacy,
        Riley Martin Chapter, ca. 1922.

Filson Historical Society, Louisville, Ky.
> Minutes of the Annual Conventions of the United Daughters of the Confederacy, 1904–54

Fromkin Memorial Collection, University of Wisconsin–Milwaukee, Golda Meir Library
> Halpin Whitney, Bruce Barton's Babblings

Harry Ransom Humanities Center, University of Texas, Austin
> Edgar Lee Masters Papers / Lincoln the Man File

Henry Rosenberg Library, Galveston, Tex.
> William Pitt Ballinger Papers

Herbert Hoover Institution on War, Revolution and Peace, Stanford University
> Sidney Hook Collection

Herbert Hoover Presidential Library, West Branch, Iowa
> Charles C. Tansill Papers

Houston Metropolitan Research Center. Unidentified letter, Old Vault Collection, Houston, Tex.
> MS 113, April 26, 1865

Joseph Mark Lauinger Memorial Library, Georgetown University, Washington, D.C.
> David Rankin Barbee Papers

Kentucky Historical Society, Thomas D. Clark Center for Kentucky History, Frankfort
> Mary Singleton Slack, "Causes That Led to the War between the States." Paper read before the Albert Sidney Johnston Chapter of the United Daughters of the Confederacy, Louisville, Ky., March 16, 1904.

Margaret I. King Library, Special Collections and Digital Programs, University of Kentucky, Lexington
> Cassius M. Clay Papers
> Leeland Hathaway Papers
> John Hunt Morgan Papers
> William H. Townsend Papers
> John C. Wardlaw Papers

Papers of Jefferson Davis, Jefferson Davis Association, Rice University, Houston, Tex.
> Jefferson Davis Papers

Southern Historical Collection, University of North Carolina Library, Chapel Hill
> Oliver R. Barrett Papers
> Laurence Foushee London Papers

Texas State Archives, Austin
> Andrew Jackson Hamilton Papers

Vanderbilt University, Jean Heard Library, Nashville, Tenn.
> Frank J. Owsley Papers
> John Crowe Ransom Papers

Virginia Historical Society, Richmond
> William Roane Aylett Papers
> Blanton Family Papers
> Clayton Family Papers
> Eggleston Family Papers
> Grinnan Family Papers
> Albert Hill Hudgins Papers
> King and Queen County Historical Society Papers
> Lee Family Papers
> Minutes of Grand Camp of Confederate Veterans, Robert E. Lee Camp no.
> 1, Richmond
> Miscellaneous Lincoln, unprocessed pamphlets of Marvin Mobley

NEWSPAPERS

Arkansas Gazette
Atlanta Daily World
Bangor Daily Whig & Courier
Boston Journal
Chicago Defender
Chicago Tribune
Cleveland Morning Daily Herald
Congregationalist
Daily Evening Bulletin (San Francisco)
Daily Inter-Ocean (Chicago)
Dallas Herald
Daily Mississippian
Flake's Bulletin (Galveston)
Galveston Daily News
Galveston Tri-Weekly News
Houston Chronicle
Houston Daily Telegraph
Houston Tri-Weekly Telegraph
Lexington Herald-Leader (Kentucky)
London Times
Louisville Courier Journal
Lowell Daily Citizen and News
Memphis Commercial-Appeal
Miami Herald
Milwaukee Daily Sentinel
Morning Oregonian (Portland)

Negro World
New Orleans Times-Picayune
New York Amsterdam News
New York Times
News-Observer-Chronicle (Raleigh)
North American (Philadelphia)
Pittsburgh Courier
Richmond Enquirer and Examiner
Richmond Times-Dispatch
Scioto Gazette (Chillicothe, Ohio)
Southern Vindicator (Pine Bluffs, Ark.)
Southwestern Christian Advocate (New Orleans)
St. Louis Globe-Democrat
Texas Republican (Marshall)
True Issue (La Grange)
Wall Street Journal
Washington Post
Washington Times
Weekly State Gazette (Austin)

PERIODICALS

American Spectator
Chronicle of Higher Education
Chronicles: A Magazine of American Culture
Confederate Veteran
Dissent
Intercollegiate Review
Journal of Libertarian Studies
Land We Love (Journal)
Libertarian Forum
Libertarian Papers
Nation
National Review
New Left Review
New Republic
Newsweek
New York Review of Books
Rothbard-Rockwell Report
Southern Churchman
Southern Historical Society Papers

Southern Magazine
Southern Partisan
Southern Review
Time
Tyler's Quarterly Historical and Genealogical Magazine

PUBLIC DOCUMENTS

U.S. Congress. *Congressional Record.* 74th Cong., 2d sess., 1936. Vol. 80, pt. 6.
The War of the Rebellion: A Compilation of the Official Records of the Union and Confederate Armies. 130 vols. Washington, D.C.: Government Printing Office, 1880–1901.

BOOKS AND PAMPHLETS

About the Ludwig von Mises Institute. Pamphlet. Auburn, Ala.: Ludwig von Mises Institute, 2010.
Adams, Charles. *When in the Course of Human Events: Arguing the Case for Southern Secession.* Lanham, Md.: Rowman and Littlefield, 2000.
Alexander, Michelle. *The New Jim Crow: Mass Incarceration in the Age of Colorblindness.* Rev. ed. New York: New Press, 2012.
Allitt, Patrick. *The Conservatives: Ideas and Personalities throughout American History.* New Haven: Yale University Press, 2009.
Alperovitz, Gar. *America beyond Capitalism: Reclaiming Our Wealth, Our Liberty, and Our Democracy.* 2d ed. Takoma Park, Md.: Democracy Collaborative Press and Dollars and Sense, 2011.
Amar, Akhil Reed. *America's Constitution: A Biography.* New York: Random House, 2005.
Anderson, Benedict. *Imagined Communities.* London: Verso Books, 1983.
Anderson, Dwight G. *Abraham Lincoln: The Quest for Immortality.* New York: Alfred A. Knopf, 1982.
Anderson, Gary Clayton. *The Conquest of Texas: Ethnic Cleansing in the Promised Land, 1820–1875.* Norman: University of Oklahoma Press, 2005.
Anderson, John Q., ed. *Brokenburn: The Journal of Kate Stone, 1861–1868.* Baton Rouge: Louisiana State University Press, 1955.
Andrews, Eliza Frances. *The War-Time Journal of a Georgia Girl.* New York: D. Appleton, 1908.
Angle, Paul M. *A Shelf of Lincoln Books: A Critical Selective Bibliography of Lincolniana.* New Brunswick, N.J.: Rutgers University Press, 1946.
Arnhart, Larry. *Darwinian Natural Right: The Biological Ethics of Human Nature.* Albany: State University of New York Press, 1998.

Arsenault, Raymond. *The Sound of Freedom: Marian Anderson, the Lincoln Memorial, and the Concert That Awakened America.* New York: Bloomsbury Press, 2009.

Ashworth, John. *Slavery, Capitalism, and Politics in the Antebellum Republic.* Vol. 2: *The Coming of the Civil War, 1850–1861.* Cambridge, U.K.: Cambridge University Press, 2007.

Aslan, Reza. *How to Win a Cosmic War: God, Globalization, and the War on Terror.* New York: Random House, 2009.

Ayers, Edward L. *The Promise of the New South: Life after Reconstruction.* New York: Oxford University Press, 1992.

Bacevich, Andrew. *American Empire: The Realities and Consequences of U.S. Diplomacy.* Cambridge, Mass.: Harvard University Press, 2002.

Baker, Julie P., and T. Lindsay Baker, eds. *Till Freedom Cried Out: Memories of Texas Slave Life.* College Station: Texas A&M University Press, 1997.

Barbee, David Rankin. *An Excursion in Southern History, Briefly Set Forth in the Correspondence between Senator A. J. Beveridge and David Rankin Barbee.* Pamphlet. Richmond, Va.: Langbourne M. Williams, 1928.

Barnes, Harry Elmer, ed. *Perpetual War for Perpetual Peace: A Critical Examination of the Foreign Policy of Franklin Delano Roosevelt and Its Aftermath.* Caldwell, Idaho: Caxton Printers, 1953. Available online at Mises.org.

Barnhart, Terry A. *Albert Taylor Bledsoe: Defender of the Old South and Architect of the Lost Cause.* Baton Rouge: Louisiana State University Press, 2011.

Barton, Bruce. *The Man Nobody Knows.* Indianapolis: Bobbs-Merrill, 1925.

Basler, Roy P. *The Lincoln Legend: A Study in Changing Conceptions.* 1935. Reprint. New York: Octagon Books, 1969.

Basler, Roy P., Lloyd A. Dunlap, and Marion Dolores Pratt, eds. *The Collected Works of Abraham Lincoln.* 9 vols. New Brunswick, N.J.: Rutgers University Press, 1953.

Bates, Finis L. *The Escape and Suicide of John Wilkes Booth, or The First True Account of Lincoln's Assassination Containing a Complete Confession by Booth, Many Years after the Crime.* Memphis: Historical Publishing Company, 1907.

Baum, Dale. *The Shattering of Texas Unionism: Politics in the Lone Star State during the Civil War Era.* Baton Rouge: Louisiana State University Press, 1988.

Beale, Howard K., ed. *The Diary of Gideon Welles.* 3 vols. New York: W. W. Norton, 1960.

Becker, Carl L. *The Declaration of Independence: A Study in the History of Political Ideas.* New York: Harcourt Brace, 1922.

Beeth, Howard, and Cary D. Wintz, eds. *Black Dixie: Afro-Texan History and Culture in Houston.* College Station: Texas A&M University Press, 1992.

Belz, Herman. *Abraham Lincoln, Constitutionalism, and Equal Rights.* New York: Fordham University Press, 1998.

Bender, Thomas. *A Nation among Nations.* New York: Hill and Wang, 2006.

Bennett, Lerone, Jr. *What Manner of Man: A Biography of Martin Luther King, Jr., 1929–1968.* Chicago: Johnson Publishing, 1968.

———. *Forced into Glory: Abraham Lincoln's White Dream.* Chicago: Johnson Publishing, 1999.

Bernstein, Patricia. *The First Waco Horror: The Lynching of Jesse Washington and the Rise of the NAACP.* College Station: Texas A&M University Press, 2005.

Blackburn, Robin. *An Unfinished Revolution: Karl Marx and Abraham Lincoln.* London: Verso Books, 2011.

Blackmon, Douglas A. *Slavery by Another Name: The Re-Enslavement of Black Americans from the Civil War to World War II.* New York: Anchor Books, 2008.

Blacknall, O. W. *Lincoln as the South Should Know Him.* Pamphlet. Raleigh, N.C.: Commercial Printing Company, 1915.

Blair, William A. *Cities of the Dead: Contesting the Memory of the Civil War South, 1865–1914.* Chapel Hill: University of North Carolina Press, 2004.

Blair, William A., and Karen Fisher Younger, eds. *Lincoln's Proclamation: Emancipation Reconsidered.* Chapel Hill: University of North Carolina Press, 2009.

Blanchard, Kenneth C., Jr., ed. *Darwinian Conservatism: A Disputed Question.* Charlottesville, Va.: Imprint Academic, 2009.

Bledsoe, Albert Taylor. *An Essay on Liberty and Slavery.* Philadelphia: J. B. Lippincott, 1856.

Blight, David W. *Race and Reunion: The Civil War in American Memory.* Cambridge, Mass.: Harvard University Press, 2001.

———. *Beyond the Battlefield: Race, Memory, and the American Civil War.* Amherst: University of Massachusetts Press, 2002.

———. *American Oracle: The Civil War in the Civil Rights Era.* Cambridge, Mass.: Belknap Press of Harvard University Press, 2011.

Blight, David W., and Brooks D. Simpson, eds. *Union and Emancipation: Essays on Politics and Race in the Civil War Era.* Kent, Ohio: Kent State University Press, 1997.

Blum, Edward J. *Reforging the White Republic: Race, Religion, and American Nationalism, 1865–1898.* Baton Rouge: Louisiana State University Press, 2005.

Boaz, David. *Libertarianism: A Primer.* New York: Free Press, 1997.

Bodnar, John. *Remaking America: Public Memory, Commemoration, and Patriotism in the Twentieth Century.* Princeton: Princeton University Press, 1992.

Bogus, Carl T. *Buckley: William F. Buckley Jr. and the Rise of American Conservatism.* New York: Bloomsbury Press, 2011.

Boritt, Gabor S. *Lincoln and the Economics of the American Dream.* Urbana: University of Illinois Press, 1978.

———, ed. *The Historian's Lincoln: Pseudohistory, Psychohistory, and History.* Urbana: University of Illinois Press, 1988.

———. *Why the Civil War Came.* New York: Oxford University Press, 1996.

———, ed. *Of the People, by the People, for the People and Other Quotations from Abraham Lincoln.* New York: Columbia University Press, 1996.

———, ed. *The Lincoln Enigma: The Changing Face of an American Icon.* New York: Oxford University Press, 2001.

———. *The Gettysburg Gospel: The Lincoln Speech Nobody Knows.* New York: Simon and Schuster, 2006.

Bradford, M. E. *The Reactionary Imperative: Essays Literary and Political.* Peru, Ill.: S. Sugden, 1990.

Brevard, Caroline Mays. *A History of Florida.* New York: American Book Company, 1904.

Bridges, Linda, and John R. Coyne Jr. *Strictly Right: William F. Buckley, Jr., and the Conservative Movement.* Hoboken, N.J.: John Wiley and Sons, 2007.

Briggs, John Channing. *Lincoln's Speeches Reconsidered.* Baltimore: Johns Hopkins University Press, 2005.

Brooks, Noah. *Washington in Lincoln's Time.* New York: Century Company, 1895.

Brown, David. *Southern Outcast: Hinton Rowan Helper and the Impending Crisis of the Civil War.* Baton Rouge: Louisiana State University Press, 2006.

Brown, David S. *Richard Hofstadter: An Intellectual Biography.* Chicago: University of Chicago Press, 2006.

Brown, Norman. *One of Cleburne's Command: The Civil War Reminiscences and Diary of Captain Samuel T. Foster, Granbury's Texas Brigade, C.S.A.* Austin: University of Texas Press, 1980.

Bruce, Dickson D. *Archibald Grimké: Portrait of a Black Independent.* Baton Rouge: Louisiana State University Press, 1993.

Brundage, W. Fitzhugh, ed. *Where These Memories Grow: History, Memory, and Southern Identity.* Chapel Hill: University of North Carolina Press, 2000.

———. *The Southern Past: A Clash of Race and Memory.* Cambridge, Mass.: Belknap Press of Harvard University Press, 2005.

Bryan, George S. *The Great American Myth.* New York: Carrick and Evans, 1940.

Buchanan, Allen. *Secession: The Morality of Political Divorce from Fort Sumter to Lithuania and Quebec.* Boulder, Colo.: Westview Press, 1991.

Buchanan, Patrick J. *Churchill, Hitler, and the Unnecessary War: How Britain Lost Its Empire and the West Lost the World.* New York: Random House, 2008.

Buckley, William F., Jr. *The Unmaking of a Mayor.* New York: Viking Books, 1966.

———. *Did You Ever See A Dream Walking? American Conservative Thought in the Twentieth Century.* Indianapolis: Bobbs-Merrill, 1970.

———. *Up from Liberalism.* 25th anniversary ed. New York: Stein and Day, 1984.

Buckley, William F., Jr., and L. Brent Bozell. *McCarthy and His Enemies: The Record and Its Meaning.* Chicago: Henry Regnery, 1954.

Buenger, Walter L. *Secession and the Union in Texas.* Austin: University of Texas Press, 1984.

Burkhalter, Lois Wood. *Gideon Lincecum, 1793–1874: A Biography.* Austin: University of Texas Press, 1965.

Burlingame, Michael. *The Inner World of Abraham Lincoln.* Urbana: University of Illinois Press, 1994.

———. *Abraham Lincoln: A Life.* 2 vols. Baltimore: Johns Hopkins University Press, 2008.

Burr, Virginia Ingraham, ed. *Secret Eye: The Journal of Ella Gertrude Thomas, 1848–1889.* Chapel Hill: University of North Carolina Press, 1990.

Burton, Orville Vernon. *The Age of Lincoln.* New York: Hill and Wang, 2007.

Bushman, Richard L. *The Refinement of America: Persons, Houses, Cities.* New York: Vintage Books, 1992.

Campbell, Randolph B. *An Empire for Slavery: The Peculiar Institution in Texas, 1821–1865.* Baton Rouge: Louisiana State University Press, 1989.

———. *Gone to Texas: A History of the Lone Star State.* Oxford: Oxford University Press, 2003.

Cantrell, Gregg, and Elizabeth Hayes Turner, eds. *Lone Star Pasts: Memory and History in Texas.* College Station: Texas A&M University Press, 2007.

Carey, George W., ed. *Freedom and Virtue: The Conservative/Libertarian Debate.* 1984. Reprint. Wilmington, Del.: ISI Books, 1998.

Carnahan, Burrus M. *Act of Justice: Lincoln's Emancipation Proclamation and the Law of War.* Lexington: University Press of Kentucky, 2007.

———. *Lincoln on Trial: Southern Civilians and the Law of War.* Lexington: University Press of Kentucky, 2010.

Carrigan, William D. *The Making of a Lynching Culture: Violence and Vigilantism in Central Texas, 1836–1916.* Urbana: University of Illinois Press, 2004.

Carter, Joseph C., ed. *Magnolia Journey: A Union Veteran Revisits the Former Confederate States.* Tuscaloosa: University of Alabama Press, 1974.

Carter, Mary, and Lloyd T. Everett, eds. *A Youth's History of the Civil War [War between the States] from 1861–1865* by R. G. Horton. 1866. Reprint. New York: Van Evrie, Horton and Company, 1925.

Carwardine, Richard J. *Lincoln: Profiles in Power.* London: Pearson Education Limited, 2003.

Carwardine, Richard J., and Jay Sexton, eds. *The Global Lincoln.* New York: Oxford University Press, 2011.

Ceaser, James W. *Nature and History in American Political Development: A Debate.* Cambridge, Mass.: Harvard University Press, 2006.

Chesebrough, David B. *"No Sorrow like Our Sorrow": Northern Protestant Ministers and the Assassination of Lincoln.* Kent, Ohio: Kent State University Press, 1994.

Christian, George L. *Abraham Lincoln.* Pamphlet. 1909. Reprint. Richmond, Va.: Richmond Press, 1927.

Cisco, Walter Brian. *War Crimes against Southern Civilians.* Gretna, La.: Pelican Publishing Company, 2007.

Clark, Kathleen Ann. *Defining Moments: African American Commemoration and Political Culture in the South, 1863–1913.* Chapel Hill: University of North Carolina Press, 2005.

Clift, G. Glenn, ed. *The Private War of Lizzie Hardin: A Kentucky Confederate Girl's Diary of the Civil War in Kentucky, Virginia, Tennessee, Alabama, and Georgia.* Frankfort: Kentucky Historical Society, 1963.

Cloyd, Benjamin G. *Haunted by Atrocity: Civil War Prisons in American Memory.* Baton Rouge: Louisiana State University Press, 2010.

Cobb, James C. *Away Down South: A History of Southern Identity.* New York: Oxford University Press 2005.

Colaiaco, James A. *Frederick Douglass and the Fourth of July.* New York: Palgrave Macmillan, 2006.

Commager, Henry Steele, ed. *The Blue and the Gray: The Story of the Civil War as Told by Participants.* New York: Fairfax Press, 1982.

Connelly, Thomas L. *The Marble Man: Robert E. Lee and His Image in American Society.* Baton Rouge: Louisiana State University Press, 1977.

Contasta, David R. *Rebel Giants: The Revolutionary Lives of Abraham Lincoln and Charles Darwin.* Amherst, N.Y.: Prometheus Books, 2008.

Cook, Robert J. *Troubled Commemoration: The American Civil War Centennial, 1961–1965.* Baton Rouge: Louisiana State University Press, 2007.

Cooke, Alistair, ed. *The Vintage Mencken.* New York: Alfred A. Knopf, 1955.

Cooper, William J., Jr. *Jefferson Davis, American.* New York: Alfred A. Knopf, 2000.

———. *Liberty and Slavery: Southern Politics to 1860.* 1983. Reprint. Columbia: University of South Carolina Press, 2000.

Cooper, William J., Jr., and John M. McCardell Jr., eds. *In the Cause of Liberty: How the Civil War Redefined American Ideals.* Baton Rouge: Louisiana State University Press, 2009.

Cox, Hank H. *Lincoln and the Sioux Uprising.* Nashville: Cumberland House, 2005.

Cox, Karen L. *Dixie's Daughters: The United Daughters of the Confederacy and the Preservation of Confederate Culture.* Gainesville: University Press of Florida, 2003.

Cox, LaWanda. *Lincoln and Black Freedom: A Study in Presidential Leadership.* Columbia: University of South Carolina Press, 1981.

Crabb, Martha L. *All Afire to Fight: The Untold Tale of the Ninth Texas Cavalry.* New York: Avon Books and Post Road Press, 2000.

Critchlow, Donald T. *The Conservative Ascendancy: How the Republican Right Rose to Power in Modern America.* 2d rev. ed. Lawrence: University Press of Kansas, 2011.

Critchlow, Donald T., and Nancy MacLean. *Debating the American Conservative Movement, 1945 to the Present.* Lanham, Md.: Rowman and Littlefield, 2009.

Cuomo, Mario M., and Harold Holzer, eds. *Lincoln on Democracy: His Own Words, with Essays by America's Foremost Civil War Historians.* New York: HarperCollins, 1990.

Current, Richard N. *Lincoln and the First Shot.* Philadelphia: J. B. Lippincott, 1963.

———. *Speaking of Abraham Lincoln: The Man and His Meaning for Our Times.* Urbana: University of Illinois Press, 1983.

———. *Lincoln's Loyalists: Union Soldiers from the Confederacy.* Boston: Northeastern University Press, 1992.

Dabney, Lewis M. *Edmund Wilson: A Life in Literature.* New York: Farrar, Straus and Giroux, 2005.

Darwin, Charles. *On the Origin of Species by Means of Natural Selection or The Preservation of Favoured Races in the Struggle for Life.* New York: Alfred A. Knopf, Everyman's Library, 2003.

Davidson, Donald. *Attack on Leviathan: Regionalism and Nationalism in the United States.* 1938. Reprint. Chapel Hill: University of North Carolina Press, 1962.

Davis, David Brion. *The Slave Power Conspiracy and the Paranoid Style.* Baton Rouge: Louisiana State University Press, 1969.

———. *Slavery and Human Progress.* New York: Oxford University Press, 1984.

———. *Inhuman Bondage: The Rise and Fall of Slavery in the New World.* New York: Oxford University Press, 2006.

Davis, Harold E. *Henry W. Grady's New South.* Tuscaloosa: University of Alabama Press, 1990.

Davis, Jefferson. *The Rise and Fall of the Confederate Government.* New York: Thomas Yoseloff, 1881.

Davis, Michael. *The Image of Lincoln in the South.* Knoxville: University of Tennessee Press, 1971.

Davis, Rodney O., and Douglas L. Wilson, eds. *Herndon's Lincoln.* Urbana: Knox College Lincoln Studies Center and University of Illinois Press, 2006.

———, eds. *The Lincoln-Douglas Debates.* Urbana: Knox College Lincoln Studies Center and University of Illinois Press, 2008.

Dawkins, Richard. *The Selfish Gene.* New York: Oxford University Press, 1976.

Denson, John V., ed. *The Costs of War: America's Pyrrhic Victories.* New Brunswick, N.J.: Transaction Publishers, 1997.

Deutsch, Kenneth L., and Joseph R. Fornieri, eds. *Lincoln's American Dream: Clashing Political Perspectives.* Washington, D.C.: Potomac Books, 2005.

Dew, Charles B. *Apostles of Disunion: Southern Secession Commissioners and the Causes of the Civil War.* Charlottesville: University Press of Virginia, 2001.

Deyle, Steven. *Carry Me Back: The Domestic Slave Trade in American Life.* New York: Oxford University Press, 2005.

Diggins, John Patrick. *The Rise and Fall of the American Left.* New York: W. W. Norton, 1992.

———. *On Hallowed Ground: Abraham Lincoln and the Foundations of American History.* New Haven: Yale University Press, 2000.

DiLorenzo, Thomas J. *The Real Lincoln: A New Look at Abraham Lincoln, His Agenda, and an Unnecessary War.* New York: Three Rivers Press, 2002.

———. *Lincoln Unmasked: What You're Not Supposed to Know about Dishonest Abe.* New York: Three Rivers Press, 2006.

Dirck, Brian R. *Lincoln and Davis: Imagining America, 1809–1865.* Lawrence: University Press of Kansas, 2001.

———. *Lincoln Emancipated: The President and the Politics of Race.* DeKalb: Northern Illinois University Press, 2007.

———. *Abraham Lincoln and White America*. Lawrence: University Press of Kansas, 2012.

Doherty, Brian. *Radicals for Capitalism: A Freewheeling History of the Modern American Libertarian Movement*. New York: Public Affairs, 2007.

———. *Ron Paul's Revolution: The Man and the Movement He Inspired*. New York: Broadside Books, 2012.

Donald, David. *Lincoln's Herndon: A Biography*. New York: Alfred A. Knopf, 1948.

———. *Lincoln Reconsidered: Essays on the Civil War Era*. New York: Alfred A. Knopf, 1956.

———. *Lincoln*. New York: Simon and Schuster, 1995.

Dower, John W. *War without Mercy: Race and Power in the Pacific War*. New York: Pantheon Books, 1986.

Duberman, Martin B. *Charles Francis Adams, 1807–1886*. Boston: Houghton Mifflin, 1961.

———, ed. *The Antislavery Vanguard: New Essays on the Abolitionists*. Princeton: Princeton University Press, 1965.

DuBose, Joel Campbell. *Alabama History*. Richmond, Va.: B. F. Johnson Publishing Company, 1915.

Dumond, Dwight L., ed. *Southern Editorials on Secession*. Gloucester, Mass.: Peter Smith, 1964.

Dunbar, Alice Moore, ed. *Masterpieces of Negro Eloquence, 1818–1913*. Mineola, N.Y.: Dover Publications, 2000.

Ecksteins, Modris. *Rites of Spring: The Great War and the Birth of the Modern Age*. Boston: Houghton Mifflin, 1989.

Edelman, Murray. *The Symbolic Uses of Politics*. Urbana: University of Illinois Press, 1985.

Elliott, Mark, and John David Smith, eds. *Undaunted Radical: The Selected Writings and Speeches of Albion W. Tourgée*. Baton Rouge: Louisiana State University Press, 2010.

Elson, Henry William. *History of the United States of America*. New York: Macmillan, 1904.

Emerson, Jason. *Lincoln the Inventor*. Carbondale: Southern Illinois University Press, 2009.

Emison, John Avery. *Lincoln Über Alles: Dictatorship Comes to America*. Gretna, La.: Pelican Publishing Company, 2009.

Escott, Paul D. *Slavery Remembered: A Record of Twentieth-Century Slave Narratives*. Chapel Hill: University of North Carolina Press, 1979.

———, ed. *W. J. Cash and the Minds of the South*. Baton Rouge: Louisiana State University Press, 1992.

———. *"What Shall We Do with the Negro?" Lincoln, White Racism, and Civil War America*. Charlottesville: University of Virginia Press, 2009.

Evans, C. Wyatt. *The Legend of John Wilkes Booth: Myth, Memory, and a Mummy.* Lawrence: University Press of Kansas, 2004.

Everett, Lloyd T. *Davis, Lincoln, and the Kaiser, Some Comparisons Compared: National and International Ethics, 1861 and 1914.* Pamphlet. Ballston, Va.: Yexid Publishing Company, 1917.

Fahs, Alice. *The Imagined Civil War: Popular Literature of the North and South, 1861–1865.* Chapel Hill: University of North Carolina Press, 2001.

Fahs, Alice, and Joan Waugh, eds. *The Memory of the Civil War in American Culture.* Chapel Hill: University of North Carolina Press, 2004.

Farber, Daniel. *Lincoln's Constitution.* Chicago: University of Chicago Press, 2003.

Faust, Drew Gilpin. *The Creation of Confederate Nationalism: Ideology and Identity in the Civil War South.* Baton Rouge: Louisiana State University Press, 1988.

————. *Southern Stories: Slaveholders in Peace and War.* Columbia: University of Missouri Press, 1992.

————. *Mothers of Invention: Women of the Slaveholding South in the American Civil War.* Chapel Hill: University of North Carolina Press, 1996.

————. *This Republic of Suffering.* New York: Alfred A. Knopf, 2008.

Fears, J. Rufus, ed. *Essays in the History of Liberty: Selected Writings of Lord Acton.* Indianapolis: Liberty Fund, 1985.

Fehrenbach, T. R. *Lone Star: A History of Texas and the Texans.* 1968. Reprint. New York: American Legacy Press, 1983.

Fehrenbacher, Don E. *Prelude to Greatness: Lincoln in the 1850's.* Stanford: Stanford University Press, 1962.

————, ed. *The Leadership of Abraham Lincoln.* New York: John Wiley and Sons, 1970.

————. *Lincoln in Text and Context: Collected Essays.* Stanford: Stanford University Press, 1987.

Fehrenbacher, Don E., and Virginia Fehrenbacher, eds. *Recollected Words of Abraham Lincoln.* Stanford: Stanford University Press, 1996.

Ferguson, Andrew. *The Land of Lincoln.* New York: Atlantic Monthly Press, 2007.

Finkelman, Paul, ed. *Defending Slavery: Proslavery Thought in the Old South.* Boston: Bedford Series in History and Culture, 2003.

Fletcher, William A. *Rebel Private: Front and Rear.* New York: Dutton Books, 1995.

Flood, Charles Bracelen. *Lee: The Last Years.* Boston: Houghton Mifflin, 1981.

————. *1864: Lincoln at the Gates of History.* New York: Simon and Schuster, 2009.

Foner, Eric. *Free Soil, Free Labor, Free Men: The Ideology of the Republican Party before the Civil War.* New York: Oxford University Press, 1970.

————. *Reconstruction: America's Unfinished Revolution, 1863–1877.* New York: Harper and Row, 1988.

————. *A Short History of Reconstruction, 1863–1877.* New York: Harper and Row, 1990.

——. *The Story of American Freedom.* New York: W. W. Norton, 1998.

——. *Forever Free: The Story of Emancipation and Reconstruction.* New York: Alfred A. Knopf, 2006.

——, ed. *Our Lincoln: New Perspectives on Lincoln and His World.* New York: W. W. Norton, 2008.

——. *The Fiery Trial: Abraham Lincoln and American Slavery.* New York: W. W. Norton, 2010.

Foner, Philip S., ed. *The Life and Writings of Frederick Douglass.* 5 vols. New York: International Publishers, 1955.

Ford, Lacy K., ed. *A Companion to the Civil War and Reconstruction.* Malden, Mass.: Blackwell Publishing, 2005.

Forgie, George B. *Patricide in the House Divided: A Psychological Interpretation of Lincoln and His Age.* New York: W. W. Norton, 1979.

Forgue, Guy J., ed. *Letters of H. L. Mencken.* New York: Alfred A. Knopf, 1961.

Fornieri, Joseph R., and Sara Vaughn Gabbard, eds. *Lincoln's America, 1809–1865.* Carbondale: Southern Illinois University Press, 2008.

Forrest, Barbara, and Paul R. Gross. *Creationism's Trojan Horse: The Wedge of Intelligent Design.* New York: Oxford University Press, 2004.

Foster, Gaines M. *Ghosts of the Confederacy: Defeat, the Lost Cause, and the Emergence of the New South.* New York: Oxford University Press, 1987.

Francis, Samuel. *Beautiful Losers: Essays on the Failure of American Conservatism.* Columbia: University of Missouri Press, 1993.

Franklin, John Hope. *Reconstruction: After the Civil War.* Chicago: University of Chicago Press, 1961.

Fraysee, Olivier. *Lincoln, Land, and Labor, 1809–1860.* Urbana: University of Illinois Press, 1988.

Frederickson, George M. *The Inner Civil War: Northern Intellectuals and the Crisis of the Union.* 1965. Reprint. Urbana: University of Illinois Press, 1993.

——. *Big Enough to Be Inconsistent: Abraham Lincoln Confronts Slavery and Race.* Cambridge, Mass.: Harvard University Press, 2008.

Freehling, William W. *The Reintegration of American History: Slavery and the Civil War.* New York: Oxford University Press, 1994.

——. *The South vs. the South: How Anti-Confederate Southerners Shaped the Course of the Civil War.* New York: Oxford University Press, 2001.

——. *The Road to Disunion*: Vol. 2: *Secessionists Triumphant, 1854–1861.* New York: Oxford University Press, 2007.

Freeman, Douglas Southall. *Lee: An Abridgement in One Volume of the Four-Volume R. E. Lee,* by Richard Harwell. New York: Charles Scribner's Sons, 1993.

Fried, Richard. *The Man Everybody Knew.* Chicago: Ivan R. Dee, 2005.

Friedman, Milton. *Capitalism and Freedom.* 1962. Reprint. Chicago: University of Chicago Press, 1982.

Gallagher, Gary W. *The Confederate War: How Popular Will, Nationalism, and Military Strategy Could Not Stave Off Defeat.* Cambridge, Mass.: Harvard University Press, 1997.

———. *Lee and His Generals in War and Memory.* Baton Rouge: Louisiana State University Press, 1998.

———. *Causes Won, Lost, and Forgotten: How Hollywood and Popular Art Shape What We Know about the Civil War.* Chapel Hill: University of North Carolina Press, 2008.

Gallagher, Gary W., and Alan T. Nolan, eds. *The Myth of the Lost Cause and Civil War History.* Bloomington: Indiana University Press, 2000.

Garrett, William Robertson, and Albert Virgil Goodpasture. *History of Tennessee: Its People and Institutions.* Nashville: Brandon Printing Company, 1900.

Gates, Henry Louis, Jr., ed. *Lincoln on Race and Slavery.* Princeton: Princeton University Press, 2009.

Geary, James. *Geary's Guide to the World's Great Aphorists.* New York: Bloomsbury, 2007.

Gellner, Ernest. *Nations and Nationalism.* Oxford: Blackwell Publishing, 1983.

Genovese, Eugene D. *Roll, Jordan, Roll: The World the Slaves Made.* New York: Vintage Books, 1972.

———. *The Political Economy of Slavery: Studies in the Economy and Society of the Slave South.* 1961. Reprint. Middletown, Conn.: Wesleyan University Press, 1989.

———. *The Southern Front: History and Politics in the Cultural War.* Columbia: University of Missouri Press, 1995.

———. *A Consuming Fire: The Fall of the Confederacy in the Mind of the White Christian South.* Athens: University of Georgia Press, 1998.

Genovese, Eugene D., and Elizabeth Fox Genovese. *The Mind of the Master Class: History and Faith in the Southern Slaveholder's Worldview.* Cambridge, U.K.: Cambridge University Press, 2005.

Gienapp, William E., ed. *This Fiery Trial: The Speeches and Writings of Abraham Lincoln.* New York: Oxford University Press, 2002.

Gilbert, Charles Edwin. *Two Presidents: Abraham Lincoln, Jefferson Davis: Origin, Cause and Conduct of the War between the States, the Truth of History Belongs to Posterity.* Houston: By the author, 1927.

Glatthaar, Joseph T. *Forged in Battle: The Civil War Alliance of Black Soldiers and White Officers.* Baton Rouge: Louisiana State University Press, 1990.

Goldberg, Michelle. *Kingdom Coming: The Rise of Christian Nationalism.* New York: W. W. Norton, 2006.

Goldfield, David. *Still Fighting the Civil War: The American South and Southern History.* Baton Rouge: Louisiana State University Press, 2002.

Goodwin, Doris Kearns. *Team of Rivals: The Political Genius of Abraham Lincoln.* New York: Simon and Schuster, 2005.

Gopnik, Adam. *Angels and Ages: A Short Book about Darwin, Lincoln, and Modern Life*. New York: Alfred A. Knopf, 2009.

Gordon, David, ed. *Secession, State, and Liberty*. New Brunswick, N.J.: Transaction Publishers, 1998.

——. *The Essential Rothbard*. Auburn, Ala.: Ludwig von Mises Institute, 2007.

Gottfried, Paul. *Conservatism in America: Making Sense of the American Right*. New York: Palgrave Macmillan, 2007.

Gottfried, Paul, and Thomas Fleming. *The Conservative Movement*. Boston: Twayne Publishers, 1988.

Gould, Lewis L. *Alexander Watkins Terrell: Civil War Soldier, Texas Lawmaker, American Diplomat*. Austin: University of Texas Press, 2004.

Goyne, Mineta Altgelt, ed. *Lone Star and Double Eagle: Civil War Letters of a German Family*. Fort Worth, Tex.: TCU Press, 1982.

Graham, John Remington. *A Constitutional History of Secession*. Gretna, La.: Pelican Publishing Company, 2002.

Grear, Charles D., ed. *The Fate of Texas: The Civil War and the Lone Star State*. Fayetteville: University of Arkansas Press, 2008.

Greenberg, Kenneth S. *Honor and Slavery: Lies, Duels, Noses, Masks, Dressing as a Woman, Gifts, Strangers, Humanitarianism, Death, Slave Rebellions, the Proslavery Argument, Baseball, Hunting, Gambling in the Old South*. Princeton: Princeton University Press, 1996.

Grimshaw, Anna, ed. *The C. L. R. James Reader*. Oxford: Blackwell, 1992.

Grimsley, Mark. *The Hard Hand of War*. Cambridge, U.K.: Cambridge University Press, 1995.

Guelzo, Allen. *Abraham Lincoln: Redeemer President*. Grand Rapids, Mich.: William B. Eerdmans Publishing, 1999.

——. *Lincoln's Emancipation Proclamation: The End of Slavery in America*. New York: Simon and Schuster, 2004.

——. *Lincoln and Douglas: The Debates That Defined America*. New York: Simon and Schuster, 2008.

——. *Abraham Lincoln as a Man of Ideas*. Carbondale: Southern Illinois University Press, 2009.

——. *Lincoln: A Very Short Introduction*. New York: Oxford University Press, 2009.

Hague, Euan, Heidi Beirich, and Edward H. Sebesta, eds. *Neo-Confederacy: A Critical Introduction*. Austin: University of Texas Press, 2008.

Haidt, Jonathan. *The Righteous Mind: Why Good People Are Divided by Politics and Religion*. New York: Pantheon Books, 2012.

Halbwachs, Maurice. *On Collective Memory*. Translated by Lewis A. Coser. Chicago: University of Chicago Press, 1992.

Hale, Douglas, ed. *The Third Texas Cavalry in the Civil War*. Norman: University of Oklahoma Press, 1993.

Hale, Grace Elizabeth. *Making Whiteness: The Culture of Segregation in the South, 1890–1940.* New York: Vintage Books, 1998.

Hanchett, William. *The Lincoln Murder Conspiracies.* Urbana: University of Illinois Press, 1983.

Harding, Vincent. *There Is a River: The Black Struggle for Freedom in America.* New York: Harcourt Brace Jovanovich, 1981.

Harlan, Louis R., ed. *The Booker T. Washington Papers.* Urbana: University of Illinois Press, 1972.

Harrell, Carolyn L. *When the Bells Tolled for Lincoln: Southern Reaction to the Assassination.* Macon, Ga.: Mercer University Press, 1997.

Harris, Thomas M. *The Assassination of Lincoln: A History of the Great Conspiracy.* Boston: American Citizen Company, 1892.

Harris, William C. *With Charity for All: Lincoln and the Restoration of the Union.* Lexington: University Press of Kentucky, 1997.

——. *Lincoln's Last Months.* Cambridge, Mass.: Harvard University Press, 2004.

Hart, Jeffrey. *The Making of the American Conservative Mind: National Review and Its Times.* Wilmington, Del.: ISI Books, 2005.

Harwell, Richard Barksdale, ed. *Kate: The Journal of a Confederate Nurse.* Baton Rouge: Louisiana State University Press, 1959.

Haworth, Alan. *Anti-Libertarianism: Markets, Philosophy, and Myth.* London: Routledge, 1994.

Hayek, Friedrich A. *The Road to Serfdom.* 1944. Reprint. Chicago: University of Chicago Press, 1976.

Henderson, John N. *Davis and Lincoln.* Pamphlet published under the auspices of Camp Robertson Confederate Veterans, August 9, 1894.

Herndon, William H. *Abraham Lincoln, Miss Anne Rutledge, New Salem, Pioneering, and the Poem: A Lecture.* 1866. Reprint. LaVergne, Tenn.: Kessinger Publishing, 2010.

Hill, Daniel Harvey. *Young People's History of North Carolina.* Charlotte: Stone and Barringer Company, 1907.

Hirschman, Albert O. *The Rhetoric of Reaction: Perversity, Futility, Jeopardy.* Cambridge, Mass.: Harvard University Press, 1991.

Hobson, Fred. *Serpent in Eden: H. L. Mencken and the South.* Baton Rouge: Louisiana State University Press, 1974.

Hofstadter, Richard. *The American Political Tradition and the Men Who Made It.* New York: Alfred A. Knopf, 1948.

Hogan, Jackie. *Lincoln, Inc.: Selling the Sixteenth President in Contemporary America.* Lanham, Md.: Rowman and Littlefield, 2011.

Hogeland, William. *Inventing American History.* Cambridge, Mass.: MIT Press, 2009.

Holmes, Stephen. *The Anatomy of Antiliberalism.* Cambridge, Mass.: Harvard University Press, 1993.

———. *Passions and Constraint: On the Theory of Liberal Democracy*. Cambridge, Mass.: Harvard University Press, 1995.

Holzer, Harold. *Lincoln Seen and Heard*. Lawrence: University Press of Kansas, 2000.

———. *Lincoln at Cooper Union: The Speech That Made Abraham Lincoln President*. New York: Simon and Schuster, 2004.

———. *Lincoln, President-Elect: Abraham Lincoln and the Great Secession Winter, 1860–1861*. New York: Simon and Schuster, 2008.

———, ed. *The Lincoln Anthology: Great Writers on His Legacy from 1860 to Now*. New York: Library of America, 2009.

Holzer, Harold, Gabor S. Boritt, and Mark E. Neely Jr. *The Lincoln Image: Abraham Lincoln and the Popular Print*. New York: Charles Scribner's Sons, 1984.

Hook, Sidney. *The Hero in History*. 1943. Reprint. New York: Cosimo Classics, 2008.

Hoppe, Hans-Hermann. *Democracy, the God That Failed: The Economics and Politics of Monarchy, Democracy, and Natural Order*. New Brunswick, N.J.: Transaction Publishers, 2011.

Horne, Gerald. *The White Pacific: U.S. Imperialism and Black Slavery in the South Seas after the Civil War*. Honolulu: University of Hawaii Press, 2007.

Horsman, Reginald. *Race and Manifest Destiny: The Origins of American Racial Anglo-Saxonism*. Cambridge, Mass.: Harvard University Press, 1981.

Horton, Carol A. *Race and the Making of American Liberalism*. New York: Oxford University Press, 2005.

Horwitz, Tony. *Confederates in the Attic: Dispatches from the Unfinished Civil War*. New York: Pantheon Books, 1998.

Howe, Daniel Walker. *The Political Culture of the American Whigs*. Chicago: University of Chicago Press, 1979.

———. *Making the American Self: Jonathan Edward to Abraham Lincoln*. New York: Oxford University Press, 2009.

Huebert, Jacob H. *Libertarianism Today*. Santa Barbara, Calif.: Praeger, 2010.

Hummel, Jeffrey Rogers. *Emancipating Slaves, Enslaving Free Men: A History of the American Civil War*. Chicago: Open Court Press, 1996.

Jaffa, Harry V. *Crisis of the House Divided: An Interpretation of the Issues in the Lincoln Douglas Debates*. Chicago: University of Chicago Press, 1959.

———. *A New Birth of Freedom: Abraham Lincoln and the Coming of the Civil War*. Lanham, Md.: Rowman and Littlefield, 2000.

———. *How to Think about the American Revolution*. Claremont, Calif.: Claremont Institute, 2001.

———. *American Conservatism and the American Founding*. Claremont, Calif.: Claremont Institute, 2002.

———. *Crisis of the Strauss Divided: Essay on Leo Strauss and Straussianism, East and West*. Lanham, Md.: Rowman and Littlefield, 2012.

Janney, Caroline E. *Burying the Dead but Not the Past: Ladies' Memorial Associations and the Lost Cause*. Chapel Hill: University of North Carolina Press, 2008.

Jividen, Jason. *Claiming Lincoln: Progressivism, Equality, and the Battle for Lincoln's Legacy in Presidential Rhetoric.* DeKalb: Northern Illinois University Press, 2011.

Johannsen, Robert W. *Lincoln, the South, and Slavery: The Political Dimension.* Baton Rouge: Louisiana State University Press, 1991.

Johnson, Ludwell. *Division and Reunion: America, 1848–1877.* New York: John Wiley and Sons, 1978.

Johnson, Paul. *Modern Times: The World from the Twenties to the Eighties.* New York: Harper and Row, 1983.

Jones, Alfred Haworth. *Roosevelt's Image Brokers: Poets, Playwrights, and the Use of the Lincoln Symbol.* Port Washington, N.Y.: National University Publications, Kennikat Press, 1974.

Jones, Daniel Stedman. *Masters of the Universe: Hayek, Friedman, and the Birth of Neoliberal Politics.* Princeton: Princeton University Press, 2012.

Jones, Howard. *Abraham Lincoln and a New Birth of Freedom.* Lincoln: University of Nebraska Press, 1999.

Jordan, Terry G. *German Seed in Texas Soil: Immigrant Farmers in Nineteenth-Century Texas.* Austin: University of Texas Press, 1996.

Judis, John B. *William F. Buckley, Jr.: Patron Saint of the Conservatives.* New York: Simon and Schuster, 1988.

Kachun, Mitch. *Festivals of Freedom: Memory and Meaning in African American Emancipation Celebrations, 1808–1915.* Amherst: University of Massachusetts Press, 2003.

Kammen, Michael. *Mystic Chords of Memory: The Transformation of Tradition in America.* New York: Vintage Books, 1991.

Kantrowicz, Stephen. *Ben Tillman and the Reconstruction of White Supremacy.* Chapel Hill: University of North Carolina Press, 2000.

Kaplan, Fred. *Lincoln: The Biography of a Writer.* New York: HarperCollins, 2008.

Karp, Walter. *The Politics of War: The Story of Two Wars Which Forever Altered the Political Life of the American Republic.* 1979. Reprint. New York: Franklin Square Press, 2003.

Kauffman, Michael W. *American Brutus: John Wilkes Booth and the Lincoln Conspiracies.* New York: Random House, 2004.

Kendall, Willmoore, and George W. Carey. *The Basic Symbols of the American Political Tradition.* Baton Rouge: Louisiana State University Press, 1970.

Kennedy, David. *Freedom from Fear: The American People in Depression and War, 1929–1945.* New York: Oxford University Press, 1999.

Kennedy, James Ronald, and Walter Donald Kennedy. 1991. Reprint. *The South Was Right!* Gretna, La.: Pelican Publishing Company, 1994.

Kerby, Robert L. *Kirby Smith's Confederacy: The Trans-Mississippi South 1863–1865.* New York: Columbia University Press, 1972.

Kimball, Roger, and Hilton Kramer, eds. *Counterpoints: 25 Years of the New Criterion on Culture and Arts.* Chicago: Ivan R. Dee, 2007.

Kimmel, Stanley. *The Mad Booths of Maryland.* New York: Bobbs-Merrill, 1940.

King, Grace, and John R. Ficklen. *History of Louisiana.* New Orleans: L. Graham Company, 1893.

Kirk, Russell. *The Conservative Mind: From Burke to Eliot.* Chicago: Regnery Books, 1953.

Klein, Naomi. *The Shock Doctrine: The Rise of Disaster Capitalism.* New York: Henry Holt, 2007.

Korngold, Ralph. *Two Friends of Man: The Story of William Lloyd Garrison and Wendell Phillips and Their Relationship with Abraham Lincoln.* Boston: Little, Brown, 1950.

Krannawitter, Thomas L. *Vindicating Lincoln: Defending the Politics of Our Greatest President.* New York: Rowman and Littlefield, 2008.

Kristol, Irving. *Reflections of a Neoconservative.* New York: Basic Books, 1983.

Krugman, Paul. *The Conscience of a Liberal.* New York: W. W. Norton, 2007.

LaFeber, Walter. *The New Empire: An Interpretation of American Expansion.* 1963. Reprint. Ithaca: Cornell University Press, 1998.

Lamon, Ward Hill. *The Life of Abraham Lincoln.* 1872. Reprint. Lincoln: University of Nebraska Press, 1999.

Lankford, Nelson, ed. *An Irishman in Dixie: Thomas Connolly's Diary of the Fall of the Confederacy.* Columbia: University of South Carolina Press, 1988.

Lasch, Christopher. *The True and Only Heaven: Progress and Its Critics.* New York: W. W. Norton, 1991.

Lassiter, Matthew D., and Joseph Crespino. *The Myth of Southern Exceptionalism.* New York: Oxford University Press, 2010.

Lawson, Melinda. *Patriot Fires: Forging a New American Nationalism in the Civil War.* Lawrence: University Press of Kansas, 2002.

Lee, Susan Pendleton. *Lee's School History of the United States.* Richmond, Va.: B. F. Johnson Publishing Company, 1895.

———. *Lee's School History of the United States with Questions and Summaries for Reviews and Essays.* Richmond, Va.: B. F. Johnson Publishing Company, 1896.

———. *Lee's Primary School History of the United States.* Richmond, Va.: B. F. Johnson Publishing Company, 1897.

Leonard, Elizabeth. *Lincoln's Avengers: Justice, Revenge, and Reunion after the Civil War.* New York: W. W. Norton, 2004.

Levine, Bruce. *Half Slave and Half Free: The Roots of the Civil War.* New York: Hill and Wang, 1992.

Lewis, Lloyd. *Myths after Lincoln.* 1929. Reprint. New York: Press of the Readers Club, 1941.

Lincecum, Jerry Bryan, Edward Hake Phillips, and Peggy A. Redshaw, eds. *Gideon Lincecum's Sword: Civil War Letters from the Texas Home Front.* Denton: University of North Texas Press, 2001.

Lincoln, Abraham, and Orville Hickman Browning. *Abraham Lincoln and Mary Owen[s]: Three Letters.* . . . Springfield, Ill.: Barker's Art Store, 1922.

Lind, Michael. *What Lincoln Believed: The Values and Convictions of America's Greatest President.* New York: Doubleday, 2004.

Litwack, Leon. *Trouble in Mind: Black Southerners in the Age of Jim Crow.* New York: Vintage Books, 1998.

Livingston, Donald. *Philosophical Melancholy and Delirium: Hume's Pathology of Philosophy.* Chicago: University of Chicago Press, 1998.

Loewen, James M., and Edward H. Sebesta, eds. *The Confederate and Neo-Confederate Reader: The Great Truth about the "Lost Cause."* Jackson: University Press of Mississippi, 2010.

Long, David E. *The Jewel of Liberty: Abraham Lincoln's Re-election and the End of Slavery.* Mechanicsburg, Pa.: Stackpole Books, 1994.

MacIntyre, Alisdair. *After Virtue:* Notre Dame, Ind.: University of Notre Dame Press, 1984.

MacLean, Nancy. *Freedom Is Not Enough: The Opening of the American Workplace.* Cambridge, Mass.: Harvard University Press, 2006.

Magill, Mary Tucker. *Magill's First Book in Virginia History.* Lynchburg, Va.: J. P. Bell Company, 1908.

Magness, Phillip W., and Sebastian N. Page. *Colonization after Emancipation: Lincoln and the Movement for Black Resettlement.* Columbia: University of Missouri Press, 2011.

Malik, Kenan. *From Fatwa to Jihad: The Rushdie Affair and Its Aftermath.* Brooklyn: Melville House Publishing, 2010.

Malvasi, Mark G. *The Unregenerate South: The Agrarian Thought of John Crowe Ransom, Allen Tate, and Donald Davidson.* Baton Rouge: Louisiana State University Press, 1997.

Manber, Jeffrey, and Neal Dahlstrom. *Lincoln's Wrath: Fierce Mobs, Brilliant Scoundrels and a President's Mission to Destroy the Press.* Naperville, Ill.: Sourcebooks, 2005.

Marsden, George M. *Fundamentalism and American Culture.* New York: Oxford University Press, 1980.

Marshall, Anne E. *Creating a Confederate Kentucky: The Lost Cause and Civil War Memory in a Border State.* Chapel Hill: University of North Carolina Press, 2010.

Marten, James. *Texas Divided: Loyalty and Dissent in the Lone Star State, 1856–1874.* Lexington: University Press of Kentucky, 1990.

Martin, Isabella D., and Myrta L. Avary, eds. *A Diary from Dixie.* New York: D. Appleton and Company, 1905.

Martin, James J. *Men against the State.* Colorado Springs: Ralph Myles, 1970.

Martin, Peter. *Samuel Johnson: A Biography.* Cambridge, Mass.: Belknap Press of Harvard University, 2009.

Masters, Edgar Lee. *Spoon River Anthology*. 1915. Reprint. Cutchogue, N.Y.: Buccaneer Books, 1986.

———. *Lincoln: The Man*. 1931. Reprint. Columbia, S.C.: Foundation for American Education, 1997.

Masters, Roger D. *The Nature of Politics*. New Haven: Yale University Press, 1989.

Masur, Louis P. *Lincoln's Hundred Days: The Emancipation Proclamation and the War for the Union*. Cambridge, Mass.: Harvard University Press, 2012.

Mayer, Henry. *All on Fire: William Lloyd Garrison and the Abolition of Slavery*. New York: St. Martin's Press, 1998.

Mayfield, Janis Boyle, ed. *My Eighty Years in Texas*. Austin: University of Texas Press, 1971.

McCaleb, Walter Flavius, ed. *The Memoirs of John H. Reagan: With Special Reference to Secession and the Civil War*. New York: Neale Publishing Company, 1906.

McCaslin, Richard B. *Tainted Breeze: The Great Hanging at Gainesville, Texas, 1862*. Baton Rouge: Louisiana State University Press, 1994.

McClintock, Russell. *Lincoln and the Decision for War*. Chapel Hill: University of North Carolina Press, 2008.

McCrary, Peyton. *Abraham Lincoln and Reconstruction: The Louisiana Experiment*. Princeton: Princeton University Press, 1978.

McCurry, Stephanie. *Confederate Reckoning: Power and Politics in the Civil War South*. Cambridge, Mass.: Harvard University Press, 2010.

McMichael, Kelly. *Sacred Memories: The Civil War Monument Movement in Texas*. Denton: Texas State Historical Association, 2009.

McPherson, James M. *The Struggle for Equality: Abolitionists and the Negro in the Civil War and Reconstruction*. Princeton: Princeton University Press, 1964.

———. *The Negro's Civil War: American Blacks Felt and Acted during the War for the Union*. New York: Vintage Books, 1965.

———. *Battle Cry of Freedom: The Civil War Era*. New York: Oxford University Press, 1988.

———. *Abraham Lincoln and the Second American Revolution*. New York: Oxford University Press, 1990.

———, ed. *"We Cannot Escape History": Lincoln and the Last Best Hope of Earth*. Urbana: University of Illinois Press, 1995.

———. *Drawn with the Sword: Reflections on the American Civil War*. New York: Oxford University Press, 1996.

———. *Is Blood Thicker than Water? Crises of Nationalism in the Modern World*. New York: Vintage Books, 1998.

———. *This Mighty Scourge: Perspectives on the Civil War*. New York: Oxford University Press, 2007.

———. *Tried by War: Abraham Lincoln as Commander in Chief*. New York: Penguin Books, 2008.

McPherson, James M., and William J. Cooper, Jr., eds. *Writing the Civil War: The Quest to Understand.* Columbia: University of South Carolina Press, 1998.

McPherson, Tara. *Reconstructing Dixie: Race, Gender, and Nostalgia in the Imagined South.* Durham: Duke University Press, 2003.

Mencken, H. L. *Prejudices: A Selection.* Selected, with introduction, by James T. Farrell. New York: Vintage Books, 1962.

Meriwether, Elizabeth Avery. *Facts and Falsehoods concerning the War on the South, 1861–1865.* Memphis: Spence Hall Lamb, 1904.

———. *Recollections of 92 Years, 1824–1916.* 1916. Reprint. McLean, Va.: EPM Publications, 1994.

Miller, William Ian. *The Anatomy of Disgust.* Cambridge, Mass.: Harvard University Press, 1997.

Miller, Randall M., Harry S. Stout, and Charles Reagan Wilson, eds. *Religion and the American Civil War.* New York: Oxford University Press, 1998.

Minor, Charles L. C. *The Real Lincoln: From the Testimony of His Contemporaries.* Facsimile ed. Richmond, Va.: Everett Waddey Company, 1904.

Mises, Ludwig von. *Human Action: A Treatise on Economics.* 1949. Reprint. Auburn, Ala.: Ludwig von Mises Institute, 1998.

———. *Theory and History.* 1957. Reprint. Auburn, Ala.: Ludwig von Mises Institute, 2007.

———. *Socialism: An Economic and Sociological Analysis.* 1951. Reprint. Auburn, Ala.: Ludwig von Mises Institute, 2010. http://mises.org/books/socialism/contents .aspx (accessed 1/21/2013).

Mitgang, Herbert, ed. *Lincoln as They Saw Him.* New York: Collier Books, 1962.

Moneyhon, Carl H. *Texas after the Civil War: The Struggle of Reconstruction.* College Station: Texas A&M University Press, 2004.

Moore, Mrs. M. B. *The Geographical Reader for the Dixie Children.* Raleigh, N.C.: Branson, Farrar, and Company, 1863.

Moretta, John Anthony. *William Pitt Ballinger: Texas Lawyer, Southern Statesman, 1825–1888.* Austin: Texas State Historical Association, 2000.

Moss, William, ed. *Confederate Broadside Poems: An Annotated Descriptive Bibliography.* Westport, Conn.: Meckler, 1988.

Murphy, Lawrence R., and Ron Tyler, eds. *The Slave Narratives of Texas.* Austin: State House Press, 1997.

Murphy, Paul V. *The Rebuke of History: The Southern Agrarians and American Conservative Thought.* Chapel Hill: University of North Carolina Press, 2001.

Napolitano, Andrew P. *The Constitution in Exile: How the Federal Government Has Seized Power by Rewriting the Supreme Law of the Land.* Nashville: Thomas Nelson Publishers, 2006.

Nash, George H. *The Conservative Intellectual Movement in America since 1945.* New York: Basic Books, 1976.

——. *Reappraising the Right: The Past and Future of American Conservatism.* Wilmington, Del.: ISI Books, 2009.

Neely, Mark E., Jr. *The Abraham Lincoln Encyclopedia.* New York: McGraw-Hill, 1982.

——. *The Fate of Liberty: Abraham Lincoln and Civil Liberties.* New York: Oxford University Press, 1991.

——. *The Last Best Hope: Abraham Lincoln and the Promise of America.* Cambridge, Mass.: Harvard University Press, 1993.

——. *The Union Divided: Party Conflict in the Civil War Era.* Cambridge, Mass.: Harvard University Press, 2002.

——. *The Boundaries of American Political Culture in the Civil War Era.* Chapel Hill: University of North Carolina Press, 2005.

——. *The Civil War and the Limits of Destruction.* Cambridge, Mass.: Harvard University Press, 2007.

——. *Lincoln and the Triumph of the Nation.* Chapel Hill: University of North Carolina Press, 2011.

Neely, Mark E., Jr., Harold Holzer, and Gabor S. Boritt. *The Confederate Image: Prints of the Lost Cause.* Chapel Hill: University of North Carolina Press, 1987.

Neff, John R. *Honoring the Civil War Dead: Commemoration and the Problem of Reconciliation.* Lawrence: University Press of Kansas, 2005.

Neuhaus, Richard John. *The Naked Public Square: Religion and Democracy in America.* Grand Rapids, Mich.: William B. Eerdmans, 1984.

Nevins, Allan, and Milton Thomas, eds. *The Diary of George T. Strong.* 4 vols. New York: Octagon Books, 1974.

Nichols, David A. *Lincoln and the Indians: Civil War Policy and Politics.* Urbana: University of Illinois Press, 1978.

Nichols, John. *The "S" Word: A Short History of an American Tradition . . . Socialism.* London: Verso, 2011.

Nicolay, John G., and John Hay. *Abraham Lincoln: A History.* 10 vols. New York: Century Company, 1890.

Nock, Albert Jay. *Our Enemy, the State.* 1935. Reprint. Caldwell, Idaho: Caxton Printers, 1950.

Noll, Mark A. *The Civil War as a Theological Crisis.* Chapel Hill: University of North Carolina Press, 2006.

——. *God and Race in American Politics: A Short History.* Princeton: Princeton University Press, 2008.

Norton, Anne. *Leo Strauss and the Politics of American Empire.* New Haven: Yale University Press, 2004.

Novick, Peter. *That Noble Dream: The "Objectivity Question" and the American Historical Profession.* Cambridge, U.K.: Cambridge University Press, 1998.

——. *The Holocaust in American Life.* Boston: Houghton Mifflin, 1999.

Nunn, W. C. *Texas under the Carpetbaggers.* Austin: University of Texas Press, 1962.

Oakes, James. *The Ruling Race: A History of American Slaveholders*. 1982. Reprint. New York: W. W. Norton, 1998.

——. *The Radical and the Republican: Frederick Douglass, Abraham Lincoln, and the Triumph of Antislavery Politics*. New York: W. W. Norton, 2007.

——. *Freedom National: The Destruction of Slavery in the United States, 1861–1865*. New York: W. W. Norton, 2012.

Oates, Stephen B. *With Malice toward None: The Life of Abraham Lincoln*. New York: Harper and Row, 1977.

——. *Abraham Lincoln: The Man behind the Myths*. New York: Harper and Row, 1984.

O'Brien, Michael. *The Idea of the American South, 1920–1941*. Baltimore: Johns Hopkins University Press, 1979.

——. *Intellectual Life and the American South*. An Abridged Edition of *Conjectures of Order*. Chapel Hill: University of North Carolina Press, 2010.

Orwell, George. *1984*. New York: Harcourt Brace, 1949.

——. *Essays*. New York: Alfred A. Knopf, Everyman's Library, 2002.

Osterweis, Rollin G. *The Myth of the Lost Cause, 1865–1900*. Hamden, Conn.: Archon Books, 1973.

Paludan, Phillip Shaw. *The Presidency of Abraham Lincoln*. Lawrence: University Press of Kansas, 1994.

Paul, Ron. *Liberty Defined: 50 Essential Issues That Affect Our Freedom*. New York: Grand Central Publishing, 2011.

Pennybacker, Anna J. *The New History of Texas for Schools*. N.p.d., 1895.

Perry, Jeffrey B., ed. *The Hubert Harrison Reader*. Middletown, Conn.: Wesleyan University Press, 2002.

Perry, Lewis. *Radical Abolitionism: Anarchy and the Government of God in Antislavery Thought*. Ithaca: Cornell University Press, 1973.

Peterson, Merrill. *Lincoln in American Memory*. Oxford: Oxford University Press, 1994.

Phillips, Jason. *Diehard Rebels: The Confederate Culture of Invincibility*. Athens: University of Georgia Press, 2007.

Plain Farmer. *Abraham Lincoln, Late President of the United States, Demonstrated to be the Gog of the Bible, as Foretold by the Prophet Ezekiel in the XXXVIII and XXXIX Chapters of the Book of Prophecy*. Pamphlet. Memphis: N.p., 1868.

Pollard, Edward Alfred. *The Lost Cause: A New Southern History of the War of the Confederates*. New York: E. B. Treat and Company, 1866.

Potter, Andrew. *The Authenticity Hoax: How We Get Lost Finding Ourselves*. New York: HarperCollins, 2010.

Potter, David. *The South and the Sectional Conflict*. Baton Rouge: Louisiana State University Press, 1968.

Prokopowicz, Gerald J. *Did Lincoln Own Slaves? And Other Frequently Asked Questions about Abraham Lincoln*. New York: Pantheon Books, 2008.

Quarles, Benjamin. *Lincoln and the Negro*. New York: Oxford University Press, 1962.

Rable, George C. *But There Was No Peace: The Role of Violence in the Politics of Reconstruction*. Athens: University of Georgia Press, 1984.

———. *The Confederate Republic: A Revolution against Politics*. Chapel Hill: University of North Carolina Press, 1994.

Raimondo, Justin. *An Enemy of the State: The Life of Murray Rothbard*. Amherst, N.Y.: Prometheus Books, 2000.

Raines, C. W., ed. *Six Decades in Texas*. Austin: Ben C. Jones and Company, 1900.

Ramsdell, Charles W. *Reconstruction in Texas*. Reprint ed. Gloucester, Mass.: Peter Smith, 1964.

Randall, James G. *Lincoln and the South*. Baton Rouge: Louisiana State University Press, 1946.

———. *Lincoln the Liberal Statesman*. New York: Dodd, Mead, 1947.

Rawick, George P., ed. *The American Slave: A Composite Autobiography*. 19 vols. Westport, Conn.: Greenwood, 1972.

Reynolds, Donald E. *Editors Make War: Southern Newspapers in the Secession Crisis*. Nashville: Vanderbilt University Press, 1966.

———. *Texas Terror: The Slave Insurrection Panic of 1860 and the Secession of the Lower South*. Baton Rouge: Louisiana State University Press, 2007.

Richardson, Heather Cox. *The Greatest Nation of the Earth: Republican Economic Policies during the Civil War*. Cambridge, Mass.: Harvard University Press, 1997.

Richardson, H. Edward. *Cassius Marcellus Clay: Firebrand of Freedom*. Lexington: University Press of Kentucky, 1976.

Richardson, Rupert N., Ernest Wallace, and Adrian N. Anderson. *Texas: The Lone Star State*. 4th ed. Englewood Cliffs: Prentice-Hall, 1981.

Riddle, Donald W. *Lincoln Runs for Congress*. New Brunswick, N.J.: Rutgers University Press, 1948.

———. *Congressman Abraham Lincoln*. Urbana: University of Illinois Press, 1957.

Riggenbach, Jeff. *Why American History Is Not What They Say: An Introduction to Revisionism*. Auburn, Ala.: Ludwig von Mises Institute, 2009.

Riley, F. L. *School History of Mississippi*. N.p.p., 1900.

Ripley, C. Peter, ed. *The Black Abolitionist Papers*. 5 vols. Chapel Hill: University of North Carolina Press, 1992.

Roark, James L. *Masters without Slaves: Southern Planters in the Civil War and Reconstruction*. New York: W. W. Norton, 1977.

Robertson, James I., ed. *A Confederate Girl's Diary*. Bloomington: Indiana University Press, 1966.

Robertson, Stacey M. *Parker Pillsbury: Radical Abolitionist, Male Feminist*. Ithaca: Cornell University Press, 2000.

Robin, Corey. *The Reactionary Mind: Conservatism from Edmund Burke to Sarah Palin*. New York: Oxford University Press, 2011.

Robinson, Armstead L. *Bitter Fruits of Bondage: The Demise of Slavery and the Collapse of the Confederacy.* Charlottesville: University of Virginia Press, 2005.

Rockwell, Llewellyn H., Jr., ed., *The Irrepressible Rothbard: The Rothbard-Rockwell Report Essays of Murray N. Rothbard.* Burlingame, Calif.: Center for Libertarian Studies, 2000.

Roland, Charles. *History Teaches Us to Hope: Reflections on the Civil War and Southern History.* Edited with an introduction by John David Smith. Lexington: University Press of Kentucky, 2007.

Rosenberg-Smith, Carroll. *This Violent Empire: The Birth of an American National Identity.* Chapel Hill: University of North Carolina Press, 2010.

Rothbard, Murray N. *The Ethics of Liberty.* New York: New York University Press, 1998.

———. *For a New Liberty: The Libertarian Manifesto.* 1973. Reprint. Auburn, Ala.: Ludwig von Mises Institute, 2006.

———. *The Betrayal of the American Right.* Auburn, Ala.: Ludwig von Mises Institute, 2007.

Rowland, Dunbar, ed. *Jefferson Davis, Constitutionalist: His Letters, Papers, and Speeches.* 10 vols. New York: J. J. Little and Ives Company, 1923.

Royster, Charles. *The Destructive War: William Tecumseh Sherman, Stonewall Jackson, and the Americans.* New York: Vintage Books, 1991.

Rubin, Anne Sarah. *A Shattered Nation: The Rise and Fall of the Confederacy, 1861–1868.* Chapel Hill: University of North Carolina Press, 2005.

Rubin, Paul H. *Darwinian Politics: The Evolutionary Origin of Freedom.* New Brunswick, N.J.: Rutgers University Press, 2002.

Rugemer, Edward Bartlett. *The Problem of Emancipation: The Caribbean Roots of the American Civil War.* Baton Rouge: Louisiana State University Press, 2008.

Russell, Herbert K. *Edgar Lee Masters: A Biography.* Urbana: University of Illinois Press, 2001.

Rutherford, Mildred Lewis. *Jefferson Davis and Abraham Lincoln.* N.p., 1916.

———. *Contrasted Lives of Jefferson Davis and Abraham Lincoln—Jefferson Davis: The Home of a Christian Gentleman; Abraham Lincoln: The Home of an Unbeliever.* Athens, Ga.: Mildred Lewis Rutherford, 1927.

Sandel, Michael. *Justice: What's the Right Thing to Do?* New York: Farrar, Straus, and Giroux, 2009.

Sands, Eric C. *American Public Philosophy and the Mystery of Lincolnism.* Columbia: University of Missouri Press, 2009.

Savage, Kirk. *Standing Soldiers, Kneeling Slaves: Race, War, and Monument in Nineteenth-Century America.* Princeton: Princeton University Press, 1997.

Schivelbusch, Wolfgang. *The Culture of Defeat: On National Trauma, Mourning, and Recovery.* New York: Henry Holt, 2001.

Schneider, Thomas E. *Lincoln's Defense of Politics: The Public Man and His Opponents in the Crisis over Slavery.* Columbia: University of Missouri Press, 2006.

Schott, Thomas E. *Alexander H. Stephens of Georgia: A Biography.* Baton Rouge: Louisiana State University Press, 1988.

Schulz, Kathryn. *Being Wrong: Adventures in the Margin of Error.* New York: Harper-Collins, 2010.

Schwartz, Barry. "The Reconstruction of Abraham Lincoln." In *Collective Remembering,* edited by David Middleton and Derek Edwards, 81–106. London: Sage Publications, 1990.

———. *Abraham Lincoln and the Forge of National Memory.* Chicago: University of Chicago Press, 2000.

———. "The New Gettysburg Address: A Study in Illusion." In *Rediscovering Abraham Lincoln,* edited by John Y. Simon and Harold Holzer, 160–86. New York: Fordham University Press, 2002.

———. *Abraham Lincoln in the Post-Heroic Era: History and Memory in Late Twentieth-Century America.* Chicago: University of Chicago Press, 2008.

Schwartz, Thomas F., ed. *"For a Vast Future Also": Essays from the Journal of the Abraham Lincoln Association.* New York: Fordham University Press, 1999.

Scrugham, Mary. *The Peaceable Americans of 1860–61: A Study in Public Opinion.* New York: Columbia University, 1921.

———. *Force or Consent as the Basis of American Government: The Debate on the Subject by the Author and Attorney W. H. Townsend.* Pamphlet. Lexington, Ky.: Lexington Chapter of the United Daughters of the Confederacy, n.d.

Sebesta, Edward H. "Neo-Confederate Ideology in the Texas History Standards." In *Politics and the History Curriculum: The Struggle over Standards in Texas and the Nation,* edited by Keith A. Erekson, 148–68. New York: Palgrave Macmillan, 2012.

Sehlinger, Peter J. *Kentucky's Last Cavalier: General William Preston, 1816–1887.* Frankfort: Kentucky Historical Society, 2004.

Sellers, Charles. *The Market Revolution: Jacksonian America, 1815–1846.* New York: Oxford University Press, 1992.

Shea, John Gilmary, ed. *The Lincoln Memorial: A Record of the Life, Assassination, and Obsequies of the Martyred President.* New York: Bunce and Huntington, 1865.

Shenk, Joshua Wolf. *Lincoln's Melancholy: How Depression Challenged a President and Fueled His Greatness.* Boston: Houghton Mifflin, 2005.

Sherman, William Tecumseh. *Memoirs.* 2 vols. New York: D. Appleton, 1875.

Shively, Charles, ed. *The Collected Works of Lysander Spooner.* 6 vols. Weston, Mass.: M and S Press, 1971.

Shone, Steve J. *Lysander Spooner: American Anarchist.* Lanham, Md.: Lexington Books, 2010.

Silber, Nina. *The Romance of Reunion: Northerners and the South, 1865–1900.* Chapel Hill: University of North Carolina Press, 1993.

Silverthorne, Elizabeth. *Ashbel Smith of Texas: Pioneer, Patriot, Statesman, 1805–1886.* College Station: Texas A&M University Press, 1982.

Simms, William Gilmore. *The History of South Carolina.* Columbia, S.C.: State Company Printers, 1917.

Simon, John Y., Harold Holzer, and Dawn Vogel, eds. *Rediscovering Abraham Lincoln.* New York: Fordham University Press, 2002.

———, eds. *Lincoln Revisited: New Insights from the Lincoln Forum.* New York: Fordham University Press, 2007.

Singal, Daniel Joseph. *The War Within: From Victorian to Modernist Thought in the South, 1919–1945.* Chapel Hill: University of North Carolina Press, 1982.

Sitkoff, Harvard. *A New Deal for Blacks: The Emergence of Civil Rights as a National Issue.* Vol. 1: *The Depression Decade.* New York: Oxford University Press, 1978.

Smith, David Livingstone. *Less than Human: Why We Demean, Enslave, and Exterminate Others.* New York: St. Martin's Press, 2011.

Smith, John David. *An Old Creed for a New South: Proslavery Ideology and Historiography, 1865–1918.* 1985. Reprint. Carbondale: Southern Illinois University Press, 2008.

Smith, Rogers M. *Civic Ideals: Conflicting Visions of Citizenship in U.S. History.* New Haven: Yale University Press, 1997.

Spurlin, Charles D., ed. *The Civil War Diary of Charles A. Leuschner.* Austin, Tex.: Eakin Press, 1992.

Stampp, Kenneth. *The Peculiar Institution: Slavery in the Antebellum South.* New York: Vintage Books, 1956.

———. *The Era of Reconstruction, 1865–1877.* New York: Alfred A. Knopf, 1965.

Steers, Edward, Jr. *Blood on the Moon: The Assassination of Abraham Lincoln.* Lexington: University Press of Kentucky, 2001.

———. *Lincoln Legends: Myths, Hoaxes, and Confabulations Associated with Our Greatest President.* Lexington: University Press of Kentucky, 2007.

Steiner, Mark E. *An Honest Calling: The Law Practice of Abraham Lincoln.* DeKalb: Northern Illinois University Press, 2006.

Stenner, Karen. *The Authoritarian Dynamic.* New York: Cambridge University Press, 2005.

Stephens, Alexander H. *A Constitutional View of the Late War between the States; Its Causes, Character, Conduct and Results.* 2 vols. Philadelphia: National Publishing Company, 1868 and 1870.

Stewart, James Brewer. *Holy Warriors: The Abolitionists and American Slavery.* New York: Hill and Wang, 1976.

Stout, Harry S. *Upon the Altar of the Nation: A Moral History of the Civil War.* New York: Viking Press, 2006.

Strauss, Leo. *Natural Right and History.* Chicago: University of Chicago Press, 1953.

Striner, Richard. *Father Abraham: Lincoln's Relentless Struggle to End Slavery.* New York: Oxford University Press, 2006.

Strozier, Charles B. *Lincoln's Quest for Union: Public and Private Meanings.* New York: Basic Books, 1982.

Strunsky, Rose. *Abraham Lincoln*. New York: Macmillan, 1914.

Sundquist, Eric J., ed. *The Oxford W. E. B. Du Bois Reader*. New York: Oxford University Press, 1996.

Tagg, Larry. *The Unpopular Mr. Lincoln: The Story of America's Most Reviled President*. New York: Savas Beatie, 2009.

Tavris, Carol, and Elliot Aronson. *Mistakes Were Made (but Not by Me): Why We Justify Foolish Beliefs, Bad Decisions, and Hurtful Acts*. New York: Harcourt Books, 2007.

Thomas, Benjamin. *Portrait for Posterity: Lincoln and His Biographers*. New Brunswick, N.J.: Rutgers University Press, 1947.

———. *Abraham Lincoln*. New York: Alfred A. Knopf, 1952.

Thompson, C. Bradley, and Yaron Brook. *Neoconservatism: An Obituary for an Idea*. Boulder, Colo.: Paradigm Publishers, 2010.

Tidwell, William A. *April '65: Confederate Covert Action in the American Civil War*. Kent, Ohio: Kent State University Press, 1995.

Tilman, Rick. *Ideology and Utopia in the Social Philosophy of the Libertarian Economists*. Westport, Conn.: Greenwood Press, 2001.

Topping, Simon. *Lincoln's Lost Legacy: The Republican Party and the African American Vote, 1928–1952*. Gainesville: University Press of Florida, 2008.

Townsend, Stephen A. *The Yankee Invasion of Texas*. College Station: Texas A&M University Press, 2006.

Townsend, William H. *Lincoln and the Bluegrass: Slavery and Civil War in Kentucky*. Lexington: University of Kentucky Press, 1955.

Trefousse, Hans L. *Andrew Johnson: A Biography*. New York: W. W. Norton, 1989.

———. *"First among Equals": Abraham Lincoln's Reputation during His Administration*. New York: Fordham University Press, 2005.

Tripp, C. A. *The Intimate World of Abraham Lincoln*. New York: Free Press, 2005.

Turner, James. *Without God, without Creed: The Origins of Unbelief in America*. Baltimore: Johns Hopkins University Press, 1985.

Turner, Thomas Reed. *Beware the People Weeping: Public Opinion and the Assassination of Abraham Lincoln*. Baton Rouge: Louisiana State University Press, 1982.

Twelve Southerners. *I'll Take My Stand: The South and the Agrarian Tradition*. 1930. Reprint. Baton Rouge: Louisiana State University Press, 1977.

Tyler, Lyon Gardiner. *John Tyler and Abraham Lincoln: Who Was the Dwarf? A Reply to a Challenge*. Richmond, Va.: Richmond Press, 1929.

Vidal, Gore. *Lincoln*. New York: Random House, 1984.

———. *United States: Essays, 1952–1992*. New York: Random House, 1993.

Wakelyn, John L., ed. *Southern Pamphlets on Secession: November 1860–April 1861*. Chapel Hill: University of North Carolina Press, 1996.

Walsh, John Evangelist. *The Shadows Rise: Abraham Lincoln and the Anne Rutledge Legend*. Urbana: University of Illinois Press, 1993.

Walther, Eric H. *The Fire-Eaters*. Baton Rouge: Louisiana State University Press, 1992.

——. *The Shattering of the Union: America in the 1850s.* Lanham, Md.: SR Books, 2004.

——. *William Lowndes Yancey and the Coming of the Civil War.* Chapel Hill: University of North Carolina Press, 2006.

Warren, Robert Penn. *The Legacy of the Civil War: Meditations on the Centennial.* New York: Vintage Books, 1964.

——. *Jefferson Davis Gets His Citizenship Back.* Lexington: University Press of Kentucky, 1980.

Watson, Robert P., William D. Pederson, and Frank J. Williams, eds. *Lincoln's Enduring Legacy: Perspectives from Great Thinkers, Great Leaders, and the American Experiment.* Lanham, Md.: Rowman and Littlefield, 2011.

Watterson, Henry. *The Compromises of Life and Other Lectures and Addresses.* New York: Fox, Duffield and Company, 1903.

Weaver, Richard M. *Ideas Have Consequences.* Chicago: University of Chicago Press, 1948.

——. *The Ethics of Rhetoric.* Chicago: Regnery, Gateway, 1953.

——. *The Southern Tradition at Bay: A History of Postbellum Thought.* Washington, D.C.: Regnery, Gateway, 1968.

Weber, Jennifer L. *Copperheads: The Rise and Fall of Lincoln's Opponents in the North.* New York: Oxford University Press, 2006.

Webster, Richard. *Why Freud Was Wrong: Sin, Science, and Psychoanalysis.* New York: Basic Books, 1995.

Weicek, William M. *The Sources of Antislavery Constitutionalism in America.* Ithaca: Cornell University Press, 1977.

Weiss, Nancy J. *Farewell to the Party of Lincoln: Black Politics in the Age of FDR.* Princeton: Princeton University Press, 1983.

White, Jonathan W. *Abraham Lincoln and Treason in the Civil War: The Trials of John Merryman.* Baton Rouge: Louisiana State University Press, 2011.

White, Ronald C. *Lincoln's Greatest Speech: The Second Inaugural.* New York: Simon and Schuster, 2002.

——. *Abraham Lincoln: A Biography.* New York: Random House, 2009.

Wiggins, William H. *O Freedom! Afro-American Emancipation Celebrations.* Knoxville: University of Tennessee Press, 1987.

Wiley, Bell Irvin, ed. *Fourteen Hundred and 91 Days in the Confederate Army: or Camp Life Day by Day, of the W.P. Lane Rangers.* Jackson, Tenn.: McCowat-Mercer Press, 1954.

Williams, Ben Ames, ed. *A Diary from Dixie by Mary Chesnut.* Boston: Houghton Mifflin, 1949.

Williams, Frank J. *Judging Lincoln.* Carbondale: Southern Illinois University Press, 2002.

Williams, T. Harry. *Lincoln and the Radicals.* Madison: University of Wisconsin Press, 1941.

Williams, William Appleman. *America Confronts a Revolutionary World, 1776–1976.* New York: William Morrow, 1976.

———. *Empire as a Way of Life: An Essay on the Causes and Character of America's Present Predicament along with a Few Thoughts about an Alternative.* New York: Oxford University Press, 1980.

———. *The Tragedy of American Diplomacy.* 1959. Reprint. New York: W. W. Norton, 1984.

Williamson, Joel. *The Crucible of Race: Black-White Relations in the American South since Emancipation.* New York: Oxford University Press, 1984.

Wills, Garry. *Lincoln at Gettysburg: The Words That Remade America.* New York: Simon and Schuster, 1992.

———. "Henry Adams on Lincoln." In *Lincoln Revisited,* edited by John Y. Simon, Harold Holzer, and Dawn Vogel, 297–310. New York: Fordham University Press, 2007.

Wilson, Charles Reagan. *Baptized in Blood: The Religion of the Lost Cause, 1865–1920.* Athens: University of Georgia Press, 1980.

Wilson, Clyde N., ed. *A Defender of Southern Conservatism: M. E. Bradford and His Achievements.* Columbia: University of Missouri Press, 1999.

———. *From Union to Empire: Essays in the Jeffersonian Tradition.* Columbia, S.C.: Foundation for American Education, 2003.

Wilson, David Sloan. *Darwin's Cathedral: Evolution, Religion, and the Nature of Society.* Chicago: University of Chicago Press, 2002.

———. *Evolution for Everyone: How Darwin's Theory Can Change the Way We Think about Our Lives.* New York: Delacorte Press, 2007.

Wilson, Douglas. *Honor's Voice: The Transformation of Abraham Lincoln.* New York: Alfred A. Knopf, 1998.

Wilson, Edmund. *Patriotic Gore: Studies in the Literature of the Civil War.* New York: Farrar, Straus, and Giroux, 1962.

Wilson, Frances. *John Wilkes Booth: Fact and Fiction of Lincoln's Assassination.* Boston: Houghton Mifflin, 1929.

Wilson, Rufus Rockwell. *Lincoln in Caricature.* New York: Horizon Press, 1953.

Winchell, Mark Royden. *Where No Flag Flies: Donald Davidson and the Southern Resistance.* Columbia: University of Missouri Press, 2000.

Winger, Stewart. *Lincoln, Religion, and Romantic Cultural Politics.* DeKalb: Northern Illinois University Press, 2003.

Winkle, Kenneth J. *The Young Eagle: The Rise of Abraham Lincoln.* Dallas: Taylor Trade, 2001.

Wise, John S. *The End of an Era.* Boston: Houghton Mifflin, 1899.

Witt, John Fabian. *Lincoln's Code: The Laws of War in American History.* New York: Free Press, 2012.

Wolfe, Alan. *The Future of Liberalism.* New York: Alfred A. Knopf, 2009.

———. *Political Evil: What It Is and How to Combat It.* New York: Alfred A. Knopf, 2011.

Wolff, Jonathan. *An Introduction to Political Philosophy*. Rev. ed. New York: Oxford University Press, 2006.

Wood, William D. *Reminiscences of Reconstruction in Texas*. N.p.p., 1902.

Woods, Thomas E., Jr. *The Politically Incorrect Guide to American History*. Washington, D.C.: Regnery Publishing, 2004.

Woodson, Carter Godwin. *The Mis-Education of the Negro*. 1933. Reprint. N.p.: Seven Treasures Publications, 2010.

Woodward, C. Vann. *The Strange Career of Jim Crow*. 3d rev. ed. New York: Oxford University Press, 1974.

———, ed. *Mary Chesnut's Civil War*. New Haven: Yale University Press, 1981.

Wooster, Ralph A. *Civil War Texas: A History and a Guide*. Austin: Texas State Historical Association, 1994.

———. *Lone Star Blue and Gray: Essays on Texas in the Civil War*. Austin: Texas State Historical Association, 1995.

Wyatt-Brown, Bertram. *Southern Honor: Ethics and Behavior in the Old South*. New York: Oxford University Press, 1982.

Yoo, John. *Crisis and Command: The History of Executive Power from George Washington to George W. Bush*. New York: Kaplan Publishing, 2009.

Zuckert, Catherine, and Michael Zuckert. *The Truth about Leo Strauss: Political Philosophy and American Democracy*. Chicago: University of Chicago Press, 2006.

ARTICLES AND ESSAYS

Adler, Constance. "The House That Dr. Calhoun Built." *Gambit Weekly* 22, February 27, 2001.

Anderson, David. "Down Memory Lane: Nostalgia for the Old South in Post–Civil War Plantation Reminiscences." *Journal of Southern History* 71 (February 2005): 105–36.

Arnhart, Larry. "Biopolitical Science." In *Evolution and Morality*, edited by James E. Fleming and Sanford Levinson, 221–65. New York: New York University Press, 2012.

Bailey, Fred Arthur. "The Textbooks of the 'Lost Cause': Censorship and the Creation of Southern State Histories." *Georgia Historical Quarterly* 75 (Autumn 1991): 507–33.

———. "Free Speech at the University of Florida: The Enoch Marvin Banks Case." *Florida Historical Quarterly* 71 (July 1992): 1–17.

———. "Free Speech and the 'Lost Cause' in Texas: A Study of Social Control in the New South." *Southwestern Historical Quarterly* 97 (January 1994): 453–77.

———. "Mildred Lewis Rutherford and the Patrician Cult of the Old South." *Georgia Historical Quarterly* 77 (Autumn 1994): 509–35.

———. "Free Speech and the Lost Cause in the Old Dominion." *Virginia Magazine of History and Biography* 103 (April 1995): 237–66.

———. "The Best History Money Can Buy: Eugene Campbell Barker, George Washington Littlefield, and the Quest for a Suitable Past." *Gulf South Historical Review* 20 (Autumn 2004): 28–48.

———. "M. E. Bradford, the Reagan Right, and the Resurgence of Confederate Nationalism." In *Painting Dixie Red: When, Where, Why, and How the South Became Republican,* edited by Glenn Feldman, 291–313. Gainesville: University Press of Florida, 2011.

Banks, Enoch Marvin. "A Semi-Centennial View of Secession." *Independent* 70, February 9, 1911, 299–303.

Barbee, David Rankin. "The Line of Blood: Lincoln and the Coming of the War." *Tennessee Historical Quarterly* 16 (March 1957): 3–54.

Barnett, Randy E. "Was Slavery Unconstitutional before the Thirteenth Amendment? Lysander Spooner's Theory of Interpretation." *Pacific Law Journal* 28 (1997): 977–1014.

Barnhart, Terry A. "Albert Taylor Bledsoe: The Political Creed of an Illinois Whig, 1840–48." *Journal of Illinois History* 3 (Spring 2000): 3–30.

Barr, John M. "The Tyrannicide's Reception: Responses in Texas to Lincoln's Assassination." *Lincoln Herald* 91 (Summer 1989): 58–63.

———. "If Lincoln Had Lived: Texans Reconsider Lincoln's Assassination." *Lincoln* 91 *Herald* (Winter 1989): 151–54.

———. "African American Memory and the Great Emancipator." In *Lincoln's Enduring Legacy: Perspectives from Great Thinkers, Great Leaders, and the American Experiment,* edited by Robert P. Watson, William D. Pederson, and Frank J. Williams, 133–64. Lanham, Md.: Rowman and Littlefield, 2011.

Beaty, Josephine Powell. "Lines Written for Memorial Day." *Historian* 3 (Spring 1941): 233–43.

Beck, Warren A. "Lincoln and Negro Colonization in Central America." *Abraham Lincoln Quarterly* 6 (September 1950): 162–83.

Bell, Walter F. "Civil War Texas: A Review of the Historical Literature." *Southwestern Historical Quarterly* 109 (October 2005): 205–32.

Berkeley, Kathleen. "Elizabeth Avery Meriwether, 'An Advocate for Her Sex': Feminism and Conservatism in the Post–Civil War South." *Tennessee Historical Quarterly* 43 (1984): 390–407.

Blackburn, Robin. "Lincoln and Marx: The Transatlantic Convergence of Two Revolutionaries." *Jacobin* 7–8 (Summer 2012): 48–51.

Blanchard, Kenneth C., Jr. "Natural Right and *The Origin of Species.*" *Perspectives on Political Science* 39 (January–March 2010): 12–18.

Blassingame, John W. "Using the Testimony of Ex-Slaves: Approaches and Problems." *Journal of Southern History* 41 (November 1975): 473–92.

Bledsoe, Albert Taylor. "The Great Error of the Eighteenth Century." *Southern Review* 5 (January 1869): 1–18.

———. "Alexander Hamilton." *Southern Review* 6 (July 1869): 1–31.

———. Review of *The Life of Abraham Lincoln, from His Birth to His Inauguration as President,* by Ward Hill Lamon. *Southern Review* 26 (April 1873): 328–64.

Blight, David W. "For Something beyond the Battlefield." *Journal of American History* 75 (March 1989): 1156–78.

Blount, Louise Foster. "Captain Thomas William Blount and His Memoirs." *Southwestern Historical Quarterly* 39 (July 1935): 1–14.

Boate, Edward Wellington. "The True Story of Andersonville Told by a Federal Prisoner." *Southern Historical Society Papers* 10, nos. 1–2 (January–February 1882): 25–32.

Boritt, Gabor S. "*Punch* Lincoln: Some Thoughts on Cartoons in the British Magazine." *Journal of the Abraham Lincoln Association* 15 (Winter 1994): 1–22.

Bradford, M. E. "Lincoln's New Frontier: A Rhetoric for Continuing Revolution, Part I." *Triumph* 6 (May–June 1971): 11–13, 15–17.

———. "Lincoln's New Frontier: A Rhetoric for Continuing Revolution, Part II." *Triumph* 6 (June 1971): 15–17.

———. "The Heresy of Equality: Bradford Replies to Jaffa." *Modern Age* 20 (Winter 1976): 62–77.

———. "Dividing the House: The Gnosticism of Lincoln's Political Rhetoric." *Modern Age* 23 (Winter 1979): 10–24.

———. "The Lincoln Legacy: A Long View." *Modern Age* 24 (Autumn 1980): 355–63.

———. "It's George Will Who's Being Shrill." *Washington Post,* December 12, 1981, A13.

———. "On Remembering Who We Are: A Political Credo." *Modern Age* 26 (Spring 1982): 144–52.

———. "Against Lincoln: My Dissenting Views." *American Spectator* 17 (December 1984): 37–39. Reprinted as "Against Lincoln: An Address at Gettysburg." In *The Historian's Lincoln: Pseudohistory, Psychohistory, and History,* edited by Gabor S. Boritt. Chicago: University of Illinois Press, 1988.

———. "Lincoln and the Language of Hate and Fear: A View from the South." *Continuity* 9 (Autumn 1984): 87–108.

———. "Bradford and Jaffa: Once More on Lincoln." *American Spectator* 18 (June 1985): 25–27.

———. "With the Lion and the Eagle." *Southern Partisan* 5 (Autumn 1985): 20–21.

———. "Lincoln's Republican Rhetoric: The Development of a Political Idiom." *Old Northwest* 14 (Spring 1990): 185–211.

———. "From the Family of the Lion." *Chronicles: A Magazine of American Culture* 15 (December 1991): 30–31.

Braeman, John. "Albert J. Beveridge and Demythologizing Lincoln." *Journal of the Abraham Lincoln Association* 25 (2004): 1–24.

Brook, Daniel. "Unreconstructed: The Federal Government Builds a Shrine to Its Archenemy." *Harper's Magazine* (May 2012): 40–41.

Brown, Sterling A. "Unhistoric History." *Journal of Negro History* 15 (April 1930): 134–61.

Browne, William Hand. Review of *The Life of Abraham Lincoln, from His Birth to His Inauguration as President,* by Ward Hill Lamon. *Southern Magazine* 4 (September 1872): 368–74.

Buchanan, Allen. "Toward a Theory of Secession." *Ethics* 101 (January 1991): 322–42.

———. "Theories of Secession." *Philosophy and Public Affairs* 26 (Winter 1997): 31–61.

Buchanan, Patrick J. "Mr. Lincoln's War: An Irrepressible Conflict?" *Chronicles: A Magazine of American Culture* 21 (October 1997): 13–22.

Cain, Marvin R. "Lincoln's Views on Slavery and the Negro: A Suggestion." *Historian* 26 (1964): 502–20.

Carney, Court. "The Contested Image of Nathan Bedford Forrest." *Journal of Southern History* 67 (August 2001): 601–30.

Case, Sarah H. "The Historical Ideology of Mildred Lewis Rutherford: A Confederate Historians New South Creed." *Journal of Southern History* 68 (August 2002): 569–628.

Childs, Herbert Ellsworth. "Agrarianism and Sex: Edgar Lee Masters and the Modern Spirit." *Sewanee Review* 41 (July–September 1933): 331–43.

Chomsky, Carol. "The United States–Dakota War Trials: A Study in Military Injustice." *Stanford Law Review* 43 (November 1990): 13–98.

Clampitt, Brad R. "The Breakup: The Collapse of the Confederate Trans-Mississippi Army in Texas." *Southwestern Historical Quarterly* 108 (April 2005): 499–534.

Cleven, N. Andrew N. "Some Plans for Colonizing Liberated Negro Slaves in Hispanic America." *Journal of Negro History* 11 (January 1926): 35–49.

Coffey, Shelby, III. "Gore Vidal's Lincoln Log." Review of *Lincoln: A Novel,* by Gore Vidal. *Washington Post Book World* 24, June 10, 1984, 1.

Commager, Henry Steele. "Myths, Morals and a House Divided." *New York Times,* April 29, 1962, 309.

Conant, Eve. "Rebranding Hate in the Age of Obama." *Newsweek,* May 4, 2009, 31–33.

Coski, John M. "Early 20th Century Pamphlets and Correspondence Present a Dissenting View of Lincoln." *Museum of the Confederacy Magazine* (Winter 2009): 9–12.

Crouch, Barry. "A Spirit of Lawlessness: White Violence; Texas Blacks, 1865–1868." *Journal of Social History* 18 (Winter 1984): 217–32.

Crouthamel, James L. "The Springfield Race Riot of 1908." *Journal of Negro History* 45 (July 1960): 164–81.

Current, Richard N. "Fiction as History: A Review Essay." *Journal of Southern History* 52 (February 1986): 77–90.

Dabney, Rev. R. L., D.D. "Memoir of a Narrative Received of Colonel John B. Baldwin, of Staunton, Touching the Origin of the War." *Southern Historical Society Papers* 1, no. 6 (June 1876): 443–55.

Daniel, John W. "Life, Services and Character of Jefferson Davis." *Southern Historical Society Papers* 17 (January–December 1889): 113–59.

Davidson, Donald. "The New South and the Conservative Tradition." *National Review* (September 1960): 141–46.

————. "Mirror for Artists." In *I'll Take My Stand: The South and the Agrarian Tradition,* by Twelve Southerners. 1930. Reprint. Baton Rouge: Louisiana State University Press, 1977.

Davis, David Brion. "The Enduring Legacy of the South's Civil War Victory." *New York Times,* August 26, 2001.

De Leon, Edwin. "Ruin of Reconstruction of Southern States." *Southern Magazine* (May 1874): 17–41, 287–309.

Draper, Robert. "It's Just a Texas Governor Thing." *New York Times Magazine,* December 6, 2009, 30–32.

Du Bois, W. E. B. "The Lie of History as It Is Taught Today (1960)." In *W. E. B. Du Bois: A Reader,* edited by Andrew G. Paschal, 115–20. New York: Collier Books, 1993.

Edgley, Alison. "Chomsky's Political Critique: Essentialism and Political Theory." *Contemporary Political Theory* 4 (2005): 129–53.

Egerton, Douglas R. "'Its Origin Is Not a Little Curious': A New Look at the American Colonization Society." *Journal of the Early Republic* 5 (Winter 1985): 463–80.

Fairclough, Adam. "Civil Rights and the Lincoln Memorial: The Censored Speeches of Robert R. Moton (1922) and John Lewis (1963)." *Journal of Negro History* 82 (Autumn 1997): 408–16.

Faust, Drew Gilpin. "Altars of Sacrifice: Confederate Women and the Narratives of War." *Journal of American History* 76 (March 1990): 1200–1228.

Feller, Daniel E. "Libertarians in the Attic: A Tale of Two Narratives." *Reviews in American History* 32 (June 2004): 184–95.

Fielding, Ellen Wilson. "Honest, Yes, but No Pushover." Review of *Lincoln: A Novel,* by Gore Vidal. *Wall Street Journal,* June 27, 1984, 32.

Fleming, Thomas. "Lincoln's Tragic Heroism." *National Review,* December 8, 1989, 38–40.

————. "From White House to Blockhouse." *Chronicles: A Magazine of American Culture* 21 (October 1997): 10–12.

————. "Rendering unto Lincoln." *Chronicles* 33 (February 2009): 10–11.

Foner, Eric. "Lincoln, Bradford, and the Conservatives." *New York Times,* February 13, 1982.

————. "*Review of Forced into Glory: Abraham Lincoln's White Dream,* by Lerone Bennett, Jr." *Los Angeles Times Book Review,* April 9, 2000.

Forbes, Ella. "African-American Resistance to Colonization." *Journal of Black Studies* 21 (December 1990): 210–23.

Foster, Gaines M. "Guilt over Slavery: A Historiographical Analysis." *Journal of Southern History* 56 (November 1990): 665–94.

Frederickson, George M. "A Man but Not a Brother: Abraham Lincoln and Racial Equality." *Journal of Southern History* 41 (February 1975): 39–58.

Freeman, Samuel. "Illiberal Libertarians: Why Libertarianism Is Not a Liberal View." *Philosophy and Public Affairs* 30, no. 2 (Spring 2001): 105–51.

————. "Capitalism in the Classical and High Liberal Traditions." *Social Philosophy and Policy* 28, no. 2 (2011): 19–55.

Fritzsche, Peter. "Specters of History: On Nostalgia, Exile, and Modernity." *American Historical Review* 106 (December 2001): 1587–1618.

Gannett, Lewis. "The Anne Rutledge Story: Case Closed?" *Journal of the Abraham Lincoln Association* 31 (Summer 2010): 21–60.

Gaughan, Anthony. "Woodrow Wilson and the Legacy of the Civil War." *Civil War History* 43 (September 1997): 225–42.

———. "Woodrow Wilson and the Rise of Militant Interventionism in the South." *Journal of Southern History* 65 (November 1999): 771–808.

Glazer, Lee, and Susan Key. "Carry Me Back: Nostalgia for the Old South in Nineteenth-Century Popular Culture." *Journal of American Studies* 30 (April 1996): 1–24.

Grimké, Archibald H. "Abraham Lincoln and the Fruitage of His Proclamation." *American Missionary* 63, no. 2 (February 1909): 51–53.

———. "Charles Sumner." American Negro Academy, Washington, D.C., 1911.

Grow, Matthew J. "The Shadow of the Civil War: A Historiography of Civil War Memory." *American Nineteenth Century History* 4 (Summer 2003): 77–103.

Guelzo, Allen C. "How Abe Lincoln Lost the Black Vote: Lincoln and Emancipation in the African American Mind." *Journal of the Abraham Lincoln Association* 25 (Winter 2004): 1–22.

———. "Hardly: The Democratic Nominee Is No Latter-Day Lincoln." *National Review,* September 29, 2008, 22–24.

———. "Our Lincoln: Obama, He Was Not." *National Review,* February 23, 2009, 25–28.

———. "Nullification Temptation." *National Review,* February 21, 2011, 28–30.

———. "Does Lincoln Still Belong to the Ages?" *Journal of the Abraham Lincoln Association* 33 (Winter 2012): 1–13.

———. Review of *Colonization after Emancipation: Lincoln and the Movement for Black Resettlement,* by Phillip W. Magness and Sebastian N. Page. *Journal of the Abraham Lincoln Association* 34, no. 1 (Winter 2013): 78–87.

Hacker, J. David. "A Census-Based Count of the Civil War Dead." *Civil War History* 57, no. 4 (December 2011): 307–48.

Haidt, Jonathan, Paul Rozin, Clark McCauley, and Sumio Imada. "Body, Psyche, and Culture: The Relationship between Disgust and Morality." *Psychology and Developing Societies* 9 (1997): 107–31.

Hall, James O. "Pink Parker's Tombstone." *Civil War Times Illustrated* 18 (July 1983): 134–35.

Hart, Jeffrey. "M. E. Bradford: RIP." *National Review,* March 29, 1993, 19–20.

Harwell, Richard B. "Confederate Anti-Lincoln Literature." *Lincoln Herald* 53 (Autumn 1951): 22–40.

Hayek, F. A. "The Intellectuals and Socialism." *University of Chicago Law Review* (Spring 1949): 417–33.

Hayes-Bautista, David. "Southwest's Mexican Roots: The Untold Stories: Mexicans, Lincoln, and Obama." *Los Angeles Eastside Sun* 63, no. 48, February 12, 2009, 1–2.

———. "Southwest's Mexican Roots: The Untold Stories: Mexicans, Lincoln, and Obama (Continued)." *Los Angeles Eastside Sun* 63, no. 49, February 19, 2009, 1–2.

Herndon, William H. "Analysis of the Character of Abraham Lincoln." *Abraham Lincoln Quarterly* 1, no. 7 (September 1941): 343–83.

———. "Analysis of the Character of Abraham Lincoln." *Abraham Lincoln Quarterly* 1, no. 8 (December 1941): 403–41.

———. "Facts Illustrative of Mr. Lincoln's Patriotism and Statesmanship." *Abraham Lincoln Quarterly* 3 (December 1944): 178–203.

Herrick, Sophia Bledsoe. "Albert Taylor Bledsoe." *Virginia University Alumni Bulletin* 6 (May 1899): 1–6.

Heyse, Amy Lynn. "The Rhetoric of Memory-Making: Lessons from the UDC's Catechism's for Children." *Rhetoric Society Quarterly* 38 (October 2008): 408–32.

Hill, Michael, and Thomas Fleming. "The New Dixie Manifesto: States' Rights Shall Rise Again." *Washington Post,* October 29, 1995.

Hitchens, Christopher. "The Man Who Made Us Whole." *Newsweek,* January 10, 2009.

Horne, Gerald. "Toward a Transnational Research Agenda for African American History." *Journal of African American History* 91 (Summer 2006): 288–303.

Howe, Irving. "Edmund Wilson and the Sea Slugs." *Dissent* (1963): 70–74.

Hughes, Richard T. "A Civil Theology for the South: The Case of Benjamin M. Palmer." *Journal of Church and State* 25 (1983): 447–67.

Hunter, R. M. T. "The Peace Commission of 1865." *Southern Historical Society Papers* 3, no. 4 (April 1877): 168–76.

Huston, James L. "The Experiential Basis of the Northern Anti-Slavery Impulse." *Journal of Southern History* 56 (November 1990): 609–40.

Hutter, W. H., and Ray H. Abrams. "Copperhead Newspapers and the Negro." *Journal of Negro History* 20 (April 1935): 131–52.

Jacobs, Wilbur R. "National Frontiers, Great World Frontiers, and the Shadow of Frederick Jackson Turner." *International History Review* 7 (May 1985): 261–70.

Jaffa, Harry. "Lincoln and the Cause of Freedom." *National Review* 17, September 21, 1965, 827–28, 842.

———. "Lincoln's Character Assassins." *National Review,* January 22, 1990, 34–38.

———. "In Abraham's Bosom." *National Review* 45, April 12, 1993, 50–51.

Janda, Lance. "Shutting the Gates of Mercy: The American Origins of Total War, 1860–1880." *Journal of Military History* 59 (January 1995): 7–26.

Janney, Caroline E. "Written in Stone: Gender, Race, and the Heyward Sheperd Memorial." *Civil War History* 52 (June 2006): 117–41.

———. "'One of the Best Loved, North and South': The Appropriation of National Reconciliation by LaSalle Corbett Pickett." *Virginia Magazine of History and Biography* 116 (January 2008): 370–406.

———. "War over a Shrine of Peace: The Appomattox Peace Monument and Retreat from Reconciliation." *Journal of Southern History* 77, no. 1 (February 2011): 91–120.

Jones, Malcolm. "Who Was More Important: Lincoln or Darwin?" *Newsweek,* July 7–14, 2008, 30–34.

Jost, John J., Christopher M. Federico, and James L. Napier. "Political Ideology: Its Structure, Functions, and Elective Affinities." *Annual Review of Psychology* 60 (2009): 307–37.

Kammen, Michael. "The Problem of American Exceptionalism: A Reconsideration." *American Quarterly* 45 (March 1993): 1–43.

Kaplan, Sydney. "The Miscegenation Issue in the Election of 1864." *Journal of Negro History* 34 (1949): 274–343.

Kendall, Willmoore. "Source of American Caesarism: Review of Harry V. Jaffa." *National Review* 7, November 7, 1959, 461–62.

———. "Equality: Commitment or Ideal?" *Phalanx* 1 (Autumn 1967): 95–103.

Kidd, Henry. "Richmond Air Corps." *Confederate Veteran* 51 (July–August 2003): 56.

King, Richard H. "The South and Cultural Criticism." *American Literary History* 1 (Autumn 1989): 699–714.

Kirk, Russell. "The Measure of Abraham Lincoln." *Month* 2 (April 1954): 197–206.

Klement, Frank. "'Brick' Pomeroy: Copperhead and Curmudgeon." *Wisconsin Magazine of History* 35 (Winter 1952): 106–13.

———. "Copperheads and Copperheadism in Wisconsin: Democratic Opposition to the Lincoln Administration." *Wisconsin Magazine of History* 42 (Spring 1959): 182–88.

Kolchin, Peter. "Whiteness Studies: The New History of Race in America." *Journal of American History* 89 (June 2002): 154–73.

Kramer, Paul A. "Empires, Exceptions, and Anglo-Saxons: Race and Rule between the British and United States Empires, 1880–1910." *Journal of American History* 88 (March 2002): 1315–53.

———. "Race-Making and Colonial Violence in the U.S. Empire: The Philippine-American War as Race War." *Diplomatic History* 30 (April 2006): 169–210.

LaFeber, Walter. "The Constitution and United States Foreign Policy: An Interpretation." *Journal of American History* 74 (December 1987): 695–717.

———. "The World and the United States." *American Historical Review* 100 (October 1995): 1015–33.

———. "The Post September 11 Debate over Empire, Globalization, and Fragmentation." *Political Science Quarterly* 117 (Spring 2002): 1–17.

Landess, Thomas H. "The Dark Side of Abraham Lincoln." *Southern Partisan* 5 (Autumn 1985): 18–22.

———. "Andrew Lytle, RIP." *Intercollegiate Review* (Spring 1996): 52–54.

Lapham, Lewis H. "Ignorance of Things Past: Who Wins and Loses When We Forget American History." *Harper's Magazine* (May 2012): 26–33.

Lasch, Christopher. "The Anti-Imperialists, the Philippines, and the Inequality of Man." *Journal of Southern History* 24 (August 1958): 319–31.

Lears, T. Jackson. "The Concept of Cultural Hegemony: Problems and Possibilities." *American Historical Review* 90 (June 1985): 567–93.

Lehmann-Haupt, Christopher. Review of *Lincoln: A Novel,* by Gore Vidal. "Books of the Times." *New York Times,* May 30, 1984, C20.

Livingston, Donald. "The Litmus Test for American Conservatism." *Chronicles: A Magazine of Culture* 25 (January 2001): 17–18.

Lockett, James D. "Abraham Lincoln and Colonization: An Episode That Ends in Tragedy at L'Ile a Vache, Haiti, 1863–1864." *Journal of Black Studies* 21 (June 1991): 428–44.

Lowenthal, David. "Past Time, Present Place: Landscape and Memory." *Geographical Review* 65 (January 1975): 1–36.

Lynn, Kenneth S. "The Right to Secede from History." *New Republic,* June 25, 1962, 21–24.

Lytle, Andrew Nelson. "The Lincoln Myth." Review of *Lincoln: The Man,* by Edgar Lee Masters. *Virginia Quarterly Review* 7 (October 1931): 620–26.

———. "The Hind Tit." In *I'll Take My Stand: The South and the Agrarian Tradition,* by Twelve Southerners, 1930. Reprint. Baton Rouge: Louisiana State University Press, 1977.

———. "They Took Their Stand: The Agrarian View after Fifty Years." *Modern Age* 24 (Spring 1980): 114–20.

Magness, Phillip W. "Benjamin Butler's Colonization Testimony Reevaluated." *Journal of the Abraham Lincoln Association* 29 (Winter 2008): 1–28.

Majewski, John. "Review of *The Real Lincoln,* by Thomas J. DiLorenzo." *Ideas on Liberty* 55 (April 2003): 60–62.

Masur, Kate. "The African American Delegation to Abraham Lincoln: A Reappraisal." *Civil War History* 56 (June 2010): 117–44.

McPherson, James M. "Abolitionist and Negro Opposition to Colonization during the Civil War." *Phylon* 26 (4th quarter 1965): 391–99.

———. "Lincoln the Devil." *New York Times Book Review,* August 27, 2000.

McRae, Elizabeth Gillespie. "Caretakers of Southern Civilization: Georgia Women and the Anti-Suffrage Campaign, 1914–1920." *Georgia Historical Quarterly* 82 (Winter 1998): 801–28.

Medford, Edna Greene. "Imagined Promises, Bitter Realities: African Americans and the Meaning of the Emancipation Proclamation." In *The Emancipation Proclamation: Three Views (Social, Political, Iconographic),* by Harold Holzer, Edna Greene Medford, and Frank J. Williams, 1–47. Baton Rouge: Louisiana State University Press, 2006.

Mencken, H. L. "The Sahara of the Bozart." *Prejudices: A Selection.* Selected, with introduction by James T. Farrell. New York: Vintage Books, 1962.

———. "Birth of Order." In Edgar Lee Masters, *Lincoln: The Man.* 1931. Reprint. Columbia, S.C.: Foundation for American Education, 1997.

Meyer, Frank S. "Review of *Freedom under Lincoln*, by Dean Sprague." *National Review* 17, June 15, 1965, 520.

———. "Lincoln without Rhetoric." *National Review* 17, August 24, 1965, 725.

———. "Again on Lincoln." *National Review* 18, January 25, 1966, 71 and 85.

———. "Richard M. Weaver: An Appreciation." *Modern Age* 14 (Summer–Autumn 1970): 243–48.

Miller, William Lee. "Lincoln's Profound and Benign Americanism, or Nationalism without Malice." *Journal of the Abraham Lincoln Association* 22 (Winter 2001): 1–13.

Mitgang, Herbert. "Was Lincoln Just a Honkie?" *New York Times,* February 11, 1968.

Monroe, Dan. "Lincoln the Dwarf: Lyon Gardiner Tyler's War on the Mythical Lincoln." *Journal of the Abraham Lincoln Association* 24 (Winter 2003): 32–42.

Morel, Lucas E. "Lincoln, Race, and the Spirit of '76." *Perspectives on Political Science* 39 (January–March 2010): 3–11.

Neely, Mark E., Jr. "Lincoln and the Indians." *Lincoln Lore,* no. 1627 (September 1973): 1–4.

———. "Lincoln and the Indians (Continued)." *Lincoln Lore,* no. 1628 (October 1973): 1–4.

———. "Abraham Lincoln's Nationalism Reconsidered." *Lincoln Herald* 76 (Spring 1974): 12–28.

———. "Miscegenation: Broad Farce or Political Dirty Trick?" *Lincoln Lore,* no. 1635 (May 1974): 1–4; no. 1636 (June 1974): 1–4.

———. "American Nationalism in the Image of Henry Clay: Abraham Lincoln's Eulogy on Henry Clay in Context." *Register of the Kentucky Historical Society* 73 (January 1975): 31–60.

———. "Lincoln Historiography: News and Notes." *Lincoln Lore,* no. 1647 (May 1975): 1–4.

———. "Emancipation: 113 Years Later." *Lincoln Lore,* no. 1653 (November 1975): 1–4.

———. "Pale-Faced People and Their Red Brethren." *Lincoln Lore,* no. 1686 (August 1978): 1–4.

———. "Abraham Lincoln and Black Colonization: Benjamin Butler's Spurious Testimony." *Civil War History* 25 (1979): 77–83.

———. "Lincoln and the Hateful Poet." *Lincoln Lore,* no. 1696 (June 1979): 1–4.

———. "The Lincoln Theme since Randall's Call: The Promises and Perils of Professionalism." *Papers of the Abraham Lincoln Association* 1 (1979): 10–70.

———. "A Progressive Admiration: Theodore Roosevelt and Abraham Lincoln." *Lincoln Lore,* no. 1707 (May 1980): 1–3.

———. "Can a Hero Survive Psychoanalysis?" *Lincoln Lore,* no. 1737 (November 1982): 1–4.

———. "The Emancipation Proclamation as an Act of Foreign Policy: A Myth Dispelled." *Lincoln Lore,* no. 1759 (September 1984): 1–4.

———. "Lincoln's Lyceum Speech and the Origins of a Modern Myth." *Lincoln Lore,* no. 1776 (February 1987): 1–4.

———. "Lincoln's Lyceum Speech and the Origins of a Modern Myth (Continued)." *Lincoln Lore,* no. 1777 (March 1987): 1–4.

———. "Lincoln Gored by Television." *Lincoln Lore,* no. 1787 (January 1988): 1–4.

———. "Colonization and the Myth That Lincoln Prepared the People for Emancipation." In *Lincoln's Proclamation: Emancipation Reconsidered,* edited by William A. Blair and Karen Fisher Younger. Chapel Hill: University of North Carolina Press, 2009.

———. "Lincoln, Slavery, and the Nation." *Journal of American History* 96 (September 2009): 456–58.

Nora, Pierre. "Between Memory and History: Les Lieux de Mémoire." *Representations* 26 (Spring 1989): 7–24.

Norman, Matthew D. "An Illinois Iconoclast: Edgar Lee Masters and the Anti-Lincoln Tradition." *Journal of the Abraham Lincoln Association* 24 (2003): 43–57.

———. "The Other Lincoln-Douglas Debate: The Race Issue in a Comparative Context." *Journal of the Abraham Lincoln Association* 31 (2010): 1–21.

Novak, William J. "The Myth of the 'Weak' American State." *American Historical Review* 113 (June 2008): 752–72.

Nutter, W. H., and Ray H. Abrams. "Copperhead Newspapers and the Negro." *Journal of Negro History* 20 (April 1935): 131–52.

Oakes, James. "The War of Northern Aggression." *Jacobin* 7–8 (Summer 2012): 45–47.

Obama, Barack. "What I See in Lincoln's Eyes." *Time,* July 4, 2005, 74.

Onuf, Peter S. "'To Declare Them a Free and Independent People': Race, Slavery, and National Identity in Jefferson's Thought." *Journal of the Early Republic* 18 (Spring 1988): 1–46.

Owsley, Frank J. "Irrepressible Conflict." In *I'll Take My Stand: The South and the Agrarian Tradition,* by Twelve Southerners. 1930. Reprint. Baton Rouge: Louisiana State University Press, 1977.

Paludan, Phillip Shaw. "Lincoln and Colonization: Policy or Propaganda?" *Journal of the Abraham Lincoln Association* 25 (Winter 2004): 23–37.

———. "Lincoln and Negro Slavery: I Haven't Got Time for the Pain." *Journal of the Abraham Lincoln Association* 27 (Summer 2006): 1–23.

Patten, Allen. "Democratic Secession from a Multinational State." *Ethics* 112 (April 2002): 558–86.

Payne, Walter A. "Lincoln's Caribbean Colonization Plan." *Pacific Historian* 7 (May 1963): 65–72.

Pearce, Colin D. "Libertarianism Ancient and Modern: Reflections on the Strauss-Rothbard Debate." *Interpretation* 38 (2010): 73–94.

Pessen, Edward. "How Different from Each Other Were the Antebellum North and South?" *American Historical Review* 85 (December 1980): 1119–49.

Pickett, LaSalle Corbett. "President Lincoln: Intimate Personal Recollections." *Lippincott's Monthly* (May 1906): 555–60.

Pinkser, Matthew. "Lincoln Theme 2.0." *Journal of American History* 96 (September 2009): 417–40.

Planck, Gary R. "Abraham Lincoln and Black Colonization: Theory and Practice." *Lincoln Herald* 72 (Summer 1970): 61–77.

Potter, David M. "The Historians Use of Nationalism and Vice Versa." *American Historical Review* 67 (July 1962): 924–50.

Pratt, Harry E. "Albert Taylor Bledsoe: Critic of Lincoln." *Illinois State Historical Society* 41 (1934): 153–83.

Pressly, Thomas J. "Emancipating Slaves, Enslaving Free Men: Modern Libertarians the Interpret United States Civil War, 1960s–1990s." *Civil War History* 46 (2000): 254–65.

Prokopowicz, Gerald J. "Rethinking Lincoln: Lerone Bennett's White Dream." *Lincoln Lore,* no. 1864 (Spring 2001): 2–3.

Quimby, Rollin W. "Lincoln's Character as Described in Sermons at the Time of His Death." *Lincoln Herald* 69 (Winter 1967): 179–85.

Ramsdell, Charles W. "Lincoln and Fort Sumter." *Journal of Southern History* 3 (August 1937): 259–88.

Randall, J. G. "Has the Lincoln Theme Been Exhausted?" *American Historical Review* 41 (January 1936): 270–94.

"Reexamining the Racial Record of Abraham Lincoln." *Journal of Blacks in Higher Education,* no. 29 (Autumn 2000): 126–31.

Reid, Brian Holden. "Review of *On the Road to Total War: The American Civil War and the German Wars of Unification, 1861–1871,* by Stig Forster and Jorg Nagler." *Journal of Military History* 62 (July 1998): 631–32.

Reid, R. L. "Louisiana and Lincoln's Assassination: Reactions in a Southern State." *Southern Historian* 6 (Spring 1985): 20–27.

Rockwell, Llewelyn H., Jr. "The Case for Paleo-Libertarianism." *Liberty* 3 (January 1990): 34–37.

———. "Down with the Presidency." *Chronicles: A Magazine of American Culture* 21 (October 1997): 27–32.

Roland, Charles. "The South of the Agrarians." In *History Teaches Us to Hope: Reflections on the Civil War and Southern History.* Edited by John David Smith. Lexington: University Press of Kentucky, 2007.

Ross, Dorothy. "Lincoln and the Ethics of Emancipation: Universalism, Nationalism, Exceptionalism." *Journal of American History* 96 (September 2009): 379–99.

Rothbard, Murray N. "The Negro Revolution." *New Individualist Review* (Summer 1963): 29–37.

Rozin, Paul, Jonathan Haidt, and Clark McCauley. "Disgust." In *Handbook of Emotions,* edited by M. Lewis and J. M. Haviland Jones, 637–53. New York: Guilford Press, 2000.

Sandage, Scott A. "A Marble House Divided: The Lincoln Memorial, the Civil Rights Movement, and the Politics of Memory, 1939–1963." *Journal of American History* 80 (June 1993): 135–67.

Sandefur, Timothy. "How Libertarians Ought to Think about the U.S. Civil War." *Reason Papers* 28 (Spring 2006): 61–83.

Scheips, Paul J. "Lincoln and the Chiriquí Colonization Project." *Journal of Negro History* 4 (October 1952): 418–53.

Scialabba, George. "A Great Deal of Work." *Nation,* January 16, 2008.

Schlesinger, Arthur, Jr. "In Defense of Government." *Wall Street Journal,* June 7, 1995, A14.

Schoonover, Thomas. "Misconstrued Mission: Expansionism and Black Colonization in Mexico and Central America during the Civil War." *Pacific Historical Review* 49 (November 1980): 607–20.

Schwartz, Barry. "Mourning and the Making of a Sacred Symbol: Durkheim and the Lincoln Assassination." *Social Forces* 70 (December 1991): 343–64.

———. "Memory as a Cultural System: Abraham Lincoln in World War II." *American Sociological Review* 61 (October 1996): 908–27.

———. "Collective Memory and History: How Abraham Lincoln Became a Symbol of Racial Equality." *Sociological Quarterly* 38 (Summer 1997): 469–96.

———. "Postmodernity and Historical Reputation: Abraham Lincoln in Late Twentieth-Century American Memory." *Social Forces* 77 (September 1998): 63–103.

———. "The Limits of Gratitude: Lincoln in African American Memory." *OAH Magazine of History* (January 2009): 27–32.

Schwartz, Barry, and Howard Schuman. "History, Commemoration, and Belief: Abraham Lincoln in American Memory, 1945–2001." *American Sociological Review* 70 (April 2005): 183–203.

Scrugham, Mary. "Force or Consent as the Basis of American Government." *Confederate Veteran* 32, no. 10 (October 1924): 376–78.

Sen, Amartya. "The Boundaries of Justice: David Hume and Our World." *New Republic,* December 29, 2011, 23–26.

Shaw, Stephanie J. "Using the WPA Ex-Slave Narratives to Study the Impact of the Great Depression." *Journal of Southern History* 69 (August 2003): 623–58.

Shear, Michael D., and Peter Whoriskey. "Lincoln Statue Heightens Old Pains." *Washington Post,* April 6, 2003.

Sheperd, William G. "Shattering the Myth of John Wilkes Booth's Escape." *Harper's Magazine* (November 1924): 700–719.

Silverman, Jason H. "In Isles beyond the Main: Abraham Lincoln's Philosophy of Black Colonization." *Lincoln Herald* 80 (Autumn 1978): 115–22.

Simon, John Y. "Abraham Lincoln and Anne Rutledge." *Journal of the Abraham Lincoln Association* 11 (1990): 13–34.

Smith, John David. "Black Images of Lincoln in the Age of Jim Crow." *Lincoln Lore,* no. 1681 (March 1978): 1–4.

———. "Black Intellectuals as Activists in the Age of Jim Crow." *Reviews in American History* 22 (June 1994): 328–34.

———. "The Enduring Myth of Forty Acres and a Mule." *Chronicle of Higher Education,* February 21, 2003, 10–11.

Sneed, Edgar P. "A Historiography of Reconstruction in Texas: Some Myths and Problems." *Southwestern Historical Quarterly* 72 (April 1969): 435–48.

Sparks, Randy J. "John P. Osterhout, Yankee, Rebel, Republican." *Southwestern Historical Quarterly* 90 (July 1986): 111–38.

Spindel, Donna J. "Twentieth-Century Slave Narratives Reconsidered." *Journal of Interdisciplinary History* 27 (Autumn 1996): 247–61.

Steele, Brian. "Thomas Jefferson, Coercion, and the Limits of Harmonious Union." *Journal of Southern History* 74 (November 2008): 823–54.

Steen, Ralph W. "Texas Newspapers and Lincoln." *Southwestern Historical Quarterly* 51 (January 1948): 199–212.

Stephenson, William Holmes. "Charles W. Ramsdell: Historian of the Confederacy." *Journal of Southern History* 26 (November 1960): 501–25.

Stewart, James Brewer. "Reconsidering the Abolitionists in an Age of Fundamentalist Politics." *Journal of the Early Republic* 26 (Spring 2006): 1–23.

Streifford, David M. "The American Colonization Society: An Application of Republican Ideology to Early Antebellum Reform." *Journal of Southern History* 45 (May 1979): 201–20.

Strickland, Arvarh E. "The Illinois Background of Lincoln's Attitude toward Slavery and the Negro." *Journal of the Illinois State Historical Society* 56 (1963): 474–94.

Sunstein, Cass R. "Constitutionalism and Secession." *University of Chicago Law Review* 58 (Spring 1991): 633–70.

Sutherland, Daniel. "Abraham Lincoln, John Pope, and the Origins of Total War." *Journal of Military History* 56 (October 1992): 567–86.

Teillard, Dorothy Lamon. "Lincoln in Myth and Fact: A Striking Instance of the Effort to Make History Conform to Respectability—How the First Fact-Life of Lincoln Was Received." *World's Work* 21 (February 1911): 14040–44.

Thelen, David. "Memory and American History." *Journal of American History* 75 (March 1989): 1117–29.

Thomas, Emory M. "Rebel Nationalism: E. H. Cushing and the Confederate Experience." *Southwestern Historical Quarterly* 73 (January 1970): 343–55.

Turner, Thomas Reed. "Review Essay: *'Right or Wrong God Judge Me': The Writings of John Wilkes Booth,* edited by John Rhodehamel and Louise Taper; *When the Bells Tolled for Lincoln: Southern Reaction to the Assassination,* by Carolyn Harrell." *Journal of the Abraham Lincoln Association* 20 (Summer 1989): 80–89.

Veyser, Harry C. "Murray Rothbard: In Memoriam." *Intercollegiate Review* (Autumn 1995): 41–45.

Vorenberg, Michael. "Abraham Lincoln and the Politics of Black Colonization." *Journal of the Abraham Lincoln Association* 14 (Summer 1993): 23–45.

Voss, Frederick S. "Adalbert Volck: The South's Answer to Thomas Nast." *Smithsonian Studies in American Art* 2 (Autumn 1988): 67–87.

Wallstein, Peter, and Valerie Bauerlein. "Haley Keeps Taking the Southern Test." *Wall Street Journal,* June 22, 2010.

Walther, Eric H. "The Fire-Eaters and ~~Seward~~ Lincoln." *Journal of the Abraham Lincoln Association* 32 (Winter 2011): 18–32.

Warren, Robert Penn. "Edmund Wilson's Civil War." *Commentary* (August 1962): 151–58.

Weaver, John. "Chaplain's Comments: Lincoln and the Emancipation Proclamation." *Confederate Veteran* 5 (2002): 61.

Weaver, Richard M. "Up from Liberalism." *Modern Age* 3 (Winter 1958–59): 21–32.

Weber, Jennifer L. "Was Lincoln a Tyrant?" *New York Times,* March 25, 2013. http://opinionator.blogs.nytimes.com/2013/03/25/was-lincoln-a-tyrant/ (accessed 4/4/2013).

Wei-Siang Hsieh, Wayne. "Total War and the American Civil War Reconsidered: The End of an Outdated 'Master Narrative.'" *Journal of the Civil War Era* 1 (September 2011): 394–408.

Wesley, Charles H. "Lincoln's Plan for Colonizing the Emancipated Negroes." *Journal of Negro History* 4 (January 1919): 7–21.

White, William W. "The Disintegration of an Army: Confederate Forces in Texas, April–June, 1865." *East Texas Historical Journal* 26 (Autumn 1988): 40–47.

Whitney, Halpin. "Bruce Barton's Babblings." *Southern Methodist,* September 1, 1926.

Wilentz, Sean. "Who Lincoln Was." *New Republic,* July 15, 2009, 24–47.

———. "States of Anarchy." *New Republic,* April 29, 2010, 5–6.

Will, George F. "A Shrill Assault on Mr. Lincoln." *Washington Post,* November 29, 1981.

Williams, Walter L. "United States Indian Policy and the Debate over Philippine Annexation: Implications for the Origins of American Imperialism." *Journal of American History* 66 (March 1980): 810–31.

Wilson, Clyde. "Lost Causes Regained: The Achievements of M. E. Bradford." In *A Defender of Southern Conservatism: M. E. Bradford and His Achievements,* edited by Clyde N. Wilson. Columbia: University of Missouri Press, 1999.

———. "The Treasury of Counterfeit Virtue." *Chronicles: A Magazine of American Culture* 33 (February 2009): 14–16.

———. "Society before Government: Calhoun's Wisdom." *Chronicles: A Magazine of American Culture* (July 2011): 14–17.

Wilson, Edmund. "Abraham Lincoln: The Union as Religious Mysticism." *New Yorker,* March 14, 1953, 116–36.

Woodward, C. Vann. "History from Slave Sources." *American Historical Review* 79 (April 1974): 470–81.

Wooster, Ralph A. and Robert Wooster. "A People at War: East Texas during the Civil War." *East Texas Historical Journal* 28 (Spring 1990): 3–17.

Worley, Ted R. "The Story of Alfred W. Arrington." *Arkansas Historical Quarterly* (Winter 1955): 315–39.

Wyatt-Brown, Bertram. "The Mask of Obedience: Male Slave Psychology in the Old South." *American Historical Review* 93 (December 1988): 1228–52.

Yetman, Norman R. "The Background of the Slave Narrative Collection." *American Quarterly* 19 (Autumn 1967): 534–53.

———. "Ex-Slave Interviews and the Historiography of Slavery." *American Quarterly* 36 (Summer 1984): 181–210.

Zengerle, Jason. "Paleo Wacko: The Roots of Rand Paul's Radicalism." *New Republic,* June 24, 2010, 5–6.

Zilversmit, Arthur. "Lincoln and the Problem of Race: A Decade of Interpretations." *Papers of the Abraham Lincoln Association* 2 (Summer 1980): 22–45.

Zoellner, Robert H. "Negro Colonization: The Climate of Opinion Surrounding Lincoln, 1860–65." *Mid-America: A Historical Review* 42 (July 1960): 131–50.

MANUSCRIPTS, CONFERENCE PAPERS, AND ADDRESSES

Bailey, Fred Arthur. "M. E. Bradford and the Resurgence of Confederate Nationalism." MS, in author's possession.

Barr, John M. "The Tyrannicide's Reception: Texans Respond to Lincoln's Assassination." Master's thesis, University of Houston–Clear Lake, 1988.

Clampitt, Brad R. "Morale in the Western Confederacy, 1864–1865: Home Front and Battlefield." Ph.D. diss., University of North Texas, 2006.

Demaree, David. "'A Gentleman, in Substance at Least': Lincoln's Relationship with Gentility in America." Paper read at Lincoln without Borders Conference, Shreveport, La., October 22, 2009.

Everett, Lloyd T. "Living Confederate Principles: A Heritage for All Time." Address delivered at the reception of the Washington Camp of the Confederate Veterans, Washington, D.C., February 14, 1914.

Frank, Edwin G. "The Meriwethers of Memphis and St. Louis." Master's thesis, University of Memphis, 1999.

Hays, Willard Murrell. "Polemics and Philosophy: A Biography of Albert Taylor Bledsoe." Ph.D. diss., University of Tennessee, 1971.

Horton, James Oliver, and Lois E. Horton. "The Man and the Martyr: Abraham Lincoln in African American History and Memory." Forty-fifth Annual Fortenbaugh Memorial Lecture. Gettysburg, Pa.: Gettysburg College Civil War Institute, 2008.

Jividen, Jason R. "Woodrow Wilson's Abraham Lincoln." Paper prepared for the Western Political Science Association Annual Meeting, Las Vegas, March 8, 2007.

Maas, David. "The Battle over Lincoln's Soul." Paper read at Lincoln Conference on Illinois History, Springfield, Ill., October 2, 2009, 1–21. MS in author's possession.

———. "An Unlikely Couple? Abraham Lincoln and Martin Luther King." Paper read at Lincoln without Borders Conference, Shreveport, La., October 22, 2009.

McClure, John M. "Men in the Middle: Freedmen's Bureau Agents in Lexington, Virginia, 1865–1869." Master's thesis, Virginia Commonwealth University, 2003.

Peatman, Jared Elliott. "Virginians Respond to the Gettysburg Address." Master's thesis, Virginia Tech University, 2006.

Read, James H. "Francis Lieber, Abraham Lincoln, and the American Contribution to International Law." Paper read at Lincoln without Borders Conference, Shreveport, La., October 23, 2009.

Sandefur, Timothy. "Texas Lincoln Talk." Paper read at Lone Star College–Kingwood, Houston, September 20, 2012.

Smith, Rogers M. "Emancipators' Dilemmas: The Lincoln Legacy and Struggles for African-American and Women's Rights, 1895–1945." Paper read at Wepner Symposium, Springfield, Ill., October 20, 2012.

Stockwell, Mary. "Lincoln's Bridge to the World: Woodrow Wilson." Paper read at Lincoln without Borders Conference, Shreveport, La., October 23, 2009.

Striner, Richard. "Lincoln, the Roosevelt's, and Herbert Croly's America." Paper read at Lincoln without Borders Conference, Shreveport, La., October 22, 2009.

Walther, Eric H. "The Course to Freedom: The Fire-Eaters and Secession." Master's thesis, Louisiana State University, 1984.

Wells, Cheryl A. "Mourning the President: British North American Reactions to Abraham Lincoln's Assassination." Paper read at Lincoln without Borders Conference, Shreveport, La., October 22–24, 2009.

ONLINE SOURCES

Abbeville Institute. Website. AbbevilleInstitute.org.

Adams, Paul. "Amelia Barr in Texas, 1856–1868." *Southwestern Historical Quarterly* online 49, no. 3 (January 1946). www.tsha.utexas.edu/publications/journals/ (accessed 8/24/2006).

American Presidency Project. Website. www.presidency.ucsb.edu.

Antiwar.com. Randolph Bourne Institute. Website. www.antiwar.com.

"AOL Lincoln Poll: What Does It Mean?" Council of Conservative Citizens, December 27, 2007. http://cofcc.org/2007/12/aol-lincoln-poll-what-does-it-mean/ (accessed 8/2/10).

Arnhart, Larry. DarwininianConservatism.com (accessed 8/14/2010).

Ashbrook Center. Ashland University. Website. Ashbrook.org.

Avlon, John. "Return of the Confederacy." *Daily Beast,* February 25, 2010. www .thedailybeast.com/articles/2010/02/25/return-of-the-confederacy.html (accessed 5/24/2010).

Barnett, Randy E. Website. LysanderSpooner.org (accessed 8/11/2010).

Beirich, Heidi. "Infighting at Sons of Confederate Veterans Leads to Calls for Leader's Resignation." *Intelligence Report,* no. 127 (Autumn 2007). www.splcenter.org/ get-informed/intelligence-report/browse-all-issues/2007/fall/dogfight (accessed 6/2/2012).

Beirich, Heidi, and Mark Potok. "The Ideologues: Who Are the Intellectuals Who Form the Core of the Modern Neo-Confederate Movement? And What Exactly Do They Think?" *Intelligence Report,* no. 116 (Winter 2004). www.splcenter.org/get-informed/intelligence-report/browse-all-issues/2004/winter/the-ideologues?page=0,0 (accessed 6/2/2012).

Benen, Steve. "Polling Secession." *Washington Monthly,* "Political Animal" blog, May 6, 2009. www.washingtonmonthly.com/archives/individual/2009_05/018062.php (accessed 6/1/2012).

Blackburn, J.K.P. "Reminiscences of the Terry Rangers," pts. 1–2. *Southwestern Historical Quarterly* online 22, nos. 1–2. www.tshaonline.org/shqonline/toc/vol-022-1115 (accessed 9/1/2006).

Bloom, Harold. "The Central Man." *New York Review of Books,* July 19, 1984. www.nybooks.com/articles/archives/1984/jul/19/the-central-man/?pagination=false (accessed 6/22/2010).

Blow, Charles. "Escaping Slavery." *New York Times,* January 4, 2013. www.nytimes.com/2013/01/05/opinion/blow-escaping-slavery.html (accessed 1/6/2013).

Blumenthal, Max. "Lobbyist for the Lost Cause." *Nation,* August 29, 2005. www.thenation.com/article/lobbyist-lost-cause (accessed 5/14/2012).

Boaz, David. "Up from Slavery: There's No Such Thing as a Golden Age of Lost Liberty." *Reason,* April 6, 2010. http://reason.com/archives/2010/04/06/up-from-slavery (accessed 6/30/2010).

Chait, Jonathan. "Why Romney Loves the States and Hates the Feds." *New York Magazine,* April 19, 2012. http://nymag.com/daily/intel/2012/04/why-romney-loves-the-states-and-hates-the-feds.html (accessed 5/5/2012).

Citizens' Councils. CitizensCouncils.com.

Citizens for Tax Justice. "Who Pays Taxes in America?" April 4, 2012. http://ctj.org/ctjreports/2012/04/who_pays_taxes_in_america.php (accessed 5/7/2012).

Claremont Institute. Website. Claremont.org.

Conason, Joe. "Joe Wilson's Confederate Cronies." *Truthdig,* September 16, 2009. www.truthdig.com/report/item/20090916_joe_wilsons_dixie_partisans/ (accessed 5/14/2012).

Deslatte, Melinda. "Southern States Low-Key for Lincoln Bicentennial." Sons of Confederate Veterans website, February 10, 2009. www.sonsofconfederateveterans.blogspot.com/2009/_02_02_archive.html (accessed 6/30/2010).

Dickerson, John. "Bob's Big Oy!" *Slate,* April 7, 2010. www.slate.com/articles/news_and_politics/politics/2010/04/bobs_big_oy.html (accessed 6/30/2010).

DiLorenzo, Thomas J. "An African-American Icon Speaks Truth to the Lincoln Cult." LewRockwell.com, January 12, 2008. www.lewrockwell.com/dilorenzo/dilorenzo139.html (accessed 3/13/2012).

———. "Will Ron Paul Destroy the 'Party of Lincoln'?" LewRockwell.com, January 4, 2012. http://lewrockwell.com/dilorenzo/dilorenzo224.html (accessed 1/21/2012).

Douglass, Frederick. "Oration in Memory of Abraham Lincoln." Speech delivered at the Unveiling of the Freedmen's Monument in Memory of Abraham Lincoln, Lincoln Park, Washington, D.C., April 14, 1876. TeachingAmericanHistory.org. http://teachingamericanhistory.org/library/index.asp?documentprint=39 (accessed 12/26/2012).

Drum, Kevin. "Soaking the Poor, State by State." *Mother Jones,* February 3, 2012. www.motherjones.com/kevin-drum/2012/02/soaking-poor-state-state (accessed 5/7/2012).

Elias, Paul. "John Yoo, Former Justice Department Lawyer, Protected from Torture Lawsuit, Rules Appeals Court." *Huffington Post,* May 2, 2012. www.huffingtonpost.com/2012/05/02/john-yoo-torture-bush-administration-jose-padilla_n_1471587.html (accessed 5/31/2012).

"(Former) John Wilkes Booth Monument, Troy, Alabama." ExploreSouthernHistory.com. www.exploresouthernhistory.com/boothmonument.html (accessed 3/30/2013).

Gamble, Richard M. Review of *The Real Lincoln: A New Look at Abraham Lincoln, His Agenda, and an Unnecessary War,* by Thomas J. DiLorenzo. *Independent Review* 7 (Spring 2003): 611–14. www.independent.org/publications/tir/article.asp?a=79 (accessed 5/26/2010).

Greenhouse, Linda. "The Supreme Court: Homosexual Rights; Justices, 6–3, Legalize Gay Sexual Conduct in Sweeping Reversal of Court's '86 Ruling." *New York Times,* June 27, 2003. www.nytimes.com/2003/06/27/us/supreme-court-homosexual-rights-justices-6-3-legalize-gay-sexual-conduct.html?pagewanted=all&src=pm (accessed 1/5/2013).

Guelzo, Allen C. "Prudence, Politics, and the Proclamation." Heritage Foundation, *First Principles Series Report on Political Thought,* no. 14, August 17, 2007. www.heritage.org/research/reports/2007/08/prudence-politics-and-the-proclamation (accessed 11/9/2012).

———. "Abraham Lincoln or the Progressives: Who Was the *Real* Father of Big Government?" Heritage Foundation, *Special Report,* no. 100, February 10, 2012. www.heritage.org/research/reports/2012/02/abraham-lincoln-was-not-the-father-of-big-government (accessed 5/19/2012).

Haddigan, Lee. "How Anticommonism 'Cemented' the American Conservative Movement in a Liberal Age of Conformity, 1945–64." *Libertarian Papers* 2, no. 7 (2010): 1–18. http://libertarianpapers.org/articles/2010/lp-2-7.pdf (accessed 4/26/2010).

Hampson, Rick. "200 Years Later, a More Complex View of Lincoln." *USA Today,* February 24, 2009. http://usatoday30.usatoday.com/news/nation/2009-02-10-lincoln_N.htm (accessed 3/4/2012).

Hawkins, John. "An Interview with Ron Paul." *Right-Wing News,* March 31, 2010. http://rightwingnews.com/interviews/an-interview-with-ron-paul/ (accessed 5/19/2012).

Handbook of Texas Online. Texas State Historical Association. www.tshaonline.org/handbook/online.

Healy, Gene. "The Cult of the Presidency." *Reason* (June 2008). http://reason.com/archives/2008/05/12/the-cult-of-the-presidency (accessed 6/25/2010).

"Hesiod." "McCain Campaign Paid $50,000 to a White Supremacist." DailyKos .com, February 15, 2008. www.dailykos.com/story/2008/02/15/457290/-McCain-Campaign-Paid-50-000-to-a-White-Supremacist (accessed 5/7/2012).

Hoemann, George H. American Civil War Homepage. "Declaration of the Causes of Secession." http://sunsite.utk.edu/civil-war/reasons.html (accessed 6/28/2010).

Houston Public Library. Online newspaper collection database. www.houston library.org/newspapers.

Hummel, Jeffrey Rogers. "Review of *The Politically Incorrect Guide to American History,* by Thomas E. Woods, Jr." *Journal of Libertarian Studies* 20, no. 2 (Spring 2006): 65–86. http://mises.org/journals/jls/20_2/20_2_4.pdf (accessed August 28, 2010).

Kantor, Myles. "Murray Rothbard's Copperhead Abolitionism: An Inquiry into Libertarian Ethics." Mises.org, March 15, 2002. http://mises.org/pdf/asc/2002/asc8-kantor.pdf (accessed May 4, 2010).

Kirchik, James. "Angry White Man: The Bigoted Past of Ron Paul." *New Republic,* January 8, 2008. www.tnr.com/article/politics/angry-white-man (accessed 5/19/2010).

Krannawitter, Thomas L. "Dishonest about Abe: Review of *The Real Lincoln,* by Thomas J. DiLorenzo." http://www.claremont.org/publications/crb/id.736/article_detail.asp (accessed 12/26/2013).

Kreptul, Andrei. "The Constitutional Right of Secession in Political Theory and History." *Journal of Libertarian Studies* 17 (Autumn 2003): 39–100. Mises.org. http://mises.org/journals/jls/17_4/17_4_3.pdf (accessed 8/28/2010).

Lamberton, Lance. "Abraham Lincoln." *Libertarian Forum* (March–April 1979): 2. Mises.org. http://mises.org/journals/lf/1979/1979_03-04.pdf (accessed 9/1/10).

Landess, Thomas H. "Mel Bradford, Old Indian Fighters, and the NEH." Lew Rockwell.com, April 25, 2003, 1–6. www.lewrockwell.com/orig4/landess1.html (accessed 9/25/2009).

Levine, Bruce. "Review of *We Have the War upon Us: The Onset of the Civil War, November 1860–April 1861,* by William J. Cooper." *Civil War Book Review* (Autumn 2012). www.cwbr.com/index.php?q=5261&field=ID&browse=yes&record=full&searching=yes&Submit=Search (accessed 1/2/13).

Lewrockwell.com. Website.

Lizza, Ryan. "Leap of Faith: The Making of a Republican Front-Runner." *New Yorker,* August 15, 2011. www.newyorker.com/reporting/2011/08/15/110815fa_fact_lizza (accessed 1/12/2013).

Livingston, Donald W. "Secession and the Modern State." December 1996. www .lrainc.com/swtaboo/taboos/dwliv01.html (accessed 9/9/2009).

———. "A Moral Accounting of the Union and the Confederacy." *Journal of Libertarian Studies* 16, no. 2 (Spring 2002): 57–101. http://mises.org/journals/jls/16_2/16_2_4.pdf (accessed 8/28/2010).

———. "What Is 'Secession'?" *Vermont Commons* (November 2005). www.vtcommons .org/journal/issue-7-november-2005/donald-livingston-what-secession (accessed 9/9/2009).

———. "David Hume and the Conservative Tradition." *Intercollegiate Review* 44 (Autumn 2009): 30–41. www.firstprinciplesjournal.com/articles.aspx?article=1312 (accessed 1/20/2013).

Ludwig Von Mises Institute. Website. Mises.org.

Maass, Alan. "Lincoln at 200." *CounterPunch,* February 13–15, 2009. www.counter punch.org/2009/02/13/lincoln-at-200/ (accessed 9/24/2012).

Machan, Tibor. "Lincoln, Secession, and Slavery." Cato Institute "Commentary," June 1, 2002. www.cato.org/publications/commentary/lincoln-secession-slavery (accessed 5/20/2012).

"McAllister and Quinn Endorse Gingrich." Press release. FITSNews.com, January 20, 2012. www.fitsnews.com/2012/01/20/mcalister-and-quinn-endorse-gingrich/ (accessed 5/14/2012).

McGee, Robert W. "Secession Reconsidered." *Journal of Libertarian Studies* 11, no. 1 (Autumn 1994): 11–33. Reprinted at https://mises.org/journals/jls/11_1/11_1_2.pdf (accessed 8/28/2010).

McKinley, James, Jr., "Texas Governor's Secession Talk Sparks Furor." *New York Times,* April 17, 2009. www.nytimes.com/2009/04/18/us/politics/18texas.html (accessed 6/1/2012).

McNally, Terence. "There Are More Slaves Today than at Any Time in Human History." Alternet.org, August 24, 2009. www.alternet.org/story/142171/there_ are_more_slaves_today_than_at_any_time_in_human_history (accessed 12/16/2012).

Mercer, Illana. "'Taking America Back' Starts with Taking Lincoln Down." WorldNetDaily.com, February 12, 2003. www.wnd.com/news/article.asp?ARTICLE_ ID=30992 (accessed 7/29/2010).

Miller, John J. "America's Greatest Play: Arthur Miller Didn't Write It." *National Review,* February 18, 2005. http://old.nationalreview.com/miller/miller2005 02180801.asp (accessed 5/23/2012).

Moser, Bob. "Conflicts Arise over Lincoln Statue in Richmond, Va., Cemetery." *Intelligence Report,* no. 110 (Summer 2003). www.splcenter.org/get-informed/intelli gence-report/browse-all-issues/2003/summer/lincoln-reconstructed?page=0,0 (accessed 7/29/2010).

Napolitano, Andrew P. "The Presidency and Mythology." LewRockwell.com, February 22, 2011. www.lewrockwell.com/napolitano/napolitano23.1.html (accessed 1/20/2012).

Owens, Mackubin T. "Abraham Lincoln Saved the Union, but Did He Really Free the Slaves?" Ashbrook.org, March 2004. http://ashbrook.org/publications/oped-owens-04-guelzo/ (accessed 5/20/2012).

Paul, Ron. "Federal Courts and the Imaginary Constitution." LewRockwell.com, August 12, 2003. www.lewrockwell.com/paul/paul120.html (accessed 1/5/2013).

——. "The Trouble with the '64 Civil Rights Act." LewRockwell.com, July 3, 2004. www.lewrockwell.com/paul/paul188.html (accessed 5/21/2012).

Payne, John. "Rothbard's Time on the Left." *Journal of Libertarian Studies* 19, no. 1 (Winter 2005): 7–24. http://mises.org/journals/jls/19_1/19_1_2.pdf (accessed 10/11/2011).

Pew Research Center. "Civil War at 150: Still Relevant, Still Divisive." PEWResearch. org, April 8, 2011. www.pewresearch.org/pubs/1958/civil-war-still-relevant-and-divisive-praise-confederate-leaders-flag (accessed 5/25/2012).

Richman, Sheldon L. "The Anti-War Abolitionists: The Peace Movement's Split over the Civil War." *Journal of Libertarian Studies* 5 (Summer 1981): 327–40. Mises .org, "Literature Library." http://mises.org/journals/jls/5_3/5_3_7.pdf (accessed 8/28/2010).

Robin, Corey. "Fragmented State, Pluralist Society: How Liberal Institutions Promote Fear." *Missouri Law Review* 69, no. 4 (Autumn 2004): 1061–93. http://law .missouri.edu/lawreview/files/2012/11/robin.pdf (accessed 1/31/2012).

Rockwell, Llewellyn, Jr. "King Lincoln" Archive. LewRockwell.com. www.lewrock well.com/orig2/lincoln-arch.html (accessed 4/20/2013).

——. "Murray N. Rothbard Library and Resources." LewRockwell.com. www .lewrockwell.com/rothbard/rothbard-lib.html (accessed 4/20/2013).

RonPaul.com. "Hearings." House Financial Services Committee, Subcommittee on Domestic Monetary Policy and Technology, 112th Cong. www.ronpaul.com/ congress/hearings/ (accessed 8/27/11).

"Ron Paul Newsletters." *New Republic.* www.tnr.com/article/politics/ron-paul-newsletter# (accessed 1/3/2012).

Roosevelt, Theodore. "The Heirs of Abraham Lincoln." February 12, 1913. Teaching AmericanHistory.org. http://teachingamericanhistory.org/library/index.asp? document=1140 (accessed 3/2/10).

Rothbard, Murray N. Introduction to *Vices Are Not Crimes* by Lysander Spooner. 2d ed. Cupertino, Calif.: Tanstaafl, 1977. www.mises.org/books/vicescrimes.pdf.

——. "Generalissimo Washington: How He Crushed the Spirit of Liberty." 1979. Excerpted from *Conceived in Liberty.* Auburn, Ala.: Ludwig von Mises Institute, 2011. www.lewrockwell.com/rothbard/rothbard171.html (accessed 9/1/10).

——. "A Strategy for the Right." *Rothbard-Rockwell Report,* March 17, 1992. http:// mises.org/daily/3931 (accessed 5/20/2010).

——. *Egalitarianism as a Revolt against Nature and Other Essays.* 2d ed. Auburn, Ala.: Ludwig von Mises Institute, 2000. Available at Mises.org, "Literature Library." http://mises.org/books/egalitarianism.pdf (accessed 5/22/2012).

Sanchez, Julian, and David Weigel. "Who Wrote Ron Paul's Newsletters?" *Reason,* January 16, 2008. http://reason.com/archives/2008/01/16/who-wrote-ron-pauls-newsletter (accessed 8/26/2010).

Sandefur, Timothy. "Liberty and Union: Now and Forever." *Liberty* 16 (July 2002): 33–39. www.libertyunbound.com/node/175 (accessed 5/17/12).

———. "Springtime for Jeff Davis and the Confed'racy." "Freespace" blog, April 19, 2011. http://sandefur.typepad.com/freespace/2011/04/springtime-for-jeff-davis-and-the-confedracy.html (accessed 4/25/2011).

———. "Make Sure the Tables Are Turned the Right Way." "Freespace" blog, March 6, 2012. http://sandefur.typepad.com/freespace/2012/03/make-sure-the-tables-are-turned-the-right-way.html (accessed 5/21/2012).

Schulten, Susan. "Barack Obama, Abraham Lincoln, and John Dewey." http://www.law.du.edu/documents/denver-university-law-review/schulten.pdf (accessed 12/28/2013).

Sebesta, Edward H. "Letter to President Barack Obama." "Arlington Confederate Monument Report" blog, May 8, 2009. http://arlingtonconfederatemonument.blogspot.com/2010/03/2009-letter-to-president-obama.html (accessed 7/20/2010).

———. "An Overview of the Neo-Confederate Movement." TempleOfDemocracy.com, October 9, 2011, 1–25. www.templeofdemocracy.com/overview.pdf (accessed 11/4/11).

Sons of Confederate Veterans. Website. SCV.org.

Southern Poverty Law Center. Website. SPLCenter.org.

Sowell, Thomas. "Trashing Our History." Townhall.com, August 11, 2005. http://townhall.com/columnists/thomassowell/2005/08/11/trashing_our_history_lincoln/page/full/ (accessed 10/13/2009).

Spooner, Lysander. "Forced Consent." 1873. Molinari Institute. http://praxeology.net/LS-FC.htm (accessed 8/12/2010).

Stromberg, Joseph R. "The War for Southern Independence: A Radical Libertarian Perspective." *Journal of Libertarian Studies* 3, no. 1 (Spring 1979): 31–53. https://mises.org/document/1690/The-War-for-Southern-Independence-A-Radical-Libertarian-Perspective (accessed 8/28/2010).

———. "William Appleman Williams: Premier New Left Revisionist." AntiWar.com, "The Old Cause" blog, November 16, 1999. www.antiwar.com/stromberg/s111699.html (accessed 6/25/2010).

———. "Harry Elmer Barnes (1898–1968): Progressive and Revisionist." AntiWar.com, "The Old Cause" blog, February 7, 2000. www.antiwar.com/stromberg/s020700.html (accessed 6/18/2010).

———. "War, Peace, and the State." LewRockwell.com, ongoing. www.lewrockwell.com/stromberg/stromberg23.html (accessed 12/28/2009).

Sturdevant, Lori. "Secession Gaining Fans in MN GOP." *Star Tribune,* April 12, 2010. www.startribune.com/opinion/90659669.html (accessed 5/25/2012).

Terris, Ben. "Scholars Nostalgic for the Old South Study the Virtues of Secession, Quietly." *Chronicle of Higher Education,* December 6, 2009. http://chronicle.com/article/Secretive-Scholars-of-the-Old/49337/ (accessed 1/18/2013).

Wall, Richard. "A Hegelian at Gettysburg: Woodrow Wilson and the Perfect Union." LewRockwell.com, April 10, 2008. www.lewrockwell.com/wall/wall35.html (accessed 34/2010).

Walsh, David A. "What Is the Least Credible History Book in Print?" History News Network, July 16, 2012. http://hnn.us/articles/what-least-credible-history-book-print (accessed 12/16/2012).

Watner, Carl. "The Radical Libertarian Tradition in Antislavery Thought." *Journal of Libertarian Studies* 3 (1979): 299–329. https://mises.org/document/1704/The-Radical-Libertarian-Tradition-in-Antislavery-Thought (accessed 8/28/2010).

Welch, Matt. "More Details on the Increasingly Bitter Koch/Cato Lawsuit and Feud." *Reason,* "Hit and Run" blog, March 7, 2012. http://reason.com/blog/2012/03/07/more-details-on-the-increasinly-bitter-k (accessed 5/30/2012).

Wheeler, Samuel P. "Psychic Lincoln?" *Lincoln Studies: Abraham Lincoln and the American Civil War.* http://lincolnstudies.blogspot.com/2007/12/psychic-lincoln.html (accessed 4/14/2012).

Wilkins, Steve. "Yes, Mr. Minnery, Lincoln, Like Satan, 'Knew' Scripture but 'Dishonest Abe' Was No Christian." AmericanView.com, January–May 2007. http://archive.theamericanview.com/index.php?id=800 (accessed 11/3/2011).

Williams, Walter. "The Civil War Wasn't about Slavery." *Jewish Review,* December 2, 1998. www.jewishworldreview.com/cols/williams120298.asp (accessed 5/11/2012).

Willis, Ellen. "What's the Matter with Tom Frank (and the Lefties Who Love Him)?" *Situations: Project of the Radical Imagination* 1, no. 2 (2006): 5–20. http://ojs.gc.cuny.edu/index.php/situations/article/view/30/26 (accessed 3/19/2013).

Yan, Holly, and Gabriella Schwartz. "GOP Candidates Caught in Slavery Controversy." CNN.com, "Political Ticker" blog, July 11, 2011. http://politicalticker.blogs.cnn.com/2011/07/11/gop-candidates-caught-in-slavery-controversy/?hpt=po_bn2 (accessed 8/27/11).

INDEX